SQL Server® 2008
Administration

SQL Server® 2008 Administration

Real World Skills for MCITP Certification and Beyond

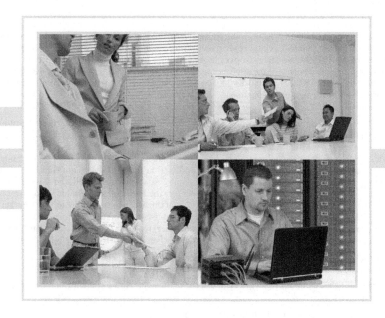

Tom Carpenter

WILEY

Wiley Publishing, Inc.

Acquisitions Editor: Jeff Kellum
Development Editor: Denise Santoro Lincoln
Technical Editors: Acey Bunch and Mitchel Sellers
Production Editor: Elizabeth Ginns Britten
Copy Editor: Kathy Grider-Carlyle
Editorial Manager: Pete Gaughan
Production Manager: Tim Tate
Vice President and Executive Group Publisher: Richard Swadley
Vice President and Publisher: Neil Edde
Media Project Manager 1: Laura Moss-Hollister
Media Associate Producer: Josh Frank
Media Quality Assurance: Shawn Patrick
Book Designers: Judy Fung, Bill Gibson
Compositor: Craig Johnson, Happenstance Type-O-Rama
Proofreader: Word One, New York
Indexer: Ted Laux
Project Coordinator, Cover: Lynsey Stanford
Cover Designer: Ryan Sneed

Library of Congress Cataloging-in-Publication Data
Carpenter, Tom.
SQL server 2008 administration : real world skills for MCITP certification and beyond / Tom Carpenter.—1st ed.
    p. cm.
Includes bibliographical references and index.
ISBN 978-0-470-55420-3 (papen/cd-rom : alk. paper)
978-0-470-64940-4 (ebk); 978-0-470-64942-8 (ebk); 978-0-470-64941-1 (ebk)
1. Electronic data processing personnel—Certification. 2. Microsoft software—Examinations—Study guides. 3. SQL server. I. Title.
QA76.3.C34845 2010
005.4'476—dc22
                            2010004720

Dear Reader,

Thank you for choosing *SQL Server 2008 Administration: Real World Skills for MCITP Certification and Beyond*. This book is part of a family of premium-quality Sybex books, all of which are written by outstanding authors who combine practical experience with a gift for teaching.

Sybex was founded in 1976. More than 30 years later, we're still committed to producing consistently exceptional books. With each of our titles, we're working hard to set a new standard for the industry. From the paper we print on to the authors we work with, our goal is to bring you the best books available.

I hope you see all of that reflected in these pages. I'd be very interested to hear your comments and get your feedback on how we're doing. Feel free to let me know what you think about this or any other Sybex book by sending me an email at nedde@wiley.com. If you think you've found a technical error in this book, please visit http://sybex.custhelp.com. Customer feedback is critical to our efforts at Sybex.

Best regards,

Neil Edde
Vice President and Publisher
Sybex, an Imprint of Wiley

I dedicate this book to my family and God—the two most important relationships in my life. Thanks for all you do.

Acknowledgments

I would like to acknowledge the members of my amazing family, who continue to find the energy to support me during long writing projects. Tracy, I love you and appreciate the unending patience you've shown during the writing process. Faith, Rachel, Thomas, and Sarah, you are the most amazing children any father could hope to lead. I would also like to thank Denise Santoro Lincoln, one of the most proficient editors I've had the chance to work with. She is certain to make any book she touches better. Additionally, I'd like to thank Jeff Kellum for allowing me to write my first Sybex book. I've been an admirer of Sybex books for many years and am proud to have my name on the cover of one. Of course, I must acknowledge all of my training attendees and consulting clients. They have provided me with the greater depth of knowledge required to write a book like this.

About the Author

Tom Carpenter is a consultant and trainer based in Marysville, Ohio. He is the founder and current Senior Consultant for The Systems Education and Consulting Company (SysEdCo). SysEdCo provides training on Microsoft technologies, wireless networking, security, and IT professional development. Tom is the author of several books on topics ranging from wireless network administration to SQL Server database administration and optimization. Tom holds several certifications including MCITP: SQL Server 2008 Database Administrator, CWNA, CWSP, Project+, and several additional Microsoft certifications. He spends every spare moment he can with his amazing wife and children.

Contents at a Glance

Contents

Table of Exercises

Introduction

Administering SQL Server 2008 is no simple task. As database management systems go, SQL Server 2008 is one of the most complex solutions available today. Offering more than just straightforward database management, SQL Server 2008 also includes data management for data transfer and transformation; data distribution through replication; and high availability through database mirroring and server clustering. The modern database administrator (DBA) must understand all of these components and more to successfully administer an efficient and secure data facility, and this book has been written for just such a DBA.

This book was written from two perspectives. First, it covers the most important administrative tasks that the DBA in organizations of all sizes will need to perform. These are covered with a real-world focus on SQL Server 2008 administration. Second, it covers the MCITP: Database Administrator 2008 exam objectives, 70-432 and 70-450, through the written pages of the book and the videos and practice exams on the included DVD. Whether you're preparing for these exams or preparing for life as a DBA, you'll find this book a useful reference.

Who Should Read This Book

As you can probably tell by the title of this book, *SQL Server 2008 Administration: Real World Skills for MCITP Certification and Beyond,* this book is primarily aimed at two groups: those seeking real-world SQL Server database administration knowledge and those preparing for the MCITP Database Administrator exams. Yet a third group may benefit from reading this book as well. Following are some descriptions of those who will find this book useful:

- DBAs looking for a reference for common administrative tasks. Everything from backing up your databases to securing them is covered in this book. You'll find coverage of the extra SQL Server 2008 components such as SQL Server Integration Services and SQL Server Reporting Services as well.

- Exam candidates preparing to take the MCITP: Database Administrator 2008 exams: 70-432 TS: Microsoft SQL Server 2008, Implementation and Maintenance and/or 70-450 PRO: Designing, Optimizing and Maintaining a Database Administrative Solution Using Microsoft SQL Server 2008. You'll find that all of the objectives are covered when you use the complete training kit this book provides, which includes the book, the practice exams on the included DVD, and the video training. It's important to note that what you hold in your hands is more than just a book. The DVD includes video training and memory-jogging flashcards, as well as practice exams and more, to help you master the objectives of both MCITP exams.

- Programmers will also find value in this book. This book does not contain programming guidance or detailed explanations of the T-SQL language or CLR code; however, it does provide the programmer with a reference to the SQL Server 2008 functionality and how to install and manage the SQL Server that may just be used as the backend for their data-driven applications.

As you can see, this book is useful to several groups. I have worked as a systems engineer creating applications, which access SQL Servers, so I know the value of a good administration book sitting on my shelf, and I've striven to write this book with that in mind. I've also taken the 70-432 and 70-450 exams, so I understand the stresses related to preparing for these challenges and the inside information needed to pass them. And although I could have provided the exam information in a series of bulleted lists, I wrote this book from a practical perspective instead, because I feel that this approach makes the information easier to remember and it certainly makes it more valuable for your real life outside of the exam.

What You Will Learn

As you progress through this book, you will go from understanding what SQL Server 2008 has to offer to your organization to implementing it with all the bells and whistles it provides. You'll learn to select the appropriate hardware for your servers and then install SQL Server 2008 right the first time. Then you'll move on to learn how to use the administration tools from both the graphical user interface (GUI) of Windows and the command-line interface (my favorite place to be).

Next, you'll learn how to design and implement database design solutions for SQL Server 2008. During this process, you'll learn all about normal forms and database optimization and the many terms you'll need to understand to master database administration and design. You'll learn to create databases with the SQL Server Management Studio and with T-SQL code. Of course, part of the optimization process will be to implement indexes, so I'll make sure you really understand what they are and how they work to improve the performance of your database queries. You'll also learn to enforce rules and data standards by using triggers, stored procedures, and other advanced administration solutions.

Once your database is in place, you'll need to provide ongoing support for that database. One of the first things you must implement is a working backup and recovery plan. You'll learn how to do this by first learning to create jobs, operators, and alerts. Then you'll learn to perform performance analysis and optimization and how to take advantage of the new Declarative Management Framework (DMF), also known as Policy-Based Management (PBM). And, of course, you'll learn to back up and restore your databases. The primary focus of this ongoing administration process will be to standardize, automate, and update so that your workload is reduced over the long haul.

Once you have the maintenance plans in place, it's time to think seriously about security, which is a very important issue for databases, networks, and anything else of value. There are three chapters in this section. First, you'll learn about security threats and vulnerabilities. You'll then move on to learn about authentication and encryption in detail. Finally, I'll provide you with several best practices for securing a SQL Server 2008 environment.

The final section of the book is three chapters long and addresses SQL Server 2008 high availability and data distribution. You'll learn about failover clustering, database mirroring, database snapshots, and data replication in these chapters.

Throughout the book, you'll find real-world exercises that walk you through the processes required to implement and support commonly used features of SQL Server 2008. You'll also find notes and warnings scattered throughout the book to help you understand more detailed concepts. Additionally, real-world scenarios provide you with insights into the daily life of a DBA or database consultant.

This book was written to address the complete collection of tasks the DBA will be required to perform in the real world, while also covering all exam topics so readers can pass their MCITP exams. Each section offers real-world exercises so you can learn with hands-on tasks. I have also provided videos of some of these exercises as well. These are available on the book's DVD.

Yet it's also important that you remember what this book is not; this book is not a programming reference. My goal here is not to teach you everything about the T-SQL language. That would require a 700+ page volume itself and is well beyond the scope of this book. However, I have good news for you: If you are new to T-SQL you will find an introduction to the T-SQL language and some code examples in the demonstration and training videos on the DVD that is included with this book. Additionally, you can visit www.TomCarpenter.net to find blog posts related to SQL Server and other technologies. In these posts, I often cover T-SQL best practices and optimization techniques.

What You Need

The exercises in this book assume that you are running SQL Server 2008 on Windows Server 2008 or later. If you are using Windows Server 2003 R2 or previous versions, the exercises should work in most cases; however, they were only tested on Windows Server 2008.

If you do not have a Windows Server 2008 machine, you might want to create a virtual machine so that you can go through every exercise in the book. Here are your options:

- You can download Microsoft's Windows Virtual PC from www.microsoft.com/windows/virtual-pc.

- You can also download a trial version of Windows Server 2008 from http://www.microsoft.com/windowsserver2008/en/us/trial-software.aspx and install it as a virtual machine within Windows Virtual PC. I recommend a machine with 4GB of RAM to perform virtualization.

- If your machine does not meet the requirements of Windows Virtual PC, you may be able to use the VMWare Player 3.0 found at www.vmware.com.

You will also need the SQL Server 2008 media for installation. If you do not have a licensed copy of SQL Server 2008, you have two choices.

- First, you can download a trial version from Microsoft's website at www.microsoft.com/SQLserver/2008/en/us/trial-software.aspx.

- Second, you can purchase the Developer Edition of SQL Server 2008. It usually costs between $50 and $70 and is exactly the same as the Enterprise Edition except for the licensing. The Developer Edition license allows you to develop solutions but not deploy them. For example, you cannot implement a production database server for your users with the Developer Edition; however, you can work through every exercise in this book using it.

What Is Covered in This Book

SQL Server 2008 Administration: Real World Skills for MCITP Certification and Beyond is organized to provide you with the information you need to effectively administer your SQL Server 2008 instances. The following list provides an overview of the topics covered in each chapter.

Part I—Introducing SQL Server 2008

Chapter 1—**Understanding SQL Server's Role:** In this chapter, you will learn about the role of a database server and the various roles SQL Server 2008 can play in your organization.

Chapter 2—**Installing SQL Server 2008:** Master the SQL Server installation process by actually doing it in this chapter. You will install a named instance and also learn how to install a default instance. Each step of the installation process is covered in detail.

Chapter 3—**Working with the Administration Tools:** Take a tour of the administration tools provided with SQL Server and Windows Server and learn to use them to keep your SQL Servers running smoothly.

Chapter 4—**SQL Server Command-Line Administration:** This chapter teaches you how to use the command line and Windows PowerShell for SQL Server 2008 administration. You'll learn to use the SQLCMD command and also how to use the general command-line commands that ship with Windows itself.

Part II—Designing Database Solutions

Chapter 5—**Database Concepts and Terminology:** It's time to begin learning the theory behind database systems. You'll learn all the important terms and what they mean. This chapter lays a foundation for the following chapters of the book.

Chapter 6—**ERD and Capacity Planning:** Have you heard of entity relationship diagramming? In this chapter, you learn what it is and how to use it by using common tools and free tools available on the Internet. You'll also learn to estimate the capacity needs for a given database specification.

Chapter 7—Normalization: Enough Is Enough: Normalization is an important process and this chapter teaches you how to use it to optimize your database designs.

Part III—Implementing Database Solutions

Chapter 8—Creating SQL Server Databases: You will learn to create databases using the SQL Server Management Studio as well as T-SQL code in this chapter. This is where the theory meets reality in the SQL Server database system.

Chapter 9—Creating Tables: In order to create well-performing tables, you must understand data types. This chapter provides a reference of data types in SQL Server 2008 and how to choose the best data type for any situation. You'll also learn the difference between a heap and a clustered index.

Chapter 10—Indexes and Views: Trainers like to talk about them. DBAs like to implement them. Now, you will learn what they really are and how they improve the performance of your databases. What are they? Indexes, of course. You'll also learn about views and the benefits they provide.

Chapter 11—Triggers and Stored Procedures: Triggers and stored procedures are often used to centralize business rules or business logic. This chapter introduces the concepts and provides examples of both.

Chapter 12—Implementing Advanced Features: SQL Server 2008 provides some advanced functionality right out-of-the-box, and this chapter introduces these capabilities with coverage of SQL Server Analysis Services, SQL Server Reporting Services, and SQL Server Integration Services.

Part IV—Administration and Maintenance

Chapter 13—Creating Jobs, Operators, and Alerts: Now that your databases are in place, it's time to maintain them. In this chapter, I introduce the Standardize, Automate, and Update (SAU) model of administration and provide steps for creating jobs, operators, and alerts.

Chapter 14—Performance Monitoring and Tuning: This chapter introduces you to the performance maintenance tools available in Windows Server and SQL Server 2008. You'll learn how to track down performance problems and improve the responsiveness of your servers.

Chapter 15—Policy-Based Management: Also known as the Declarative Management Framework. This chapter teaches you how to implement Policy-Based Management from the ground up.

Chapter 16—Backup and Restoration: This final general administration chapter will focus on the very important task of backing up and restoring your databases. You'll learn about the different backup types and how to implement them. You'll also learn about the importance of recovery testing and recovery procedures.

Part V—SQL Server Security

Chapter 17—Security Threats and Principles: When administering databases, you are often managing the most valuable asset in modern organizations. For this reason, I take a very serious approach to security when it comes to SQL Server 2008. This chapter begins the security journey by evaluating threats and vulnerabilities in a SQL Server 2008 networked environment.

Chapter 18—Authentication and Encryption: Continuing from Chapter 17, this chapter moves on to the topics of authentication and encryption. You'll learn how authentication helps to protect your environment and about the authentication options SQL Server provides. You'll also learn to implement and manage encryption in SQL Server databases.

Chapter 19—Security Best Practices: In this third and final chapter on security, you'll learn several best practices to help you maintain the security of your environment. You'll learn to perform surface area reduction and auditing in this chapter.

Part VI—High Availability and Data Distribution

Chapter 20—SQL Server Failover Clustering: SQL Server 2008 supports the failover clustering feature of Windows Server, and this chapter introduces you to the topic of clustering and how it is implemented in a SQL Server 2008 environment.

Chapter 21—Database Mirrors and Snapshots: Database mirroring was brand new in SQL Server 2005, and it has been enhanced in SQL Server 2008. This chapter provides instruction for implementing database mirroring and database snapshots for point-in-time data recovery and analysis.

Chapter 22—Implementing Replication: The final chapter in the book introduces the features of SQL Server replication. You'll learn about the different replication types and how to implement them. You'll also learn how to configure subscribers to receive the replicated data.

Appendixes

Appendix A: Appendix A provides an objectives map for exam 70-432 and exam 70-450. If you are studying for the exams, use this Appendix to find the portion of the book that covers the objectives you are studying currently.

Appendix B: Appendix B tells you all about the additional bonus materials, including what's on it, system requirements, how to use it, and troubleshooting tips.

Glossary: The final element of the book is the Glossary. You'll find definitions of important terms related to SQL Server 2008 and the role of a DBA. If you're preparing for the exams, be sure to read the Glossary on the morning of the exam. This action will ensure your understanding of the most important topics covered.

Additional Bonus Material

With this book, we are including quite an array of training resources. The bonus material include sample videos, bonus exams, and flashcards to help you study for certification candidates. The resources are described here:

Sample Videos   Throughout the book, I have included numerous hands-on exercises showing you how to perform a variety of tasks. For some of these tasks, I have also included Camtasia video-walkthrough. Look for the CD icon for exercises that include video walkthroughs.

The Sybex Test Engine   Since this book is also a supplement for MCITP: SQL Server 2008 DBA candidates, we have also included two bonus exams, one practice exam for TS: Microsoft SQL Server 2008, Implementation and Maintenance (70-432) and one for IT Pro: Designing, Optimizing and Maintaining a Database Administrative Solution Using Microsoft SQL Server 2008 (70-450).

Sybex Flashcards   The "flashcard" style of question offers an effective way to quickly and efficiently test your understanding of the fundamental concepts.

 To download the bonus materials, visit booksupport.wiley.com, and plug in the book's ISBN: 9780470554203. From there, click on ISBN, and then download the zip file to your hard drive.

How to Contact the Author

If you have any questions on your certification or administration journey, please contact me. My email address is carpenter@sysedco.com, and I always respond when I receive an email from a reader. More than a decade ago, I sent an email to a well-known author and he responded. I was shocked because I had never gotten a response from any other author I'd written. I told myself then that, if I ever had the chance to write a book, I would respond to any and all email messages that I received. When I respond to your email, just remember that you have Mark Minasi to thank, since he was the author who responded to me. If you don't hear back within a few days, please email me again. You know how spam filters are! This is my seventh book, and I still love hearing from my readers.

Finally, if you ever get the chance to attend one of my seminars on SQL Server or any other topic, please let me know you've read my book. I always enjoy speaking with my readers face-to-face and learning how to improve the books as well as how they have helped the reader. My speaking schedule is posted at www.SysEdCo.com and I look forward to seeing you at a future event.

Introducing SQL Server 2008

Chapter

1

Understanding SQL Server's Role

TOPICS COVERED IN THIS CHAPTER:

- ✓ What Is Information Technology?
- ✓ An Introduction to Databases
- ✓ Database Servers
- ✓ Database Applications
- ✓ New Features in SQL Server 2005 and SQL Server 2008
- ✓ Core SQL Server Features

Microsoft SQL Server 2008 is a database management system that provides enterprise-class features for organizations of all sizes. If you are tasked with administering a SQL Server, you need to understand the various roles it can play within an organization. This understanding comes best by studying from the foundation up, and this chapter provides that foundation. From this foundation, you will move through this book to learn how to administer the essential aspects of SQL Server 2008. In addition, the contents of exams 70-432 (Microsoft SQL Server 2008, Implementation and Maintenance) and 70-450 (PRO: Designing, Optimizing, and Maintaining a Database Administrative Solution Using Microsoft SQL Server 2008) are covered throughout the book.

The first major topics you'll tackle in this chapter are the concepts of *information technology* and the role a database or database system plays within this concept. Next, you'll look at databases in more detail and gain an understanding of fundamental concepts that apply to *all* databases, not just SQL Server databases. Once you've sufficiently covered the general database concepts, you'll investigate database servers and applications. Finally, you'll explore SQL Server's features and the roles SQL Server can play in modern organizations.

What Is Information Technology?

Many organizations differentiate between Information Systems (IS) and Information Technology (IT). In general, IS deals with software and system development, and IT is concerned with technology management. Certainly, IT is the collection of technologies and resources used to manage information. Organizations place great value on their information, as they should, and they expect the IT group to manage this information well. It is essential that those of us who work in IT remember the "I" stands for *information* and that our primary responsibilities are to collect, retain, distribute, protect, and when appropriate destroy that information. When a single group is responsible for these tasks, consistency is accomplished and security can be achieved.

The Importance of IT

Consider an organization that manufactures and sells the components used to make fishing lures. These components are used by many different fabricators and distributors. What would happen if a competing company stole the customer database of the world's top fishing lure company? The results could be catastrophic. However, if the company's IT department creates and uses the proper information-protection mechanisms, the event could be mitigated or the theft itself could be prevented.

 Most people pronounce SQL Server as "sequel server" and the SQL language as "ess-cue-el." Throughout this book, the term "SQL Server" will refer to Microsoft's database server product in general. When a discussion is applicable only to a specific version of SQL Server, the appropriate version number, such as SQL Server 2000, will be specified.

Finally, I pronounce SQL Server as "sequel server" and I pronounce the SQL language as "ess-cue-el." You'll notice this based on the articles ("a" versus "an") that I use. I have reasons for my pronunciations, but we'll reserve those for a later chapter.

Although losing a database to a competitor is an extreme example of why an IT department is needed, there are many day-to-day problems and issues that arise within a company that are best handled by the IT department. For instance, customer service professionals aren't as productive or effective when they cannot access data (information distribution) when they need it to answer customers' question. Customers may become impatient if their questions aren't sufficiently addressed, and they could very well choose a different provider. An effective IT department helps everyone within a company manage information so each team can be successful.

Effective IT solutions enable the five key responsibilities of information management to be accomplished. These five key responsibilities are

Information Collection   Database systems and applications are used to collect information from users. Well-coded applications validate data integrity and ensure that only valid users can enter or modify information.

Information Retention   A good information storage system provides effective storage and backup mechanisms. You'll learn about SQL Server's backup solutions in Chapter 16, "Backup and Restoration."

Information Distribution   The right people need the right information at the right time, and information distribution solutions allow for this. Examples include replication, mirroring, Integration Services packages, and more.

Information Protection   There are many different types of information with varying degrees of priority and confidentiality. In most organizations, only certain users should have access to certain information. Security solutions from authentication to storage encryption should be used to protect valuable data. Additionally, coding best practices should be followed in order to prevent the opening of accidental back doors into your information stores.

Information Destruction   Sometimes information needs to be destroyed. Your IT solutions should account for this and ensure that a nonrecoverable method is used to destroy the data when it is required.

These five facets of information management must be included in any IT plan. SQL Server databases can assist with these processes. Although SQL Server features and capabilities can be integrated with client solutions and network infrastructure solutions to do so, SQL Server cannot provide all of the best solutions alone. An authentication system, such as Microsoft's Active Directory, will be needed to provide secure authentication. Additionally, although SQL Server integrates with Windows Server Active Directory domains to provide stronger authentication, if the SQL Server is not integrated with a Windows domain and the client computers are running non-Windows operating systems, you may be required to implement a VPN or IPSec association with the SQL Server before the users can authenticate. This VPN solution can be implemented using Microsoft's RRAS service or a third-party product.

The Components of IT

In today's computing environments, three core components exist in the IT puzzle:

- Client solutions
- Network infrastructure solutions
- Information storage solutions

Although these components can be broken down further, this chapter will focus on these three. These core components will be discussed further throughout this book as you learn about SQL Server and how to deploy and administer it in any environment.

Figure 1.1 shows these core components of IT. You can break down the components into separate groupings:

- Client solutions include desktop computers, laptops or notebooks, portable devices, and even telephones in Voice over IP implementations.
- Network infrastructure solutions include switches, routers, and network communications services. Network communications services allow communications to take place on the network, such as DNS, DHCP, authentication services, and so on.
- Information storage solutions include databases, file servers, and networked storage such as Network Attached Storage (NAS) and Storage Area Networks (SANs).

FIGURE 1.1   The core components of IT

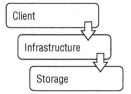

Understanding how SQL Server operates within these three areas is crucial for the modern database administrator (DBA). Unlike DBAs in the past, today's DBA must understand the basics of the operating system on which the database solution runs, the fundamentals of network communications, and the clients that talk to the database server. Gone are the days of simply replacing a dumb terminal if a user cannot communicate with the database (or at least those days are far less common for most of us).

When you implement advanced SQL Server features, such as database mirroring, you need to understand how to determine if a communication problem is caused by an internal configuration error or a problem in the network infrastructure between the two SQL Servers involved. Even if you're not responsible for repairing the network infrastructure, you'll need to know when to contact the network administrator at the very least.

Many support professionals work in small organizations (or small groups within larger organizations), and they must be able to support practically everything that has a wire in their buildings. Of course, this means they need to understand everything in the communication chain from the database server to the client and back again. For this reason, this book will teach you more than just how to work with SQL Server. It will explain how SQL Server works with your other systems, including Windows clients, non-Windows clients, and other servers.

Introduction to Databases

The word "data" is defined as meaningful information, and it can include words, numbers, letters, and binary information such as images. The word "base" means foundation or place. Simply put, a database is a place to put your data. If you're looking for a more technical definition of a database, it would go something like this: A computer database is a (usually) structured collection of information stored according to a defined model and accessible through standard or proprietary database communications languages.

 If you've been working with databases for many years, you may choose to skip over this section and move on to the section titled "SQL Server's Role." However, if you do read this section, you may be surprised and learn a few things. This choice is yours.

Make sure you don't confuse the database with the database management system. The "Database Servers and Applications" section will cover this in more detail. For now, just remember that the database is separate from the database management system and it can usually be transferred from one computer running the compatible database management system to another computer running the same.

Types of Databases

The *database model* defines the way in which the data is stored. Most modern databases use the relational model, but other models do exist. In general terms, the database model is the type of database. Two primary types are still in use today: flat-file and relational databases.

Flat-File Databases

All of the information in a *flat-file database* is stored in a single storage container. When stored in a database, information regarding customer orders might look something like Figure 1.2.

FIGURE 1.2 A table of flat-file databases

OrderID	CustomerNum	CustomerName	Phone	Email
23	413	Dale Thomas	937-555-0135	DaleThomas4532@company.net
27	413	Dale Thomas	937-555-0135	DaleThomas4532@company.net
36	413	Dale Thomas	937-555-0135	DaleThomas4532@company.net
42	413	Dale Thomas	937-555-0135	DaleThomas4532@company.net

Here are a few key points to consider regarding flat-file databases:

Flat-file databases result in high levels of data redundancy. If you examine Figure 1.2, you can see redundancy in action. Note that the name Dale Thomas is repeated for each line item, as well as the customer number, phone number, and email address. If a separate table were used to store the customer information, this redundancy could be avoided.

Flat-file databases cost more when data is added. Because flat-file databases result in more redundancy, the system simply must write more information when data is added. When referring to an information system, the term "cost" can mean dollars and cents or it can mean resource costs (CPU, memory, etc.). In this case, the costs are resource costs. You cannot ask a system to do more without consuming more resources within that system.

Working with flat-file databases may be easier for some users. This point is actually a positive characteristic of flat-file databases, and it is one of the many reasons you create views in relational databases. Flat-file databases are often easier for users to work with because all of the data is in one location. Consider the two SQL statements in Listing 1.1. (Don't worry if you don't fully understand SQL yet; you will learn more about it in Chapters 8 through 12.) Although the increased complexity of the relational database query may seem trivial, consider what it might look like if you have to join five or more tables together to retrieve the needed information. Because all of the data is in a container in the flat-file format, no join statements are needed, and all of the data is easily accessed by decision-support professionals or business managers who may not understand the complexities of relational queries.

Listing 1.1: SQL Statement Examples

```
--This first query is on a relational database
SELECT dbo.Products.ProductID, dbo.Products.ProductName,
       dbo.Sales.OrderID, dbo.Sales.Quantity, dbo.Sales.Price
FROM dbo.Products
INNER JOIN dbo.Sales ON dbo.Products.ProductID = dbo.Sales.ProductID;

--This second query retrieves the same information from a flat-file database
SELECT dbo.Sales.ProductID, dbo.Sales.ProductName,
       Dbo.Sales.OrderID, dbo.Sales.Quantity, dbo.Sales.Price
FROM dbo.Products;
```

This simplification is one of the driving factors behind many views that are created and behind many of the decisions that are made when online analytical processing (OLAP) databases are implemented. OLAP databases are usually read (far more read operations are performed as opposed to write operations), and they may benefit from a flattened model; however, even with OLAP databases, it is still common to have multiple tables. The tables may simply be less *normalized* (understood as more redundant) than those for an online transaction processing (OLTP) database that processes large numbers or writes to the data.

 Normalization is defined as the process used to ensure that relational data is stored in a manner that removes or reduces anomalies in data modifications. The process also results in a reduction in redundancy within the data store. Normalization will be covered in more detail in Chapter 7, "Normalization: Enough Is Enough."

Relational Databases

Relational databases store information in separate containers called tables. Each table represents a single entity, although *denormalized relational databases* may not always do so. You'll learn about normalization in Chapter 7; for now, you just need to know that a relational database is a collection of entity containers (tables) that are related to one another in various ways.

When you convert the data in Figure 1.2 to a relational database model, the results should be similar to those shown in Figure 1.3. Notice that the Customers table is related to the Sales table so that the customer information is entered only once. In each order, the customer ID is used to reference everything about the customer. You could further optimize this database by breaking the Sales table into two tables: Sales and Items. The Sales table would contain the header information for the sale (sale date, sale ID, customer ID, etc.) and the Items table would list the details for each item purchased (product ID, price, quantity, etc.).

FIGURE 1.3   The sales and items tables interact in a relational structure.

OrderID	CustomerNum	ProductID	Quantity	UnitPrice
23	413	45	12	12.45
27	413	32	6	14.97
36	413	78	53	3.78
42	413	98	13	12.17

CustomerNum	CustomerName	Phone	Email	City
413	Dale Thomas	937-555-0135	DaleThomas4532@company.net	Marysville
414	Amie Freeman	405-555-9090	Amie_F@company.net	Urbana
415	Tracy Mathys	417-555-0078	Tracy@thenet.com	Austin
416	Jose Ramos	913-555-1616	JoseRamos@company.net	Elk City

The relational model provides several benefits:

Relational databases can be indexed and optimized more efficiently.   Relational databases can be indexed and optimized more efficiently because you are dealing with smaller units of information in each data store (each table). For example, you can index the Customers table uniquely for retrieving common columns of information and you can index the Sales table uniquely for retrieving common columns of information retrieved from the Sales table. If the two tables were crammed together into a single flat structure, you would have to ask which is more important: customer columns or sales columns. You can only create so many indexes before you start hurting more than you help.

Relational databases consume less space to store the same information as flat-file databases.   Because the redundancies have been removed, a relational database requires less space to store the same information as a flat-file database. For example, consider Figure 1.2 again. The customer ID, customer name, phone number, and email address must be added every time Dale Thomas places an order; however, with the structure in Figure 1.3, only the customer ID must be added with each order. You are, therefore, dealing with one column instead of four. You can see how the relational structure saves on storage space.

Relational databases can handle more concurrent users more easily.   Because data is broken into logical chunks, relational databases can handle more concurrent users more easily. With the data store represented in Figure 1.2, even if the user only wants the sales-specific information with no information about the customer, all of the data must be locked in some way while the user retrieves the information. This behavior prevents other users from accessing the data, and everyone else must wait in line (what a database system usually calls a *queue*). The relational model is better because one user can be in the Sales table while another is in the Customers table. Of course, modern database systems go even further and usually allow locking at the data page or even the row (record) level.

Relational databases are more scalable.   Because they allow for more granular tweaking and tuning, relational databases *scale* better. They store more information in less space. They allow more users to access the data more quickly. These benefits are all realized in SQL Server 2008 databases.

Of course, the fact remains that a relational database that is heavily normalized (with extreme reductions in redundancy) may be much more difficult for users to utilize. For example, it is not uncommon to see the typical customer record build from four or more underlying tables in modern relational databases. This structure means that the users have to join the four or more tables together to retrieve that typical customer record. One of the key decisions a DBA makes is determining just how normalized a database needs to be. That question is addressed in Chapter 7.

Weighing the Benefits of Using a Local or Server-Based Database

In addition to the flat-file versus relational database debate, the value of local databases versus server-based databases needs to be considered. Developers must continually decide which to use, and IT support professionals in general must also make this decision frequently. For example, when a vendor tells you that you can run their application with a locally installed database for a single user or with a SQL Server server-based database for several users, you must choose between the two.

Additionally, you may have to choose between using a database intended for local use (i.e., Access) and a database intended for server-based access (i.e., SQL Server) when just a few users need access to the data. Some organizations have successfully implemented Microsoft Access databases for 5 to 10 people and others have faced tremendous difficulties allowing just 2 or 3 users to share a Microsoft Access database. Databases that are designed primarily for local access simply do not scale well, and when multiple users need access to the data, implementing a server-based database system is usually a better multiuser solution.

Understanding Local Databases

A local database, such as Microsoft Access or FileMaker Pro, is completely stored on the user's machine or a network share the user can access. When using local file storage, the application that accesses the database uses a local data access engine to talk to the database file. No network communications occur. When using storage on a network share, the database file is still treated as a local file from the perspective of the database application. The networking functionality in Windows is handled in a different part of the operating system called Kernel mode.

Truly local databases are good from one perspective: they do not consume network bandwidth. If only one user needs access to the data, local databases are often the way to go. The good news is that Microsoft provides a free version of SQL Server for this scenario called SQL Server Express 2008. In addition, Microsoft provides the SQL Server Compact Edition for use on mobile devices such as PDAs. The 2008 version of the Compact Edition adds support for desktop applications running on Windows as well as web applications. The features of these free editions are similar to those of the SQL Server 2008 Standard Edition as long as you are using small databases, and you can use a solution you are familiar with for both your local databases and your server-based databases.

So, why use Microsoft Access or any other single-user database system today? For many organizations, the built-in forms engine in Microsoft Access is enough to justify continued use of the tool, while other IT departments simply don't have any use for it. Of course, you can use Microsoft Access to build forms, queries, and reports against a backend SQL Server database as well. The latter option is probably the best use of Microsoft Access today. And, yes, Microsoft Access can be used as a frontend for local SQL Server 2008 Express databases, although you will probably have to design the database in SQL Server Management Studio Express 2008.

Understanding Server-Based Databases

The benefits of server-based databases can be grouped into three primary categories:

- Data availability
- Data integrity
- Data security

Data Availability

Users need access to data when they need it. Although this may seem obvious, this point is often overlooked when developers build database solutions. Data availability can be considered from two viewpoints:

- Data persistence or existence
- Data access efficiency

From the perspective of data persistence, you need to ensure that your data is stored safely, is backed up properly, and is accessible to the appropriate users. To accomplish this, data that must be accessed by multiple users should be stored in a network location. Of course, Microsoft Access databases can be stored in a network location; however, depending on the database in question, fewer than five users may be able to access that data concurrently. The power of server-based databases really shines in this area in that many server-based databases can handle hundreds or even thousands of users accessing the data concurrently. Local databases simply cannot match this scale.

Although network storage ensures that the data is accessible, the storage engine used by the server-based database will ensure that the data is stored safely. SQL Server uses transaction logs to help in this area. Active transaction logs are used to recover from minor failures, and backed up transaction logs may be used to recover from major mistakes or failures. Either way, the server system establishes solid data storage processes to make sure the data gets into the database properly.

The last element of data existence is backup. The backup features of a server-based database system are usually far more extensive than those of local databases. In fact, most local databases are backed up at the file level only. The entire file is copied to a backup location, and the data is backed up in this simple way. This simple method may seem beneficial, but it is missing an important feature: the ability to back up the database while a user is connected to it. Server-based systems usually provide this feature. For example, SQL Server allows online backups of the data that is in the database. This feature allows backups to occur even in 24x7 shops, and it is essential to modern database systems.

For the data to exist or persist, regardless of the calamity, all three of these factors must be in place:

- The data must be appropriately stored when it is initially entered.
- The data must be backed up to protect against catastrophic failures.
- The data must be available when users want it.

SQL Server provides for all three factors.

The next element of data availability is access efficiency. It's one thing to say that users can get to the data they need. It is quite another to say that they can get to it in a timely fashion. Server-based database systems have much more complex locking algorithms, which allow them to handle many more users more quickly than a local or single-user database system. SQL Server can lock an entire table, a single data page (which may contain one or more rows), or a single row (record). In addition, SQL Server can use different lock types. For example, a shared lock can be acquired for data reads. This type of lock allows other users to read the same data without waiting for the first user's shared lock to release. Of course, exclusive locks can also be used when modifying data to ensure data integrity.

From the perspective of data availability for multiuser applications, there is just no comparison between a proper server-based database system like SQL Server and an intended single-user database system like Microsoft Access. When you need the data to be available to the right users at the right time and multiple users must access the same data, server-based systems win every time.

Data Integrity

For the purposes of this book, *data integrity* is defined in a different way than in most resources. Data integrity means that the data could be what it should be. Notice that the definition reads *could be* what it should be and not that it *is* what it should be. There is a simple reason for this definition: it is impossible to guarantee that all data is what it is supposed to be even with excellent data integrity policies and procedures. Why? Because of the human element.

Most of the time, data is entered by humans and not by machines. As long as the programming is accurate, you can predict with certainty what a machine will do or generate in relation to data output; however, humans are not so predictable.

For example, imagine a company has a website form that a user must fill out in order to retrieve a white paper from the company. In that form, they ask the user to enter his or her email address and they require that the email address field include data that is formatted like an email address (i.e., it has some characters followed by the @ sign, followed by more characters, and then a period and at least two more characters). Will every user enter their valid email address? Of course not! Users will often use completely fabricated addresses to avoid receiving spam from the company.

The company may decide to send a link to the email address in order to download the white paper. Will this force users to enter email addresses where the company can actually reach them? Not really. They could simply use something like 10MinuteMail.com or any of the dozens of free email servers. Yes, users really hate spam that much.

In the end, websites usually settle for something that looks like an email address. They may try emailing the link just to see if it is a valid email address, but there is no way to know if it is the user's real email address. So, the outcome is simple. The email address could be what it should be, but you don't know that it is what it should be.

For some data elements, there may be methods to guarantee the data is accurate. For email addresses and many other similar data elements, you have to accept reality. However, this acquiescence does not mean that you give up on data integrity. It simply means that you employ data integrity measures that are worth the effort and stop there.

In the area of data integrity, there is not a tremendous difference between local database systems and server-based systems. For example, SQL Server offers triggers and Access offers macros. SQL Server offers stored procedures and, again, Access offers macros. SQL Server offers data types (to ensure that numbers are numbers, for example) and so does Access. The line is not as clear-cut here, but you will find that SQL Server 2005 and 2008 triggers and stored procedures offer much more power than Access macros, thanks to the ability to run .NET code. Earlier versions of SQL Server used extended stored procedures, which were basically DLL files called by the SQL Server. This ability to run code developed in advanced languages is one of the separating factors between SQL Server and Microsoft Access in the area of data integrity. In addition, SQL Server has the Transact-SQL language, which is more powerful than the SQL version used in Microsoft Access.

In this context, data integrity is viewed from the perspective of accuracy. Data integrity can also be considered from a security or storage consistency perspective. From a security perspective, data integrity ensures that no malicious changes are made to the data. From a consistency perspective, it ensures that the data is not corrupted under normal data processing or storage operations. In Chapters 17 through 19, you'll learn about SQL Server security solutions. In Chapter 14, you'll learn how to analyze the integrity of the stored data.

Data Security

Information is valuable, and for most organizations this information is stored primarily in two types of locations. The first type of location is a data file such as a spreadsheet, presentation, or typed document. The second type of location is a server-based database. While databases are ultimately stored in files, the access methods for spreadsheets, presentations, and word processor documents differ. Server-based databases provide enhanced security for these databases. Figure 1.4 illustrates the difference between local or single-user database security and server-based database security.

In the example in Figure 1.4, notice that the Access database requires users to have permissions on the database file itself. If a user wants to open an Access database from a network location, the user must have a minimum of Read permissions on the MDB file that holds the database. This presents a security concern in that many network operating systems allow a user with Read access to a file to copy that file to their own computer or removable media such as a USB thumb drive.

FIGURE 1.4   Comparing Microsoft Access and SQL Server database security

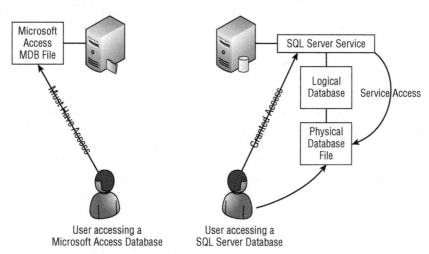

Notice the difference in Figure 1.4 in the represented access to a SQL Server database. The user is given access to talk to the SQL Server service, but the user is given no access to the data files themselves. This configuration means the user can access the data only through provided applications. If a user with Read access wanted to copy all of the data to a thumb drive, he or she would have to export the data. Such behavior could be easily logged and prevented through the use of security features built into SQL Server.

For example, access to data could occur only through stored procedures. With such a configuration, users are not given direct access to the tables. They are given access only to execute stored procedures. The stored procedures execute as a different user than the calling user so they can access the data on the user's behalf. A data access model that relies solely on stored procedures could ultimately make it impossible for nonadministrative users to make a copy of the entire data set. The stored procedures would not only limit the data returned with each execution, but they may further look for nonstandard use and disallow a given account access to the data until further investigation has been done or some acceptable time has passed.

A more passive security method would be the simple logging of any SELECT statements (basic database statements used mostly to read information) that read all of the data in a given table. For example, the system could watch for nonfiltered SELECT statements (statements without a WHERE clause) and log the username, the time of execution, and the actual statement. This log could be sent to security personnel who audit data access. Additionally, the system could disallow more than one nonfiltered SELECT statement in a given window of time against multiple tables.

These actions do not need to be taken for every database. In fact, they should not be taken for most. However, these brief examples illustrate the power derived from an intermediary data access method that could be used if a very sensitive database must be placed online. The SQL Server service acts as the intermediary between the client and the database. As the man-in-the-middle, SQL Server can provide many different data protection mechanisms. In Chapters 17 through 19, you'll learn about the most important security techniques at your disposal.

Important Database Terms

As you learn about programming and SQL Server, you will encounter many terms related to SQL Server implementation and management. It is important that you understand the definitions for these terms as used in this book. Many terms have more than one definition, and it is important that you understand the meaning poured into the words in context. Some of these terms are basic, and some are more complex, but you will see them appearing again and again throughout this book and as you read articles, white papers, and websites related to the work of a DBA. The following section will define these common terms used in the world of databases and specifically SQL Server:

Table/Record set/Relation   In relational database design, a table is not something at which you sit down to eat. Rather, a *table* is a container for data describing a particular entity. Tables are sometimes called record sets, but the term *record set* usually references a result set acquired by a SELECT statement that may include all or a portion of the table data. The formal name for a table is a *relation*. All of the entries in the table are related in that they describe the same kind of thing. For example, a table used to track LCD projectors describes projectors. All entries are related to projectors.

Column/Field/Domain   In order to describe the entity represented in a table, you must store information about that entity's properties or attributes. This information is stored in *columns* or *fields* depending on the database system you're using. SQL Server calls them columns, and Microsoft Access calls them fields, but they are the same thing. For example, the LCD Projectors table would include columns such as Brand, Model, SerialNum, and Lumens. Note that these properties all describe the projector. The term *domain* is used to reference a type of property or attribute that may be used throughout the database. For example, you may consider City, LastName, and eMail to be domains. To ensure domain integrity, you would enforce the same data type, constraints, and data entry rules throughout the database for these domains.

Record/Row/Tuple   A collection of columns describing or documenting a specific instance of an entity is called a *record*. Stated simply, one entry for a specific unit in the LCD

Projectors table is a record. Records are also called rows in many database systems and by many DBAs. The formal term for a record is a *tuple* (usually pronounced /too-pel/, but some argue for /tyoo-pel/).

Index   An *index* is a collection of data and reference information used to locate records more quickly in a table. SQL Server supports two primary index types: clustered and non-clustered. Clustered indexes are similar to a dictionary or telephone book. Nonclustered indexes are similar to those found at the back of a book. For now, it's enough to know that they can be used to increase database performance and that they can equally decrease database performance when used improperly. You will learn about them in detail in Chapter 10, "Indexes and Views."

View   One of the most over-explained objects in databases is the view. Here's the simple definition: a *view* is a stored SQL SELECT statement. That's really all it is. Views are used to make data access simple, to abstract security management, and to improve the performance of some operations. The most common use of views is the simplification of data access.

SQL   *SQL* is the database communications language managed by the ANSI organization. It is a vendor-neutral standard language that is supported at some level by nearly every database product on the planet. SQL Server implements a customized version of SQL called Transact-SQL, or T-SQL for short.

Stored Procedure   When you want to process logical operations at the server instead of the client, stored procedures can be used. A *stored procedure* is either a collection of T-SQL statements or a compiled .NET stored procedure in SQL Server 2008. Earlier versions of SQL Server supported and recommended extended stored procedures, which were really just DLLs called by the SQL Server. Stored procedures are used to centralize business rules or logic, to abstract security management, or to improve performance. Other reasons exist, but these are the big three motivators.

Trigger   A trigger is like a dynamic stored procedure. A *trigger* is a group of T-SQL statements that is executed automatically when specified events occur. For example, you may want to launch a special procedure anytime someone attempts to execute a DROP TABLE (delete a table) statement. The trigger could either back up the table before deleting it or simply refuse to delete the table.

Concurrence   *Concurrence* is defined as acting together. In the database world, a system either supports multiple concurrent users or it does not. *Concurrency* is a single word that says a database system supports multiple users reading and writing data without the loss of data integrity.

DBA   A *DBA* is a database administrator. A DBA is the person who installs the routers and switches, implements the network operating system, builds the user databases, configures the client computers, programs the telephone system, troubleshoots production and security problems, and, oh yeah, works with databases on occasion. But seriously, you live in a new world of IT. Today, most IT professionals must wear multiple hats. This reality means that DBAs usually have to know about the database server service, the server operating system, and even a bit about the network infrastructure across which users communicate with the database system. It's a brave new world.

Remember, these are the basic terms that will appear throughout your experiences with databases, regardless of the database system with which you are working. Be sure you know what these terms mean. You'll learn about many more database terms as you read the rest of this book.

Database Servers and Applications

Now that you've learned the fundamental concepts of a database, it's time to investigate server-side databases and database applications in a bit more detail. Let's immediately clear up one thing:

The database is not the database server and the database server is not the database.

It's not uncommon for a DBA to say, "I have to restart the SQL Server database." What he really means is that he needs to restart the SQL Server service, which manages access to the database. The database is separate from the database management system. SQL Server is the database management system. Databases may be detached from one SQL Server instance and then attached to another. In fact, you can attach Excel spreadsheets, Access databases, and virtually any data source that you can connect to with ODBC (open database connectivity) to a SQL Server as a linked server object. Once the link is made, the SQL Server service can manage access to that data source (via the ODBC or other connection type) for your users. ODBC is a standard database access method used by many database management systems.

To help you better understand the relationship that applications have with a database server, the following section will explain the three kinds of database applications:

- Localized
- Client/server (single tier)
- N-tier (multiple client/server relationships)

Database Application Types

The three primary kinds of applications are localized, client/server, and n-tier applications. Localized applications will not be covered in detail here because our primary focus is on running SQL "Servers" and not SQL Server on the clients. However, you should know that a localized application usually talks to a local install of SQL Server using a protocol called shared memory. The name says it all: the local application talks to the local SQL Server installation (usually SQL Server Express) without using the network interface card.

Client/Server (Single Tier)

Client/server implementations, also called single tier, involve a client application communicating directly with the database in most cases. An example of a client/server application is a Microsoft Access frontend that communicates with a SQL Server 2008 backend database. The SQL Server database is the server, and Microsoft Access is the client. Technically, an Excel data import from a SQL Server is a client/server application. Figure 1.5 shows an example of this model.

FIGURE 1.5   A simple implementation of client/server technology with a client accessing a single server directly

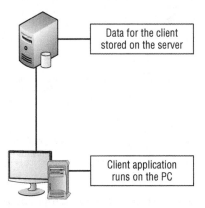

Data for the client stored on the server

Client application runs on the PC

Figure 1.5 shows an application communicating with a SQL Server. Notice that the user interacts with the application as if everything is installed on her local machine. In fact, as long as the network is working and the database server is available, the user will usually feel as if the data is indeed in her computer. Of course, as you add more users—without increasing servers or the single server's capacity—she will likely notice a drop in performance; however, this drop should be minimal as long as the database server is well maintained and upgraded as needed.

N-Tier (Multiple Client/Server Relationships)

An n-tier application is an application that requires multiple levels (tiers) of communication in order to accomplish meaningful work. For example, a SharePoint server farm that includes one server for the database and another server for the website is an n-tier application or, more specifically in this case, a two-tier application. The user communicates with the web server (tier one) and the web server communicates with the database on the user's behalf (tier two). The n in n-tier is simply replaced with the number of links in the communication chain.

Figure 1.6 shows the SharePoint implementation visually. You can see the links or tiers in the application. Such an implementation provides several benefits. First, developers can change the database without necessarily rewriting all of the code at the web server. This benefit assumes that a standard data access method was used between the web server and the database. Second, the developers can completely change the look and feel of the application without changing any of the data. In 3-, 4-, and more-tier implementations, the solution is even more componentized and the result is greater flexibility in the solution over time.

FIGURE 1.6   An n-tier application using a SharePoint server to access a backend database server

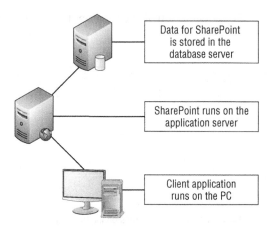

Finally, n-tier applications are easier to scale. Single-tier applications are notoriously difficult to scale. Everything is resting on a single server. If the performance of the database becomes too slow, you are very limited in what you can do. With an n-tier application, you can distribute the data across several servers on the backend and absolutely nothing changes from the users' perspectives. No wonder developers love to use this model. It's not without its faults, but it certainly has its benefits.

SQL Server's Role

You are finally ready to explore how SQL Server 2008 fits into all of this discussion of database technologies. To help you understand the roles SQL Server 2008 can play in your organization, this section will begin by explaining the major new features in the product. These new features are explored from two perspectives. First, the new features since SQL Server 2005 are covered. If you're already familiar with SQL Server 2005 in some detail, this section may be all you need. Next, the new features that SQL Server 2005 introduced and that, of course, are still in SQL Server 2008, will be discussed. This latter coverage is very important. Many organizations are moving directly from SQL Server 2000 and skipping SQL Server 2005 altogether. That decision is certainly acceptable as long as you can ensure compatibility with your applications. But compatibility was also an important consideration for those who upgraded from SQL Server 7.0 or 2000 to SQL Server 2005 a few years ago.

Finally, the roles SQL Server can play based on these new features will be discussed. You'll learn about enterprise databases, departmental databases, reporting servers, ETL servers, analysis servers, and more. So let's jump into these exciting new features.

New Features Since SQL Server 2005

If you are upgrading from SQL Server 2005 to SQL Server 2008, the features covered in this section will be of great interest to you. The features are either brand new or greatly enhanced. In order to make the coverage simpler, the features are separated into two categories: management features and development. This book is primarily focused on management or administration of SQL Server 2008, so more information about the management enhancement features is provided; however, it is practically impossible to manage a SQL Server without doing some development or without understanding the components, languages, and processes used by developers. For this reason, the development features will be covered here and throughout the rest of the book, although less exhaustively.

All of the features mentioned here will be discussed in more detail in later chapters. The intent here is to help you understand the roles SQL Server 2008 can play in an organization based on the enterprise-class feature set it provides. The features listed here will indeed be covered in more detail, but it doesn't stop there. Many other new features will be introduced as you read through the book. For example, the new backup compression ability will be featured. Where has this feature been for 15 years?

New Management Features

The management features in SQL Server 2008 are among the most talked-about new features. From policy-based management to the Resource Governor, SQL Server 2008 has definitely provided the major capabilities needed for large multiserver enterprise implementations. These features include:

- Policy-based management
- Configuration servers
- The Resource Governor
- Transparent data encryption
- Performance data collectors

Policy-Based Management

Policy-based management (PBM) allows for the configuration of SQL Server services through policies. This new functionality means that DBAs can configure pools of SQL Servers together rather than having to configure each server individually. Of course, PBM is most useful for environments with 10 or more servers, but it may provide benefits to smaller organizations as well.

To use PBM, policies are grouped into facets that are configured as conditions and applied to targets. For example, the Surface Area facet can be used to disable the `xp_cmdshell` extended system stored procedure, and then this policy can be applied to every server or a selection of servers. A *policy,* in the PBM world, is defined as a condition enforced on one or more targets.

Configuration Servers

Configuration servers are special SQL Servers that are used to centrally configure other servers. Any SQL Server 2008 instance can be converted to a configuration server. Once the configuration server is implemented, two primary tasks can be performed: centralized management of PBM and multiserver queries. The centralized management of PBM with a configurations server causes PBM to provide functionality similar to group policies in a Windows domain. From one central server, you can configure all of your SQL Servers based on configuration groups.

The multiserver query feature is exceptional. With this feature, you can execute a query from the configuration server to be run against all of the servers in a configuration group. For example, if you need to create a table in a database that has been replicated or simply duplicated to seven different servers, a configuration server would allow you to execute the code to create that table on all seven servers at the same time. Figure 1.7 illustrates the concept of the multiserver query.

FIGURE 1.7   An example of multiserver queries with the user querying one server that queries three other servers in turn

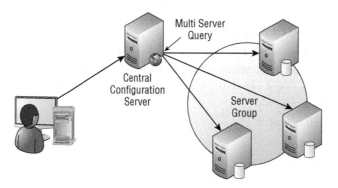

The Resource Governor

The new Resource Governor is used to impose limits on workloads based on the user requesting the work, the application requesting the work, or the database against which the work is performed. Workloads can be assigned priorities so that, for example, a single user's actions do not prevent other users from completing necessary work. With previous versions of SQL Server, DBAs could use the Windows System Resource Manager (WSRM) on Enterprise Editions of Windows Server to perform similar operations. Now, the feature is built into SQL Server and has more granular control over the resources in relation to SQL Server.

Transparent Data Encryption

SQL Server 2005 first introduced encryption into the SQL Server Database Engine. The only problem was that existing applications could not use it because the application had to call both the encrypting and decrypting routines. SQL Server 2008 takes this to the next level with transparent data encryption (TDE). To use TDE, you must still generate the appropriate encryption keys and enable encryption for the database; however, these steps are taken at the server by the DBA, and the developers will not have to change anything in their applications. The encryption and decryption happens automatically, and the data is accessed in the same way as unencrypted data.

The TDE feature provides storage encryption. The data is decrypted by the SQL Server and then transferred to the client. Do not confuse this with transit encryption or communications encryption. In order to encrypt the communications between the SQL Server and the client, you will still usually need to implement IPSec or a VPN protocol.

Performance Data Collectors

The next major management feature is the performance data collectors. *Data collectors* are simply the tools used to collect performance information about your server. Historical performance data can be automatically stored in a management data warehouse, allowing the DBA to review historical performance data at any time. The process of collecting the data is as follows:

1. SQL Server Agent schedules and launches the Data Collector component.

2. The Data Collector component launches the needed SSIS package.

3. The SSIS package collects the performance data and stores it in the management data warehouse.

As you can see, Microsoft has taken advantage of existing technologies from earlier versions of SQL Server to build the Data Collector engine. You could have accomplished something similar in earlier versions of SQL Server by collecting performance data using the System Monitor and configuring it to automatically store the data in a SQL Server table; however, the built-in tools to accomplish this are much more integrated in SQL Server 2008.

New Development Features

The development enhancements in SQL Server 2008 are also important. As a DBA, you may never write a single line of code that gets compiled into an application or you may be a "programming DBA." Many times programmers/developers must manage their own SQL Servers. However, even if you do not write the code, it is useful to understand its basic structure so that you can better troubleshoot problems in SQL Server-based applications. The development features new to SQL Server 2008 are included here.

Developer Tool Improvements

The SQL Server 2008 Query Editor, which is still built into the SQL Server Management Studio, now supports IntelliSense capabilities. This means that the Query Editor can complete entire words for you representing functions, keywords, variables, and more. If you find yourself testing scripts in the Query Editor, this feature will prove priceless. Additionally, an error list feature similar to that in Visual Studio has been incorporated into the Query Editor. When the editor detects errors, they will appear (see Figure 1.8) and you can click on the instance to see the error and find help to repair it.

FIGURE 1.8   Errors listed in the Error List dialog

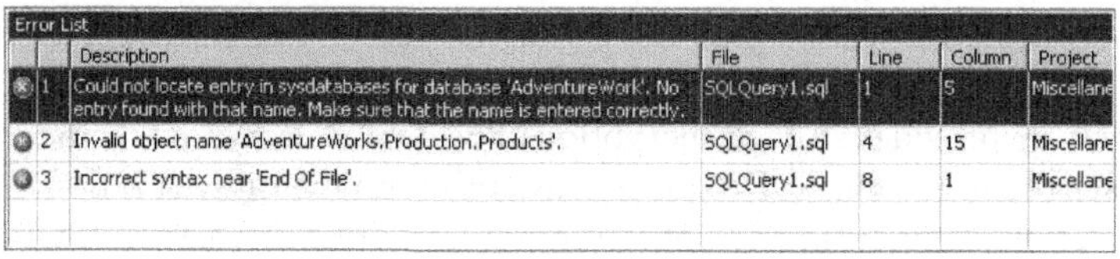

	Description	File	Line	Column	Project
1	Could not locate entry in sysdatabases for database 'AdventureWork'. No entry found with that name. Make sure that the name is entered correctly.	SQLQuery1.sql	1	5	Miscellane
2	Invalid object name 'AdventureWorks.Production.Products'.	SQLQuery1.sql	4	15	Miscellane
3	Incorrect syntax near 'End Of File'.	SQLQuery1.sql	8	1	Miscellane

Change Data Capture

Developers have been writing triggers and stored procedures for years in order to capture data changes. When a user modifies a record, for example, the trigger fires and saves to a History table a copy of what the data looked like before the modification. SQL Server 2008 Enterprise and Developer editions now support a feature called Change Data Capture. It is easily enabled for the entire database or a specific set of tables. Once enabled, historical states of the data can be queried.

Data Type Changes

SQL Server 2008 provides several data type enhancements and changes. The date and time data types have been upgraded with a new `datetime2` data type. The `datetime2` data type supports a broader range of dates and greater accuracy. The new `hierarchyid` data type is used to reference the position of items in a hierarchy, such as an employee's position in an organizational chart. Finally, the new `filestream` data type allows data to be stored on the NTFS files system outside of the database data files but managed by SQL Server like other data types.

New Report Designer

SQL Server 2005 introduced the Report Builder, but SQL Server 2008 takes this to the next level with the Report Designer. The Report Designer takes on the look and feel of Microsoft Office 2007, including the Ribbon bar. Charting has also been enhanced, and a new *tablix* data region that looks oddly similar to a Pivot table, although that name never seems to appear in Microsoft's documentation related to the tablix.

Sparse Columns

When Windows 2000 was released in 1999, Microsoft implemented sparse files in the NTFS file system. These files consumed 0 literal bytes on the drive, although they appeared to consume from 1 byte to terabytes of space. Now, sparse columns have been added to the feature set of SQL Server 2008. Sparse columns are most useful for columns that may have excessive records with NULL values. When the value is NULL, the column will consume 0 bytes in the data pages. Sparse columns can help you fit a few more bytes of data into that 8,060 byte limit imposed by SQL Server.

LINQ to SQL Provider

Microsoft developed the Language Integrated Query (LINQ) feature for .NET development some time ago; however, there was no direct support for it in SQL Server 2005 and earlier. SQL Server 2008 implements a LINQ to SQL provider, which means that developers can write queries in standard .NET code (instead of embedded SQL variables), and the SQL Server will take care of translating the request into T-SQL that the server can process.

New Features Since SQL Server 2000

If you are upgrading from SQL Server 2000 to SQL Server 2008, you will get all of the new features covered in the previous section, but you will also acquire all of the features that were first introduced in SQL Server 2005. Moving from SQL Server 2005 to SQL Server 2008 is like climbing a three- or four-rung stepladder; significant changes have occurred, but they are not massive. However, moving from SQL Server 2000 to 2008 is like climbing 35 to 40 rungs on a ladder. As you will see, SQL Server 2005 introduced drastically different administration tools, an entirely new way of thinking about custom stored procedures, and the ability to mirror databases, just to name a few changes. Like SQL Server 2008's features, the features can be divided into management and development enhancements.

New Management Features in SQL Server 2005

The new management features in SQL Server 2005 were many. This section focuses on a few key features, including:

- New management tools
- Database Mail
- Dedicated administrator connection
- SQL Server Integration Services
- Database snapshots
- Database mirroring
- Failover clustering for Analysis Services
- Online indexing
- Security enhancements
- Reporting services

New Management Tools

The new management tools introduced in SQL Server 2005 and enhanced in SQL Server 2008 were very welcome additions. The tools did not simply upgrade what was available in SQL Server 2000; they completely replaced them. The Enterprise Manager (shown in Figure 1.9) and Query Analyzer (shown in Figure 1.10) were both replaced with the SQL Server Management Studio (SSMS).

FIGURE 1.9 The SQL Server 2000 Enterprise Manager used in earlier versions of SQL Server

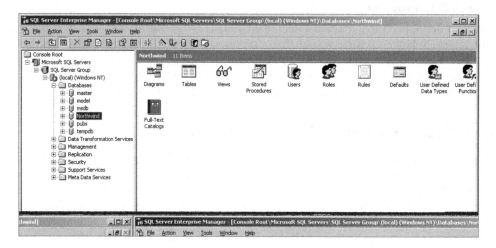

FIGURE 1.10 The Query Analyzer from SQL Server 2000

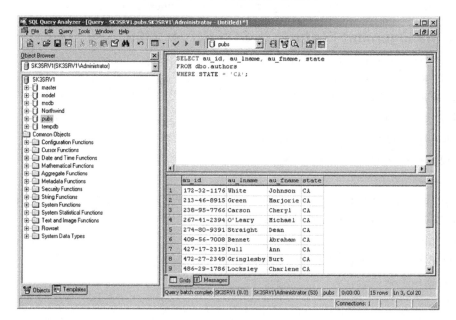

SSMS, as depicted in Figure 1.11, incorporates a query window into the management environment. Now, instead of switching between the Enterprise Manager and the Query Analyzer during testing and optimization efforts, you can use one tool to get the job done.

FIGURE 1.11   The new built-in Query Editor in SSMS

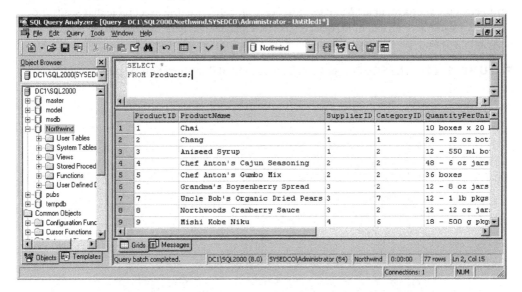

Of course, everything is not perfect in the new management tools—at least for those of us who used the earlier tools extensively. One example is the Object Browser in the Query Analyzer that shipped with SQL Server 2000. The Object Browser allowed you to easily browse through T-SQL functions to locate the one you needed by category. SSMS does not support this same Object Browser; however, it does offer Dynamic Help, but this feature requires that you remember the function name. You can always create a Books Online (the SQL Server help system) favorite link to the T-SQL functions page, but you might miss the Object Browser just the same.

Database Mail

In versions of SQL Server before SQL Server 2005, sending mail from the server was an arduous task. Oddly, you had to install Outlook on the server (although standard documentation suggested only the need to install "a MAPI client"). Not because SQL Server used Outlook to send email, but because you had to install Outlook to get a needed Control Panel applet for the configuration of SMTP accounts. By putting Outlook on the server, you were creating yet one more component to update and secure. The old way can be summarized by saying it was kludged at best.

SQL Server 2005 solved the problem by introducing Database Mail. Database Mail provides direct sending of SMTP mail messages. This component can be used to send email from your jobs or applications. The actual sending component runs outside of the memory space of SQL Server, and it simply checks in with the SQL Server periodically to see if messages are waiting to be sent. The Service Broker component is used to queue the mail messages. Configuring Database Mail is as simple as stepping through a wizard (see Figure 1.12) and entering the parameters for your available SMTP servers. For your reference, the executable that sends the mail is `DatabaseMail90.exe` in SQL Server 2005. The new Database Mail solution is both more efficient and less annoying than the older SQL Mail alternative.

FIGURE 1.12   The SQL Server 2005 Database Mail Configuration Wizard

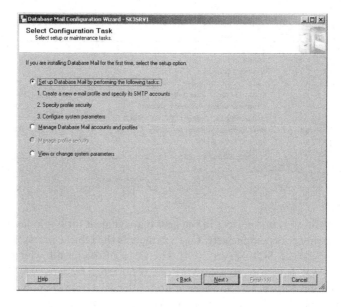

Dedicated Administrator Connection

The dedicated administrator connection (DAC) allows you to connect to a SQL Server system that is not responding to normal connections. The DAC is available through the new SQLCMD command-prompt tool and can only be initiated by the members of the sysadmin server role. Once connected, you can execute standard diagnostic commands, such as basic DBCC commands and potentially data-query commands.

SQL Server listens for DAC connections on a different TCP port than that which is used for normal connections. The default instance of SQL Server usually listens on TCP port 1433, but the DAC listens on TCP port 1434 by default.

SQL Server Integration Services

Data Transformation Services (DTS) provided you with an extraction, transformation, and loading (ETL) tool in SQL Server 2000. The tool was simple and to the point. This simplicity, however, also meant that it lacked the power for more advanced ETL procedures. With

SQL Server Integration Services (SSIS), you have one of the most powerful ETL toolsets in existence and certainly one of the best bundled ETL toolsets available with any database management system. With SSIS, you can do everything you did in DTS (you can even run an old DTS package if necessary) and a whole lot more. Figure 1.13 shows the SSIS interface.

FIGURE 1.13   SQL Server Integration Services showing a sample project

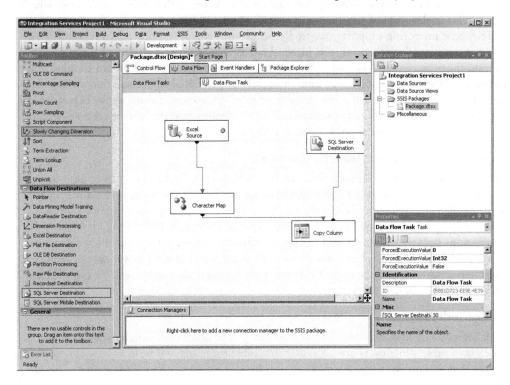

Database Snapshots

Database *snapshots* allow you to capture a point-in-time view of your entire database. The snapshots are created using sparse files on NTFS volumes, so they are created very quickly. In fact, the initial snapshot file contains 0 bytes of actual data. Before information changes in the database, the old information is copied into the snapshot file. This implementation allows several snapshots to exist at the same time without a tremendous burden on the server. Snapshots are useful for several practical functions including:

- Viewing and reporting on data as it existed at a point in the past
- Selectively restoring data to a specific point in time, such as restoring the Customers table to the state it was in before a user accidentally set everyone's email address to the same value
- Reverting the entire database to the state in the snapshot

Database Mirroring

If you want to configure a warm or hot standby server, database mirroring is a potential solution. Standby servers are covered in detail in Chapter 21, "Database Mirrors and Snapshots." Database mirroring allows you to mirror one database or several databases from one SQL Server onto another. The primary server will receive all changes, and those changes are then immediately transferred to the mirror database server transactionally (based on changes and not simply accesses). The latency is very low with database mirroring, which means that in the event of a failure very little data should be lost.

Database mirroring supports two implementations: warm standby and hot standby. In warm standby implementations, the mirror database cannot automatically be promoted to become the primary database. Some DBA intervention will be required. In hot standby implementations, the mirror database can automatically be promoted to become the primary database. However, to implement a hot standby mirroring solution, a third server is required. The third server is known as the *witness server*. It ensures that the mirror server does not promote itself unless the primary server is really down.

Failover Clustering for Analysis Services

Failover clustering provides fault tolerance for SQL Server. Earlier versions of SQL Server supported failover clustering for the database ending, but it was not supported for the other services. With the release of SQL Server 2005, failover clustering was supported for SQL Server Analysis Services (SSAS) as well. SSAS is used for data warehousing, data analysis, and various data management and storage operations. Failover clustering allows one server to act as the primary server and another server to automatically take over should the primary server fail. In addition to SSAS, failover clustering is also supported for Notification Services and Replication servers.

Online Indexing

SQL Server 2005 first introduced online indexing. The concept is simple: you can create an index on a table while users are accessing that table for reads and writes. This new feature means that you do not have to wait for a non-busy window to create indexes. In previous versions of SQL Server, it was common to schedule index creation during down times, such as 12 A.M. to 5 A.M. The only problem was that it was very difficult to find an inactive time window in 24x7 shops.

Consultants often spend a large portion of their consulting time optimizing existing databases. One key optimization strategy is the creation of indexes (and the deletion of unneeded indexes). The ability to create indexes on the fly without the need for down time is priceless. Not just to consultants, but to their clients as well. They no longer have to carefully schedule consulting windows or prepare a mirror server that matches their production server for performance testing. A performance analysis can usually be scheduled to run on the server while users are accessing the data, and then that information can be analyzed offline. Next, proper indexes can be created, and the performance analysis can be run again to determine if the desired outcome was accomplished. You'll learn all about this process in Chapter 14, "Performance Monitoring and Tuning."

Security Enhancements

Many security enhancements were introduced in SQL Server 2005, including:

Storage Encryption   Data can be encrypted in the database. SQL Server 2005 requires that the application be aware of the encryption and implement code to both encrypt and decrypt the data. Storage encryption helps protect your data if the backup media is stolen or an attacker otherwise steals the entire database file.

Password Policies for SQL Logins   SQL logins have been a negative issue for SQL Server for years. The authentication process is not the most secure, and it is hampered even more by the use of weak passwords. Password policy association allows you to require that users' passwords meet the policy requirements established in the Windows domain or on the local server. Users can be required to select passwords greater than a specified length and requiring complexity in character types.

Separated Owners and Schemas   Before SQL Server 2005, if you made a user the owner of a table, that table was placed in the user's schema. You would end up with table names such as fred.sales and jose.marketing. Needless to say, this structure was less than ideal. Because of this functionality, most DBAs chose to use the dbo schema for everything and, therefore, ensured that the dbo owned everything. With the release of SQL Server 2005, schemas became useable—in a practical way—for the first time. A user can own a table, and that table can remain in the assigned schema.

Surface Area Configuration Tool   The Surface Area Configuration tool is used to lock down a SQL Server installation. The tool allows you to control the SQL Server services and enable or disable features as needed. Figure 1.14 shows the Surface Area Configuration for Features interface.

FIGURE 1.14   The Surface Area Configuration for Features dialog box

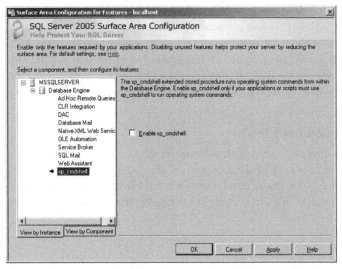

Reporting Services

Reporting Services was first introduced as an add-on for SQL Server 2000. The product did not come on the SQL Server 2000 distribution CDs, but was an after-the-fact download or could be purchased on a CD. As the name implies, Reporting Services provides reporting features for your database deployments. Be careful not to be fooled by the fact that Reporting Services "comes with" SQL Server 2005 and later. You must license the product separately from your SQL Server deployment. Each Reporting Services server requires SQL Server licenses—either per processor or a server license plus client access license (CAL) for each user who accesses the reports.

What's new in SQL Server 2005's implementation of Reporting Services (other than the fact that it comes on the CD or DVD now)? First, a new reporting tool is included. The Report Builder application provides simplified report creation for users. Because the Report Builder uses concepts familiar to those who use Microsoft Office 2003 and earlier, the learning curve is reduced. You can format, preview, print, and publish reports from the Report Builder.

New Development Features in SQL Server 2005

The enhancements for those developing applications for SQL Server were also important in the release of SQL Server 2005. They are briefly covered here and will be covered in the appropriate locations throughout the book as well.

.NET Integration

The integration of .NET and CLR capabilities into SQL Server means that developers can code stored procedures, triggers, and functions in the many modern languages supported by .NET. Additionally, the integration of .NET into the memory space of SQL Server improves performance and provides improved security.

Transact-SQL Changes

Every version of SQL Server has introduced changes to the T-SQL language. Sometimes these changes add support for new commands and capabilities, and sometimes they remove support for older commands that are no longer needed or for which Microsoft simply chose to end support. SQL Server 2005 makes improvements in the area of error handling, support for new database engine features (such as database snapshots), and recursive query capabilities.

Enhanced Development Tools

The development tools that ship with SQL Server 2005 are a huge leap over what was available in SQL Server 2000. Most developers used third-party tools or extra Microsoft tools to get the job done. Now, many developers find that the tools built into SQL Server 2005 provide sufficient capabilities to accomplish their objectives. The new Business Intelligence

Development Studio (BIDS) is a key component among these development tools. Figure 1.13 on page 29 shows the BIDS environment while developing an SSIS solution.

HTTP Endpoints

SOAP is a communications protocol used to allow applications to interact based on XML data. If you wanted to implement an HTTP endpoint for use with SOAP development in SQL Server 2000, you had to install Internet Information Services (IIS) on the SQL Server. SQL Server 2005 introduces HTTP endpoints. These endpoints can be created without requiring IIS on the server, and they are more secure by default. For example, you can control which stored procedures are permitted for execution through the endpoint.

XML Support Improvements

The XML support in SQL Server 2000 was minimal. You could store XML data in columns with a text data type, but your application had to retrieve the data as text and then parse it as XML. No support existed for direct querying of the XML data within the SQL Server. However, you were able to return SELECT statement results sets as XML using the FOR XML clause. SQL Server 2005 takes XML support to the next level. You can store the data in an XML data-typed column, and you can use the XQuery subset of the SQL/T-SQL language in order to retrieve only the XML values you require. Chapter 9, "Data Types and Table Types," will cover the XML data type in more detail.

Service Broker

You're probably used to databases working in a synchronous manner. The client submits a request to the SQL Server and waits for the server to respond. The server receives the request from the client and processes it as quickly as the current workload allows and then responds to the client. This traditional database communications model does not scale well when a customer submits an order at a website and that order must update an inventory system, a shipment system, a billing system, and a website tracking system. Service Broker provides asynchronous communications without the need for building the entire core communications engine. It provides queuing, queue processing, and other services that allow a more scalable application.

Notification Services

If you've used SQL Server for any amount of time, you've probably used operators and had notifications sent to you when a backup completes or when a job fails. Notification Services provides this concept to your users. For example, Notification Services provides the framework to allow a sales representative to subscribe to a change in pricing. Imagine a customer who is ready to buy 50,000 units of item number 2043978 as soon as the price drops below $0.70 per unit. The salesperson can configure a notification so that she is notified immediately when the price drop takes place.

Core Features of SQL Server

In addition to the special features introduced with SQL Server 2005 and 2008, core features have existed in the product going all the way back to SQL Server 6.5 and earlier. These important features include:

Support for Concurrent Users   Support for concurrent users is provided using worker threads and connections. Each connection receives its own process ID and can be managed individually (for example, a single connection can be killed). The number of concurrent users that can be supported will be determined by the resources available in the server—for example, as memory, processors, network cards, and hard drives.

Transactional Processing   Transactional processing ensures that the database maintains consistency. For example, in a banking application, you would not want to allow a transfer from savings to checking to take place in such a way that the money is removed from savings but doesn't make it into checking. Transactional processing ensures that the entire transaction is successful or none of the transaction components are allowed. Transactions can be implicit or explicit, and all changes are treated as transactions.

Large Database Support   SQL Servers support large databases. SQL Server 2000 allowed database sizes as large as 1,048,516 terabytes, which is equivalent to 1 exabyte in size, which is very large. Of course, finding hardware that can handle a database that size is a different story. Interestingly, according to Microsoft's documentation, the maximum allowed database size was reduced in SQL Server 2005 and 2008 to 524,272 terabytes. This size constraint is still very large at 524 petabytes, so it will not likely be a problem soon. Very few databases exceed 5 terabytes in size today.

Advanced Storage Mechanisms   The storage mechanisms provided by SQL Server allow databases to be stored in single files or multiple files. The database can be spread across multiple files located on multiple storage volumes. By using filegroups, the DBA can control on which file which tables will be placed. The storage mechanisms are far more advanced than those available in a simple database system such as Microsoft Access.

Large Object Support   Large objects, up to 2GB, can be stored in SQL Server databases. Depending on the application, it may be better to store the large objects (LOBs) outside of the database and simply reference them in the database; however, internal storage is supported. You can store large amounts of text (up to 2GB) in the text data type. You can store any binary data in the image data type, which also allows up to 2GB of data to be stored in a single record.

Replication   Sometimes you need to distribute your data to multiple locations. You may need to provide localized reporting servers at branch offices, or you may need to aggregate new data from several remote offices into a central reporting server. Whatever the motivation behind data distribution, SQL Server offers replication as a solution. SQL Server 6.5 supported basic replication features. With each version since then, more capabilities have been added. For example, SQL Server 2005 added support for replication over the HTTP protocol and SQL Server 2008 adds a new graphical tool for creating peer-to-peer replication maps and an enhanced version of the Replication Monitor tool.

These core features, and more, have been with SQL Server for well over 10 years, and they continue to evolve and improve. They have a tremendous impact on the roles that SQL Server can play within your organization and can help you decide between it and other database systems—particularly single-user database systems.

 Many people have been waiting for SQL Server 2008 to upgrade their SQL Server 2000 installations. If you're one of those people, don't forget about the features that were deprecated in SQL Server 2005; they may be gone now in SQL Server 2008. To locate such features, search for *SQL Server 2005 deprecated features* in your favorite search engine. Several sites provide information about these removed features.

SQL Server Roles

Now that you've explored the many features and capabilities of databases in general and SQL Server specifically, let's quickly explore the roles that SQL Servers can play in your organization. This section will cover the following roles:

- Enterprise database servers
- Departmental database servers
- Web database servers
- Reporting servers
- ETL servers
- Analysis and decision support servers
- Intermediary servers
- Standby servers
- Local databases

This list may be longer than you expected, but believe it or not it's not exhaustive. More roles exist, but these are the most common roles played by SQL Servers.

Enterprise Database Servers

Enterprise database servers provide data access to the entire organization. These servers usually house enterprise resource planning (ERP) applications, customer resource management (CRM) applications, and other applications that are accessed by individuals from practically every department in the organization. The databases tend to be very large and must usually be distributed across multiple servers.

As an example, consider a SharePoint implementation that is used as a company portal. Each department may have a section on the SharePoint server, but the portal is there for the entire company. With an implementation this large, the SharePoint installation would most likely be a farm-based installation with one or more backend SQL Servers. This implementation qualifies as an enterprise database server implementation.

Common SQL Server features and concepts used on enterprise database servers include:

- Failover clustering

- Log shipping or database mirroring

- 64-bit implementations for increased memory support

- Replication

- Encryption

- Third-party backup software

- ETL packages

- Reporting Services

- Windows domain membership

- RAID or SAN data storage

Departmental Database Servers

Many times an application is needed only for a single department. For example, the engineering group may need a database server for the management of their drawings or the marketing group may need a database server to track their marketing efforts. While this information could be stored in an enterprise server, if the server will be heavily used by the department, it may be more efficient to use a dedicated server. The hardware may be identical to that which is commonly implemented for enterprise servers. The only difference is usually the number of users who access the server.

Departmental servers tend to utilize features and concepts such as:

- Built-in backup software

- Log shipping or database mirroring

- Reporting Services

- Windows domain membership

- RAID data storage

Web Database Servers

Web database servers are used to provide data for websites. The data is frequently replicated or otherwise merged into the web database server from other internal servers. Web database servers are usually less powerful than enterprise servers, with the obvious exception of web-based companies such as eBay or Amazon.com.

Web database servers tend to utilize features and concepts such as:

- Built-in backup software
- Reporting Services
- RAID data storage
- Explicitly no Windows domain membership

Reporting Servers

Dedicated reporting servers are used to gather report information from enterprise, departmental, and other database servers. A dedicated reporting server usually houses the reporting databases locally, but accesses all other data from remote database servers.

Reporting servers tend to utilize features and concepts such as:

- Built-in backup software
- Reporting Services
- Raid data storage
- Windows domain membership

ETL Servers

Dedicated ETL servers are used to perform nightly or periodic data moves, data transformations, and even data destruction. Due to licensing costs, dedicated ETL servers are usually found only on very large scale deployments. Many smaller deployments simply use SSIS on existing database servers.

Analysis and Decision Support Servers

Analysis, or decision support, servers are used by business analysts to determine the state of operations within an organization. Analysis servers may run Microsoft's Analysis Services or they may run third-party tools as well. These servers get their data from other servers in the environment. Depending on the size of deployment, the transaction processing servers may send data to a warehouse from which the analysis servers retrieve it or the data may be housed entirely within the analysis server.

Intermediary Servers

Intermediary servers are becoming more common. These servers exist between two or more servers. An example of an intermediary server is a replication distributor server. The distributor sits between the publisher and the subscriber. The subscriber pulls information from the distributor that was first pulled by the distributor from the publisher. A model that deploys intermediary servers can often scale to be much larger than a single-server model.

Standby Servers

Standby servers include log-shipping receiver servers, database mirror servers, and any server that is not actively used unless the primary server fails. Standby servers fall into three primary categories: cold standby, warm standby, and hot standby. These standby solutions are categorized by two factors.

The first factor is the latency of updates. A hot standby server receives updates at the same time as (or within seconds of) the primary server. A warm standby server may receive updates within minutes, and a cold standby server may receive updates only every few hours.

The second factor is the amount of time it takes to bring the standby server online. A hot standby server comes online immediately when the primary server fails. A cold standby server will never come online without manual intervention. A warm standby server may require manual intervention or it may simply delay before coming online.

Local Databases

The final role that SQL Server plays is the local database role. Many assume that only SQL Server Express Edition is used as a local database; however, due to the size constraints of SQL Server Express (the maximum database size is 4GB), some applications require SQL Server Standard Edition to be installed for a local database. The good news is that no client access licenses will be required; the bad news is that there is some expense, which is the price of the SQL Server Express Edition.

 Real World Scenario

Enterprise Databases and 64-Bit Computing

When choosing the role of your SQL Server implementation, remember to also choose the proper edition. I was working with an organization that used SQL Server for a very large database application. Both performance and stability problems were prevalent, and we had to find a solution. I went through the normal performance and configuration analysis procedures and found no significant changes that could be made with the existing hardware.

In the end, we decided to upgrade the system to a 64-bit server running Windows Server 2003 Enterprise Edition 64-bit. We also installed the 64-bit version of SQL Server 2005. What do you think happened? If you guessed that both the performance problems and the stability problems disappeared, you are correct. The culprit was, as it often is, memory—and the 64-bit version provided us with much more memory to utilize. Don't forget this when considering your implementation.

At the same time, it is important to ensure that your applications will run on a 64-bit installation of SQL Server. Many application vendors still develop extended stored procedures, which are basically DLL files called by the SQL Server. If these DLLs are provided only in 32-bit versions, they may or may not work with a 64-bit edition of SLQ Server. Yes, there is much involved, but selecting the right edition and bit level is very important. Chapter 2, "Installing SQL Server 2008," explores this choice in even more detail.

Summary

The goal of this chapter was to lay a solid foundation on which to build the information contained in the rest of this book. You learned about the role played by databases in general and the specific roles that Microsoft recommends for SQL Server. You also learned the definitions of several important terms and concepts and found out what features were introduced in SQL Server 2005 and 2008. Now you're ready to move on to the next chapter and begin installing and working with SQL Server.

Chapter Essentials

Information Technology's Many Components   Database servers make up one part of Information Technology (IT); however, they are a very important part. After all, they are the permanent locations where most of our data is stored.

Databases' Many Flavors   Both server-based and local databases are common. Server-based databases provide advanced features such as support for concurrent users, improved security, and improved availability.

SQL Server's Evolution   Over the years the SQL Server product line has evolved and matured into a very stable and feature-rich database solution. SQL Server 2005 was a big upgrade over SQL Server 2000, and SQL Server 2008 takes the product to even greater heights.

SQL Server's Many Roles   From enterprise servers to local databases, the SQL Server product can be utilized throughout an organization. Choosing the appropriate edition for the intended role is essential for performance and stability.

Chapter

2

Installing
SQL Server 2008

TOPICS COVERED IN THIS CHAPTER:

- ✓ Installation Planning, Architecture, and Data Access

- ✓ Configuring Service Accounts

- ✓ Installing a Default Instance

- ✓ Installing Named Instances

- ✓ Installing to a Cluster

- ✓ Installing Extra Features

- ✓ Upgrading from Previous Versions

- ✓ Removing an Installation

Installing SQL Server 2008 is really a very painless task; however, it is important that you plan the installation well.

A poorly planned installation may result in security, stability, and functional problems. To help you avoid these problems and due to its importance, this chapter will cover installation planning first.

Once a plan is in place, you'll need to learn how to install a default instance, a named instance, and even a clustered installation of SQL Server 2008, so these will be covered next. Then the installation of additional features within an instance will be addressed, and the chapter will wrap up with an explanation of the upgrade, migration, and removal options.

All of these should provide you with complete coverage for installing SQL Server 2008 and beginning your use of this product. In addition, the installation will provide you with the foundation needed to test and develop solutions based on the remaining chapters in this book.

Installation Planning

Installation planning can be divided into two broad topics: understanding the SQL Server 2008 architecture and the installation planning process. Both topics are addressed in this section.

SQL Server 2008 Architecture

You can't really plan the implementation of a technology you do not understand. Imagine trying to build a car without understanding the components used to build one. You would probably end up with some sort of vehicle, but it probably wouldn't run well or for very long. SQL Server 2008 is no different. You must understand how it works in order to make it work efficiently. For this reason, the architecture of SQL Server 2008 will be presented from a logical perspective in this section. Later chapters will address physical processes that take place under the hood, such as data file structures, log file access, and other such topics. Here, the goal is to understand how SQL Server works so you can ensure an effective implementation; however, it is important to realize that the best performing installs take into account the many concepts that are addressed throughout this book. The good news is that most servers can be optimized after the installation, if required.

So, how does SQL Server 2008 work? To understand the answer to this question, you must understand the following concepts:

- Database system components
- Data access methods
- Data write methods
- Deployment features

As each concept is addressed, remember that you are being shown a bird's eye view of the architecture to help you understand the basic operations of the database system. As you read through the rest of this book, you'll be going deeper and deeper into the true physical actions that take place in memory and on the disk system; however, the concepts covered here remain true and the remaining chapters simply provide much more detail.

Database System Components

Figure 2.1 shows the basic components involved in a typical SQL Server 2008 application. As you can see, database access is more complex with a server-based system than the access provided by a single-user system. The following components must be understood:

- Database server
- SQL Server services
- Logical databases
- Data files
- Transaction logs
- Buffer memory

FIGURE 2.1   SQL Server logical architecture

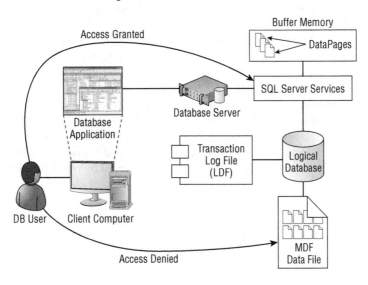

Database Server

The database server will run a compatible version of Windows Server. SQL Server 2008 supports several versions of Windows Server, and it operates differently depending on the version of Windows Server used. Windows XP and later clients, as well as Windows Server 2003 and later servers, can all run SQL Server 2008. However, enhanced security features are available when you install SQL Server 2008 on a Windows Server 2008 or later server. If you choose to install the database management system on Windows Server 2003 or Windows XP, the operating systems must be running Service Pack 2 or higher. Like Windows Server 2008, SQL Server 2008 will install and run on Windows Vista, and it has been tested on Windows 7 with success; however, at the time of Windows 7's release, Microsoft had not suggested official support for that platform.

In addition to selecting the proper operating system, you must ensure that the users requiring access to the SQL Server have access to the Windows server. Think of this structure as a layered approach. Before the users can access a database, they must have access to the SQL Server service. Before the users can access the SQL Server service, they must have access to the server. Three layers protect your database and, when configured properly, can provide functionality that supports multiple databases used by different users on the same instance in the same server.

The most important thing to remember is that the users must have access to the database server first and then the database services. Starting with Windows 2000 Server, Windows servers have supported a Group Policy right named *Access this computer from the network*. The policy is still in Windows Server 2008 and the users who need access to the databases stored on a server must be granted this right. You can grant the right through Windows groups so that you are not required to add each individual user.

SQL Server Services

Several services are used to provide the various functions of SQL Server. The two most frequently used are the SQL Server service (also known as the database engine) and the SQL Server Agent service. The SQL Server service for the default instance is named MSSQLSERVER in SQL Server 2008 and is sometimes more completely called the SQL Server Database Services service. The service shows up as SQL Server (MSSQLSERVER) in the Services management tool, but the name MSSQLSERVER is assigned to the service by default and used with the NET STOP command at the command line. When you run multiple instances of SQL Server, each instance runs its own services. The SQL Server service is named MSSQL$*Instance_Name* for a named instance and shows up in the Services management tool as SQL Server (*Instance_Name*). Figure 2.2 shows these services running with a default instance and a named instance, which is named Marketing. The core functionality of SQL Server data storage and retrieval is performed by the SQL Server service.

FIGURE 2.2   The SQL Server services are displayed.

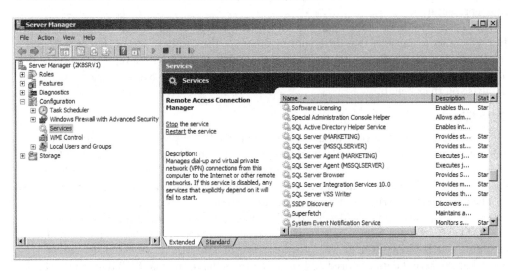

The SQL Server Agent service is used to monitor the databases and database server. It is also used to automate maintenance and administration tasks through the use of jobs. The SQL Server Agent service is named SQL Server Agent (MSSQLSERVER) for the default instance and SQL Server Agent (*instance_name*) for named instances.

As depicted in Figure 2.1, all user database access occurs through the SQL Server service. Users do not have direct access to the physical data files that store the databases. These MDF (master data file) files are accessed by the SQL Server service on behalf of the users. Because the users do not have access to the physical data file, the system is more secure than a single-user database system that does require the user to have access to the database files.

Logical Databases

The database is referenced as a logical database in Figure 2.1. The reasons for this are twofold. First of all, a database may be stored as one physical file or as several. To reduce confusion, the database that the users access may be referred to as the *logical database*. The database appears to be a single entity, and the users are unaware of the actual storage method used for the data. You can refer to this apparent single entity as a database or as a logical database; both terms are acceptable. Modern databases are frequently built from several underlying files.

Secondly, users never access the actual database. They feel as if they are accessing the database, but they are actually communicating with the SQL Server service, which is representing the database to the users based on the users' permissions and not based on what is literally in the database. For example, some users may only be able to read data through views that have been implemented by the DBA. To these users, the database "looks like" the representation provided by the views; however, a real physical database exists beneath this representation.

If you prefer to think of the database without this logical conceptualization, that is fine. Just remember to consider that different users may see the database very differently. Also, remember that users never access the database, but they interact with a representation of the database provided to them by the SQL Server service and the SQL Server service accesses the database on their behalf.

Data Files

The actual data stored in your database must be placed on a physical disk somewhere. SQL Server uses a default data file extension of .MDF for the master data file and .NDF for additional databases. Databases always use one MDF file and may use one or more NDF files. The MDF file contains the schema information or the structure for the database objects.

The data files are structured using pages and extents. A data page is 8 kilobytes (8,192 bytes) in size and provides up to 8,060 bytes for an individual record consisting of standard data types. When eight pages are grouped together, they form an extent. The result is a 64KB extent. SQL Server allocates space in data files on an extent-by-extent basis, but the actual data is stored and retrieved from the individual 8KB data pages. The extents can be uniform (the entire extent belongs to a single table or index) or mixed (the extent is shared among up to eight different tables or indexes).

For now, this description is sufficient. Chapters 5, 6, and 8 will explain the storage engine in detail because a database designer must understand how SQL Server stores and retrieves data, if he is to implement a well-performing database. At this time, however, it is simply important that you remember the following fact: SQL Server database data is never modified directly in the physical database files.

You will understand this statement better after you learn about buffer memory in the next few pages, but it is very important that you understand this concept. Without this understanding, you'll never be able to grasp how SQL Server uses transaction logs for automatic recovery or how to best optimize a database. If you assume data modifications are made directly in the data file, you may focus solely on hard drive performance; however, when you know that data modifications happen in memory and understand how that buffer memory is used, you will know that memory optimization can often have a greater impact on database performance.

Transaction Logs

Transaction logs are used by every database attached to a SQL Server instance. If you've worked with SQL Server for awhile, you may have heard the rumor that simple recovery databases do not use a transaction log. This statement is not correct. Even databases in the Simple Recovery model use a transaction log; they simply wrap around to the beginning of the log and overwrite the oldest transactions instead of preserving them between backups. Why does a Simple Recovery database still use a transaction log? To answer this question, examine the three primary benefits of a transaction log-based database system.

Database Atomicity   *Atomicity* is a database system term that means all tasks in a transaction are completed successfully or no task is performed. The transaction log assists with atomicity in that every step in the transaction is entered in the transaction log, but if a step fails all previous steps can be removed (rolled back). The transaction log is essential because many transactions may be too large to completely perform in memory.

Automatic Recovery   Automatic recovery occurs when the SQL Server service starts. During startup, the service looks in the transaction log for any transactions that are completely entered in the log, but have not been committed. Data is only committed to the physical MDF file when a checkpoint occurs. The automatic recovery process uses checkpoints and transaction commits to determine which transactions should be executed again (rolled forward) and which should be ignored (rolled back).

Disaster Recovery   Disaster recovery is a manual process performed by an administrator. Assuming your data (MDF and NDF files) is on one physical drive and your transaction log (LDF file) is on another physical drive, you can restore to the point of failure. This restoration is accomplished by using the transactions in the current transaction log that were executed since the last backup.

As you can see, the transaction log is very important. In the later section titled "Data Write Methods," you'll discover more details about the role played by the transaction log.

Buffer Memory

The buffer memory or buffer pool is used to store data in RAM so that it can be read from and written to. A buffer is a storage location in RAM that can hold a single 8KB data or index page. When data is accessed and the data already exists in the buffer pool, access is much faster. When data is accessed and the data does not exist in the buffer pool, buffers must be requested in the buffer pool (this request may result in some buffers being flushed to free space for the requested data) and the pages must be loaded from the physical data files into the assigned buffers.

Data Access Methods

Now that the major components in the SQL Server logical architecture have been defined, it's time to explore the way in which data is accessed. For this explanation, assume that a user executed the following SQL statement against a database located on a SQL Server 2008 server:

```
SELECT CustomerID, FirstName, LastName, eMail
FROM Sales.Customers
WHERE LastName = 'Smith';
```

Assume that 1,200 records match this query and are spread across 750 data pages. Furthermore, assume that none of the needed pages are in memory. SQL Server uses the following high-level steps to retrieve the data for the user:

1. Locate the pages containing the matching records and read the pages into buffers.

2. Read the records from the pages and return them to the user as a result set or record set.

Notice that the pages are not removed from memory after the data is transferred to the user. The pages are left in the buffers until the buffers are needed for other pages. This behavior allows future reads of the same pages without the need to load the pages from disk. For example, imagine the following SQL statement was executed immediately after the previous one:

```
SELECT CustomerID, FirstName, LastName, eMail, Phone
FROM Sales.Customers
WHERE LastName = 'Smith' and FirstName = 'John';
```

This statement would need data that is located in the same pages as the previous statement. While all pages would not be required, all required pages would already be in the buffers assuming the buffers had not been required for an intermediate statement. Performing data access in this manner dramatically improves the performance of read operations.

Data Write Methods

Data write operations work much the same way as data read operations—at least in the initial stages. For example, imagine the following SQL statement is executed against a database:

```
UPDATE Sales.Customers
SET Phone = '937-555-1029'
WHERE CustomerID = 63807;
```

Remember, data modifications are never performed directly against the physical data files. Therefore, the first step is reading the data into the buffers just like a data read operation. Once the appropriate pages are loaded into the buffers, the data changes are made in the buffer memory. Next, the transaction is recorded in the transaction log. Believe it or not, the data write is complete.

Now, you may be wondering how the data gets back into the actual data files on disk and, if so, your curiosity is well founded. At this point, the data is in memory and the transaction is in the log, but the data file has not been updated. However, keep in mind that you have only modified a value in a specific column for a specific customer. Furthermore, remember that the page is retained in memory so that the data is available for future reads and writes. You have not created the demand for any new data pages at this point.

The key to understanding how the data is updated in the data files is found in SQL Server actions called a checkpoint and lazy writes. Any page that has been modified is designated as a *dirty page*. When a checkpoint occurs, the SQL Server service processes the pages in the buffer memory buffers. Dirty pages are written back out to the data files during a checkpoint and are designated as not dirty pages. The buffers holding the dirty pages before the checkpoint are not cleared or freed for use at this time.

The lazy writer and workers are responsible for freeing buffers so that sufficient buffers are available as needed by applications. The lazy writer sleeps much of the time, but when it wakes, it evaluates the free buffers and, if they are not sufficient, writes dirty pages to disk so that the buffers can be freed. The lazy writer uses an algorithm that is dependent on the size of the buffer pool to determine sufficient free buffers. In addition, the workers (processes that work with data) are also responsible for writing dirty pages and freeing buffers. When a worker accesses the buffer pool, it is also assigned 64 buffers to analyze. Any buffered pages in those 64 buffers that are not worth keeping in memory are written to the disk or discarded depending on whether they were dirty pages or not. Dirty pages are always written to disk before they are discarded.

As you can see, it is quite a myth that dirty pages are only written to disk when a checkpoint occurs. Indeed, if the server has massively more memory than it requires for the attached databases, dirty pages may only be written to disk during checkpoints, but it is far more common that dirty pages are written to disk by all three processes: checkpoints, lazy writer actions, and worker actions. The primary purpose of checkpoints is to make sure that dirty pages are written to disk frequently enough so that the autorecovery process completes in a timely fashion should the SQL Server service require a restart for any reason.

Deployment Features

Several features and configuration options must be considered to effectively plan and deploy a SQL Server installation. These features and options include:

- SQL Server components
- Multiple instances
- TCP ports
- Installation options

SQL Server Components

When you install SQL Server 2008, you have the option of installing several components. You will need to understand these components and what they offer in order to determine whether they are needed for your installation or not. The most important components include the database engine, Integration Services, administration tools, Analysis Services, Reporting Services, full-text search, and Books Online—all of which are discussed in the following list:

Database Engine   This is the core of SQL Server. Without the database engine, you can't really do much so you will install this with every instance. The database engine provides access to your databases.

Integration Services   The Integration Services component is the extraction, transformation, and loading (ETL) toolset provided by SQL Server. With this service, you can move data from one server to another and massage the data (transform or modify it in some way) during the process. Additionally, database maintenance plans depend on Integration Services from SQL Server 2005 and higher.

Administration Tools   You may not want to install the administration tools, such as SQL Server Management Studio and Visual Studio for SQL Server, on the server itself. However, it is often convenient to have the tools installed on the server so that you can access them locally if needed.

Analysis Services   The Analysis Services (AS) component is one of those special components of SQL Server that warrants its own book. For now, it's enough to know that AS is used to perform business intelligence work and for data warehousing operations.

Reporting Services   Reporting Services provides a report generation service for your SQL Server (and possibly other) databases. Larger organizations usually choose to install dedicated reporting servers, but smaller organizations may opt to install Reporting Services on one or more servers used as standard database servers as well.

Full-Text Search   The full-text search feature allows for searching of large and small text data types. Normal `WHERE` clause searches are limited to string-based patterns. Full-text search performs word searches and understands language elements. For example, inflection forms can be searched such as tooth and teeth, while only specifying teeth. Additionally, searches can be performed for words close to one another and the results ranked based on how close together the words are.

Books Online   Books Online is the famous, and sometimes infamous, electronic help for SQL Server. The SQL Server 2008 Books Online is, of course, larger than its predecessor and according to Microsoft weighs in at 240MB. If you've ever downloaded an eBook, you know that a 200MB eBook is huge and SQL Server 2008 Books Online is just that. However, it is searchable and you can usually find what you need after several search attempts and forward and backward clicks.

Multiple Instances

SQL Server 2008 supports multiple instances on the same machine. In fact, you can run SQL Server 2000, 2005, and 2008 all on the same server at the same time. In some upgrade and migration scenarios, this multiversion configuration may be desired. All instances share certain components such as the Books Online, but each instance has its own set of executables. Several reasons exist for installing multiple instances. The following reasons represent the most common:

Service Pack Compatibility   You can install several instances of SQL Server 2008 on the same physical host and install different service packs. For example, one vendor may require Service Pack 1 (SP1) at a minimum, while another does not yet support SP1. You could install one instance with SP1 and the other without it and support both applications on the same server.

SQL Server Version Compatibility   Similar to the service packs, you may need to run multiple versions of SQL Server on the same physical host. If you have an internal application that does not work on SQL Server 2008, you can run it in a SQL Server 2000 or 2005 instance and run other applications in a SQL Server 2008 instance on the same server.

Policy Compliance   Many organizations have security policies that require limiting user access to database services. In fact, the policy could state something like, *"A single database service shall provide access only to databases that share a common set of users."* A policy such as this may force you to create separate instances to house different databases accessed by different users without requiring multiple physical servers.

Testing and Development   Building test and development labs can be expensive. With multiple instances, a single physical host can house several instances for various development projects. These instances can be used for testing different service packs, SQL Server versions, and code bases for the supported applications.

Global Service Settings   Finally, any time you must implement one global service setting for one application and a different value for the same setting for another application, you will be required to either implement separate instances or separate physical hosts. Of course, implementing separate instances would be cheaper. An example global setting is the authentication mode. You cannot have one database using Windows authentication and another database using Mixed authentication within the same instance.

 Real World Scenario

Why So Many Instances?

I can't move on from this discussion of multiple instances without addressing a common question I've received from training attendees over the years. Here's the question: Why in the world do SQL Server 2005 and 2008 support up to 50 instances?

The motivation behind the question is obvious today, but we must travel through time in order to understand why such a large allowance is built into the system. First, let's travel back to the year 2000. SQL Server 2000 was released to manufacturers on August 9, 2000. This version of SQL Server supported up to 11 instances on a single server. At the time, this seemed like a lot, since servers were commonly less than 10 percent as powerful as they are today (remember that many of the early servers used to run SQL Server 2000 were purchased from 1998 to 2000). In fact, the minimum requirement for SQL Server 2000 was a 166MHz Pentium with 64MB RAM.

The thought of running 11 instances of SQL Server 2000 on a server in the year 2000 would cause most DBAs to cringe or even cry out in pain; however, the thought of running 11 instances today on a quad processor quad core server (16 total cores) wouldn't even cause the same DBAs to blink. Microsoft ended mainstream support for SQL Server 2000 in April of 2008; extended support will continue until April of 2013. With mainstream support, both security updates and nonsecurity hotfixes are provided to everyone. During extended support, only those who purchase an extended support contract get the nonsecurity hotfixes.

Here's the point: If SQL Server 2000 support is lasting until 2013, how long will SQL Server 2008 support last? Well, support is currently promised through the year 2019. Imagine what a new server will look like then. Will it have eight cores in each of 16 processors at a price similar to that of today's quad/quad servers? Will it use 20GBps solid state drives providing 250 terabytes of storage per drive? I can't guarantee it, but I won't say no. Maybe now you can see why 50 instances just might be possible in the very near future.

TCP Ports

Another flexible configuration option is the TCP port on which SQL Server listens for incoming connections to the databases. A default instance of SQL Server uses port 1433 by default, but this can be changed. Named instances use a dynamically assigned port, but it can be changed as well. You use the SQL Server Configuration Manager to configure the TCP ports for installed instances.

 Be very thoughtful when changing the TCP port. If you are not also the network administrator, you should check with her to verify that the new port will function properly on the network. Many networks block communications using deep packet inspections, and a port other than 1433 might not work properly or the administrator may need to adjust the network configuration.

Installation Options

Several options are available for the installation of each instance. You can choose the installation directory for the instance and the shared components. You can configure the service accounts for improved security, and you can choose to enable the new filestream support. The filestream feature allows for the storage of large external data sets so that the MDF and NDF files do not become unnecessarily large. In the past, DBAs stored videos, large drawings, and other binary large objects (BLOBs) outside of the database and simply stored a reference to the file location inside the database. This structure resulted in difficulty for management of the database and the application. With the filestream feature, both database management and application updates become easier.

Installation Planning Process

A SQL Server 2008 installation planning process consists of three phases.

Phase 1   In the first phase, server use analysis should be performed. It is in this phase that the planning team determines the various ways in which each server will be utilized. The output of phase 1 should be a plan document (usually an Excel spreadsheet listing each server and the databases that will run on the server with details about each database) that can be used as the input for phase 2.

Phase 2   This phase involves requirements analysis. In this phase, the planning team determines the hardware requirements based on the server use analysis report document. The output of phase 2 should be an amended plan document that now includes the hardware requirements for the servers to be deployed.

Phase 3   Finally, in phase 3, the plan is finalized with projected deployment dates for each server. Plans normally include testing start and completion dates, implementation start and completion dates, and post-installation user interview dates. This complete plan ensures that all activities are scheduled and they are, therefore, more likely to be performed.

The following sections cover these three phases in more detail.

Phase 1: Server Use Analysis

Assuming you have existing databases deployed as SQL Server or some other type of database, you'll begin your installation planning by analyzing existing servers. But before you begin, two considerations must be made. The first consideration is the structure and size of the database itself. The second is the utilization of that database. If you are analyzing only SQL Server 2000 or 2005 database servers, you can use a tool from the SQL Server 2008 disc. The tool is the Installed SQL Server Features Discovery Report, and it will create a report (see Figure 2.3) of the installed SQL Server instances and features.

To run the tool, follow these steps:

1. Insert the SQL Server 2008 disc.

2. Click Tools on the left menu of the Installation Center.

3. From here, click Installed SQL Server Features Discovery Report.

FIGURE 2.3 Installed features report

Microsoft SQL Server 2008 Setup Discovery Report

Product	Instance	Instance ID	Feature	Language	Edition	Version	Clustered
Sql Server 2000	SQL2000		SQL Server	1033	Enterprise Edition	8.4.2039	No
Sql Server 2000	SQL2000		Replication Support	1033	Enterprise Edition	8.4.2039	No
Sql Server 2000	SQL2000		Full-Text Search	1033	Enterprise Edition	8.4.2039	No
Sql Server 2000	SQL2000		Debug Symbols	1033	Enterprise Edition	8.4.2039	No
Sql Server 2000	SQL2000		Performance Counters	1033	Enterprise Edition	8.4.2039	No
Sql Server 2000			Enterprise Manager		Tools	8.00.194	No
Sql Server 2000			Profiler		Tools	8.00.194	No
Sql Server 2000			Query Analyzer		Tools	8.00.194	No
Sql Server 2000			DTC Client Support		Tools	8.00.194	No
Sql Server 2000			Conflict Viewer		Tools	8.00.194	No
Sql Server 2000			Client Connectivity		Tools	8.00.194	No
Sql Server 2000			Books Online On Disk		Tools	8.00.194	No
Sql Server 2000			Debugger Interface		Tools	8.00.194	No
Sql Server 2000			DTS		Tools	8.00.194	No
Sql Server 2005	MSSQLSERVER	MSSQL.1	Database Engine Services	1033	Enterprise Edition	9.00.1399.06	No
Sql Server 2005	MSSQLSERVER	MSSQL.1	SQL Server Replication	1033	Enterprise Edition	9.00.1399.06	No
Sql Server 2005	MSSQLSERVER	MSSQL.1	Full-Text Search	1033	Enterprise Edition	9.00.1399.06	No
Sql Server 2005	MSSQLSERVER	MSSQL.1	SharedTools	1033	Enterprise Edition	9.00.1399.06	No

The following information should be gathered during the first phase:

- Database server instance information such as the instance name, version of SQL Server, service pack level, and important configuration settings
- Databases attached to each instance and information such as database size, features used, and storage structure
- Database utilization including number of users and minimum, maximum, and average query sizes

Once you've collected this information, you may want to create an Excel (or any spreadsheet application) spreadsheet that can be used to track this information and the added information collected and developed throughout the next two phases.

Phase 2: Hardware Requirements Analysis

Hardware requirements must be considered from two perspectives:

- Minimum requirements
- Implementation requirements

The minimum requirements provide an absolute baseline below which you know you cannot install SQL Server; however, these minimum requirements are seldom enough for any implementation. So, what is the DBA to do? Start with the minimum requirements and then calculate the additional demands you will place on the system.

Minimum Requirements

SQL Server 2008 has different minimum requirements depending on the edition you select. Table 2.1 lists the hardware requirements for each edition.

TABLE 2.1 Hardware Requirements

Edition	Processor	Memory	Storage Space
Enterprise/Developer	1.0GHz 32-bit/1.4GHz 64-bit	512MB	280MB to 1.8GB
Standard	1.0GHz 32-bit/1.4GHz 64-bit	512MB	280MB to 1.8GB
Workgroup	1.0GHz 32-bit/1.4GHz 64-bit	512MB	280MB to 1.7GB
Express	1.0GHz 32-bit/1.4GHz 64-bit	256MB	280MB to 1GB
Web	1.0GHz 32-bit/1.4GHz 64-bit	512MB	280MB to 1.7GB

If your organization chooses to implement SQL Server Enterprise Edition for all instances, you are starting with a minimum baseline of a 1GHz processor with 512MB of RAM. Next, you'll need to calculate additional demands.

Calculating Additional Demands

When calculating demands above the minimum requirements, you should do two things. First, calculate the expected workload and then multiple this by 1.5 to determine the needs for a given server. For example, assume the following figures:

- 80 concurrent users
- 16 queries per minute
- 23 kilobyte average query size
- 4 gigabyte database with 55 percent data utilization

Before you start to calculate the demands, you need to understand the terminology. *Concurrent users* is a reference to the number of users connected to the database at a given time. The *average query size* can be used in conjunction with the concurrent users and the *queries per minute* to calculate the workload in a given window of time.

In the previous example, the figures result in $80 \times 23 \times 16$ or 29,440 kilobytes or 28.75 megabytes per minute. This is not an intensive workload for a server, but it also does not factor in the overhead required to manage the 80-user processes. Each user connection consumes between 40KB and 50KB. With only 80 users, the memory overhead is only about 400KB or less than half a megabyte. Unless you have more than 500 concurrent connections, you will not usually worry about calculating the connection overhead.

Two important decisions will eventually be made based on these memory and size calculations. First, you must choose the amount of RAM for the server, which you'll calculate in a moment. Second, you must ensure that you have the drive I/O capabilities and the network throughput capabilities to handle the workload. In this example, drive and network capabilities will be no problem. In fact, this example would allow for a 10Mbps NIC (network interface card) and just a single SATA hard drive, if you're strictly considering the needs of this application.

Now, examine the 55 percent data utilization figure. This calculation simply means that, out of the 4 gigabytes of data, about 2 gigabytes is actually used regularly. Therefore, if this is the only instance and database on the server and you can provide about 3GB of RAM, the server should work quite well. Remember, if you are running Enterprise edition, you need 512MB of RAM as a minimum. If you add 2.5GB for the SQL Server to use for this database, you should achieve relatively good performance.

You're probably wondering about the processor at this point. Well, that's a different set of calculations. You need to factor in the processor utilization during an average query operation on a given processor speed and, from there, you can determine the processor requirements. For example, imagine that your 23 kilobyte average query runs and the processor is at 10 percent utilization with a 1GHz processor. If you have 16 such queries that you need to run per minute and the queries each take about 5 seconds to run (just an arbitrary number for your calculations here, but you can get the exact number using tools you'll learn about in Chapter 14), you'll have at most two to three queries running at the same time. The result would be a maximum of 30 percent utilization, not factoring in operating system level scheduling and multitasking, which would likely be at 5 to 10 percent utilization.

Now, let's look at your resulting numbers:

- 1GHz processor 40 percent utilized

- 3GB of RAM

- 10Mbps NIC (certainly, you should go with 100Mbps minimum today)

- SATA hard drive

And now it's time for a reality check. Most organizations have minimum standards for hardware. Additionally, you always want to make room for the future, so you'll calculate new numbers by a factor of 1.5 (rounded up to common values) and utilizing common current organizational minimums (these will likely change during the life of this book):

- 1.6GHz dual-core processor

- 6GB RAM

- 1Gbps NIC

- Three SATA drives in a RAID 5 array

This resulting server configuration will work very well for a 4GB database on a SQL Server 2008 implementation. Additionally, it represents common minimum hardware allowances for many organizations.

 In many cases, you will be implementing SQL Server 2008 databases for vendor-provided applications. When you are implementing these databases, you can usually inform the vendor of the total expected users and the ways in which these users will utilize the system. The vendor can usually calculate the needed hardware once this information is provided.

Phase 3: Complete the Implementation Plan

Phase 1 provided you with an inventory of existing database servers that could be upgraded or migrated to SQL Server 2008. Phase 2 provided you with the hardware specifications for the individual database applications. In phase 3, you can look at those requirements and determine which databases can be housed on shared servers and even in shared instances. Once you've determined this, you can select the appropriate servers to upgrade or migrate first, second, third, and so on. You may take months or years to complete the process of upgrading all databases or, in smaller organizations, you may complete the entire process in a weekend.

Managing Permissions

One last issue must be addressed before you begin installing the SQL Server 2008 instances that are required in your organization. You must determine the permissions with which the services will run. The permissions granted to the services will be dependent on the service account used. All SQL Server services must run in a context in order to access resources on the local machine or the network.

Service Account Options

You have three options when configuring service accounts:

Network Service   The Network Service option runs the SQL Server services with permissions to access the network as the computer account. You may choose to use this option in a lab environment, but it should never be used in production (in this context, the term "production" refers to a system used by active users for real and useful data).

Local System   Like the Network Service option, the Local System option is far too powerful to be used in a production setting; however, you may choose this as an easy installation choice in a lab environment.

Windows Account   This is the preferred choice for production SQL Servers. When a SQL Server is installed in a Windows domain, a domain service account will be used. When installed on a stand-alone server, a local Windows account will be used.

In addition to using Windows accounts for the SQL Server services, you should use a separate account for each service. Yes, this configuration requires more work, but it is more secure as you'll soon see.

The Argument for Differentiation

In the world of information and system security, an important principle known as least privilege is often cited. *Least privilege* simply means that a subject (a user or process) can do no more than is needed to perform the required functions of that subject. For example, if a user needs to be able to read the data in a particular network share, the user is given read-only access and not modify access. The only way to accomplish least privilege is to determine the permissions and rights needed by a subject and then either directly assign the permissions and rights to that subject or place the subject in a group that possesses only the necessary permissions and rights.

Now, SQL Server includes several services and here's an important reminder: not all of the services are required by all installations. This statement can be true only if the services perform different functions. Indeed they do. The SQL Server service provides access to the data. The SQL Server Agent service supports jobs and database monitoring. The Reporting Service is used to talk to the SQL Server service and generate reports. The point is simple. Each service performs different functions and should run in the contexts of different accounts (differentiation) in order to implement least privilege.

The process to configure least privilege and differentiation for a new SQL Server installation is simple:

1. Create the separate Windows accounts for each service.

2. Configure these accounts to be used during installation.

3. Test the installation to ensure that all necessary permissions are available.

Some database applications will require more permissions than are granted to the service account during installation. This is particularly true when the database application uses external application code or a multitier implementation model. Always check with the vendor and ensure that the service account is given the minimum permissions required and no more. By combining this practice with differentiation, you'll achieve a more secure implementation.

Installing a Default Instance

The preceding sections explained the installation planning process. At this point, you will be walked through a typical installation. Along the way, the options available will be explained and you will be told when you might want to change the default settings. However, you will find that the default settings work in most situations when you intend to install a single instance on a server.

Getting a Trial Copy of SQL Server 2008

If you do not have a licensed copy of the Enterprise Edition of SQL Server 2008, search for "SQL Server 2008 trial download" at the Google search engine and follow the link to the Microsoft website that references Trial Software. Download the SQL Server 2008 120-day trial of Enterprise Edition and burn to a disc. You can do the same thing to download the Windows Server 2008 trial software. This exercise assumes you've installed Windows Server 2008 already.

SQL Server 2008 can be installed on Windows Server 2003 machines running SP2 or higher and on later server operating systems such as Windows Server 2003 R2 and Windows Server 2008. In this example, you will be installing the database system on a Windows Server 2008 Enterprise Edition server. To begin the installation, follow these steps:

1. Insert the DVD and open My Computer.

2. From here, double-click the DVD-ROM drive to begin the installation.

3. If the installation does not begin when you insert or double-click the DVD-ROM drive, you may need to run the SETUP.EXE application directly on the disc.

At this point, if you were installing SQL Server 2008 on a Windows Server 2003 machine without the .NET 3.5 Framework, the installation would immediately prompt you with an update message. However, the needed update is included on the SQL Server 2008 installation disc, so you can simply click OK to allow it to update your machine. Because the server is running Windows Server 2008 and is up-to-date, you can see the screen in Figure 2.4. This screen is now called the SQL Server Installation Center.

FIGURE 2.4   The SQL Server Installation Center

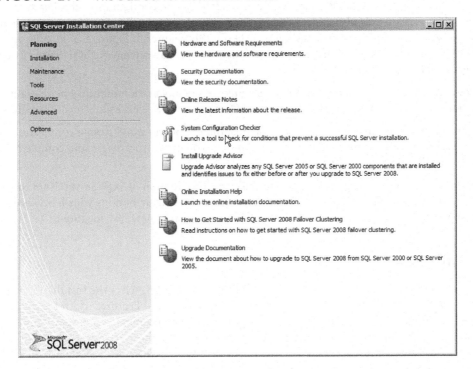

SQL Server Installation Center Tasks

From the SQL Server Installation Center, you can perform several tasks. You can do far more than simply install SQL Server 2008. The following tasks can be performed:

Planning   The planning tasks include reviewing documentation, system configuration analysis, and installing the upgrade advisor. The system configuration analysis task evaluates your current configuration to make sure nothing will hinder the installation. The upgrade advisor may be used on a machine running an earlier version of SQL Server in order to detect potential upgrade issues.

Installation   While this option may seem obvious since this is a setup program, several installation tasks may be performed. A stand-alone instance of SQL Server may be installed or a clustered installation may be launched from here. You can also add a node to an existing cluster or search for updates for the SQL Server products.

Maintenance On the Maintenance page, you may upgrade from one edition of SQL Server 2008 to another. For example, you could upgrade from Standard Edition to Enterprise. You may also repair a damaged installation or remove a node from a cluster.

Tools The Tools page allows you to launch the same system configuration checker as the Planning page. You may also run a new installation tool, the installed SQL Server Features Discovery Report. This report was shown earlier in this chapter in Figure 2.3. Finally, you may choose to convert SQL Server Integration Services packages from the SQL Server 2005 format to the 2008 format.

Resources The Resources page is filled with links to documentation that may be relevant to your installations. You can also review the SQL Server 2008 license agreement from here.

Advanced On the Advanced page, you may install SQL Server 2008 from a configuration file. This feature allows for automated installations. You may also prepare and complete cluster installation from this page.

Options The Options page allows you to select the distribution of SQL Server 2008 to install. You may choose x86, x64, or ia64 depending on the distributions your hardware will support. You can also redirect the installation engine to a new disc location.

Installation

Because you are installing a default instance of SQL Server 2008, select the Installation page and choose the New SQL Server Stand-Alone Installation or Add Features to An Existing Installation option. When this option is selected, a brief flash of a command prompt will usually appear and then quickly disappear. This behavior is normal as the SQL Server Installation Center is shelling out to the proper routine to perform the installation.

The next useful screen is the Setup Support Rules screen shown in Figure 2.5. When you click the Show Details button, you'll see that your server has passed all the rules. These rules must be met in order to install SQL Server 2008. For example, the server cannot be in a state where a reboot is pending and the account credentials that launched the installation must be those of an administrator.

When you click OK, the next stage of the installation begins. The first thing you have to do is choose whether to install a free evaluation edition or provide a product key to install a licensed product. Enter the product key and then click Next. Then agree to the license text and click Next. This takes you to the screen shown in Figure 2.6. This is the prerequisites screen and only the Setup Support Files are required. Click on Install to install the needed support files.

Do not be alarmed if at several points during the installation the installation program seems to have left the screen and you've been returned to the SQL Server Installation Center. This behavior, while a bit unorthodox, is normal.

FIGURE 2.5   The Setup Support Rules screen

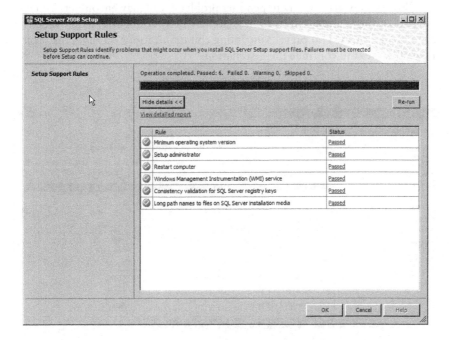

FIGURE 2.6   The Setup Support Files screen

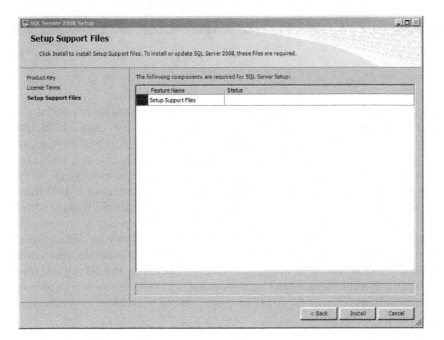

After the Setup Support Files are installed, you will be presented with the screen in Figure 2.7. This screen warns of any impending problems you may encounter. You can see the warning about the Windows firewall. It is not currently configured to allow traffic on TCP port 1433, and this would prevent incoming communications on that port. You can fix this later, so click Next to continue the installation.

FIGURE 2.7   Potential installation issues

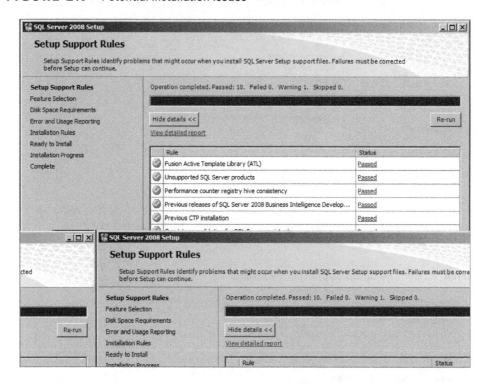

Now you are finally at the point where you can choose the installation options you want for this server. Figure 2.8 shows several features that are selected to install. In fact, the only features not being installed at this point are Analysis Services, Reporting Services, and the Microsoft Sync Framework. These features can be useful. They simply will not be needed on this particular server. You can also change the shared features directory, but the example leaves this at the default so that all instances look to the same location for these files.

The next screen is titled Instance Configuration and it provides the functionality to choose between a default and a named instance. You can also specify an instance ID and view installed instances to ensure that you do not create a duplicate named instance. The instance unique folder or directory can also be specified. In this example, you'll install a default instance and accept all of the default options. Therefore, the default instance ID will be MSSQLSERVER. Because this server's name is 2k8SRV1, you will be able to connect to the default instance on the server by connecting to \\2k8SRV1. After choosing the default instance, click Next.

FIGURE 2.8   The Feature Selection screen

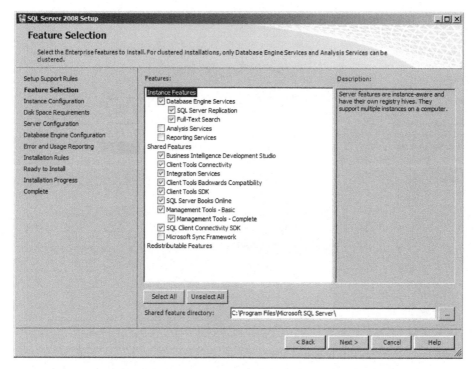

The next screen shows the disk space requirements. The installation chosen here will require 2,402MB of storage space. The example has plenty more than that, so click Next to continue the installation.

Figure 2.9 shows the next screen. The Server Configuration screen is where you set up the service accounts. Two accounts were created before the example installation began. Because they are Windows domain accounts and the example could have several SQL Servers, service account names that reflect the server and the purpose of the account were chosen. The SQL Server service on the 2k8SRV1 server will log on with the 2k8srv1sqldef account. The sqldef portion indicates that this is the service account for the default SQL Server instance on that server. Notice that the SQL Server Agent will log on with the 2k8srv1sqldefagent account. The account names may be longer, but they are more meaningful than names like SQL1, SQL2, and SQL3. However, you will need to discover a naming convention that works for you. No requirement is imposed on you other than the Windows domain account-name character-length limit. Windows accounts can be longer than 100 characters, but if you keep the character length to 20 or less the names will be easier to use. Many logon dialogs throughout Windows systems only allow 20 character usernames even though the backend will allow for longer names.

FIGURE 2.9   The Server Configuration screen

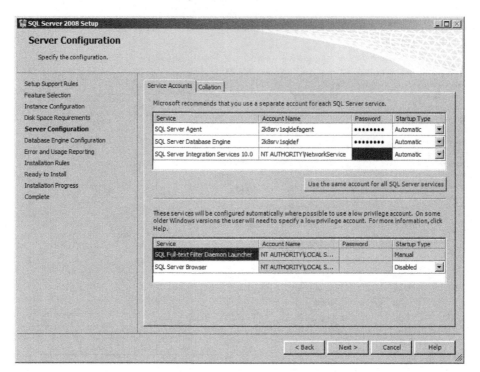

If you do not have the permissions needed to create the Windows accounts, you may need to request these accounts in advance of the installation. Any Active Directory administrator should be able to create these accounts for you. For a standard installation, simply ask them to create accounts and add them to no groups. The exception is the SQL Server Agent account. This account should be added to the Pre-Windows 2000 Compatible group in the domain. The account must also be granted local permission to log on as a service on the local server. The SQL Server installation process will assign the needed permissions automatically.

Based on the information provided in "The Argument for Differentiation" section earlier in this chapter, you should create separate accounts for each service. Additionally, you should typically configure the SQL Server service and the SQL Server Agent service to start up automatically. If you are running named instances, you will also want the SQL Server Monitor service to start up automatically.

After you've configured the service accounts, you could also click on the Collation tab shown in Figure 2.9 and modify the collation settings. It's handy that Microsoft made the collation settings an "as needed" interface element, because you accept the default chosen collation most of the time anyway. The collation ensures that the proper language, sort order, and character set are utilized. On most servers, the Windows locale settings are what you need for the SQL Server installation and that is the default chosen collation. Without changing the collation settings, click Next.

The Database Engine Configuration screen is shown in Figure 2.10. Here, you can choose the authentication mode, configure the data directories, and choose whether to enable filestreams or not. The authentication modes will be covered in more detail in Chapter 18, "Authentication and Encryption," but for now, choose Mixed Mode so you can access both Windows logins and SQL logins throughout this book. Set the SA password to a strong password because the SA account is very powerful (it stands for system administrator). Because you're installing with an administrator account, you can click the Add Current User button to add a valid administrator account, which is needed to perform the actual installation.

FIGURE 2.10   The Database Engine Configuration screen

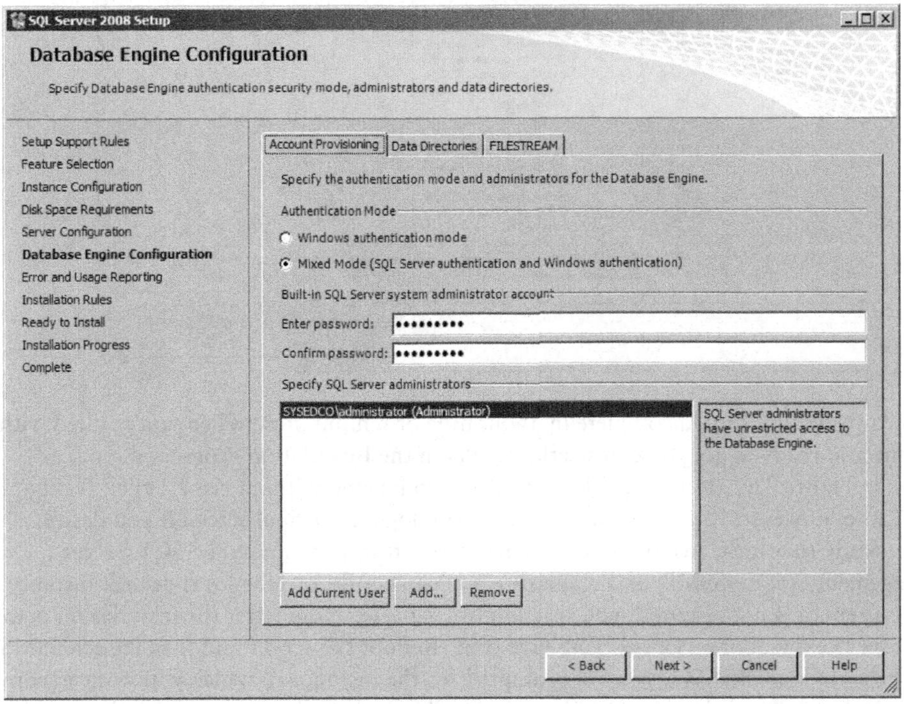

Accept the default on the Data Directories tab, as these settings can be reconfigured at any time. Finally, accept the default of not enabling filestreams at this time. With these settings in place, click Next.

The next screen requests permission to send error reports to Microsoft or a corporate reporting server. If you do not wish to do either, accept the defaults of not reporting errors and click Next. Based on the installation options you've chosen, the setup routine evaluates the potential for problems. The example server passes all tests. When yours passes, you can click Next again.

Finally, you'll see the screen in Figure 2.11, which is the Ready to Install dialog that provides a summary of the features and settings you've chosen to deploy for this installation. Once you are satisfied that everything is correct, click Install to begin the process. The installation will take a few minutes, so go get a cup of coffee.

FIGURE 2.11   Installation summary

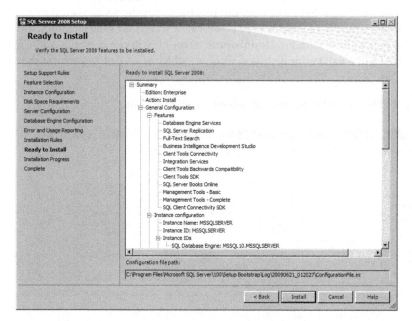

The installation should complete in about nine or ten minutes. When you're filled with caffeine and ready to go, you can see the results in the Installation Progress dialog, as shown in Figure 2.12. If it looks like everything completed without errors, click Next and then Close; however, you can view an installation log on the final screen if you desire. You're ready to test the installation now. To do this test, just launch the SQL Server Management Studio (SSMS) and make sure you can connect to the local default instance. While a reboot is not required, you should always perform one after the installation of a major service or set of services if you have time. Reboot the server and then launch SSMS.

When you launch SSMS, you are prompted for the instance to which you want to connect. The local default instance and logon with Windows authentication was chosen for the example. Windows authentication uses the administrator credentials with which you are currently logged on. The local Administrators group is automatically given access to the SQL Server installation, so you will be able to connect to the server and quickly see the screen shown in Figure 2.13. In the figure, the databases container is expanded and a query has been executed against one of the databases.

FIGURE 2.12   The installation is complete.

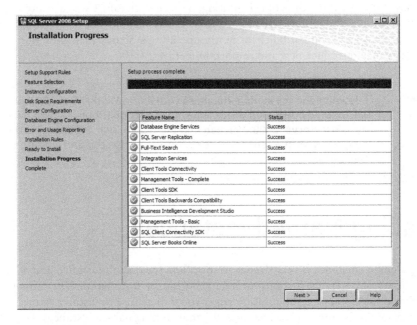

FIGURE 2.13   SSMS connecting to the installed instance

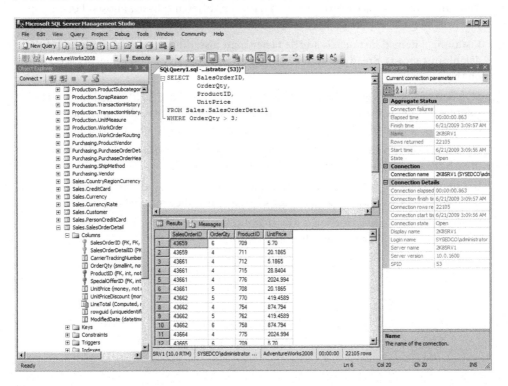

In addition to testing the functionality of the installation, you may want to consider checking for updates. At the time of this writing, Service Pack (SP) 1 was already available for SQL Server 2008 and SP 2 was scheduled to be released soon. The SPs often fix bugs in the system and also add compatibility for newer operating systems (such as Windows 7). In addition, they may introduce new and important features.

I downloaded the sample database (AdventureWorks) from CodePlex, Microsoft's open source site. They no longer distribute sample databases with SQL Server 2008. You can find the SQL Server 2008 sample databases by visiting http://sqlserversamples.CodePlex.com and clicking Sample Databases.

Installing Named Instances

Installing a named instance is very similar to installing the default instance. Exercise 2.1 provides the step-by-step instructions for a named instance installation. The primary difference is that on the Instance Configuration page, you will choose to install a named instance and provide a unique name for the instance. When installing named instances, keep the following facts in mind:

- You can install instances with the same name on different physical hosts. For example, you can have a \\server1\marketing instance and a \\server2\marketing instance.

- Installing a named instance is a little faster than installing the default instance, if the default instance is already installed. This is because the shared components are already on the machine.

- SQL Server 2008 Express Edition should always be installed as a named instance. Express Edition is used mostly as a local database and this installation recommendation ensures that multiple applications can run their own instances of the database.

- Remember that you are allowed to install 50 instances with SQL Server 2008 Enterprise Edition and only 16 instances with all other editions.

- If a single instance of SQL Server 2008 is to be installed on a server and the instance is not using Express Edition, the instance should be installed as a default instance.

- Some applications are written in a way that disallows the use of named instances. Always check with your application vendor or developer.

If you have trouble installing drivers for Windows Server 2008 on a desktop computer used for evaluation, download the vendor's Vista drivers. They usually work.

EXERCISE 2.1

Installing a Named Instance

In this exercise, you will install a named instance of SQL Server 2008. The following instructions will walk you through the installation of a named instance. The resulting instance name will be Sales.

1. Boot the Windows Server 2008 operating system and log on as an Administrator.

2. Insert the SQL Server 2008 Enterprise Trial disc.

3. If the installation does not start automatically, open Computer from the Start menu and double-click the SQL Server 2008 installation disc drive.

4. Once the SQL Server Installation Center loads (see Figure 2.4 earlier in this chapter), click Installation on the left side of the page.

5. Select New SQL Server Stand-Alone Installation or Add Features to an Existing Installation.

6. If all the Setup Support Rules passed, click OK to continue the installation. Otherwise, resolve the problem indicated and then restart the installation.

7. Click the Install button to install the Setup Support files needed to perform the installation. Wait patiently for this process to complete.

8. You are now in the actual installation process and should see a screen warning you if any potential problems exist that could hinder a successful installation (see Figure 2.7 earlier in this chapter). Address any displayed issues and then click Next.

9. Choose to Perform a New Installation and click Next.

10. If you are using a licensed version, enter the product key; otherwise, choose the Enterprise Evaluation and click Next.

11. Read and accept the license terms and click Next.

12. Install the features selected in the following image (if this is not the first instance you've installed, the shared components will show gray checkmarks instead of black).

EXERCISE 2.1   *(continued)*

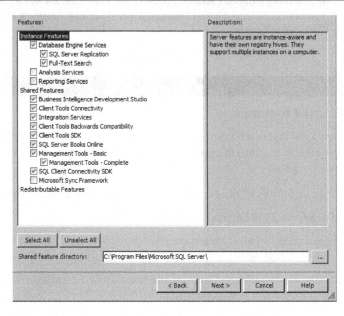

13. Once you've checked the appropriate boxes, click Next.

14. You can now choose the Instance options. Install a named instance with the name and ID of **Sales,** as in the following image:

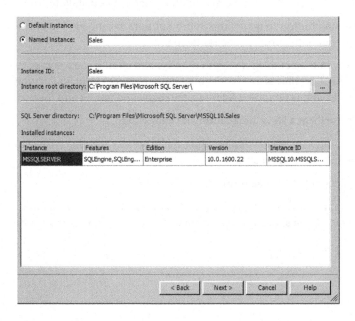

15. Once your installation screen looks like the one in the preceding image, click Next.

16. Assuming you have sufficient drive space on the Disk Space Requirements screen, click Next.

17. On the Server Configuration screen, configure both the SQL Server Agent and the SQL Server Database Engine to run as NT AUTHORITY\SYSTEM. Remember, this is a lab. In a production environment, these services should run as Windows accounts. Make sure both services are set as Startup Type = Automatic (see Figure 2.9 earlier in this chapter). When the configuration of the services is complete, click Next.

18. On the next screen, set the authentication mode to Mixed so you can work with SQL logins for testing. Enter a secure password for the SA account, but do not forget it because you may need it to connect to the SQL Server instance for troubleshooting purposes. Click the Add Current User button and then click Next.

19. Do not send any report information. Simply click Next.

20. As long as the Installation Rules show no errors, click Next. Otherwise, you may need to analyze the errors and potentially restart this exercise.

21. On the Ready to Install screen, click Install to begin the installation of the named instance.

After a few minutes, the installation will complete. You can test the installation by opening SQL Server Management Studio and ensuring that you can connect to the named instance.

Installing to a Cluster

If high availability is important for your database server instance, clustering is an excellent choice. Clustering and the steps required to implement it are covered in detail in Chapter 20, "Server Clustering"; however, a brief overview is presented here.

Clustering is a technology that allows more than one physical server to be available for processing a single application. For example, you may implement a SQL Server instance that primarily runs on SERVER32, but SERVER33 is prepped and ready to take over the instance should SERVER32 fail. SQL Server 2008 can be installed to a failover cluster.

In order to implement a SQL Server cluster, several things must be in place. First, you must have the Windows Clustering service installed and configured properly. SQL Server clustering actually uses the underlying Windows Clustering service. The Windows Clustering service implements a shared IP address for a group of one or more servers (called nodes) participating in the cluster. Only one node is servicing the clients at any given time.

Second, you must provide shared storage for the cluster nodes. If the active node fails, the failover node can only take over the operations if it can access the most current data. This external data may be directly attached external SCSI or even a storage area network (SAN).

Next, you must install SQL Server 2008 as a cluster install. This can be done with the installation program, as you will see in Chapter 20. You can install one node at a time and you can also perform enterprise installations.

Installing Extra Features

It is not uncommon to install SQL Server 2008 only to realize that you missed a component. You can run the installation programs as many times as you need to to install additional components. For example, you may choose not to install Reporting Services when you first set up the database server. After running the server for six months, several users ask you to provide a reporting solution. You analyze the server and determine that it is only 36 percent utilized and decide that it can also support Reporting Services.

At this point you really have two options. You could run the installation program and add features (Reporting Services) to the existing instance or you could install a new instance dedicated to Reporting Services. Valid arguments exist for both options in different situations. As the DBA, you'll need to evaluate the situation and then respond as needed. If the reporting users are not the same users that regularly access and modify the production database, you might want to install Reporting Services in its own instance. It is common to have business analysts who report against data that they do not create.

In addition to the features available from within the installation program, you may choose to download add-ons for SQL Server. You can download several items from the Microsoft websites including:

- Sample databases

- End-to-end example applications

- Service-specific samples (Reporting Services, Integration Services, etc.)

These samples and more can be downloaded from `http:\\sqlserversamples.codeplex` `.com`. If you're trying to grasp how you might use a feature of SQL Server, these sample projects can be very useful. Because they are open source, they can also act as a starting point for new projects you may be required to build.

Upgrading from Previous Versions

So far, only clean installations have been considered. The installations were not dependent on existing versions of SQL Server. In many cases, you can install a clean installation and then migrate the databases over from the previous installation. However, you sometimes need to perform an in-place upgrade. Several options are available. The following section addresses upgrades first and then provides a brief overview of the migration processes used to move databases from older versions of SQL Server over to SQL Server 2008.

Handling Upgrades

Upgrading an application on a client computer is risky business. Upgrading a server that is accessed by many users is downright scary. However, much of the concern can be removed by following two important best practices.

- Always perform a full backup of your databases (including the system databases used by SQL Server) before beginning the upgrade process.

- You should attempt to discover as many potential problems as you can before you start the upgrade.

Upgrading from SQL Server 2000 to 2008

The upgrade from SQL Server 2000 to 2008 is the upgrade most likely to result in application problems. More SQL Server 2000 features have been removed in SQL Server 2008 than SQL Server 2005 features. For this reason alone, you are likely to experience application problems. It's important to look for the use of deprecated features in the current SQL Server 2000 application and database. Finding the deprecated features that were either dropped when SQL Server 2000 was released or dropped between the 2000 and 2005 release can be a bit difficult.

Two sources, however, are helpful. In the SQL Server 2000 Books Online, you can read about features that were in 6.5 and 7.0 that were no longer in SQL Server 2000. In the SQL server 2005 Books Online, you can read the Installation section and look for the Backwards Compatibility section. Here, the deprecated featured are listed. If your application uses any of these features, it will fail in those areas.

You may also use the Upgrade Advisor to see if it can detect any problems in your databases or applications. Remember, however, that the Upgrade Advisor looks at the database and may not have access to analyze all of your application code. You will need to ensure the code is compatible.

Upgrading from SQL Server 2005 to 2008

When you need to find the features that were in SQL Server 2005, but are no longer in SQL Server 2008, your job is much easier. You can run the SQL Server 2005 profile and monitor for Deprecated Features and specifically for the deprecated features under final notice. These features will no longer exist in SQL Server 2008. The good news is that you can have your users run against the existing SQL Server 2005 database as they normally do. All the while, you're monitoring the access to look for these deprecated features. If you find any, you'll have to either rewrite the code for that section of the application or contact the vendor and request an upgrade or a patch.

Understanding Migrations

Migrations are different from upgrades. *Upgrades* are accomplished by installing on top of the existing deployment. *Migrations* are accomplished by performing clean installations and then moving the databases over to the newly installed servers. The clean installations may be named instances on the older server as well.

Migrations are usually simpler than upgrades from a pure database access point of view. However, the feature deprecation issue is still a concern. Whether you upgrade the SQL Server 2000 database to 2008 or copy a database from a 2000 instance to a 2008 instance, you still have to deal with application compatibility issues. That said, migrating a database from SQL Server 7.0 (or earlier) is possible, but you can only upgrade to SQL Server 2008 from a SQL Server 2000 or higher installation.

Migrating from SQL Server 7.0 to 2008

The trick to migrating a SQL Server 7.0 database over to a SQL Server 2008 instance is to migrate it to a SQL Server 2000 instance first. That's right. You simply have to attach the database to a SQL Server 2000 instance and it will be automatically converted to a SQL Server 2000 database. Now, you can detach the database from SQL Server 2000 and attach it directly to SQL Server 2008 in order to migrate it to the new server. However, you *must* still ensure that the database works with SQL Server 2008. Just because you can attach it doesn't mean that all the stored procedures and application code will function properly.

Migrating from SQL Server 2000 and 2005 to 2008

As you might have guessed while reading the previous paragraph, you can migrate a 2000 database over to a 2008 server by simply attaching the database to the 2008 server. Yes, you can use the Copy Database Wizard and it may make things simple for a beginning DBA, but eventually, you'll need to learn how to manually detach and attach databases. SQL Server 2005 databases are migrated in the same way. Attaching and detaching databases is covered in Chapter 8, "Creating SQL Server Databases."

Removing an Installation

You're probably thinking that a section devoted to removing an installation seems to be unneeded. However, improper database removals do occur. In most cases, the mistakes were easy ones to avoid. When you run the Uninstall feature in Add/Remove Programs or simply Programs in Control Panel, pay close attention to these issues:

- Be sure to back up the databases before removing the instance. The Uninstall program doesn't usually delete the databases, but some administrators act too quickly and delete them manually without proper backups.

- Make sure you select the proper instance to uninstall. Because SQL Server supports multiple instances, it's easy to accidentally uninstall the wrong instance.

- Test the remaining instances to make sure they are still operating properly. For example, you may delete one instance and accidentally delete a few shared components with it.

As long as you pay close attention to these reminders, you should find success when removing SQL Server instances.

Summary

This chapter provided the information you needed to install a default or named instance of SQL Server 2008. Of greater importance, you learned how to effectively plan an installation. In addition, upgrades and migrations were covered so that you can implement SQL Server 2008 in an environment where SQL Server 2000 or 2005 already exists. Finally, you learned the simple process used to remove an installation.

Chapter Essentials

Installation Planning   Planning an installation includes discovering current server utilization levels, determining hardware requirements for the new SQL Server 2008 servers, and formulating a time-based plan for implementation.

SQL Server Architecture   It is essential that you understand the architecture of any product if you are to implement it successfully. The SQL Server architecture includes the database system components, data access methods, data write methods, and deployment features.

Data Access   The data access model, in SQL Server, is based on memory buffers. Data is read into the memory buffer and is not removed until space is needed. This behavior increases the likelihood that requested data will already exist in memory and, therefore, improves performance.

Configuring Service Accounts   The SQL Server service accounts should be least privilege accounts. You should not run a production server using the Network Service or System accounts. Windows Domain accounts are the preferred service authentication method.

Installing a Default Instance   Default instances are accessed using UNC paths or IP addresses such as \\SERVER1 or \\10.10.13.89. Some applications require that the database instance used by the application be a default instance.

Installing Named Instances   Named instances are usually accessed using UNC paths such as \\SERVER1\Marketing or \\DB3\Sales. You can install up to 50 instances of SQL Server 2008 Enterprise Edition or up to 16 instances of any other edition.

Installing to a Cluster   When installing a SQL Server 2008 cluster, you must first install and configure the Windows Clustering Service. All nodes in the cluster must have access to shared storage.

Installing Extra Features   Extra features can be installed by running the installation program again. For example, you can install Analysis Services days, weeks, or years after the initial installation. You can also download additional components from Microsoft's various websites. These downloaded components are often free.

Upgrading from Previous Versions   When upgrading from a previous version of SQL Server, it is important that you look for deprecated features. Deprecated features come in two forms: those that will be deprecated in some future version and those that will not exist in the next version. You can also migrate databases from any previous version of SQL Server as long as you have the right versions of SQL Server to install for the detach, attach, detach, attach processes necessary.

Removing an Installation   When removing an installation of SQL Server, perform a backup, make sure you remove the right instance, and verify that the remaining instances are functioning properly after the removal completes.

Chapter

3

Working with the Administration Tools

TOPICS COVERED IN THIS CHAPTER:

- ✓ SQL Server Configuration Manager

- ✓ SQL Server Management Studio

- ✓ SQL Server Business Intelligence Development Studio

- ✓ SQL Server Profiler

- ✓ SQL Server Books Online

- ✓ Windows Server Administration for the DBA

One of Microsoft's strengths, when compared to many other software vendors, is in the area of GUI-based administration tool development. For example, the SQL Server tools have been among the best built-in tools available with any database system for many years. The SQL Server 2008 GUI (graphical user interface) administrative tools have been enhanced since the release of SQL Server 2005 with several very important improvements. This chapter focuses on the GUI tools provided with SQL Server 2008 and the Windows Server operating system. As a DBA, you must learn to navigate through and use these tools as efficiently as possible.

Database administration is more complex today than it used to be. The DBA must be able to administer the database management system (DBMS), the databases, and the server on which the DBMS runs. In the early days of computerized databases, the operating system on which the DBMS ran was a very small footprint OS. Today, even Linux-based DBMS packages are 10 times more complex to manage than the DBMS of old when managing databases with the MS-DOS system required less than 1MB of hard drive space for a minimal install. For that matter, I remember typing in the code for a database system on my Commodore 64 that fit on a single floppy (and, yes, I do mean floppy) disk.

Because DBMS solutions have become so complex, this chapter will cover two categories of tools. First, it will present the SQL Server administration tools, such as the SQL Server Management Studio and the SQL Server Profiler. Second, it will cover some of the basic administration tasks you'll need to understand from a Windows Server perspective. These tasks will include user account management, file system management, and network configuration management.

SQL Server Configuration Manager

The SQL Server Configuration Manager (SSCM) is your one-stop shop for the many options you have when configuring the SQL Server services and protocols. If you need to change the logon account used by a service, this is the place to do it. If you need to disable or enable a protocol for use by a service, this is the place to do that too. In fact, you can perform any of the following tasks from the SSCM:

- Stop and start the SQL Server services
- Change service login information

- Enable or disable network protocols
- Configure aliases on client computers
- Enable or disable protocol encryption for client connections
- Enable or disable filestream support for a SQL Server instance

This section will cover the basic tasks you can perform in the SSCM and then it will walk you through the most common of these tasks.

Overview of the SSCM

It is very important that you perform account maintenance tasks from within SSCM. If you use the Services node in Computer Management, which is built into all Windows Servers starting with Windows Server 2003, you risk disrupting service functionality. When you change a service account from within SSCM, the process ensures that all permissions are granted to the newly assigned account that are needed for a default install of SQL Server and for most SQL Server-based applications. If you change the account settings from within the Services node in Computer Management, you get no such benefit. The service will usually fail to start when you change the account from within Computer Management. The only exception to this would be when you assign an Administrator account to the service and this practice is certainly not recommended.

In addition to account maintenance tasks, you'll use SSCM to configure supported protocols. Several protocols are supported including:

- TCP/IP
- Shared Memory
- Named Pipes
- Virtual Interface Adapter

TCP/IP   Most SQL Servers that are implemented as servers will use TCP/IP. The TCP/IP protocol suite is, without question, the most widely supported protocol solution in use today. The default instance of SQL Server runs on TCP port 1433, if you've accepted the default settings during installation and have not reconfigured these settings after the installation. You must know the port on which SQL Server is listening in order to configure firewalls to allow for communications with the SQL Server. This issue is discussed in more depth later in the section titled "Network Configuration Administration."

Shared Memory   The preceding TCP/IP definition used the phrase "most SQL Servers that are implemented as servers will use TCP/IP." This phrasing may seem odd to you because the product is called SQL Server after all. However, many developers use SQL Server Express Edition as a local database for their applications. In these cases, the Shared Memory protocol is most often used. Shared Memory is a very simple protocol that requires no configuration because all communications happen within the memory of the local machine. The Shared Memory protocol may also be used on test servers for development and other testing purposes.

Named Pipes   Named Pipes is an older protocol that is being used less and less in SQL Server implementations. This transition is mostly due to the excessive overhead incurred when using Named Pipes for communications. Even though TCP/IP has management overhead, the overhead is not as bandwidth intensive as Named Pipes. Local Named Pipes, functioning within the local computer only, may still serve a purpose; however, if Shared Memory is available, this latter option is more efficient still.

Virtual Interface Adapter   The Virtual Interface Adapter (VIA) protocol is used for high-speed connections within data centers. Specialized VIA hardware is required and Microsoft does not provide detailed instructions for working with such hardware. You will have to rely on your hardware vendor for assistance with the configuration of any VIA-based implementation.

Ultimately, the vast majority of SQL Server 2008 server installations will use TCP/IP. It is important that the SQL Server clients have a route to the server and that the route provides sufficient bandwidth. If you provide SQL Server performance tuning services to your clients, you may find that the network infrastructure itself is quite often the real bottleneck in the communications process. If you're using older switches and routers—even if they do support 100Mbps links—they may not have sufficient RAM and processing speed to keep up with intensive database communications. Many database applications communicate with the database server several times just to display a single screen that the user may only access for a few seconds. If several dozen users use the application at the same time...well, you get the picture. The routers and switches between the clients and the server are suddenly very busy.

Figure 3.1 shows the interface for the SSCM utility. As you can see, it uses a traditional Microsoft Management Console (MMC) type interface with a left pane for component or function selection and a right pane for access to specific tasks and objects. The nodes in the left pane allow you to configure three main components: SQL Server Services, SQL Server Network Configuration, and SQL Native Client Configuration.

FIGURE 3.1   The SQL Server Configuration Manager interface

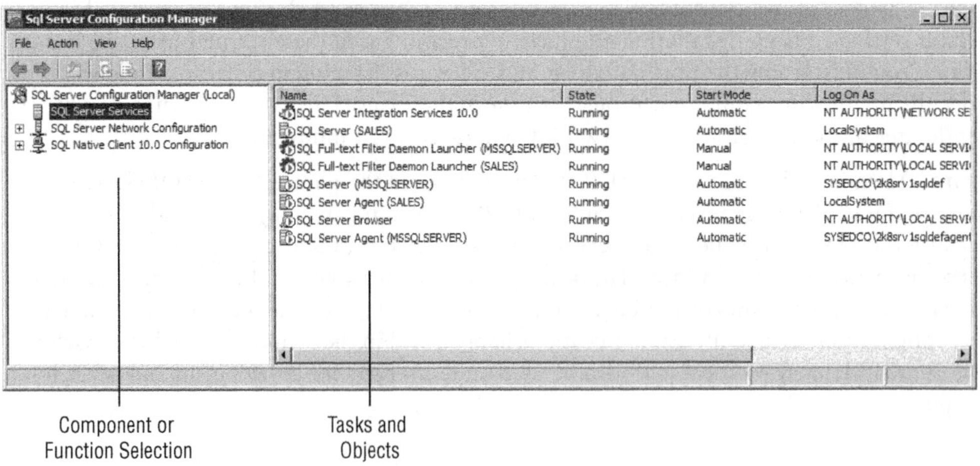

Component or Function Selection   Tasks and Objects

Performing Common SSCM Tasks

You will perform several tasks using SSCM. At times you will need to stop a service or refresh (stop and restart) a service; the SSCM tool will provide access to all of the SQL Server services. You may also need to reconfigure a service. For example, you may need to change the account a service uses to log on or you may need to change a service startup mode so that it starts automatically. In addition, you may need to enable or disable protocols.

Starting and Stopping Services

Starting and stopping SQL Server services is a simple task from within the SSCM tool. Exercise 3.1 steps you through the process of starting and stopping services.

EXERCISE 3.1

Starting and Stopping Services

In this exercise, you will stop and start a SQL Server service using the Configuration Manager.

1. Click Start ➢ Programs (or All Programs) ➢ Microsoft SQL Server 2008 ➢ Configuration Tools ➢ SQL Server Configuration Manager.

2. Click the SQL Server Services node in the left pane, as in the following image.

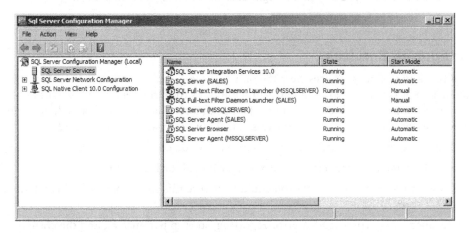

3. Right-click the SQL Server (MSSQLSERVER) service in the right pane and select Stop, as in the following image.

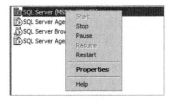

EXERCISE 3.1 *(continued)*

4. If the SQL Server Agent service is running, you will be prompted to allow that service to be stopped as well. Click Yes. Once the service is stopped, the icon will change. Note the difference between the icon in the image before step 2 above and the icon in the following image.

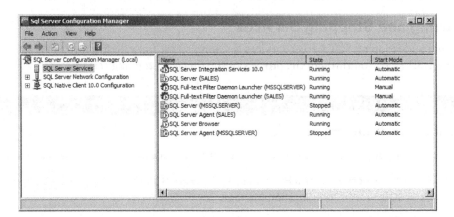

5. To start a service, you will simply right-click the service and select Start.

Configuring Services

If starting and stopping services were the only tasks you could perform in SSCM, it wouldn't be of much use; you can perform these tasks from the Services node within Computer Management. Indeed, you can do much more. One key task you will perform in SSCM is service configuration. Parameters you choose to configure may include:

The service account that is used by the service to log on

The start mode for the service (Automatic, Manual, or Disabled)

Filestream support (you knew you could configure this somewhere after installation, didn't you?)

Advanced properties, such as error reporting, startup parameters, and the crash dump directory

Exercise 3.2 details the steps you need to go through to configure service properties.

EXERCISE 3.2

Configuring Service Properties

In this exercise, you will confirm that the SQL Server (MSSQLSERVER) default instance is configured for automatic startup. You will also enable error reporting.

1. Launch the SQL Server Configuration Manager by selecting Start ≻ All Programs ≻ Microsoft SQL Server 2008 ≻ Configuration Tools ≻ SQL Server Configuration Manager.

2. Click the SQL Server Services node in the left pane.

3. Right-click the SQL Server (MSSQLSERVER) item in the right pane and select Properties.

4. On the Service tab, select Automatic for the Start Mode and click the Apply button.

5. On the Advanced tab, select Yes for Error Reporting and click the Apply button as shown in the following image.

6. Click OK. Note the message indicating that a restart is required in order for the Error Reporting change to be enabled.

7. Right-click on the SQL Server (MSSQLSERVER) item in the right pane and select Restart to refresh the service.

At this point, Error Reporting is enabled and the service is configured to start automatically when the operating system starts.

Configuring Protocols

SQL Server–supported protocols can be configured from two perspectives on the servers or the clients:

- You can configure the server protocols used by the server service to listen for incoming connections. If a SQL Server installation receives a connection from another machine, it is acting as the server.

- You can configure the SQL Native Client protocols for use when connecting to a SQL Server as a client. For example, if one SQL Server connects to another SQL Server to retrieve data, the connecting or retrieving server is acting as a client.

Server protocols are configured in the SQL Server Network Configuration node. SQL Server Native Client protocols are configured in the SQL Server Native Client 10.0 Configuration node. In addition, you can configure aliases for the SQL Server Native Client. *Aliases* allow you to connect to a named instance on a server using a simple name rather than having to connect to the server with a longer UNC path like \\SQLServer1\ Marketing. For example, Figure 3.2 shows the configuration of an alias named Mkt that points to the server instance at \\192.168.23.46\Marketing on TCP port 1478. Creating an alias is as simple as expanding the SQL Server Native Client 10.0 Configuration node and then right-clicking on the Aliases node and selecting New Alias. Exercise 3.3 provides step-by-step instructions for protocol configuration.

FIGURE 3.2   Creating an alias

Verify Protocol Requirements

Make sure you do not need a protocol before you disable it. Always check with your application vendor if you are unsure or use a Network Protocol analyzer to see if any activity is occurring that uses the protocol in question.

EXERCISE 3.3

Configuring Protocols

In this exercise, you will ensure that TCP/IP is enabled for the SQL Server Network Configuration and that Named Pipes is disabled in the SQL Server native client. Both settings will be configured for the SQL Server (MSSQLSERVER) default instance.

1. Launch the SQL Server Configuration Manager by selecting Start ➢ All Programs ➢ Microsoft SQL Server 2008 ➢ Configuration Tools ➢ SQL Server Configuration Manager.

2. Click the SQL Server Network Configuration node in the left pane.

3. Double-click on Protocols for MSSQLSERVER in the right pane.

4. Ensure that TCP/IP is set to Enabled. If it is not, double-click TCP/IP and set the value for Enabled to Yes. Note that the IP Addresses tab can be used to select which IP addresses should be used for SQL Server on a server with multiple NICs or multiple IP addresses associated with a single NIC.

5. Click OK.

6. Click the SQL Server Native Client 10.0 Configuration node in the left pane.

7. Double-click on the Client Protocols item in the right pane.

8. If Named Pipes is Enabled, double-click it and select No for the Enabled property and then click OK.

The SQL Server Configuration Manager is a very simple tool to use, but it is important that you use it carefully. It is the tool that determines what protocols are in use and on what IP addresses the SQL Server listens. These settings are very important.

WMI Scripting and the SSCM

Windows Management Instrumentation (WMI) is fully supported for SQL Server configuration management. You can use it to read the configuration settings and even configure certain SQL Server settings. In most cases, this is done with VBScript scripts. To create a VBScript script file, follow these general instructions:

1. Open the Notepad application.

2. Type the code into the Notepad editing window.

3. Save the file with a file name having a .VBS extension to create a VBS file.

As an example script, consider the following VBScript code:

```
set wmiObject = GetObject(
"WINMGMTS:\\.\root\Microsoft\SqlServer\ComputerManagement10"
```

```
)
for each prop in wmiObject.ExecQuery(
"select * from SqlServiceAdvancedProperty
where SQLServiceType = 1 AND PropertyName = 'VERSION'"
)
WScript.Echo prop.ServiceName & " " & prop.PropertyName &
": " & prop.PropertyStrValue
Next
```

The first thing this code example does is create a wmiObject and then query that object to get the name and version number for each instance of SQL Server installed. Next, the service name and the version value are echoed to the screen. If you enter this code into a VBS file and then double-click on the VBS file, you'll see the results. The point is simple: with a little scripting, you can accomplish a lot using WMI.

Microsoft is committed to assisting overworked IT professionals with the automation of their environments. WMI scripting is just one way in which they are doing this. As you'll see in the next chapter, Windows PowerShell can also be used with the SQL Server snap-in for PowerShell.

SQL Server Management Studio (SSMS)

SQL Server 2005 introduced the new SQL Server Management Studio (SSMS). When compared with the Enterprise Manager, which was used in earlier versions of SQL Server, the SSMS interface provides many enhancements. Much like the Enterprise Manager, the vast majority of actions taken in SSMS are really just calls to the database engine using Transact-SQL code. At least two benefits arise from this architecture.

First, you can learn to automate administrative tasks by capturing the actions when a Script button is not available or by viewing the code directly when a Script button is available. Second, you can discover which settings are stored in the Registry (and some still are) and which settings are stored in the internal configuration tables (system tables). When settings are stored in the Registry, the SSMS application must call for Registry access instead of the normal T-SQL code.

Overview of the SSMS

Like most Windows applications, the SSMS interface has a menu bar across the top as well as a toolbar area, as shown in Figure 3.3. The panes, such as the Object Explorer shown on the left, can be docked or undocked; and they can be located on the left, top, right, bottom, or middle of the screen. There's a common joke about needing a 30-inch widescreen LCD for all administrators; however, it's only a joke if your budget will not allow it. A 28-inch screen is useful for most administrative tasks. The larger screen space (sometimes called screen real estate) allows more information to be on the screen at the same time. You will need to have a minimum resolution of 1024×768 for many dialogs to function as designed in SSMS.

FIGURE 3.3   The SSMS interface

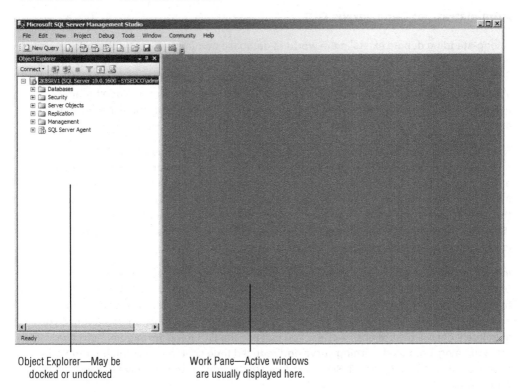

Object Explorer—May be   Work Pane—Active windows
docked or undocked   are usually displayed here.

The SSMS tool is used for the vast majority of SQL Server 2008 administrative tasks. The major tasks include:

Configuring database engine properties

Creating, altering, securing, and deleting databases, tables, views, and other database objects

Creating and working with jobs, operators, and alerts

Performing backups with the built-in backup toolset

Reporting on server performance and operations

Monitoring server activity and managing connections

As you can see, the list is long and quite complete. With SQL Server 2008, very few tasks require you to write administrative code as a DBA. However, the writing of such code is yet another capability within SSMS. In fact, it has been improved with a new error-tracking feature and better Intellisense support.

Real World Scenario

Administration: Code versus GUI

A long-standing debate exists in the world of database administration. On the side of coding, you have the DBAs who insist that administration through code is the only proper administration method or that it is the best method. On the side of GUI administration, you have the DBAs who ask why they should spend all that time writing code for an action they can perform in less than one minute. In my opinion, both sides have valid arguments.

First, administration through code provides several benefits. You can save the code and use it as documentation for work performed. You can make small changes to the code at a later time and reuse it to accomplish a similar task. You may gain a better understanding of the inner workings of the SQL Server Database Engine. Finally, you can administer the server from any client that can execute Transact-SQL code against the server. Clearly, the benefits are many. However, two major drawbacks exist for the beginning DBA: the learning curve is greater and the time cost is higher.

In fact, the drawbacks of code-based administration are the primary benefits of GUI-based administration. It's also true that the benefits of code-based administration have been the drawbacks of GUI administration for many years. However, SQL Server 2005 and now SQL Server 2008 changed all that. With Microsoft's GUI management tools, you absolutely get the best of both worlds. You can use the GUI to perform administrative tasks (gaining a reduced learning curve and reduced time cost) and use the built-in Script button to save the action as a T-SQL code file. That's right! You don't have to sacrifice one for the other.

In the past, with Enterprise Manager (SQL Server 2000 and earlier), you could script objects after they were created, but you could not configure an object (such as a database) in the GUI and generate a script to create it in the first place. The benefit of generating the script first and then creating the object from the script is that you can add T-SQL parameters that may not be easily available in the GUI.

SSMS is a real-world, powerful tool for the modern DBA. You can script all you want and you can use the GUI while still saving code as documentation, reusing code with slight modifications, improving your understanding of the database internals, and administering the server from any client (as long as you can access your SQL code repository or have learned coding through experience). Can you tell that I like the SSMS toolset?

Performing Common SSMS Tasks

The first thing you'll need to do in SSMS is configure it to your liking. This means adjusting fonts, determining default window layouts, and adjusting other important global settings. To configure global settings, click the Tools menu and select Options. You'll be presented with a dialog like the one in Figure 3.4.

FIGURE 3.4   The SSMS Options dialog

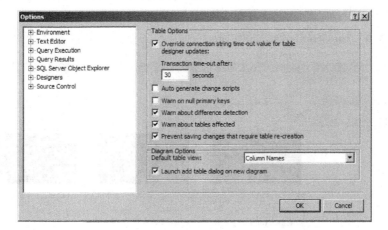

As you can see, you have several configuration options including:

Environment. Startup window layouts, tabbed interfaces versus multiple document interfaces (MDI), fonts and text colors, keyboard shortcut schemes, and options for Help configuration.

Text Editor. File extensions mapped to editor configurations, statement completion options, editor tab and status bar configuration settings.

Query Execution. Configure the batch separator keyword (that's right, you could use something instead of GO), stipulate the number of rows a query is allowed to return before the server cancels the query, and configure advanced execution settings such as deadlock priorities and transaction isolation levels.

Query Results. Specify that query results are presented as a grid, text, or file, and configure various parameters for the different kinds of result sets.

SQL Server Object Explorer. Change the top n number of records to a value greater or less than 1,000, and configure options for automatic scripting of objects such as tables or entire databases.

Designers and Source Control. Configure settings for the table designer, the maintenance plan designer, and source control management.

Look through these various options and make sure the environment is configured so that it is optimized for the way you work. For example, you could start SSMS with the Environment set to open the Object Explorer and the Activity Monitor automatically on startup. This will make your SSMS screen look like Figure 3.5 on initial startup. You may not like this configuration, however, but that's the beauty of the tool: you can configure it as you like it. Most beginning DBAs prefer an interface similar to the one in Figure 3.5, but as you work with the tool, you may realize that activity monitoring is a very small part of your job and you may want the initial screen to show different views that relate more to your common daily routines.

FIGURE 3.5   Tom's preferred SSMS startup

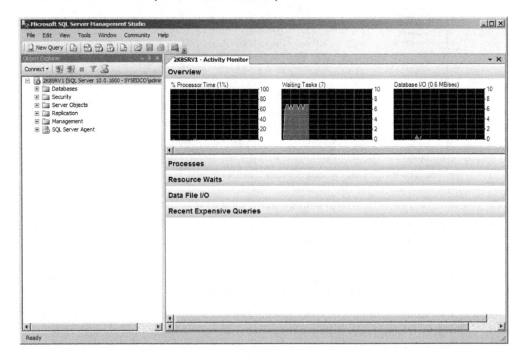

In the following sections, you will learn to configure the various windows in SSMS. You will launch a New Query window and view the error list, which is a new feature in SQL Server 2008. You will also look at reports against the AdventureWorks database. Finally, you will learn to script a task that is configured in the GUI interface.

If you have not already done so, you will need to download and install the AdventureWorks database before performing this exercise. Chapter 2, "Installing SQL Server 2008," provides instructions for acquiring the AdventureWorks database.

Loading SSMS and Working with Windows

The first thing you'll need to do to configure SSMS is launch it from the Microsoft SQL Server 2008 program group. Then you can configure and work with windows within the application. Exercise 3.4 steps you through this process.

EXERCISE 3.4

Initial SSMS Configuration

1. Log on to the Windows server as an Administrator.

2. Launch SQL Server Management Studio by clicking Start ➢ All Programs ➢ Microsoft SQL Server 2008 ➢ SQL Server Management Studio.

3. You will be presented with a connection dialog like the one in the following image. Select the appropriate server (the default instance in this case) and choose Windows Authentication to allow your administrative credentials to pass through.

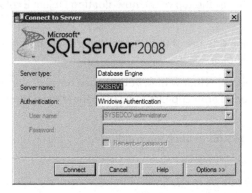

4. Click the Connect button when everything is configured appropriately in the Connect to Server dialog box.

5. To modify the status of the Object Explorer window (also called a pane or panel), click the Windows Position button, which looks like an arrow pointing down, in the upper-right corner of the Object Explorer window.

EXERCISE 3.4   *(continued)*

6. Select Floating from the list and notice that the window is now released from the rest of the SSMS interface as in the following image.

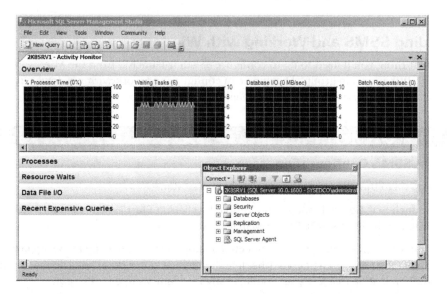

7. Right-click the title bar at the top of the now-floating Object Explorer window and select Dockable.

8. Left-click and drag the title bar of the Object Explorer window and notice that several docking indicators appear.

9. Drag the Object Explorer window until your mouse hovers over the left docking indicator and a blue shaded area appears indicating that the windows will be docked there.

10. Release the mouse button to dock the window.

You can add more windows to the SSMS interface from the View menu. For example, if you select View ➢ Other Windows ➢ Web Browser, you can open a web browser inside of the SSMS interface. If you've opened a web browser window in SSMS, please click the X in the upper-right corner of the web browser windows to close it before continuing.

Query Editor Windows and Error Lists

The Error List view is a new feature of the Query Editor in SQL Server 2008, and it is very helpful in tracking down problems. Exercise 3.5 shows how to launch a New Query window and use the Error List view as well.

EXERCISE 3.5

Opening a New Query Window and Viewing the Error List

1. Click the New Query button or press Ctrl+N to open a Query Editor window, as shown in the following image.

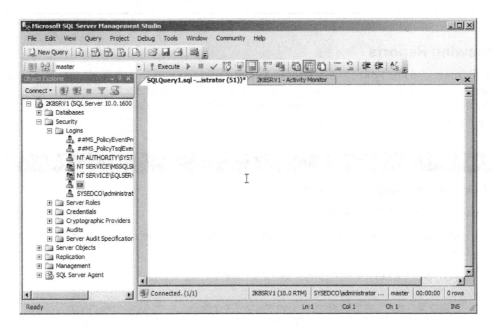

2. Enter the following code into the Query Editor window:

```
USE master;
CREATE Database test;
USE test;
```

3. The word test in the USE test; line of code will be underlined in red on your screen, which indicates an error.

4. Click View ➢ Error List to view the cause of the error as shown in the following image.

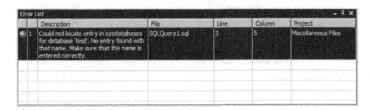

5. To close the Query Editor, click the X in the upper-right corner of the SQLQuery1.sql window and choose No when the Save Changes dialog appears.

6. Click the X in the upper-right corner of the Error List window to close the window.

In case you would like to resolve the problem in the previous code snippet, you would insert a GO directive between the CREATE Database statement and the USE test statement.

Viewing Reports

SQL Server 2005 first introduced integrated predesigned reports into the SSMS interface. SQL Server 2008 has improved on these reports and increased the number of reports. However, the method for accessing the reports has also changed. To view database reports, perform the steps in Exercise 3.6.

EXERCISE 3.6

Viewing Predesigned Reports

1. Expand the Databases node in the SSMS Object Explorer.

2. Right-click on the AdventureWorks database and select Reports ➤ Standard Reports ➤ Disk Usage.

3. View the report in the right panel as shown here.

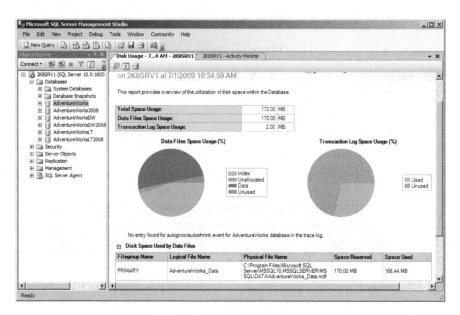

4. Close the report by clicking the X in the upper-right corner of the report window.

You can view any report on any database by repeating the steps listed here and replacing AdventureWorks with the intended database and Disk Usage with the intended report. You can also view server-level reports by right-clicking the root server node and selecting Reports.

Scripting Administrative Tasks

One of my favorite features, first introduced in SQL Server 2005, is the ability to generate scripts for administrative tasks. These scripts provide documentation of the actions taken and may be used to repeat the actions at a later time. Exercise 3.7 makes these steps simple.

EXERCISE 3.7

Administrative Task Scripts

1. In the Object Explorer's Databases node, right-click on the AdventureWorks database and select Properties.

2. Select the Options page in the Database Properties - AdventureWorks dialog.

3. Change the Recovery model value to Full, as in the following image.

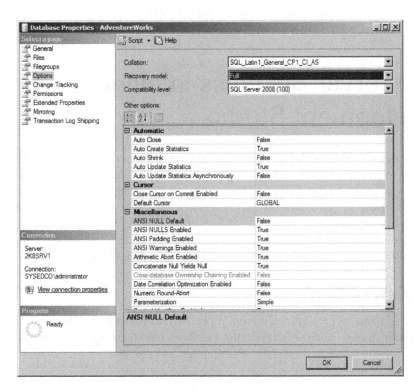

4. Do not click OK. Instead, click the Script button and you may see some brief screen flashing behind the Database Properties - AdventureWorks dialog. This behavior is normal.

5. Click Cancel to close the dialog.

6. You should see a Query Editor window with code similar to the following:

```
USE [master]
GO
ALTER Database [AdventureWorks] SET RECOVERY FULL WITH NO_WAIT
GO
```

7. Execute the code by clicking the Execute button or by pressing F5 on the keyboard.

At this point, the AdventureWorks database is running in the Full recovery model (don't worry, you'll learn all about it in Chapter 16, "Backup and Restoration"), and you've learned how to generate a script from within an administrative GUI dialog.

You may want to spend some more time exploring SSMS. As long as you are on a test machine, you really can't do any damage so go ahead and explore its many features.

SQL Server Business Intelligence Development Studio

The SQL Server Business Intelligence Development Studio (lovingly known as BIDS to reduce the mouthful) is used for Reporting Services, Analysis Services, and Integration Services projects. In this book, you will focus on core administration of SQL Server so most of the content will be related to Integration Services. However, Chapter 12, "Implementing Advanced Features," will introduce you to Reporting Services and Analysis Services. Integration Services will be covered in detail in Chapters 12, 13, and 21. For now, let's look at the basic features and interface provided by the BIDS application.

Overview of BIDS

BIDS is used to create projects of different types. BIDS is basically a slimmed-down version of Visual Studio (Microsoft's premium software-development environment) designed specifically for working with SQL Server components such as Reporting Services and Integration Services. With a default installation, you can create any of the following project types:

Analysis Services Project   The Analysis Services projects are used to contain and manage the resources used for an Analysis Services database. An Analysis Services project can be created based on an existing database or by using the Analysis Services template.

Import Analysis Services 2008 Database   This is the method used to create an Analysis Services project from an existing SQL Server 2008 Analysis Services database. The process reads the database and builds a project automatically.

Integration Services Project   An Integration Services project contains the various files and objects used to manage an Integration Services package. The package may include several steps to be taken against data sources and destinations.

Integration Services Connections Project Wizard   This alternative to the Integration Services Project option allows you to step through a wizard while creating the Integration Services Project. The wizard assists you in creating connections to data sources and destinations.

Report Server Project   The Report Server project contains objects for Reporting Services reports. One or more reports may be contained within a project.

Report Server Project Wizard   The Report Server Project Wizard option results in the same Reporting Services project as the simpler Report Server Project option. The difference is that the wizard holds your hand as you make key decisions about the report.

Report Model Project   Report Models are used to abstract the underlying data so that users can easily build reports on the data. Report Models are created and published to Reporting Services servers.

In addition to the concept of projects, BIDS supports solutions (as does SSMS). A *solution* is a collection of one or more projects. For example, you may create a solution that includes an Analysis Services project, an Integration Services project, and a Reporting Services project. The Analysis Services project may be used to manage and accommodate data used by the Integration Services project to provision a data store used by the Reporting Services project. This is the way solutions are intended to be used: Projects that "solve" a problem are grouped together.

Figure 3.6 shows the BIDS interface. As you can see, it is very similar to the SSMS interface. It supports the floating or docked windows and even includes an error-tracking interface much like the Query Editor in SSMS.

Performing Common BIDS Tasks

The most common tasks a DBA performs in BIDS are managing projects and creating Integration Services packages. For DBAs who also create and manage reports, the Report Server projects may also be used; for DBAs who must work with data warehouses, business intelligence, and the like, Analysis Services projects will be used. The primary focus of this book is on the implementation and administration of the core SQL Server functionality, so this section will walk you through working with projects and creating a basic Integration Services package.

FIGURE 3.6   The BIDS interface

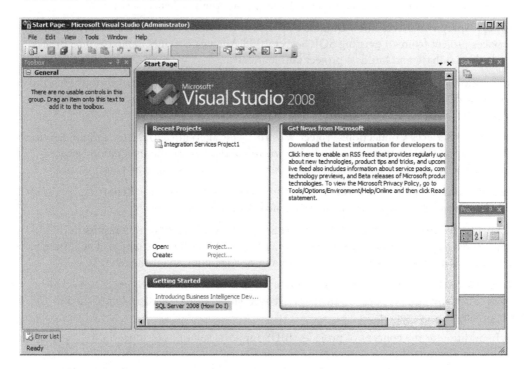

Working with Projects and Solutions

Solutions are a bit confusing to beginners working in BIDS. This is because the File menu does not contain a New Solution option. However, projects exist in solutions. Because you cannot create a new solution directly and projects are said to exist in solutions, many users get confused. The key to clearing out the cobwebs is to notice what the New Project dialog presents. Take a look at Figure 3.7 and notice the last field labeled *Solution Name*. This is where you create a new solution.

Once you've created a single project solution, you can add new projects to it. If you open a solution and then click File ➤ New ➤ Project, the New Project dialog changes to allow for the creation of new projects within an existing solution. Notice the difference in Figure 3.8.

When you have multiple projects in a single solution, the Solution Explorer window looks similar to what you see in Figure 3.9. You can easily move from one project to another and the solution is a useful way to bring related projects together into one location for management and utilization.

FIGURE 3.7   Creating a new project and solution

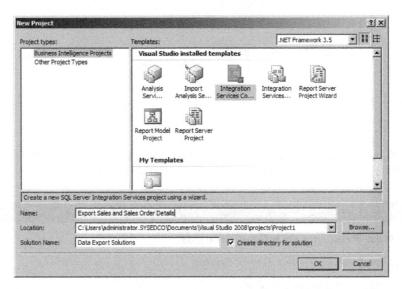

FIGURE 3.8   Adding a project to an existing solution

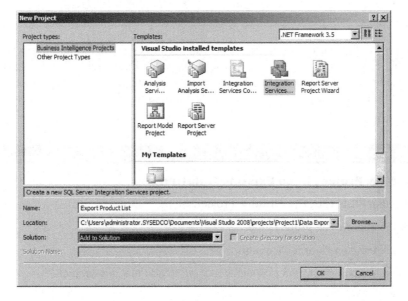

FIGURE 3.9   Solution Explorer with multiple projects

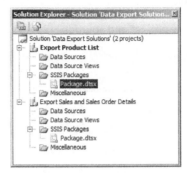

One of the primary tasks you'll perform in BIDS is creating a project and one or more solutions. Exercise 3.8 walks you through the simple steps used to perform these tasks.

EXERCISE 3.8

Create a New Project and a New Solution

1. From within BIDS, click File ➤ New ➤ Project.

2. Select the appropriate project type.

3. Provide a name, storage location, and solution name.

4. Click OK.

Sometimes you'll have an existing solution and need to create additional projects within that solution. For example, you may have a solution called Engineering Database Projects. You may need to add a Reporting Services project or an Integration Services project to this existing solution. Exercise 3.9 provides the steps required to add a project to an existing solution.

EXERCISE 3.9

Create a New Project in an Existing Solution

1. From within BIDS, click File ➤ New ➤ Project.

2. Select the appropriate project type.

3. Provide a name and storage location.

4. Choose the existing solution to which you want to add the new project.

5. Click OK.

If you need to delete a project from a solution, you'll need to perform the steps in Exercise 3.10. You may need to delete a project if the project no longer serves your needs or if you've replaced it with a newer project. It's not uncommon to create a new version of a project before deleting the old version. This way you can continue using the old version until the new version is complete and fully tested.

EXERCISE 3.10

Delete a Project from a Solution

1. From within BIDS, ensure that the Solution Explorer window is open by selecting View ➢ Solution Explorer or pressing Ctrl+Alt+L.

2. In the Solution Explorer window, right-click the project you want to delete and select Remove.

3. Click OK to accept that the project will be removed.

4. Save or discard changes in the Save Changes dialog that appears by selecting Yes to save changes or No to discard them.

Creating Integration Services Packages

SQL Server Integration Services (SSIS) packages allow you to perform ETL tasks—among many others. ETL stands for extract, transform, and load. You may need to extract data from one source, transform (also called massage by some) the data in some way, and then load it into a destination. Or you may simply read the data, transform it, and then write it back into the source. Whatever the ETL needs, SSIS is the solution in SQL Server. SSIS allows you to create packages that perform hundreds of potential data-related tasks. BIDS is used to create these SSIS packages.

In fact, SSIS is so powerful that many organizations have purchased SQL Server Standard Edition just to get the SSIS component for their other database servers, such as MySQL or Oracle. There's no question that SSIS is powerful; however, this power does come at a cost and that cost is in the area of complexity. SSIS is so complex that very large books are devoted to covering the topic. For now, you will just learn to export some data from a database. In Chapter 12, you'll dive a little deeper into what SSIS can do.

You have two basic options for creating an SSIS package. You can either run a wizard that creates the package for you or you can manually create the package step-by-step using BIDS. Of course, wizards are easier to use, but they are also less powerful. However, you'll start with the easy task of creating an export package by using a wizard. Exercise 3.11 steps you through the process of using the Import and Export Wizard.

EXERCISE 3.11

Using the Import and Export Wizard

1. Launch the Import and Export Wizard by clicking Project ➤ SSIS Import and Export Wizard. When you do this, a Welcome dialog box appears. Just click Next to move on from the Welcome dialog and you'll see a screen like the following:

2. In the preceding image, the defaults were accepted with the exception of the database, where AdventureWorks was chosen. You could also choose a remote server or a different client. For example, clients are provided for Oracle, Microsoft Access, Microsoft Excel, and many other data sources. With the AdventureWorks database selected, click Next.

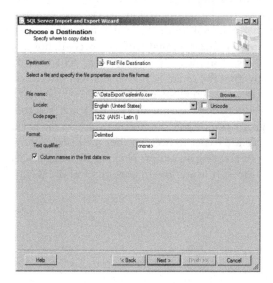

3. The preceding image shows how to configure the Choose a Destination screen. The data is being exported to a flat file named C:\ DataExport\salesinfo.csv. A column delimiter was chosen, which means that the delimiting character can be selected later in the wizard. The Column Names in the First Data Row option is also selected, which will provide a quality data source for importing into other systems. With these settings in place, you can click Next to move on from the Choose a Destination screen.

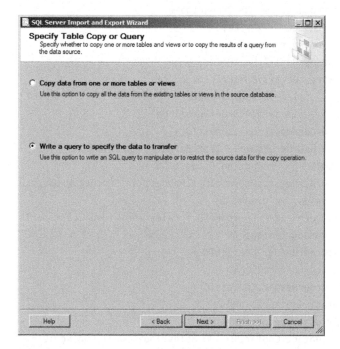

4. In the Specify Table Copy or Query dialog, choose to Write a Query to Specify the Data to Transfer. This will allow you to easily pull just the data you need. With this option selected, click Next. The next screen asks you to provide a source query. You can load one from a file or type the query manually. Enter the following query:

```
SELECT     Sales.SalesOrderHeader.SalesOrderID,
Sales.SalesOrderHeader.OrderDate,
Sales.SalesOrderHeader.DueDate,
Sales.SalesOrderHeader.Status,
Sales.SalesOrderHeader.AccountNumber,
Sales.SalesOrderHeader.PurchaseOrderNumber,
Person.Contact.ContactID,
```

```
Person.Contact.FirstName,
Person.Contact.LastName,
Person.Contact.EmailAddress,
Person.Contact.Phone,
Sales.SalesOrderDetail.SalesOrderDetailID,
Production.Product.ProductID,
Production.Product.Name AS ProductName,
Production.Product.ListPrice,
Sales.SalesOrderDetail.OrderQty,
Sales.SalesOrderDetail.UnitPrice,
Sales.SalesOrderDetail.UnitPriceDiscount
FROM          Sales.SalesOrderHeader
INNER JOIN    Sales.SalesOrderDetail ON
Sales.SalesOrderHeader.SalesOrderID =
    Sales.SalesOrderDetail.SalesOrderID
    INNER JOIN    Production.Product ON
Sales.SalesOrderDetail.ProductID = Production.Product.ProductID
INNER JOIN Sales.Individual ON
Sales.SalesOrderHeader.CustomerID = Sales.Individual.CustomerID
INNER JOIN Person.Contact ON
Sales.SalesOrderHeader.ContactID =
Person.Contact.ContactID AND
Sales.SalesOrderHeader.ContactID =
Person.Contact.ContactID AND
Sales.Individual.ContactID =
    Person.Contact.ContactID AND Sales.Individual.ContactID =
    Person.Contact.ContactID;
```

5. Don't worry too much about the T-SQL code for now. Just know that you are pulling data from several tables and aggregating it together for your users. The code you use in real-world scenarios would be very different because you would be dealing with your specific databases and the data you need to export. This query is one of the most complicated areas in the wizard. You could use the GUI Query Designer to write the query and then copy and paste it here. To use the GUI Query Designer, open a New Query windows, right click in the window, and select Design Query in Editor. The following image shows the wizard dialog with the query in place. You can click the Parse button to ensure that the code is correct and without syntax errors. Once you are sure the query is correct, click Next.

6. The Configure Flat File Destination screen allows you to change the column delimiter, but you will accept the default of a comma. Commas are supported by most data applications that can import a delimited file. In fact, most delimited files are either known as comma-delimited or tab-delimited files. For example, Microsoft Excel supports automatic importing of comma-delimited data stored in CSV files. This screen also allows you to edit mappings so that you can exclude some columns or rename the destination if desired. You can even preview the data to make sure it looks the way it should. Leave the options at their defaults as shown in the following image and click Next.

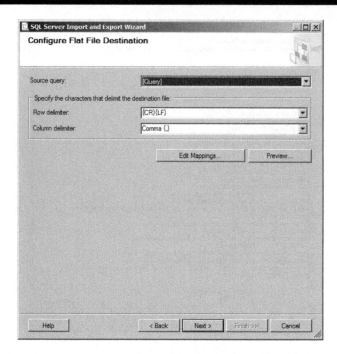

7. The final screen is a summary screen that indicates the choices you've made. It gives you a final chance to go back and make changes. Because everything is configured the way you need it, click Finish. Hopefully, the report will indicate that the export function was created successfully. If it does, you can click Close to exit the wizard.

Once the wizard completes, you'll notice a new package resting in your project. The package is usually named something useless like Package 1 or Package 2 or something like that. You may want to right-click it and select Rename to give it a more meaningful name. The example was renamed ExportCSVSales, and you can see the result in Figure 3.10.

Notice that the Data Flow tab was selected in Figure 3.10 so you can see the items that are used by the wizard. That seemingly lengthy wizard used only two data flow items: a data source and a data destination. The data source is the T-SQL query and the data destination is the flat file. What was the transformation in this case? It was the aggregation of data from multiple underlying tables. They've been combined into one flat data source.

If you want to test the package, you can click the Debug menu and select Start Debugging or press the F5 key on your keyboard. The debugging results are shown in Figure 3.11. When you debug a package, you hope to see all green boxes in the end. If you do, you can click the Debug menu and select Stop Debugging or press Shift+F5.

FIGURE 3.10   Viewing the package created by the wizard

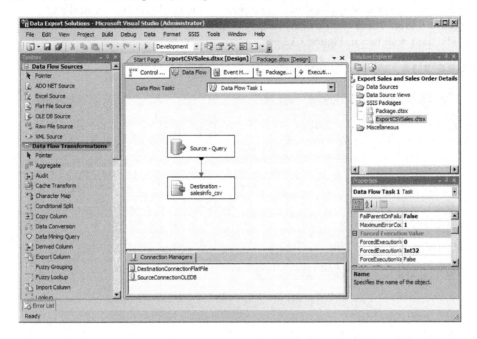

FIGURE 3.11   Debugging the package

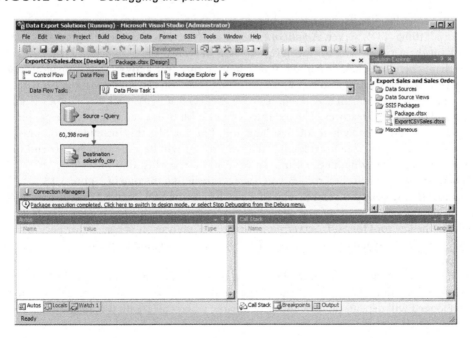

The last step is to look at the package output from the debugging session. If you followed along on a test server, you should have a file named `salesinfo.csv` in the `C:\ExportData` folder. When you navigate to that folder, you can open the file to view the contents. The data is shown in Figure 3.12 as it appears in Notepad.

FIGURE 3.12   Viewing the CSV data

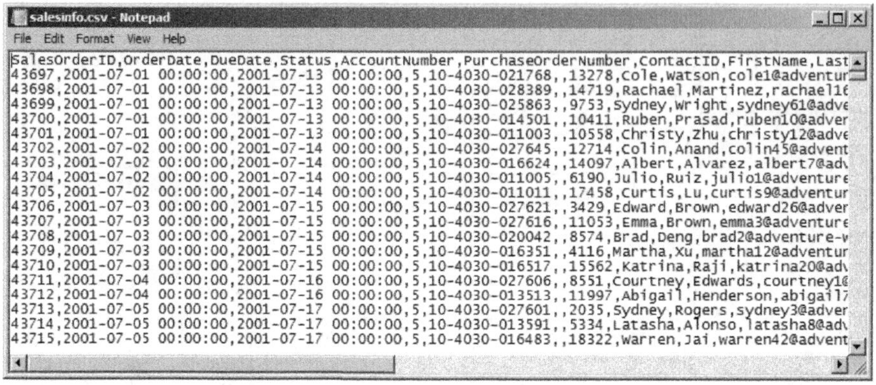

SQL Server Profiler

The SQL Server Profiler (from here on simply called Profiler) is like a network packet analyzer for all things SQL Server. A *network packet analyzer* is a software program that reads packets off the network wire for low-level analysis. In reality, the SQL Server Profiler is even better than a network packet analyzer. It not only captures the activity that transpires based on network requests, but it also captures everything else. You can monitor for general activity, such as T-SQL statement execution, or more advanced activity, such as deadlock occurrences and deprecated features. The interface can be a bit overwhelming to some people because it is a blank slate when you first launch it. But don't let this intimidate you into running away. As you'll see in later chapters, the Profiler will become your best friend for troubleshooting, analyzing, and optimizing your SQL Server installations.

When you first launch the Profiler, you'll see a screen like the one in Figure 3.13. Looking at this screen, you can see why so many beginning SQL Server DBAs simply click the X in the upper-right corner and never look back; however, this is a big mistake. The Profiler is the key tool for SQL Server monitoring and analysis. It is perfect for performance tuning, application troubleshooting, and simply learning more about the inner workings of SQL Server.

To make something happen in the Profiler, you need to create something called a trace. A *trace* is a collection of logged information stored in a file or a database table. The information logged will depend on the choices you make when you create the trace.

FIGURE 3.13   The SQL Server Profiler default interface

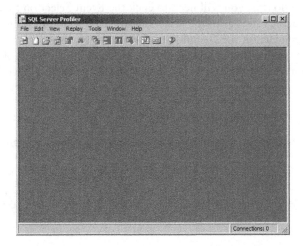

When you select File ➢ New Trace, the server and service to which you want to connect must be provided. Once the connection is established, you may configure the trace properties which include the trace name, the template used or a blank template, the file or table name in which to save the trace, and the trace stop time for when you want the trace to stop automatically. Figure 3.14 shows these basic settings. You should know that you can create a trace without specifying a file or table name to indicate that you only want to retain the trace in the server's memory. This is useful for quick analysis when you do not need to save the trace log.

FIGURE 3.14   Basic Profiler trace settings

In addition to the basic settings, you may also choose to customize the events you want to log. If you want to do this, you will need to click the Event Selection tab. You will be presented with a screen similar to the one in Figure 3.15 assuming you've chosen the Standard (default) template on the General tab. Notice the Show All Events and Show All columns check boxes in the lower-right corner. If you check one or both of these check boxes, you will be amazed at the amount of information that can be logged or traced by the Profiler.

FIGURE 3.15   Event selection in a Profiler trace

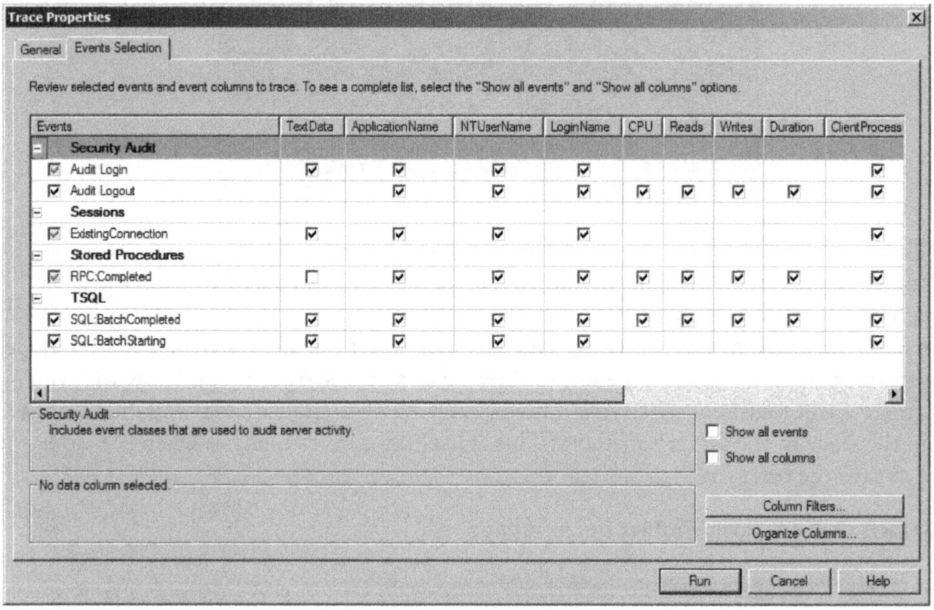

Because so many events and columns exist, it's good to know that you can also filter on the Event Selection tab. Clicking the Column Filters button will bring up the dialog shown in Figure 3.16. From here, you can filter on any column value and you can look for either matches ("like") or mismatches ("not like"). This feature can be used to monitor only events triggered from a specific application, a specific user, a specific computer (by host name), and more.

Once you have created the trace settings, you can click the Run button and the trace will begin to run immediately. Figure 3.17 shows a trace running, which uses the Standard (default) template and no custom event selections of filters. The SSMS was launched after the trace started, and all of the captured events shown in Figure 3.17 were generated. While this is a simple example, it does reveal the power of the tool. Additionally, you can see the options available while a trace is running.

FIGURE 3.16   Event filtering in a Profiler trace

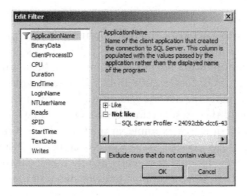

FIGURE 3.17   Capturing SSMS startup events

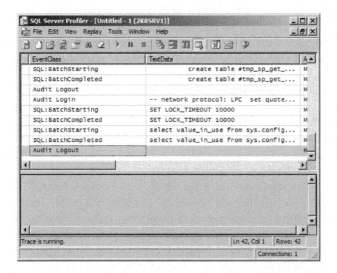

Here's the good news. If you create a trace, but forget to specify the file or table name, you can save the trace anyway. Just stop the trace once you've captured everything you need to capture and then select File ➢ Save As to choose among tables, trace files, or XML trace files.

You'll revisit the Profiler in Chapter 14, "Performance Monitoring and Tuning." In that chapter, you will learn how to trace deadlocks, capture performance traces, and correlate performance logs to Profiler traces.

Books Online

SQL Server has shipped with the most exhaustive online help system of any Microsoft product for several versions now. The online help is called Books Online, and it can be installed from the distribution media (CD or DVD) or it can be downloaded and installed separately. If you search for **SQL Server 2008 Books Online download** at Google.com, the first search result link is usually the newest version waiting for download.

Make sure you download the latest version. Books Online may be updated several times during the life of a given version. For example, at the time of this writing, the most recent version of the SQL Server 2005 Books Online was November 2008 and the SQL Server 2000 Books Online had been updated as recently as July 2007. Clearly, Microsoft corrects errors, adds information, and changes support policies stated in the documentation, so you want to use the most recent copy available.

You may be wondering why a book about SQL Server database administration would bother to cover Books Online. The answer is simple: Books Online is your immediate reference that is always with you on your laptop or desktop computer. You can use it to quickly locate information such as data type descriptions, sample code, and high-level overviews of how various technologies work. The major difference between Books Online and this book is that this book provides you with real-world experience, while Books Online supplies only the cold hard facts. This is as online help should be, but please note that Books Online's examples are usually limited at best.

You should also note that Books Online has some extremely helpful features that most people don't even use. For example, favorites are extremely useful. You can create direct links to pages you'll need again and again, such as the Data Types (Transact-SQL) page or the massive Glossary page. Once you've added a page to your favorites, you can navigate to that page again without having to search for it.

Additionally, you can integrate online searching with Books Online. This way you retrieve the Books Online information plus information at Microsoft TechNet and MSDN. The odds of finding helpful information increase dramatically when integrating with online content; however, you can also easily disable this when working in an area without online access. Simply click the Tools menu and select Options. From here, select the Online child node within the Help node and choose Try Local Only, Not Online.

Finally, the Books Online interface provides a web browser built right into the tool. You can navigate to your favorite SQL Server website or blog using this feature. Once you have loaded the website, you can add it to your favorites. As Figure 3.18 demonstrates, the website will be listed right alongside the internal Books Online links.

FIGURE 3.18   Website favorites and Internal favorites

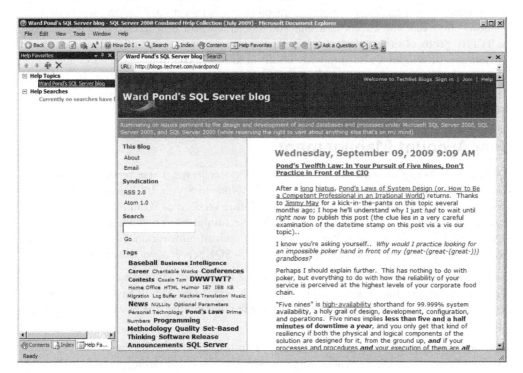

Windows Server Administration for the DBA

In order to configure a SQL Server properly, you will need to understand the basics of Windows Server account management. Each service should run in the context of either a local Windows account or a Windows Domain (Active Directory) account. If you are not a Windows administrator (in that you do not belong to the local Administrators group or the Domain Admins group), you may need to solicit the help of someone who has the appropriate privileges. Either way, you'll need to know the appropriate settings for the user accounts used by the SQL Server services.

Next, you'll need to understand the basics of file management. At least two important skills must be acquired: folder management and permission management. You'll need to know how to create folders for data storage and backups. You'll also need to know how to configure permissions so that the data stored in the folders is properly secured.

Finally, you must understand the basics of network configuration within a Windows environment. This is basically the same regardless of whether it's a Windows server or a Windows client that you are configuring. You'll need to know how to configure and verify the TCP/IP protocol suite including DNS settings and network communications. Newer distributions of Windows also ship with a built-in firewall. You must understand how to configure the Windows firewall to allow for communications with SQL Server. In fact, the SQL Server 2008 installation process warns you about the Windows firewall, if it is not configured to allow such communications.

User Account Management

SQL Server 2008 can run on several versions of Windows Server. These versions include Windows Server 2003, Windows Server 2003 R2, Windows Server 2008, and Windows Server 2008 R2. In addition, it will likely run on future versions of Windows Server. For this reason, it is difficult to provide the exact steps for use administration; however, as a SQL Server 2008 DBA, you may be called on to perform such administration. The following items should be considered when creating user accounts for SQL Server services and users:

Use separate accounts for each service.   By using a unique account for each service, you allow for the application of least privilege. No SQL Server service will have more power than it needs. If a service is exploited through some vulnerability, the power of the attacker is reduced.

Implement strong password policies for users.   This is more of a Group Policy setting, but you should ensure that the users accessing your sensitive data have strong passwords. You should use at least six characters for the length and have multiple character types (i.e., upper-case, lowercase, and numbers). Of course, longer passwords are even more secure, but you will rarely need passwords longer than 10 characters. If you think you do, you might actually need a different authentication solution such as biometrics or smart cards.

Use the same user account for domain login and SQL Server login.   Security topics are addressed in full in Chapters 17 through 19, but it is important that you use as few SQL logins as possible. If the user logs into the Windows domain, but uses another login for access to the SQL Server that is a SQL login, you may be unnecessarily exposing yourself to the risk of password hacks.

Use groups for simplified management.   You can add a Windows group as a SQL Server principal. A *principal* is simply an entity that can be given access to resources. For example, both users and groups are principals. When you add a group as a security principal, you automatically provide all members of that group with access to the SQL Server.

File System Management

Another important Windows-level administration task is file system management. This includes the configuration of drives and storage locations as well as the management of permissions. For SQL Server, you will need to provide reliable and efficient storage for the database files and the log files. The database files should be stored on a sufficiently large drive that can grow as needed. The definition of sufficiently large will vary for every database. Some databases are only a few megabytes in size, while others are several terabytes. The log files should be stored on drives with write caching disabled as much as possible. This ensures that the transactions are really written to the log when the SQL Server Database Engine thinks they are.

Permissions are also important. You do not want your SQL Server database files and logs located in a folder with Read permissions granted to Everyone. (In Windows systems, Everyone is a literal internal group that includes even those who have not logged on.) Remember, the only accounts that need access to the database files and logs are the accounts used by the SQL Server services and accounts used by administrative personnel. Consider configuring permissions so that the service accounts have the needed access and all domain admins have full control access to the folder. Domain Admins is also a group that exists in all Windows domains. Domain admins are automatically members of the local Administrators group on every machine in the domain. Chapter 19, "Security Best Practices," covers permissions as they relate to SQL Server 2008 in depth.

You can perform file administration tasks from either the GUI interface or the command line. In the GUI interface, it's as simple as right-clicking the file or folder and selecting Properties. In the Properties dialog, you should click the Security tab. Figure 3.19 shows an example of this interface in Windows Server 2008. From here you can add or remove users or groups and grant or deny the appropriate permissions.

FIGURE 3.19   Working with permissions

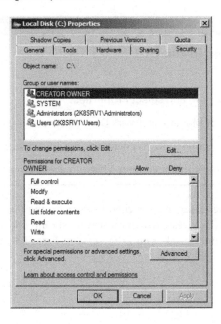

From the command line, you can use the CACLS command. This command supports adding and removing permissions and even supports directory recursion. Command-line tools are useful because they can be scripted to automate routine tasks.

Network Configuration Administration

The final Windows-level administration task set this chapter will cover is network configuration. If the network settings are configured improperly, it doesn't matter how well your SQL Server is running. No one will be able to access it. Five main tasks are important for network configuration:

- Configuring TCP/IP
- Verifying TCP/IP
- Verifying DNS
- Verifying TCP/IP communications
- Configuring the Windows firewall

Configuring TCP/IP

In most cases, you will use the GUI interface to configure TCP/IP settings; however, the NETSH command can be used from the command line as well. On a Windows Server 2008 server, you access the IP address settings in the GUI by following the procedure in Exercise 3.12.

EXERCISE 3.12

Configuring IP Settings in the GUI

1. Click the Start menu.

2. Right-click the Network item and select Properties.

3. In the left Task list, select Manage Network Connections.

4. Right-click the network connection you want to configure and select Properties.

5. Double-click the Internet Protocol version 4 item to access the settings.

Once you've accessed the IP settings reached by performing the steps in Exercise 3.12, you can configure a static IP address, which all servers should use, as well as other settings like the default gateway, subnet mask, and DNS servers. Figure 3.20 shows this dialog.

FIGURE 3.20　The TCP/IP configuration

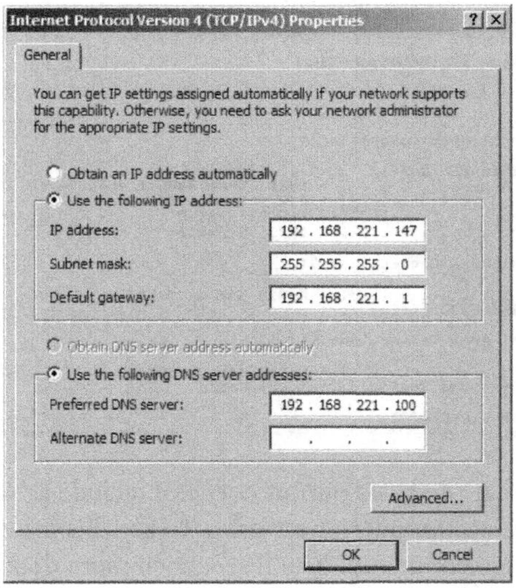

Verifying TCP/IP

The simplest way to verify TCP/IP settings in any Windows system is to visit the command prompt. To get to the command prompt, follow the steps in Exercise 3.13.

EXERCISE 3.13

Opening the Windows Command Prompt

1. Click the Start menu and select Run.

2. Type **cmd** into the Open field and click OK or press Enter.

3. At the newly opened command prompt, type **COLOR /?**

That last step is a little bonus. You can use the COLOR command any time to change your background and foreground colors in a command prompt. For example, you might like to capture command prompt screens with a white background and a black foreground, so you will issue the COLOR f0 command.

To view the TCP/IP configuration and ensure that everything is configured appropriately, use the IPCONFIG command. If you type **IPCONFIG** and press Enter, you will receive basic information about the IP configuration for your network connections, as shown in Figure 3.21.

FIGURE 3.21   Basic IPConfig output

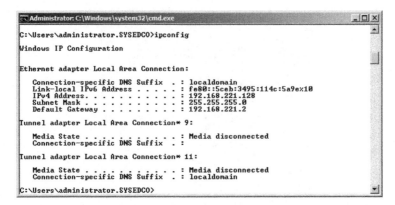

You may have noticed that the basic output does not include DNS settings. DNS settings are extremely important in modern networks. To see this information, plus a lot more, use the IPCONFIG /ALL command. You'll see much more detailed output like that in Figure 3.22.

FIGURE 3.22   Detailed IPConfig output

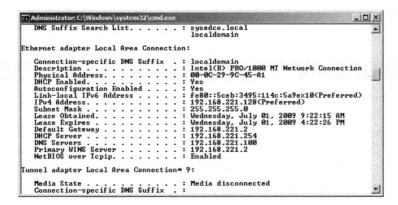

In addition to IPCONFIG, you can use the NETSH command to view IP configuration information. Type **NETSH INTERFACE IP SHOW CONFIG** and press Enter. You'll receive similar information to that revealed by IPCONFIG. NETSH is, however, more powerful in that it can be used to actually reconfigure IP settings as well.

Verifying DNS

As stated previously, DNS is extremely important in today's networks. This importance is not just related to the Internet, although that is important in and of itself; however, it is also related to internal services. For example, Microsoft's Active Directory Domain Services (ADDS) depends heavily on DNS. Clients use DNS to locate domain controllers. Servers use DNS to find domain controllers configured for specific tasks and more. Clearly, DNS must be working properly.

The simplest test you can perform is to open your browser and attempt to connect to a website based on the domain name. For example, if you can connect to www.SysEdCo.com, it means you were able to resolve the domain name to the IP address and DNS resolution is working for the Internet.

You may also use the command prompt tool, NSLOOKUP. NSLOOKUP allows you to perform queries against DNS servers in order to ensure that DNS is operating appropriately. If you simply type **NSLOOKUP** and press Enter, you will be placed in a special command-line interface where you can type either IP addresses or host names to perform lookups. Figure 3.23 shows the results from simply typing www.sysedco.com into this special interface.

FIGURE 3.23   Verifying DNS with NSLOOKUP

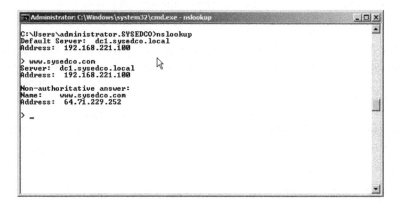

Verifying TCP/IP Communications

If you know you have the configuration right and DNS is configured appropriately, you can perform tests that will verify the proper functionality of TCP/IP communications across your network. Three primary command-line tools can be used for this:

- PING
- TraceRT
- PathPING

PING

PING is the most commonly used of the three. It provides a simple interface that is used to check the liveliness of a remote host. In order for PING to work, the remote host must allow incoming ICMP requests. Many machines are configured with firewalls today, which do not allow pinging by default. If ICMP is supported, you can ping the remote machine with the simple command:

```
PING ip address or hostname
```

For example, if you want to test the IP address 10.10.47.17, you would type:

PING 10.10.47.17

If you know the hostname, but not the IP address, and hostname resolution is working properly on your machine, you can type something like:

PING server13

The hostname of server13 will be resolved to the IP address, and then the IP address will be tested for a response. PING is very useful for quick and basic testing, but what do you do if the PING command fails and you know that the remote machine does allow incoming ICMP requests? Then you may need to move on to the TraceRT tool.

TraceRT

TraceRT is used to test each connection along the path to a destination. For example, you may be communicating with a server that is three network routers away from you and the communications suddenly stop working. You ping the server, but get no response. This, alone, does not verify that the server is the problem. It could be some device in the path. If you execute **TraceRT** *IP address* from a command prompt, you can find the router that is down. You may also find that all routers are working fine, which indicates that the server itself is really down.

PathPING

PathPING is PING's and TraceRT's newest sibling. This command not only tests the devices along the path, but it generates reports to help you determine network communications problems such as latency and intermittent problems. Figure 3.24 shows a PathPING operation against www.sysedco.com. To use PathPING, simply execute **pathping** *IP address*.

FIGURE 3.24 PathPING in action

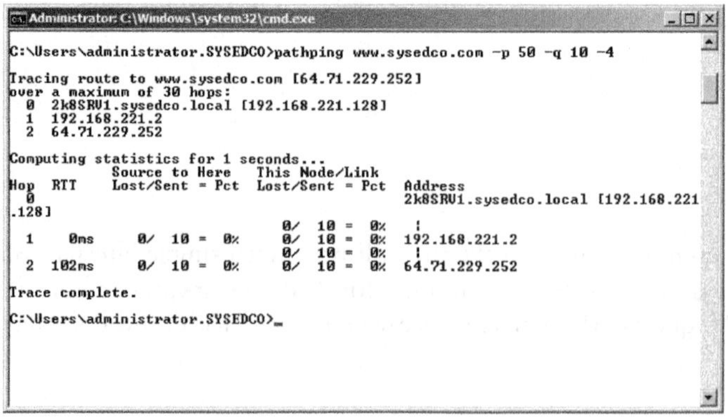

Configuring the Windows Firewall

When you install SQL Server 2008, you may receive warnings that the firewall is not properly configured to support the services. Indeed, the Windows firewall does not allow incoming connections on TCP port 1433 by default, and this is the port that a default instance of SQL Server uses. You may be required to open up the appropriate firewall ports for SQL Server to function properly. The steps vary from one version of Windows Server to another, but the steps in Exercise 3.14 will work in Windows Server 2008.

EXERCISE 3.14

Configuring the Windows Firewall

1. Click Start and select Control Panel.

2. Open the Windows Firewall applet.

3. Click Change Settings.

4. Click the Exceptions tab.

5. Click Add port and configure the settings as shown in this image.

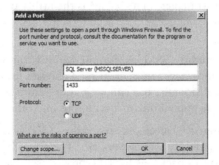

6. Click OK in the Add Port dialog and then OK in the Windows Firewall windows.

While these steps allow communications into the default instance of the SQL Server Database Engine, they do not accommodate named instances. You will need to use the SSCM (covered earlier in this chapter) to locate the dynamic port and then allow that port through the firewall. However, the basic process is the same once you know the port that should be allowed.

Summary

In this chapter, you toured the various GUI administration tools provided with SQL Server 2008. You began by looking at the SQL Server Configuration Manager (SSCM) and using it to manage services, service accounts, and protocols. Next, you used the SQL Server Management Studio (SSMS), the primary administration tool for SQL Server. You learned to configure the SSMS interface and use the scripting options so that you can document and automate administrative tasks.

The SQL Server Business Intelligence Development Studio (BIDS) was explored next. You learned about solutions and projects and how to create, manage, and delete them. Next, the SQL Server Profiler was introduced. You learned to create a trace of SQL Server activity using this tool. You next saw Books Online and some of its little-used features. Finally, Windows Administration was covered from the perspective of the DBA.

Chapter Essentials

SQL Server Configuration Manager The SSCM is the utility of choice for service management in SQL Server. Use it to change service accounts, modify startup parameters, and stop or start a SQL Server service.

SQL Server Management Studio SSMS is the core administration tool for the SQL Server environment. You can perform tasks from creating databases to building stored procedures right inside of this tool. Additionally, you can script out administrative tasks so you can both learn the scripting code and automate it with jobs and other automation techniques.

SQL Server Business Intelligence Development Studio BIDS is used for Integration Services, Analysis Services, and Reporting Services. The most common use for a core DBA is to create Integration Services packages for ETL procedures. However, the tool is flexible enough to serve the needs of business intelligence authors and report managers as well.

SQL Server Profiler The Profiler is the cool under-the-hood tool for SQL Server DBAs. If you want to know what's happening, this is the tool to use. You can capture deadlocks, SQL statements, and more with this powerful tool.

Books Online Books Online is just what it sounds like: a bunch of books on your computer. The content is massive, but thankfully a search engine is provided.

Windows Server Administration for the DBA As a SQL Server DBA, you may be expected to perform Windows administration tasks. These tasks will likely include user account management, file and folder management, and network configuration. You should know about the tools and techniques related to each of these three administrative task sets.

Chapter

4

SQL Server Command-Line Administration

TOPICS COVERED IN THIS CHAPTER:

- ✓ Introducing the Command Prompt
- ✓ General Commands
- ✓ Batch Files
- ✓ Mastering SQLCMD
- ✓ Introducing Windows PowerShell
- ✓ Using SQL Server PowerShell Extensions
- ✓ Windows Scripting Host

Why would anyone want to use the command line to administer SQL Server when Microsoft's GUI tools are so convenient? This question comes up quite frequently when DBAs and other IT professionals are being coached on automation concepts in a Microsoft environment. This chapter is focused on answering that question through demonstration, but for now consider that the command line provides an interactive environment where you can enter many different commands and redirect output to any location (file, printer, or screen) that you desire. In addition, you can automate most command-line commands using batch files.

This chapter will begin by discussing commands, starting with the built-in command line (also called the command prompt) and the different ways you can customize and use it. Then it will discuss the general commands that are common to all command-prompt operations. These commands allow you to navigate the drive systems, communicate with the operating system, and analyze the network. Finally, it will cover the topic of batch files in case you ever want to automate using the command line.

Once the general command-line topics are under your belt, you'll move on to the SQL Server–specific tools. You'll see a demonstration of the SQLCMD tool and also a special tool specifically designed for SQL Server Express Edition. After the normal command-line tools have been covered, you'll dive into the Windows PowerShell interface. You'll learn the basics of working with Windows PowerShell and then the specifics of the SQL Server extensions. Finally, you'll get a brief introduction to script writing for SQL Server using Windows Scripting Host.

Are you ready to experience the coolest Windows and SQL Server administration methods on the planet? If so, read on. If you are an expert at the Windows command line, you may want to skim much of the chapter, but be sure to read the "Batch Files" section if you are not familiar with the use of batch files. If you are also an expert in batch file programming, you may want to just focus on the "Mastering SQLCMD" section, although it's definitely a good idea to scan the other material as a refresher and you may even learn a new tip or two that can make you a more efficient server and database administrator.

Introducing the Command Prompt

The Windows command prompt is not what many people think it is. It is not DOS running on top of Windows. In Windows 3.1, it was indeed the same COMMAND.COM that provided the interface at the DOS command prompt; however, Windows NT changed the way you interact with the command-prompt interface by providing CMD.EXE as an alternative to COMMAND.COM. The CMD.EXE shell interface has several advantages over COMMAND.COM, including:

- CMD.EXE runs as a true 32-bit interface to the Windows NT through Windows Server 2008 R2 operating systems. COMMAND.COM is still there, but it should never be used unless you must support a very old 16-bit DOS application that requires it.

- You have full support for long file names. COMMAND.COM still uses the older 8.3 file-naming convention with the exception of Server 2008, where it emulated long file names for the 16-bit interpreter.

- COMMAND.COM is more memory and processor intensive because it requires NTVDM.EXE (NT Virtual DOS Machine) to be loaded.

The good news is that CMD.EXE supports practically every one of the internal command-interpreter commands that COMMAND.COM supports. Internal commands are those commands that do not require an external executable. For example, DIR is a directory listing command that is embedded in the CMD.EXE and COMMAND.COM interpreters. However, commands like XCOPY and TREE are external commands that can be executed from the command prompt. Figure 4.1 shows the CMD.EXE command prompt with the background color set to white and the foreground color set to black.

FIGURE 4.1   The Windows command prompt

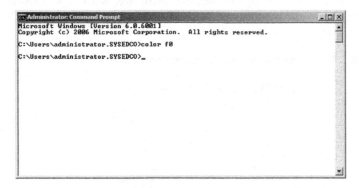

You can launch the command prompt in one of several ways.

- Click Start ➢ All Programs ➢ Accessories ➢ Command Prompt.
- Click Start ➢ Run and then type **CMD** and press Enter.
- Assign a shortcut key to the Command Prompt Start Menu shortcut. To do this, follow these steps:

   1. Click Start ➢ All Programs ➢ Accessories.

   2. Right-click the Command Prompt item and select Properties.

   3. On the Shortcut tab, enter the desired shortcut key (Ctrl+Alt + ` [this is the back-tick key] is a good one because it is not commonly used by other applications).

   4. Click OK.

Once you've entered the desired shortcut key, you have a fast way of getting to the command prompt. You may have been pressing Ctrl+Esc and then pressing R (for run), typing **CMD**, and pressing Enter for years. Now, you can just press Ctrl+Alt + ` and you're there.

The command prompt can be customized in several ways. To see the options, click the icon in the upper-left corner of the Command Prompt window and select Properties. From there, you can configure four sets of parameters: general options, fonts, screen layout, and colors.

If you right-click the title bar and select Defaults instead of Properties, you will be able to configure the properties for all CMD sessions you initiate. The Properties menu item is used to configure settings for the current windows and the Defaults item is used to configure defaults for all CMD sessions.

General Command-Prompt Options

In Windows Server 2008, the Options tab provides several general configuration options for the command prompt, as shown in Figure 4.2. The Cursor Size section of the dialog box allows you to do exactly what it says: change the cursor size. When typing longer commands, some people find the default small cursor to be difficult to locate on the screen. You can use a medium or large cursor to resolve this issue.

FIGURE 4.2   The command prompt's general options

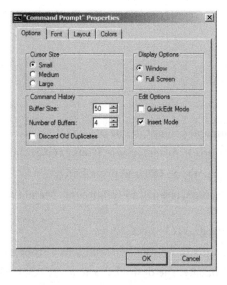

The next section on the Options tab is the Display Options section. Here you can control whether the command prompt runs in a windowed interface or full screen. You may want to set this to Window and then use the Alt+Enter shortcut to jump to Full Screen when desired. If you've never tried this, go ahead and launch a command prompt (CMD.EXE) on and Windows 2000 or higher system and press Alt+Enter. You will be taken to a full-screen display. Press Alt+Enter again and you'll be taken back to the Window display. With the proper setup, you can press Ctrl+Alt +` and then immediately press Alt+Enter and you'll be sitting at a full-screen command-prompt interface. That's living.

You can also configure the Command History buffer from the Options tab. When you allow for larger buffer sizes and more buffers, you enable the ability to scroll back through more historic commands with the up and down arrow keys. Leaving this at 50 is a good setting if you seldom need to go back in your previous command list any further than that. The number of buffers value determines how many processes can have their own buffer memories.

This last option is hard to understand without further explanation. If you run a CMD session and then type **CMD** and press Enter from within that session, you launch another CMD process within the first. You can then type **CMD** and press Enter again to launch a third process. If you allow for only two buffers, you will notice that the third instance of CMD does not support the up and down arrow keys. If you rarely launch more than a second instance inside of a CMD window, you can just leave this at its default of 4.

The last setting you can configure in the Command History section is the Discard Old Duplicates option. If you check this box, the Command History buffer will retain only one copy of an executed command. For example, if you type CLS to clear the screen and you type it five times, it will exist in the history only once. The box is not checked by default.

The final section of the Options tab is the Edit Options section. If you enable the Quick Edit feature, you will be able to copy from the command prompt and paste into it. More importantly, it enables copy-and-paste functions using the mouse. It works a little oddly for most people, but you will simply highlight the text that you want to copy from the command-prompt screen and then right-click. Immediately, the text is copied to the Clipboard. Now you can paste it where you need it—either in the command prompt or another Windows application.

Font Settings

The font settings are important for readability. Figure 4.3 shows that you have two basic choices. You can use raster fonts in an $n \times n$ resolution, or you can use the Lucida Console font and then choose the font size. The latter option is most useful on high-resolution displays. You can make the font size much larger so that it is very easy to work with and read. The Bold Fonts option is not available in Figure 4.3 because the Raster Fonts option is selected. Bold fonts are available only when you choose the Licida Console font. The Selected Font: Terminal section simply shows a sample of what the command line (terminal) would look like with the chosen options on the tab.

FIGURE 4.3 Command-prompt font settings

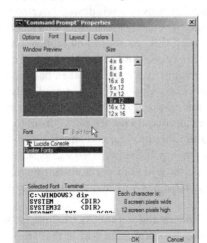

Screen Layout

The Screen Layout tab is very important. You may run commands that scroll on and on for hundreds or even thousands of lines. If you want to scroll back through that information, you will need to increase the screen buffer size. This option is found on the Screen Layout tab shown in Figure 4.4. You can also change the screen width in both characters and display. The maximum screen buffer size is 9,999 lines. If you run a command with more output than this, you will have to redirect the output to a file for later viewing. You'll see how to do that in the subsection titled "Redirecting Output" in the "General Commands" section later in this chapter.

FIGURE 4.4 Command-prompt screen layout

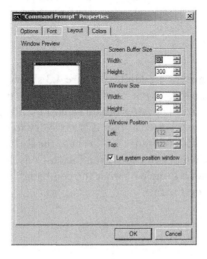

Color Choices

Finally, there is the fun customization option: the Color tab. In addition to being fun, color settings can be very practical. For example, all of the command-prompt captures for this book use a white background so that you can read them better. However, many people set the colors to match their favorite team, to match a traditional console they're used to (green on black is wildly popular), or to simply ease their eyestrain. Whatever your motivation, you can set the colors on the Colors tab as shown in Figure 4.5.

FIGURE 4.5   The command prompt's Colors tab

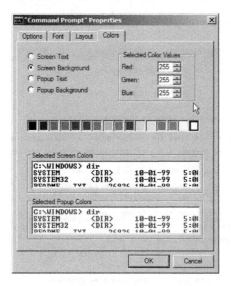

General Commands

Now that you have the command prompt configured for your purposes, you can begin working with it. Several general commands must be understood for basic navigation and operation. These commands fall into the following categories and will be discussed in depth in this section:

- Directory and folder navigation
- Directory and folder listing
- Screen management
- Displaying information
- Redirecting output
- Administrative commands

Directory and Folder Navigation

One of the first skill sets you need to master for command-prompt utilization is directory or folder navigation. The debate over whether folders are directories or directories are folders will be avoided here, but the term *directory* will be used because you are working with the command prompt.

At the command prompt, you use the CD or ChDir command to change directories. CD is short for change directory as is ChDir. Both commands work the same way, so you will most likely use the CD command instead of the ChDir command. Figure 4.6 shows the output of the CD /? command, which lists the help for the command.

FIGURE 4.6   CD command Help

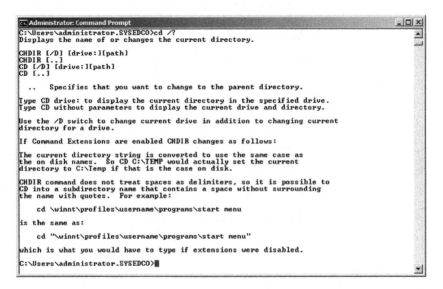

The CD command is very easy to use in simple situations. For example, if you are in the C:\Program\Files\Microsoft SQL Server directory and you want to change to the C:\Windows\System32 directory, you would enter the following command. (Please note that {Enter} indicates that you should press the Enter key.)

CD\Windows\System32 {Enter}

However, if you need to change to the directory on another drive, you would need to issue a more complex command, but it's still easy to use. Assuming you are in a directory on the C: drive and you want to change to the D:\x86 directory on the SQL Server 2008 DVD ROM, you would enter the following command:

CD /D D:\x86

If you want to change back to the C: drive, you would simply enter this command:

C:

While these commands allow for basic directory and drive navigation, here are some power tips that will help you get around faster:

Moving Up Through the Directory Tree   You can easily move up one directory level. If you are in the C:\Windows\System32 directory and you want to navigate to the C:\Windows directory, simply type **CD ..** and press Enter. Now, change back to the System32 directory by typing **CD System32**. Go to the root of the C: drive with the following command: **CD ..\..** and press Enter. Notice that your prompt now indicates that you are in the root of the drive. Please note that you can always jump to the root of the current drive by typing **CD** and pressing Enter.

Changing Directories on the Short   The bane of long directory names is that you have to type those long names to get around at the command prompt; but you can use a wildcard character to change directories. For example, if you type **CD \Prog*\Microsoft SQ*** and press Enter with a default installation of SQL Server, you will be taken to the C:\ Program Files\Microsoft SQL Server directory. Try it, you might like it. You do have to type enough information so that the request gets the folder you want. For example, if you type **CD \Prog*\Microsoft S*** and press Enter, you may end up in C:\Program Files\ Microsoft SDKs instead.

All of the concepts presented in this section relating to directory and folder navigation are demonstrated in Figure 4.7.

FIGURE 4.7   Directory navigation commands

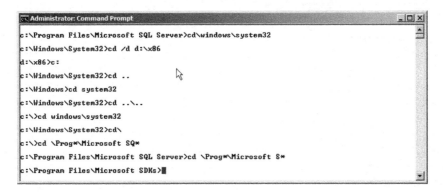

Directory and Folder Listing

If you could only move around at the command prompt and do nothing else, it would be rather pointless. So let's take this to the next level and begin looking at how you view the information stored in these directories or folders that you can access with the CD command. When you want to view the directory structure of your hard drives, the best command to use is the TREE command. When you want to view the files on your drives, the best command available out-of-the-box is the DIR command. Both the TREE command and the DIR command can list directories without files. The TREE command defaults to listing directories only; the DIR command defaults to listing directories and files. Both the TREE and DIR commands will be discussed in the following sections.

The *TREE* Command

The TREE command presents the directories in a tree form that makes it very readable. For example, execute (which means type it and press Enter) the following command at a command prompt:

```
TREE /A "C:\Program Files\Microsoft SQL Server"
```

Your output will look something like the listing in Figure 4.8, assuming you've installed the operating system and SQL Server 2008 to the C: drive with default installation locations. The /A switch told the TREE command to use ASCII characters. The ASCII characters are more readable by most text editors. When you redirect the TREE command output to a text file, it makes it easier to read. You'll see how to redirect output in the section titled "Redirecting Output" later in this chapter.

FIGURE 4.8   Using the TREE command

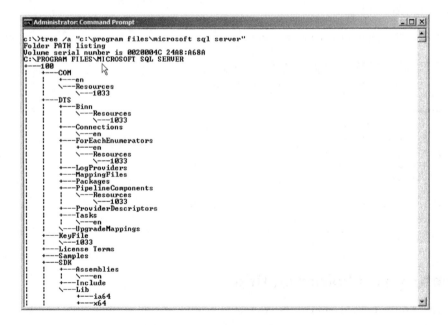

If you want to force the TREE command to list files as well, simply use the /F switch with the command. Remember, you can always execute the TREE /? command to get help. Figure 4.9 shows the beginning of the output from the TREE command when using the /F switch.

FIGURE 4.9   Listing files with the Tree command

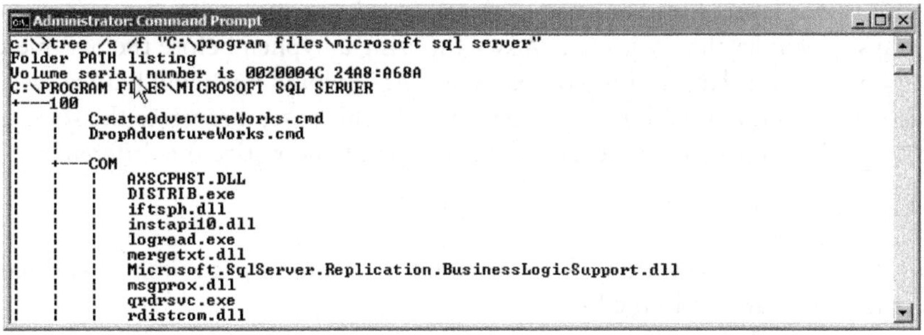

The *DIR* Command

The DIR command is more commonly used than the TREE command. It provides many more options for file and directory selection and also includes sorting parameters and display options. Figure 4.10 shows just how flexible the command is with the many switches it supports.

FIGURE 4.10   DIR command options

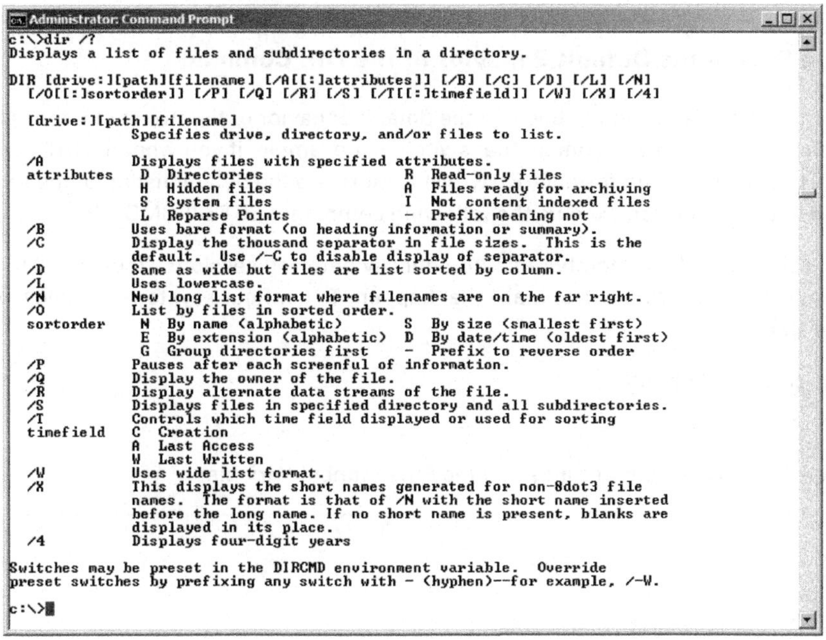

As you can see in Figure 4.10, you can customize and select the output in several ways. For example, if you want to list files by size, you can use the /O:S switch. When you want to list only files and not directories, you can use the /A:-D switch. If you execute the following command, you can see the results:

```
DIR /O:S /A:-D C:\Windows
```

The result is that larger files are listed at the end of the listing and directories are not listed. Always remember that, with the /A switch, using a hyphen before the parameter means you do not want that option. For example, /A:-H would not show hidden files. This hyphen also changed the behavior of the /O switch. In this case, it reverses the sort order that the /O switch specifies. Run the following command and notice the difference:

```
DIR /O:-S /A:-D C:\Windows
```

As you can see, things now look a little different. If you ran the command as listed, the largest files now appear first in the list.

Another important DIR command switch is the /S option. With this switch, you can list all of the files and directories (or just the files or just the directories) under a starting location. For example, the following command will dump a directory listing of the entire hard drive:

```
DIR C:\ /S
```

You should play around with this DIR command in order to become comfortable with it. You will be using it frequently as you work with the command prompt.

Making a Switch the Default Behavior of the *DIR* Command

If you want a particular switch to become the default behavior of the DIR command, simply set the DIRCMD variable to contain that switch. For example, if you want the DIR command to use the bare listing format (/B), which is more like the default listing of the LS command in Linux, you can execute the following command: SET DIRCMD=/B.

However, this will not be remembered automatically between sessions. You'll need to set the system variable in Windows to make that happen. To configure system variables, follow these steps:

1.   Right-click My Computer.

2.   Select Properties.

3.   Click Advanced System Settings and the Environment Variables.

Screen Management

Command-prompt screen management includes color management and clearing the screen. You'll look at the latter first.

Clearing the Screen

Clearing the screen is accomplished with the CLS command. CLS does not support any switches or parameters. When you execute the CLS command, the prompt moves to the upper left of the screen and all content is removed. It's important to remember that CLS clears the screen buffer and not just what is displayed on the screen. Once you execute a CLS command, you can no longer get back to the previously displayed information. The CLS command does not remove the Command History buffer.

Color Management

Color management can be performed in three ways:

- You can configure it in the command prompt's properties as you learned previously in this chapter.
- You can launch the CMD.EXE shell with a special switch to set the colors.
- You can use the COLOR command.

Since you looked at the color options in properties earlier, you do not need to revisit them now. Instead, consider the following steps that can be used to launch a command prompt in the color scheme of your choosing:

1. Click Start and select Run.
2. Type CMD /T:1f and press Enter.

When you run this command, you should see a command prompt with a dark blue background and a white foreground. The command syntax is simple:

```
CMD /T:{background color code}{foreground color code}
```

Table 4.1 shows the valid color codes. For example, to set the background color to dark green and the foreground color to yellow, you would type **CMD /T:2E**. This combination is not very pleasant for some, but other people in a northern state seem to be fond of it because it is very close to the Green Bay Packers' team colors.

The COLOR command works in much the same way as the /T switch with the CMD shell. Execute COLOR {background color code}{foreground color code} by typing these commands at the command prompt. For example, the command COLOR 17 sets the color scheme to one that is very reminiscent of the good old Commodore 64 days.

TABLE 4.1   Command Prompt Color Codes

Color	Code
Black	0
Blue	1
Green	2
Aqua	3
Red	4
Purple	5
Yellow	6
White	7
Grey	8
Light Blue	9
Light Green	A
Light Aqua	B
Light Red	C
Light Purple	D
Light Yellow	E
Bright White	F

Displaying Information

Most command-prompt commands show information as output; however, some commands are designed specifically for showing information. These commands are TYPE, ECHO, and SET. As you move closer to writing batch files for SQL Server administration, it's important that you understand these commands.

The *TYPE* Command

The TYPE command, as you may have guessed, is used to TYPE the contents of a file onto the screen. It is mostly used with simple text documents. As an example, if you want to see the contents of the Autoexec.bat file in the root of the C: drive on a default Windows Server 2008 installation, execute the following command:

```
TYPE C:\autoexec.bat
```

You will see one line of text typed to the screen, which reads, "REM Dummy file for NTVD." The file exists only to make NTVDM feel at home as it emulates DOS for 16-bit DOS and Windows 3.1 applications. Like CLS, the TYPE command has no switches. The only command-line parameter passed to the TYPE command is the file you want to display on the screen.

Even though the TYPE command does not support any switches, you should know about a method that will allow you to deal with long text files that scroll off the screen when listed by the command. For example, if you've installed SQL Server to the default locations as a default instance, execute the following commands at a command prompt:

```
CD \Program Files\Microsoft SQL Server\MSSQL10.MSSQLSERVER\MSSQL
TYPE Log\ErrorLog
```

If you are using a default size command-prompt window, some of the text scrolled right off the top of the screen. Of course, you can use the scroll bar to scroll backward, but you can also do the following. Still in the C:\Program Files\Microsoft SQL Server\MSSQL10 .MSSQLSERVER\MSSQL directory, execute the following command:

```
TYPE Log\ErrorLog | more
```

That vertical line is the piping symbol (Shift+\ on most keyboards). You are telling the command prompt to feed the results of the TYPE command into the MORE command. The MORE command simply takes any amount of input and displays it one screen or one line at a time. When you are viewing output with the MORE command, you can proceed one line at a time by pressing Enter or one screen at a time by pressing the space bar.

The *ECHO* Command

When you want to output text to the screen or a file, you can use the ECHO command. In most cases, it is used to display information on the screen from within batch files (as you'll see later in the "Batch Files" section), but it can also be used to dump information to a text files. The syntax is simple:

```
ECHO {message}
```

As you can see, *message* is the text you want to output. For example, if you what to display the classic "Hello World!" to the screen, you would execute:

```
ECHO Hello World!
```

If you want to output a blank line (carriage return), you would execute:

```
ECHO.
```

Notice that there is no space between the keyword ECHO and the period. If you put a space between them, a period will be echoed to the output.

You can also display the contents of a variable. Several system variables exist by default on Windows servers and clients, such as ComputerName, UserName, and UserDomain. To ECHO the contents of a variable to the output, surround the variable name with percent signs (%). Here's an example that includes hard-coded text with system variables:

```
ECHO The computer name is %ComputerName% and the user is %UserDomain%\%UserName%.
The current time is %Time% and the current date is %Date%.
```

The code line above is typed as one line, although it will wrap in your command-prompt display.

This rather long command results in the following output on my Windows Server 2008 machine:

```
The computer name is 2k8SRV1 and the user is SYSEDCO\administrator. The current
time is 14:09:07.05 and the current date is Fri 07/03/2009.
```

When you want to place text into a file, you will use the ECHO command with the redirection capabilities of the command prompt. The redirection capabilities allow you to redefine the output. Instead of going to the screen, it can be output to a file for example.

The ECHO commands covered so far are represented in Figure 4.11.

FIGURE 4.11   ECHO commands

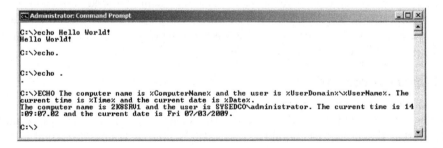

The *SET* Command

The SET command is used to show the contents of variables and also to configure or set the contents. You can create new variables or change the contents of existing variables. To display all of the current variables for the session, execute the one-word command SET. You will see a listing similar to the following:

```
ALLUSERSPROFILE=C:\ProgramData
APPDATA=C:\Users\administrator.SYSEDCO\AppData\Roaming
CommonProgramFiles=C:\Program Files\Common Files
COMPUTERNAME=2K8SRV1
ComSpec=C:\Windows\system32\cmd.exe
FP_NO_HOST_CHECK=NO
HOMEDRIVE=C:
HOMEPATH=\Users\administrator.SYSEDCO
LOCALAPPDATA=C:\Users\administrator.SYSEDCO\AppData\Local
LOGONSERVER=\\DC1
NUMBER_OF_PROCESSORS=2
OS=Windows_NT
PATHEXT=.COM;.EXE;.BAT;.CMD;.VBS;.VBE;.JS;.JSE;.WSF;.WSH;.MSC
PROCESSOR_ARCHITECTURE=x86
PROCESSOR_IDENTIFIER=x86 Family 6 Model 23 Stepping 7, GenuineIntel
PROCESSOR_LEVEL=6
PROCESSOR_REVISION=1707
ProgramData=C:\ProgramData
ProgramFiles=C:\Program Files
PROMPT=$P$G
PUBLIC=C:\Users\Public
SESSIONNAME=Console
SqlSamplesDatabasePath=C:\Program Files\Microsoft SQL Server\MSSQL10.MSSQLSERVER\
SqlSamplesSourceDataPath=C:\Program Files\Microsoft SQL Server\100\Tools\Samples\
SystemDrive=C:
SystemRoot=C:\Windows
TEMP=C:\Users\ADMINI~1.SYS\AppData\Local\Temp
TMP=C:\Users\ADMINI~1.SYS\AppData\Local\Temp
USERDNSDOMAIN=SYSEDCO.LOCAL
USERDOMAIN=SYSEDCO
USERNAME=administrator
USERPROFILE=C:\Users\administrator.SYSEDCO
windir=C:\Windows
```

The PATH variable was removed from this listing to save space, but this is an otherwise typical listing of default variables on a Windows system. You can display any of these variables using the ECHO command or the SET command. You learned to use the ECHO command earlier in this chapter. With the SET command, you type SET and then the variable name to display the contents. To demonstrate, if you execute SET SystemRoot, you will see the following output on a standard install to the C: drive:

```
Systemroot=C:\Windows
```

You can also create your own variables. User variables are mostly used with batch files. To create a variable, use the following syntax:

```
SET {unique name}={value}
```

In this instance, *unique name* is equal to a variable name that is not in use and value is equal to the value you wish to store. As an example, if you want to store the value AdventureWorks in the variable DBname, you would execute the following:

```
SET DBname=AdventureWorks
```

Now you can use the DBname variable with command-prompt commands and in batch files. Variable names are not case sensitive, so the command ECHO %dbname% will work exactly like the command ECHO %DBname%.

When you create variables like this, they will remain in scope (be available for use) only during the current command-line session. When you close the session, all variables created during the session are lost because they are stored in the memory of that session. These temporary variables are most useful within batch files.

Redirecting Output

Up to this point, you have explored several commands and methods of interacting with the operating system at the command prompt. Now, you need to move to the next step, which explores changing the default output to a file or even another application.

Three redirectors exist at the Windows command line:

- The piping symbol (|)
- The greater-than sign (>)
- Two greater-than signs (>>)

Each works differently and you must understand their use to ensure proper functionality in your commands or batch files.

Redirecting to Another Application Using the Piping Symbol (|)

The piping symbol is the key to application redirection. You read about this earlier when you piped the output of the TYPE command through the MORE command. You can accomplish other creative things with the piping symbol as well. To demonstrate this, perform the following steps on a machine running the SQL Server services:

1. Start the command prompt.
2. Execute TASKLIST /SVC.
3. Scroll through the list and notice the lines that reference MSSQL.
4. To list only the lines with MSSQL, execute TASKLIST /SVC | FIND /I "mssql".

You should see output for the command suggested in step 4 that resembles Figure 4.12. The purpose here is not to master the TASKLIST or FIND commands, but to see the way you can feed the output of the TASKLIST command into the FIND command to filter your results.

FIGURE 4.12   Piping output from one command into another

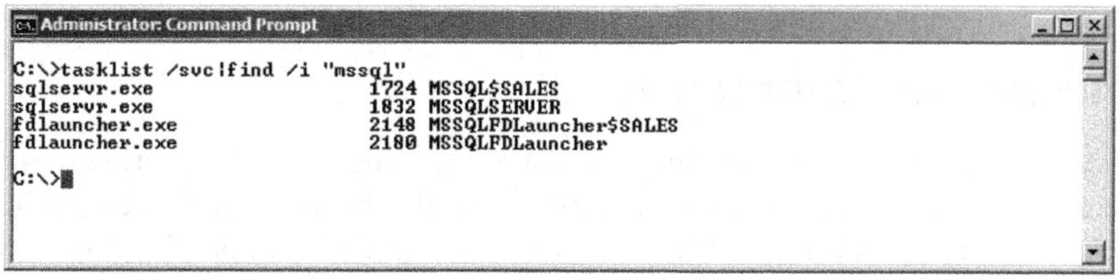

Redirecting to an Output File Using the Greater-Than Sign (>)

Sometimes you just need to save the output of a command into a file. You may do this to create logs or to more easily view the output in a text editor. When you want to create a new file or overwrite an existing file, use one greater-than sign as the redirector. Execute the following command to see how this works:

```
IPCONFIG /ALL > C:\IPSETUP.TXT
```

Now, you can open the file C:\IPSETUP.TXT in any text editor (Notepad would work) and view the output. Remember, if the file exists, a single greater-than sign will overwrite it. If the file does not exist, it will be created.

Appending to an Output File Using Two Greater-Than Signs (>>)

Sometimes you want to create a running log. To do this, you will need to append to an existing file or create a new one if you're just starting the log. Using two greater-than signs will do the trick. Execute the following three statements to see it in action:

```
ECHO This is the first line in the log. >> c:\echolog.txt
ECHO This is the second line. >> c:\echolog.txt
ECHO This is the third and final line. >> c:\echolog.txt
```

Now, open the file C:\echolog.txt in a text editor. You will see three lines in the file, assuming it did not exist before you executed these three commands. If you have used a single greater-than sign in each of the three statements, you would only see the text, "This is the third and final line." Be very careful with the output redirector. A common mistake is the overwriting of existing files instead of appending to them when creating running logs.

All of the information presented so far in this chapter has been foundational to SQL Server administration at the command line. The good news is that this information is beneficial for all Windows administration and not just SQL Server. When you read the Batch Files section in just a few pages, you will see clearly how all of this fits into SQL Server administration. Everything you've learned will be brought together into a useful batch file that can be used to perform several administrative tasks. For now, move on from the internal operations of the command prompt to look at a few administrative commands you'll need to understand.

Administrative Commands

Windows Systems provide several commands that are specific to administration tasks. These commands allow you to perform tasks that may also be performed in the GUI, but they often provide more features and simpler interfaces. Several command-prompt commands can be used to perform tasks such as starting and stopping SQL Server services, defragmenting single data files, viewing network statistics, and copying data. While these are not the only four tasks you can perform, they are common tasks performed on SQL Servers. All four will be covered in the next few sections.

Starting and Stopping SQL Server Services

The NET command provides an interface to the Windows services. You can use this tool to stop and start services. For example, if you have a default installation of the default instance of SQL Server, you can stop the SQL Server Database Engine with the following command:

```
NET STOP MSSQLSERVER
```

To stop a named instance, you will execute NET STOP service_name. The service ID for an instance can be seen in the SQL Server Configuration Manager. However, you are working with the command prompt and you want to do everything from the commands prompt. On a Windows Server 2008 server running SQL Server, execute the following command:

```
TASKLIST /SVC |FIND /I "sql"
```

The results of the preceding command will show all of the services for all instances of the SQL Server Database Engine service and the SQL Server Agent service, as well as a few other SQL Server services. Figure 4.13 shows the output of the command. Notice that two instances of SQLSERVR.EXE are running. SQLSERVR.EXE is the database engine service. The first listed instance is named MSSQL$SALES and it is a named instance. The second listed instance is named MSSQLSERVER and it is the default instance.

FIGURE 4.13   SQL Server service list at the command prompt

It is important to note that two instances of the SQL Server Agent are also running. The SQL Server Agent depends on the database engine. If you execute the command provided previously, NET STOP MSSQLSERVER, while the SQL Server Agent is running, the following prompt will result:

```
The following services are dependent on the SQL Server (MSSQLSERVER) service.
Stopping the SQL Server (MSSQLSERVER) service will also stop these services.

SQL Server Agent (MSSQLSERVER)

Do you want to continue this operation? (Y/N) [N]:
```

If you are attempting to automate the service closure, this prompt could be problematic. You have two basic options for dealing with the prompt. First, you could stop the SQL Server Agent for the instance before stopping the database engine for the instance. Second, you could use an old trick to answer the question automatically. Execute the following command and the SQL Server Database Engine and Agent for the MSSQLSERVER instance will be stopped:

```
NET STOP MSSQLSERVER /Y
```

You can see the results of this command in Figure 4.14. The command simply answers the prompt with a "Y" for yes. The result is that the SQL Server Agent service is stopped first and then the database engine service is stopped. Some commands do not allow you to answer the prompt with a /Y option, but the NET commands do, and that is very helpful in cases such as this.

FIGURE 4.14 Automatically responding to a NET Stop prompt

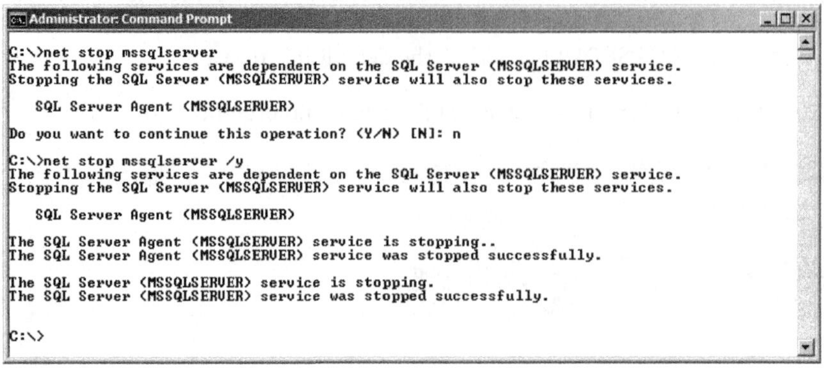

```
Administrator: Command Prompt                                            _ □ ×
C:\>net stop mssqlserver
The following services are dependent on the SQL Server (MSSQLSERVER) service.
Stopping the SQL Server (MSSQLSERVER) service will also stop these services.

   SQL Server Agent (MSSQLSERVER)

Do you want to continue this operation? (Y/N) [N]: n

C:\>net stop mssqlserver /y
The following services are dependent on the SQL Server (MSSQLSERVER) service.
Stopping the SQL Server (MSSQLSERVER) service will also stop these services.

   SQL Server Agent (MSSQLSERVER)

The SQL Server Agent (MSSQLSERVER) service is stopping..
The SQL Server Agent (MSSQLSERVER) service was stopped successfully.

The SQL Server (MSSQLSERVER) service is stopping.
The SQL Server (MSSQLSERVER) service was stopped successfully.

C:\>
```

Of course, you can also start services with the command prompt. The following statements will restart the previously stopped services:

```
NET START MSSQLSERVER
NET START SQLSERVERAGENT
```

Notice that you first start the SQL Server Database Engine and then the Agent service. This order is important because the Agent depends on the database engine.

Defragmenting Single Files

Windows servers have built-in volume defragmentation abilities. They do not have a single file defragmenter. The SysInternals toolset provides an excellent solution to this missing feature. The program is called Contig and, since Microsoft purchased SysInternals, it is available for download from the Microsoft website. To download any of the SysInternals tools, navigate to http://TechNet.Microsoft.com/en-us/SysInternals.

Once you've arrived at the SysInternals TechNet site, click on the File and Disk Utilities link and then the link for the Contig page. Here you can read about the utility and its command-line switches. You can also download the free utility from this page.

If you extract the Contig.zip file into the C:\Windows folder (or your system folder location), it will be located in the system path. This will give you the ability to run the Contig program from any directory at the command line.

SQL Server databases may become fragmented at the storage level. This fragmentation should not be confused with internal index fragmentation. In this case, the physical storage on the drive sectors is being referred to; if the physical files become fragmented, the performance of the database will be diminished. You can use `Contig` to check for fragmentation with the following command:

```
CONTIG -A {database file name}
```

Note that *database file name* represents the `*.mdf` file that is used for physical storage of the database. Some databases have both `*.mdf` and `*.ndf` files and all files should be checked for fragmentation. Figure 4.15 shows the output of the `Contig` command when run against the AdventureWorks physical data file on the example test server. In this case, the data file is stored in one fragment and does not require defragmenting.

FIGURE 4.15   Analyzing fragmentation with `Contig`

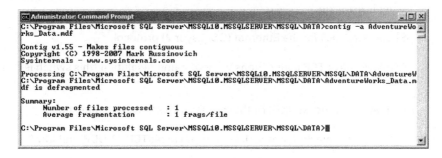

To defragment a file, execute the following command:

```
CONTIG {file name}
```

In this case, `file name` is the name of the file to be defragmented. You can also use wildcards as in:

```
CONTIG *.mdf
```

The latter command would defragment all `*.mdf` files in the current folder.

Before you can defragment a database file, the file must be unlocked. The SQL Server service locks the data files for all active databases. You can either detach the database from the SQL Server service or stop the SQL Server service to defragment the physical database. In most cases, physical defragmentation is only needed with direct attached storage (DAS) and, even then, only once or twice per year. Of course, this defragmentation interval depends on the database usage and the storage location. If a single volume (whether a true single drive or RAID) is completely dedicated to a single database, physical fragmentation may not be an issue.

Viewing Network Statistics

At times, you will want a quick way to view the current network utilization and various statistics related to network communications. You can use advanced third-party GUI tools to accomplish this, but basic network statistics are available via the command line's NETSTAT command. The NETSTAT command syntax is as follows:

```
netstat[-a] [-e] [-n] [-o] [-pProtocol] [-r] [-s] [Interval]
```

The command-line switches are listed in Table 4.2.

TABLE 4.2   The Command-Line Switches

Switch	Action
-a	Displays the active TCP connections and TCP or UDP ports on which the computer is listening.
-e	Shows statistics for the Ethernet (OSI Layer 2) protocol.
-n	Displays active TCP connections without name resolution (this switch is faster than -a)
-o	Displays the process ID (PID) that requested each open connection.
-pProtocol	Filters to the selected protocol. Options include: TCP, IP, UDP, and ICMP.
-r	Shows the current IP routing table.
-s	Generates statistics for the connections, such as packets sent and received.
Interval	Places NETSTAT in auto-repeat mode. The statistics will be regenerated and display every n seconds according to the value entered.

NETSTAT may be used for several purposes. For example, if you want to see which processes have open connections, you can execute the following:

```
netstat -n -o
```

Assuming an active connection is in place, you will receive output similar to that in Figure 4.16. Notice that the PID is 2424. Now, to identify the process, you can use the previously covered TASKLIST command like this:

```
tasklist /FI "PID eq 2424"
```

The /FI switch indicates that a filter follows. The filter of PID eq 2424 indicates that you only want to display tasks with a PID of 2424. The results of this command are shown in Figure 4.17.

FIGURE 4.16   Finding PIDs for active connections

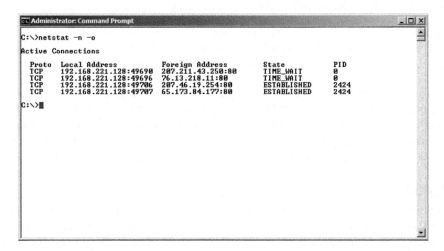

FIGURE 4.17   Matching PIDs with process names

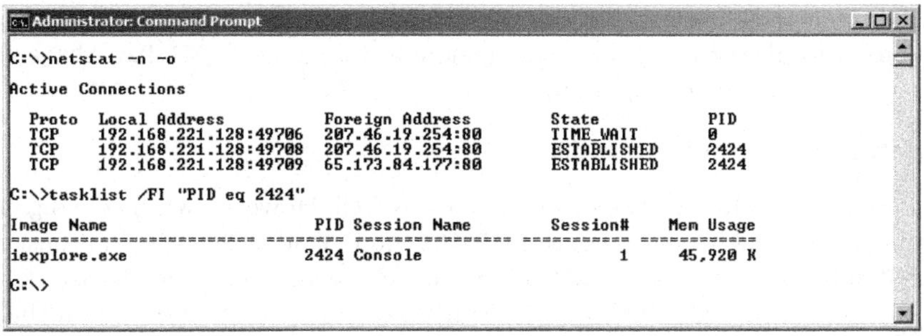

In addition to process location, you can simply view the statistics for networking in general or a protocol in specific. You should become familiar with this command because it can provide fast information for troubleshooting connections on your SQL Server. For example, you may want to check a PID for the server to determine whether it is active within the network stack. To do this, first locate the SQL Server Database Engine process ID with this command:

```
tasklist /fi "imagename eq sqlservr.exe" /svc
```

This command filters for processes based on the `sqlservr.exe` file and displays the service name. The output should be similar to the following:

```
Image Name                      PID Services
sqlservr.exe                   1724 MSSQL$SALES
sqlservr.exe                   2156 MSSQLSERVER
```

Now that you know the default instance (MSSQLSERVER) is PID 2156, you can check for connections to that PID. The `NETSTAT` command can be used to look for such connections. By executing `netstat -o -n`, you will display the connections and this display includes the PID for each connection. If PID 2156 shows up in the list, someone is connected to the SQL Server instance from a remote location. If it does not, no current connections exist.

Copying Data

In many cases, you'll need to perform simple file copy operations. For such scenarios, the traditional `COPY` command works fine. However, you may need more advanced copy features and this will drive you to use `ROBOCOPY`. Both commands are built into all Windows Server 2003 servers and newer versions and can be used to transfer database files, data export files, and any other data files from one drive to another or from one server to another.

The `COPY` command is very simple. For example, to copy a file named `data.csv` from a directory on the local server to a share on a remote server named `\\DC1\DataShare` with verification, execute the following command:

```
copy c:\data\data.csv \\dc1\datashare /v
```

You can use wildcards with the copy command as well. However, when copying more than one file, it is probably best to use the `ROBOCOPY` command. `ROBOCOPY` is a robust copy utility for Windows-based systems. `ROBOCOPY` is available only from the resource kit tools previous to Vista and Server 2008. Now, Vista, Windows 7, and Server 2008 include `ROBOCOPY` right out-of-the-box. To discover the many switches and features of `ROBOCOPY`, at the Windows Server 2008 command prompt, type **ROBOCOPY /?** and press Enter.

As an example, to copy the same `data.csv` file to the same share that was used with the `COPY` command previously, while logging the copy process information to `copylog.txt`, execute the following:

```
robocopy c:\data \\dc1\datashare data.csv /log:c:\copylog.txt
```

The output of this command can be seen in Figure 4.18. As you can see from this example, the `ROBOCOPY` command is certainly more complex than the `COPY` command. You must specify the source directory, then the destination directory, and then any files you want to copy, if you do not want to copy everything in the directory. However, this increased complexity brings with it much more power.

FIGURE 4.18 ROBOCOPY output and log

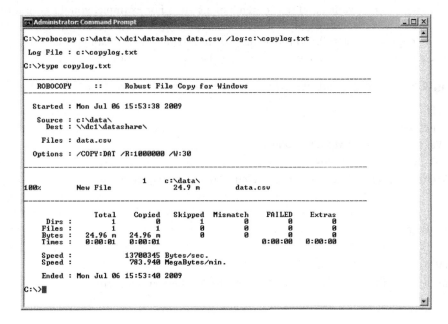

Batch Files

At this point, you have either gained a fundamental understanding of how to work with the command prompt from the preceding pages of this chapter or you came to this chapter with basic command-prompt skills already. Either way, it's time to put these skills to use with batch files. A batch file is exactly what it sounds like: a file that contains a batch (or collection) of command-prompt commands. You simply type the batch files in a text editor (like the infamous Notepad) and then save them with a .BAT extension. Exercise 4.1 will walk you through creating a batch file, but first, you should understand some basic commands that are useful within batch files.

Using Logic (*IF* and *GOTO*)

One of the most important tasks you will need to perform in batch files is decision making. The IF statement is the most commonly used. The following syntax is provided for IF statements at the command prompt:

```
if [not] errorlevel number command [else expression]
if [not] string1==string2 command [else expression]
if [not] exist FileName command [else expression]
```

As you can see, several methods of execution are available. You can check for the existence of a file, an error value, and the contents of a string. For example, you may want to execute a particular command only if the server is running Windows Server 2008, which is actually Windows version 6.0. Consider the code in Listing 4.1 (you can type this into your favorite code editor or Notepad and save it as verbat.bat if you desire).

Listing 4.1 The verbat.bat file, which checks for Windows version 6.0

```
@ECHO OFF
VER > version.txt
FIND "Version 6.0" version.txt >NUL
IF ERRORLEVEL 1 GOTO WrongV
ECHO Right version. This system is using the following version:
VER
ECHO.
GOTO CLEANUP

:WrongV
ECHO Wrong version. This system is using the following version:
VER
ECHO.
GOTO CLEANUP

:CLEANUP
DEL version.txt
:END
```

The first line, @echo off, cleans up the output of the batch file so that the executed command displays results, but not the command itself. The second line redirects the output of the ver command to a file named version.txt. Next, the find command looks for the string Version 6.0 in the file. If the string is not found, the ERRORLEVEL value will be 1. If the string is found, the IF statement will do nothing and the batch file will continue from there.

Assuming it is Windows Server 2008, the batch file simply outputs the fact that it is the right version and executes the ver command again, but this time it allows the output of the ver command to show. The ECHO. line simply displays a blank line before returning to the command prompt.

If the operating system is not Windows Server 2008, the IF statement forces batch processing to jump to the :WrongV position. From here, the user is informed that it is the wrong version and the actual version is displayed. Both the right version and wrong version routines rely on the :CLEANUP section to delete the *version.txt* file when all processing is done.

As a side note, notice that the output of the FIND command in the third line of the batch file is thrown out. This is a great trick. The output is redirected to NULL. The command still runs and the ERRORLEVEL value is set appropriately, but the user does not see it.

This batch file represents just one way to perform different actions depending on the operating system version. The main focus here is on understanding the IF statement.

Passing Data

Batch files are very useful for repeating static commands that you must perform again and again. But they can also be useful as dynamic tools. To use batch files in a more dynamic way, you'll have to understand how to pass command-line parameters to the batch file and how to read them within the batch file.

As with any other program you execute at the command line, parameters are passed to batch files by placing the parameters after the batch file name. For example, you can extend the previous batch file used to check for a specific version so that it accepts input like this:

```
verbat.bat "Version 6.0"
```

The string Version 6.0 will become parameter 1 and is referenced in the batch file as %1. You can use more than one command-line parameter and they are referenced as %1, %2, %3, and so on. Consider Listing 4.2, which is the updated version of the verbat.bat file that supports command-line parameters.

Listing 4.2 Updated verbat.bat with support for command-line parameters

```
@ECHO OFF
VER > version.txt
FIND %1 version.txt >NUL
IF ERRORLEVEL 1 GOTO WrongV
ECHO Right version. This system is using the following version:
VER
ECHO.
GOTO CLEANUP

:WrongV
ECHO Wrong version. This system is using the following version:
VER
ECHO.
GOTO CLEANUP

:CLEANUP
DEL version.txt
:END
```

Notice that the only change is in line 3. The %1 variable is placed after the FIND command instead of the hard-coded "Version 6.0" information. The batch file still runs, but you could also check for version 6.1 or 5.1 or any other version you desire.

In the same way that you use command-line parameter variables, you can access system variables. You can access variables created before the batch file was launched, and you can also create variables for use within the batch file. This functionality is achieved using the SET command discussed previously in this chapter.

Including Comments

Once you begin creating batch files, you are likely to create dozens or even hundreds of them. You may need to modify a batch file months or years later. Another administrator may need to modify a batch file. In both cases, including comments in your files can greatly improve manageability.

The following two lines of code do not cause any actions to take place, but they are stored as comments if placed in a batch file:

```
REM Batch file created by Tom Carpenter: carpenter@sysedco.com
REM Purpose: To export data and copy it to three different locations.
```

The REM statement, short for remark, is simple and takes only one parameter: the comment to be stored in the file. If you type the two REM statements shown and execute them, nothing will happen. That is the intended design. Be sure to use REM statements in your batch files to make updates easier down the road.

Now that you understand the basic building blocks of a batch file, you are ready to create a batch file from scratch. Exercises 4.1, 4.2, and 4.3 will walk you through the process. Exercise 4.1 provides the steps needed to prepare your system for the batch file to work.

EXERCISE 4.1

Preparing Your System for the Batch File

In this exercise, you will create the ExportDir, BackupDir, and BatchDir folders, which are the folders used by the Export.bat batch file created in Exercise 4.2.

1. Launch the command prompt.

2. Type CD\ and press Enter to return to the root of the C: drive.

3. Execute the following three commands:

    ```
    MD ExportDir
    MD BackupDir
    MD BatchDir
    ```

    These commands create the directories (folders) needed for Exercises 4.2 and 4.3.

4. Change to the BatchDir folder by executing CD BatchDir.

In Exercise 4.2, you will create the actual batch file used to export data from the SQL Server AdventureWorks database. You will use the Edit command mode application, just to spice things up a bit. You could alternatively use Notepad or your favorite code editor as well.

Create the Batch File

1. Type **EDIT Export.bat** and press Enter.

2. Enter the following batch file code into the Editor window so that it looks similar to the image shown after the code:

```
@echo off
REM This batch file will export data to the C:\ExportDir directory.
REM You must specify the backup file name when you run the batch file.
REM
REM For example: export.bat backup1.dat
REM
IF "%1"=="" GOTO NoName

ECHO.
ECHO Export.bat version 1.0
ECHO.
ECHO Exporting data...
SQLCMD -d AdventureWorks -Q "SELECT * FROM Sales.SalesOrderDetail" -o c:\
ExportDir\export.csv
ECHO.
ECHO Copying data...
copy c:\ExportDir\export.csv c:\BackupDir\%1 /v /y >null
IF NOT ERRORLEVEL 1 GOTO ENDGOOD
GOTO ENDBAD
:NoName
ECHO.
ECHO Export.bat version 1.0
ECHO.
ECHO You must provide a file name for the backup at the command line.
ECHO For example:
ECHO.
ECHO export.bat backup1.dat
ECHO.
ECHO.
```

EXERCISE 4.2 *(continued)*

```
GOTO END

:ENDBAD
ECHO.
ECHO An error occurred!
ECHO.
GOTO END

:ENDGOOD
ECHO.
ECHO The process completed without error on %DATE% at %TIME%.
ECHO.
:END
```

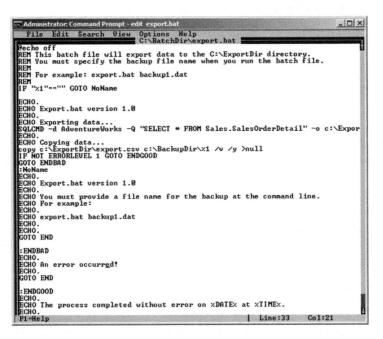

3. Save the file by pressing Alt+S.

4. Before you exit the editor, take some time to inspect the code. Can you predict how it will run and what features it will offer?

5. Exit the Edit program by pressing Alt+X.

Now that you've created the batch file, you're ready to run it and see it in action. Exercise 4.3 steps you through this process.

EXERCISE 4.3

Running the Batch File

1. To see the built-in Help routine, run Export.bat without any parameters, like this:

    C:\BatchDir\Export.bat

    Note the Help that is displayed.

2. Now run the batch file with the parameter backup1.dat like this:

    C:\BatchDir\Export.bat backup1.dat

3. You should see results similar to those in the following image:

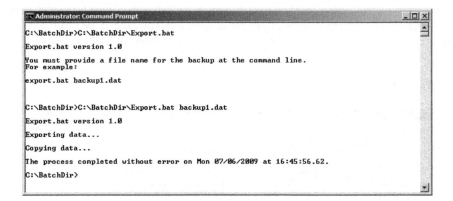

4. Now look at the contents of the ExportDir directory by executing the following command:

    DIR C:\ExportDir

5. You should see a file named export.csv. Look at the contents of the BackupDir directory by executing the following command:

    DIR C:\BackupDir

6. You should see a file named backup1.dat.

These exercises walked you through creating a simple batch file. This batch file could be extended in many ways, including:

- Add a command-line option for the export file name.
- Add code to check for the existence of the backup file.
- Clean up the ExportDir file after the backup is complete.

These ideas represent just a few of the options. The power of batch files is limited only by the tools at your disposal and your creativity.

Mastering SQLCMD

In Exercises 4.1, 4.2, and 4.3, you were introduced to the SQLCMD utility. This command-prompt utility is used to interact with the SQL Server. SQLCMD supports dozens of switches as shown in Figure 4.19. Pay close attention to these switches as they are case-sensitive. For example, the -S switch specifies the server to which you want to connect, but the -s switch specifies the column separator for output. As another example, the -Q switch is used to run the specified query and exit, while the -q switch runs the query and remains in the SQLCMD interactive mode prompt.

FIGURE 4.19   SQLCMD switches

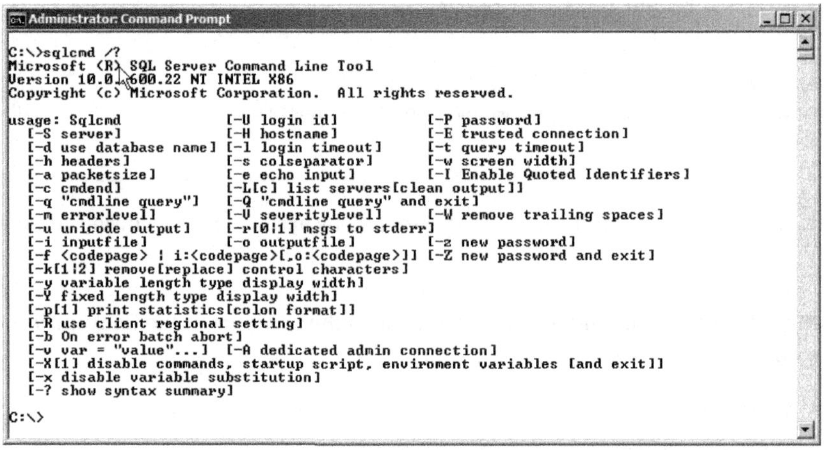

The simplest way to use SQLCMD is to sit at the SQL Server console and log on as an administrator. From there, you launch a command prompt, type **SQLCMD**, and press Enter. You will see an interactive prompt like the one shown in Figure 4.20. A USE command was entered to switch to the AdventureWorks database and then a DBCC CHECKTABLE command was used to analyze the Production.Product table. Interactive mode allows you to perform the same administrative tasks you would usually do from the query windows inside of SSMS, but you don't have the extra bloat of the GUI engine slowing you down.

FIGURE 4.20   SQLCMD in interactive mode

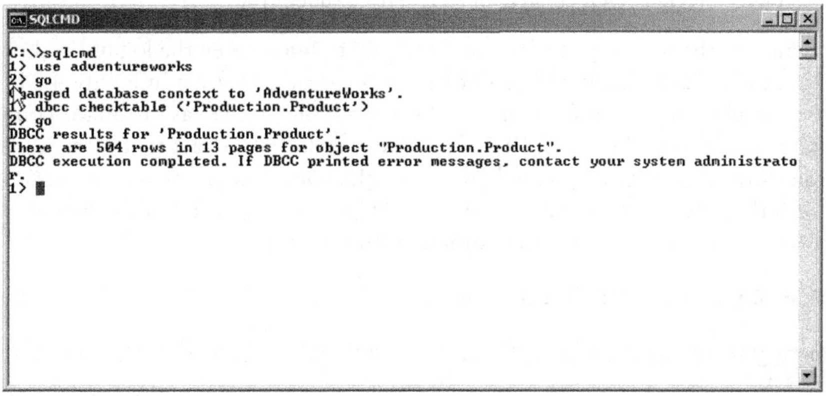

Interactive mode can be used with the local server by simply typing and pressing Enter, but it can also be used with remote servers. For example, if you wanted to administer the default instance on a server named SQL1, you would execute the following command to enter interactive mode on that server:

```
SQLCMD -S SQL1
```

This command assumes you are logged on with an account that has administrative privileges on the SQL1 server. If you are not logged on with such an account and the SA account is available on SQL1, you could use a command like this:

```
SQLCMD -S SQL1 -U sa -P sapassword
```

Of course, you would replace sapassword with the actual password of the sa account.

SQLCMD can also be used in a scripted noninteractive mode. You can do this in one of two ways:

- Inline queries
- Input file-based queries

For inline queries, you use the -Q switch. For input file-based queries, you use the -i switch. For example, to run a DBCC CHECKDB command against AdventureWorks on the local server, you can execute the following statement:

```
SQLCMD -Q "DBCC CHECKDB (AdventureWorks)"
```

The results of the database check will be displayed on the screen, and you will be taken back to a standard command prompt. You can redirect the output to a text file with the following modified statement:

```
SQLCMD -Q "DBCC CHECKDB (AdventureWorks)" -o C:\dbcc.log
```

Now, change to the root of your drive and type **dbcc.log** to open the log file in the default viewer. On most systems, the log file will open in Notepad as shown in Figure 4.21. The point here is simple: you can perform practically any administrative task from the command prompt that you can from the SSMS GUI. This power is due to the fact that most administrative tasks performed in SSMS actually launch T-SQL code. Take the power of SQLCMD and couple it with the general command-prompt knowledge you've gained in this chapter and you have a powerful set of automation and administration tools.

FIGURE 4.21   Viewing the SQLCMD output log

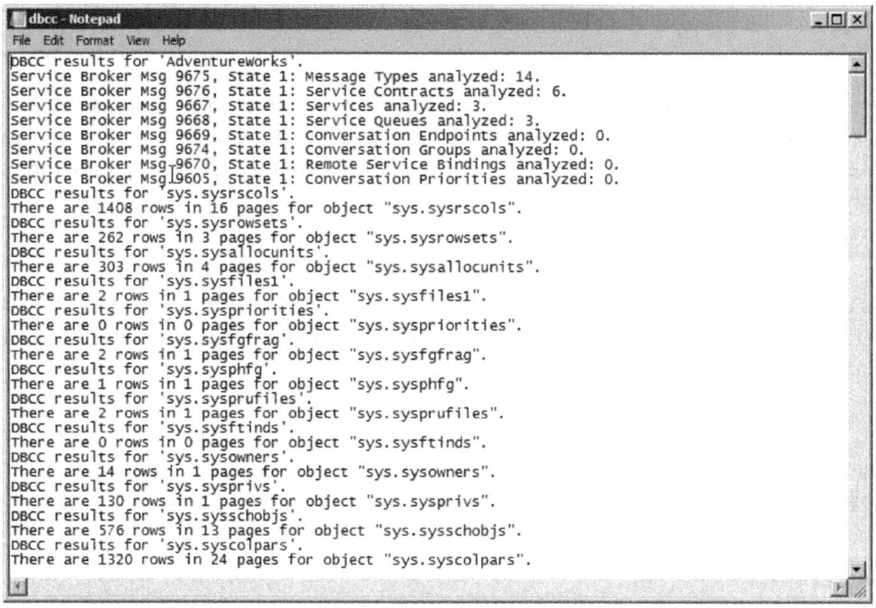

🌐 **Real World Scenario**

Command Prompt Automation

I once worked on a project for a company located in the Midwestern United States. As a parts supplier for thousands of clients, they provided an online interface for their customers to track and place orders. Several of the managers wanted to have data waiting for them in their email inboxes every morning. Thankfully, they all needed the same data set.

While I could have used SQL Server Integration Services (SSIS) to create a complex package for this purpose, I took the easier route, but—more importantly—the route that the internal support staff could manage. No one on the internal staff knew how to work with SSIS or had the time to learn it. This is why, for years now, I've spoken often of my pleasure at the flexibility SQL Server provides for automation. You can do it with batch files, WSH scripts, SSIS packages, and jobs.

In the end, I created a simple batch file that called SQLCMD to dump the data in a comma-separated format (using the −s switch). The next step in the batch file was a call to Blat (an excellent freeware command-line emailing tool). Blat sent the emails off to the managers automatically. Because the format was CSV, the managers could easily open the data in Excel and manipulate it to their hearts' desire. This batch file was then scheduled to run every morning at 6~AM on the server.

Here's the best part: About a year after the batch file was created, the managers called the internal support staff to indicate that they needed another column in the output file. No problem. The support professional simply opened the batch file, modified the query in the line that invoked SQLCMD, and saved the file. No SSIS knowledge was required and the edit was done in under 60 seconds. Flexibility. I love flexibility.

Introducing Windows PowerShell

Up to this point, you have focused on the standard built-in command prompt provided by CMD.EXE. In recent years, Microsoft began shifting their focus to a new command-line interface called PowerShell. They are certainly still committed to traditional command-prompt utilities as is evidenced by the new utilities in Windows 7 and Windows Server 2008 R2; however, the PowerShell engine is the secret behind many new administration tools. For example, the System Center Virtual Machine Manager makes calls to PowerShell to get its work done. So does the Exchange 2007 administration tool. There is sure to be more of this as Microsoft continues to evolve PowerShell.

Windows PowerShell is a command-line interface that is focused on scripting and the power to accomplish administrative tasks with consistency. Command-prompt commands may use dashes for switches or they may use forward slashes and even double dashes. This inconsistency can make it more difficult to master. Windows PowerShell is focused on providing a consistent interface across all utilities and administration tasks.

On most servers, you will need to download and install Windows PowerShell as it is not installed by default. To download PowerShell, go to www.Microsoft.com and search for "PowerShell download." This will change with Windows 7 and Windows Server 2008 R2, but for those using older systems, a download is still required. You can either search for Windows PowerShell at Microsoft's website or download it through Windows Updates. Once you've installed it, you can launch the Windows PowerShell from the Start menu. It will look something like the screen in Figure 4.22.

FIGURE 4.22   The Windows PowerShell interface

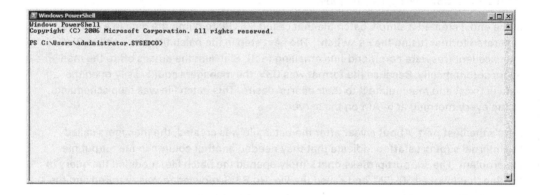

Using SQL Server PowerShell Extensions

In order to take advantage of PowerShell for SQL Server administration, you'll need to download the Microsoft Windows PowerShell Extensions for SQL Server. The extensions add a PowerShell provider that allows navigation through a SQL Server instance much like browsing through a directory structure. Additionally, it will install several *cmdlets* (command lets—something like applets in the Control Panel) that allow for tasks such as converting data from one structure to another and invoking commands against the SQL Server.

Once you've downloaded the extensions (which you'll find best by visiting Microsoft. com and searching for Microsoft SQL Server 2008 Feature Pack), the installation process is simple. First, you must ensure that you have the SQL Server Management Objects installed. They are available on the same page as the PowerShell Extensions for SQL Server. Next, you will launch the installation file (at the time of this writing, it is named `PowerShellTools.msi`) and step through the wizard to perform the installation.

When the installation completes, you will need to execute a special command to open a SQL Server–ready PowerShell window. The command to execute is `sqlps`.

You should run it from the Start ➤ Run option, but you can also execute it from a command prompt, if you have one open continually. In fact, when you execute `sqlps` from a Command Prompt window, PowerShell runs in the same window. This integration is excellent. When you're done with the PowerShell work, you can simply type **EXIT** and press Enter to return to your previous command-prompt session.

One of the coolest features of the SQL Server extensions for PowerShell is the ability to navigate the SQL Server services as if they were a directory structure. Figure 4.23 shows this in action. Notice that the Default instance and the Sales instance show up with directory listings invoked by the `DIR` command.

FIGURE 4.23   Navigating SQL Server in PowerShell

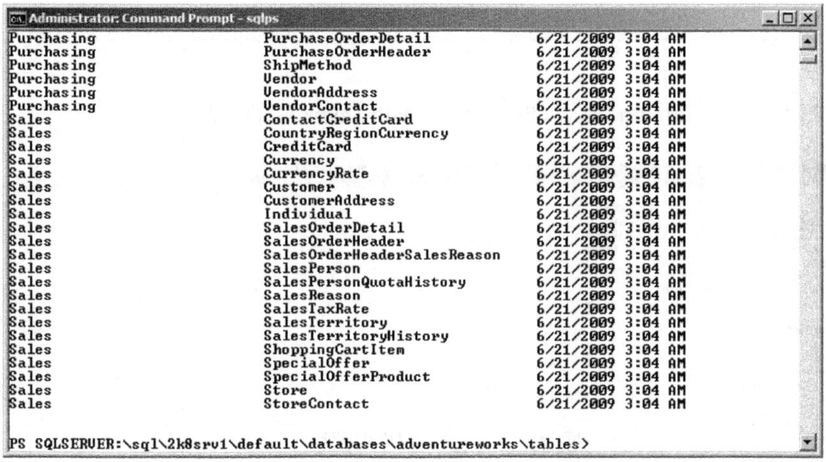

Of course, simply browsing around in the database doesn't provide a lot of power alone. The `Invoke-SQLCMD` cmdlet is where the real power is. With this cmdlet, you can do the same tasks that you perform in `SQLCMD` at the regular command prompt. Figure 4.24 shows the execution of a simple query against the AdventureWorks database. Figure 4.25 shows the results of running a `DBCC CHECKTABLE` command against the Production.Product table. Notice the use of the `-verbose` switch when running `DBCC`. This switch is required to see the results of the `DBCC` command.

FIGURE 4.24 Executing queries with Invoke-SQLCMD

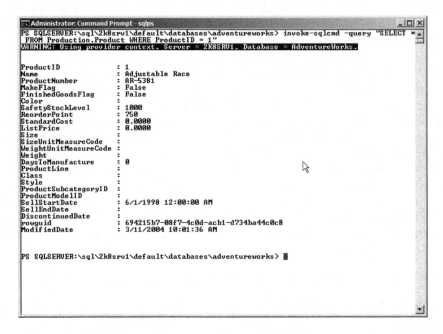

FIGURE 4.25 Running DBCC CHECKTABLE with Invoke-SQLCMD

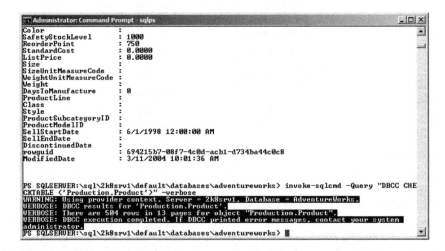

For more information on the Windows PowerShell and the SQL Server Extensions for PowerShell, search for SQL Server 2008 PowerShell at http://www.Microsoft.com.

Windows Scripting Host

If the command prompt and Windows PowerShell are not enough for you, the Windows Scripting Host (WSH) engine may do the trick. It is beyond the scope of this book to attempt a tackle of WSH in its entirety, but Microsoft's website is filled with valuable information about WSH and scripting options. This section will provide one example with some comments, but it won't try to teach you WSH scripting here because that is a multi-hundred-page topic by itself.

The following example code can be saved to a file, such as checkspace.vbs, and executed:

```
strServerName = "."
strDBName = "AdventureWorks"

Set objSQLSrv = CreateObject("SQLDMO.SQLServer")
objSQLSrv.LoginSecure = True
objSQLSrv.Connect strServerName

Set objDB = objSQLServer.Databases(strDBName)
WScript.Echo "Space Left (Data File + Transaction Log) for DB " &_
 strDBName & ": " & objDB.SpaceAvailableInMB & "(MB)"
```

This script is a modified version of the script found in the Microsoft Script Repository. You will need to install SQL Server 2008 Backward Compatibility in order to use this script and any other script that uses the SQL DMO (data management objects). Figure 4.26 shows the execution of the checkspace.vbs script using the CSCRIPT command-line tool.

FIGURE 4.26   Running a VBScript WSH script

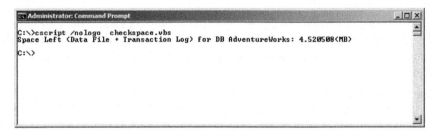

If you look back at the code, it's not extremely complex. First, you establish that the server is the local machine. The dot indicates the local machine. Next, configure the database to be AdventureWorks. To check the space left on any other database, you would simply change the name here in line 2. The next thing the script does is establish a SQL DMO connection to the SQL Server instance. Finally, you use the property SpaceAvailableInMB to retrieve the free space.

Certainly, this script is more complex than batch files, but you can do many complex things with WSH. If you want to learn more about it, be sure to visit the Microsoft Script Center at `http://www.microsoft.com/technet/scriptcenter`.

Summary

In this chapter, you were introduced to the many ways in which the command line and scripts can be used to manage and administer your SQL Servers. You learned to launch and customize the command line (`CMD.EXE`) and you learned to navigate at the command-prompt interface. Next, you learned several administration commands that are essential for managing SQL Servers. After this, batch files were introduced and you created a batch file that can export data from a SQL Server database. Finally, you were introduced to the new PowerShell and Windows Scripting Host.

Chapter Essentials

Introducing the Command Prompt   The Windows command prompt is a valuable tool for administration, troubleshooting, and automation. The most efficient Windows administrators know the command-prompt interface well.

General Commands   In order to use the command prompt, you must have several commands memorized and mastered. These commands include `DIR`, `CD`, `COPY`, `ROBOCOPY`, `CLS`, `ECHO`, and `TYPE`, among others.

Batch Files   When you want to automate mundane or routing tasks, batch files are frequently an excellent solution. With batch files, you can make decisions, execute dozens or hundreds of commands, and quickly modify them without any requirements for compilation.

Mastering `SQLCMD`   With the command prompt's fundamentals under your belt, you moved on to the `SQLCMD` utility. This is the primary utility for communicating with the SQL Server in both SQL Server 2005 and 2008. You can communicate with SQL Server 2000 servers as well.

Introducing Windows PowerShell   Windows PowerShell is Microsoft's new command-line interface with more powerful scripting and greater consistency. The SQL Server 2008 PowerShell Extensions enhance PowerShell to provide better support for SQL Server administration.

Using SQL Server PowerShell Extensions   When using the SQL Server PowerShell Extensions you gain two core benefits. First, you have the ability to navigate the SQL Server objects as a directory structure. Second, you are provided with several cmdlets—Invoke-SQLCMD being one of the most important—for SQL Server administration.

Windows Scripting Host   Windows Scripting Host (WSH) provides a scripting engine that uses runtime compilation to interact with and administer practically any Windows component. This interaction does include SQL Server 2008.

Designing Database Solutions

Chapter

5

Database Concepts and Terminology

TOPICS COVERED IN THIS CHAPTER:

✓ Relational Database Theory

✓ Database Design Processes

✓ Business: Purpose and Requirements

✓ Users: Performance and Usability

✓ Modeling: Simple and Logical

✓ Project Management for the DBA

Now that your SQL Server is up and running, you need to make sure you fully understand the database concepts and terminology introduced in Chapter 1, "Understanding SQL Server's Role," before you create your databases. If you create databases without understanding the concepts covered in this chapter, you risk needing to change your databases later on, which is often time-consuming and frustrating. It is much easier to create a database right in the first place than it is to restructure it later. For this reason, this chapter and the next two will focus on database design concepts as they relate to SQL Server 2008.

In order to successfully build a database and communicate the functionality of that database to others, it is important to have a shared language. This chapter begins by explaining the differences between data and information. Once this foundation is built, you'll move on to explore additional terms used in relational database design. This information will help you understand the process and create databases that perform well. Next, you'll be introduced to the database design process called the BUM process. Don't worry; you'll see why it's called BUM as you read on. It is not a negative spin on database design, but a simplified model for ensuring good design. The three-phase design model is simple to remember, but ensures that the proper steps are taken as you lead up to the actual database build process. After stepping through the three-phase design process, the project management methodology used at The Systems Education Company will be explained. The methodology is mature, proven, and simple. Best of all, you can use it for your projects without buying anything. It's a concept, not a tool.

It's time to dive right in.

Relational Database Theory

You do not have to be a relational-database design guru to administer and implement SQL Server 2008 servers and databases, but having a solid foundational understanding of relational database theory will help you make better decisions when creating databases. In this section, you will delve deeper into the concepts of data, information, tables, and table components. You'll also explore the common relationship types that exist between database tables.

Data

Data should not be confused with information. For example, the following list represents data:

- 45908

- Thomas

- 43.27

When you look at this list, you cannot be certain what it represents. Is 43.27 a price, a percentage, or simply a precise value? Is the value 45908 a zip code or a number representing some other piece of information?

Data is meaningless until it is organized into information. The goal of a database system is to store data so that users can retrieve information. In fact, the data is often stored by several different users or processes who, individually, have no idea how the final information set will be presented. Data becomes meaningful information when it is placed in context.

Information

Information is one of the most valuable assets of organizations today. As a DBA, your goal is to securely store data that can be presented to users and systems as meaningful information. An Information Technology (IT) professional is one who ensures that information is stored, maintained, retrieved, and potentially destroyed properly. IT professionals must deal with the information from the database to the end user. This is the main reason that DBAs must have a much broader knowledge base today than they did in the past. Of course, they must know the database system extremely well. But they must also understand the fundamentals of the network infrastructure technologies and the endpoint (user-accessed computing devices) systems as well.

Consider Table 5.1, which lists the data shown in the preceding section in its information context. Notice that 45908 is the Customer ID, Thomas is the LastName, and 43.27 is the AvgOrdQty (average order quantity). If you guessed these domains for the data values shown earlier, that's great; however, you can clearly see that data without context is not information. If the data set does not inform, it's not information.

TABLE 5.1   Data in Context

Customer ID	First Name	Last Name	eMail	AvgOrdQty
45908	Dale	Thomas	Dale.Thomas@company.internal	43.27

Tables

Information must be stored in a manner that maintains the data and the data context. You must be able to store the data so that it can be retrieved as information. Database tables provide this functionality. Table 5.1 shows a portion of a database table. Because the table stores the data in named columns (context), you can retrieve the data and understand its intended meaning. You can be informed by the data set and, therefore, the data set is information.

As indicated previously, the people who actually enter the data may not see the big picture. If a customer calls a company and indicates that she wants to update her profile with a new email address, the customer service representative may launch a form that asks for a Customer ID and the new email address like the one in Figure 5.1. This customer service representative is dealing with a very small information set: the Customer ID and its associated email address. A user with the ability to retrieve the entire customer record can see the full context. Not only does the email address belong to the Customer ID, but it also belongs to the named individual who is associated with that Customer ID.

FIGURE 5.1   Simple data entry form

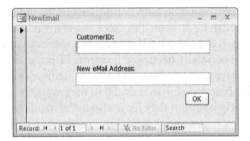

Table Components

Database tables are storage containers for data values that represent an entity. An entity is sort of like a noun: it can be defined as a person, place, thing, or idea. The following are examples of entities that might be represented in a table:

- Customers
- Device status
- Products
- Orders
- Stock values
- Company cars
- Servers
- Clients
- Employees

As you can see, many objects and actions can be defined as entities. These entities are defined by their properties or attributes. The Device Status table may store information about a piece of manufacturing equipment. The equipment may report health and production values to a database system for tracking and reporting. Attributes of the Device Status entity may include internal temperature, parts per minute, uptime, active state, and last maintenance time, among others. Figure 5.2 shows how this table might look with additional columns.

FIGURE 5.2   Device Status sample table

ID	Time	Temp	PPM	Uptime	Active	LatMaint
1	10:01	32	7	2:34	1	2/2/2009
2	10:02	31.3	5	2:35	1	2/2/2009
3	10:03	32.4	8	2:36	1	2/2/2009
4	10:04	32.2	7	2:37	1	2/2/2009

When you create a database table, you begin by defining the attributes of the entity that the table represents. If the table is to store customer records, typical attributes might be chosen from the following:

- Customer ID
- First name
- Last name
- Address
- City
- State
- Zip
- Work phone
- Mobile phone
- Home phone
- Email
- Status

These attributes are examples, and your scenario may demand additional attributes. You will discover both the entities and the attributes of those entities during the design process. The entities and attributes will be determined based on business requirements and user needs.

In SQL Server, the entity is the table and the attributes are the columns. If you access the table designer in SSMS, you will see this clearly. Figure 5.3 shows the table design window for an existing table (Production.Product) in the AdventureWorks sample database. You can see the column names and the data types selected in the center of the screen. Below that are the column properties. Each attribute (column) has its own set of attributes (properties).

However, the column properties define the integrity and domain requirements for the data values where the columns themselves define the attributes of the entire object or entity.

FIGURE 5.3   SSMS table designer

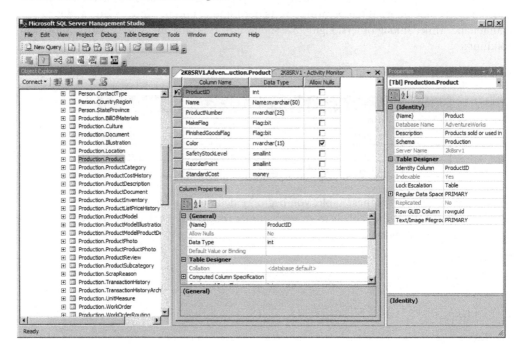

In addition to the table itself, it is important to understand special table containers and properties. The table containers, which give a logical structure to your tables, are called schemas. The table properties are identity columns and keys. The following sections explain all three.

Schemas

If you look to the right in Figure 5.3, you'll see the Properties window. The table properties are shown in this window. One of the table properties you'll need to understand is the schema. In SQL Server, a *schema* is defined as a container that provides a logical security boundary for database objects. In versions of SQL Server prior to 2005, the schema was intertwined with the user objects. If a user owned a table, the table was in the user's schema. This behavior resulted in odd scenarios like having a table named Fred.Sales or Amy.Customers. With the release of SQL Server 2005, schemas were separated from users. Now, Amy can own the Customers table and it can stay in the dbo schema or be placed in another schema. Most DBAs still use the dbo schema for all objects, which is the default; however, larger databases and specific security requirements may justify the use of more complex schema structures.

Identity Columns

Another specific table property is the identity column. An *identity column* is a special attribute that is automatically calculated for the table. It is meant to act as a record identifier that does not require user input. The table represented in Figure 5.2 is a perfect table for an identity column. The ID attribute serves one purpose: to identify the unique record. Notice that it simply increments by one for each new record. Rather than requiring the application to calculate this, you can ask the database server to do it for you. Without the identity column, developers would insert data into the table represented in Figure 5.2 like this:

```
INSERT INTO dbo.DeviceStatus (
ID, Time, Temp, PPM, Uptime, Active, LastMaint
)
VALUES (5, 10:05, 32.1, 7, 2:38, 2/2/2009);
```

With the identity column, the ID column would be dropped from the column list and the ID value of 5 would be removed from the values resulting in the following code:

```
INSERT INTO dbo.DeviceStatus (
Time, Temp, PPM, Uptime, Active, LastMaint
)
VALUES (10:05, 32.1, 7, 2:38, 2/2/2009);
```

The benefit of the latter over the former is that the developers do not have to determine the next available ID value. The value is calculated automatically.

Keys

One final table component that must be understood is the key. A *key* is a unique identifier for a record. A key may be an identity column, which generates the keys automatically, or it may be a standard column requiring user or system input. Two key types are most commonly used: primary and foreign.

A *primary key* is the unique identifier for records in the current table. The primary key may be defined as a single column or the combination of multiple columns. Multicolumn primary keys usually result in decreased database performance. When retrieving a single record from a table, the primary key is usually used as the filter. Consider the following T-SQL statement that could be executed against the table represented in Figure 5.2:

```
SELECT ID, Temp, PPM FROM dbo.DeviceStatus WHERE ID = 3;
```

This statement would retrieve one record and one record only. The WHERE clause of the SELECT statement filters to the ID column value of 3. The ID column is the primary key, which means that the value in each record is unique and only one or zero records will match a given single value.

In most cases, the primary key column will also be the clustered index column. The clustered index dictates the ordering of the data and that the data should be stored in a branching tree index structure. The result is faster retrieval of records filtered on the primary key column.

 Indexes are a very important factor in database performance. For this reason, they are covered in detail in Chapter 10, "Indexes and Views."

The *foreign key* is really a primary key from one table referenced in another table. Stated differently, if a table references the primary key of another table it is called a foreign key in the referencing table. If Table_A has a primary key named ProductID and Table_B references the ProductID value of Table_A, ProductID is a foreign key in Table_B.

Foreign keys are used to build relationships. When two tables are related to each other, they are said to have a relationship. Several relationship types exist and they will be covered in the next section, but it is important to remember that, in most cases, the foreign key is the building block for these relationships.

Relationship Types

Tables may be related to one another in three primary ways:

- One-to-one
- One-to-many
- Many-to-many

The following sections describe each relationship type.

One-to-One

In a one-to-one relationship, one record in one table matches one and only one record in another table. Figure 5.4 shows an example of a one-to-one relationship. Notice that the Employees table and the Compensation table both have the same primary key column, which is the EmployeeID column. For each record in Employees exactly one record exists in Compensation. The relationship is built on the shared EmployeeID value.

FIGURE 5.4 One-to-one diagram

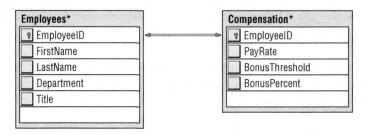

You can query the joined results with the following statement:

```
SELECT      Employees.EmployeeID,
            Employees.FirstName,
            Employees.LastName,
            Employees.Department,
            Employees.Title,
            Compensation.PayRate,
            Compensation.BonusThreshold,
            Compensation.BonusPercent
FROM        Employees
INNER JOIN  Compensation ON Employees.EmployeeID = Compensation.EmployeeID;
```

The reasons for creating a one-to-one relationship usually fall into one of three categories:

- Database system constraints
- Improved security
- Improved performance

SQL Server limits row or record sizes to 8,060 bytes for tables that contain standard data types only. Exceptions exist for large objects (Image and Text data types, for example) and variable-length columns (nVarChar and VarBinary, for example), but all other data types are constrained by this size limit. While the example presented in Figure 5.4 would not be forced by this constraint, tables containing dozens of columns can certainly reach the limit. In such cases, you may have no choice but to vertically partition the table by splitting it into two tables that can then be joined together at query time.

Security may be improved if the data in one of the tables is more sensitive. In our example, the Compensation table data is probably more sensitive than the data that is in the Employees table. You can implement security at the column level, but it is often easier to partition the data into separate tables and then apply the appropriate permissions at the table level.

Finally, performance is a common motivator. Imagine that 5,000 queries are run each day against the Employees table. Further, imagine that only 230 queries are run against the Compensation table. If the two tables were stored as one, the 5,000 queries would probably suffer a performance hit. Some DBAs will vertically partition tables like this simply to gain a performance advantage. Chapter 9, "Data Types and Table Types," will explain why, in most instances, fewer columns equal better performance.

One-to-Many

The one-to-many relationship is probably the most common relationship type. Figure 5.5 shows a one-to-many relationship between the Sales.Customer table and the Sales.SalesOrderHeader table in the AdventureWorks database. Notice the lazy eight (that's just a nickname for it; it's really an infinity symbol) on the right side of the line joining the tables. This identifier means that the table on that side of the relationship is the "many" table and the table on the other side (the side with the key indicator) is the "one" table.

FIGURE 5.5   One-to-many diagram

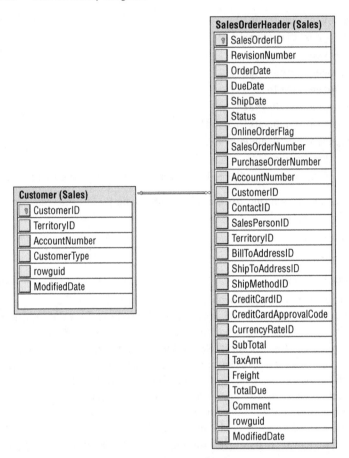

One-to-many relationships are heavily used in modern databases. They allow you to enter a multiple action entity once and reuse it again and again. A customer may buy from you one time or he may make hundreds of purchases. You can see all of the orders placed by a given customer by executing a query based on the following construct:

```
SELECT     desired_columns
FROM       Customers
INNER JOIN Orders
ON Customers.CustomerID = Orders.CustomerID WHERE CustomerID = id_value;
```

The following is an actual SELECT statement against the diagrammed tables in Figure 5.5:

```
SELECT     Sales.Customer.CustomerID,
           Sales.Customer.AccountNumber,
           Sales.SalesOrderHeader.SalesOrderID,
           Sales.SalesOrderHeader.OrderDate
```

```
FROM        Sales.Customer
INNER JOIN  Sales.SalesOrderHeader
ON Sales.Customer.CustomerID = Sales.SalesOrderHeader.CustomerID
WHERE       Sales.Customer.CustomerID = 227;
```

Figure 5.6 shows the results of this query in the SSMS query window. Notice that the only orders shown are those for CustomerID 227, and the CustomerID and AccountNumber values are being pulled from the Sales.Customer table, while all other values are retrieved, using the one-to-many relationship, from the Sales.SalesOrderHeader table.

FIGURE 5.6   Querying data in a one-to-many scenario

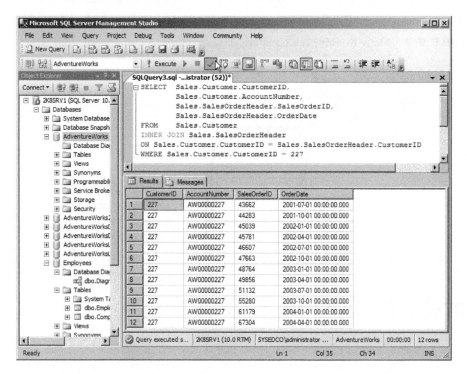

Many-to-Many

The final relationship type is the many-to-many relationship. Technically, the many-to-many relationship is really two coordinated one-to-many relationships combined into a centralized linking table. This final relationship type is used least often, but it serves tremendous value when it is needed. If you have two groups called GroupA and GroupB and several of the entities in GroupA are related to several of the entities in GroupB while the same is true in reverse, such that several of the entities in GroupB are related to several of the entities in GroupA, you need a many-to-many relationship.

Here are a couple of examples of where a many-to-many relationship could be useful:

Authors to books—Several authors can contribute to a single book and multiple books could be authored by a single author.

Students to classrooms—Several students are likely to be in one class and several classes are likely to have the same students.

To create many-to-many relationships, you need a special table called a linking table or a junction table. The linking table serves the sole purpose of bringing the other two tables together. Figure 5.7 shows an example of a many-to-many relationship scenario. Notice that Tom Carpenter is the author of a CWSP book, but so is Richard Dreger. Tom is the author of two books and the CWSP book is authored by two authors. Tom has authored many books and the CWSP book has many authors. The result is a many-to-many relationship.

FIGURE 5.7 Many-to-many relationship

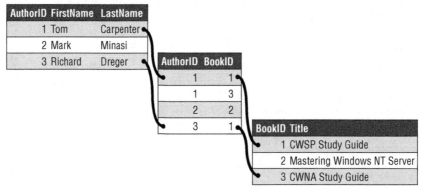

Database Design Processes

With the nuts and bolts of relational database theory covered in the first few pages of this chapter and in Chapter 1, it's time to move on to the database design process. Several database design processes exist and some methods are more generic than others. For example, many DBAs will use the Systems or Software Development Lifecycle (SDLC) as the foundation for their database design process. Others use a simple two-phase model of requirements analysis and then logical design. This section will review some of the common design processes available to you and then share a successful process used after years of consulting work and practical design challenges related to SQL Server databases.

Of the many design models available, the most commonly used ones and the one used at The Systems Education Company are:

- Systems Development Lifecycle (SDLC)
- Database Lifecycle (DBLC)
- Business, User, Model (BUM)

Systems Development Lifecycle (SDLC)

The Systems Development Lifecycle (SDLC) is a systems design and implementation model that usually passes through several sequential phases, including:

1. Planning
2. Requirements gathering
3. Conceptual and logical design
4. Physical design
5. Construction and testing
6. Implementation and deployment
7. Maintenance/ongoing support

If you consider the responsibilities of the DBA at each of these phases, they would map out something like this:

1. Select a database system and assign database designers and administrators.
2. Determine the needed user data screens (views) and identify entities.
3. Develop the conceptual and logical data models (usually use ERD tools).
4. Determine physical database model based on the database system selected.
5. Create a test lab and implement the database.
6. Create production databases and import or convert existing data.
7. Tune, tweak, and maintain the database system.

Clearly, the SDLC model can be used as a database design flow model. In many cases, the DBA will be working alongside network engineers, server administrators, and project managers and will need to perform specific operations during different phases of a project. It is not uncommon for a project manager to use the SDLC model for her project, and it is helpful for you to understand it for that reason. For more free information related to the SDLC, refer to the Department of Justice SDLC Guidance document found at http://www.usdoj.gov/jmd/irm/lifecycle/table.htm.

Database Lifecycle (DBLC)

The Database Lifecycle (DBLC) model is usually broken into six phases that occur in sequential order. They can be used by a DBA working as a task manager in a larger project or even as the sole project methodology for implementing a database solution. The six phases are as follows:

1. Initiation

2. Design

3. Build and load

4. Test

5. Implementation

6. Operations

Here is a brief description of each phase so you'll understand them more fully:

Initiation   During the Initiation phase, the DBA evaluates the organization's position and the requirements for the specific database in question. This phase may take a few hours or a few weeks depending on the size of the project and the cooperation of the stakeholders. Sometimes it can be difficult to get a return phone call or email from some important stakeholders. The result of the Initiation phase should be a document or set of documents clearly defining the scope of the project and the key stakeholders.

Design   In the Design phase, the conceptual, logical, and physical database designs are created. The conceptual design includes screens, forms, and user interface elements. These elements may or may not be the responsibility of the DBA. The logical and physical design will most likely be the responsibility of the DBA. During the logical design tasks, the DBA will use either formal entity relational modeling/design (ERD) tools or simple modeling concepts, but the concern is not with actual implementation constructs for a real database system. With the logical design complete, the DBA begins to evaluate how to implement the logical design in the physical system. In this case, this means a SQL Server database. The result of the Design phase is the documentation for exactly how the database will be implemented in SQL Server.

Build and Load   During this third phase, you build the database in a test environment and load it with real or test data. This can take from a few minutes to a few days depending on the size of the database and the tools you have for data generation. If you work on projects that require the development of custom script for data generation, you might like to use the EMS Data Generator for SQL Server found at http://www.sqlmanager.net. With this tool, you can generate millions of records with excellent variability in a short amount of time. The result of the Build and Load phase is a test environment that can be used for the activities of the fourth phase.

Test   The Test phase is very straightforward. The database is tested for usability, performance, security, and expandability. You must ensure that the proper data is provided and that it is provided in a timely manner. Of course, it must be secured and you want to make sure you can expand the database in the future. You don't necessarily need to plan for adding new columns or tables, but you must plan for the ultimate size of the database after months or years of utilization. The result of the Test phase will either be the finalization of the original database design that entered into the phase or the finalization of a modified design based on problems detected in the phase.

Implementation   The fifth phase, which is truly part of the design process, is the Implementation phase. In this phase, you implement the production server and database and allow importing of existing data or the generation of data required. The result of this phase is an active database solution used by production users.

Operations   The sixth phase of the DBLC model is not really a phase of the design process, but rather the results of the design process. The term *operations* refers to the day-to-day process of administering the database solution. Traditional tasks include database backup, indexing, re-indexing, managing security, implementing jobs, and upgrading servers and services.

Business, User, Model (BUM)

After years of experience, you'll probably become a believer in simplification without sacrifice. Simplification reduces cost, increases efficiency, and lowers the learning curve. You never want to oversimplify, but you always want to simplify. Based on this thinking, the BUM database design process was developed. BUM stands for Business, Users, and Model. It is a simple three-phase process that results in a database system that meets the business and user needs.

 I started The Systems Education and Consulting Company (SysEdCo) in 1997 and it became quickly apparent that standardized processes would help us better serve our clients. We developed the BUM design process to make certain that all the bases were covered when developing a new database solution. This section briefly explains the model so that you can understand what one may look like in your organization or so that you can build on this model. Either way, I'm glad to provide you with this information, which has helped us improve our database design processes over the years.

Here's a list of the three phases along with descriptions for each:

Business   In the Business phase, you determine the purpose and requirements of the database.

Users   During the Users phase, you investigate performance requirements and usability issues.

Modeling   Finally, the Modeling phase is where you document the logical and physical database implementation plan as one.

Some hard-core DBAs were probably just shocked by the indication that the logical and physical models are developed as one process or task. Don't worry. If you want to do them separately, you can. If you know the database system in which you will be implementing the database, you can go right into the physical database design at the same time. If you need to generate a higher-level logical design from that physical design at some point in the future, you can.

BUM is a database design model, so after the design is complete, you'll enter a testing phase where the design is implemented in a lab and users work with the system. They can be observed to improve the database design during this testing phase before final implementation.

Business: Purpose and Requirements

In the Business phase of the database design model, you are focused on determining the purpose of the database and the business-level requirements. Some groups choose to create a mission statement or a purpose statement at this point. The following template was created for a purpose statement when creating a database: You will create a database that serves the *list group or groups here* and allows them to *list business processes here*, which results in *list benefits here*.

This template may not work for every scenario, but it should fit well in most situations.

With the purpose defined, you need to gather business requirements. The following list provides some samples of these requirements:

- Order fulfillment must take place within a single database solution.

- All sales information must be tracked in this database.

- The database must provide separation of data so that an unauthorized user is never granted access to a table that contains data the user is not authorized to view.

- Customer records must only exist for contacts that purchased at least one item. All others should be stored as contacts.

- All orders must be linked to a customer and a sales person.

- The database system must be available 24/7.

- The database must be recoverable within a 30-minute window should an unexpected failure occur.

You may generate a much longer list during your database design process, but the point is to ensure that the resulting database meets the high-level business demands. This sample list also shows that, in the real world, database design is about more than entity discovery and relationship diagramming. The DBA must consider issues like high availability, backup and restore, and security.

The outputs of the Business phase will include:

Database Design Plan—A high-level document listing the purpose of the database, the DBAs and key stakeholders, and the business objectives. This document will usually be from three to five pages in length. It is not a plan; it is a guide from which a plan will be developed.

Other Documents—Several other documents may be developed during this first phase including a responsibility matrix (who is responsible for what), a business objective link document (how does this database help achieve current major objectives), etc.

Users: Performance and Usability

As you enter the Users phase of the BUM model, you will begin to evaluate how the users will use the database and the performance needs of the users. Consider asking the following questions of the eventual database users:

- Will you be running ad hoc queries (queries that you build on-the-fly) or will you only perform actions provided by an application? If they don't know the answer to this question, ask if they will be generating custom reports against the data in the database.

- How many transactions will you be making in a day? If they don't understand this, ask them what their job is in relation to this data and what processes they go through. Then ask how many times they go through each process daily.

- From where will you be accessing the database? If the users will access the database from remote locations, special security considerations must be made. Additionally, careful attention should be given to the size of result sets.

- During what hours will you be accessing it? The hours of access will often dictate your backup and maintenance windows. If you know that the database will be unused from 10 P.M. to 6 A.M. on most days, you can schedule automated maintenance for this window of time.

- How many total users will need access to the database? This question may have been answered already in the Business phase, but it will be helpful in making design decisions (such as what indexes to create) and hardware selection.

These questions are a sampling of the kind of questions you'll need to ask the users. The answers will reveal the way in which the users will use the database or, at least, the way they think they'll use it. During the testing of the database design, you may discover changes that must be made. People are seldom aware of every step they'll take to complete a task, which is why observing the users during testing is essential.

In addition to ensuring usability factors, it is also important that the database perform well. Determining how many users access the database concurrently and from where will be a starting point; however, it's also important to remember the answer to some of the other questions. For example, if you asked the users how many times they go through a process in a day and they answered 100 to 120 times, you must ensure the system will allow them to do this. If the database is unresponsive and it delays the process by one minute during an iteration, it will cost the employees two hours of time each day. You may decide to partition the data, implement multiple servers with replication, or simply purchase more powerful servers, but you must meet the performance needs as well as the usability needs.

The result of the Users phase will be an updated set of documents from the Business phase and, likely in the real world, a whole new set of meetings with management to talk about the users' needs and how they will be implemented.

Modeling: Simple and Logical

With the business and user objectives and requirements defined, you're ready to begin modeling a solution. You can use formal relational diagramming techniques, or you can use any number of solutions that work for you. Following is a list of common tools used in database modeling:

- Visio diagrams
- ER/Studio from Embarcadero
- ConceptDraw Pro
- Toad Data Modeler
- xCase
- Open System Architect

Open System Architect is an open source ERD toolset that will be explored in Chapter 6, "ERD and Capacity Planning." This product is covered in more depth simply because it is readily available to anyone who wants to use it. The product is open source, so the price is free. You can use it at home or at work to learn database modeling or to perform full database modeling tasks on a day-to-day basis.

Although the common argument for first designing the logical model of a database and then implementing the physical model is fully understandable, based on the modern tools available, the value of doing so is not great. In the past, you could reuse the logical model to implement the database on any database system. Today, these tools can read in a database from an existing physical implementation and create a logical model. Then, you can apply the logical model to a different physical database system. For this reason, designing for the database system you are using immediately (physical design) and then generating a logical design from this implementation is encouraged at The Systems Education Company. It's faster and you still end up with the logical design for portability to other platforms.

The result of the Modeling phase is a logical and physical design for database implementation. With the modern tools available to use, you can implement the physical design with the click of a button. In the next chapter, you'll walk through modeling a small database using the Open System Architect. You will see how the logical and physical designs are accomplished in one process instead of two.

Real World Scenario

Automatic Logical Design

I was working on a project in early 2009 that required moving several databases from Microsoft Access into SQL Server 2005. The organization wanted to perform some remodeling tasks on the databases as they were moved to the new system. In order to accomplish this, I created ODBC data sources for connection to each Access database. Then I automatically generated a physical model from the existing databases with Open System Architect.

With the physical models created, it was a simple process to generate logical models from them. At this point, I remodeled the databases at the logical level and then generated new physical models, still using the open source Open System Architect program.

With the new physical designs in place, I created the databases on a test SQL Server with a few simple clicks in the menus. Don't misunderstand, it takes a while to become comfortable with any program, but the point is clear: Modern applications make logical and physical modeling much easier and in many cases they make it automatic.

Project Management for the DBA

Project management is an important skill set for the DBA to possess. The task management and time management components are essential to timely operations. The average DBA does not require a Project Management Professional (PMP) certification or an MBA in Project Management; however, basic project management skills will help you ensure you deliver what the users need when they need it.

The Systems Education Company uses a project management methodology developed specifically for IT projects. It is named Method4D. The methodology breaks IT implementation projects into four distinct phases:

- Define
- Design
- Deliver
- Determine

Each of these phases involves inputs, processes, and outputs. The utilization of the methodology helps to ensure that the projects are implemented and managed effectively so that they come in on time and within budget as often as possible (risk always exists). To illustrate the fundamentals of effective project management, a high-level overview of this methodology will be presented. If you would like to learn more about it, you can visit the company website at www.SysEdCo.com. The methodology is freely available and documented at the website. The following sections discuss the phases in greater detail than the simple list provided previously.

The Define Phase

The Define phase is the first of the four phases. In this phase, the project is clearly and concisely defined. The goal here is not to develop a detailed project plan with all the tasks included, but rather to develop a concise project definition and provide a project charter to the sponsor or decision maker for approval and guidance throughout the remaining phases.

The inputs to phase 1 are minimal and they include:

- A project idea
- A project proposal

Sadly, many projects are launched without much forethought. In some cases, you are fortunate enough to have a well-designed project proposal at the beginning. The project proposal will include the major goals of the project and possibly a rough definition. It is far more common to start the Define phase with a basic idea from the mind of a manager instead of this nice proposal document. As an example, you may be approached by the company president with the following statement, "Could you implement a database for us?" This kind of request is usually all that you have as the input to the Define phase.

The good news is that this is exactly why the Define phase exists. Taking the input of a simple idea, you can execute selected processes that result in a well-defined project. The processes used in the Define phase include:

- Define the project
- Evaluate the project

Defining the project involves user and manager interviews that result in a better understanding of what is required. This process takes you from, "Can you implement a database for us?" to "We will implement a database that provides transaction processing and reporting services for the new process management initiative." Do you see the difference? The first question is a simple idea. The second statement is a concisely detailed project definition. The project definition states the following requirements for the database implementation:

- Transaction processing is required. The database is not read only.
- Reporting services will be needed.

Does this definition state the specific technologies to be used or the tables required? No. You will not usually want to constrain yourself to a specific technology or design at this point. Such details will be provided in the Design phase.

Creating a Project Definition

This definition is the result of the first process used in the Define phase. To be clear, the project definition is to implement a database that provides transaction processing and reporting services for the new process management initiative.

A good project definition accomplishes three tasks:

1. It will clearly define what your project is about.

2. It will be easily understood by anyone involved in the project.

3. It will act as a baseline for decisions.

When a stakeholder comes to you asking for a change to the project, you can go back to the definition and ask your project team how the requested change fits within the definition.

Making a Project Evaluation

The second process used in the Define phase is project evaluation. This process includes cost evaluations, existing database reviews, and possibly requirements analysis. The goal of this process is to ensure that the project is feasible. If the project doesn't make sense for the organization, it is far better to abandon the project in the Define phase than in the Design or Deliver phases.

Understanding a Project Charter

The output of the Define phase is a project charter. *Project charters* include several pieces of information and usually fit on one to three printed pages. The sponsor is often asked to sign the charter as a method of green lighting the project. Project charters may include the following information:

- Project name
- Potential start date
- Rough order estimate of duration
- Rough order estimate of cost
- Project manager name
- Project sponsor name
- Key project team members
- Project definition
- Major project deliverables
- Roles and responsibilities

Using Rough Order Estimates

The rough order estimates (sometimes called rough order of magnitude estimates) are very simple estimates that can be off by 50 percent or more. You should be sure to make this clear to the project sponsor and let her or him know that more accurate estimates will be provided after project planning within the Design phase. With many databases, the project will be small enough that the sponsor will not require a budget estimate. The last process in the Define phase is usually the creation of rough order estimates. In the Design phase, you will create more accurate estimates for the work tasks.

The Design Phase

The Design phase is where the detailed project plan is born. Without a thorough project plan and scope document, the project is almost certain to fail or at least not meet expectations. You've heard the wise saying: If you fail to plan, you plan to fail. The inputs to the Design phase include:

- Project charter
- Past projects
- Group knowledge

The most important input to the Design phase is the project charter. This document will help the team focus on the actual desired outcomes during project planning. Past projects also provide valuable insights. These projects may reveal costs, procedures, and potential problems that your project plan will need to address. Finally, group knowledge will be provided by the project team and key stakeholders. This knowledge includes technical knowledge, but it also includes knowledge of business processes.

The project management processes used in the Design phase include:

- Task discovery
- Resource selection
- Time estimation
- Schedule creation
- Budget development
- Risk analysis

After performing these processes, you will generate the key output of the Design phase: a project plan. The project plan will consist of the following common elements. Please note that all project charter information is updated according to the Design phase process results.

- Work breakdown structure (WBS)
- Budget
- Schedule

- Resource assignments
- Hardware acquisition plan
- Risk response plan

Your project plan may have more or less information, but this is a rough guideline to the items that should be included in the plan.

The Deliver Phase

The Deliver phase is where the work gets done. The input to this phase is the project plan, and the processes include execution and control.

Of course, execution can be considered from two perspectives. The first perspective is that of the task worker, who sees execution as doing the work. The second perspective is that of the project manager, who sees execution as monitoring the work. In smaller organizations, it is very common for the project manager to also be the task worker.

Control implies that the project should be constrained within the boundaries of the plan as much as possible. This activity includes monitoring of the budget, the schedule, and the scope. The scope is defined as the promised deliverables of the project.

The desired output of the Deliver phase is the accomplishment of the definition provided all the way back in the Define phase. In addition, actual project schedules, budgets, and deliverables should be documented.

The Determine Phase

You will know when it's time to move to the Determine phase because it only happens when all of the technical work is done. Now that your database exists, the Determine phase takes the original schedule, budget, and scope and compares them to the actual schedule, budget, and scope. The primary goal of the Determine phase is to evaluate the project with two major objectives in mind:

- Ensure that the project charter has been fulfilled.
- Learn lessons for future projects.

The greatest long-term value usually comes from creating a lessons-learned analysis. These lessons will benefit future projects and, over time, your project management skills and methodologies will mature resulting in greater project success rates.

It is very tempting to skip the Define and Design phases of a project. It is also tempting to avoid the Determine phase. However, it is in these three phases that project management succeeds or fails in the big picture. If you always jump right into the work or quickly move on to the next project without considering the lessons learned in the current one, you are not truly utilizing project management.

Summary

The database design process you select will be used to keep you focused during the defining and planning phases of your database development project. You can use common industry models, such as the SDLS and DBLC, or you can use the BUM model referenced in this chapter. Whatever model you choose, the main point is to have a structures process set that can be matured over time.

As a DBA, you may work under the umbrella of a larger project and the entire project management methodology may not apply to you. For example, you may be given the specifications for a database and be asked to implement it without any involvement in the design of those specifications. While this may not be the best use of your expertise, it is reality. However, if you find yourself installing a new SQL Server for one or more databases, it's time to pull out a good project management methodology and start to work.

As a final note on project management as a DBA, consider that the database design process (whether it be SDLC, DBLC, or BUM) is not equal to the project management methodology. The project management methodology sits as an umbrella over the database design and implementation. In fact, the database design process will likely begin toward the end of the Define phase or very early in the Design phase. It will usually be completed before the Determine phase. The point is that database design fits into project management and is not a competing concept or process.

Chapter Essentials

Relational Database Theory   Tables are the building blocks of relational databases. The tables may be related to each other in one of several relationship types, including one-to-one, one-to-many, and many-to-many. Primary and foreign keys are usually used to establish relationships.

Database Design Processes   Several database design processes exist. The SDLC and DBLC models are popular. The BUM model is used at The Systems Education Company. You may decide to develop your own model as well. The key is to have a model that can be matured (changed and corrected over time as needs change) as you employ it during different projects.

Business: Purpose and Requirements   Defining the purpose for your database helps you to maintain focus throughout the design and implementation process. Establishing business requirements early ensures that the database satisfies the demands of the organization.

Users: Performance and Usability   Involving the users in the design process helps reduce resistance to the database solution at implementation. It ensures that the users receive a system that performs well and meets their needs.

Modeling: Simple and Logical   By modeling the logical and physical design of the database together, you reduce design time without sacrificing quality. The end result is an earlier implementation date and happier users and managers.

Project Management for the DBA   Project management is about answering four key questions in sequence. Should you do it? How will you do it? How are you doing? How did you do? The Method4D methodology is just one of many project management methodologies that can be used to manage a database implementation—or any other IT project, for that matter.

Chapter

6

ERD and Capacity Planning

TOPICS COVERED IN THIS CHAPTER:

✓ Planning a Database

✓ Understanding Entity Relationship Diagramming

✓ Building an Entity Relationship Diagram (ERD)

✓ Capacity Planning

In the preceding chapter, you explored the basic components of the database design process. In this chapter, you will learn about the specific steps involved in planning a database. First, you'll learn about the steps that lead up to the logical design. These steps include user surveys, evaluation of business processes, and the development of use cases or activity descriptions.

Next, you'll study an overview of the entity relationship diagramming toolset. The icons and connectors will be presented with their features and attributes. With the description complete, you'll move on to creating an actual entity relationship diagram. You'll walk through the process of creating a diagram in Visio, and then you'll work through an exercise creating the same diagram in the Open System Architect open source application.

The final topic in this chapter will provide an overview of the capacity planning process. Here, the coverage will be specific to SQL Server, but the concepts could be applied to any database.

Planning a Database

Although the primary focus of this chapter is on diagramming your database, you cannot really create a diagram until you know what you're trying to accomplish. The three important database planning tasks you'll need to perform are

- User surveys

- Evaluating business processes

- Developing use cases

The topics covered in this section take place in the Business and User phases of the BUM model covered in the previous chapter.

To simplify the learning process, you will build a basic database used to track books for the example book collection. The business processes will be very simple. This database will be planned and modeled throughout this chapter.

User Surveys

User surveys can be performed in order to determine how users will utilize the database and what data they will need to store in the database. For example, you are creating a database to catalog some personal books, and the user will enter book names into the Book Collection Database you'll create later in this chapter. In this type of situation, you need to consider the following questions:

How many books do you have in your collection?

Answer: Approximately 2,300.

What information do you plan to store related to each book?

Answer: Title, author, copyright, binding, condition, publisher, category, estimated value, and location.

Do you want to store images of the books?

Answer: No.

How often will you be adding new books?

Answer: Weekly.

How often will you be removing books?

Answer: Weekly.

How many adds or removes do you plan to make?

Answer: About 10.

Will any other users access the database?

Answer: Three users in total.

What kind of reports will you need?

Answer: Books by category, books by copyright year, books by value, and books by author.

Can you think of anything else?

Answer: No.

Because this is a simple database, the process is not complicated. Table 6.1 represents the information collected from the user. You can use this information later as you model the database.

TABLE 6.1   Book Collection Database Information

Input	Value
Database purpose	To track books in a collection
Largest table	2,300 records
Domains or columns required	Title Author Copyright Binding Condition Publisher Category Estimated value Location
Images required	No
Add/remove rate	Weekly
Add/remove number	10
Total users	3
Report types	Books by category Books by copyright year Books by author Books by value

With large databases, the user survey process can take weeks or months. You may have to perform Intranet-based surveys, email-based surveys, and focus group surveys. It's not uncommon to gather hundreds of columns and dozens of inputs that you will need to consider as you model a database.

Evaluating Business Processes

Business processes are the end-to-end activities that result in service or product delivery. When planning a database, you should consider the business processes that will touch the database. For example, if you are creating a database to track sales activity, you may need to address the following business processes:

- Adding and fulfilling a new sale
- Providing a refund for an old sale
- Modifying a sale in the fulfillment process

How do these processes interact with the database and what information do they need? Business process mapping is beyond the scope of this book, but it is a valuable skill set for the modern DBA to possess. *Business process mapping* is the process of gathering business process information and steps and then documenting this collected data in a visual or logical manner. Many different tools and techniques are available for business process mapping, and you may find them very useful. *Business Process Mapping: Improving Customer Satisfaction, 2nd Edition* (Wiley, 2009) is an excellent resource on this topic.

 Real World Scenario

Business Process Mapping for the Books Database

I was once involved in a database project that you might call the "Books Database from Hell." It was, indeed, a books database project, but on a very grand scale for a local library system. The goal was to create a database that tracked the life of every book. The database was intended to answer questions such as who checked a certain book out, how long they had it, and so on. The problem was that process mapping was not performed and much of the necessary data was not accounted for in the database design plans. We had missed some things like the fact that multiple books were often checked out during one transaction (of course) and that the collection of books a customer checks out can tell a story about what that customer is trying to learn or achieve. I wish had known then what I know now about developing requirements through business process mapping.

My experiences creating that library database taught me how real-world database requirements are revealed only by investigating the business processes. While we are using the Books database being developed in this chapter and the next, it is important to consider the required processes.

At minimum, the following processes would be performed against the example database:

- Add new books
- Update existing books
- Remove books

Now, you need to ask yourself a couple of questions:

- What do these actions look like?
- What is involved in completing them?

Let's explore the first action, adding a new book.

When adding a new book, the first step is to gather the information about the book. This information includes the book's title, author, copyright, binding, page count, and more.

For each of these elements, a column would need to exist in our database; otherwise, we could not complete the business process.

Imagine that we also wanted to store pictures of the books. In this scenario, we would need to scan the book cover or take a digital picture and then transfer the image to the computer. Now we have to consider the impact on the database. How will we store the images? Should they be stored as binary large objects in the database files, or should they be stored externally using the file system?

Are you beginning to see how an investigation of the business processes reveals the requirements of the database? In addition to gaining a better understanding of the database requirements, business process analysis can also result in process improvements. As you map the flow of the process, you will often see redundant steps, unneeded steps, or missing steps. These problems can be addressed and the business will be better for it.

Developing Use Cases

A *use case* is the description of a system's actions based on requests or inputs from outside the system. For example, adding a new book to the database may be a use case. Use cases can be complicated and detailed or they can be simple two or three sentence descriptions. Because this book is primarily focused on SQL Server 2008 administration, the simple version will be used here. The following is an example use case for the simple database you're building in this chapter:

```
1.1 - Add Book
Actor: DB Data Writer
Description: A new book is added to the database.
Basic flow: If the publisher is new, update the publisher table;
    if the author is new, update the author table;
    add the book to the books table; response to the user with
    a successful outcome.
```

Notice that the use case has an ID, name, *actor* (the person or system taking the action), description, and basic flow. If these elements are included, they will provide the basic information needed to model and build the database. More advanced use cases may also factor in error processing and alternative paths based on different outcomes at each step in the flow process. For example, if the author is new, you would update the author table, but what if the book category is new? You would also need to update the category table.

Advanced use case solutions may include these branching options in the use case or simply refer to other use cases. As an example, in the use case for adding a book, you may simply say if the author is new, execute the add author use case.

Understanding Entity Relationship Diagramming

With the early stage business analysis complete, you're ready to move on to the actual modeling of the database. An entity relationship diagram (ERD) is a logical representation of your database that presents just such a model. An ERD is a logical model and may also be a physical model. A logical model is not system specific. Stated differently, the logical model is not unique to any specific database system, such as SQL Server or Oracle. The physical model specifies exactly how a logical model would be implemented within a specific system. You would need a different physical model for SQL Server than you would for Oracle.

You cannot store data in an ERD, nor can you retrieve data from an ERD. However, the ERD will provide you with a tool used in several beneficial ways:

- Use the ERD for team discussions to ensure that all needed data is included in the database model.
- Use the ERD as you work with users to ensure that you have mapped their needs to your database plan.
- Use the ERD to automatically generate a physical model for your target database system, if the ERD tool in use supports this feature.

The Open System Architect tool is used in Exercise 6.4 later in this chapter. This open source tool will work for all three benefits outlined in the preceding set of bullets. You can create the logical design for planning and discussions and then automatically generate the physical design for an Oracle, ODBC, MySQL, or SQL Server implementation. Then you can actually create the database automatically.

The simplest way to understand an ERD is to look at one. Figure 6.1 shows a basic ERD for the Book Collection Database you are building in this chapter. In the next section, "Building an ERD," you will walk through the process to create the ERD in Figure 6.1 using Microsoft Visio. You will create the same ERD using Open System Architect in Exercise 6.1 as well.

Tables are used in databases, and *entities* represent those tables in an ERD drawing. In Figure 6.1, each large square filled with column names is an entity. You should also note the lines connecting the entities. One end of each line looks like a crow's foot, and the other end has a straight line through it. The crow's foot represents a *many* connection, and the straight line represents a *one* connection. This means that the straight line end is the one end and the crow's foot end is the many end of a one-to-many relationship.

FIGURE 6.1   ERD for the Book Collection Database

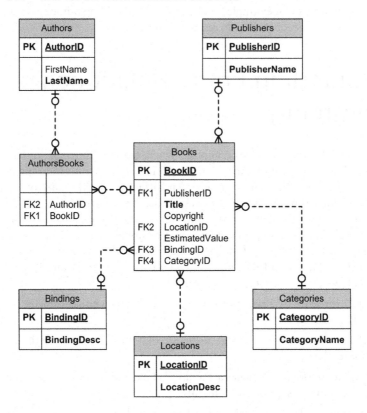

The "O" at each end represents zero or *x*. On the many side of the relationship, the "O" means zero or more. On the one side of the relationship, the "O" means zero or one. These options can be adjusted per your needs. For example, ERD drawings can use symbols to represent one or more, zero or more, zero or one, exactly one, and so on.

Because this ERD represents a simple database (although you might have been surprised by the number of tables required for this basic database), you do not see any examples of one-to-one relationships. However, if you look closely at Figure 6.1, you'll see a many-to-many relationship. (As a hint, look at the AuthorsBooks entity.) The AuthorsBooks entity is actually used to link the Authors table with the Books table in a many-to-many relationship.

To be clear, this is cheating. In the ERD drawing, you would normally just show the many-to-many relationship as it is shown in Figure 6.2. However, when you use Visio, you can go ahead and add the linking table because it cannot generate the physical model (and therefore the linking table).

FIGURE 6.2   Many-to-many relationship in an ERD

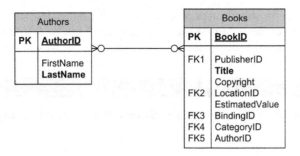

The ERD model, or logical database modeling in general, uses icons, boxes, lines, and indicators to represent the logical parts and pieces that comprise a database, such as:

- The entities usually map to tables
- The relational connectors map to relationships
- The attributes map to columns and so on

For more information about ERD concepts and tools, refer to *Beginning Database Design Solutions* (Wrox, 2008) by Rod Stephens. Although this book utilizes the Chen notation instead of the Barker notation (because Visio and Open System Architect use the Barker or crow's feet notation), the concepts are the same.

Building an ERD

Now that you have the basics of ERD modeling down, you can begin creating ERD models. You'll create the model shown in Figure 6.1 using Microsoft Visio in the next few pages.

> If you do not have a license for Visio or another ER diagramming tool, you may want to consider using Open System Architect (OSA), which will be discussed later in the chapter.

You can approach the creation of a logical ER diagram from two angles. First, you can document the primary entities and then the supporting entities. In the example database, you would create the Books entity first and then the Authors, Publishers, Bindings, Locations, and Categories entities. Alternatively, you can create the supporting entities first and then the primary entities. The approach is preferential, but you should follow any best practices specified in the software documentation. The example uses the primary entities first approach.

Creating an ERD in Visio

Microsoft Visio (Visio for short) supports creating ER diagrams, but you have to set everything up just right to get the results you see in Figure 6.1. Exercise 6.1 will prepare the Visio drawing environment to create the ER diagram for the Book Collection Database.

Preparing the Visio Environment for Entity Relationship Diagramming

1. Launch Visio.

2. Choose the Database Model Diagram template from the Software and Database category.

3. Select either US or Metric units (the example uses US) and click Create, as in the following image:

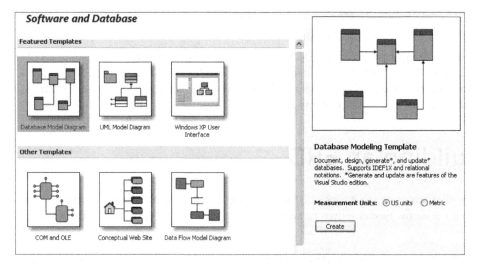

4. To implement Crow's Feet notation (Barker notation), select Database ➢ Options ➢ Document from the menus.

5. Click the Relationship tab, as shown in the following image:

6. Ensure that the Crow's feet check box is checked and click OK.

7. Developer mode must be enabled. Click the Tools menu and select Options.

8. Click on the Advanced tab.

9. Ensure that Run in Developer mode is checked and click OK.

With these steps taken, you are ready to begin creating the ER diagram. The first entity that you will create is the Books entity. This entity will require the following attributes or columns:

- BookID
- Title
- Copyright
- EstimatedValue

At this point, you will not create the foreign keys for the other entities. They will be added to the Books entity automatically when you create the relationships. This behavior is important to remember when working in Visio, but it may not be the way your chosen ER diagramming software works.

To create the Books entity, perform the steps in Exercise 6.2.

EXERCISE 6.2

Creating the Visio Entity Relationship Diagram

1. From the Entity Relationships shapes container, drag the Entity object onto the drawing canvas and drop it. A Database Properties window will appear below the drawing canvas.

2. In the Database Properties window, select the Definition category.

3. Enter **Books** as the Physical name and accept the default Conceptual name value. The results should be similar to those shown in the following image.

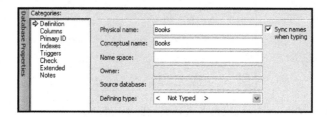

4. Click the Columns category to add the necessary attributes.

5. Add the attributes so that they look similar to the following image. Notice that BookID is set as the Primary Key.

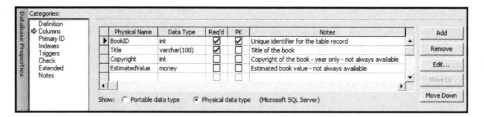

6. Click on the drawing canvas to deselect the Books entity. The drawing canvas should be similar to the following image.

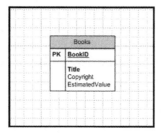

Once Exercise 6.2 is completed, the Books entity is created within the Visio drawing. You can add each of the other entities using the same process. The simplified steps for adding an entity are as follows:

1. Drag an entity object onto the drawing canvas.
2. Enter the Physical name in the Definition category screen.
3. Enter the attributes (columns) in the Columns category screen.

You can add entity objects for the remaining entities using the parameters in Table 6.2. Once completed, the resulting ER diagram would look like Figure 6.3.

TABLE 6.2   Entity Parameters

Entity Physical Name	Columns/Attributes
Authors	AuthorID, FirstName, LastName
Publishers	PublisherID, PublisherName
Categories	CategoryID, CategoryName
Locations	LocationID, LocationDesc
Bindings	BindingID, BindingDesc
AuthorsBooks	AuthorID, BookID

FIGURE 6.3   All entities created without relationships

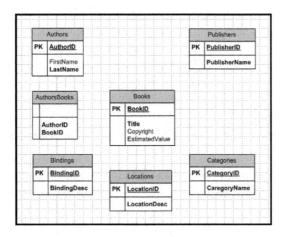

The next step is to create the relationships between the entities, as shown in Exercise 6.3.

EXERCISE 6.3

Creating Relationships Between Entities

Begin this exercise by relating the Publishers entity to the Books entity. To create the relationship, follow these steps:

1.   Drag a Relationships object onto the drawing canvas. The relationships object looks like the lines shown in the following image.

2.   Drag the end without the circle to the center of the Publishers entity and release it when the Publishers entity is outlined in red. The result should look something like this.

3.   Drag the other end of the relationship (the end with the circle) to the center of the Books entity and release it when the Books entity is outlined in red. The results should look something like this.

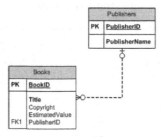

4.   Note that the PublisherID has been added automatically as a foreign key in the Books entity.

At this point, the relationship has been created and the exercise is complete.

In the steps in Exercise 6.3, the end of the relationship with the circle is the *many* end, and the end with the two lines is the *one* end in a one-to-many relationship. Now, you need to create one-to-many relationships between the following entities:

- Categories (one) to Books (many)

- Locations (one) to Books (many)

- Bindings (one) to Books (many)

- Books (one) to AuthorsBooks (many)

- Authors (one) to AuthorsBooks (many)

Regarding the last two bullet points, remember that you are building the linking table into your ER diagram. You could alternatively create a many-to-many relationship link directly between the Books and Authors entities. The inclusion of the linking table is purely based on preference. By following the same steps used to create the relationship between Publishers and Books, you've created the remaining relationships outlined in these bullet points. The simple steps for creating a relationship in Visio ER diagrams are as follows:

1. Drag a relationship object onto the drawing canvas.

2. Drag the appropriate ends of the relationship over the appropriate entities and release when the entities are outlined in red.

With all of the relationships created, you have the original ER diagram represented in Figure 6.1. Figure 6.4 shows the diagram within the context of the Visio application. The most important thing to remember about this process is that the foreign keys (FKs) in the Books entity were added automatically during the creation of the relationships. This Visio behavior makes the process much easier.

FIGURE 6.4   The Books Collection ERD in Visio

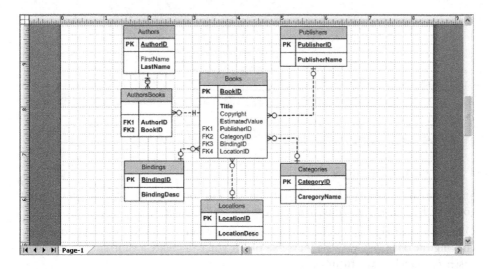

Creating an ERD in OSA

If you do not have a license for Visio or another ER diagramming tool, you may want to consider using Open System Architect (OSA). It is a new ER diagramming application that runs on Windows and Linux. The help system is not thorough, but you can usually find out how to get the job done within the GUI interface. Exercise 6.4 will now step you through creating the same ER diagram using OSA that you just built in Visio.

Downloading and Installing OSA

Before you can perform the exercises related to OSA, you will need to download and install OSA on your machine. You will find the download pages at `http://www.codebydesign.com`. When you download, install, and run it, you will see a screen like the one in Figure 6.5.

FIGURE 6.5 Open System Architect

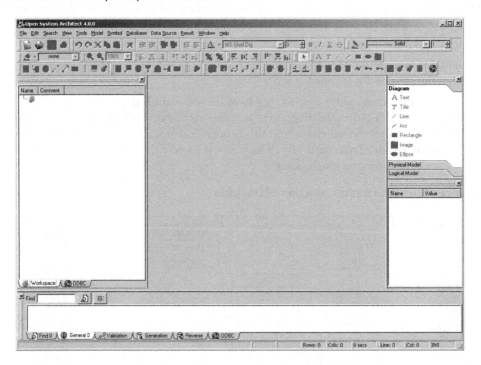

To install OSA, follow these steps:

1. Smply unzip the file to a folder of your choice. This open source application does not come with an installer program at the time of this writing.

2. Once you've unzipped the file into a folder, you can launch OSA by either double-clicking the `OpenSystemArchitect.exe` file or you can create a shortcut to make it easier to launch in the future.

3. To create a shortcut, right-click on your desktop and select New ➤ Shortcut.

4. Follow the prompts to add a shortcut to the `OpenSystemArchitect.exe` file in the folder into which you unzipped it.

If you receive errors about missing `msvcr71.dll` or `msvcp71.dll` files, you may need to either install the Microsoft .NET Framework 1.1 Redistributable Package or you can download the individual files from `www.dll-files.com`.

Creating an ER Diagram in OSA

In this section, you will use the Open System Architect open source application to create the ER diagram for the Book Collection Database. You will start by creating an ERD file in Exercise 6.4.

EXERCISE 6.4

Creating an ER File

1. Launch the OSA application from a shortcut you've created or by double-clicking on the executable file.

2. Click File ➤ New.

3. Select Logical Model in the New dialog and click OK.

4. Fill out the Logical Model properties dialog, similar to the one shown here.

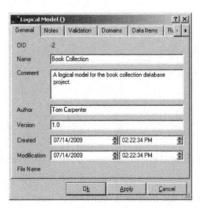

5. Click OK.

6. Click File and select Save.

7. Enter a file name, such as **BookCol**, and click Save.

You now have an empty model file and a drawing canvas you can use to add entities. OSA is different than Visio, however, so you will have to manually add both the internal attributes/columns and the foreign keys. Exercise 6.5 leads you through this process.

EXERCISE 6.5

Creating the Entities

1. Click the Tools menu and select Entity.

2. Click and drag to draw an entity on the drawing canvas.

3. Double-click the entity you've drawn to edit the properties. Please note that you can move the mouse to the edges of the various dialogs in OSA to resize them. They usually display in a low resolution by default, and you will have to resize them to view the information you need.

4. Use the value *Books* in both the Name and the Code fields on the General tab, as in the following image.

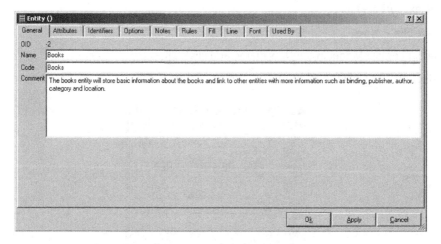

5. Click on the Identifiers tab and click the New button (the first button on the left side of the dialog toolbar).

6. Enter **BookID** as the value for both the Name and the Code fields. Check the Primary check box and click OK.

7. Add three more new identifiers, using the procedures in steps 5 and 6, with the Name and Code fields equal to **LocationID**, **CategoryID**, **PublisherID**, and **BindingID**.

Do not check the Primary check box for these four IDs because they represent foreign keys. When complete, the Identifiers tab should look similar to the following.

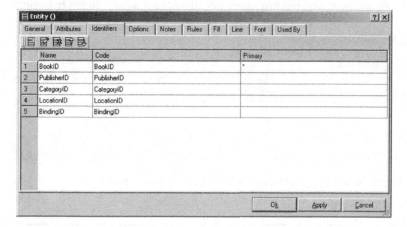

8. Click on the Attributes tab.

9. Click the New Data Item button (the last or right-most button on the dialog toolbar).

10. Enter the Name and Code value of **Title** on the General tab.

11. Click the Data Type tab.

12. Choose VARCHAR(n) as the data type and enter the value of **100** in the arguments field, as in the following image.

13. Click OK.

14. Using the basic steps 9 through 13, add two more attributes with Name/Code values of **Copyright** and **EstimatedValue**. Choose the data type of INTEGER for both attributes. When complete, the Attributes tab should look similar to the following image.

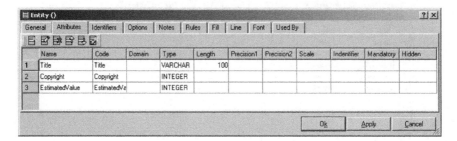

15. Select the Fill tab and choose the color White for the fill color.

16. Click OK to save the entity.

Your drawing canvas should now look something like that shown in Figure 6.6. If the entity box does not display all of the attributes or identities, simply move the cursor over one of the corners and click-and-drag to resize the box.

FIGURE 6.6 The Books entity shown in OSA

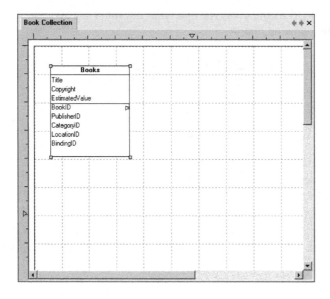

Now you will need to create the remaining entities using the same basic steps taken to create the Books entity. Use Table 6.3 as your guide. If the identity is referenced as Primary, you must remember to check the Primary check box when creating the identity.

TABLE 6.3 Entities

Entity Name/Code	Identities	Attributes
Publishers	PublisherID (Primary)	PublisherName (VARCHAR(50))
Authors	AuthorID (Primary)	FirstName (VARCHAR(30)), LastName (VARCHAR(50))
Categories	CategoryID (Primary)	CategoryName (VARCHAR(30))
Locations	LocationID (Primary)	LocationDesc (VARCHAR(25))
Bindings	BindingID (Primary)	BindingDesc (VARCHAR(20))
AuthorsBooks	AuthorID (Foreign), BookID (Foreign)	

After creating all of the required entities, the diagram should look something like the one in Figure 6.7.

FIGURE 6.7 All entities created in OSA

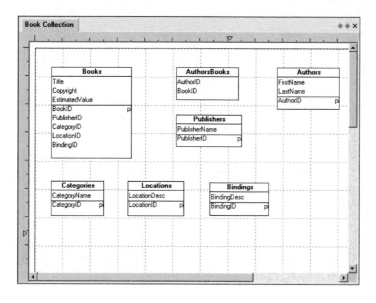

Now that the entities have been created, the only remaining task is to connect them using relationships. To relate the entities to one another properly, follow the steps in Exercise 6.6:

EXERCISE 6.6

Creating Relationships

1. Click the Tools menu and select Relationship.

2. Move your mouse over the Books entity, and notice that the Books entity becomes outlined in purple. Click-and-drag over the Publishers entity until the Publishers entity is outlined in purple and then release. A relationship will be created between the two entities.

3. Do the same thing from AuthorsBooks to Books. Click Tools ≻ Relationship, hover over AuthorsBooks, and then click-and-drag over Books and release.

4. Do the same thing from AuthorsBooks to Authors.

5. Create the relationship from Books to Categories, then from Books to Locations, and finally from Books to Bindings.

After completing these steps, your ER diagram should look similar to the one in the following image:

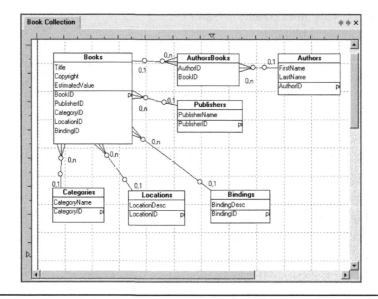

Here are a few tips to "beautify" the results:

- To change the location of the text labels (for example, the values 0,1 or 0,n), click the relationship line and then look for the small green square near the label. Click that square and drag it to the location you desire for the label.

- To align entities with other entities, use the Ctrl key to select multiple entities and then use the alignment buttons.

- Be consistent with your color choices.

As one final tip related to OSA, you can quickly generate a SQL Server–compatible physical model. To do this, follow these steps:

1. Save the ER diagram you've created in this exercise by clicking File ➢ Save.

2. Click the Model menu and select Create Physical Model.

3. Choose Physical Model (MS SQL) in the New dialog and click OK.

Just like that, you've created a model that is compatible with SQL Server capabilities.

Capacity Planning

After you've created the logical model and, potentially, the physical model, you'll need to ensure that you have a server that can support the resulting database. This demand forces the sometimes arduous task of capacity planning and analysis. However, the task doesn't have to be difficult, although it is repetitive when done manually. To perform capacity planning, you must estimate the size of every table and index in your database. The process for table size estimation varies slightly depending on whether you are estimating the size of a table without a clustered index (known as a *heap*) or a table with a clustered index.

In order to perform capacity planning, you will need to know the following facts about your tables and indexes:

- How many columns are in the table, and what data types are used?

- Is the table a heap or a clustered index?

- On what columns are nonclustered indexes created and what columns are included in the nonclustered indexes?

- How many rows will exist in the table?

Once you've collected this information for each table and index in your planned database, you can begin capacity planning. Exercise 6.7 provides steps for estimating the size of a table stored as a clustered index.

Estimating the Size of a Clustered Index

Remember that a table with a clustered index column is actually stored as a clustered index instead of a heap. To estimate the size of a clustered index, you must first calculate the space required for the leaf level (the data location). To do this, follow these steps:

1. Calculate the space required for fixed-length columns (int, char, bigint, money, etc.), which you'll call fixed_length_space. This calculation is performed by calculating the space required for each fixed-length column and then adding them all together. For example, three char(10) columns would require 30 bytes of space.

2. Calculate the space required for variable-length columns (varchar, nvarchar, etc.), which you'll call variable_length_space. This calculation is performed with the following formula: *total_variable_size_per_row = 2 + (number_of_variable _columns × 2) + maximum_variable_columns_size + 4*. For example, with a row containing three variable columns and the largest variable column being 50 bytes, the calculation is *2 + (3 × 2) + 50 + 4 = 62 bytes*.

3. Calculate the size of the null bitmap (an internal tracking mechanism used in SQL Server), which you'll call null_bitmap_space. The null bitmap is calculated with the following formula: *null_bitmap = 2 + ((number_of_columns + 7) / 8)*. For example, with a row containing 17 columns, the null bitmap calculation would be *2 + ((17 + 7) / 8) = 5 bytes*. If the result of the formula is not a whole number, discard any remainder rather than rounding up.

4. Calculate the total row size, which you'll call row_space. This calculation is performed by using the following formula: *fixed_length_space + variable_length_space + null_bitmap_space + 4*. Four bytes are used for the row overhead for each row.

5. Determine the number of rows that can fit in a data page, which you'll call rows_per_page. The formula is *8,096 / (row_space + 2)*. The two extra bytes are used for the row entry in the page slot array (tracking of the row in the page header).

6. Calculate the number of pages required to store all rows, which you'll call pages_required. The formula is *pages_required = total_estimated_num_rows / rows_per_page*. The results should be rounded up to the next whole number.

7. To determine the drive space required for this clustered index leaf-level data, multiply the number of pages times 8 kilobytes. If, for example, the number of pages is 10,000, you would need 80,000 kilobytes or just under 80 megabytes to store the leaf-level data for the table.

At this point, you know how much space is required for the leaf-level data, but you are not yet finished. You must now estimate the space required for the index information. To calculate the space required for the index information:

8. Calculate the index row size. The formula is *fixed_length_space* + *variable_length_ space* + *null_bitmap_space* + 1 + 6. The extra 1 byte is for the row overhead space and the extra 6 bytes are for the pointer to the leaf-level page where the referenced row is stored. The fixed_length_space, variable_length_space and null_bitmap_ space will be calculated using the formulas used in steps 1, 2, and 3 of this exercise.

9. Calculate the number of index rows per page. The formula is the same as that used in step 6.

10. Calculate the total number of pages required. An easy formula to use is (t*otal_ estimated_num_rows* / *rows_per_page*) + *50* × (*total_estimated_num_rows* / 1,000). This formula avoids complex logarithmic functions, but will be accurate to within a few megabytes even for a multigigabyte table.

11. To determine the drive space required by the index pages, multiple the total number of required pages by 8KB.

At this point, you can estimate the space required for the clustered index. Simply add the space required for the leaf-level pages to the space required for the index pages and you have your total.

To estimate the size of a heap, you would perform only steps 1 through 7 in Exercise 6.7. To make sure you understand the process, walk through the calculations for a simple table stored as a clustered index in Exercise 6.8.

Estimating the Size of a Clustered Index Table

In this exercise, you will estimate the size of a clustered index table. Assume the table has the following data columns:

- CustomerID, int
- FirstName, varchar(30)
- LastName, varchar(40)
- phone, char(10)

In addition, assume that the CustomerID column is the primary key and the clustered index for the table. Estimate that the table will contain 10,000 rows. To estimate the size:

1. Based on the process in Exercise 6.7, the first step is to calculate the fixed-length column space, which could include the CustomerID and the phone columns. Because the CustomerID is an int data type, the size is 4 bytes per row. The char(10) data type used for the phone column is 10 bytes per row. The total space required for the fixed-length columns is 14 bytes per row.

2. The next step is to calculate the size of the variable-length columns. There are two variable-length columns with a maximum length of 40 bytes for the LastName column. The formula to calculate the variable length space for this small table is

    $2 + (2 \times 2) + 40 + 4 = 50$

3. Now that you know that the variable-length columns will require an average of 50 bytes per row, you're ready to calculate the null bitmap space. Because the table has four columns, the formula is

    $2 + ((4 + 7) / 8) = 3$

    Remember to discard the remainder so the null bitmap is 3 bytes.

4. Now, you can calculate the row size with the following problem:

    $14 + 50 + 3 + 4 = 71$ bytes per row

5. The row size will average 71 bytes. Now you can calculate the number of rows per page by dividing 8,096 by 73 (*71 + 2* bytes for row tracking) to get 111 (remember to round up for this calculation). Because you have 10,000 rows, you can calculate the number of required 8 kilobyte pages by dividing the number of rows per page into 10,000 and rounding up again for a total of 91 pages totaling 728 kilobytes of storage space.

    The 728 kilobytes accounts for the leaf-level pages of the clustered index table. Next, you must calculate the size of the index pages (the non-leaf pages). This process was explained in steps 8 through 11 of Exercise 6.7.

6. You have a single-column clustered index on the CustomerID column. Therefore, no variable-length columns factor into the index page requirements. Therefore, you must calculate only the null bitmap space to process the row size estimation formula. The null bitmap for the index pages will be calculated with the following formula:

    $2 + ((1 + 7) / 8) = 3$

7. To calculate the row size, add the null bitmap to the 4 bytes for the `integer` data type used by the CustomerID column. You also add in the row overhead (1 byte) and the pointer to the leaf-data page (6 bytes). The following formula is used:

    $4 + 3 + 1 + 6 = 14$ bytes

8. Now that you know each row requires 14 bytes, the next step is to determine how many rows can fit on a page. To determine this, use the following formula:

    $8,096 / (14 + 2) = 506$

9. Finally, using the noncomplicated, no-need-for-logarithms, easier-than-Microsoft's-method formula, you can estimate the space consumed by the index with the following formula:

   $(10,000 / 506) + 50 \times (10,000 / 1000) = 69$

10. If you need 69 pages for the index information, the result is a total space consumption of 69 times 8 kilobytes or 552 kilobytes for the index information. The last calculation is simple: add the space for the leaf pages to the space for the index information and you'll get your total. Add 728 kilobytes and 552 kilobytes to reach a total space requirement of 1,280 kilobytes or approximately 1.2 megabytes.

If you want to perform capacity analysis for several dozen tables and indexes, you will be busy for quite some time. For this reason, you should consider using either third-party tools that can perform the estimations for you or the Microsoft DataSizer tool that will be covered next. One such third-party tool is ER/Studio available for demo at http://www.embarcadero.com.

In addition to the manual and possibly time-consuming process, Microsoft provides a great little spreadsheet template known as the DataSizer. If you search Microsoft's website for SQL Server DataSizer Tool, you should find it available for download. The URL is rather long and sometimes prone to change, so using the search feature is the best way to find it. To use the Excel spreadsheet, you will need to know the space consumed by different data types. As this is beyond the scope of this book, you should review the information in Books Online. Please, don't do this manually, however. Download the DataSizer and you can copy the existing Heap or Clustered worksheets for each table your database contains. Then fill in the data and you're done.

Although the SQL Server DataSizer tool was originally designed for SQL Server 7, as long as your tables are using common data types such as int, varchar, and char, it should work fine for common day-to-day usage.

Figure 6.8 shows the DataSizer tool with the information plugged in for the Books table in the database designed in this chapter. You can see that the table will consume approximately 330 kilobytes or one third of a megabyte.

FIGURE 6.8   Using the DataSizer tool

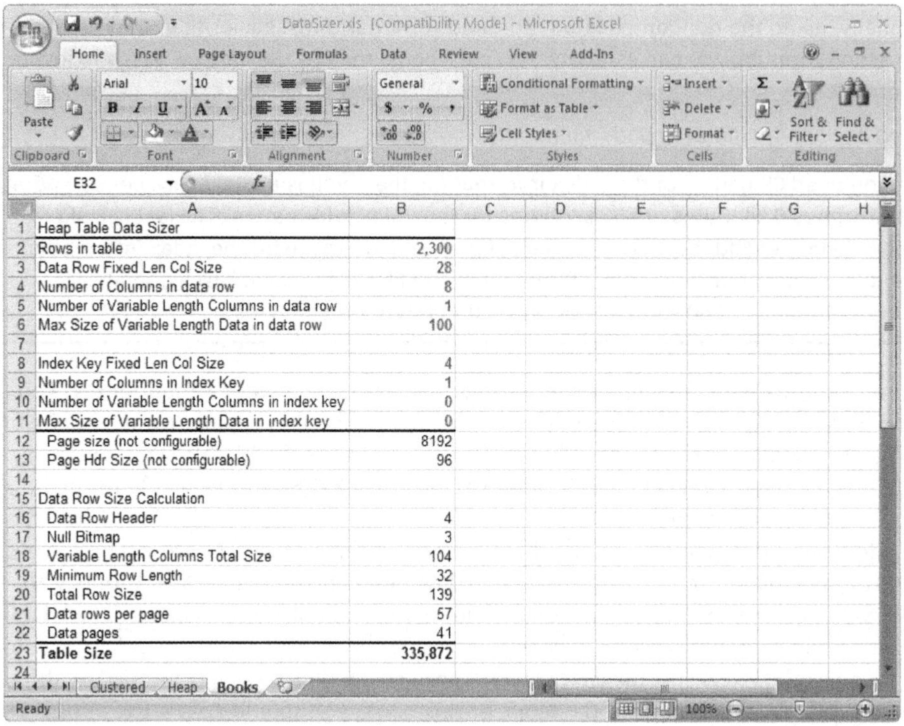

Summary

In this chapter, you learned the important steps required to plan a database. You began by looking at business requirements analysis. Business process mapping can be used to determine the requirements of a database because it results in step-by-step procedures required to fulfill a business-related action.

Entity relationship diagramming (ERD) was explained to help you understand logical and physical database models. Logical database models are not system specific, and physical models are specific to a selected database solution, such as SQL Server or MySQL.

Next, you explored using ERD tools. The first tool used was Microsoft's commercial diagramming tool, Visio. With Visio you can create graphically compelling ER diagrams and help is readily available. The second tool used was the OSA tool. Because OSA is open source, you can download it and use it without any licensing fees; however, the downside is that it lacks proper documentation.

Finally, you learned the basics of capacity planning. Capacity planning is all about size estimation. Estimating table sizes, index sizes, and heap sizes is important. Without these estimations, you'll have no way to predict future growth and the need for increased live storage or backup storage space.

Chapter Essentials

Planning a Database   It is important to gather information from the users of the database. If you try to plan the database on your own, you will perform a lot of refactoring and table modifications late in the project.

Understanding Entity Relationship Diagramming   ER diagramming is used to logically represent a database. The model can be used to discuss the database and to look for missing information before you create the database and other valuable tasks. ER diagrams can use several different notation schemes.

Building an ERD   An ERD can be built using Visio and many other tools. In this chapter, you looked at creating an ERD with both Visio and an open source tool called Open System Architect.

Capacity Planning   Once the database model is completed, you can then perform capacity planning. Capacity planning involves estimating the size of the end database.

Chapter 7

Normalization: Enough Is Enough

TOPICS COVERED IN THIS CHAPTER:

- ✓ Normalization Defined
- ✓ Normal Forms
- ✓ Normalizing a Database
- ✓ Denormalizing a Database
- ✓ Designing for Performance
- ✓ Designing for Availability
- ✓ Designing for Security

In this chapter, the final database theory topics are discussed. These topics will give you the information you need to design the proper database for your specific situation. If you need a database that supports fast read operations, you'll learn the best levels of normalization for such a database. If you need a database that allows for faster add and modify operations, you'll learn to apply normalization for this purpose as well.

Normalization is addressed first because it is one of the most important concepts in database design. You will learn the definition of normalization itself, and then move on to the normal forms, normalizing a database by example, and denormalizing a database. Then the performance factors related to database design will be presented. Many databases perform poorly because they are designed poorly. Understanding good design will, almost by itself, cause your databases to perform better. Why? Because you will automatically make decisions that improve the operations of your database. The chapter will follow this up with a discussion on availability. You will see how availability does not always equal performance and how you will often have to choose between the two. Finally, security will be discussed from a design perspective so you will be well prepared to deal with security questions and issues that may come up during the design phase of a database project.

Normalization Defined

Normalization is the process used to ensure that a database is properly designed according to relational database principles. The term is best understood by considering what you are attempting to avoid as a database designer or administrator. Common database problems can be all but eradicated through the process of normalization. These problems that present themselves in poorly designed relational databases, such as duplicating data, creating improper data relationships, and constraining data entry, must either be addressed during the design process or through reparations after the database is in production. Needless to say, it is much easier to deal with the problems before the database is actually implemented. You can think of these problems as abnormalities or as anomalies. Just a few of these problems are outlined in the following list:

Duplicate Data   Duplicate or redundant data results in poor database performance for many databases. For example, if a database is used to store sales information and the entire customer information set is stored in each record for each sale, the result is a much larger database. Not only is the database larger, but each record is larger than necessary too. This increased record size causes slower writes in every situation, and it may cause slower reads as well.

Improper Data Relationships   When unrelated data is stored in a record, managing the data becomes difficult. If you want to delete the customer record but not the sales information referenced in the preceding paragraph, you would need to manually process each and every record to delete all instances of a given customer. This work is not only time-consuming, but it also introduces an increased likelihood for error. The problem is born of improper data relationships. The customer is not the sale and the sale is not the customer. They should be stored separately in an OLTP database.

Data Entry May Be Constrained   One common mistake in relational database design is the implementation of table structures that include columns like Item1, Item2, Item3, and so on. What happens when the data entry employee needs to enter a fourth item into a table that stops at Item3? The situation cannot be accommodated unless the data entry employee enters multiple items in a single column, which results in the loss of data integrity.

These problems, and others not listed, can be categorized as three potential anomaly types:

Insert Anomalies   An insert anomaly usually occurs when improper data relationships are designed within a single table. An example would be a sales table that contains the customer ID, customer name, and customer address information, while no separate customers table exists. You cannot add a new customer to this database without entering a sale into the sales table. This is an insert anomaly.

Delete Anomalies   Delete anomalies are the mirror of insert anomalies. Continuing with the preceding example, if the last sale for a given customer is deleted, all information about that customer is also deleted. You could delete the information about the sale only if you specifically deleted the sales column values while leaving the customer column values. Because the table is a sales table, the result would be an orphaned sales ID value used only to locate the customer information.

Update Anomalies   Update anomalies also occur due to redundant information entry. If a customer calls and informs the data entry employee that a new address should be associated with the company, every sales record must be updated. If only one sales record is updated, future sales could be shipped to the wrong address.

These problems and anomalies are possible because the data is not stored in the most effective way. To help database designers implement better tables, Dr. E. F. Codd, a systems engineer and scientist heavily involved in database system solutions during the 1960s and 1970s, defined three normal forms: first normal form, second normal form, and third normal form. Over the years, several other normal forms have been developed as well, and the most commonly accepted normal forms are defined in the later section of this chapter titled "Really, Really Normal Forms." However, most database designers target the third normal form, which is covered in the later section of this chapter titled "Third Normal Form," and then implement other normal forms only as they are needed.

Based on this information, you can see that normalization is the process used to create a good database design that removes the potential for anomalies or problems. To make something normal is to make it standard. The normalization process is about designing databases according to standards that improve database operations and remove or reduce the potential for anomalies.

Normal Forms

As just discussed, several normal forms exist. Most databases will perform well if the designer ensures that they meet the third normal form. For this reason, the first, second, and third normal forms will be discussed in detail. Other normal forms, including Boyce-Codd, fifth, and domain-key, will also be briefly defined.

First Normal Form

The entry level of normalization is called *first normal form (1NF)*. A database that does not meet 1NF cannot be called normalized. A database that does meet the requirements of 1NF is normalized, but it is said to be in the first normal form or state. The primary requirement of 1NF is that all tables contain unique records. Stated differently, no table can contain duplicate records.

While different authorities have suggested slightly different formal definitions of 1NF, the following definition should suffice for most databases: An entity or table is in the first normal form if it contains no repeating groups or columns and each group or column contains only a single value, which may be nothing or NULL.

From this definition, you can summarize the requirements of 1NF as follows:

- No two rows in a table can be identical.
- No row can contain repeating columns.
- No column in a row can contain multiple values.

Some 1NF definitions require the following additional characteristics:

- Each column must be uniquely named.
- Each column must have only one data type.
- The order of the rows and columns must not be constrained.

However, SQL Server automatically provides these last three characteristics. You cannot create a table with two columns using the same name. Each column can have only one data type, and the order of the columns does not matter. Because SQL Server takes care of the latter three for you automatically, you only have to be concerned about the first three: no identical rows, no repeating columns, and no multivalued columns.

One of the best ways to understand normalization is to look at the problems corrected by its utilization. Table 7.1 shows a potential data table for a database. Notice that it allows duplicate records, uses multiple values in the Categories column, and also uses repeating columns (Category1, Category2, Category3).

TABLE 7.1 Books Table Without Normalization

Title	Authors	Publisher	Category1	Category2	Category3
CWSP Study Guide	Tom Carpenter, Richard Dreger, Grant Moerschel	McGraw-Hill	Security	Wireless	Networking
CWNA Study Guide	David Coleman, David Westcott	Sybex	Wireless	Networking	Certification
CCNA Study Guide	Todd Lammle	Sybex	Cisco	Networking	Certification
CWNA Study Guide	David Coleman, David Westcott	Sybex	Cisco	Networking	Certification

Let's look at the problems with the structure in Table 7.1. First, it has duplicate records—that is, the second and fourth rows are identical. In order to resolve this problem, you need to know why the table exists. In this case, assume the table exists to track an inventory of books and their locations. Furthermore, assume that the second row references a book stored in a location called *storage* and the fourth row references the same book stored in a location called *library*. In addition, assume that the second row references a hard-cover copy of the book and the fourth row references a soft-cover copy. In the end, there are several ways to resolve the issue:

Add a new column to track the book binding. This would solve the problem shown in Table 7.1; however, you need to think about the future. What if another hard-cover book is added to your inventory? You would be right back in the situation you're in now: duplicate rows.

Add a new column to track the book binding and a column to track quantity. This solution is better because it allows you to increment the quantity without adding a new record. Indeed, it would accomplish 1NF from the perspective of removing duplicates.

Add a unique key column. This is the most common solution to duplicate records. If every record has a unique key (also known as a primary key), it is impossible to have duplicate records; however, if the unique key is the only unique value in two or more existing records, you may still experience problems. Therefore, it's best to combine the unique key for a book with other solutions.

For now, let's solve the unique record dilemma with the new table structure presented in Table 7.2. Notice that a BookID column exists and serves as the primary key column and a Binding and Location column has also been added to provide extra unique information.

TABLE 7.2 Duplicate Records Problem Solved

BookID	Title	Authors	Binding	Publisher	Location	Category1	Category2	Category3
1	CWSP Study Guide	Tom Carpenter, Richard Dreger, Grant Moerschel	Soft-cover	McGraw-Hill	Storage	Security	Wireless	Network-ing
2	CWNA Study Guide	David Coleman, David Westcott	Hard-cover	Sybex	Storage	Wireless	Network-ing	Certifica-tion
3	CCNA Study Guide	Todd Lammle	Soft-cover	Sybex	Library	Cisco	Network-ing	Certifica-tion
4	CWNA Study Guide	David Coleman, David Westcott	Soft-cover	Sybex	Library	Wireless	Network-ing	Certifica-tion

Yet even after you change the table, you have another problem with your Books table in the multivalued column named Authors. 1NF does not allow columns with more than one value equating to the domain. Stated differently, you can't list multiple objects (in this case, authors) in one entry. In order to be in 1NF, you must solve this problem. The only solution that will meet the requirements is the creation of a new table. By creating a table named Authors and linking it to the Books table, you can move closer to 1NF.

An additional dilemma is presented as soon as you create the Authors table, however. To see this problem, consider the Authors table shown in Table 7.3. While this table tracks the authors perfectly, how will you link them to the books? You cannot create an AuthorID column and add multiple IDs for multiauthor books. This action would result in the same problem you started out trying to solve.

TABLE 7.3   Authors Table

AuthorID	FirstName	LastName
1	Tom	Carpenter
2	Rich	Dreger
3	Grant	Moerschel
4	David	Coleman
5	David	Westcott
6	Todd	Lammle

The solution is to create a many-to-many relationship using a linking or junction table. Table 7.4 shows the linking table named AuthorsBooks. The final step is to simply remove the Authors column from the Books table. Users can then build a list of books by author (for Tom Carpenter, as an example) using a SELECT statement like the following:

```
SELECT * FROM Books WHERE BookID IN(SELECT BookID FROM AuthorsBooks WHERE
AuthorID = 1);
```

You can also use more complicated SELECT statements based on joins. Joined statements can pull information from both the Authors table and the Books table. The same SELECT statement provided here only pulls actual displayed data from the Books table.

TABLE 7.4   AuthorsBooks Linking Table

AuthorID	BookID
1	1
2	1
3	1
4	2
4	4
5	2
5	4
6	3

The Books table, however, is still not normalized to 1NF. The next problem is the repeating Category column. You must find a way to prevent this column from repeating. Can you guess the solution? That's right. You need to create another many-to-many relationship. A Categories table will be linked with the Books table using a BooksCategories linking table. Finally, the Category1, Category2, and Category3 columns will be removed from the Books table.

This example would be much simpler if you knew that you had only one copy of each book in inventory; however, because multiple books could exist (soft-cover, hard-cover, staple binding, etc.), you must build these many-to-many relationships. If you had multiple copies of each binding type, you would also need to add a Quantity column to the Books table.

Remember, to ensure that your tables are in 1NF, they must not allow duplicate records, multivalued columns, or repeated columns. If these requirements are met with a SQL Server table, it will be in 1NF.

Second Normal Form

Second normal form (2NF) builds on the foundation of 1NF. Therefore, a table that is not in 1NF cannot be in 2NF. In addition to this requirement, all of the non-key columns must depend on the key columns. Stated differently, all non-primary key columns must depend on the primary key in a SQL Server table (a primary key can be comprised of multiple columns). The requirements of 2NF can be summarized as follows:

- The requirements of 1NF must be met.
- All columns must depend on the complete primary key.

You cannot use the Books table to consider 2NF because it has a single-column primary key. A table with a single-column primary key is automatically in 2NF. To help you understand 2NF, consider Table 7.5.

TABLE 7.5 AuthorTopics Table

Author	Topic	CityState
Tom	Windows Server	Marysville, OH
Tom	Wireless	Marysville, OH
Tom	SQL Server	Marysville, OH
Tom	VoIP	Marysville, OH
Rich	Wireless	Washington, DC
Jim	Wireless	Xenia, OH

When you analyze the AuthorTopics table, you can see that Author cannot act as the primary key because it appears more than once. Also, Topic cannot act as the primary key because duplication exists in this column as well. The only option is to use a joined primary key of Author and Topic. Indeed, Tom/Wireless is a unique combination in the table. However, this table is not in 2NF even though it is in 1NF. Why? The table is not in 2NF because the CityState column depends on only part of the primary key, the Author column value.

To prevent update anomalies, such as changing Marysville, OH, to some other city and state combination should Tom relocate for just one record, the table must be placed in second normal form. To do this, simply split the data into two tables. One table will contain the Author and Topic columns and the other table will contain the Author and CityState columns. Update anomalies will be reduced, and a simple query like the following can be used to join the data together when needed:

```
SELECT AuthorTopic.Author,
  AuthorTopic.Topic,
  AuthorLocation.CityState
FROM AuthorTopic
INNER JOIN AuthorLocation
ON AuthorTopic.Author = AuthorLocation.Author;
```

Of course, this example assumes that no two authors would ever have the same name. A better and more enduring solution would be to add an Authors table to track the author-specific information (location, birth date, deceased date, etc.) and a separate AuthorTopics table to track the topics about which each author writes.

Remember, a table with a single-column primary key that is in 1NF is automatically in 2NF. A table with a multicolumn primary key should be further evaluated to ensure that all non-key columns depend on the entire primary key and not just a part of it.

Third Normal Form

Third normal form (3NF) requires that a table be in 2NF and that all non-key columns in the table depend on the primary key directly. The non-key columns cannot have transitive dependence upon the primary key. Transitive dependence indicates that a non-key column (column A) depends on another non-key column (column B) that depends on the primary key, but column A does not depend directly on the primary key. Based on this information, a table must meet the following requirements to be in 3NF:

- The table must meet 2NF requirements.

- All non-key columns must be directly dependent on the primary key.

To help you understand the application of 3NF, consider the Books table from the earlier discussion of 1NF as represented in Table 7.6. Notice the addition of a PublisherID column. The table is currently normalized to 2NF, but it is not in 3NF. Can you find the reason why the table is not in the third normal form?

TABLE 7.6 Books Table in 2NF, But Not 3NF

BookID	Title	Binding	PublisherID	PublisherName	Location
1	CWSP Study Guide	Soft-cover	2	McGraw-Hill	Storage
2	CWNA Study Guide	Soft-cover	1	Sybex	Storage
3	CCNA Study Guide	Hard-cover	1	Sybex	Library
4	CWNA Study Guide	Hard-cover	1	Sybex	Library

If you said that the PublisherName column is transitively dependent on the BookID via the PublisherID, you are correct. In order to place this table in the third normal form, the PublisherName column must be separated into another table. In that table, you could track the PublisherID, PublisherName, and any other values related to a single publisher entity. The PublisherID values can remain in the Books table without losing 3NF because that column is a key column (however, it is a foreign key column in the Books table).

The Books table should look like the representation in Table 7.7, assuming you need to track the items listed so far in this chapter. A separate table would be used to track the Bindings, Publishers, and Locations (as well as the earlier extracted Authors and Categories tables). Notice that the only non-key column in the table is the Title column. Title is directly dependent on BookID—the primary key—and if you design the other tables properly, you'll have a database in 3NF.

TABLE 7.7 Recommended Books Table Structure

BookID	Title	BindingID	PublisherID	LocationID
1	CWSP Study Guide	1	2	2
2	CWNA Study Guide	1	1	2
3	CCNA Study Guide	2	1	1
4	CWNA Study Guide	2	1	1

Really, Really Normal Forms

You may decide that, for some databases, 3NF is not enough. In such cases, you can take the database to more rigid normal forms. The remaining commonly used normal forms are fourth normal form (4NF) and Boyce-Codd form (BCNF). Just in case you are wondering, Boyce and Codd are the systems engineers who developed BCNF.

A table must meet the following requirements to be in Boyce-Codd form (BCNF):

- The table must meet 3NF requirements.

- The table must not have multiple overlapping candidate keys.

A candidate key is one or more columns that, when combined, form a unique identifier for the rows or records in the table. You could say that the column is in the running for the office of primary key. It's a candidate, but it's up to the database designer whether it is used as the unique identifier or not.

A table must meet the following requirements to be in fourth normal forms (4NF):

- The table must meet BCNF requirements.

- The table does not contain an unrelated multivalued dependency.

These normal forms strengthen the normalization provided by 3NF; however, most databases in 3NF will also meet Boyce-Codd and fourth normal forms. The reason for this is simple: the steps taken to implement first, second, and third normal forms usually result in the eradication of design errors that would prevent Boyce-Codd or fourth normal form. To understand this, consider the entity represented in Table 7.8.

TABLE 7.8   3NF Table Without Boyce-Codd (BCNF)

Customer	ProductCategory	SalesRepresentative
ABC Enterprises	Widgets	J. Cline
XYZ Limited	Fridgets	L. Vasquez
GHI Unlimited	Gidgets	S. Barnet
ABC Enterprises	Fridgets	L. Vasquez
GHI Unlimited	Widgets	J. Cline

In this table, the customer purchases from multiple categories, but each category is sold by a single sales representative. Therefore, the Customer column and the ProductCategory column are used together to form the primary key. However, the SalesRepresentative column also limits the valid values in the ProductCategory column and the SalesRepresentative determines ProductCategory. This makes ProductCategory a determinant column, but it is not a key and that means the table is not in BCNF even though it is in 3NF.

So, how do you implement the data in Table 7.8 while ensuring a database meets BCNF? Easy, you split it into two tables. One table will track the customer-to-product category relation and another will track the sales representative-to-product category relation. However, most DBAs would have created this structure long ago when analyzing normal forms 1 through 3. It is still important that you analyze the database after 3NF to ensure that you are not implementing tables that are not compliant with BCNF or 4NF.

A table is in fourth normal form if it is in BCNF and it does not contain an unrelated multivalued dependency. Consider Table 7.9 to help you understand 4NF.

TABLE 7.9   BCNF Table Without 4NF

Musician	Instrument	Show
Tom Carpenter	Piano	Over the Rainbow
Dale Thomas	Electric Guitar	Singin' in the Rain
Tracy Dee	Piano	Singin' in the Rain
Rachel Thomas	Drums	Over the Rainbow
Tom Carpenter	Bass Guitar	Singin' in the Rain
Tom Carpenter	Acoustic Guitar	Over the Rainbow

Notice that all three columns must be used to form a primary key (it's the only way to ensure uniqueness). Is this table in 1NF? Yes, there are no duplicate rows, and columns are not repeated. Also, no column contains multiple values. Is it in 2NF? Yes, because the entire row is the primary key; therefore, all non-key columns are dependent on the key—because there are no non-key columns. Is it in 3NF? Yes, it is. For the same reason it is in 2NF—there are no non-key columns. It is in BCNF because Show does not determine Instrument, but Musician does determine Instrument and Musician does determine Show.

So where is the problem in Table 7.9 that keeps it from meeting the requirements of 4NF? The concept of a musician playing in a show is a separate concept from a musician playing an instrument. It assumes there is a relationship between the instrument and the show when, in fact, there is not. Tom Carpenter plays the piano, bass guitar, acoustic guitar, and a few other instruments; and he is attending the show Over the Rainbow. What's the solution? Place the information in appropriately separate tables. You can create a Musician-to-Instrument table and another Musician-to-Show table.

Normalizing a Database

In order to ensure you understand the concept of normalization, you're going to work through the process from start to finish. In this case, assume that a user has a spreadsheet with several data columns on a single worksheet and she wants it converted to a SQL Server database. Because the data has been tracked in Excel for years, it is flat and doesn't even meet the requirements of 1NF. To accomplish 3NF for this database, first establish 1NF and then ensure 2NF and 3NF.

The columns included in the worksheet are as follows:

- CustomerID
- FirstName
- LastName
- Address
- City
- State
- Zip
- Phone
- Email
- ProductID
- ProductName
- ListPrice
- Quantity
- UnitPrice
- SalesRepID
- SalesRepName
- SalesRepCommission

As you might have guessed, the Excel worksheet has acted as a rudimentary tool for tracking sales by customer and sales representative. The worksheet is growing unmanageable in its current Excel storage format. Every time the user needs to modify a phone number or an address for a customer, she has to update dozens or hundreds of rows. The goal of this exercise is to implement a database that is in at least 3NF and can track the same information.

Building a 1NF Table from the Excel Worksheet

Because this data is stored in a single Excel worksheet, you can think of it as a single table. Currently, this table includes 17 columns. The first goal is to reach 1NF. To do this simply, look for separate entities represented in the data. When you look at the list of 17 columns in the current Excel worksheet, you come up with the following entities:

- Customers
- Products
- SalesReps
- Orders

If you accept these entities, the 17 columns of data need to be divided among them. Table 7.10 provides a starting point.

TABLE 7.10 Columns Assigned to Entities

Entity	Columns
Customers	CustomerID, FirstName, LastName, Address, City, State, Zip, Phone, email
Products	ProductID, ProductName, ListPrice
SalesReps	SalesRepID, SalesRepName
Orders	Quantity, UnitPrice

Now that you've assigned the columns to tables, it's time to create primary keys. In order to achieve 1NF, each row in each table must have a primary key. The Customers entity already has a primary key of CustomerID. In addition, the Products entity can use ProductID as the primary key and the SalesReps entity can use the SalesRepID. For the Orders entity, you must create one. The most obvious name is OrderID.

In order to know what a customer has ordered, you must also add some information to the Orders entity or table. You need to add a ProductID, which will be a foreign key pointing to the Products table. Additionally, you need to add a CustomerID and a SalesRepID (to bring everything together). With this complete, you have the table descriptions shown in Table 7.11. The table is in 1NF at this point, assuming it is acceptable to say that the full name of a sales representative is a single value (in reference to the SalesRepName column).

TABLE 7.11   Table Descriptions in 1NF

Table Name	Columns
Customers	CustomerID, FirstName, LastName, Address, City, State, Zip, Phone, email
Products	ProductID, ProductName, ListPrice
SalesReps	SalesRepID, SalesRepName
Orders	OrderID, CustomerID, SalesRepID, ProductID, Quantity, UnitPrice

Ensuring Data Is in 2NF and 3NF

In this case, 2NF is easy. All tables have a single-column primary key (CustomerID, ProductID, SalesRepID, and OrderID) and the tables are in 1NF; therefore, the tables are in 2NF. However, the tables are not all in 3NF. Look closely at the Orders table. CustomerID is dependent on the OrderID (the customer placed the order) and SalesRepID is dependent on the OrderID (the sales representative made the sale). The ProductID may or may not be dependent on the OrderID directly. It really depends on whether a single order can be made for multiple products or not. If you assume that it can, you must change the tables.

Assuming multiple products can be purchased on a single order, you can leave the Customers, Products, and SalesReps tables as they are. However, you must extract the product data out of the Orders table and place it in another table. When you do this, you end up with something like the table descriptions in Table 7.12.

TABLE 7.12   The Final Table Descriptions in 3NF

Table Name	Columns
Customers	CustomerID, FirstName, LastName, Address, City, State, Zip, Phone, email
Products	ProductID, ProductName, ListPrice
SalesReps	SalesRepID, SalesRepName
Orders	OrderID, CustomerID, SalesRepID
OrderItems	OrderID, OrderItemID, ProductID, Quantity, UnitPrice

Now the database is in 3NF (it's actually in 4NF, but that's because of the data structure and not because of anything you've done in particular). This database can be created and should work very well for OLTP operations.

Denormalizing a Database

After a dozen pages or so explaining how and why to normalize your databases, it may seem odd to begin discussing denormalization. After all, why would you want to intentionally structure a database that could be susceptible to anomalies? If you think back to the anomalies that were discussed, they all had to do with data modifications (inserts, updates, and deletes). Read anomalies or unexpected results rarely occur. You usually just get the data you ask for when querying a database. That which is sometimes called a read anomaly is more often a programming error in the application code. When users—particularly decision support staff—must perform ad hoc queries (custom queries built on-the-fly) against your data, working with denormalized data can be much easier.

Think about the tables built in the preceding section. You ended up converting a single Excel worksheet into five separate tables. If you wanted to query the data in the database and have it look like the old Excel worksheet, you would need a query like the following:

```
SELECT Customers.CustomerID, Customers.FirstName,
   Customers.LastName, Customers.Address,
   Customers.City, Customers.State, Customers.Zip,
   Customers.Phone, Customers.email, Orders.OrderID,
   OrderItems.OrderItemID, OrderItems.ProductID,
   Products.ProductName, Products.ListPrice,
   OrderItems.Quantity, OrderItems.UnitPrice,
   SalesReps.SalesRepID, SalesReps.SalesRepName
FROM SalesReps
INNER JOIN Customers
INNER JOIN Orders
   ON Customers.CustomerID = Orders.CustomerID
   ON SalesReps.SalesRepID = Orders.SalesRepID
CROSS JOIN Products
INNER JOIN OrderItems
   ON Products.ProductID = OrderItems.ProductID;
```

You could take some coding shortcuts (like using aliases for the table names), but this query is still required. However, if the data were denormalized for reporting and analysis purposes, the same data could be placed in a single table again. Then the user could query the data with something like this:

```
SELECT * FROM flat_orders;
```

Yes, it is really that big of a difference. In most cases, data is denormalized in order to simplify access for users and, in some scenarios, it may also improve performance. However, you must be very careful about denormalizing databases that are used to perform data modifications. The introduction of insert, update, and delete anomalies may be too great to tolerate.

> Here's a great tip. Reports are usually very read intensive and very write light. For this reason, it's often helpful to create a dedicated reporting database and to denormalize the data as it is loaded into the reporting database. You get the best of both worlds: improved performance and simpler access for your users.

Designing for Performance

As you design a database, it is important to keep performance issues in mind. Two major problems occur when a database performs poorly. First, users are less productive as they wait on the database during heavy processing times. Second, some users just stop using the database—particularly if the data entered in the database is also written on printed forms. They may just decide to file it and forget it. To ensure proper design for performance, make sure you consider the following factors at a minimum:

Utilization   Consider how the data will be used. Will it be used for mostly reads or mostly writes? If the use will be entirely reads, you may tolerate 1NF or even ignore many rules of 1NF. If the use will be partly or mostly reads, normalization will become more important.

Capacity   It's also important to consider how large the data set will be come. For flat data, the larger the database becomes the slower it gets. This is also true for relational data (normalized data), but it can usually handle larger databases better due to the fact that the data is less redundant.

Constraints   You have to remember that a database system, like SQL Server 2008, still has limits. For example, if you create a table with 100 columns and each column contains a fixed-length data type, you may run into a constraint of SQL Server. The maximum size of a record with all fixed-length standard data types (non-large objects) is 8,060 bytes. You must remember this when designing your databases.

In addition to the constraints imposed by the database management system, you may choose to impose constraints for performance benefits. If you vertically partition a table (i.e., split it into two tables) for performance reasons, you are not doing it to comply with some level of normalization. Instead, you're partitioning the table to separate frequently used data from infrequently used data. It may be better to purchase more powerful hardware, but sometimes that's just not in the budget.

Designing for Availability

Performance is not the only factor that the DBA must consider. The database should perform well—but, with a limited budget, performance must be balanced with availability. Availability means that the database and, therefore, the data is there when you need it. Performance means that you can get the data fast.

But what is more important, performance or availability? The answer is unique to each scenario. If you are given a limited budget and told that the database should be available 99.99 percent of the time between 8 A.M. and 6 P.M., you can't throw all your money into one really fast server. You will have to ensure availability through features like replication, database mirroring, log shipping, and failover clustering. This scenario may mean that performance is sacrificed to some extent. Chapters 20 through 22 will provide more information on availability.

However, it is important to realize that frequently you can improve the performance of a SQL Server database without purchasing new hardware. Performance tuning and optimization will be covered in Chapter 14, "Performance Monitoring and Tuning." In that chapter, you'll see that you have many options for improving the performance of your databases by telling SQL Server how to better access the data.

 Real World Scenario

Balancing Performance and Availability

Sometime in late 2008, I was working on a project for a government agency that involved SQL Server 2005 servers. The project budget had been established by, of course, a non-technical individual who didn't understand what it would take to get the system up and running. I was asked to provide a recommendation document for the SQL Server portion of the project. I was given $25,000 for licensing.

At first, $25,000 may seem like a lot of money; but when you start factoring in client licenses, it gets eaten up really fast. In addition, the hardware for the solution had to come out of the same budget. In fact, depending on the licensing, the costs for SQL Server could consume the $24,000 of the budget in the first 60 seconds of planning.

Here's the biggest problem: one week into the project, I had the proposal nearly complete only to receive an email from the project manager. He had forgotten to mention that we needed to implement two servers for high availability. I was planning to buy a dual-socket server (two physical processors) with 8GB of RAM that was going to cost about $6,500. Now, my SQL Server licensing for the two servers would have been around $20,000 alone (two servers multiplied by two sockets). In the end, we had to settle for less powerful servers that would meet today's needs but leave a lot of uncertainty about 12 months into the future.

Of course, today, we are 12 months into the future and you'll never guess what happened last month—or maybe you will. I received a phone call from the client indicating that the servers aren't performing up to their needs. They want me to come in and see if I can tweak them to get any more performance out of them. I'll do my best, but I sure am glad that I indicated in the recommendation for their project that the servers would not provide acceptable performance beyond six to ten months. The call came right on schedule.

Don't worry...this kind of thing won't happen to you.

Designing for Security

The third and final design factor is security. As the DBA, you must ensure that your data is safe from theft, damage, and destruction. This can be accomplished in several ways.

First, you can control who has access to your database server. This is accomplished by granting access only to users who need it. While that may sound obvious, it's surprisingly common to see DBAs adding the Domain Users group or the Everyone group in an attempt to "ease the burden" of SQL Server administration. Of course, this behavior is not recommended.

Second, you can control what the users have access to once they have entered the database server. This is accomplished at the database level. You may choose to give some users write access and others read-only access. You can even control access at the column level. For example, you can allow the users in the HR department to see employee pay information from the Employees table, while only allowing other employees to see contact information from the same table.

Chapters 17 through 19 will give you all the information you need to design and implement secure SQL Server 2008 databases.

Summary

In this chapter, you learned about the final and certainly very important database-design concept of normalization. In the end, normalization is mostly about eradicating redundancies; however, the principles used to get there are actually focused on removing the likelihood of write anomalies. Write anomalies usually result in bad or missing data, and that's never good for any database.

You learned about the different levels of normalization that are commonly defined in the database design knowledge domain. With each level, you explored how to achieve it in a given database. To make the process as easy for you as possible, you stepped through converting a flat, denormalized Excel worksheet into a normalized database table.

Finally, you explored the three key areas of design: performance, availability, and security. Regardless of the entity relationship diagramming methodology or database design system you choose to utilize, you must remain focused on providing the levels of performance, availability, and security required of the project.

Chapter Essentials

Normalization Defined   Normalization is the process used to optimize the structure of a database in order to minimize data anomalies. Once you've designed and normalized a few databases, you'll usually find that you normalize as you design.

Normal Forms   Several normal forms exist, but most DBAs agree that third normal form (3NF) is the minimum requirement for standard OLTP databases. You may be able to tolerate or even desire to go beyond 3NF, but it is not usually needed.

Normalizing a Database   The process of normalizing a database to 3NF involves three simple and obvious steps: move to 1NF, ensure 2NF, and move to 3NF if necessary. Many times a database in 1NF is automatically in 2NF and 3NF simply because it does not contain complex data structures.

Denormalizing a Database   DBAs often denormalize data in order to make it easier for users to access that data. You can help the users by requiring fewer tables to gather the needed results. In some scenarios, denormalization even results in improved performance.

Designing for Performance   When designing for performance, you must consider utilization, capacity, and constraints. How will the users use the database? How big will the database become? What limits are imposed by the database management system?

Designing for Availability   At times, you must decide between performance and availability. You can have both, but it is often more expensive. If you require availability more than instant response times, you may purchase two less powerful servers and configure them in a cluster. Performance and availability are not the same thing.

Designing for Security   Security is important for databases. Information is one of the most valuable assets in modern organizations. You must protect your data from theft, damage, and destruction.

Implementing Database Solutions

Chapter 8

Creating SQL Server Databases

TOPICS COVERED IN THIS CHAPTER:

- ✓ SQL Server Databases
- ✓ Database Storage
- ✓ Database Options and Properties
- ✓ Creating Databases in the GUI
- ✓ Creating Databases with T-SQL
- ✓ Creating Databases with PowerShell
- ✓ Attaching and Detaching Databases
- ✓ Database Snapshots

The ultimate purpose of any SQL Server 2008 system is to provide data services. The services provided may be more advanced than simple database provisioning, but all SQL Server functions relate to data in one of several ways, including:

- Direct data access
- Data replication
- Reporting against data
- Analyzing data
- Data monitoring
- Creating data
- Providing data redundancy

What do all of these functions have in common? The word "data," of course. Because the database is the core of all SQL Server 2008 functionality, this chapter will cover the details of creating databases. First, you'll learn about the SQL Server databases known as system databases and the way in which data is stored. Then you'll explore the options and properties available for databases.

With the foundations covered, you'll move on to create databases in several ways. First, you'll master the GUI database creation tools. Second, you will use T-SQL (the SQL Server variant of the SQL language) to create a database. Finally, you'll create a database with the new Windows PowerShell interface to SQL Server 2008.

Having created some databases, you'll learn two advanced techniques related to the databases: attaching and detaching a database. These techniques are very useful when moving or copying databases from one SQL Server instance to another. The last topic of the chapter is database snapshots. Snapshots were first introduced in SQL Server 2005, and they provide an excellent solution to common problems in data reporting and recoverability.

SQL Server Databases

SQL Server is a database management system, so it's essential that the DBA understand the types of databases it supports. Two broad categories exist. First, you have the system databases, which are used by SQL Server and the SQL Server services and functions. Second, you have the user databases, which are used to store the intentional data—the data for which you've implemented SQL Server in the first place. This section discusses both.

System Databases

Four system databases exist in SQL Server 2008, and this is unchanged from previous versions. The system databases contain configuration information about the SQL Server services and the various user databases, which are attached to the database server. The system databases should be understood from at least three perspectives:

- Functionality
- Storage
- Backup

The four system databases are the master, MSDB, model, and tempdb databases. As each of these is described in this section, you'll be offered recommendations for storage and backup.

Master Database

The master database, as its name implies, is the primary configuration database for SQL Server. The SQL Server service uses the master database. The tables in the system databases, including the master database, are called system tables. The system tables are used to track the server parameters and information about every user and every database within the system.

The master database is stored in the `master.mdf` file, and the transaction log is stored in `masterlog.ldf`. It is standard practice to leave the master database in the default storage location, which is `C:\Program Files\Microsoft SQL Server\InstanceName\MSSQL\Data`. Because the database is small, sharing the drive with the SQL Server instance and the operating system is not usually a performance issue.

If the master database is corrupted, you will not be able to start the database system with your user databases attached. You would first have to restore the database from a backup and then restart the system. You'll walk through the steps required to back up and restore the master database in Chapter 16, "Backup and Restoration." Clearly, it is essential that you perform regular backups of the master database. You should back it up nightly because the database files are small (usually less than 20MB) and the backup happens very quickly.

NOTE   You will learn how to create backup jobs in Chapter 16. These jobs are used to automate the backup procedures so that you do not have to hold the server's hand through the backup process.

MSDB Database

While the master database is used by the SQL Server service, the MSDB database is used by the SQL Server Agent service. Of course, all data access goes through the database engine and, therefore, through the SQL Server service; however, the data stored in the MSDB database is stored for the SQL Server Agent service. The data in the MSDB database includes:

- Scheduled jobs
- Job parameters including steps and alerts
- Alerts
- Operators

The MSDB database is stored in the same directory as the master database. The file name for the data file is `MSDBData.mdf,` and the file name for the log file is `MSDBLog.ldf,` as you can see in Figure 8.1. The best practice is to leave the MSDB database in the default location.

FIGURE 8.1   The default data store including the system databases

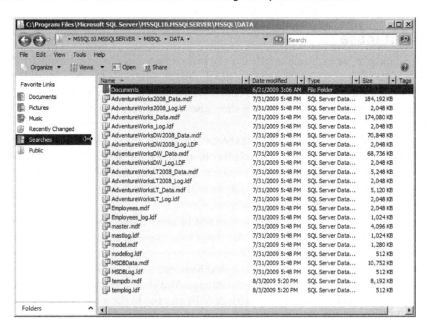

The MSDB database should also be backed up nightly (or once each day). Jobs, alerts, and operators are managed on a continual basis. If you do not back up the MSDB database, you'll lose these changes. A typical MSDB database is between 10 and 25 megabytes, even with dozens of jobs. This small size results in a short backup window, so daily backups are not a major problem. In fact, the backup process for both the master and the MSDB databases usually takes less than one minute.

Model Database

The model database is a database that wears weird clothes and walks funny. (That joke goes over much better in a live training class.) Anyway, the model database—like the master database—is just what it sounds like. It is a model for new databases. If you want all new databases to have a particular property set to a specific value, set that value in the model database. For example, later in this chapter you will learn to use the CREATE DATABASE statement in T-SQL. If you type a simple statement such as **CREATE DATABASE mydb** and execute it, a new database named mydb will be created. How does SQL Server know the many settings for this new database that were not specified? It gets them from the model database.

The model database is stored in the same location as the master and MSDB. It should remain in that storage location in most cases.

The model database will not require daily backups for most installations because it is not modified as frequently as the master and MSDB databases. However, the model database is usually very small (less than 10 megabytes) and it may be easier for you to simply back it up in the same job you use to back up the master and MSDB databases. Adding the model database to the backup may add 15 to 20 seconds to the backup window.

Tempdb Database

The tempdb database is the fourth and final managed system database. Think of the tempdb database as a scratch pad or a temporary holding place for data processing. The tempdb database is used automatically by the SQL Server database engine to process large queries and data modifications that cannot be handled entirely in memory. It may also be used by programmers. For example, a programmer could execute the following code to utilize the tempdb database:

```
SELECT * INTO #tmp_table
FROM Production.Product;
```

This statement would copy all of the data in the Production.Product table into a temporary table named #tmp_table. The temporary table could now be queries with code like the following:

```
SELECT *
FROM #tmp_table;
```

Notice that the database didn't have to be specified. SQL Server sees that the table name begins with a pound sign (#) and automatically knows to look for it in the tempdb database. If you create a table and start the name with a pound sign, it will always be stored in the tempdb database. Figure 8.2 shows the code samples combined and running in SSMS.

The tempdb database is stored in the same location as the other system databases by default. You may leave it there, if your system is performing well. If your system uses the tempdb database excessively and performance is suffering, you may consider moving it to another location. To check the size of the tempdb database, execute the following code:

```
USE tempdb
exec sp_helpfile
```

FIGURE 8.2   Using the tempdb database in code

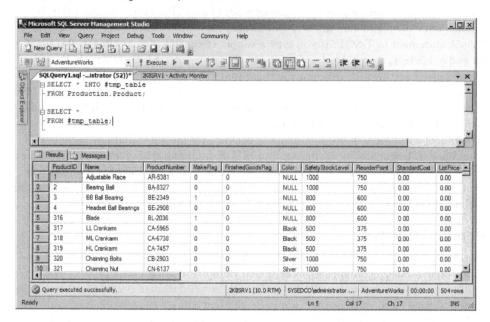

You should see results similar to those shown in Figure 8.3. Note the size of the tempdb .mdf and tempdb.ldf files. In Figure 8.3, these files are roughly 99 megabytes and 6.5 megabytes, respectively. If you decide to move the tempdb database to another drive, you will need to execute code similar to that in Listing 8.1. In this case, the code is moving the tempdb database file and log file to the G: drive and placing them in the tempdata folder.

FIGURE 8.3   Viewing the size of the tempdb database and log file

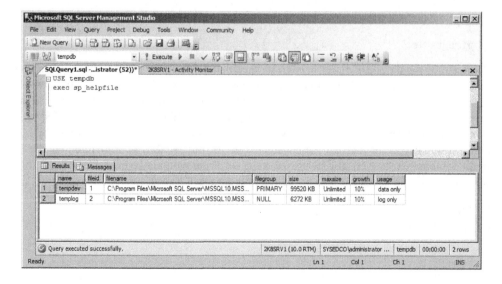

Listing 8.1: Moving the tempdb database to a different drive and folder

```
USE master
GO
ALTER DATABASE tempdb MODIFY FILE(NAME = tempdev,
        FILENAME = 'G:\tempdata\tempdb.mdf');
GO
ALTER DATABASE tempdb MODIFY FILE (NAME = templog,
        FILENAME = 'G:\tempdata\templog.ldf');
GO
```

As for backing up the tempdb, it's simply not necessary. The tempdb database is re-created every time the SQL Server service starts. Any data placed in the tempdb database should be considered volatile. It will not be retained during system reboots or service restarts.

The tempdb database is created based on the model database. If you want to have a particular object exist in the tempdb database at all times, you have two options:

- Create the object in the master database. This action results in the object being placed in the tempdb database automatically. It is not recommended, however, because the model is also used to create all other databases.

- Create the object using a startup stored procedure. Startup stored procedures run automatically every time the SQL Server service starts. This action is recommended.

User Databases

The user databases are defined as databases used by users. The databases may be used directly or indirectly. For example, a user may access one database, but in order for that database to respond properly to the user, the directly accessed database must retrieve information from yet another database. Whether accessed directly or indirectly, the database is still used by the user.

As an example of a user database, think about the typical customer databases used in many organizations. The database would contain tables for customers, organizations, possibly sales persons, and other information related to the customers. The point is that a user database is not a system database. A user database is used by users to store business or personal data, and a system database is used to store information about the SQL Server database system itself.

You cannot create a system database—not really. You can create a database that stores "system information" for your application, but that doesn't really qualify it as a system database. You can create as many user databases as you need. Your only limits with SQL Server 2008 Standard Edition and higher are drive space and the ability of the server to keep up with all the databases.

Database Storage

SQL Server databases are stored in files. That much is obvious. However, what may not be immediately apparent is that you can use more than one file with a database. Additionally, you can use filegroups to organize these files. This section will cover the concepts of files and filegroups, so that you can make good decisions for the storage of your databases. Additionally, it will address transaction logs and make some recommendations for the storage of the logs and the default sizes you should implement.

Database Data Files

The default extension for the single data file used with a small database is `.mdf`. MDF stands for master data file. Every database has one and only one MDF file. The MDF file contains the database schema information (the structure of the database) and the properties configured for that database. Of course, it also contains data.

If you want to create more than one file for data storage, the additional files will use the NDF extension. For example, if your master data file is named `data1.mdf`, you may choose to name a second file `data2.ndf`.

 I have no idea what the n stands for in NDF. While teaching a class on SQL Server 2000 several years ago, an attendee who was aware that I grew up in West Virginia said that it might stand for 'nuther data file. Maybe he's correct. Microsoft hasn't told us. My best guess is that n was simply the next letter in the alphabet after m.

Why create multiple data files? Two primary reasons exist. First, you can back up a single data file. This is not usually recommended because it becomes more difficult to keep the entire database synchronized during recovery, but it is possible. Second and more commonly used, you can create multiple data files in order to improve performance.

 While you can create multiple files and place them on multiple physical disks to improve performance, I don't recommend it as the optimal performance enhancement procedure. In most cases, you're better off placing a single file on a RAID 5 array than you are spreading the files across single disks. Of course, exceptions exist, but hardware-based RAID is usually best.

If you create multiple data files in the same filegroup, SQL Server will stripe the data across those files proportionally. "Proportionally" simply means that SQL Server will stripe an amount of data onto each file based on the free space left in the file so that both files reach the full state at the same time. For example, if one file has 100MB of free space and the other has 50MB of free space, the 100MB file will receive twice as much data on every write. Figure 8.4 illustrates the use of multiple files in a single filegroup.

FIGURE 8.4 Using more than one file in a single filegroup

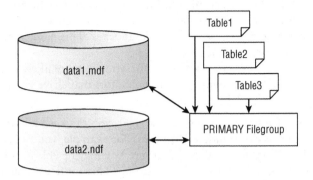

Notice in Figure 8.4 that all of the tables are stored in the same filegroup in spite of the fact that multiple files exist. Stated differently, tables (and other objects) are stored in filegroups by assignment. You cannot assign an object to be stored in a specific file. If multiple files exist in a filegroup, the tables assigned to that filegroup will be striped across the files rather than stored in a single file.

Database Filegroups

Filegroups provide you with control over object placement. For example, if you want a customers table to be stored on the E: drive and an orders table to be stored on the F: drive, you accomplish this using filegroups, as shown in Exercise 8.1.

EXERCISE 8.1

Creating Multiple Filegroups

1. Create a filegroup for the customers table and assign one or more files located on the E: drive to that filegroup.

2. Create the customers table and place it in the filegroup on the E: drive. You can also move a table to a different filegroup at a later time.

3. Create another filegroup and assign one or more files located on the F: drive to the second filegroup.

4. Create or move the orders table into the second filegroup.

The results of these steps are that the customers table is on the E: drive and the orders table is on the F: drive. This is the power of filegroups.

By default, the Primary filegroup exists for all databases. If you want only one filegroup, use the Primary filegroup for everything. You can create additional filegroups according to your needs. Most DBAs choose to name a second filegroup Secondary, but this is not a requirement. You may decide to place all your tables in the Primary filegroup and place all indexes in a separate filegroup that uses files storage on a separate disk. In such a case, it may be better to name the filegroup something like Indexes. This name makes it clear that the filegroup is used for the storage of indexes.

If you are building a very large database (VLDB), you are more likely to take advantage of multiple files and multiple filegroups. Several motivators may drive you to use this dispersed storage structure with a VLDB, including:

Smaller Backup Sizes   If you design the database right, you can keep all synchronized data in single filegroups while having multiple filegroups. For example, you can store the orders table and the OrderDetails table in a single filegroup. You may be able to store the SalesReps and CustomerServiceReps table in a separate filegroup. This configuration (taken to more complex levels) allows you to back up part of the database (one of the filegroups) during one backup window and another part during another backup window. Such implementations can be useful with VLDBs because the backups can take hours.

Improved Performance   Imagine that you've created a database with three filegroups. The files in each filegroup are stored on a separate and dedicated RAID 5 array. You have three RAID 5 arrays for the storage of your data. This configuration will result in exceptional drive performance—even for a VLDB.

An additional important point about filegroups is related to backups. If you store table data in one filegroup and the indexes for that table in another filegroup, you can no longer back up the filegroups separately. The reason is simple: if you back up such a structure separately, you cannot restore a synchronized data set (both the tables and the indexes). This is an important fact to keep in mind if you're optimizing a database by spreading the data around in multiple file groups. Placing the data in one filegroup and the indexes in another is a common performance trick, but you should be aware of the limitations it imposes on backups.

Transaction Logs

While data files use MDF and NDF extensions, transaction logs use the LDF extension. You can create multiple transaction log files for a database, but they are not used like multiple data files. The transactions are not striped across the multiple log files in any way. Instead, the transactions are written to the first log file until it is full. When the first log file is full, the transactions will begin to overflow into the second log file and so on. For heavily used databases (thousands of transactions per hour), you may decide to implement a second log file just to make sure the database does not run out of transaction storage space between backups.

Transaction logs should be stored on separate physical disks from the data files. By default, the transaction log will be stored with the data files. You must change this configuration manually during the creation of the database. Exercise 8.2, later in this chapter, provides the steps required for creating a database. During these steps, you would indicate that the transaction log should be stored in a separate location from the database files. The only time you should store the transaction log on the same drive as the data files is when you are implementing a read-only database. In a read-only database implementation, the transaction log doesn't matter. In all other implementations, it is essential that the transaction log be stored on a separate physical disk. There is a reason this point has been repeated, as you will soon see.

If the data files and the transaction log are stored on the same physical disk and the disk fails, you can recover only to your most recent backup. Assume you have a database that you back up nightly at 12 A.M. and the data files and log file are stored on the same physical disk. Further assume that 2,500 transactions are performed against that database in a typical work day. Now, the data storage drive fails at 4:50 P.M.—just 10 minutes before the end of the work day. In this scenario, about 2,500 transactions will be unrecoverable. Why? Because you lost the data and the transaction log.

If the transaction log were stored on a separate physical disk from the data files, you could first back up the tail log (the transactions in the transaction log since the nightly backup) and the restore from the nightly backup and finally restore from the tail log backup. This procedure would take you right back to the point of failure. You would lose no transactions and your job would be secure.

 Notice that I've used the phrase "separate physical disk" repeatedly throughout this section. You should not store the transaction log on a separate volume on the same physical disk. Make sure the log is stored on a truly separate physical disk—preferably a RAID 5 array.

In addition to the fault-tolerance provided, storing the transaction log on a separate physical disk can also increase the performance of the database. The data files can be read from one disk at the same time the log file is being written on another disk. When you spread activity across multiple physical disks, you nearly always improve performance.

Database Options and Properties

SQL Server databases have dozens of properties that can be configured. These properties control the functionality and features of the database. If you are implementing a database for a vendor-provided application, you will usually be given specific instructions for the configuration of the database. When you have these instructions, you won't have to decide what setting to use for a given option. However, you may also need to create databases for internal use by applications that are also developed internally. With internal applications, you'll need to understand the options and properties and how they impact the database.

Five properties comprise the most commonly configured database properties. Most of the other properties are simply left at their default settings. In this section, you'll review the five properties most frequently altered, which are

- Autogrowth

- Recovery Model

- Compatibility Level

- Auto Shrink

- Restrict Access

A table will describe many more properties. Of course, deciding which files the database is stored in is essential when you are creating a database. Because the files and filegroups were covered in the preceding section, you will not revisit them here. You can consider the files and filegroups essential items—they must always be configured. The preceding top-five list should be considered the top-five optionally configured properties.

Autogrowth

The autogrowth property allows you to configure the database so that it will grow automatically as needed. The autogrowth feature supports both percentage-based growth and fixed-size growth. If you configure the database to grow by 10 percent, for example, it will grow by 10 percent of its size at each growth point. If you configure the database to grow by a fixed amount, it will grow the same amount each time.

You can also configure a maximum file size. If you set a maximum file size and the database reaches that size, it will automatically go into read-only mode. For this reason, leaving the maximum file size as unrestricted is recommended. This recommendation does not mean that you're leaving the server to run out of drive space. Instead, configure an alert to watch for a free-space threshold on the data storage drive. If the free space falls below the defined threshold, an email is sent to the administrator so that action may be taken. This recommendation is most useful on a database server with multiple databases. It can be very difficult to determine the appropriate maximum file sizes for several databases so that they all reach their maximum at relatively the same time. By watching for low free space, you solve the problem. Chapter 13, "Creating Jobs, Operators, and Alerts," provides the steps for creating a drive space alert.

A full database (one that has reached the maximum size) will usually generate an event with the Event ID of 3758. If you see this event in your Event Viewer log files on the server, check the mentioned database. You have several options when a database is full:

- Add additional files to the database. This can be useful when you are adding new drive storage and want to span the data across the new drive.

- Archive old data in the database. If you cannot add new drive space, this is an option, assuming you can remove older data from the system without preventing users from accomplishing their objectives.

- Free space on the storage drive by deleting other information and then extend the allowed size of the database files. If you cannot archive old data or add new storage, you may have to free space from the drive by deleting non–database-related files that happen to be stored on the same drive.

Recovery Model

The recovery model determines how the transaction log is used. Because the transaction log is the key to recovering to the point of failure, this setting is one of the most important settings for any database. Three choices are available:

- Simple
- Bulk-Logged
- Full

Simple Recovery Model

The first choice, *simple recovery model*, means that the transaction log is used for data changes, but the transactions are lost at each checkpoint. As changes are made to the data, the changes take place in buffer memory. Once the change is made in buffer memory, the transaction is written to the transaction log. Every so often, a checkpoint occurs. When the checkpoint occurs, the dirty pages are written from buffer memory to the data file and the transaction log is truncated. The term *truncated* means that the data is removed from the log, but the log size is not reduced.

The first thing that stands out in the preceding paragraph is the shattering of a common myth about SQL Server and the simple recovery model. It is commonly said that the simple recovery model does not use the transaction log, but this statement is false. The transaction log is still used (it helps to recover from a power failure or any other sudden system crash), but it is not retained for backups. You do not—and cannot—back up the transaction log for a database in the simple recovery model.

The simple recovery model is useful for test databases, lab environments, development databases, and even production databases that are read-only. Additionally, if the only changes that are ever made to the database are done using bulk scripts once each day or once each week, you may consider using the simple recovery model on these databases. Because all of the changes are made using scripts, the imported data should still be available. In other words, you can restore the database from a backup and then rerun the scripts in sequence.

The recommendation to use the simple recovery model for a production read-only database or a database that is updated only through bulk scripts assumes that the database is never updated by individual users. If the database is updated by individual users, you will not be able to resynchronize the data after a restore when using the simple recovery model.

Bulk-Logged Recovery Model

The *bulk-logged recovery model* is the in-between model. It's not as basic as the simple recovery model, and it doesn't provide the complete transaction logging of the full recovery model. Like the simple recovery model, some misunderstandings exist in relation to the functionality of the bulk-logged recovery model. This misinformation can be heard at conferences and found in books and articles. The incorrect statement usually goes something like this: "If you use the bulk-logged recovery model, you cannot recover to a point in time anymore." As you'll see, that statement is not necessarily true.

When in the bulk-logged recovery model, the transaction log is still used; however, for certain types of actions—bulk actions—minimal logging is performed. These actions include several things as represented by the following list:

- SELECT INTO statements
- Some INSERT INTO statements that use a SELECT statement to provide the data values
  - When the OPENROWSET(BULK…) function is used
  - When data totaling more than an extent (64KB) is inserted and the TABLOCK hint is used
- BULK INSERT operations
- Write actions performed by the BCP command-line program
- When using the WRITE clause with an UPDATE statement
- Index creation (CREATE INDEX), modification (ALTER INDEX), or deletion (DROP INDEX)

Now, when a bulk action occurs, the action is logged to the transaction log. It is noted that it occurred and in the database, for each extent that was modified by the bulk action, the Bulk Changed Page (BCP) bit for that extent is set to 1. All extents have a bit value of 0 on the BCP if a bulk action has not modified their data.

Here's where the interesting part comes in. When you back up the transaction log for a database that is in the bulk-logged recovery model, the transaction log is not backed up alone. Instead, every extent with a BCP bit of 1 is also backed up with the log. By performing this extra action, an administrator can use the SQL Server backup tools to restore the database, including the bulk transactions.

What about the point-in-time recoveries? If the database is in the bulk-logged recovery model and no bulk actions have occurred since the last full backup, the database can be restored to any point-in-time. If, however, a bulk action has occurred and you desire to restore data as it existed during the bulk action, you will run into problems. You must create a new backup of the transaction log to enable more restore points. Even with a bulk action, you may restore to any point-in-time before the bulk action or any point-in-time after the bulk action as long as additional transaction log backups have been created.

Full Recovery Model

The final option in the recovery model is the *full recovery model*. The full recovery model logs every single transaction to the log. A transaction is a change. Any time a change occurs on a database in the full recovery model, an entry is added to the transaction log. If a read operation occurs, nothing is entered in the transaction log because no change has occurred. The vast majority of production databases operate in the full recovery model during normal operations.

 **Real World Scenario**

Strategic Use of the Bulk-Logged Recovery Model

Although most databases do run in the full recovery model, this does not mean that you cannot take advantage of the bulk-logged recovery model. Some databases should simply operate in this model. It really depends on the recoverability needed for the database.

In addition to the databases that should run in bulk-logged mode all the time, you may want to take strategic advantage of this mode for certain operations. For example, I was consulting with a company that had a 65GB database. Every night, they ran a batch job that imported more than 3GB of data into the existing database and then archived from 2GB to 3GB of data. After the data import and archive, a full backup was performed. The batch process was taking close to two hours and they needed to reduce the window of operation so that more time could be made available for additional automated jobs.

I configured the job to first switch the database to the bulk-logged recovery model and then perform the bulk import of the data. In this case, the time to import the data was reduced by about 35 percent, which took the entire operation window down to about 80 minutes. If you decide to use a similar procedure, be sure to verify that you've accomplished a performance gain. In rare scenarios, it may take longer to import the data in bulk-logged mode. Also, make sure you switch back to the full recovery model right before doing the full backup.

Compatibility Level

The *compatibility level* setting has become more important in the last two versions of SQL Server (SQL Server 2005 and 2008). This setting allows you to make the database a little more compatible with older applications. It is not guaranteed to make an older application work with a newer version of SQL Server, but it may just do the trick.

The compatibility level can be set to one of three levels in SQL Server 2008:

100 – SQL Server 2008 compatibility level

90 – SQL Server 2005 compatibility level

80 – SQL Server 2000 compatibility level

For the most part, the compatibility level setting really just disables new keywords and also allows some older T-SQL syntax that is no longer supported. For example, a database with a compatibility level of 90 will allow the creation of tables or columns named

MERGE, CUBE, or ROLLUP without the use of special delimiters. These names are not allowed in compatibility level 100 (the default for all newly created databases in SQL Server 2008) because they are now reserved words.

If you attach a database from an earlier version (SQL Server 2000 and 2005 databases can be attached to SQL Server 2008 servers), the compatibility level is automatically set to the required value for that version. A SQL Server 2000 database would be set to 80, and a SQL Server 2005 database would be set to 90. The same is true if you upgrade to SQL Server 2008 from one of these earlier versions.

The compatibility level setting should be used only as an interim solution. Eventually, Microsoft will stop supporting level 80 and then level 90 and so on. Ultimately, the applications must be updated to support the newer functionality in SQL Server 2008 and later editions.

Auto Shrink

Auto shrink is used a lot, so it is mentioned in the list; however, it shouldn't be used—at least in a production situation. Auto shrink will shrink the data and transaction log files when space becomes available within the file. The problem with this is that shrinking the files is an intensive process. The way auto shrink works is simple, but it is very processor-intensive. When free space is provided, auto shrink will automatically shrink the database files by removing data. The problem is that the database files must grow again when new data is added. Then when more data is removed, the files shrink, only to grow again when more data is added. Do you see the cycle and why it is so performance-hindering? The best practice is to perform all shrinking operations manually. Microsoft discourages the use of auto shrink on production databases.

When you are optimizing a SQL Server, one of the first things to look for is auto shrink. By turning it off, you will usually get an immediate overall performance boost. To see the boost, you would normally need to compare an entire day's performance against another entire day's performance before the auto shrink feature is disabled.

If this option causes so many problems, why do people enable it? This is more easily answered by describing a scenario than with a detailed explanation. At some point, a well-meaning DBA goes to a server and notices that the database file has grown very large. He realizes that he has not archived any data in a long time, so he archives about half of the data into a completely separate server. Afterward, he notices that the file size has not been reduced. He remembers the auto shrink feature and turns it on. A little later, the database file is smaller and he has accomplished his goal. To prevent this from happening again, he simply leaves the auto shrink feature enabled. The end result of this action is a continued decrease in performance for that database.

Third-party vendor support personnel also seem to like to tell customers to turn auto shrink on as a solution to various problems. Remember this when making your help calls. Realize that the support staff is telling you to configure the system in a way that is easier to support and that removes problems without considering the impact on performance. However it becomes enabled, it should really be disabled in the vast majority of deployments. If a vendor tells you to turn on auto shrink, you can simply turn it back off after the support call and everything will work fine. Some other action the vendor requested is usually the true solution for the problem. To learn how to shrink a file manually (or in an automated job), search for **DBCC SHRINKFILE** in Books Online. Alternatively, you can search for **DBCC SHRINKDATABASE**.

> It is always important to consider vendor support. If the vendor indicates that they will not support their application with auto shrink turned off, you will have to leave it on and find some other way to enhance the overall performance of your system. You may be able to counter the performance loss incurred with auto shrink by storing the database files on a very fast RAID array. As the full details of using auto shrink are beyond the scope of this chapter, please search for **DBCC SHRINKFILE** and **auto shrink** in Books Online to learn more.

Restrict Access

The final option is one you might find yourself using a lot. *Restrict access* allows you to control who has rights to a database at any given time, from allowing only one person into the database to granting only administrative personnel access or opening it up to everyone. This option is wildly helpful when you need to gain exclusive access to the database for administrative purposes. To configure the restrict access option, set it to one of the following:

MULTI_USER   This setting is the default. In this mode, any valid user may connect to and use the database.

SINGLE_USER   In this mode, any single user can connect to and use the database.

RESTRICTED_USER   In this mode only administrative personnel and the database owner may connect to and use the database.

If you attempt to change a database to SINGLE_USER or RESTRICTED_USER mode while users who would be considered invalid users in these modes are connected, by default the command will wait for infinity to pass or for all users to get out of the database, whichever happens first. However, you can force everyone off the SQL Server so that you can work on it alone. The following T-SQL statement allows you to do this:

```
ALTER DATABASE Sales
    SET SINGLE_USER
    WITH ROLLBACK AFTER 360
```

This command tells the SQL Server to set the database to SINGLE_USER mode, but to allow the current transactions 360 seconds to complete. Any transactions that are not committed after 360 seconds will be rolled back. After 360 seconds (and maybe a few more seconds to perform the changeover), the Sales database will be in SINGLE_USER mode and the user that executed the command will be the single user allowed in the database.

More Database Properties

The top-five properties represent common attributes you must configure. However, it is important for you to have a basic understanding of the remaining properties so that you can choose the right options when required. Table 8.1 lists the properties not yet covered and that are available when creating databases from the GUI interface.

TABLE 8.1   Database Properties Defined

Property/Option	Definition	Recommendations
Auto Close	If this option is set to TRUE or ON, the database will be closed and unavailable when the last user exits the database.	Useful for various exclusive administrative tasks.
Auto Create Statistics	If this option is set to the default of TRUE or ON, the SQL Server Query optimizer ensures that statistics are created for columns referenced in WHERE clauses.	Used to improve query performance.
Auto Update Statistics	Statistics are updated automatically when the table data changes. The default is ON.	Helps maintain performance by keeping statistics up-to-date.
Auto Update Statistics Asynchronously	When set to TRUE or ON, queries that trigger an automatic update of statistics do not wait for the statistics to be updated before running.	Value is FALSE or OFF by default, but in some scenarios query response may be improved by setting this to TRUE or ON.
Close Cursor on Commit Enabled	When set to TRUE or ON, any cursors used within transactions are closed when the transaction completes.	The default of FALSE or OFF usually allows for better performance, particularly when Default Cursor is set to Global.
Default Cursor	Optional values include LOCAL or GLOBAL. When set to LOCAL, cursors are available only to the calling routine. When set to GLOBAL, any routing from within the calling connection can access the cursor.	The best setting is determined by the application. Set this according to vendor or developer specifications.

TABLE 8.1   Database Properties Defined *(continued)*

Property/Option	Definition	Recommendations
ANSI NULL Default	Determines whether NULL values are allowed in columns by default.	To comply with ANSI SQL-92, this should be set to TRUE or ON; however, you should check with your application vendor or developer.
ANSI NULLS Enabled	Specified that comparisons with NULL values result in UNKNOWN—the ANSI SQL-92 standard response.	When set to OFF or FALSE, two compared NULL values result to TRUE instead of UNKNOWN.
ANSI Padding Enabled	When set to ON (TRUE), strings are padded to be of equal length when compared. When set to OFF (FALSE), they are not.	Set this according to vendor or developer specifications.
ANSI Warnings Enabled	When set to ON (TRUE), warnings are issued when divide by zero errors occur.	Usually set to FALSE. Check with your vendor or developer.
Arithmetic Abort Enabled	When set to ON (TRUE), queries abort if an arithmetic overflow or divide by zero occurs.	Set this according to vendor or developer specifications.
Concatenate NULL Yields NULL	When set to ON (TRUE), concatenating two strings results in NULL if either string is NULL. When set to OFF (FALSE), a NULL string is treated as an empty string.	Set this according to vendor or developer specifications.
Cross-database Ownership Chaining Enabled	When set to ON (TRUE), the database can be either the source or the target of a cross-database ownership chain.	Set this according to vendor or developer specifications.
Date Correlation Optimization Enabled	When set to ON (TRUE), SQL Server maintains correlation statistics between related tables that have datetime columns.	Set this according to vendor or developer specifications.
Numeric Round Abort	When set to ON (TRUE), an error is generated if precision is lost when calculating an expression.	Set this according to vendor or developer specifications.

TABLE 8.1 Database Properties Defined *(continued)*

Property/Option	Definition	Recommendations
Parameterization	When set to SIMPLE (the default), SQL Server attempts to parameterize simple query parameters in WHERE clauses. When set to FORCED, most literals are parameterized.	Leave this setting at SIMPLE for databases that are performing well. For poorly performing databases, change the setting to FORCED and monitor performance over time.
Quoted Identifiers Enabled	When set to ON (TRUE), identifiers for objects like tables and columns may be surrounded by quotation marks. Literals must be surrounded by single quotes, if set to ON.	Set this according to vendor or developer specifications.
Recursive Triggers Enabled	When set to ON (TRUE), triggers can call themselves. Default setting is OFF (FALSE).	Set this according to vendor or developer specifications.
Trustworthy	When set to ON (TRUE), allows the EXECUTE AS statement to be used for impersonation while accessing resources outside the database.	The best practice is to set Trustworthy to OFF (FALSE) and use certificates or digital signatures for external authentication. Enabling Trustworthy could introduce a vulnerability within your database.
Page Verify	Detects page problems caused by I/O errors, which can result in a corrupt database. Values include CHECKSUM, TORN_PAGE_DETECTION, and NONE.	Configure this to either CHECKSUM or TORN PAGE DETECTION for most databases; otherwise, set this according to vendor or developer specifications.
Broker Enabled	Enables or disables the Service Broker for the database.	Leave the setting at FALSE unless you need to use the Service Broker in the specific database.
Database Read Only	Places the database in read-only mode. The value cannot be changed if any users are in the database.	Normally set to FALSE.
Encryption Enabled	When set to ON (TRUE), the database allows transparent data encryption.	Set this according to vendor or developer specifications.

You will notice that many definitions in Table 8.1 indicate that an option can be set to ON or TRUE or OFF or FALSE. The reason for this is simple. In the GUI, you set the option to TRUE or FALSE. In T-SQL code, you set the option to ON or OFF. You'll have to ask Microsoft why.

Creating Databases in the GUI

With the database options and storage structures covered, you're ready to create a database. In this chapter and the next two, you'll be creating and working with the Books database—the database you designed in Chapter 6, "ERD and Capacity Planning." In Exercise 8.1, you'll create the database that you'll use again in Chapter 9, "Data Types and Data Tables," for table creation and in Chapter 10, "Indexes and Views," for index creation. To ensure that the exercises in Chapters 9 and 10 work, make sure you follow the instructions in Exercise 8.1 exactly.

Creating a database in the GUI (graphical user interface) is a simple process. You can get to the GUI interface by right-clicking either the Databases node or an existing database and selecting New Database. You'll be presented with a screen similar to the one in Figure 8.5.

FIGURE 8.5   The New Database window used to create databases from the GUI

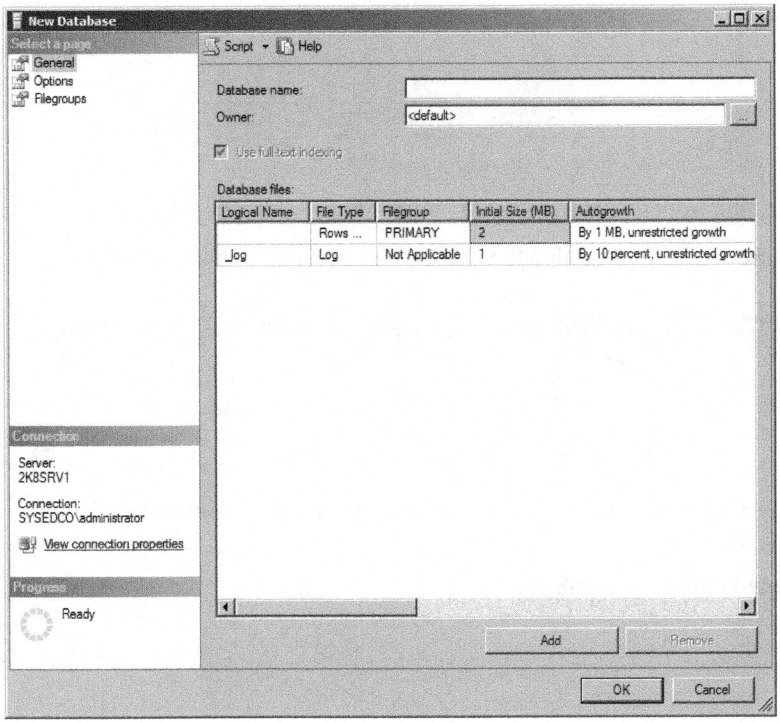

In Exercise 8.2, you'll be creating a database named Books that is stored in a single data file with a single transaction log file.

EXERCISE 8.2

Creating the Books Database in the GUI

This exercise walks you through the process of creating a database named Books using the GUI interface. You will create a database that is stored in a single file. The database will be set to the Simple recovery model so you can see where to configure this option.

Begin by launching the New Database dialog and following these steps:

1. Launch the SSMS and connect to your SQL Server default instance.

2. Right-click the Databases contained in the Object Explorer and click New Database.

3. In the dialog that appears, enter the database name value of **Books**.

4. Set the initial size for the Books data file to 5MB, as shown in the following image:

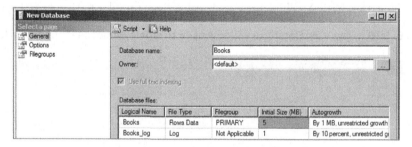

5. To select the Options page in the left corner of the window, click it.

6. Set the Recovery Model value to Simple, as shown in the following image:

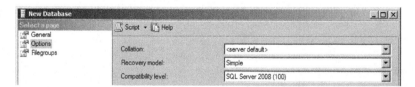

7. Click the Filegroups page to select it. Notice that one filegroup named Primary exists. Make no changes.

8. Click OK to create the database.

At this point, the New Database window will briefly display the text "Executing" in the lower-left corner and then close. If you open the Databases container, you'll now see a database named Books similar to that shown in the following image.

Creating Databases with T-SQL

Creating databases with Transact-SQL (T-SQL) is a bit more complicated. You will need to understand the syntax of the CREATE DATABASE statement before you begin. However, you can learn the syntax easily by using the GUI New Database interface that you used in Exercise 8.1 to set up the new database. Then, instead of clicking OK to create the database, as you did in step 9, you can click the Script button to generate a T-SQL script that would create the database for you. Figure 8.6 shows the Script button's options, and Figure 8.7 shows the very script that would be created for the Books database created in Exercise 8.1.

FIGURE 8.6   The Script button's options used to generate T-SQL scripts

FIGURE 8.7 The automatic script generated from the Script button

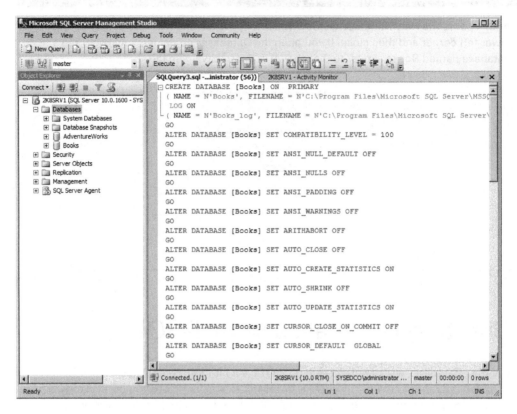

Don't let the script in Figure 8.7 scare you if you're unfamiliar with T-SQL. It's really not as complicated as it looks. The CREATE DATABASE command uses the following syntax:

```
CREATE DATABASE database_name
    [ON
        [PRIMARY] [<filespec> [ ,...n]
        [, <filegroup> [ ,...n ]]
    [LOG ON {<filespec> [ ,...n ]}]
    ]
    [COLLATE collation_name ]
    [WITH <external_access_option>]
]
[;]
```

Even this syntax may seem overwhelming at first, but with a little explanation it will become clear. To provide a very simple example, start with the following code:

```
CREATE DATABASE Books;
```

This command will create a database that is basically a duplicate of the model, but it will be named Books. Because the command does not specify any options for the database, all of the default options and those specified in the model database are used.

Now, consider the following code that is just a bit more complex:

```
CREATE DATABASE Books
ON  PRIMARY(
    NAME = 'Books',
    FILENAME = 'D:\DataStore\Books.mdf',
    SIZE = 5120KB, FILEGROWTH = 1024KB
    )
LOG ON(
    NAME = N'Books_log',
    FILENAME = E:\LogStore\Books_log.ldf',
    SIZE = 1024KB,
    FILEGROWTH = 10%
    );
```

OK, so it was more than just a bit more complex, but it is easier to understand than you might imagine. You still have the `CREATE DATABASE Books` portion of the statement, but what do the other portions do? The clause `ON PRIMARY` indicates that the afterward mentioned file name should be assigned to the `PRIMARY` filegroup. The logical name of the file is `Books`, and the literal name is `Books.mdf` located in the `D:\DataStore` folder.

Next, the transaction log is specified with the `LOG ON` clause. The transaction log is never part of a filegroup, so you do not specify one. The logical name of the log is `Books_log` and the literal name is `Books_log.ldf` located in the `E:\LogStore` folder. The size of the data file is 5MB and the size of the log file is 1MB. The data file will grow by increments of 1MB, and the log file will grow by increments of 10 percent.

You may also desire to change a database option after it has been created. For example, you may want to switch from the simple recovery model to the bulk-logged recovery model. The following T-SQL statement would switch to the bulk-logged recovery model:

```
ALTER DATABASE Books
SET RECOVERY BULK_LOGGED
WITH NO WAIT;
```

To change back to simple, execute the following statement:

```
ALTER DATABASE Books
SET RECOVERY SIMPLE
WITH NO WAIT;
```

You may have noticed that the code snippet listed previously seems to be three statements. Well, in SQL, spaces and carriage returns entered between keywords do not matter. The code is listed this way to make it easier to read. The following statement will work in exactly the same way as the preceding one:

```
ALTER DATABASE Books SET RECOVERY SIMPLE WITH NO WAIT;
```

The ALTER DATABASE command is used anytime you want to change a database setting. The ALTER DATABASE clause is always followed by the database name that you want to modify. In most cases, you use the SET keyword to indicate the option (in this case RECOVERY) that you want to configure. The WITH keyword is sometimes used to provide extra options for the statement. As an example, the preceding code uses the WITH NO WAIT clause to indicate that the database server should not wait until users are disconnected from the database to take the action.

 **Real World Scenario**

Creating Databases: GUI versus T-SQL

Even though you may decide to create most of your databases in the GUI (because it is faster), you may still want to generate the T-SQL code. The code provides you with documentation of exactly how that database was created. If you ever need to re-create it, you can do it easily by executing the saved code.

Additionally, if you make permanent changes to the database options, you should also generate code for these changes. Save the code in the same folder with the original database-creation script, and then you can run the scripts in sequence to create a new database that perfectly mirrors the production database.

I was working with one company that wanted to have a documentation system for their DBAs. At first, they planned to have an elaborate documentation method where the DBAs would fill out forms in order to indicate every option they chose when creating or altering a database. Thankfully, I was able to encourage them to use a simple code-management tool and store the T-SQL script in this tool. Now, when anyone wants to know what changes have been made to the database, they simply have to look in the code repository.

The bad news is that this solution, as with any other documentation solution, still depends on the users. If the DBAs do not generate the scripts and upload them to the repository, it's all for naught. The good news is that, at last check, the company that implemented this solution was still keeping up with its documentation. I can't emphasize enough how important that is.

Creating Databases with PowerShell

One of the great new features in SQL Server 2008 is the PowerShell extension that interacts with the SQL Server. In order to create a database in PowerShell, you'll first need to create a PowerShell script that you can call. Listing 8.2 provides just such a script for you.

Listing 8.2: The CreateDB.ps1 script code

```
# Get the command line options passed to the script
Param($dbInstance, $dbName)

[System.Reflection.Assembly]::LoadWithPartialName("Microsoft.SqlServer.Smo")
$dbServer = new-object Microsoft.SqlServer.Management.Smo.Server ($dbInstance)
$db = new-object Microsoft.SqlServer.Management.Smo.Database


"Now creating database $dbName..."
$db = new-object Microsoft.SqlServer.Management.Smo.Database ($dbServer, $dbName)
db.Create()
```

If you place the code in Listing 8.2 in a Notepad document and save it as `CreateDB.ps1` in the `C:\Windows\system32` folder, you'll be able to run it from the PowerShell command prompt, using:

```
CreateDB.ps1 -dbName Books2
```

This command executes and creates a database named Books2 in the default instance on the local server. Figure 8.8 shows the command running in Windows PowerShell. Note that, while the script can work with a parameter named `dbInstance`, it is not required if you are creating a database in the default instance.

FIGURE 8.8   Running the CreateDB.ps1 script

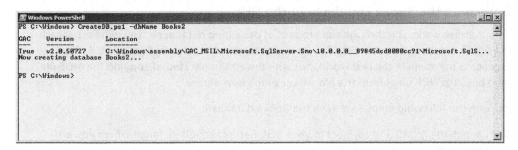

On some systems, the PowerShell scripting may need to be configured to allow an unsigned script such as the one in Listing 8.2 to run. Execute the following command at the PowerShell prompt to let unsigned scripts run on your machine (be sure that you have properly secured your environment before allowing unsigned scripts to run):

```
Set-ExecutionPolicy Unrestricted
```

Instead of allowing unrestricted scripting, you could also implement certificates. To learn more, run the following command at the PowerShell prompt:

```
get-help about_signing
```

Attaching and Detaching Databases

Sometimes you want to attach a database that was previously created on one server to another SQL Server. This task is an easy process, but you should be aware of a few facts before you attempt to do this:

- If you attach a SQL Server 2000 or 2005 database to a SQL Server 2008 server, you can no longer attach that database to the previous versions. Always make a copy of the database file before attaching it to the newer version server.

- When you detach a database from a server, it will no longer be available to users. This fact just makes sense, but it's important to remember.

- Attaching a database to a new server does not automatically give access to all previous users from the old server. These users may need to be added to the new server.

With these important facts in mind, Exercise 8.3 walks you through detaching the Books database created in Exercise 8.1.

EXERCISE 8.3

Detaching the Books Database in the GUI

This exercise walks you through the process of detaching databases. You will first detach the Books database from the SQL Server and then attach it again in Exercise 8.4. The process is the same in the real world, but with the additional step of copying the MDF file (and possible NDF files) from the old server to the new server.

Perform the following steps to detach the Books database:

1. Launch the SSMS and connect to your SQL Server default instance where you created the Books database in Exercise 8.2.

2. Expand the Databases container in Object Explorer so you can see the Books database, as in the following image:

3. Right-click on the Books database and select Tasks ➤ Detach.

4. In the Detach Database dialog, select Drop Connections and Update Statistics and then click OK:

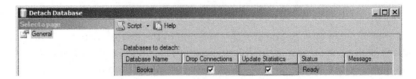

5. The database should be gone from your databases container.

Now that the database has been removed, you can navigate to the data storage location and see that the database files are still there. The detach process does not delete the database.

Exercise 8.4 walks you through the process of attaching the Books database again. You can also attach the Books database to a different server by first copying the MDF database file to another server and then performing the actions in Exercise 8.4.

Attaching the Books Database in the GUI

Perform the following steps to attach the Books database:

1. Right-click on the Databases container and select Attach.

2. In the Attach Database dialog, click the Add button to add the Books.mdf file.

3. In the Locate Database Files dialog, select the Books.mdf file, as shown in the following image and click OK.

EXERCISE 8.4 *(continued)*

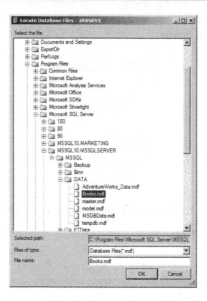

4. Notice that you can change the storage location in the lower portion of the Attach Database dialog, as shown in the following image. Change nothing, simply click OK to attach the Books database to the SQL Server instance again.

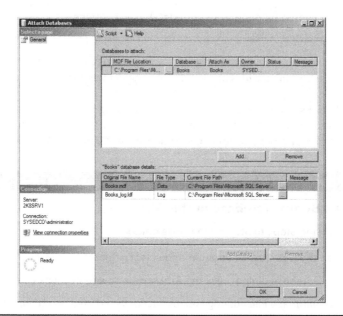

At this point, you should see the Books database back in the Databases list. Remember, it's really not any more difficult to attach a database from a different server. You simply copy the database files over to the new server and then attach the files.

Database Snapshots

Database snapshots were first introduced with the release of SQL Server 2005. The *snapshots* allow you to save the state of your data at the point in time when the snapshot was taken. Snapshots are created with the CREATE DATABASE T-SQL command. Microsoft has not released a GUI interface for the creation of snapshots for one simple reason: The vast majority of database snapshots will be taken using automated scripts. Most DBAs want snapshots of their data at various points in time throughout the day. The best way to accomplish this is through T-SQL scripts.

In the following sections, you'll see the T-SQL commands used to create database snapshots. You'll also look at the command used to drop a snapshot and the command used to revert to a snapshot. All of these examples will be based on the AdventureWorks sample database.

Creating Snapshots

Creating snapshots is achieved with the CREATE DATABASE … AS SNAPSHOT command. The syntax is as follows:

```
CREATE DATABASE database_snapshot_name
    ON
        (
        NAME = logical_file_name,
        FILENAME = 'os_file_name'
        ) [ ,...n ]
    AS SNAPSHOT OF source_database_name
[;]
```

Two important things must be understood. First, the NAME value should be equal to the logical name of the database file and not the snapshot file. Second, the FILENAME value should be equal to the actual physical path and file name of the snapshot file—most DBAs use an .ss extension as in AdventureWorks.ss. If the database has multiple files, you'll need to list each file in parentheses individually. The following code provides an example of a database snapshot for a database with multiple files:

```
CREATE DATABASE DataBaseSS
    ON
        (
        NAME = DataFile1,
```

```
FILENAME = 'C:\Snapshots\Data1.ss'
),
(
NAME = DataFile1,
FILENAME= 'C:\Snapshots\Data2.ss')
AS SNAPSHOT OF DatabaseName;
```

Now, to make this real, let's create a snapshot of the AdventureWorks sample database. If you execute the following code in a query window in SSMS, a snapshot will be created immediately:

```
CREATE DATABASE AWSS
    ON
        (
        NAME = AdventureWorks_Data,
        FILENAME = 'C:\Program Files\Microsoft SQL
        Server\MSSQL10.MSSQLSERVER\MSSQL\Data\AdventureWorks_data_1800.ss'
        )
AS SNAPSHOT OF AdventureWorks;
```

After the code executes, you can refresh the Database Snapshots container, and the new AWSS snapshot should be displayed as in Figure 8.9.

FIGURE 8.9   The AWSS snapshot displayed after creating it with the T-SQL code

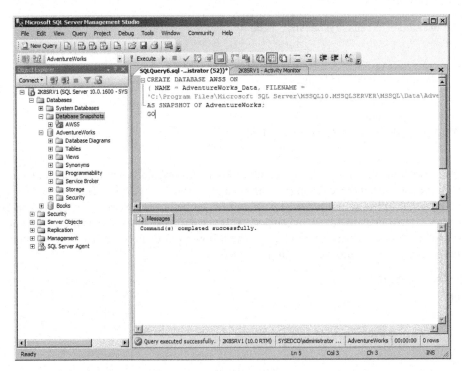

Now that the snapshot has been created, you can query it just as you would any other database. For example, the following code changes to the AWSS snapshot context and then queries the Production.Product table:

```
USE AWSS;
GO
SELECT *
FROM Production.Product;
```

If you execute this code in a query window, you will see results as if you were querying a database.

You should keep a few points in mind related to snapshots:

- Snapshots do not take long to create and are not resource intensive at the point of creation. Sparse data files are used so the snapshot is created quickly.

- After the snapshot is created, any pages that are about to be modified in the database will be copied into the snapshot just before they are modified. This is how the snapshot system works.

- You can create multiple snapshots on the same database at the same time.

To demonstrate that you can create multiple snapshots on the same database at the same time, execute the following code while noting that the snapshot database name and the physical file name are different from the previous execution:

```
CREATE DATABASE AWSS1
    ON
        (
        NAME = AdventureWorks_Data,
        FILENAME = 'C:\Program Files\Microsoft SQL
        Server\MSSQL10.MSSQLSERVER\MSSQL\Data\AdventureWorks_data_1801.ss'
        )
AS SNAPSHOT OF AdventureWorks;
```

After executing this code, refresh your Database Snapshots container and you'll notice the new snapshot named AWSS1.

Reverting to Snapshots

One of the most beneficial uses of snapshots is data protection. Have you ever had a user accidentally delete all of the customers in his or her district? Have you ever accidentally deleted a lot of data? A lot of DBAs have. If you have jobs scheduled to create snapshots every 30 minutes or every 60 minutes, you will always be able to revert the database back to a recent state very quickly.

Before you jump in and start reverting to snapshots, know this: You must drop all snapshots except the one to which you want to revert before the reversion process can be a success. This means that if you want to revert to the AWSS snapshot, you must first drop the AWSS1 snapshots. The following simple code will do the trick:

```
DROP DATABASE AWSS1;
```

If you execute the preceding single line of code and then refresh your Database Snapshots container, you should notice that you're back down to one snapshot. Now, you can revert to that snapshot. To revert to a snapshot, you use the RESTORE DATABASE command as follows:

```
RESTORE DATABASE AdventureWorks
FROM Database_Snapshot = 'AWSS';
```

Notice that the logical name of the snapshot is used. It's really that simple. The most important thing to remember about reverting to snapshots is that you must first drop all other snapshots that are based on the same database.

Summary

In this chapter, you learned about the system and user databases that exist in a SQL Server system. You learned about files and filegroups and how they can be used to enhance the performance of SQL Server 2008 databases. You also learned about the system databases and how they should be stored and backed up periodically. Next, you explored the many configuration options available for databases through the use of properties and some of the more important ones you should be aware of.

After exploring the fundamental concepts of database creation in SQL Server, you then created databases using the GUI, T-SQL, and the Windows PowerShell command prompt. You next learned to detach and attach databases. Finally, you learned about database snapshots and how to create them and revert to them in the event of a problem.

Chapter Essentials

SQL Server Databases   SQL Server supports system and user databases. The system databases are master, MSDB, model, and tempdb. The two most important system databases are master and MSDB.

Database Storage   Databases are stored in files that are assigned to filegroups. Multiple files in a single filegroup are used to enhance performance through data striping. The striping provided through the use of multiple files is not as efficient as hardware-based RAID 0 or RAID 5 striping. Multiple filegroups are used to give the DBA control over "what goes where." In addition to the data storage files, the transactions are stored in transaction log files for recoverability. The transaction logs can be used to recover from a server outage or to restore data when the data file storage fails. The transaction logs should always be stored on separate physical drives from the data files in order to ensure complete recoverability.

Database Options and Properties   SQL Server databases have dozens of options. Several options, including the auto shrink option, have caused problems for many DBAs. This option should always be set to OFF or FALSE for production databases. If auto shrink is enabled, it can greatly reduce the performance of some databases. Five additional properties are valuable as well. These include autogrowth, the recovery model, the compatibility level, auto shrink, and the option to restrict access.

Creating Databases in the GUI   In the GUI, creating a database is as simple as providing a name and choosing the options. You do not have to know T-SQL syntax or write fancy PowerShell scripts. However, you can use the Script button to generate scripts that will create your database. The Script button is both an excellent learning aid and an excellent method for documenting your work.

Creating Databases with T-SQL   In T-SQL, you use the CREATE DATABASE statement to create a database. The simplest statement is CREATE DATABASE *db_name*. When this simple statement is executed, SQL Server will create a database exactly like the model database with the name you specify. However, you can also configure any database parameter with T-SQL including files, filegroups, and database options.

Creating Databases with PowerShell   In order to create databases with PowerShell you first need to create a script that takes advantage of the SQL Server Management Objects. Then you can call the script anytime you need it. You may have to implement script signing or set scripts to Unrestricted in order to run the scripts.

Attaching and Detaching Databases   Attaching and detaching databases is an excellent method you can use to move a database around among your servers. You can detach a database from one server, copy the database files to another server, and then attach the files to the new server. If you've implemented a storage area network, you may be able to detach databases from one server and attach them to another server without the middle copying process.

Database Snapshots   Database snapshots are used to take a picture of your database at a point in time. The snapshots are created very quickly as NTFS sparse files are used. When the actual database pages are about to be changed, SQL Server first copies the pages out to the snapshot so that the original data can be retrieved from the snapshot. The entire database can be reverted to the snapshot state if you must recover the data from a past point. Snapshots are created with the CREATE DATABASE ... AS SNAPSHOT command. Databases are reverted to the state in a snapshot with the RESTORE DATABASE ... FROM Database_Snapshot command.

Chapter

9

Creating Tables

TOPICS COVERED IN THIS CHAPTER:

- ✓ Data Types
- ✓ Collations
- ✓ Creating Tables
- ✓ Data Partitioning

The first step to implementing a working SQL Server database is to create the actual database files, as you learned in Chapter 8, "Creating SQL Server Databases." The second action, which is the creation of the tables within the database, is equally important. Without the tables, the database would have no containers for data and would serve no purpose.

In this chapter, you will learn how to create tables in your SQL Server databases. You'll begin by learning about the different data types that can be used in tables and how to choose the right data types for your needs. Then you'll learn about collations and what they offer to your databases and applications. With these foundational concepts covered, you'll then go through the process of creating a table using the GUI tools and then another table using the T-SQL CREATE TABLE statement.

The final topic of this chapter will be data partitioning. This needs to be covered as well because sometimes you have too much data to be placed in a single container even though it makes logical sense to do so. Performance may suffer if all of the data is located in a single container. Partitioning provides one solution to this issue, and you'll learn what it is and how to use it in the final section of this chapter.

Data Types

Choosing the right data type is an important step in creating efficient tables. If you choose the wrong data type for a column, your data integrity and system performance may suffer. The beginning of data integrity is the use of proper data types. Exceptional system performance depends on the right data types.

Consider a table used to track customer records for United States–based customers. Imagine that the DBA set the data type for the zip code column to char(50). Two major problems will exist because of this action. First, every record will consume 50 bytes for the zip code column alone (each record would consume 100 bytes if the nchar(50) data type were used). If the table has 200,000 records in it, the DBA has wasted a lot of storage space. Just multiply 50 times 200,000 and you'll see that the records are consuming 10,000,000 bytes (just under 10 megabytes) for the zip code column by itself.

If the DBA had used the integer data type, four bytes would be consumed for each record's zip code column. The result would be the consumption of less than one tenth of the space that the char(50) data type would use. Now, an integer data type can hold any number ranging from -2^{31} ($-2,147,483,648$) to $2^{31}-1$ ($2,147,483,647$). Clearly, this data type can hold the traditional U.S. five-digit zip codes as well as the new +4 zip codes. The integer data type is a much better decision from a storage perspective.

From an integrity perspective, the char(50) data type fails miserably. What do all zip codes have in common? The answer is simple: they are comprised of numbers only—no letters are used in the U.S. This fact means that the char(50) data type will allow values that could not possibly be U.S. zip codes. For example, a data entry operator could enter the value **67gh87-ghyt** and, without additional checks in place such as triggers or constraints, the database system would allow it. If the integer data type were used, numbers would be the only characters allowed. The data type is the beginning of data integrity.

Additionally, the right data type can allow for expansion. For example, if you choose an integer data type for a column that contains numbers up to 1,000,000, the column can expand to contain values of more than 2,000,000 if needed. Expansion must be carefully considered. You do not want to configure every column based on expansion alone. If you do, you'll end up with columns requiring twice the database space needed for the actual data.

The zip code column is just one column that could be used in a customer tracking table. If every column were configured whimsically, you could end up wasting hundreds of megabytes of storage space and diminishing the performance potential of the system drastically. To prevent this, you must understand the different data types from several perspectives:

- Data type categories
- Data types
- Deprecated data types

The following section, titled "Data Type Categories," will cover these perspectives so that you can make effective decisions when building tables in SQL Server 2008.

WARNING   If you have to change the data type after you've created the table and entered data into the table, you may have to delete or change the existing data. The data in the column must meet the new data type's requirements or the column cannot be set to that data type. For this reason, data types should be carefully selected during the design and implementation phases.

Data Type Categories

The following phrases may sound odd to the ear, but you need to be aware of the types of data types. All data is not the same. Data types can be broken into several categories or types of types:

- Numerics
- Date and time
- Character and unicode character strings
- Binary strings
- Special data types

Numerics

The *numerics* category includes both exact numbers and approximate numbers. The approximate numeric data types include floating point and real. Approximate numeric data types are not as accurate as exact numerics, but they are useful in specific computational functions. Check your vendor literature for your application before using the float or real data types. Table 9.1 provides information about numeric data types.

TABLE 9.1 Numeric Data Types

Data Type	Value Ranges	Storage Size
Tinyint	0 to 255	1 byte
Smallint	−32,768 to 32,767	2 bytes
Int	−2,147,483,648 to 2,147,483,647	4 bytes
Bigint	−9,223,372,036,854,775,808 to 9,223,372,036,854,775,807	8 bytes
Bit	0 or 1	With 8 or fewer bits in a table, 1 byte; from 9 to 16 bits, 2 bytes; etc.
Decimal	$-10^{38} + 1$ to $10^{38} - 1$	Depends on precision; from 5 to 17 bytes; see Books Online for more information
Smallmoney	−214,748.3648 to 214,748.3647	4 bytes
Money	−922,337,203,685,477.5808 to 922,337,203,685,477.5807	8 bytes
Float	−1.79E+308 to −2.23E−308, 0 and 2.23E−308 to 1.79E+308	Depends on the value of the mantissa used to store the float number
Real	−3.40E + 38 to −1.18E - 38, 0 and 1.18E − 38 to 3.40E + 38	4 bytes

Date and Time

The *date and time* category contains data types for storing time-specific information. SQL Server 2008 introduces the new date data type, which includes only the date and not the time. Additionally, SQL Server 2008 still supports the `time`, `datetime`, and `datetimeoffset` data types.

Table 9.2 lists the Date and Time data types, their formatting structures, value ranges, and storage size.

TABLE 9.2   Date and Time Data Types

Data Type	Format	Value Ranges	Storage Size
Time	hh:mm:ss[.nnnnnnn]	00:00:00.0000000 to 23:59:59.9999999	3 to 5 bytes
Date	YYYY-MM-DD	0001-01-01 to 9999-12-31	3 bytes
Datetime	YYYY-MM-DD hh:mm:ss[.nnn]	1753-01-01 to 9999-12-31	8 bytes
Datetime2	YYYY-MM-DD hh:mm:ss[.nnnnnnn]	0001-01-01 00:00:00.0000000 to 9999-12-31 23:59:59.9999999	6 to 8 bytes
Smalldatetime	YYYY-MM-DD hh:mm:ss	1900-01-01 to 2079-06-06	4 bytes
Datetimeoffset	YYYY-MM-DD hh:mm:ss[.nnnnnnn] [+|-]hh:mm	0001-01-01 00:00:00.0000000 to 9999-12-31 23:59:59.9999999 (in UTC or Coordinated Universal Time)	8 to 10 bytes

Character and Unicode Character Strings

The *character strings* and *unicode character strings* are used to store exactly what they sound like they would store: character data. The difference between the two categories is that the unicode character strings include character set information with each entry, and the character strings do not. The result is that unicode character strings consume twice as much space as character strings; however, Microsoft still recommends the use of `unicode` data types because they are more transferable to different character sets. Both variable and fixed-length character data types are available. You will find the character data types listed in Table 9.3.

TABLE 9.3 Character Data Types

Data Type	Value Ranges	Storage Size
Char	From 0 to 8000 characters	1 byte per character (fixed)
Varchar	From 0 to 8000 characters	Data length + 2 bytes
nChar	From 0 to 8000 characters	2 bytes per character (fixed)
nVarchar	From 0 to 4000 characters	Data length x 2 + 2 bytes
Text (to be removed; use Varchar(max) instead)	From 0 to 2 billion characters	Up to 2 gigabytes (1 byte per character)
nText (to be removed; use nVarchar(max) instead)	From 0 to 1 billion characters	Up to 2 gigabytes (2 bytes per character)
Varchar(max)	From 0 to 2 billion characters	Data length + 2 bytes
nVarchar(max)	From 0 to 1 billion characters	Data length + 2 bytes

Binary String

Binary string data types can be used to store binary data such as images, executables, or any data that is not simply a number, date, or text value. Binary data can be up to 2 gigabytes in size and includes text as well as nontextual data. Technically, the text and ntext data types, though listed in the character strings and unicode character strings category in Books Online, are binary data types. The image data type allows for the largest amount of binary data not intended for text storage. Binary data types are described in Table 9.4.

TABLE 9.4 Binary Data Types

Data Type	Value Ranges	Storage Size
Binary	From 0 to 8000 bytes	1 byte per binary byte (fixed)
Varbinary	From 0 to 8000 bytes	1 byte per binary byte + 2 bytes
Varbinary (max)	From 0 to 2 billion bytes	1 byte per binary byte + 2 bytes
Image (to be removed; use Varbinary(max) instead)	From 0 to 2 billion bytes	1 byte per binary byte

Special Data Types

The *special data types* or what Books Online calls *other data types* category includes unique identifiers, time stamps, and cursors—among other data types. With the exceptions of sql_variant and XML, the special data types are not used to store user information. The sql_variant data type can contain data of any other data type. It is not recommended for production use for both performance and integrity reasons. The XML data type is used to store XML content. Table 9.5 provides a reference of the special data types.

TABLE 9.5   Special Data Types

DataType	Use	Storage
Cursor	Stored procedure and application development; not used as a column data type	No storage required
HierarchyID	Used to represent a position in a hierarchy	Storage varies depending on the hierarchy tree size and the number of child nodes
SQL_Variant	Used when a programmer is lost and doesn't know how to select the best data type	Varies depending on the actual data entered
Table	Stored procedure and application development; not used as a column data type	No storage required
Timestamp	Used for automatic timestamp generation in a database	8 bytes
Uniqueidentifier	A globally unique identifier (GUID) that may be generated or manually created	16 bytes
XML	For storage of XML data up to 2 gigabytes in size	From 0 bytes to 2 gigabytes depending on stored data

WARNING   When choosing an integer data type (int, smallint, tinyint, or bigint), remember to plan for the future. If you choose tinyint today, make sure it will handle the data requirements a year from now. You can easily change the data type from a smaller integer to a larger integer because the data will still be accurate for that data type; however, you usually learn of the need for the change only after users begin experiencing data entry errors.

Deprecated Data Types

If you are creating a brand new table today and you do not have specific requirements imposed by an application, you want to avoid using deprecated data types. The following data types have been deprecated in SQL Server 2008 and will be removed in some future version:

text   Use VarChar(max) instead. VarChar(max) provides the same 2 gigabytes of storage as the traditional text data type.

ntext   Use nVarChar(max) instead. nVarChar(max) provides up to 1 gigabyte of storage, because 2 bytes are required for each character.

image   Use VarBinary(max) instead. VarBinary(max) provides the same 2 gigabytes of binary storage as the image data type.

Avoid using these three data types going forward. If you use them in a newly developed system, you risk that system's compatibility with future versions of SQL Server.

Collations

Data *collations* define the rules by which data is compared, sorted, and presented. Most English-speaking people know that the letter *B* comes before the letter *F* in the English alphabet and that the letter *X* comes after the letter *M,* but most English-speaking people do not know the order of the letters (characters) used in the Hebrew alphabet. SQL Server must be able to sort data in any language that it supports. Collations allow it to perform this action.

Additionally, the collations allow the server to determine how best to display information in cooperation with the client application. The character set defines the presentation. The character set on the database server should match that used by the client applications. The database server will store a code representing the character. The code is matched with the collation to determine what is actually displayed. If the collation (think language or regional settings) is different on the server than it is on the client, display problems can result.

Collations also determine sort order preferences. For example, the words *bat* and *Bat* may appear to be the same word—with the exception of the capital letter *B* on the latter— but they may be treated differently depending on the collation's sort order preference. When an uppercase preference is used, *Bat* always sorts before *bat*. When no preference is used, the results will be random. Your application may demand a sort order preference, and you should be careful to select the proper collation.

An additional functional factor related to collations is the way in which SQL Server displays dates. If you use a collation aimed at the United States database market, you'll see dates in the year/day/month format. The date format is important because users expect to see dates in the way they are used to seeing them.

Finally, collations determine case sensitivity during comparisons. For example, using the LIKE and NOT LIKE operators in a SELECT statement depends on the collation. If the collation is case sensitive, the following code would not return records with the value of 'all' in the number column:

```
SELECT *
FROM Product
WHERE Number LIKE 'all';
```

The collation can be configured at three levels in a SQL Server 2008 DBMS:

- Configure the collation at the *server instance* to specify a collation to be used by default for all databases and columns.
- Configure the collation at the *database level* to override the default server instance collation.
- Configure the collation at the *column level* to override the default database level or server instance collations.

As this list demonstrates, you have flexibility in configuring the collation. However, a DBA should exercise caution in applying collations at ever more granular levels. When you have a database with several different collations on different columns, it makes it more difficult to manage and application developers may also find it more difficult to develop applications. Always let the business needs drive the decision, but attempts should be made to minimize the number of different collations used in a single-server instance.

Configuring Server Instance Collations

The server instance collation is configured during the installation of SQL Server 2008. It is best to know the proper collation before installation and configure it properly during the installation. With that said, the real world is not always best and things change. If you must change the server instance collation, you can do it by rebuilding the master database. For safety reasons, always back up the master database before rebuilding it. The following command can be used to rebuild the master database and specify a collation:

```
setup.exe /QUIET /ACTION=REBUILDDATABASE /INSTANCENAME=instance
/SQLSYSADMINACCOUNTS=admin_account /SAPWD=password /SQLCOLLATION=new_collation
```

The rebuild setup command should be run from the installation media at a command prompt. The SQLCOLLATION option is the key to changing the collation. Detailing a full list of the valid collation names (for use in place of new_collation) is beyond the scope of this book, but if you would like to see that information, just search for **Windows Collation Name** in SQL Server 2008 Books Online.

Configuring Database Collations

Like the server instance collation, the database collation is usually configured during the creation of the database. In fact, the server instance collation is usually just accepted as the default collation for the database. However, you can change the database collation at a later time by performing a somewhat tedious procedure.

First, you can change the database collation for all future additions by using the ALTER DATABASE command, such as in the following code example:

```
ALTER DATABASE Sales COLLATE SQL_Latin1_General_CP1_CI_AS
```

However, this command will not modify the collation of existing entries in the table. From here, you have two basic options to complete the conversion of the collation: export and import the data or manually change the collation of every column in every table. If you export the data, delete the data, and then import it again, the newly imported version of the old data will have the new collation. However, this can break timestamp values on some tables, so be careful. The more time-consuming option is to manually change the collation of each character column in each table in the database. You could also write a script to perform this action if you have in-depth T-SQL scripting experience.

The moral of the story is simple: make sure you know what you want the collation to be when you create the database. However, if you find yourself in a situation where you must copy or move a database from one server to another and change the collation in the process, you now know that it is possible.

Configuring Column Collations

The final say in collations is the column level. The column-level collation can override both the database and server instance collations. Thankfully, column-level collations can be changed at any time, and the change impacts existing and future data values. Column collations may be configured using the COLLATE clause of the CREATE TABLE or ALTER TABLE statements. Additionally, the column collation may be configured in the GUI table provided by SSMS. Exercise 9.1 steps you through the process of column-collation configuration.

EXERCISE 9.1

Assigning Collations at the Column Level

In this exercise, you will create a simple table using the Table Designer and configure a collation different from the default for one column.

1. Launch the SQL Server Management Studio.

2. Expand the database named Books, which was created in Exercise 8.1.

EXERCISE 9.1   *(continued)*

3. Expand the Tables container in the Books database.

4. Right-click the Tables container and select New Table.

5. In the Table Design window, enter column information, as shown in the following image.

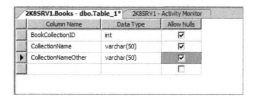

6. Click the CollectionNameOther column to select it. The Column Properties windows should look similar to the following image.

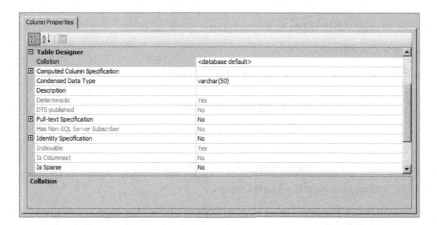

7. In the Column Properties window, click the button for the Collation property. The Collation dialog should appear.

8. Select Japanese in the Windows Collation dropdown, and check Case Sensitive under the Dictionary Sort order option, as shown in the following image.

EXERCISE 9.1 *(continued)*

9.   Click OK to save the changes to the collation for the column.

10. Click File ➢ Save Table.

11. Save the table as **Collections** by entering the table name and clicking OK.

12. Click File ➢ Close to close the Table Designer.

At this point, you have created a table named Collections with a unique collation for one column. Using the Table Designer is a simple method for completing this task.

Exercise 9.1 showed the simple process used to assign column-level collations with the Table Designer. To assign collations during table creation using T-SQL, use code like the following:

```
CREATE TABLE dbo.Collections(
    BookCollectionID int,
    CollectionName varchar(50),
    CollectionNameOther varchar(50) COLLATE Japanese_CS_AI
);
```

Notice the simple addition of the COLLATE Japanese_CS_AI clause to the CollectionNameOther column specification. The COLLATE clause is all that's required to generate a column-specific collation during table creation. It is also used to modify an existing column. For example, to assign an alternative collation to an existing column in an existing table, use the following code:

```
ALTER TABLE dbo.Collections2
ALTER COLUMN CollectionName varchar(50) COLLATE Japanese_CS_AI;
```

The complete syntax for table creation will be covered in the following section titled "Creating Tables."

 You can easily discover the name for collations without searching Books Online by creating a table with any name you desire. To do this, just apply a column-level collation to the table that meets your needs. Save the table. Right-click the table and select Design. Click the column with a custom collation, and you can see the name to use in T-SQL code for that collation.

Creating Tables

Tables can be created in SQL Server using a graphical interface or the T-SQL language. The graphical interface can be faster for complex tables, but it does not offer the flexibility of T-SQL. T-SQL is more flexible, but it does not offer the simplicity of the graphical interface. You must choose between the two methods for each table you create. When you're creating simple tables (tables containing two to five columns with no special constraint requirements), you may find it convenient to usually use T-SQL. When the table is more complicated, you may want to use the Table Designer and then export the table to a script file so that you have the T-SQL code for documentation. In general, if the table is very small, you will be more likely to use code directly; however, when the table is large or demands complex constraints or other features, you will use the Table Designer.

The following sections will present both methods. You'll first learn to create tables using the Table Designer. An exercise is provided that allows you the opportunity to create a table in the graphical interface. Next, you will learn to create tables using T-SQL.

Creating Tables with the Table Designer

If you are uncomfortable with T-SQL or simply want a quick way to create tables, the Table Designer is there to help you. With the Table Designer, you have an interface very similar to the one that many professionals have used in Microsoft Access for many years. You can specify the columns, data types, nullability, and dozens of other parameters, as shown in Figure 9.1.

FIGURE 9.1   Using the Table Designer to create tables

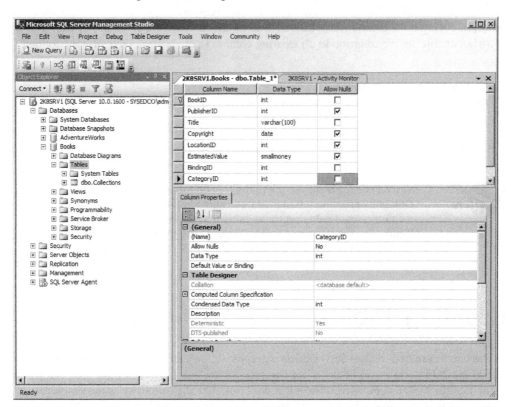

The exercises in this section walk you through the process of creating a table with the Table Designer. If you've created tables in Microsoft Access or the Table Designer in earlier versions of SQL Server, you will find the tool very similar to them. It's easy to use and simple to learn. Just don't forget that you can control even more information if you click View ➢ Properties while in the Table Designer. Figure 9.2 shows this new view.

Notice that you can configure the table name, description, and storage location (such as filegroups or partition schemes) from within the Properties window. For convenience, you might want to keep the Properties window open at all times while creating tables. (This configuration allows for easy access and helps justify your 28-inch widescreen monitor.)

In the following exercises, you will create a table in the Books database. The table will be the primary table for the database—the Books table. Along the way, you will define data types, define nullability, and identity column information. Identity columns are used to automatically generate a sequential number value for unique identification purposes. Exercise 9.2 will launch the Table Designer.

FIGURE 9.2   Displaying the Properties window in the Table Designer view

EXERCISE 9.2

Launching the Table Designer

The Table Designer is launched from within SQL Server Management Studio so the process begins there.

1. Launch the SQL Server Management Studio.

2. Expand the database named Books, which was created in Exercise 8.1.

3. Expand the Tables container in the Books database.

4. Right-click the Tables container and select New Table.

Now that you have a table, it's time to create the columns. Use the specifications detailed in Table 9.6.

TABLE 9.6 Column Specifications

Column Name	Data Type	NULL Setting
BookID	int	not NULL
Title	varchar(100)	not NULL
PublisherID	int	NULL
LocationID	int	NULL
BindingID	int	not NULL
CategoryID	int	not NULL
Copyright	date	NULL
EstimatedValue	smallmoney	NULL

You will have to repeat the following steps for each column, as shown in Exercise 9.3.

EXERCISE 9.3

Creating Columns

1. In the Table Designer, enter the column name (such as BookID) in the Column Name field.

2. Enter the data type (such as int) in the Data Type field.

3. If NULL values are not allowed, deselect the check box in the Allow Nulls column.

Column Name	Data Type	Allow Nulls
BookID	int	☑

4. Repeat this process in a new row for each column required in the table. The results should look similar to the following image:

Column Name	Data Type	Allow Nulls
BookID	int	☐
Title	varchar(100)	☐
PublisherID	int	☑
LocationID	int	☑
BindingID	int	☐
CategoryID	int	☐
Copyright	date	☑
EstimatedValue	smallmoney	☑

One of the most important attributes of any table is the primary key. The primary key defines the unique identifier for rows in the table. For the Books table, you will use the BookID column as the primary key, as shown in Exercise 9.4.

EXERCISE 9.4

Selecting a Primary Key

Follow these steps to make the BookID column the primary key.

1. Click the row selector (the gray square) to the left of the BookID row, which is the row that identifies the BookID column for the table. This action selects the row. You'll see an arrow on the row selector to indicate that the row is selected.

2. Click Table Designer ➤ Set Primary Key. You should see that the Row Selector icon changes to an arrow and a yellow key.

Specifying Column Properties

The Books table uses the BookID column as the primary key, and you do not want to generate book IDs manually. The following steps can be used to set up an identity configuration for the BookID column. The identity state will cause BookID values to be generated automatically.

1. Select the BookID column by clicking the Row Selector icon to the left of the row for the BookID entry.

2. In the Column Properties pane, scroll down until you see Identity Specification, as in the following image:

    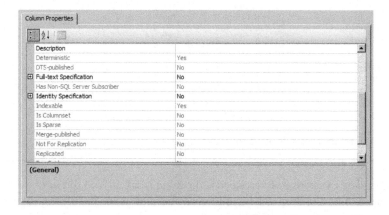

3. Expand the Identity Specification section by clicking the plus sign.

EXERCISE 9.4 *(continued)*

4. Set the Is Identity value to Yes.

5. Set the Identity Seed value to 100000 so that the first BookID will be 100000, and leave the Identity Increment value at 1 so that BookID values will increment by 1.

Identity Specification	Yes
(Is Identity)	Yes
Identity Increment	1
Identity Seed	100000

EXERCISE 9.5

Specifying Table Properties and Saving the Table

The next parameters that should be configured are the table properties. The table name and description are configured using the following steps:

1. Click View ➢ Properties or press F4 to display the Properties window.

2. In the Properties window, enter the table name value of **Books** and the Description value of **Book information table**. Notice that you can also specify the filegroup, partition scheme, and schema in the Properties window.

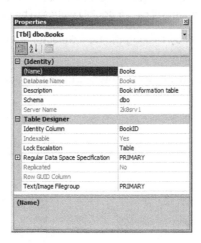

3. To save the table, click File ➢ Save or press Ctrl+S.

If you complete the steps in Exercise 9.5, the table is saved. You did not have to provide a table name because the Properties window was used to define it. In Exercise 9.6, you will generate a script to document the table.

EXERCISE 9.6

Scripting the Table for Documentation

One final step remains. If you generate a script that can be used to re-create the table, you also provide documentation for the table. The following steps can be used to create a script for the Books table:

1. If the table is still open, click File ➢ Close to close the table.

2. Right-click on the Books table in the Tables container and select Script Table As ➢ Create To ➢ File.

3. For this exercise, navigate to the Desktop and save the file as **Books_Table.sql**.

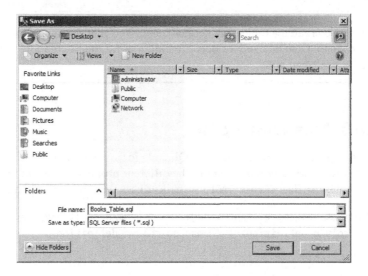

4. To view the code, click File ➤ Open ➤ File or press Ctrl+O.

5. Navigate to the Desktop and open Books_Table.sql. You should see code similar to that in the following image:

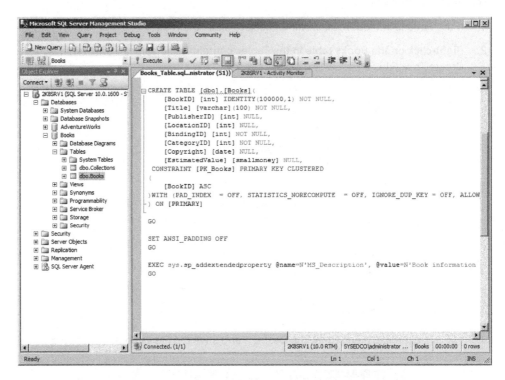

In this exercise, you created a table from scratch using the Table Designer. You also generated T-SQL code that can be used for documentation or for the re-creation of the Books table should the need ever arise.

Creating Tables with T-SQL

In Exercise 9.6, you saw how to generate T-SQL code for an existing table. The code is fairly straightforward when you understand the different properties that can be configured for tables and columns. The CREATE TABLE statement uses the following syntax:

```
CREATE TABLE [database_name.[schema_name]. | schema_name.]table_name
    ( { <column_definition> | <computed_column_definition>
```

```
            | <column_set_definition> }
        [ <table_constraint> ] [ ,...n ] )
    [ ON { partition_scheme_name ( partition_column_name ) | filegroup
        | "default" } ]
    [ { TEXTIMAGE_ON { filegroup | "default" } ]
    [ FILESTREAM_ON { partition_scheme_name | filegroup
        | "default" } ]
    [ WITH ( <table_option> [ ,...n ] ) ]
[ ; ]
```

As usual, the syntax listing looks far more complex than most CREATE TABLE commands. As an example, consider the following code, which creates the Publishers table in the Books database:

```
CREATE TABLE dbo.Publishers(
    PublisherID int IDENTITY(1,1) NOT NULL,
    PublisherName varchar(50) NOT NULL,
    CONSTRAINT PK_Publishers PRIMARY KEY CLUSTERED(
            PublisherID ASC
    )
    WITH(
        PAD_INDEX  = OFF,
        STATISTICS_NORECOMPUTE  = OFF,
        IGNORE_DUP_KEY = OFF,
        ALLOW_ROW_LOCKS  = ON,
        ALLOW_PAGE_LOCKS  = ON
    ) ON [PRIMARY]
) ON [PRIMARY];
```

The easiest way to learn about a T-SQL command, such as CREATE TABLE, is to generate the script using SSMS. Create the object in the GUI and then generate the script. You've now covered the basics of the CREATE TABLE command. If you'd like more information on this topic, search for CREATE TABLE in Books Online.

In addition to scripting a table, you can script an entire database including the tables. This technique can be helpful in analyzing a database that you did not create. Right-click the database to be scripted, select Tasks, and then select Generate Scripts. From there, you can generate detailed scripts for every element of the database.

Data Partitioning

The performance of very large tables can suffer even on the most powerful of servers. Let's define a very large table as any table that is too large to be handled efficiently by the server on which it operates. The example table could have an arbitrary number of rows, say 2,000,000, but that's all it would be—an arbitrary number. An eight-socket dual-core server with each core running at more than 2GHz while providing 32GB of RAM might handle multiple tables of 2,000,000 rows just fine. However, a single-socket dial-core server running at more than 2GHz while providing 4GB of RAM could perform very poorly with such large tables.

Whatever the size of any given table, if it is causing poor performance, you have two options when it comes to partitioning:

- You may choose to vertically or horizontally partition the table through manual or scripted operations.
- You may choose to use the table partitioning feature of SQL Server (which uses partition functions and schemes) to perform the partitioning.

The following sections discuss both options and the performance improvements you can expect from them.

Vertical and Horizontal Partitioning

Vertical partitioning involves spreading data columns across two or more tables even though they could be stored in a single table. SQL Server 2008 does not directly support vertical partitioning as a feature, but vertical partitioning can be implemented using one-to-one relationships. Vertical partitioning provides several benefits:

- You can separate seldom-used data into a different table from the frequently used data.
- More sensitive data can be separated from less sensitive data.
- Commonly grouped columns can be placed together and less commonly grouped columns can be provided to the users through the use of views.

Separating seldom-used data provides a performance boost. If 30 columns exist in a table and only 12 columns are frequently queried, the performance of the 12-column queries can be greatly improved by separating the remaining 18 columns into their own table. When the data in the 18-column table is needed, it can be aggregated with the 12-column table using simple INNER JOIN queries or predesigned views.

Separating sensitive data from less sensitive data can also provide a security benefit. Permissions can be set at the column level, but it is often easier to separate the columns out into their own table. An example of this might be an employees table that also tracks pay rates. The pay rate information could be placed in a separate table so that permission management is easier and mistakes in permission management are less likely.

Placing commonly grouped columns together is a performance strategy. When you cannot separate the columns into two simple groups—frequently used and seldom used—you may choose to place the columns into several groups based on how they are used together. With this strategy, you may have some redundancy in the database, but it may help to improve performance.

If you choose to implement vertical partitioning, your application will have to rejoin the data. The application will simply pull a portion of the data from one table and the other portion from another table. The steps for creating vertically partitioned tables are no different than any other tables. You must simply plan for the vertical partitioning and then code your data access applications to work with it using INNER JOIN statements and other such SQL requests.

Horizontal partitioning is different. In this case, the data is separated based on the value or values of a column or columns. For example, you may choose to separate the data based on date ranges, price ranges, integer ranges, or specific character-based values. The point is that rows matching specific criteria are placed in one table while rows not matching the criteria are placed in a different table. The most common example of horizontal partitioning is the removal of historic data from an active table while keeping it online in an archive table.

Neither vertical partitioning nor horizontal partitioning is automated in SQL Server 2008. Granted, you can automate them by writing your own script or application, but SQL Server does not provide functions for such partitioning. If you want to automate the partitioning of your tables, you need to leave manual table creation behind and look at partitioning with functions and schemes. Like vertical partitioning, if you choose to implement horizontal partitioning, you will need to code your data-access application so that it understands how and where to access the data. For example, the application may need to access data from the year 2008 in one table and data from the year 2010 in another table. The client understands the data partitioning, and SQL Server 2008 treats the tables as normal unpartitioned tables.

Data Partitioning with Functions and Schemes

Automated table partitioning is based on SQL Server 2008 features called partition functions and partition schemes. The partition function and scheme must exist before the table can be created as a partitioned table. Figure 9.3 shows the hierarchy of these objects.

FIGURE 9.3   The partitioning object hierarchy

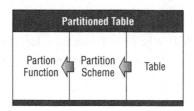

As you can see in Figure 9.3, the first object that must be created is the partition function. The scheme depends on the function, and the table depends on the scheme. The partition function is created using the CREATE PARTITION FUNCTION command. The following code is an example of a partition function command:

```
CREATE PARTITION FUNCTION PF100 (int)
AS RANGE LEFT FOR VALUES (100);
```

In this CREATE PARTITION FUNCTION command, the partition function is named PF100, and the function will specify two partitions. The first partition will contain those rows containing values of 100 or less. The second partition will contain those rows containing values of more than 100. The RANGE LEFT clause determines that the value 100 belongs to the first partition. Had RANGE RIGHT been used, the value 100 would have belonged to the second partition. Remember, this is the partition function. The scheme will associate the partition function with a set of filegroups.

The CREATE PARTITION SCHEME command is used to create the partition scheme. The following example code would use the partition function created previously:

```
CREATE PARTITION SCHEME PS100
AS PARTITION PF100
TO (FilegroupA, FilegroupB);
```

Notice that the AS PARTITION clause uses the partition function name. Because there are two partitions, two filegroups are needed. You must create the filegroups before you can run the CREATE PARTITION SCHEME command.

The beauty of automated partitioning is that SQL Server does all of the data assignments for you. When you place a table on the PS100 partition scheme, SQL Server uses the PF100 partition function to determine into which filegroup a row of data should be placed.

At this point, you're probably wondering how SQL Server knows which column should be evaluated for partition placement. The secret is in the table-creation process. You can do this partition scheme assignment from the Table Designer, but it's easier to understand when you look at the CREATE TABLE command. Consider the following code:

```
CREATE TABLE PartTable (
    PartColumn int NOT NULL,
    TextData varchar(25)
) ON PS100(PartColumn);
```

Do you see the secret revealed? When you create the table, you place it on the partition scheme—in this case, PS100. Part of the ON clause is the column identity of the partitioning column. It's really that easy.

Summary

In this chapter, you learned about database tables. First, the data types were covered. Selecting the right data type is essential to a well-performing database. The information provided in this chapter will be a helpful reference when selecting data types. The key is to select the data types that will provide integrity, performance, and expansion.

Next, collations were explored in more detail than previous chapters. You learned more about what collations are and the impact they have on the database. You also learned to create the collation configurations for the server instance, database level, and column level.

After collation, you explored table creation through both the Table Designer and the CREATE TABLE T-SQL command. The Table Designer was used to create the Books table and configure important settings like the primary key, identity columns, and data types.

Finally, you learned about table partitioning. Manual partitioning was covered first and then automated partitioning. The three automated partitioning components—partition functions, partition schemes, and partitioned tables—were introduced along with the commands used to configure each.

Chapter Essentials

Data Types   SQL Server supports many data types, and Microsoft has categorized the data types to make them easier to understand and document. Choosing the right data type is an essential step in creating well-performing databases and tables. If you choose the wrong data type, storage space may be wasted and data integrity may suffer.

Collations   Collations define the character set used for data presentation. They also define the sort order and case sensitivity of data. Collations are usually set at the server instance level, but may also be set at the database level or the column level. Column-level collations should be avoided where possible because they add complexity to database management. When no collation is specified at the column level, the database default collation is used. When no collation is specified at the database level, the server instance default collation is used.

Creating Tables   Tables may be created using the GUI with the Table Designer. The Table Designer exposes most of the parameters that can be configured through T-SQL code and can be a faster method for table creation. The T-SQL command for table creation is CREATE TABLE. The ALTER TABLE and DROP TABLE commands can be used to modify existing tables and delete tables, respectively. You can generate T-SQL code for an existing table, which is an excellent learning tool and a documentation tool as well.

Data Partitioning   Data partitioning can be performed using manual partitioning methods such as horizontal partitioning and vertical partitioning. Automated partitioning involves the creation of partition functions, partition schemes, and partitioned tables. The function must be created first, then the scheme, and finally the table. The partitioning column is defined during table creation. The partition scheme associates a function with filegroups.

Chapter

10

Indexes and Views

TOPICS COVERED IN THIS CHAPTER:

- ✓ Understanding Indexes
- ✓ Creating Basic Indexes
- ✓ Creating Advanced Indexes
- ✓ Managing Indexes
- ✓ Understanding Views
- ✓ Creating Views

In the preceding two chapters, you went through the process required to create a database and create tables in the database. This chapter takes you to the next steps: creating indexes and understanding views. Although indexes and views are two very different things, they do share one common feature: both objects are created as subsets or dependent objects that rely on underlying tables. For example, an index cannot be created by itself; it must be created on a table. In the same way a view cannot be created by itself, it must be created on another view or a table. Ultimately, all indexes and views are dependent objects in that they depend on the existence of underlying tables.

Indexes can be the difference between a database that performs well and a database that's so slow it performs like it's still in the eighties running on a Commodore 64. In this chapter, you will learn what indexes really are and how they work to optimize the performance of your databases. Next, you'll learn to create these indexes using both the SSMS GUI interface and the T-SQL CREATE INDEX command. With indexes covered, you'll move on to learn about views. Views are not usually used to enhance performance, but rather to enhance usability. However, certain types of views may indeed improve performance. This chapter will present the different types of views and explore the methods by which views can be created.

Understanding Indexes

Indexes have been enhanced again in SQL Server 2008. SQL Server 2005 first introduced a new feature called online indexing, and now SQL Server 2008 takes indexes to another level with spatial indexes, hierarchical indexes, and filtered indexes. Online indexing was a big leap forward because it allowed you to update indexes while users were utilizing those same indexes. Before SQL Server 2005, indexes had to be taken offline in order to be updated. But what are all these indexes anyway? That question will be answered in this section.

The "Indexes Defined" section of this chapter will explain the basic concepts of an index and how they improve database performance. It will then explore each of the index types provided in SQL Server 2008 and also detail when you would use each type. When you've mastered these topics, you will have the ability to optimize the performance and usability of your databases.

Indexes Defined

Database indexes have a lot in common with items you find in the real world. Think of them as the tabs on a file folder in your filing cabinet or the table of contents in a book, or even the index at the back of a book. A database index is like all of these things and, yet, it's also different. Like all of the items listed, database indexes help you find the actual thing you are seeking.

These analogies can help you understand the concept of an index. Too many DBAs define an index as something that improves the performance of a database. This definition is not necessarily accurate. Creating an index where one is not needed actually results in decreased performance of a database. Consider the file folders in a filing cabinet. If every single file were placed in a separate folder with its own tab, the benefit of the tabs would be diminished. The point of the tabs is to help you locate a subset of the files more quickly so that you can locate a specific file in that subset. Database indexes are similar. For this reason, you must understand the way indexes are used by the database management system in question.

Most SQL Server database indexes are either clustered or nonclustered indexes, and the creation of the indexes is very simple. Choosing the proper columns to index, however, is not always so simple. You must understand what an index is and how indexes are used so that you can make good choices about index creation.

What Is an Index?

A typical nonclustered index is, effectively, a separately stored copy of a database table with a limited number of table columns included. You will not read this definition in Microsoft's documentation, but it is an accurate description nonetheless. The object is technically called an index, but it can contain multiple columns just like a table, and it is stored on 8KB data pages just like a table. The only real difference is that you cannot specify an index as the direct target of a FROM clause in a SELECT statement. In fact, a clustered index is the way in which the table is stored. Stated differently, when you create a clustered index on a table, you are changing the way in which the table itself is stored; you are not creating a separately stored object from the table.

Microsoft actually acknowledges this concept in the following statement: "A table is contained in one or more partitions and each partition contains data rows in either a heap or a clustered index structure." This quote comes from the SQL Server 2008 Books Online (July 2009) article titled "Table and Index Organization." It clearly states that a table contains either a heap or a clustered index structure. The table concept or object, therefore, can be stored as either a heap or a clustered index. For this reason, it is perfectly accurate to say that an index is a table. By thinking of it this way, you should more quickly understand the concept of the index and the benefits it brings. These benefits will become clear in the next section, "How Are Indexes Used?" For now, however, it is important to keep in mind that the index is based on a separate table in all cases except the clustered index.

At this point you may be wondering, what is a heap and what does it have to do with indexes? A heap is a table without a clustered index. Think of it as a pile of unsorted clothes in the laundry room. You might hear someone say, "Look at that heap of clothes in there!" The term "heap," in this context, means a disorganized pile, and that's what a table is without a clustered index. Heaps are stored without any assigned structure for the rows. Tables stored as clustered indexes are organized according to the clustered index column. It is important that you understand the difference between a heap and a clustered index.

In addition to the facts that a table may be stored as an index and a nonclustered index is really like a separate table with a subset of the columns represented in the base table, indexes are stored differently than heaps. Heaps use two primary page types: IAM pages and data pages. Index Allocation Map (IAM) pages indicate which data pages are used by the heap. The data is then stored in those data pages. Indexes use a completely different structure.

 If you have training in programming or have a computer science degree, it is very likely that you're used to thinking of a heap as a memory allocation concept; however, Microsoft has chosen the word *heap* to refer to a table without a clustered index and so I use it here.

Indexes are stored in a B-tree structure. Many people mistakenly assume that the *B* in B-tree stands for binary, but it does not. If indexes were stored in a binary-tree structure, each branch would result in—at most—two more branches; however, a SQL Server index will start with a root node and this root node may branch out to three or more branches. Therefore, the SQL Server index structure should be thought of more like a branching tree—although Microsoft suggests that the *B* stands for *balanced,* and this is the more common industry term.

The index pages are called nodes in the B-tree structure. One root node page always exists. Between the root node and the leaf nodes, several layers or branching decisions may exist. These intermediate layers are called intermediate levels in SQL Server terminology. The end nodes are the leaf nodes, and the leaf nodes contain the actual data for clustered indexes or pointers to the data for single-column nonclustered indexes. In some Microsoft documents, the leaf level is also called index level 0. Figure 10.1 represents this B-tree structure.

FIGURE 10.1   The SQL Server B-tree index structure

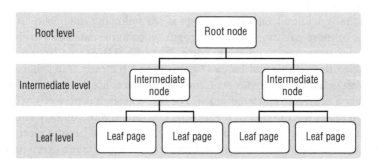

How Are Indexes Used?

Now that you understand the basic structure of an index and what it really is, let's explore how they are used. Imagine you have a data table similar to the one in Table 10.1.

TABLE 10.1   Sample Customer Data Table

CustomerID	FirstName	LastName
1	Tom	Carpenter
2	Tracy	Mathys
3	Cathy	Moyer
4	Brian	Wright
5	Jay	Galland
6	Amy	Freeman
...	...	...

Further assume that the table has 500,000 records sequentially continuing up to CustomerID 500,000 and that the table has more columns that are not shown, such as Phone, eMail, Address, City, State, etc. Let's discuss how this table would normally be accessed if it were stored as a heap—without any indexes.

Consider the following SELECT statement executed against the dbo.Customers table represented in Table 10.1:

```
SELECT * FROM Customers WHERE CustomerID = 34689;
```

This code introduces an important question that must be asked: by default, how many rows will SQL Server have to process in order to locate the row with a CustomerID value of 34689? If you answered 500,000, you are correct. Remember, this table is stored as a heap and the data order is not guaranteed in the table—even if the rows were entered in the order of the CustomerID. In addition, the SELECT statement did not use any tricks to indicate that it should stop looking after locating a single match. With the SELECT statement as it is, SQL Server will have to process each one of the 500,000 rows and answer the question, "Is the CustomerID column equal to 34689 in this row?" Clearly, this row-by-row evaluation will take a very long time.

If you do know that every row has a unique CustomerID value, you can get by with the following SELECT statement:

```
SELECT TOP 1 * FROM Customers WHERE CustomerID = 34689;
```

On average, this query would need to process 250,000 records to retrieve the proper row. That's not a shabby improvement, but it's still not as good as what you can achieve with an index.

To see the power of indexes, consider the B-tree structure in Figure 10.2. Assume that the index is a clustered index based on the CustomerID column. Figure 10.2 is not intended to represent the actual way in which this Customers table would be stored, but it does represent a typical storage structure and helps you understand the performance gain provided by a clustered index.

FIGURE 10.2   The B-tree index structure for a clustered index on the Customers table

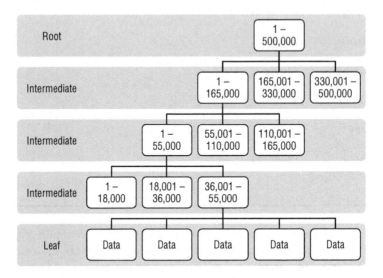

As you walk through the process of accessing CustomerID number 34689 in the B-tree structure, it becomes clear that you will not require nearly as many steps as a manual scan of the heap table requires. Notice that, after one decision, the number of potential rows has been narrowed down to 165,000. After one more decision, the pool is narrowed to 55,000 rows. In just three decisions, you're down to approximately 18,000 rows remaining. Even if you have to scan all 18,000 rows from this point—which you don't—you can say that you've reduced the number of decisions from 250,000 (using the TOP 1 trick in the SELECT statement) to just 18,003 decisions without any SELECT statement tricks.

The real picture is even better. You can jump directly to the data page that has the record and read that page into memory. There is no need to scan the entire page. This result is the reason why database gurus often tell you that you can increase the performance of a table by orders of magnitude when you create effective indexes.

In this example, you looked at the benefit of a clustered index when locating a single row based on the clustered index column. Locating multiple CustomerID values with a SELECT statement like the following also benefits from the clustered index:

```
SELECT * FROM Customers
WHERE CustomerID IN (123, 456, 789, 012, 4574, 8907, 4807, 897843);
```

In this case, you're looking for eight different customer records; however, you can still retrieve them using the B-Tree index and it will be much faster than a manual table scan (reading every row).

The next section will explain the way in which nonclustered indexes improve performance.

 WARNING   Although indexes can be extremely helpful, it is important to note that you can create too many indexes. When a DBA first learns that indexes improve performance, he will often assume that an index should be created on every column. However, if the column is not used in a filter (a WHERE clause) it will rarely improve performance.

Index Types

The type of indexes supported by SQL Server continues to grow with each new edition. SQL Server 2008 supports the following indexes for storage within the database:

- Clustered
- Nonclustered
- Spatial
- Partitioned
- XML
- Filtered

These index types are defined and explained in the following sections.

Clustered Indexes

Clustered indexes are the most important type of index for most tables. As explained in the previous section, a clustered index can reduce the decisions required to locate a specific record by a factor of many thousands. The only tables that should not have a clustered index are very small tables (those with fewer than a few hundred records). If all of the records will fit in one data page, there is certainly no use in having a clustered index on that table. However, most production tables grow to hundreds if not millions of rows, and the clustered index will greatly improve the performance of these larger tables.

When you create a clustered index on a table, the indexed column is used to structure or sort the table. The table will be ordered based on the clustered index. In the vast majority of tables, the clustered index column will be a single column and that column will usually be the record ID. For example, a customer ID or a product ID makes for a great clustered index candidate.

In most cases, the clustered index will be created on a single column. SQL Server 2008 does support creating multiple-column clustered indexes. For example, you may want to create a clustered index for a table used to track manufacturing equipment operations by combining a Time column and a Date column similar to those in Table 10.2. In this table, both the Time values and the Date values repeat; however, the combination of a time on a date will never repeat. These columns make for good clustered index candidates and the need for an extra ID column is removed, which reduces the size of the table.

TABLE 10.2 Multicolumn Clustered Index Table

Time	Date	Temperature	PPM_Rate	Uptime
09:12:30	1/1/2009	30	4	12
09:12:45	1/1/2009	31	3.5	12
...	...	...	...	...
09:12:30	1/2/2009	32	3.8	36
09:12:45	1/2/2009	31	3.6	36

When you create a primary key on a table, by default SQL Server will make that primary key the clustered index. If a clustered index is manually created before you assign the primary key, then SQL Server will not make the primary key the clustered index. It would be very rare to use a column other than the primary key as the clustered index, but it is an option.

Nonclustered Indexes

Nonclustered indexes are very different from clustered indexes. A *nonclustered index* is a separately stored index of a table. The indexed table may be a heap or a clustered index. If the indexed table is a heap, the nonclustered index uses the row identifier (RID) as the reference to the table. If the indexed table is a clustered index, the nonclustered index uses the clustered index key (the primary key value) as the reference to the table. You can create as many as 249 nonclustered indexes on a single table, but in most cases you'll create fewer than 20 to 40 percent of *n*, where *n* is the total number of columns in the table.

Nonclustered indexes are like the index at the back of a book. For example, as you are reading this book, you may decide that you want to locate information about nonclustered indexes. You can turn to the index at the back of the book and look for the keywords "non-clustered" or "index." Once you find the keyword, you will turn to the page or pages referenced in the index. Next, you will scan the page to locate the desired information.

Nonclustered database indexes are used in a similar way to the index at the back of this book. Consider the Customers table in Table 10.1 again. What if you wanted to retrieve all of the customers with a last name of Mathys? You might run a query like the following:

```
SELECT * FROM Customers WHERE LastName = 'Mathys';
```

Without a nonclustered index, you're right back to scanning every row again in order to locate the records matching the query. If you create a nonclustered index on the LastName column, everything changes for the better. Now, SQL Server can work its way through the B-tree index and locate the first row where the LastName value is equal to Mathys. Because the rows are ordered by the LastName column in the nonclustered index, the database engine can just keep reading until the row is no longer equal to Mathys.

Once a matching record is retrieved from the nonclustered index, the RID or primary key of the indexed table is provided. This key is used to then navigate through the indexed table to locate the actual matching record. If the indexed table is a heap, the performance gain is not even close to the level of that which is achieved with a clustered index.

A special kind of nonclustered index is a *covering index*, which includes all of the columns needed to service a query. The actual data is stored in the leaf pages of the covering index. For example, consider the following query:

```
SELECT CustomerID, FirstName, LastName, eMail
FROM Customers
WHERE LastName = 'Carpenter';
```

This query needs only four columns of potentially dozens available in the table. If you create an index that includes all four columns, the query will be much faster. Query performance can be improved by more than 1,000 times by creating a covering index. You should make sure that the query is run very frequently before creating a covering index for it. If you create a covering index for a query that is seldom or never run, you're just wasting space in the database. The process for creating a covering index is provided in Exercise 10.4 later in this chapter.

Spatial Indexes

Spatial indexes are special indexes used for geometric or geographic data. To use a spatial index, you must have spatial data. Spatial data is data that references geometric (width, height, etc.) or geographic (longitude, latitude, etc.) information. Spatial data columns use the geometry or geography data types. Both spatial data and spatial indexes are new in SQL Server 2008. For more information on spatial data and spatial indexes, search for **Spatial Indexing Overview** in SQL Server 2008 Books Online.

Partitioned Indexes

Partitioned indexes, like partitioned tables, are indexes stored on partitions rather than directly on filegroups. Partitioned indexes are usually used with partitioned tables. If you create an index on a table that is partitioned and do not specify otherwise, the index will automatically be partitioned to match the underlying table. You can also create a partition function and partition scheme that specifies a separate set of filegroups from the table and then place the partitioned index on the partition scheme regardless of whether the underlying table is partitioned. Many DBAs are unaware that you can store indexes separate from the table. Indeed, you can store the indexes on a separate filegroup or on a separate partition scheme.

XML Indexes

XML indexes are created for XML data columns. XML data columns contain XML data, which is highly structured and portable data formatted according to the XML (extensible markup language) specification. Two XML indexes exist: primary and secondary. The primary XML index indexes all of the XML information in the column for each row. Secondary XML indexes are used to further optimize indexing of the XML data. Secondary XML indexes come in three types:

PATH: PATH XML indexes are most useful when application queries use path expressions.

VALUE: VALUE XML indexes are most useful when application queries are value-based. A value-based query is one that seeks XML data where the value of an XML element is equal to some specified value.

PROPERTY: PROPERTY XML indexes are most useful when applications use the XML `value` method of Transact-SQL.

Filtered Indexes

The final type of index and a new type in SQL Server 2008 is the filtered index. *Filtered indexes* are useful for columns that contain a large percentage of NULL values or that have well-defined value sets. Filtered indexes are created by adding a `WHERE` clause to the `CREATE INDEX` statement when creating indexes in Transact-SQL. The steps required to create a filtered index are provided in Exercise 10.5 later in this chapter.

Filtered indexes provide several benefits including:

- Statistics are filtered as well as the row data. This fact means that the statistics are actually more accurate for a filtered index.

- Filtered indexes consume less storage space because rows not matching the `WHERE` clause (the filter) are not included in the index.

- Maintenance of the index is reduced because the index is smaller and will be updated less frequently than a nonclustered index created against the entire table.

As an example of a filtered index, consider a column that is used to store email addresses for customers. For example, a store may ask customers for their email addresses when they check out with their purchases. Many customers will choose not to provide the email address. By creating a filtered index, which does not index records with a NULL value in the email column, you will create a smaller index that performs better.

Creating Basic Indexes

Now that you understand what indexes are, how they work, and the different types of indexes, it's time to start creating some indexes. The following sections will step you through creating both clustered and nonclustered indexes.

Creating a Clustered Index

You will now create a clustered index in the most common way—by creating a primary key. In order to perform the steps in Exercise 10.1, you must first create a table in the Books database with the following code:

```
CREATE TABLE dbo.Customers (
    CustomerID int NOT NULL,
    FirstName varchar(50),
    LastName varchar(50),
    eMail varchar(60),
    Phone int,
    City varchar(40),
    State char(2),
    ZipCode int
    );
```

You can enter and execute this code in a New Query window within SSMS. Ensure that you are in the context of the Books database created in previous chapters of this book. Figure 10.3 shows the execution of this code within the Books database context.

FIGURE 10.3   Creating the Customers table for the Books database

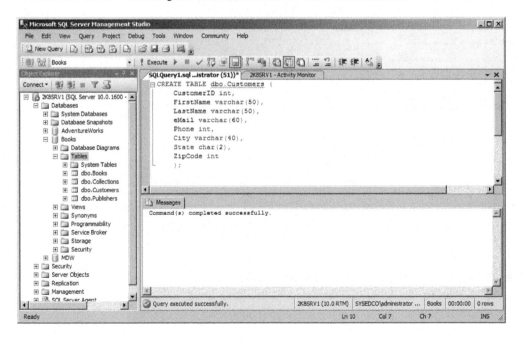

Exercise 10.1 steps you through the creation of a clustered index on a table by creating a primary key for the table.

EXERCISE 10.1

Setting the Primary Key

To configure the primary key, you will need to first open the Customers table in the Table Designer. Follow these steps:

1. Expand the Books database node and then expand the Tables node within the Books database by double-clicking on each node.

2. Right-click on the dbo.Customers table and select Design.

3. In the Table Designer, select the CustomerID column and select the Table Designer ≻ Set Primary Key menu option from the main menus. The results should look similar to those in the following image.

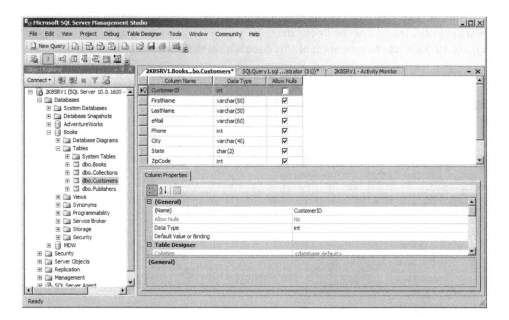

4. Click File ≻ Save Customers to save the changes to the table.

5. Close the Table Designer by clicking File ≻ Close.

After you've configured the primary key, you should verify that a clustered index exists on the table. You can do this in two ways: verify that a PK_*name* object exists in the table's indexes node or open the table in the Table Designer and verify that the CustomerID column has a yellow key assigned, or click Table Designer ➢ Indexes and Keys to view the primary key as shown in Figure 10.4.

FIGURE 10.4   Verifying the primary key for the clustered index

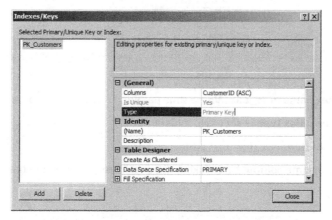

Notice that Create As Clustered is set to YES and the Type is Primary Key.

Creating a Nonclustered Index

Knowing how to create nonclustered indexes is also important. The following section steps you through the creation of two nonclustered indexes on the Customers table, building on the table that was created with the CREATE TABLE statement earlier in this section.

In order to perform this exercise, the Customers table must exist in the Books database. This table was created with the CREATE TABLE statement earlier. In Exercise 10.2, you will create a nonclustered index on the LastName column.

EXERCISE 10.2

Creating the LastName Nonclustered Index

To create the nonclustered index, follow these steps:

1. Expand the Books database node and then expand the Tables node within the Books database by double-clicking on each node.

2. Expand the dbo.Customers node by double-clicking on it and then expand the Indexes node within dbo.Customers.

3. Right-click the Indexes node and select New Index.

4. Enter the index name of *ix_LastName* (this naming convention is not required).

5. Ensure that the index type is set to Nonclustered.

6. Click the Add button.

7. Select the LastName column by checking the check box, as shown in the following image.

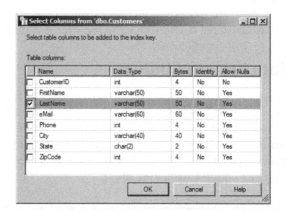

8. Click OK.

9. Verify your settings against the following image.

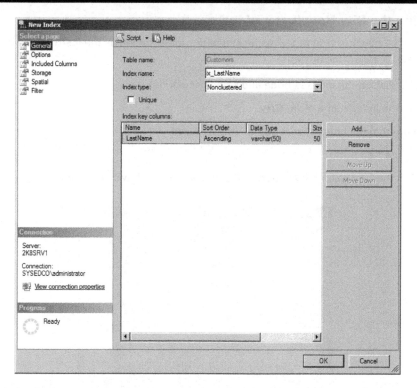

10. Click the Options page.

11. Enable the Allow Online Processing of DML Statements While Creating the Index option.

12. Click the OK button to create the index.

You should now see a nonclustered index in the Indexes node, as shown in the following image.

Exercise 10.3 provides instructions for creating a nonclustered index on the City column of the Customers database. When you are creating nonclustered indexes, consider the queries the users will perform. You will usually want to create nonclustered indexes on columns that are frequently used in the WHERE clauses of SELECT statements.

EXERCISE 10.3

Creating the City Nonclustered Index

To create the nonclustered index, while still in the same screen as the instructions in Exercise 10.2, follow these steps:

1. Right-click on the Indexes node and select New Index.
2. Enter the index name of *ix_City*.
3. Ensure that the index type is set to Nonclustered.
4. Click the Add button.
5. Select the City column by checking the check box, as shown in the following image.

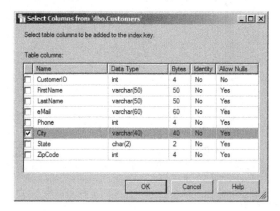

6. Click OK.
7. Click the Options page.
8. Enable the Allow Online Processing of Dml Statements While Creating the Index option. This option allows users to add data to the Customers table while the ix_City index is created.
9. Click the OK button to create the index.

    You should now see a nonclustered index in the Indexes node as shown in the following image.

Creating a Transact-SQL Index

In addition to the creation of indexes in the GUI interface, you can create indexes using Transact-SQL. The following syntax is used:

```
CREATE [ UNIQUE ] [ CLUSTERED | NONCLUSTERED ] INDEX index_name
    ON <object> ( column [ ASC | DESC ] [ ,...n ] )
    [ INCLUDE ( column_name [ ,...n ] ) ]
    [ WHERE <filter_predicate> ]
    [ WITH ( <relational_index_option> [ ,...n ] ) ]
    [ ON { partition_scheme_name ( column_name )
        | filegroup_name
        | default
        }
    ]
[FILESTREAM_ON {filestream_filegroup_name | partition_scheme_name | "NULL"}];
```

Consider the following code, which would create the same index for the LastName column that was created in Exercise 10.2:

```
CREATE NONCLUSTERED INDEX ix_LastName
ON dbo.Customers(LastName ASC)
WITH (ONLINE=ON);
```

This simple code creates a nonclustered index on the LastName column of the Customers table and sorts the index ascending. The default is to sort in ascending order so the ASC keyword can be removed and the code will still generate the same results.

Creating Advanced Indexes

Two of the most important indexes to understand in SQL Server 2008 are covering indexes and filtered indexes. Covering indexes existed in previous versions of SQL Server, but filtered indexes are new. The exercises in this section will walk you through the process of creating each type of index.

Creating a Covering Index

In this section, you will create a *covering index*, which is a special multicolumn index used to cover frequently executed queries. The Customers table must exist in the Books database. In order to perform the steps in Exercise 10.4, you should have already performed the steps in Exercises 10.1 through 10.3.

You may have noticed that users are performing many queries that look like the following:

```
SELECT CustomerID, FirstName, eMail, City
WHERE City = 'somecity';
```

You want to optimize these queries by creating a covering index that includes all of the columns required by the query. The required columns are CustomerID, FirstName, eMail, and City. Exercise 10.4 will step you through the process of creating an index to cover this query.

EXERCISE 10.4

Creating the Covering Index

To create a covering index, follow these steps:

1. Open SSMS and navigate to the Indexes node within the Customers table within the Books database.

2. Right-click on the Indexes node and select New Index.

3. Enter an index name of **cov_EmailMkt**.

4. Ensure that the index type is set to Nonclustered.

5. Click the Add button.

6. Select the City column, as in the following image (notice that the index is being structured based on the WHERE clause column).

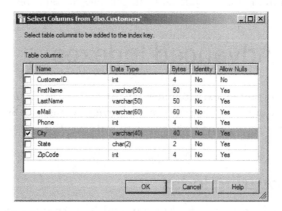

7. Click OK.

8. Click the Included Columns page.

9. Click the Add button.

10. Select the CustomerID, FirstName, and eMail columns, as in the following image.

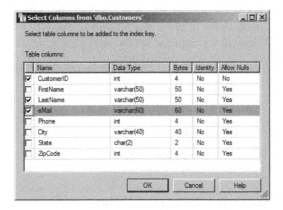

11. Click OK.

12. Click OK again to create the index.

At this point, you should see an index named cov_EmailMkt in the Indexes node of the Customers table.

Creating a Filtered Index

Now that you've explored covering indexes, Exercise 10.5 will step you through the process of creating filtered indexes. *Filtered indexes,* as discussed earlier in this chapter, are indexes that only include rows that match a filter on the column. Filtered indexes result in smaller indexes, but they should be used with caution. If you create a filtered index on a column with few NULL values and lots of variation in entered values, much of the data may be missing from the index. The result of such a scenario would often be an underperforming index. Filtered indexes are most frequently created for columns with NULL values.

In this section, you will create a filtered index. The Customers table must exist in the Books database. In order to perform the steps in Exercise 10.5, you should have already performed the steps in Exercises 10.1 and 10.2.

Creating the Filtered Index

In this exercise, you will create a filtered index. In the real world, you may have noticed that more than 35 percent of your customers do not provide their email addresses. You have a nonclustered index on the eMail column of the Customer table. You have dropped the index and want to create a new index that is filtered so that NULL email rows are not included in the index. To create the appropriate filtered index, follow these steps:

1. Open SSMS and navigate to the Indexes node within the Customers table within the Books database.

2. Right-click on the Indexes node and select New Index.

3. Enter an index name of **fix_Email**.

4. Ensure that the index type is set to Nonclustered.

5. Click the Add button.

6. Select the Email column, as in the following image.

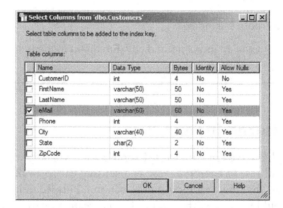

7. Click OK.

8. Select the Filter page.

9. Enter **eMail IS NOT NULL** in the Filter Expression field, as in the following image.

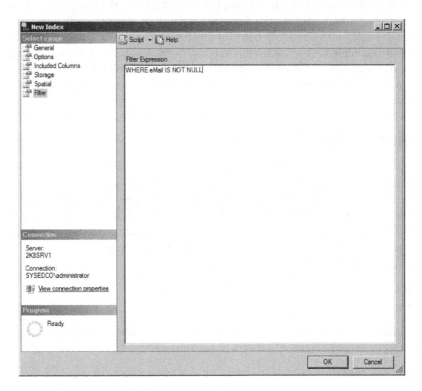

10. Click OK to create the filtered index.

At this point, you should see an index named fix_Email in the Indexes node of the Customers table.

You can also create filtered indexes with Transact-SQL code. The key addition to the CREATE INDEX statement is the WHERE clause. Just as the WHERE clause allows for filtering with SELECT statements, it allows for filtering with indexes starting in SQL Server 2008. The following code creates a filtered index on the Price column of a Products table, where the NULL prices are not included in the index:

```
CREATE NONCLUSTERED INDEX fix_Prices
ON dbo.Products (Price)
WHERE Price IS NOT NULL;
```

Managing Indexes

Indexes must be managed. You cannot simply create them and then forget they exist. For instance, you may need to delete an index if the method of data access changes. You can also disable an index temporarily in order to test performance or functionality without it. When testing is complete, you'll want to enable it. Indexes can also become fragmented and, when this happens, you'll need to either reorganize or rebuild the indexes in order to maintain acceptable levels of performance. All of these issues will be addressed in the following sections.

Dropping an Index

Indexes may be deleted at any time. The proper SQL term for object deletion or removal is *drop*. You drop databases, tables, indexes, triggers, stored procedures, and other objects. Data is deleted with DELETE commands, but objects are dropped with DROP commands. However, it is common to say you want to delete an object. In fact, if you right-click on an index in SSMS, the menu indicates that you can delete the index even though the process will call the T-SQL DROP command if you choose the menu option.

The syntax of the DROP INDEX command is as follows:

```
DROP INDEX index_name
ON table_name;
```

For example, to drop the fix_Email index created on the dbo.Customers table earlier in this chapter, you would execute the following command:

```
DROP INDEX fix_Email
ON dbo.Customers;
```

The most important thing to remember is that the syntax calls for an ON clause and not a FROM clause. It may seem more natural to drop something from something, but the syntax should be thought of as dropping something that is defined by its name and its location. In the example of the fix_Email index, the name is fix_Email and the named object is located on the dbo.Customers table.

Disabling and Enabling Indexes

Sometimes you want to disable an index instead of deleting it. You may want to test the performance of a query without the index so that you can justify the existence of the index. At any time, you can right-click on an index and select Disable in SSMS. When you do this, you will see a screen similar to the one in Figure 10.5. This will leave the definition of the index in the database, but the index will be unavailable.

Look closely at Figure 10.5. Notice the text warning indicates that you enable the index again by rebuilding it. It seems logical to think that if you disable the index with a disable option, you should be able to enable the index with an enable option. This is not the case. You must rebuild the index to enable it. Right-click the index and select Rebuild, and you will see a screen similar to the one in Figure 10.6.

FIGURE 10.5   Disabling an index within SSMS

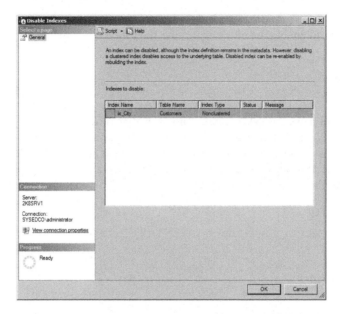

FIGURE 10.6   Enabling an index with the Rebuild option

You can also disable and enable indexes using T-SQL code. The following code would disable the ix_City index created earlier in this chapter:

```
ALTER INDEX ix_City
ON dbo.Customers
DISABLE;
```

When you want to enable the index again, use the following code:

```
ALTER INDEX ix_City
ON dbo.Customers
REBUILD;
```

Now for the bad news. In SSMS, there is no immediate indicator that an index is disabled. Even if you right-click on the index and select Properties, you will not see any indicator that the index is disabled. How then do you determine if an index is disabled or not? You can use the INDEXPROPERTY function. This T-SQL function returns information about indexes. Consider the following code:

```
ALTER INDEX ix_City
ON dbo.Customers
DISABLE;

SELECT INDEXPROPERTY
(
    OBJECT_ID('dbo.Customers'),
    'ix_City',
    'IsDisabled'
)
GO

ALTER INDEX ix_City
ON dbo.Customers
REBUILD;

SELECT INDEXPROPERTY
(
    OBJECT_ID('dbo.Customers'),
    'ix_City',
    'IsDisabled'
)
GO
```

The first ALTER INDEX command disables the ix_City index. Then the SELECT INDEXPROPERTY command reads the IsDisabled property of the ix_City index. Figure 10.7 shows the results generated when this code is executed. Notice that the first SELECT statement returns a value of 1. Next, the code rebuilds the index and then the SELECT statement returns a value of 0. The IsDisabled property is set to 1 when the index is disabled and 0 when it is not.

FIGURE 10.7   Viewing the IsDisabled property of the ix_City index in both the disabled and enabled states

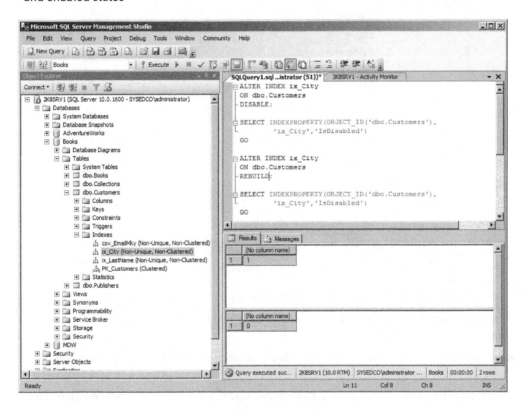

Understanding Index Fragmentation

You must be aware of one final fact about indexes. Indexes can become fragmented over time. In much the same way as the files on your hard drive become fragmented and cause poor performance, a fragmented index causes performance to suffer as well. You can check the fragmentation level on an index by right-clicking the index in question and selecting Properties. From here, click the Fragmentation page and not the Total Fragmentation. Figure 10.8 shows the fragmentation level for an index in the AdventureWorks database.

FIGURE 10.8 Viewing the fragmentation level on an index

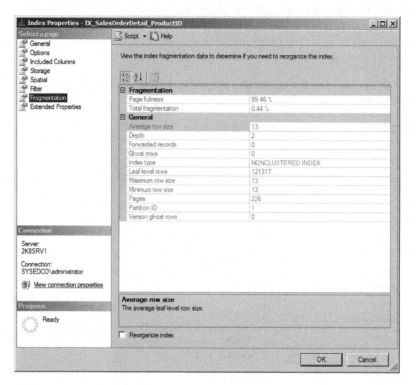

You can defragment an index in one of three ways:

Drop and re-create the index. Because the index is being re-created from scratch, it will remove excess fragmentation.

Rebuild the index. The ALTER INDEX... REBUILD statement actually drops and re-creates the index for you.

Reorganize the index. The ALTER INDEX... REORGANIZE statement attempts to do an online reorganization and lower fragmentation through this effort.

Which of these should you use? The choice is yours when making the decision between dropping and re-creating the index or rebuilding the index as the end result is the same. When choosing between rebuilding and reorganizing, Microsoft recommends that you reorganize when fragmentation is between 5 and 30 percent. Any index fragmented above 30 percent should be rebuilt.

To rebuild or reorganize an index, right-click the index in SSMS and select Rebuild or Reorganize. You can also right-click on the Indexes node in a given table and choose Reorganize All or Rebuild All to massively defragment all indexes.

In most cases, you'll want to automate index maintenance. SQL Server jobs can be used to automate the reorganizing or rebuilding of indexes. Jobs will be covered in detail in

Chapter 13, "Creating Jobs, Operators, or Alerts." You can also automate index maintenance through the use of maintenance plans. Maintenance plans will be covered in Chapter 16, "Backup and Restoration."

 Index fragmentation can sneak up on you. You can use a database for years and notice no real change in performance. Then, in a period of a few weeks, performance can be degraded drastically. This is usually caused by massive changes to the data that happen only after years of use—archives, imports, exports, etc. If you do not have automatic index maintenance in place, be sure to periodically check the fragmentation levels of the indexes.

Understanding Views

What is a view? A view is a beautiful sight that you sometimes see while driving along a road or highway. They are often marked as scenic overlooks. Someone at some point determined that large numbers of people would be interested in seeing that view, so they built a special location where cars could pull off to the side of the road and people could take in the beauty.

Of course, this section is talking about SQL Server databases and not scenic views; yet a view in a database can also be a beautiful thing—at least to your users. For example, imagine that you have a set of customer data spread across the following tables:

- Customers
- Cities
- States
- Addresses
- Websites

Now, in order to get the complete view of a customer information set, the user must join these five tables. If the user must do this each time she wants to use the tables, it will be quite frustrating. A database view aggregates this information so that it appears to be in one location. The view creates a unique collective perspective on the data. Technically, a *view* is a stored SELECT statement. However, you can do some special things with these SELECT statements stored as views, such as:

- Create an index on the view to materialize it for improved performance
- Set permission on the view as if it were a table
- Include the results of functions in the view

You can do even more than this, but this short list should begin to show the benefits of views.

When a user queries a nonindexed view, the first thing SQL Server does is run the stored SELECT statement that is the view so that the user's query can be run against that result set. For this reason, the performance of the query against the view will be less impressive than the performance of the query had it been written directly against the view's underlying tables. This fact must always be remembered when creating views. Querying a nonindexed view is never as fast as querying the underlying tables directly. Do not use nonindexed views to improve performance; use them to improve usability or to implement security abstraction.

Indexed views are simply views on which a clustered index has been created. When you create a unique clustered index on a view, you are basically indicating that you want a table to be created that matches the result set of the stored SELECT statement in the view. Indexed views perform, usually, better than direct queries against the underlying tables. This improved performance is due to the fact that the view contains only the data that is requested of the user. If the user queried the tables directly, all of the columns of data would be there and the performance would be diminished.

However, you should not haphazardly implement indexed views just because they improve the performance of the query. Indexed views always diminish the performance of updates, inserts, and deletes. The reason for this diminished performance is simple: every time you update, insert, or delete values in the underlying tables, the view must be updated as well. Therefore, indexed views are useful on mostly read tables (most operations are SELECT operations), but they can be very bad for mostly write tables (most operations are UPDATE, INSERT, or DELETE operations).

Creating Views

Views can be created in the GUI or with T-SQL. Exercise 10.6 details how to create a view in the GUI.

EXERCISE 10.6

Creating a View

To create a view in the GUI, follow these steps:

1. Expand the database in which you want to create the view, and you'll see a Views node or container.

2. Right-click on the Views container and select New View. You'll be presented with a screen similar to the one in the following image.

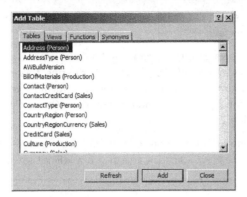

3. From here, you can select the tables, views, functions, or synonyms on which you want to base your view.

4. After you've selected the objects, click OK. Now you are presented with a screen similar to the one in the following image.

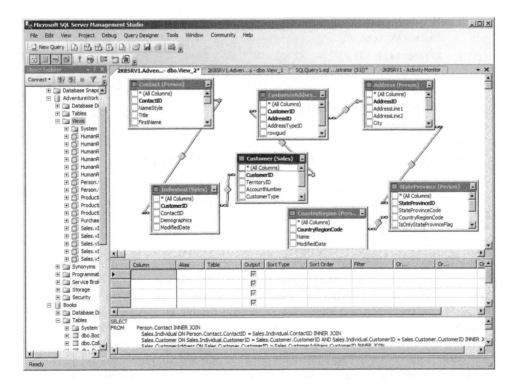

5. From here, you can select the columns you want to include in the SELECT statement that will become the view.

6. Once the columns are selected, you can use the Criteria pane to enter filtering information. If you've used Microsoft Access to build queries, this interface is very similar and will feel quite natural to you. If you're more comfortable writing the filters as WHERE clauses, use the SQL pane in the bottom of the Query Designer window to manually add the filters.

7. With the SELECT statement built, you're ready to save the view. Click File ➢ Save and provide a name for the view. Click OK and the view will be saved.

You can also create views using T-SQL. For example, the following code results in a view named vBooksPubs that uses the Books and Publishers tables from the Books database:

```
CREATE VIEW dbo.vBooksPubs
AS
    SELECT
        dbo.Books.BookID,
        dbo.Books.Title,
        dbo.Books.PublisherID,
        dbo.Books.Copyright,
        dbo.Books.EstimatedValue
    FROM dbo.Books
    INNER JOIN dbo.Publishers
    ON dbo.Books.PublisherID = dbo.Publishers.PublisherID;
```

Summary

In this chapter, you learned about indexes and views. First, you explored indexes and learned how they can help to improve the performance of a database when they are properly designed. You also learned about the different types of indexes and how to create them. Index maintenance was addressed as you discovered how to drop, disable, enable, rebuild, and reorganize indexes.

Next, you learned about views and the simplicity they introduce to data access for your users. Views allow you to aggregate data together into a virtual table so that users can more easily access that data. Additionally, views can be indexed to improve the performance of data access.

Chapter Essentials

Understanding Indexes   The key to implementing an effective indexing strategy is understanding what indexes are and how they function. Clustered indexes dictate the way in which a table should be stored. Nonclustered indexes are stored separately from the table. Filtered indexes allow you to limit the rows included in the index with standard WHERE clauses.

Creating Basic Indexes   Indexes can be created using the GUI interface or T-SQL code. The CREATE INDEX statement is used to create indexes in T-SQL. It's a good idea to save the T-SQL code used to create the index in case you ever have to re-create it again. You can generate the T-SQL code from the Script button even if you create the indexes within the GUI.

Creating Advanced Indexes   Covered indexes include all of the columns necessary to service a given SELECT statement. Covered indexes are created using the Included Columns page in the GUI. Filtered indexes use WHERE clauses to implement filtering. On the Filtered index page omit the WHERE keyword, but include the remainder of the WHERE clause. For example, WHERE email = 0 becomes email = 0.

Managing Indexes   At times you may need to temporarily disable an index. You can do this with the ALTER INDEX... DISABLE construct. To enable the index again, you will need to use the ALTER INDEX... REBUILD construct. Indexes are dropped rather than deleted in T-SQL code so the command is DROP INDEX. You should reorganize indexes fragmented between 5 and 30 percent and indexes fragmented by more than 30 percent should be rebuilt.

Understanding Views   Views are simply stored SELECT statements when they are nonindexed. Indexed views store the actual result set of the SELECT statement as an object in the database. Indexed views should not be used on tables that are heavily used for write operations. Views can be helpful in abstracting permission management (you can assign permissions to the view without having to assign permissions to each underlying table) and in simplifying data access for your users.

Creating Views   Views can be created in the GUI Query Designer or in T-SQL. The CREATE VIEW statement is used to create views with code. The Query Designer simplifies view creation because you do not have to write complex JOIN statements manually and typos are also removed from the equation.

Chapter

11

Triggers and Stored Procedures

TOPICS COVERED IN THIS CHAPTER:

✓ Triggers Defined

✓ Using Triggers

✓ Creating Triggers

✓ Understanding Stored Procedures

✓ Creating Stored Procedures

Do not let the length of this chapter fool you. Triggers and stored procedures are two of the most valuable tools available to the DBA. Because this book is focused on the DBA's role and not the application developer's role, this chapter will focus on triggers and stored procedures from the perspective of administrative tasks instead of application development. Triggers are helpful because they can save the administrator from both wasted time and problems through the automation of common monitoring and administrative tasks. Stored procedures can be used to create administrative scripts that you will run again and again, and they can also provide time-saving and error prevention benefits. This chapter will provide examples for both triggers and stored procedures so you can see first-hand the value they bring. If you are ready to see how these two SQL Server objects can be used to reduce your administrative load, read on.

Triggers Defined

A *trigger* is an action or set of actions that should be carried out if another action or event occurs. SQL Server triggers act a lot like triggers you experience in everyday life. For example, when the alarm clock goes off, it triggers the action of waking up. When the microwave bell sounds, you are triggered to open the door and pull out the hot food. When the dryer buzzer sounds, you are triggered to check the clothes in the electric dryer and see if they are ready to be removed. Database triggers work in exactly the same way. Triggers can respond to the firing event automatically or simply notify an administrator that the firing event has occurred.

For example, if you want to validate every update statement that is executed against a specific table, you can create a trigger that is fired when an update statement runs. The trigger contains the logic (code) that should be processed for every update statement. The trigger can be used for many things, as shown here:

- To ensure that the new data meets business requirements
- To prevent unauthorized users from making changes that would be difficult to enforce with permissions alone
- To make backup copies of the old data before the new data is written to the table
- To add information to additional tables that the update statement does not specify
- To notify an individual of the change if the change warrants a notification

However, because this book is for the DBA and not the programmer, it is important to focus on how triggers can be used for administrative purposes. Yet programmers will also find tremendous value in understanding the administrative side of SQL Server, so this chapter will also be helpful for those readers. So in what way can a DBA use triggers? It's all about notifications. You can use triggers to be notified when:

- Large scale deletions occur
- New users are added to the database
- Large-scale modifications occur
- Schema changes occur

Do you see a pattern? For years, triggers were used to implement auditing processes; yet even with the new auditing features included in SQL Server 2008, triggers are still beneficial and may be preferred due to their extreme flexibility.

In addition to notifications, administrators can also use triggers to:

- Prevent accidental deletions of data or tables
- Enforce naming conventions for modifications to tables or for additional tables, views, or even databases

It's true that you can enforce naming conventions with policy-based management; however, policy-based management is really only useful in larger deployments. If you run a smaller SQL Server installation base (five or fewer servers), which is the way in which SQL Server is run in most installations, you may still be better off using triggers. In the next section, "Using Triggers," you'll see several specific examples of real-world triggers that are being used in organizations.

How Triggers Differ from Stored Procedures

A trigger is very similar to a stored procedure, which is covered later in this chapter from a DBA's perspective as well, once you get past the initial CREATE TRIGGER construction. Just like stored procedures, triggers can use variables and logical constructs, and they can also access databases. In fact, triggers have two things that stored procedures do not.

- Triggers can be launched by an event without any special development requirements. The engine used to watch for the event is already there and the DBA need only create the trigger.
- Triggers have access to virtual tables that are essential to their intended operations. One virtual table is named "inserted" and the other is named "deleted." The inserted table contains the new values, and the deleted table contains the old values. These tables are available for any INSERT, UPDATE, or DELETE trigger and are called memory-resident tables because they do not exist on disk.

Types of Triggers

Triggers come in two basic types:

DML The DML triggers apply to data manipulation language events.

DDL The DDL triggers apply to data definition language events. DML and DDL are subsets of the SQL language.

DML statements include:

- SELECT
- INSERT
- UPDATE
- DELETE

In most cases, SELECT statements do not make changes, and they are not used as events to fire DML triggers. INERT, UPDATE, and DELETE statements do make changes, and they are used to fire DML triggers.

DDL statements include:

- CREATE
- ALTER
- DROP

All three DDL statements make changes, and they are used as events to fire DDL triggers. The most common DDL triggers are used to intercept improper object deletions (DROP statements), but creative uses of CREATE and ALTER triggers have also been implemented.

Within the DML category of triggers exist three trigger subtypes. The administrator must be careful in the selection of the trigger subtype:

After These execute after the firing code (INSERT, UPDATE, or DELETE statement) is fired. AFTER triggers can only be created on tables.

Instead Of These execute instead of the firing code, not before the firing code. Before triggers do not really exist, although an Instead Of trigger could be created so that it acts as a before trigger. The DBA would simply need to code the trigger to take some actions and then actually execute the code that fired the trigger in the first place. INSTEAD OF triggers can be created on tables and views.

CLR CLR (common language runtime) triggers are used when T-SQL code just can't quite get the job done. CLR triggers can be either DML or DDL, but they are mostly used when heavy mathematical operations are required or processes must be executed that cannot be executed within T-SQL code alone. CLR triggers require development using the .NET Framework provided by Microsoft.

Recursive and Nested Triggers

Triggers can also become recursive and it is important to consider how you will deal with this recursion. A *recursive trigger* is one that is fired by an event and ends up executing the same or similar code equal to the original firing event. The result is that the trigger calls itself. Of course, this structure can result in infinite recursion loops. The good news is that, by default, recursive triggers are disabled on all databases. AFTER triggers will only be able to fire themselves if the RECURSIVE_TRIGGERS option is turned on.

In addition to recursion, triggers can be nested. Trigger nesting simply means that one trigger calls another. Trigger A can call trigger B, which calls trigger C and so on. SQL Server 2008 allows up to 32 levels of trigger nesting for DML and DDL triggers. Of course, trigger nesting could result in indirect recursion; trigger A could call trigger B, which calls trigger C, which calls trigger A. You can only disable indirect recursion by setting the nested triggers option to 0 (off) with the sp_configure command. This option also disables all nested triggers, whether they cause indirect recursion or not. Figure 11.1 shows the T-SQL code used to disable recursive triggers and to disable nested triggers.

FIGURE 11.1   Disabling recursive and nested triggers on the Books database

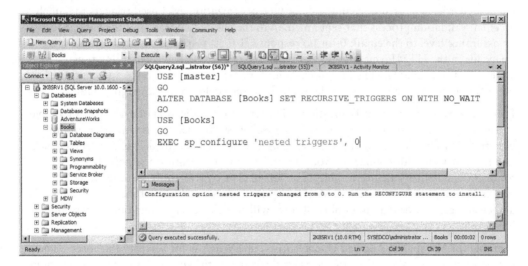

Using Triggers

Now for the fun part: using triggers. How can a DBA use triggers to make her job easier? Wouldn't it be cost effective if you could hire an administrative assistant that costs nothing each hour, but works around the clock? That's exactly what you get when you use triggers.

With triggers, you can take automatic action that you've taken manually in the past. If you have any alerts that require your intervention, however, you should look at them closely to determine how to proceed and answer these questions. Can the actions you would take in response to these alerts be automated in T-SQL code? If they can be automated, is the event a DDL or DML event? If the answer is yes to both, then you can use triggers as unpaid assistants.

To get an idea for how you can use triggers to assist you with administrative tasks, consider the following DML trigger uses:

Exporting Data When the New Data Volume Reaches a Particular Level   Imagine a user has asked you to export the 1,000 newest records when those records become available. A trigger can do the trick for you. You can create a trigger that runs with each INSERT statement. The trigger will keep a running count (in a table) of how many times it has executed and the record ID for each inserted row. When the counter reaches 1,000, all inserted rows are exported and the counter is reset to 0.

Ensuring Data Integrity Through Complex Logic   Data integrity can be enforced through data types and constraints, but triggers expose the entire T-SQL language to be used for data integrity enforcement. This fact means that DBAs can implement databases with a much higher level of assurance in the data. One organization even used triggers to launch an email validation process that sent an email to the entered address and then assigned an assurance level to the email: 0 for no response, 1 for a response based on access to an image file in the HTML email, and 2 for when the user actually clicked a link to validate the email. The trigger launched the process and triggers on another table and continued the process until a final update was made to the assurance column in the original table.

Preventing Accidental Table Truncation   The term for the deletion of every row in a table is *truncation*. In fact, a T-SQL command named TRUNCATE TABLE exists to perform this very function. Be careful, however, because users may accidentally delete all of the records in a table by using this command. You can prevent this by creating a trigger that watches for DELETE statements against a table. If no WHERE clause exists in the DELETE statement, the trigger can simply reject the action. More complex triggers could inspect the DELETE statement and ensure that fewer than n number of rows will be deleted based on your predetermined limit.

Limiting the Number of Allowed Updates in a Time Window for Security Purposes   The easiest way to think about this trigger use is through a fictitious scenario. Suppose one organization had been attacked by a malicious cracker who intended only to do harm and not to steal information. The cracker had modified data and set various columns to apparently random values. The suspect did this to more than 1,000 records in less than 10 minutes. The organization determined that a normal user would not update more than five values in one minute. A trigger was added to each table that tracked (in another table) the number of DML UPDATE statements executed by a user within a one-minute window. If the total number of updates exceeded the norm, the user's connection was killed and the specific user account was disabled in case the account was hijacked. While this is a fictitious scenario, similar situations exist in the real world and this trigger can help to prevent severe damage.

All of these examples represent real-world solutions that companies have implemented with triggers. Now, consider the following real-world DDL trigger uses:

Preventing Accidental or Intentional Table Deletion   In earlier versions of SQL Server, DBAs used a common trick to prevent table deletion: create a view on the table whether the view was needed or not. It works, but now there is a cleaner solution: create a DDL trigger that watches for a DROP TABLE command. If anyone attempts to delete a table—even if they have the proper permissions—the trigger can prevent or delay the action according to your needs.

Sending a Notification to the DBAs When Anyone Changes a Database Property   Using the strategic combination of Database Mail and triggers, you can watch for changes to the database itself. When a change is made, you can have the old option value and the new option value sent to all DBAs via email. You may also choose to log the changes in a table. The point is that you can easily implement this structure with triggers, and it will work for both SQL Server 2005 and 2008—unlike the new auditing features.

Enforcing Naming Conventions in Exactly the Same Way on Both 2005 and 2008 SQL Servers   The new policy-based management (PBM) feature of SQL Server 2008 is greater at enforcing naming conventions for your database objects; however, you may choose not to use it since the 2005 servers are unaware of the technology (they can be configured with the technology, but it is not inherently supported). If you have fewer than five servers, you will probably want to use triggers instead of PBM.

 Real World Scenario

Triggers to the Rescue

On one project, several dozen policies had to be enforced on a SQL Server database. The policies were security-related for the most part and were driven by the organization's security policy documents. The policies could be implemented in the application, but this would require updates to the application code in the clients if the policies changed. The database in question was to be used with several hundred client computers running a local application that accessed the database.

We decided to use triggers to enforce the policies. In the end, we created more than 30 triggers on the database. Some were database-level, others were server-level, and still others were table-level triggers.

Here's the interesting part. About six months after the database was implemented, the company did a major overhaul of their security policies as part of the normal periodic review process. The result of the security policy update was that many of the triggers needed modification. The good news is that the DBA was able to make the changes in a single afternoon, with only two days of testing in the lab before the changes were implemented in the production system. Had the policies been enforced through the client application, a multiweek endeavor would have been required. Triggers, clearly, are very valuable to the DBA.

Creating Triggers

Triggers are created using the CREATE TRIGGER T-SQL command. A trigger is ultimately a collection of one or more lines of T-SQL code, so a GUI tool for the creation of triggers is really not practical. The good news is that the syntax used is rather simple. The following syntax is used for trigger creation:

```
CREATE TRIGGER trigger_name
    ON { table | view | database | all server}
    WITH dml_trigger_option>
    { FOR | AFTER | INSTEAD OF } { event }
    AS
    Insert T-SQL code starting here;
```

Like most CREATE statements, the first thing you do with CREATE TRIGGER is specify a name. Next, you should indicate the trigger level of table, view, database, or server. If the trigger level is a database, table, or view, you specify ON object_name. When the trigger level is the server, you simply specify ALL SERVER.

The WITH <trigger_option> clause can include two primary different options. WITH ENCRYPTION indicates that the actual T-SQL code that is the trigger should be obfuscated or encrypted. If you use WITH ENCRYPTION, you cannot replicate the trigger. WITH EXECUTE AS 'identity_name' specifies an alternative context in which the trigger should execute.

The next option specifies the type of trigger. DDL triggers are specified as FOR or AFTER triggers, and DML triggers are specified as FOR, AFTER, or INSTEAD OF triggers. FOR is a synonym for AFTER. You can specify FOR AFTER, FOR, or AFTER and they all mean the same thing. Note that DDL triggers are always AFTER triggers, but the ROLLBACK option can be used to undo the changes before they are committed to the database.

The event that fires the trigger can be any of dozens of events. The event can be a list of events, as in AFTER UPDATE, INSERT, which would fire the trigger on either an UPDATE statement or an INSERT statement.

When deciding between AFTER and INSTEAD OF triggers for DML events, keep the following guidelines in mind:

- When you know you will rarely undo the changes, use the AFTER trigger.

- When you know you will most frequently change or disallow the action, use the INSTEAD OF trigger.

Examples of AFTER triggers are

- Logging the identity of the calling user, machine, or application

- Archiving the old data values in a separate table

- Adding the data to additional tables

Examples if INSTEAD OF triggers are

- Disallowing the deletion of objects such as tables and views
- Disallowing the update of records by most users with write access through standard UPDATE statements. In these cases, a stored procedure is usually provided as the "proper" way to update records.

The following two examples stick with the theme of using triggers for administrative purposes. The first example is a DML trigger that disallows the execution of a DELETE command that deletes more than one record. Exercise 11.1 steps you through the creation of this trigger. The second example is a DDL trigger that disallows dropping a table. Exercise 11.2 steps you through the creation of the DDL trigger.

EXERCISE 11.1

Creating a DML Trigger

In this exercise, you will create a DML trigger. The trigger will not allow a DELETE statement to execute if a WHERE clause is not specified. The trigger will be created on the Customers table in the Books database. This table was created in Chapter 10, "Indexes and Views."

To begin the process of creating the trigger, you must first launch SSMS and open a New Query window within the context of the Books database:

1. Launch SSMS.

2. Double-click on the Books database within the Databases container.

3. Click the New Query button to open a query window.

4. In the New Query window, enter the following code:

```
CREATE TRIGGER no_unfiltered_delete
ON dbo.Customers
AFTER DELETE
AS
--Begin SQL code of trigger here
IF (SELECT COUNT(*) FROM DELETED) > 1
BEGIN
    PRINT 'You cannot delete more than one record in a single action.';
    ROLLBACK TRANSACTION;
END;
```

5. Execute the code entered in step 4 to create the trigger.

EXERCISE 11.1 *(continued)*

6. If you have not entered any records, add at least two new customer records. You can execute the following code to do this:

```
INSERT INTO dbo.Customers
VALUES (
    100,
    'Joe',
    'Jackson',
    'jj@jj100jj.net',
    5551031,
    'Some City',
    'FL',
    78687
);

INSERT INTO dbo.Customers
VALUES (
    101,
    'Tina',
    'Abushala',
    'ta@ta101ta.net',
    5558970,
    'Some City',
    'FL',
    78687
);
```

7. Now attempt to execute the following code against the Customers table:

```
DELETE FROM CUSTOMERS;
```

8. The command should have failed, and you should see results similar to those in the following image:

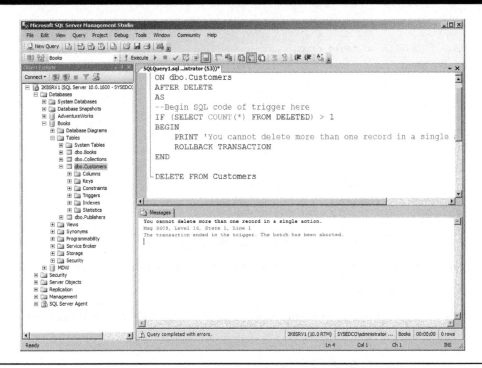

As Exercise 11.1 demonstrates, creating triggers can be simple. However, the benefits they provide are ongoing and automatic. If you want to delete the trigger, you would simply execute the statement DROP TRIGGER no_unfiltered_delete.

Exercise 11.1 shows the power of a trigger to prevent accidental deletions on a specific table at the record level. Exercise 11.2 takes this to the object level and prevents the deletion of entire tables.

EXERCISE 11.2

Creating a DDL Trigger

In this exercise, you will create a DDL trigger. The trigger will not allow a DROP statement to be executed against any table in the Books database. The trigger will be created on the Books database. The Books database must exist in order for this exercise to work properly.

To begin the process of creating the trigger, you must first launch SSMS and open a New Query window within the context of the Books database, as shown here:

1. Launch SSMS.

2. Double-click on the Books database within the Databases container.

3. Click the New Query button to open a query window.

EXERCISE 11.2   *(continued)*

4. In the New Query window, enter the following code:

```
CREATE TRIGGER no_table_drops
ON DATABASE
FOR DROP_TABLE
AS
--Begin SQL code of trigger here
PRINT
    'You cannot delete an entire table.
    In order to drop a table,
    the no_table_drops trigger must
    first be disabled.';
ROLLBACK;
```

5. Execute the code entered in step 4 to create the trigger.

6. Now attempt to execute the following code against the Customers table:

```
DROP TABLE Customers;
```

7. The command should have failed and you should see results similar to those in the following image:

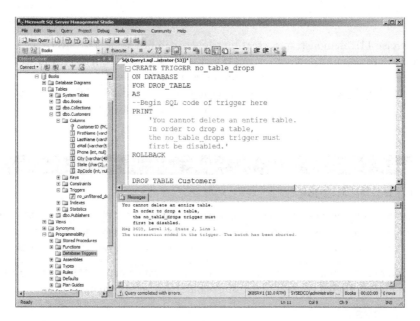

If you want to delete the trigger, simply execute the statement DROP TRIGGER no_table_drops ON DATABASE.

If you have triggers that must be disabled in order to perform administrative tasks, you have two options:

- You can use the DISABLE TRIGGER command.
- You can use the ALTER TRIGGER command.

The following code demonstrates disabling the no_unfiltered_delete trigger with the DISABLE trigger command and disabling the no_table_drops trigger with the ALTER TRIGGER command:

```
ALTER TABLE dbo.Customers
DISABLE TRIGGER no_unfiltered_delete;
GO
DISABLE TRIGGER no_table_drops
ON DATABASE;
GO
```

The following code enables both triggers again:

```
ALTER TABLE dbo.Customers
ENABLE TRIGGER no_unfiltered_delete;
GO
ENABLE TRIGGER no_table_drops
ON DATABASE;
GO
```

You can use either method (ALTER TABLE or DISABLE/ENABLE TRIGGER) with either trigger. It's really just about preference. However, if you right-click on a trigger and select Disable, SSMS uses the ALTER TABLE method behind the scenes.

Understanding Stored Procedures

Now that you have a clear understanding of triggers, let's move on to stored procedures. Microsoft often defines triggers as stored procedures that fire automatically. Of course, a stored procedure is a collection of T-SQL code that can be called upon by an application or by a user. Stored procedures provide several benefits for the developer and the DBA:

Security Abstraction Stored procedures, like triggers, support the EXECUTE AS clause so that the stored procedure can be called by one user, but run in the context of another user. This feature allows you to abstract security. For example, you could create a stored procedure used to update records. The assigned users can call the stored procedure even though they may not have UPDATE access to the target tables.

This technique forces the users to update the data according to business rules, but it also allows for simpler security management. If the users have permissions to execute the stored procedure, they have the ability to update the data.

Centralization of Business Logic   One of the most useful benefits of stored procedures is the centralization of business logic. For example, assume that a user is not allowed to increase the price of a product by more than 3 percent in the Products table. A stored procedure could be created that is used for all price updates. The logic that enforces the 3 percent rule is in the stored procedure. Coupling this with the security abstraction benefit, the user would not have UPDATE access to the Price column in the Products table; however, the user would have EXECUTE permissions on the stored procedure.

If this business logic existed in the client application, all installations of the client would have to be updated whenever the rule changed. As an example, what if the sales manager decides to restrict the rule further so that only 2 percent price adjustments are allowed to the price managers? Now, every client must be updated to support the new rule. If a stored procedure is used instead, one change in the stored procedure enforces the new rule in less than 60 to 90 seconds.

Improved Performance   Stored procedures can also improve performance. Ad hoc T-SQL statements are compiled each time they are executed. By default, stored procedures are not. The execution plan is cached and reused for each successive execution of the stored procedure. This variance in operation can result in a savings of from 10 to 50 milliseconds for each iteration of the procedure. Performance benefits are usually more apparent for SQL code that is executed dozens or even hundreds of times every few minutes.

Because this book is focused on administration, consider the following potential uses of stored procedures for the DBA (all of these examples are based on real-world stored procedures created for clients over the years):

- Standardizing SQL Server login creations by using a custom stored procedure for all user creations
- Exporting data for users without the need to learn Data Transformation Services (SQL Server 2000) or Integration Services (SQL Server 2005 and 2008)
- Disabling and enabling logins quickly
- Archiving data selectively or in mass quantities
- Creating internally standardized objects (such as triggers, tables, views, etc.) in any new database without relying on the model database

Creating Stored Procedures

Stored procedures are created with the CREATE PROCEDURE statement. The syntax used is as follows:

```
CREATE { PROC | PROCEDURE } [schema_name.] procedure_name [ ; number ]
    [ { @parameter [ type_schema_name. ] data_type }
        [ VARYING ] [ = default ] [ OUT | OUTPUT ] [READONLY]
    ] [ ,...n ]
[ WITH <procedure_option> [ ,...n ] ]
[ FOR REPLICATION ]
AS { <sql_statement> [;][ ...n ] | <method_specifier> }
[;]
```

The following example creates a stored procedure named disable_login that can be used to disable a SQL Login account and log a timestamp to the Admin_actions table in the master database:

```
CREATE PROCEDURE dbo.disableuser
    @DenyLoginName varchar(50)
AS
    DECLARE @tempstr  varchar (1024)
    SET @tempstr = 'DENY CONNECT SQL TO ' + @DenyLoginName
    PRINT @tempstr
    EXEC (@tempstr)
    INSERT INTO master.dbo.admin_actions
    VALUES(
        GETDATE(),
        'User disabled: ' + @DenyLoginName
    )
GO
```

If you want to test this stored procedure, create a table in the Master database named admin_actions with the following columns:

- actionID int NOT NULL IDENTITY (1, 1)
- actionTime datetime NULL
- actionDesc nvarchar(100) NULL

Run the stored procedure with a command like the following:

```
disable_login fred
```

This command assumes a SQL login named fred exists on the server. The following code could be used to create an enable_login stored procedure:

```
CREATE PROCEDURE dbo.enableuser
    @DenyLoginName varchar(50)
AS
    DECLARE @tempstr  varchar (1024)
    SET @tempstr = 'GRANT CONNECT SQL TO ' + @DenyLoginName
    PRINT @tempstr
    EXEC (@tempstr)
    INSERT INTO master.dbo.admin_actions
    VALUES(
        GETDATE(),
        'User enabled: ' + @DenyLoginName
    )
GO
```

Summary

In this chapter, you learned about two important administrative tools: triggers and stored procedures. You started with triggers, first seeing how they work and then seeing the different uses they have for administrative automation. You learned how to actually create triggers. Then you moved on to stored procedures and learned the benefits they provide for the developer and the DBA. You learned how to create stored procedures and saw an example of how they can be used for administrative purposes as well.

Chapter Essentials

Triggers Defined Triggers are stored procedures that are launched based on events. Triggers can be DML or DDL driven. Both INSTEAD OF and AFTER triggers are available for DML triggers, but DDL triggers can only work as AFTER triggers. However, ROLLBACK can be used to undo changes even though DDL triggers are AFTER triggers.

Using Triggers Triggers can be used as automation assistants. They can be used to prevent accidental data destruction or loss. Triggers can be used by both developers and DBAs for sometimes different purposes and sometimes shared purposes.

Creating Triggers   Triggers are created with the CREATE TRIGGER statement. Triggers can be created at three levels. The first level is the server level, and these are mostly DDL triggers. The second level is the database level, and these, too, are mostly DDL triggers. The final level is the object level (view, table, etc.), and these are mostly DML triggers, although DDL triggers may also be created at this level.

Understanding Stored Procedures   A stored procedure is a collection of T-SQL code stored in the database for use by users and applications. Stored procedures can help abstract security by using the EXECUTE AS clause. They can be used to improve performance because they do not require recompilation by default. They can also be used to centralize business rules for simple creation, enforcement, and maintenance of those rules.

Creating Stored Procedures   Stored procedures are created with the CREATE PROCEDURE statement. Stored procedures can use variables and logical constructions.

Chapter

12

Implementing Advanced Features

TOPICS COVERED IN THIS CHAPTER:

- ✓ Understanding and Installing Analysis Services
- ✓ Understanding and Installing Integration Services
- ✓ Creating a Basic Integration Services Package
- ✓ Understanding and Installing Reporting Services
- ✓ Implementing Database Mail
- ✓ Configuring Full-Text Indexing

Business Intelligence (BI) is a primary function of IT in large enterprises. Even small organizations benefit from BI processes and outputs. BI can be defined as the information used to better understand an organization's position in the marketplace. BI can also be defined as the tools, technologies, and processes used to manage and manipulate an organization's information so that the market position is better understood. BI is used to understand where an organization is today and how to move in the desired direction. BI is often used as a synonym for decision support; however, *decision support* is better stated as a feature of BI systems rather than the equivalent of a BI system.

A BI system includes multiple components. An information base must exist. The information base is used as the source of data for business decision support. In most implementations, the information base will be an aggregated data set pulled from one or more other data sources. SQL Server 2008 provides the Analysis Services component for managing this information base. This chapter will provide the fundamental steps required to install and initially configure Analysis Services.

Once the information base is in place, the users must have a way to generate reports against the information base. SQL Server 2008 provides the Reporting Services component for this purpose. Reporting Services may be installed on the same server as Analysis Services or on a different server. Additionally, you may install Reporting Services and run reports against a traditional OLTP database (Online Transaction Processing database) rather than an Analysis Services database. You will install and configure Reporting Services in this chapter.

With the information base implemented and the reporting infrastructure provided, a toolset is required to maintain the BI information base. Extraction, transformation, and loading (ETL) is the most common toolset used. SQL Server provides the Integration Services component for this purpose and other purposes as well. In this chapter, you will install and configure Integration Services and create a basic Integration Services package.

In addition to the direct BI services, this chapter provides instructions for the use of Database Mail and full-text indexing. Database Mail is used to send email from SQL Servers to administrators, users, or other computer systems. Full-text indexing allows for faster searching based on words in data columns. Both of these components can be useful for a BI system or a traditional OLTP database solution.

Understanding and Installing Analysis Services

SQL Server Analysis Services is a core BI component within the SQL Server system. Analysis Services provides the DBA with the ability to create multidimensional data structures. If you're familiar with pivot tables in Microsoft Excel, think of the multidimensional data structures as 3D pivot tables. Much as you use pivot tables to analyze large amounts of data, Analysis Services provides fast analysis of extremely large amounts of data. For example, analyzing millions of rows in several joined OLTP tables can take several minutes compared to a few seconds with an Analysis Services data source.

Analysis Services can work with data warehouses, data marts, or production operational databases.

Data Warehouses   A data warehouse is usually defined as a repository for an organization's information and is usually very large and often flat when compared to OLTP databases.

Data Marts   A data mart is a subset of the organization's data—usually provided for a department or specific decision support purpose. You can think of a data mart as one crate of content taken from the data warehouse to fulfill a specific order.

Production Operational Databases   Production operational databases are the databases used for transaction processing—also known as OLTP databases.

Analysis Services can work with an OLTP database directly, but it performs best when working against an optimized OLAP database designed specifically for information analysis. OLTP databases are designed to support optimized data processing, which includes read and write operations and assumes that many write operations will transpire. OLAP databases are designed to handle primarily read operations. In most large Analysis Services implementations, the databases directly used by Analysis Services will be OLAP databases.

Analysis Services Tools

In order to work with data in Analysis Services, you must create OLAP cubes or data mining models. An OLAP cube is a specially designed data structure that allows fast analysis of the data. Figure 12.1 represents the concepts of the data cube or multidimensional data. Think of the cube as a collection of data with multiple views provided based on the dimensions of the data. Figure 12.1 shows views by product, customer, and region.

FIGURE 12.1   OLAP cubes represented as views of data

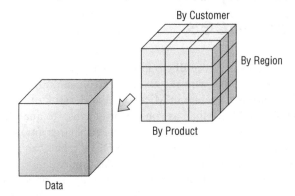

The cubed nature of the database allows for faster analysis of that data. Data mining models are used to sort data and to find patterns and relationships in that data. Both data cubes and data mining models are created in the Business Intelligence Development Studio (BIDS) and this tool is shown in Figure 12.2.

FIGURE 12.2   BIDS used to create data cubes

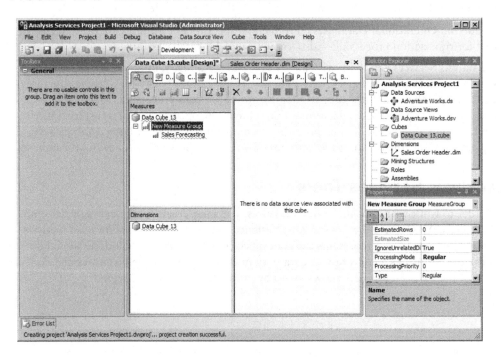

When you want to work with the data cubes and mining models, you will use SQL Server Management Studio (SSMS). Additionally, third-party tools and custom-developed applications may communicate with Analysis Services and, therefore, with the data cubes and mining models. In fact, BIDS and SSMS will only be used by administrators in most production environments. Custom applications will be used by the system users most of the time. As a DBA, you will not be required to understand the details involved in building a custom application, but you will need to provide the data platform. This requirement means that you must understand how to install and configure Analysis Services.

Analysis Services Optional Components

Analysis Services is installed using the normal SQL Server installation engine. It may be installed as the default instance or as a named instance. Analysis Services can be installed in an instance alongside other services (Integration Services, Reporting Services, etc.) or it can be installed in a dedicated instance. Before you begin installing Analysis Services, you should understand the optional components that may impact your use of the product. The following components must be considered:

Management Tools   The management tools include SSMS and command-line tools such as SQLCMD. These tools will be used primarily by the DBA and may be installed on a separate machine. In some situations, the developers may also use these tools and they may have direct access to the server's desktop for some administration purposes related to their development processes.

Business Intelligence Development Studio (BIDS)   BIDS is used primarily by developers, but may also be used by the DBA during initial setup and configuration of Analysis Services. In some organizations, the DBA is responsible for provisioning all data sources. In others, the DBA simply provides the platform and the developers build the data sources on an as-needed basis.

Software Development Kit   The SQL Server Software Development Kit (SDK) is used by developers to customize SQL Server operations or to develop custom client applications. The DBA rarely uses the SDK.

Reporting Services   Reporting Services is used to generate reports against data in production databases as well as Analysis Services databases. Many organizations set up an entirely separate server just for reporting purposes. Additionally, many organizations use third-party reporting tools, such as Crystal Reports, and have no need for Reporting Services.

Connectivity Components   The connectivity components will almost always be installed. These components allow for connectivity between client computers and the server. The components include OLEDB, ODBC, and DB-Library connectivity.

SQL Server Integration Services (SSIS)   SQL Server Integration Services (SSIS) is used to extract data from OLTP data sources, manipulate or transform that data in any way necessary, and then load the data into the Analysis Services data store. SSIS can run in the same instance as Analysis Services or you can choose to run it in a separate instance or even on a separate server.

Installing and Configuring Analysis Services

Exercise 12.1 steps you through the process of installing SQL Server Analysis Services in a named instance. The instance will be named ASvc and will include Integration Services and management components, including BIDS.

EXERCISE 12.1

Installing Analysis Services

To begin the process of installing Analysis Services, perform these steps (you must be logged in as an administrator):

1. Insert the SQL Server 2008 installation media into the server's CD or DVD drive.

2. When the AutoPlay feature activates, you should see a screen similar to the following:

3. Click Run SETUP.EXE to begin the installation. Be patient. It can take a few minutes before you see the actual installation interface.

4. In the SQL Server Installation Center screen, choose Installation.

5. Select New SQL Server Stand-Alone Installation Or Add Features to an Existing Installation. Again, be patient because it can take a while to bring up the next screen.

6. If the Setup Support Rules complete without error, click OK. Otherwise, click Show Details and evaluate the problem before proceeding.

7. When the Setup Support Files screen is displayed, click Install.

8. Once the support files are installed, you will see another Setup Support Rules processing screen. Click Next to begin the actual installation of Analysis Services.

9. On the Installation Type screen, choose Perform a New Installation of SQL Server 2008, as shown in the following image, and click Next.

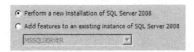

10. Enter a valid product key or choose Evaluation Mode and click Next.

11. Read the license agreement, check the acceptance box, and click Next.

12. On the Feature selection screen, check Database Engine Services and Analysis Services. Additionally, check any shared features desired if this is the first installation on the target server. Your screen should look similar to the following if you are installing SQL Server Analysis Services on a server that already contains a default instance.

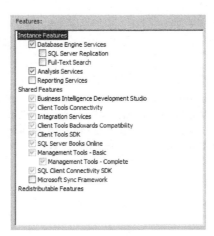

13. Click Next once you've chosen the features shown in the preceding image.

14. On the Instance Configuration screen, provide a named instance name of **ASvc**, accept all other defaults as in the following image, and click Next.

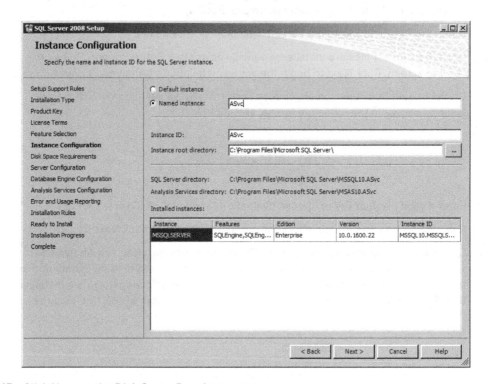

15. Click Next on the Disk Space Requirements screen.

16. On the Server Configuration screen, ensure that the SQL Server Agent, SQL Server Database Engine, and SQL Server Analysis Services services are all set to start Automatically. Because this is a lab installation, configure the account name to System for all services, as in the following image, and click Next.

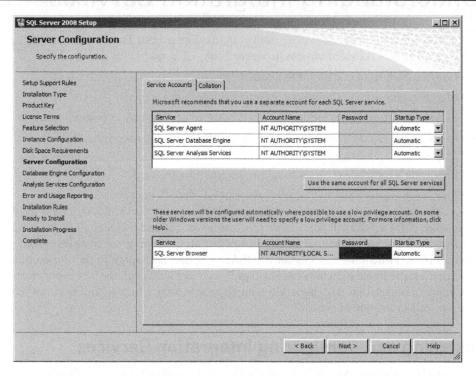

17. On the Database Engine Configuration screen, click Add Current User to add the current administrative account to the instance logins. Accept all other defaults on the Database Engine Configuration screen and click Next.

18. On the Analysis Services Configuration screen, click Add Current User and click Next.

19. Accept the defaults on the Error and Usage Reporting screen and click Next.

20. If no errors are shown on the Installation Rules screen, click Next.

21. Review the Ready to Install screen and, if you're sure you've configured the installation correctly, click Install.

The installation can take several minutes. When it is complete, you must click Next and then Close to exit the installation interface. You may want to restart the server—even though it is not required. This action will provide a refresh of the server before you begin using Analysis Services.

Understanding Integration Services

SQL Server Integration Services (SSIS) makes up the Extraction, Transformation, and Loading (ETL) tool provided with SQL Server 2008. ETL operations include:

- Copying data from one server to another

- Merging data from multiple sources into a single data location

- Extracting information, modifying it, and then returning it to its original location

- Exporting data into different formats such as Excel, comma-separated values (CSV), and Oracle databases

- Importing data while transforming it in several possible ways

This list represents just a few possible ways in which SSIS may be used.

If you've used Data Transformation Services (DTS) in SQL Server 2000, SSIS is like the big brother of DTS. SSIS offers far more processing options and includes all of the basic features of DTS as well. However, with great power often comes great complexity and SSIS can be overwhelming to a beginning DBA. Later in this chapter, in the section titled "Creating a Basic Integration Services Package," you'll walk through the process of creating a data export package that will, hopefully, simplify the interface for you and help you to prepare for your utilization of the tool.

Installing and Configuring Integration Services

Exercise 12.2 steps you through the installation of Integration Services in a named instance. You can install Integration Services as a component within an existing instance as well. If you notice that Exercise 12.2 is very similar to Exercise 12.1, it's because you use the same installation process to install an SSIS named instance as you do for an SSAS named instance. The only difference is in the features you select.

EXERCISE 12.2

Installing Integration Services

In this exercise, you will install SQL Server Integration Services as a named instance. The instance will be named ISvc and will include the Database Engine and management components.

To begin the installation process, follow these steps (you must be logged in as an administrator):

1. Insert the SQL Server 2008 installation media into the server's CD or DVD drive.

2. When the AutoPlay feature activates, click Run SETUP.EXE to begin the installation. Be patient. It can take a few minutes before you see the actual installation interface.

3. In the SQL Server Installation Center, choose the Installation page.

4. Select New SQL Server Stand-Alone Installation or Add Features to an Existing Installation. Again, be patient because it can take a while to bring up the next screen.

5. If the Setup Support Rules complete without error, click OK. Otherwise, click Show Details and evaluate the problem before proceeding.

6. When the Setup Support Files screen is displayed, click Install.

7. Once the support files are installed, you will see another Setup Support Rules processing screen. Click Next to begin the actual installation of Integration Services.

8. On the Installation Type screen, choose Perform a New Installation of SQL Server 2008 and click Next.

9. Enter a valid product key or choose Evaluation Mode and click Next.

10. Read the license agreement, check the acceptance box, and click Next.

11. On the Feature Selection screen, check Database Engine Services and Integration Services. Additionally, check any shared features desired if this is the first installation on the target server. If this is an additional installation on an existing SQL Server, any previously installed shared services will be grayed out. Your screen should look similar to the following, if you are installing SQL Server Integration Services on a server which already contains a default instance.

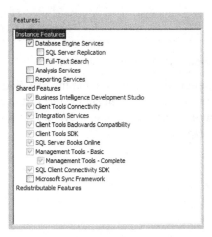

12. Click Next once you've chosen the Database Engine Services and Integration Services.

13. On the Instance Configuration screen, provide a named instance name of **ISvc**, accept all other defaults as in the following image, and click next.

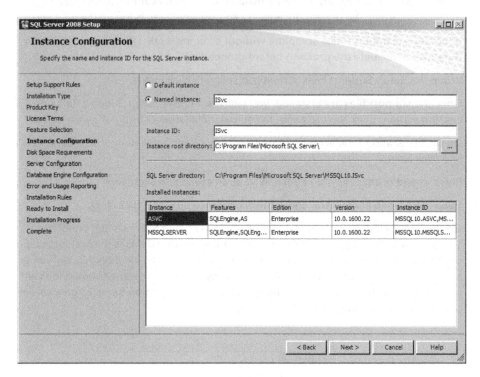

14. Click Next on the Disk Space Requirements screen.

15. On the Server Configuration screen, ensure that the SQL Server Agent and SQL Server Database Engine services are both set to start Automatically. Because this is a lab installation, configure the account name to System for both services as in the following image and click Next.

EXERCISE 12.2   *(continued)*

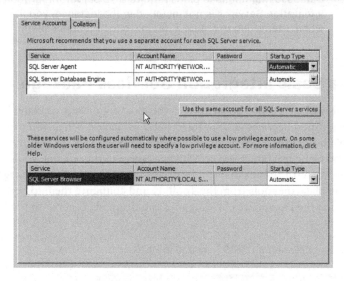

16. On the Database Engine Configuration screen, click Add Current User to add the current administrative account to the instance logins. Accept all other defaults on the Database Engine Configuration screen and click Next.

17. Accept the defaults on the Error and Usage Reporting screen and click Next.

18. If no errors are shown on the Installation Rules screen, click Next. If errors are shown, click the error line for more information and resolve any discovered issues. Most errors are related to noninstalled items that are required for the installation to proceed.

19. Review the Ready to Install screen and, if you're sure you've configured the installation correctly, click Install.

The installation can take several minutes. When it is complete, you must click Next and then Close to exit the installation interface. Even though it is not required, you might want to restart the server. This action will provide a refresh of the server before you begin using Integration Services.

In many environments, Integration Services is installed with all installations of SQL Server regardless of the instance purpose. Integration Services is widely used to automate administrative actions, so it is beneficial to have it installed with every instance.

WARNING   Database maintenance plans require SQL Server Integration Services. If Integration Services is not installed in the instance, you'll receive errors when attempting to create a database maintenance plan.

Creating a Basic Integration Services Package

Like Analysis Services, the BIDS application is the most commonly used method for creating SQL Server Integration Services (SSIS) projects and packages. When you run the Database Maintenance Plan Wizard, in SSMS, it also creates an SSIS package. Figure 12.3 shows the BIDS application being used to create an SSIS package. On the left side you see the Toolbox, which contains dozens of actions that can be performed within an SSIS package. In the center Design area, you place the tools from the Toolbox and configure them to perform as needed. Tools are placed in the Design area by dragging and dropping them onto the Design area surfaces.

FIGURE 12.3   Creating an SSIS package in BIDS

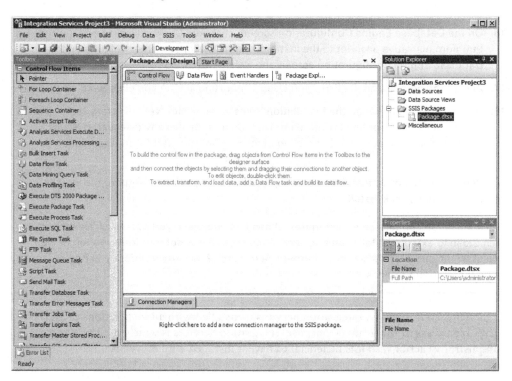

In Exercise 12.3, you will export data from the AdventureWorks database into an Excel spreadsheet. The point of the exercise is to help beginning DBAs move beyond the fear of the interface. When building SSIS packages, the BIDS interface can be a bit overwhelming, but the process of creating a package is really quite simple. It includes four primary steps:

1. You must define the Connection Managers. The Connection Managers are simply connections to the data sources and destinations used in the SSIS package.

2. You define the Data Flow data pumps and transformations. The data pumps are either data flow sources or data flow destinations. The transformations define what should be done to the data (for example, copy it from a source to a destination).

3. You should test the package to ensure proper operations. This action can be accomplished with the internal debugging tools.

4. Finally, you will save the package and potentially schedule it to run on a regular basis if needed.

That's really all there is to creating an SSIS package. In Exercise 12.3 you will create the SSIS package.

EXERCISE 12.3

Creating a Basic Integration Services Package

In this exercise, you will use BIDS to create a package that exports the Production.Product table from the AdventureWorks database into an Excel spreadsheet. This package could be created with the Export Data Wizard in SSMS; however, stepping through the process manually helps to reveal the basic components used in SSIS packages. In order to perform this exercise, you must have the default instance installed and the AdventureWorks database added to the default instance. These actions were covered in Chapter 2, "Installing SQL Server 2008," in the section titled "Installing a Default Instance."

To begin creating the package, log in as an administrator and follow these steps:

1. Launch BIDS by selecting Start ➤ All Programs ➤ Microsoft SQL Server 2008 ➤ SQL Server Business Intelligence Development Studio.

2. In BIDS, select File ➤ New ➤ Project.

EXERCISE 12.3   (continued)

3.   Choose an Integration Services Project, as shown in the following image.

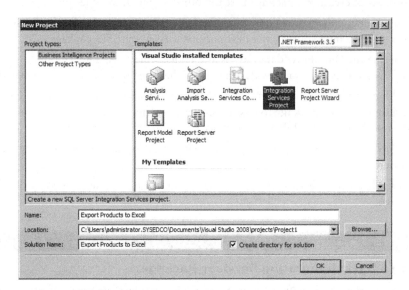

4.   Name the project **Export Products to Excel** and click OK.

5.   To add a new connection, right-click in the Connection Managers section and select New Connection.

6.   Select the OLE DB connection type and click Add.

7.   In the Configure OLE DB Connection Manager dialog, click New.

8.   Accept the default provider of SQL Server Native Client and choose the local default instance for the Server Name field. If the local default instance is not displayed, enter either **(local)** or a period to indicate the default instance. Use Windows Authentication and choose the AdventureWorks database, as shown in the following image.

EXERCISE 12.3   *(continued)*

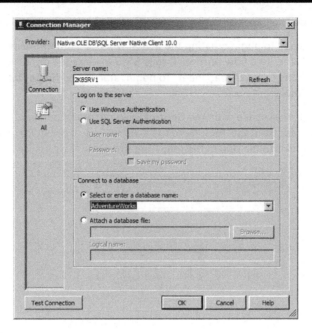

9. Click OK.

10. In the Configure OLE DB Connection Manager dialog, click OK again to save the Connection Manager for the SQL Server database.

11. Now you must create a connection to the output Excel file. Right-click in the Connection Managers section again and select New Connection.

12. Select the Excel connection types and click Add.

13. Select the location and name for the Excel file, accept the default Excel version, and check the First Row Has Column Names option, as shown in the following image.

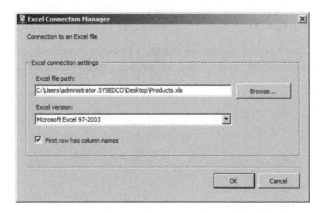

EXERCISE 12.3 *(continued)*

14. Click OK to save the Excel Connection Manager.

    You are now ready to begin creating the actual work portion of the package. This work portion is the data flow portion. It tells SSIS to copy the data from the SQL Server table to the Excel spreadsheet. To begin, start by adding a Data Flow task to your Control Flow workspace.

15. Ensure that the workspace is on the Control Flow tab and then click, drag, and drop the Data Flow task from the Toolbox to the Control Flow workspace. The workspace should look similar to the one in the following image.

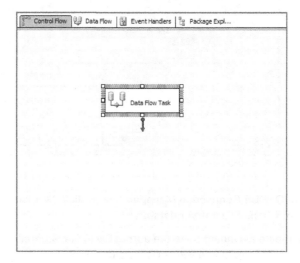

16. Double-click the new Data Flow Task to begin implementing the work of the package. The context of the workspace will change to the Data Flow tab. The Toolbox will change to show Data Flow Sources, Data Flow Transformations, and Data Flow Destinations.

17. Drag an OLE DB source object from the Data Flow Sources container to the Data Flow workspace and drop it.

18. Drag an Excel destination object from the Data Flow Destinations container to the Data Flow workspace and drop it. Your workspace should look similar to the following image.

EXERCISE 12.3 *(continued)*

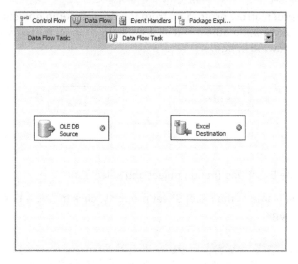

19. Drag a Copy Column task onto the workspace and drop it. You should now have the three objects you need to complete the simple export task.

20. Right-click on the OLE DB Source object and select Edit.

21. Choose the Production.Product table as the table name as in the following image and then click OK (not shown).

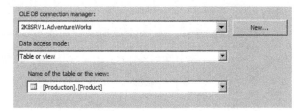

22. Click the green arrow protruding from the OLE DB Source object (the object must be selected in order to see and click on the green or red arrows) and then hover over the Copy Column object and click again to connect the two objects, as shown in the following image.

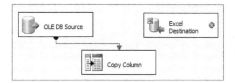

23. Now, click the green arrow protruding from the Copy Column objects and then hover over the Excel Destination object and click again to connect these two objects, as shown in the following image.

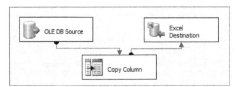

24. Right-click on the Excel Destination object and select Edit.

25. To configure the Name of the Excel Sheet property, click the New button depicted in the following image.

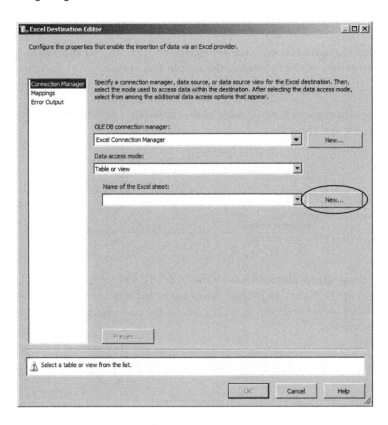

26. In the Create Table dialog that appears, change the code so that the table name is Products and accept all other defaults, as in the following image, and then click OK.

```
Create Table                                    [_][O][X]
CREATE TABLE `Products` (
    `ProductID` Long,
    `Name` LongText,
    `ProductNumber` LongText,
    `MakeFlag` Byte,
    `FinishedGoodsFlag` Byte,
    `Color` LongText,
    `SafetyStockLevel` Short,
    `ReorderPoint` Short,
    `StandardCost` Currency,
    `ListPrice` Currency,
    `Size` LongText,
    `SizeUnitMeasureCode` LongText,
    `WeightUnitMeasureCode` LongText,
    `Weight` Decimal(8,2),
    `DaysToManufacture` Long,
    `ProductLine` LongText,
    `Class` LongText,
    `Style` LongText,
    `ProductSubcategoryID` Long,
    `ProductModelID` Long,
    `SellStartDate` DateTime,

                              OK          Cancel
```

27. You'll be prompted to select the new table, click OK.

28. Click the drop-down list selector and choose Products$ from the list, as shown in the following image.

```
Name of the Excel sheet:
  Products$                              ▼    New...
```

29. Click the Mappings page to have mappings generated for you automatically and then click OK to save the configuration.

30. Click File ➢ Save Selected Items to save the package in its current state.

You now have a package that can export the data from the SQL Server table into an Excel spreadsheet. This package is a simple package, but it demonstrates the fundamental building blocks of an SSIS package: Connection Managers and Data Flows.

Troubleshooting and Debugging an SSIS Package

It's not really enough to create a package and trust that it will work. You'll also need to troubleshoot packages. The debug toolset within BIDS allows you to do this. Exercise 12.4 steps you through using the internal debug tools to verify the operations of the package created in Exercise 12.3.

EXERCISE 12.4

Troubleshooting an SSIS Package with Debug

In this exercise, you will use BIDS to verify the proper operations of the data export package created in Exercise 12.3. You will do this using the internal debug tools. To begin, open BIDS and open the Export Products to Excel project that was created in Exercise 12.3. If you have not closed the project since creating it, it should still be open in the BIDS environment.

To debug the package, follow these steps:

1. Click Debug ➢ Start Debugging. Notice that you can also press F5.

2. You hope to see results showing nothing but green boxes. If any boxes are red, you have a problem in your package and need to troubleshoot it. The following image shows the results when everything works well.

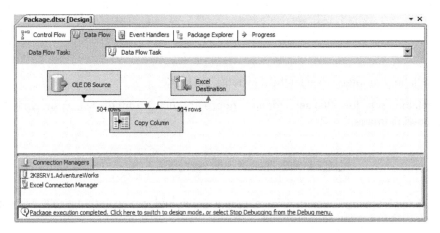

3. If you navigate to the location that you specified for the Excel destination in step 13 of Exercise 12.3, you should now see an Excel file there. Open the file and verify that the Product table data has been exported to the file.

4. In BIDS, chose Debug ➢ Stop Debugging to exit debug mode.

Scheduling Your Package to Run Automatically

Now that you know your package is working, you can schedule it to run automatically. This scheduling can be accomplished by saving the package on a SQL Server instance and then using the SQL Server Agent within that instance to run the package. Packages can be saved into multiple instances using the File ➢ Save Copy of Package As option within BIDS.

Exercise 12.5 steps you through the process of saving the package on an instance of SQL Server and then scheduling the package to run automatically. As you perform this exercise, you'll also see how you can encrypt the data for secure package access.

EXERCISE 12.5

Saving and Scheduling Packages

In this exercise, you will use BIDS to save the Product table export package into the SQL Server default instance on the same server. To save the package into a different instance, you would simply specify the server name in step 3 below.

To begin, open BIDS and the Export Products to Excel project and then take the following steps:

1. Select File ➤ Save Copy of Package.dtsx As.

2. In the Save Copy of Package dialog, specify SQL Server as the Package Location.

3. Set the *Server* to the local default instance.

4. Use Windows Authentication if you are logged on as an administrator.

5. In the Package Path field, type **/Export Products to Excel**.

6. For the Protection Level, choose Rely on Server Storage and Roles for Access Control. The dialog should look similar to the following.

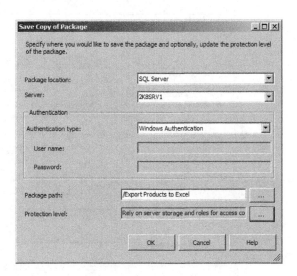

7. Click OK.

EXERCISE 12.5 *(continued)*

At this point, the package has been saved in the default instance of SQL Server 2008. Next, you need to schedule the package in SSMS. You can close BIDS if you need to lower memory consumption on the server for the next step. BIDS is not needed for the remainder of this exercise.

8. Launch SSMS, connect to the local default instance, and expand the SQL Server Agent node.

9. Right-click on the Jobs container and select New Job.

10. Name the job **Export Product Data to Excel** and then select the Steps page.

11. Click the New button to add a new step.

12. Enter the step name of **Run SSIS Export Package**.

13. For the Type, choose SQL Server Integration Services Package.

14. On the General tab, choose the local default instance for the Server.

15. For the package name, enter **\Export Products to Excel** as shown in the following image:

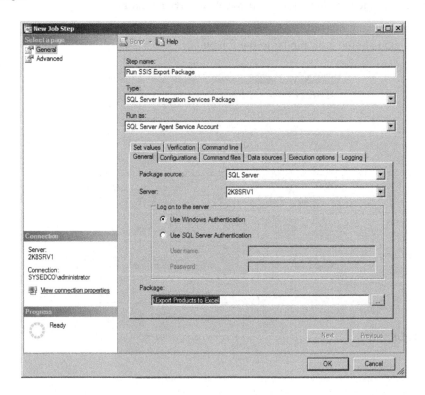

16. Click OK to add the step.

17. Select the Schedules page.

18. Click New to add a new schedule.

19. Name the schedule **6 AM Run** and set the type to Recurring.

20. Set the frequency to Daily and the time to 6:00:00 AM, as in the following image.

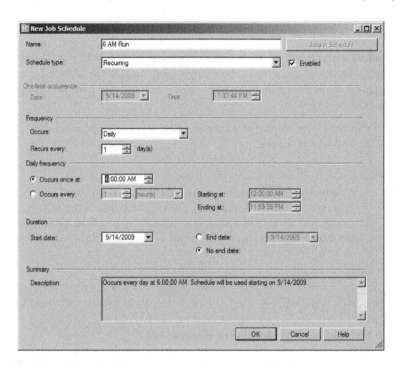

21. Click OK to save the schedule.

22. Click OK again to save the job.

Security Protection Levels

It is important that you understand the protection levels that can be configured for packages when they are saved. SSIS packages contain sensitive and nonsensitive data. You can protect only the sensitive data, all of the data, none of the data, or leave it up to the target instance to determine how data is protected. The following list provides a review of the security protection levels and descriptions of their applications.

Do Not Save Sensitive   Does not save sensitive data with the package. When a user other than the creator opens the package, sensitive values contain blanks.

Encrypt All with Password   All data in the package is encrypted using the provided password.

Encrypt Sensitive with Password   Only sensitive data is encrypted using the provided password.

Encrypt All with User Key   Uses the current user's key to encrypt the entire package. The result is that only the current user can edit the package.

Encrypt Sensitive with User Key   Uses the current user's key to encrypt the sensitive data in the package. The result is that only the current user can edit the sensitive data. Any user with access can open the package, but will have to manually enter the sensitive information needed to run the package.

Rely on Server Storage   Protection of sensitive and nonsensitive data is left to the target server in which the package is saved.

The Rely on Server Storage protection level is available only when saving packages in a SQL Server. The package is saved in the MSDB database. All protection levels are available when saving in a SQL Server, but the Rely on Server Storage protection level is not available when saving in a file.

Real World Scenario

Using SSIS Packages to Make Users Happy

Over the years, I've used SSIS and DTS packages to solve many problems; however, one of the most useful tasks I've found is very simple and makes users wonderfully happy. I've had users ask for data from large SQL Server databases (as well as other database server types) in many formats. Some want Excel, others want Access, and still others want CSV files or some cryptic format.

Using SSIS packages, you can export the data into a large variety of formats. When the users want some weird format that's really just a text file, you can usually accomplish this with some created ActiveX scripting in the job that runs the SSIS package or as a package step. I've exported data from Oracle, MySQL, SQL Server, and—yes, I have to admit— even Access into other formats.

In one recent scenario, a single user built and managed an Access database over a period of more than eight years. He was very good at working with Access and had built a rather fine database in it; however, several other users needed access to the data in that database—and sharing an Access database with more than five or six users is just asking for trouble. At the same time, the owner of the database didn't want to re-create everything based on a SQL Server backend, even though the company did have a licensed SQL Server available. So how did we solve this problem?

We created an SSIS package that pulled the data into a SQL Server database from his Access database every night and every day during lunch. We added a macro to the Access database that closed it, if it was open at 12:15 P.M. This way, the owner didn't have to remember to get out of the database so that the SSIS package could get full control to work its magic. Of course, the macro prompted him—just in case he was still working at 12:15 P.M.

The result was sufficient because the other users only needed read access to the data and 3 to 5 hours was an acceptable tolerance level for updates. This is just one example of how you can make users really happy using SSIS packages and SQL Server jobs.

Understanding and Installing Reporting Services

SQL Server Reporting Services (SSRS) is used to centrally create, manage, and distribute the reports needed within your organization. Many companies install a dedicated SQL Server just for SSRS, and others include SSRS as part of another database server installation. As long as the performance is acceptable, both methods will work well. SSRS solves the problem of reporting without requiring third-party components; however, SSRS is not as mature as third-party products such as Crystal Reports, so the DBA should consider his options carefully.

SSRS provides support for several types of reporting solutions including:

Ad Hoc Reporting   In many organizations or departments within organizations, users need to frequently generate custom reports. Ad hoc reporting provides for this business requirement. The Report Builder application is usually used by the end users in this scenario.

Managed/Controlled Reporting   Managed or controlled reporting provides prebuilt reports that users can simply run to get the information they need. If little variance exists in the reports that users require from week to week, managed reporting may work well for you. Managed reports are created with both the Report Builder (for basic reports) and the Report Designer (for more advanced reports).

Integrated Reporting   Integrated reporting allows the reports to run within business applications. Reports can execute within SharePoint servers or customized applications. Integrated reporting is also called embedded reporting.

 SQL Server 2008 no longer requires IIS to be installed on the Windows server in order to install and use Reporting Services. This saves space and resources on the server.

SSRS is installed in the same way as SSIS and SSAS—using the standard installation program from the CD or DVD media. Exercise 12.6 steps you through the process of installing a dedicated SSRS instance.

EXERCISE 12.6

Installing and Configuring Reporting Services

In this exercise, you will install SSRS in an instance named RSvc. The steps will look similar to those used to install the ASvc and ISvc instances earlier in this chapter in Exercises 12.1 and 12.2 because the same installation engine is used.

To perform the SSRS installation, follow these steps:

1. Insert the SQL Server 2008 installation media into the server's CD or DVD drive.

2. When the AutoPlay feature activates, click Run SETUP.EXE to begin the installation. Be patient because it can take a few minutes before you see the actual installation interface.

3. In the SQL Server Installation Center, choose the Installation page.

4. Select New SQL Server Stand-Alone Installation Or Add Features To An Existing Installation. Again, be patient. It can take a while to bring up the next screen.

5. If the Setup Support Rules complete without error, click OK. Otherwise, click Show Details and evaluate the problem before proceeding.

6. When the Setup Support Files screen is displayed, click Install.

7. Once the support files are installed, you will see another Setup Support Rules processing screen. Click Next to begin the actual installation of Reporting Services.

8. On the Installation Type screen, choose Perform A New Installation Of SQL Server 2008 and click Next.

9. Enter a valid product key or choose Evaluation Mode and click Next.

10. Read the license agreement, check the acceptance box, and click Next.

11. On the Feature Selection screen, check Database Engine Services and Reporting Services. Additionally, check any shared features desired if this is the first installation on the target server. Your screen should look similar to the following, if you are installing SQL Server Integration Services on a server that already contains a default instance.

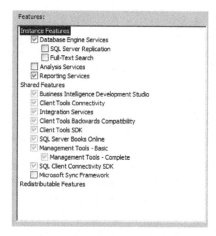

12. Click Next once you've chosen the Database Engine Services and Reporting Services. If the shared features are grayed out, it simply means they are already installed.

13. On the Instance Configuration screen, provide a named instance name of **RSvc**, accept all other defaults as in the following image, and click Next.

14. Click Next on the Disk Space Requirements screen.

15. On the Server Configuration screen, ensure that the SQL Server Agent, SQL Server Database Engine, and SQL Server Reporting Services services are set to start Automatically. Because this is a lab installation, configure the account name to System for both services, as in the following image, and click Next.

EXERCISE 12.6   *(continued)*

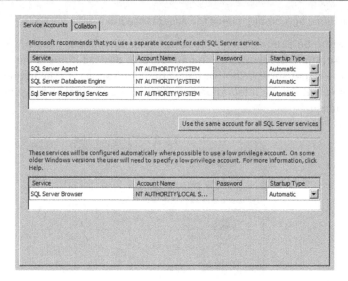

16. On the Database Engine Configuration screen, click Add Current User to add the current administrative account to the instance logins. Accept all other defaults on the Database Engine Configuration screen and click Next.

17. On the Reporting Services Configuration screen, choose to Install The Native Mode Default Configuration, as shown in the following image.

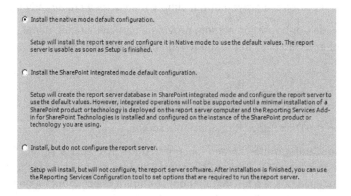

18. Accept the defaults on the Error and Usage Reporting screen and click Next.

19. If no errors are shown on the Installation Rules screen, click Next.

20. Review the Ready to Install screen and, if you're sure you've configured the installation correctly, click Install.

The installation can take several minutes. When it is complete, you must click Next and then Close to exit the installation interface.

Now that SSRS is installed, you can configure the basic settings it requires. To begin using SSRS, perform the following steps:

21. Select Start ➢ All Programs ➢ Microsoft SQL Server 2008 ➢ Configuration Tools ➢ Reporting Services Configuration Manager.

22. You'll be asked to connect to a SSRS server. Provide the named instance of RSvc and click Connect.

23. The initial screen shows the status of the SSRS service and allows you to stop and start the service.

24. Select the Web Service URL page.

25. Click the link to the web page to view the default SSRS home page. Because you have not created any reports, the page will be very basic, as shown in the following image.

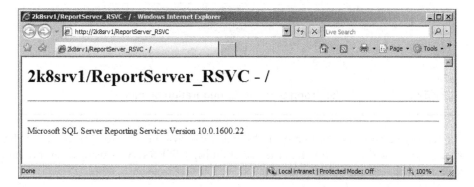

26. Close the web browser to return to the Reporting Services Configuration Manager.

27. Select the Report Manager URL page.

28. Click the link to the web page to view the Report Manager home page. You'll see a richer home page like the one in the following image (if you want to install the Report Builder, click the link on the Report Manager home page to launch the installation).

EXERCISE 12.6 *(continued)*

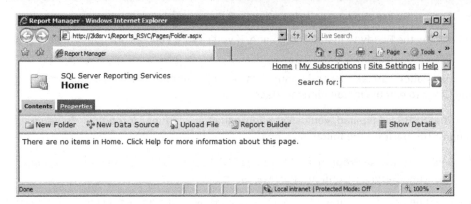

29. Close the web browser.

30. Select the Email Settings page to configure email options. Configure the email options for your SMTP server. They should look similar to those in the following image.

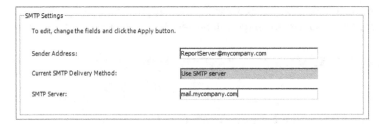

31. Click Exit to leave the Reporting Services Configuration Manager.

The Reporting Services Configuration Manager can also be used to scale out the SSRS implementation. Scaling out involves the use of multiple SSRS servers using a central data store or a distributed data store.

Implementing Database Mail

Database Mail is used to send email from the SQL Server services. SQL Server 2005 first introduced Database Mail. Before this, DBAs were forced to use SQL Mail or come up with their own solution. SQL Mail required the installation of Outlook on the servers and Database Mail does not. This fact alone makes Database Mail far more useful than SQL

Mail; however, Database Mail also supports redundancy through the use of multiple mail profiles and gives the DBA complete control over the allowed email features (attachments, retry attempts, etc.).

Database Mail can be used for many purposes including:

- Notifying administrators of alerts or problems on the server
- Notifying administrators that a job has completed with success, failure, or both
- Providing notice to users when data is modified
- Sending security alerts to administrators when new accounts are created, older accounts are changed or modified, or any other security parameter is adjusted

And these uses are just the beginning. The uses for Database Mail will vary greatly depending on the organization and the DBA, but the configuration of Database Mail is mostly the same.

In Exercise 12.7, you will perform the actions required to enable Database Mail on a SQL Server 2008 instance.

EXERCISE 12.7

Configuring Database Mail

In this exercise, you will configure Database Mail. You will create a single profile for sending email from the SQL Server instance. Additionally, you will limit the attachment size to 1MB.

To enable and configure Database Mail, follow these steps:

1. Launch SSMS and expand the Management node.

2. Right-click on the Database Mail node and select Configure Database Mail. If you are asked to enable Database Mail, click Yes.

3. Click Next to begin using the Database Mail Configuration Wizard.

    You need to choose the Set Up Database Mail option by performing the following tasks:

4. Enter a mail profile name such as **Default Mail Profile** and a description if you desire.

5. Click the Add button to add a mail profile.

6. Click the New Account button to add a new account to the profile.

7. Configure the mail accounts similar to the settings shown in the following image (replace the settings with valid settings for your SMTP account and server).

EXERCISE 12.7 *(continued)*

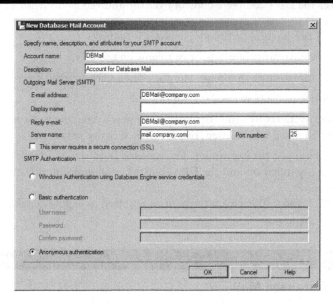

8. Click OK. The New Profile dialog should look similar to the following image.

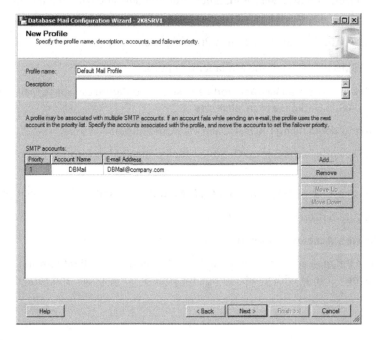

9. Click Next.

10. Enable Public and Default Profile for the profile and click Next.

EXERCISE 12.7 *(continued)*

11. Set the Maximum file size to 1,024,000 so that attachments are limited to 1MB and click Next.

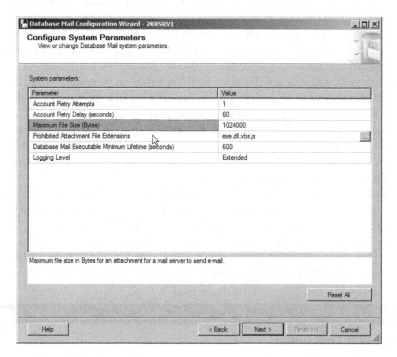

12. Click Next and review the summary and then click Finish to complete the configuration of Database Mail.

13. Test the Database Mail configuration. Right-click on the Database Mail node and select Send Test Email.

14. Enter the appropriate To: address and click Send Test Email. Click OK when complete.

With these configuration steps complete, you can configure jobs and alerts so that operators are notified appropriately.

Configuring Full-Text Indexing

SQL Server's full-text indexing feature is what you might call an "aware" indexing option. Normal clustered and nonclustered indexes are based on exact matches. Stated differently, you can only find data values that match your filter exactly. This fact is even true with the LIKE SQL operator. For example, a filter with the clause WHERE Col1 LIKE 'run%' would find values equal to run and running, but not ran. Full-text searches can also locate variant forms such as ran for run.

Additionally, full-text indexes allow for searches based on proximity. You can search for two words that are close to each other. You can also search for words based on weights with higher weighted words appearing first in the results.

Starting with SQL Server 2008, full-text indexes are stored internally within the SQL Server database. In previous versions, an external full-text catalog was created to house the full-text indexes. In addition, the full-text engine itself runs within the SQL Server memory space instead of running as a separate service.

A table can have only one full-text index, and the table must have a unique identifying column in order to create the index. Full-text index searches are performed with the CONTAINS and FREETEXT operators. For example, WHERE CONTAINS(ProdName, '"horse*"' NEAR bridle') would find values such as *horse racing bridle* or *horses' bridles*.

Exercise 12.8 walks you through creating a full-text index on the Books table in the Books database created in preceding chapters.

EXERCISE 12.8

Creating a Full-Text Index

In this exercise, you will create a full-text index on the Books table in the Books database. You will create the full-text index using the GUI Table Designer interface.

To create the full-text index:

1. Launch SSMS and expand Databases ➢ Books ➢ Storage Container.

2. Right-click on the Full Text Catalogs and select New Full-Text Catalog.

3. Enter the Full-text catalog name of **BooksFT**.

4. Set the owner to dbo.

5. Enable the Set as default catalog option and click OK.

6. Expand Databases ➢ Books ➢ Tables.

7. Right-click on the dbo.Books table and select Design.

8. Right-click on the Title column row selector and choose Fulltext Index from the pop-up menu like the one displayed in the following image.

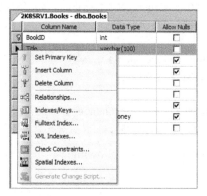

9. Click the Add button.

10. Click the Build button for the Columns property.

11. Choose the Title column and the English (United States) language, as in the following image.

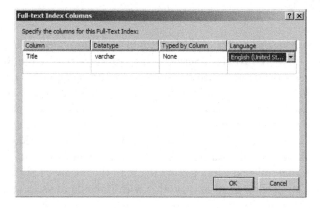

12. Click OK.

13. Click Close to complete the configuration of the full-text index and save the table changes.

After creating the full-text index in Exercise 12.8, execute the following code to add some records to the dbo.Books table (ensure that your query window is in the Books database context):

```
INSERT INTO dbo.BOOKS
    VALUES ('Real World SQL Server 2008 Database Administration',
    1, 1, 1, 1, '2009-12-01', 55.47);
INSERT INTO dbo.BOOKS
    VALUES ('CWNA/CWSP All-in-one Guide',
    1, 1, 1, 1, '2010-03-01', 67.97);
INSERT INTO dbo.BOOKS
    VALUES ('Managing at the Speed of Change',
    43, 2, 2, 12, '1994-01-01', 12.95);
```

Now, you can run a statement like the following:

```
SELECT *
FROM dbo.Books
WHERE CONTAINS(Title, 'guide');
```

If you want to see varied results, simply add more sample data to the dbo.Books table.

Summary

In this chapter, you reviewed several advanced components provided with SQL Server 2008. You installed and configured Analysis Services, Integration Services, and Reporting Services. Each installation was similar and used the same installation engine. The key was to select the appropriate options during installation. Once you installed SQL Server Integration Services, you created your first package for data export. Additionally, you worked with both Database Mail and full-text indexes. You learned that Reporting Services no longer requires IIS to be installed on the SQL Server and that Database Mail has not required Outlook on the server since SQL Server 2005 was released. You also learned that full-text indexing no longer requires external full-text catalogs starting with the release of SQL Server 2008; however, you must still create a full-text catalog within the database requiring full-text indexes.

Chapter Essentials

Understanding and Implementing Analysis Services   Analysis Services provides rapid data analysis of complex and large data systems. Analysis Services is the primary BI and decision-support component in SQL Server. It may be installed as a default or named instance, and the instance may include other SQL Server components as well. SSMS is used to manage and work with data cubes and data models, and BIDS is used to create them.

Understanding and Implementing Integration Services   SQL Server Integration Services is used to perform ETL tasks in SQL Server environments. Integration Services was first introduced with SQL Server 2005. Before this, it was known as Data Transformation Services. You install Integration Services as part of the normal SQL Server 2008 installation process.

Creating a Basic Integration Services Package   SSIS packages are creating in the BIDS application. When you create a package, you define the Connection Managers, perform tasks, and debug the package to ensure proper operations. Packages can be saved as files or as objects in the SQL Server 2008 MSDB database. Running packages from a job is a great way to schedule automatic data processing tasks.

Understanding and Installing Reporting Services   SSRS is used to generate and distribute reports for decision support professionals and other employees needing data summaries and surveys. SSRS is installed as part of an instance of SQL Server 2008 and no longer requires IIS to be installed on the Windows server. Reports can be created with the Report Designer (advanced reports) or Report Builder (basic reports).

Implementing Database Mail   Starting with SQL Server 2005, you no longer have to install Outlook on the server to send email from the SQL Server service. Database Mail simply uses an SMTP server to send email messages. It takes advantage of the Service Broker component of SQL Server to queue the email messages so that they can be delivered without adversely impacting the performance of the SQL Server. Redundant mail profiles ensure that emails will be delivered to administrative and other personnel.

Configuring Full-Text Indexing   Full-text indexing allows for filtering based on words and variations of words. SQL Server 2008 introduces internally stored full-text indexes. External catalogs are no longer required.

Administration and Maintenance

PART
IV

Creating Jobs, Operators, and Alerts

TOPICS COVERED IN THIS CHAPTER:

- ✓ Standardize, Automate, and Update
- ✓ Understanding SQL Server Jobs
- ✓ Creating T-SQL Jobs
- ✓ Creating SSIS Jobs
- ✓ Creating Windows Command Jobs
- ✓ Creating and Using Operators
- ✓ Creating and Using Alerts
- ✓ Using WSUS for SQL Server 2008

Administration and maintenance of your SQL Servers are among the most important tasks you will perform in your job as a DBA. Administration involves adding and removing objects as they are needed by the users and applications you support. It also includes configuring settings to match new and current needs throughout the lifecycle of the database server. Maintenance involves backing up databases and objects, performance tuning, and patching or updating the system. Both administration and maintenance tasks should be standardized and automated as much as possible.

In this chapter, you will first learn about the technology implementation methodology used at SysEdCo. The implementation methodology is called SAU, which stands for Standardize, Automate, and Update. It is a simple thinking tool that ensures you consider the primary aspects of technology implementation: standardization, automation, and maintenance.

Next, you'll learn to implement jobs based on T-SQL, SSIS packages, and Windows commands. You will learn to schedule jobs and plan the appropriate step types depending on your needs.

The discussion on jobs, which can notify operators and trigger alerts, will lead directly into the section on operators and alerts. In this section, you will learn how to create and use operators so that the right person or process can be notified of job results, alerts, and other important events. You will also learn to create basic alerts in the SQL Server 2008 SSMS administration tool and in the Performance Monitor of Windows.

The final topic of the chapter, WSUS, will introduce you to the need to update your SQL Servers. The update process includes the Windows server itself and the SQL Server services running on it. You'll be introduced to the gotchas related to automatic updates and the Windows Server Update Services solution for enterprise or large-scale deployments.

The Systems Education and Consulting Company (SysEdCo) was launched in July of 1997. We provide educational services and consulting services to organizations in Ohio and throughout the United States. Over the years, we've developed many different systems and processes to help us and our clients improve the way IT is implemented and managed. You can always get information about our company at http://www.SysEdCo.com.

Standardize, Automate, and Update

Over the years Systems Education and Consulting (SysEdCo) has developed SAU (Standardize, Automate, and Update), which is a simple methodology for the implementation of new technologies, such as database systems and even infrastructure solutions. The methodology is nonspecific and can be applied to any technology category. With SAU, each time a new technology is implemented, you will go through each phase of the methodology. For simpler technologies (such as the first USB memory stick), each phase may take less than a few minutes or hours. For more complex technologies (such as the very first SQL Server in an environment), the first two phases (standardize and automate) can take a week or more and the last phase (update) will likely take one or two days.

This methodology will be referred to throughout this chapter and the next three chapters as well. Right now, however, you should see how the automation and performance management features of SQL Server 2008 and Windows Server 2008 fit within the SAU methodology.

The following summary will act as an overview of the three SAU phases:

Standardize During the standardize phase, you determine the best way to configure and implement the technology. For SQL Server 2008, this might include establishing naming conventions for objects, determining security guidelines, creating templates for database creation, and coding standards for stored procedures and functions, among other things. The individual responsible for the standardize phase must be very familiar with the technology. If your organization lacks the expertise on staff, consultants may be hired or key employees can be trained on the technology so that the proper decisions can be made.

When a technology has few configuration options and operational variables, the standardize phase takes very little time. Technologies with many configuration options and operational variables can require a much greater time commitment. You may have already guessed where SQL Server 2008 fits in. It has many configuration options and operational variables and you should expect to spend a greater amount of time standardizing your configurations and operations. The benefit of this time cost is found in the most consistent production environment as consistent environments are easier to automate—hands down.

Automate Once you have standards documented for the technology, you will want to discover management automation methods. Some technologies, such as SQL Server 2008, are easier to automate than others and some technologies simply cannot be automated. Of course, if the management of a technology cannot be automated in any way, the automate phase ends quickly. When the management of a technology can be automated in several ways, the automate phase usually takes much longer; however, this time expenditure comes with great reward because less time is spent managing the technology throughout its lifecycle.

SQL Server 2008 is one of those technologies that can be automated in several ways. You can create jobs and alerts within SQL Server itself and then create triggers on databases and objects to automate many actions. SQL Server Integration Services can be used to automate many data management tasks. The new Policy-Based Management feature of SQL Server 2008 can be used to enforce configuration standards on one or 100 servers or more. Clearly, a lot of time can be spent developing management automation plans for SQL Server solutions. That's why a large part of this book, including this chapter and the next three chapters, is dedicated to the topic of administration and maintenance.

Update   The third and final phase of the SAU methodology is the update phase. In this phase, you are focused on planning the durability of the technology in question. With SQL Server 2008, this may mean implementing technologies like Windows Server Update Services (WSUS) or implementing manual update policies. Because this chapter focuses the most on automation, WSUS will be covered in the last section of the chapter.

The results of the SAU process should be a single document or collection of documents that provide the following information:

- Configuration and operational standards

- Automation methods

- Update or maintenance methods

When starting the SAU process, usually you should create three documents:

- A configuration standards document for the technology

- An operational standards and automation methods document, which lists both the expected manual administration tasks (operational—as an operator must do something) and the tasks that can be automated

- A maintenance plan document, which indicates the most efficient and cost-tolerable method for updating the solution

For a typical SQL Server 2008 implementation, the documentation will usually span 25 to 40 pages; however, this is performed only for the first SQL Server installation. All other installations are based on the same documentation, and the documentation may evolve based on experiences learned with newer implementations.

With this methodology in mind, you're ready to begin exploring the tools in SQL Server that allow for automation of administration procedures. The first tool you'll explore is the SQL Server job.

Understanding SQL Server Jobs

SQL Server jobs provide a primary tool for the automation of maintenance and data-related tasks. It is important that you understand the steps that a job can take and the properties used to configure jobs, all of which will be covered in this section. The last subsection will address common job types that you will create and standardize for your SQL Servers.

Job Steps

A SQL Server *job* is a collection of one or more steps. A *step* is a task or group of tasks that should be carried out by the job. The steps can be of any of the following types with a standard database engine implementation:

ActiveX Script   Remember the Windows Scripting Host (WSH) introduced in Chapter 4, "SQL Server Command-Line Administration"? The ActiveX Script step allows you to take advantage of WSH to perform a nearly unlimited number of tasks. You can access the Windows APIs using this step type and even WMI for lower-level monitoring and configuration.

Operating System   If you are familiar with MS-DOS or the Windows command prompt, which was covered in Chapter 4, you will likely use this step frequently—at least until you become more familiar with PowerShell. You can run batch files and other command prompt commands using this step type.

PowerShell   The new job step in SQL Server 2008 is the PowerShell job step. You can call on any PowerShell scripts using this job step. If you are familiar with PowerShell, this step type is preferred over the Operating System step type. It is more secure than the Operating System step and provides more scripting power.

Replication   The replication steps include Replication Distributor, Replication Merge, Replication Queue Reader, Replication Snapshot, and Replication Transaction-Log Reader. All five steps are used to perform actions related to SQL Server 2008 replication. Replication is covered in detail in Chapter 22, "Replication."

SQL Server Analysis Services   The SSAS steps include SSAS Command and SSAS Query. Both actions are used to interact with an SSAS server. SSAS was introduced in Chapter 12, "Implementing Advanced Features."

SQL Server Integration Services Package   The SSIS step, SQL Server Integration Services Package, is used to run a previously built SSIS package. The package should be saved in a SQL Server, and the SQL Server Agent Service Account will usually need access to the server in which the package is saved. The creation of a job step for an SSIS package is described in a later section of this chapter titled "Creating SSIS Jobs."

T-SQL Commands   Any valid T-SQL code can run in a T-SQL step. These steps are used to perform many different kinds of maintenance and administration tasks, such as integrity checks, data archiving, data moves, database backups, creation of snapshots, and more. The creation of a T-SQL job step is described in a later section of this chapter titled "Creating T-SQL Jobs."

Using these step types, SQL Server jobs are created within the SQL Server Management Studio and stored in the MSDB database. The jobs are scheduled, processed, and monitored by the SQL Server Agent service. This fact is a very important bit of knowledge. Should you need to create a job that communicates with remote servers, the SQL Server Agent service must be able to communicate with the remote servers. You must ensure that the account context in which the SQL Server Agent runs has the ability to access the remote servers.

It is important to note that jobs can both succeed or fail entirely. For that matter, the steps in a job can also succeed or fail individually. Although you can be notified of these success and failure events, in order to be notified you will need to create some operators. Operators are covered in a later section of this chapter titled "Creating and Using Operators."

Job Configuration Properties

SQL Server jobs have six property categories that can be configured through the GUI interface. Figure 13.1 shows the default screen you see when you begin to create a new job. This screen is accessed by right-clicking Jobs and selecting New Job in the Object Browser of SSMS. The six property categories are listed in the upper-left side of the image.

FIGURE 13.1 Creating a new job in SSMS with the GUI interface

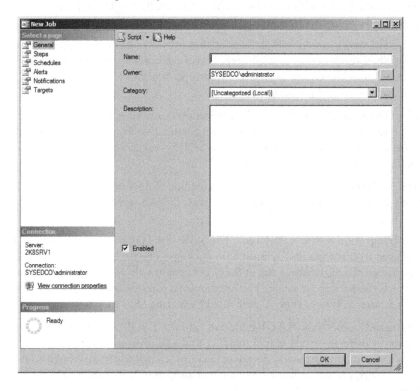

The property categories and configuration pages are

- General
- Steps
- Schedules
- Alerts
- Notifications
- Targets

Now let's discuss each of these in detail.

General Page

The General page, shown in Figure 13.1, provides access to the basic configuration parameters for the job as an object. These parameters include the job name, owner, category, description, and status (enabled or disabled). The job name should be descriptive of the job's function. For example, the backup job for the Marketing database should be named something like Marketing Database Backup.

The job category can be used to group jobs together so that they can be filtered in job history views within the Job Activity Monitor. The description provides space for more detailed information about the job and is not required; however, you may choose to use the description for several potential uses, such as listing the:

- Information about the job author or creator
- Time and date the job was created
- Purpose of the job with more details than the job name can provide
- Permissions required to execute the job
- Objects utilized by the job

During the standard SAU phase, you should standardize the use of the job description field. With such a standard, all jobs look similar and provide valuable information to future administrators.

Filling in the job owner property demands further explanation. By default, the dbo will own every job created. Of course, the dbo is a member of the sysadmin role within the SQL Server instance. The owner can manage the job much as the owner of a file on an NTFS file system can change permissions on that file. The only time you would want to change job ownership is when a user—who is not a member of the sysadmin role—needs to have management access to the job. While this need is very rare, it certainly does occur. If the new owner is not a member of sysadmin, be sure to give the owner access to any proxies that are utilized by the job steps.

Proxies, as used in SQL Server Agent jobs, are covered in Chapter 19, "Security Best Practices." For now, just know that they provide alternative, less-powerful credentials for sensitive job steps that could be hijacked in order to penetrate a server or network system. The job owner must have access to these proxy accounts, which are simply called proxies in SQL Server.

Steps Page

The Steps page is used to create the actual job steps. These job steps determine the actions that the job will take. The different step types were described in the previous section titled "Job Steps." Figure 13.2 shows the Steps page, which is used to add or insert new job steps, delete existing steps, or reorganize steps. When you click the New button to create a new step, you will be presented with a dialog similar to that in Figure 13.3.

FIGURE 13.2   The job steps page in the New Job dialog

FIGURE 13.3   Creating a new step in a job

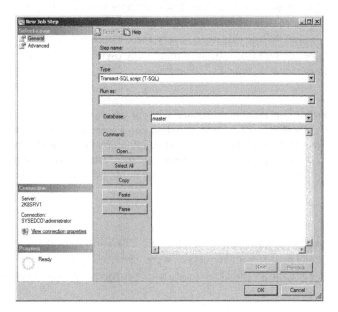

The General page of the Job Step dialog is used to configure the required settings for the step. Like the job itself, every step in the job has a name. You must also specify the step type, which can drastically alter the look of the job step dialog, as shown in Figure 13.4. When you select a SSIS step, for example, many new options—such as data sources, logging options, and the actual package selection interface—become available. In general, when you select a specific step type, the dialog will change to reflect the properties required to configure and execute that selected step type.

FIGURE 13.4   A job step of type SSIS changes the interface.

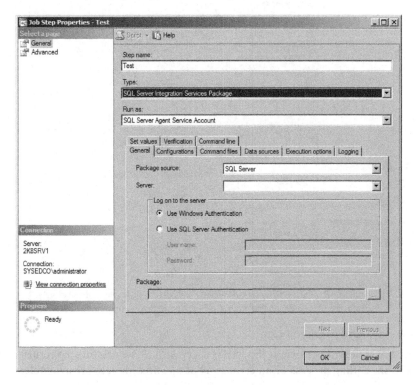

Additionally, for many step types you can specify the execution context, which is set using the Run As field. Normally, steps requiring an execution context run as the SQL Server Agent service account; however, you can change this default. In order to run the step in a different context, you must first create a proxy account, which is fully covered in Chapter 19. For now, however, it is important to note that for every step type except the Transact-SQL type, you can set a proxy.

If you must run a Transact-SQL step as a different user, you will have to use the EXECUTE AS clause within the step code itself. You would first create a stored procedure that performs the action required in the step. The stored procedure would be set to execute as a different user than the calling user. Finally, you simply need to call the stored procedure in the job step.

Alternatively, if you do not want to develop a stored procedure, you can use the Advanced page on a Transact-SQL step to specify the user context.

The Job Step dialog also includes an Advanced page, as shown in Figure 13.5.

FIGURE 13.5   Configuring advanced settings for a job step

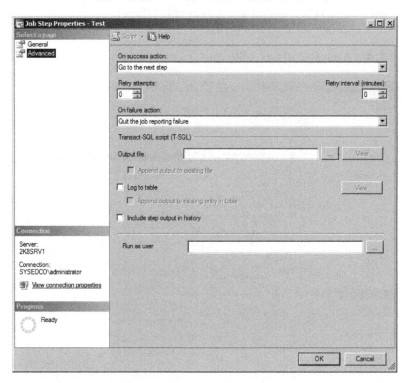

From the Advanced page, you can:

- Choose the action to perform if the step is successful. A successful step returns no errors to the calling process or an error level of 0. Three choices are available:

    - Go to next step

    - Quit the job reporting success

    - Quit the job reporting failure

    A step that runs a command reporting success when the state does not equal what you desire would report failure on success. For example, if you run a command prompt command that reports success (no errors) when a particular service is running and you don't want the service to be running if your job runs, you could quit the job reporting failure even though the step was a success.

- Determine the retry attempts. If the job step fails, you can retry multiple times before giving up entirely. By default, this parameter is set to 0 retries.

- Determine the retry interval. The retry interval determines how long to wait, in minutes, between retries. The default is 0. If you choose to enable retries, you may want to set the retry interval to 1 minute or more.

- Choose the action to perform if the step fails. A failed step returns errors or an error level of greater than 0 in most cases. The same choices exist for failed steps as those that exist for successful steps.

- Set Transact-SQL step parameters. The values in the Transact-SQL script (T-SQL) section of Figure 13.5 only apply to T-SQL steps. If the step type were PowerShell, you would see a PowerShell section instead. The options in this section vary depending on the step type.

Following is a list of the different options available on the Advanced page for the most common step types of Transact-SQL, PowerShell, Operating System, ActiveX, and SSIS.

Transact-SQL   This specifies the output file to save any output of the T-SQL script; determines a logging table, if you wish to log to a database table; indicates that the output of the script should be stored in the job history; and specifies the Run As context, if desired.

PowerShell   This specifies the output file to save any output of the PowerShell command(s); determine a logging table, if you want to log to a database table; and also indicates that the output of the commands should be stored in the job history.

Operating System   This specifies the output file to save any output of the operating system command(s); determines a logging table, if you want to log to a database table; and indicates that the output of the commands should be stored in the job history.

ActiveX   No advanced options specific to ActiveX scripts exist. Only the shared options available for all step types exist on the Advanced page.

SSIS   SSIS specifies the output file to save any output of the SSIS package; determines a logging table, if you want to log to a database table; and indicates that the output of the package should be stored in the job history.

Schedules Page

The Schedules page is used to create a data-based or a time-based schedule for the job to run. Figure 13.6 shows the Schedules page with a CPU idle schedule run configured. The schedule can be a one-time event, a recurring event, a startup event, or an idle event.

FIGURE 13.6   The Schedules page with a CPU idle schedule

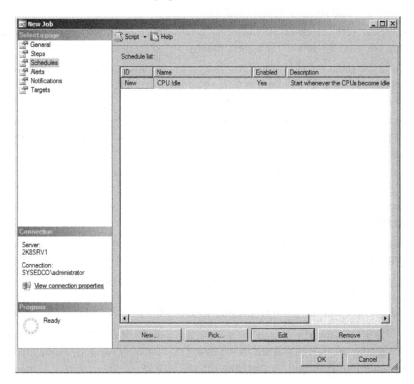

If you click the Edit button, as shown in the lower part of the screen in Figure 13.6, you can alter the schedule type. The schedule types you can choose are as follows:

One Time Scheduled Jobs   One time event jobs run once and then never run again on a schedule. The one time job is not deleted by default; however, you can configure it to be deleted after a successful run on the Notifications page. The one time job can be run manually or rescheduled at a future time.

Recurring Scheduled Jobs   Recurring jobs run on a regular schedule. The jobs can be configured to run daily, weekly, or monthly. Weekly jobs can be scheduled to run multiple times during the week. Daily jobs can be scheduled to run multiple times during the day. Monthly jobs can be scheduled to run on a specific date of each month or on the first of a given day of each month. Additionally, monthly jobs can be scheduled to run multiple times during the month.

Startup Scheduled Jobs   Jobs scheduled to run on startup run every time the SQL Server Agent service starts. This fact is very important to remember. You may think a startup job runs when the SQL Server service starts, but this is not the case.

Idle Scheduled Jobs   A job scheduled for an idle run waits for the CPU to become idle and then it launches. This type of schedule is very useful for jobs that you want to run very often for maintenance tasks. Examples include advanced data monitoring, process monitoring, user monitoring, log monitoring, or any other such task that does not require fixed intervals of operation, but should run as often as possible without hurting system performance.

Alerts Page

The Alerts page is used to create and manage alerts for a job. Alerts can monitor for SQL Server events, performance conditions, or WMI events that occur during the time window in which the job is running. You can configure alerts that monitor the server continually using independent alert objects, as discussed in the later section of this chapter titled "Creating and Using Alerts." The alerts created on the job Alerts page will be monitored only while the job is running; however, the alerts are created and configured in exactly the same way as independent alert objects, so the alert creation process will not be covered in detail here.

Notifications Page

The Notification page determines who or what is notified and in what scenarios notifications should take place. Figure 13.7 shows the Notifications page.

FIGURE 13.7   Configuring notifications for a job

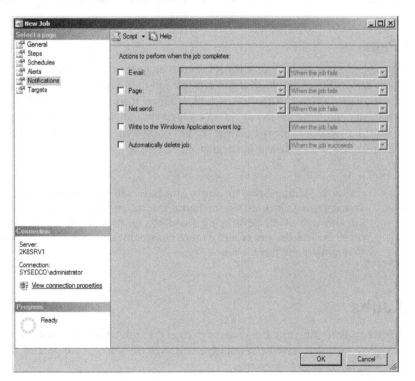

Notifications can be made for operators, which are covered in the later section of this chapter titled "Creating and Using Operators." Operators can be notified when the job succeeds, when the job fails, or simply when the job completes regardless of success or failure.

Notifications can take place by email, pager, or net send. The net send option is least useful for production notifications because the notification will be lost if the operator is not currently logged into the network. The net send option literally uses the NET SEND command that is available at the command prompt of Microsoft Windows systems going all the way back to Windows 3.x in the early 1990s. It relies on two factors for success. First, the target user must be logged into the network. Second, the machine on which the user is logged in must be running the proper service. On Windows XP and older clients, this was the Messenger service. Windows Vista and newer clients no longer support the Messenger service, and it is best to avoid sending NET SEND messages to these newer clients. In the end, the net send option is useful for initial testing at best. It should also be avoided in most live production implementations.

In addition to the operator notifications, you can send information to the Windows event logs. The event log entries will be stored in the Application log and can be viewed in the Event Viewer.

Finally, you can specify that the job should be deleted. The option to delete the job can be performed when the job completes, when it is successful, or when it fails—just like notifications.

Targets Page

On the Targets page, you can configure the job to run against or on multiple servers instead of just the local server. For example, you can create a job that backs up the master database and then configure this job to run against each SQL Server instance on your network. This way you do not have to create the job again on each server individually. To target multiple servers, you must have a central management server configured. Central management is covered in Chapter 15, "Policy-Based Management."

 Consider standardizing the format for basic job configuration settings. These settings include the job name, owner, and descriptions—as well as job step names. By developing standards for these objects and enforcing these standards, you create a more consistent environment that is easier to maintain and troubleshoot.

Typical Jobs

There is no better way to illustrate the value of SQL Server jobs than to provide some examples of typical jobs that have been implemented over the years of supporting SQL Servers. Most jobs fall into two categories:

Data Processing Jobs   The data processing jobs perform tasks such as data exports, imports, moves, deletions, archiving, and the like.

Maintenance Jobs   The maintenance jobs perform tasks such as index defragmentation (reorganizing and rebuilding), database backups, schedules administration (for example, creating new databases and database objects), and other similar tasks.

The following list details a few real-world jobs:

- A parts distributor had a customer order database that needed to have new data imported hourly. A job was created to run an SSIS package and that did the trick.

- A government client needed to have specific non-IT employees notified when particular data values changed within their SQL Server 2005 database. A job was created that ran on a CPU idle schedule to watch for the changes and then email the notifications with the `sp_send_dbmail` stored procedure, which is built into SQL Server.

- A client with a web-based application wanted to run a job every hour to ensure that no new user accounts had been added to the application database for security reasons. A job was created that compared the dbo.AppUsers table with a list of valid users. If invalid users were found, they were removed and the admin was notified.

- A manufacturing client used a machine monitoring application that checked the temperature and parts per minute (PPM) for several machines in the factory. They wanted to be notified if a machine produced lower than a specific PPM rate based on values in a table that indicated minimum PPM rates for different times of the day, and the monitoring application did not have a built-in alert engine. A job was implemented to monitor the tracking tables and send the alerts.

- A SQL Server database was used to track projects with a custom-built project management application at Systems Education and Consulting (SysEdCo). They wanted to perform four tasks: back up the database, rebuild the indexes, create a snapshot, and export several Excel reports. A single job was created that performed the backup and created the snapshot. Another job rebuilt all indexes, which ran after the backup and snapshot job. Finally, the third job exported the Excel reports and even emailed them to the inboxes of the appropriate project managers.

These five examples—a drop in the bucket compared to the jobs that can be created—provide food for thought for the types of jobs you can create with SQL Server. As you work with SQL Server yourself, you will likely discover brand new uses of the job engine that the SQL Server Agent service provides. To help you get started, the following three sections (Creating T-SQL Jobs, Creating SSIS Jobs, and Creating Windows Command Jobs) present example jobs based on real-world needs and provide step-by-step instructions for creating them.

Remember this important fact: your jobs will be easier to manage if you first develop standards for what all jobs must include. These included items may be job-naming conventions, description requirements, and ownership defaults. When you have standardized the process, you're more likely to have a consistent environment that is easier to manage. For example, when you troubleshoot problems, it is much easier without the stress of first having to figure out what actions a job performs. Standardization means reduced costs and frustrations for everyone on the support staff.

Real World Scenario

Parts Supplier Automates with Standards

A parts supplier located in Ohio was implementing several new SQL Servers for three different projects. The first project was a new, wireless inventory management system for their warehouses. The second project was a new customer website for order tracking. The final project was a new enterprise resource planning (ERP) application. All three were designed to use SQL Server and worked well on SQL Server 2005 or 2008. The organization chose to implement SQL Server 2008.

After installing and configuring the first database server, they began to create several jobs for backups and other maintenance tasks. Four different DBAs were working with the server at different times. One DBA was an independent consultant and another was from our consulting practice at SysEdCo. The other two were internal employees of the parts supplier. Each DBA was building jobs—and other objects for that matter—using his or her own opinion of how things should be done. The result, with only one server, was utter chaos.

Some tables were named with a convention of *tbl_tablename* and others were named with a convention of *data_tablename*. Still other tables were named with seeming randomness. In many cases, jobs lacked descriptions and job steps were poorly named. A standardization solution was desperately needed.

I'm happy to say that our consultant spearheaded the project to develop naming conventions, standards for jobs, and other objects and maintenance procedures. By the time the second and third database servers were installed and configured, the standards had been documented and the first server had been restructured to comply with the standards. To this day, the standards are being followed and working in the SQL Server environment is much easier.

Just recently, I worked on one of the SQL Servers in this organization and it was quite easy to understand the jobs and objects within the server. I have never seen the standardization documents for that specific SQL Server installation and I wasn't directly involved in that project. Yet, when I access the servers, I can clearly see the naming conventions used and the standards for descriptions and ownership of objects. Interestingly, I can continue to support those standards without reading them because they are clear in the objects that exist. This simplicity is a key factor that you should keep in mind when developing your own standards.

When it comes to standards for object names and descriptions and the like, our motto is clear: keep it simple, but make it work. Keeping it simple allows for inferential understanding of the standard without even reading it, in most cases. Making it work means that we must implement enough complexity to meet the needs of the situation. By combining simplicity and functionality together, you achieve minimum complexity.

Creating T-SQL Jobs

T-SQL jobs can perform just about any SQL Server–related task you desire. Most administrative actions can be performed using T-SQL commands. If you do not know the command, but you know how to do it in the GUI interface of SSMS, begin the process within the GUI and use the Script button to learn the T-SQL code. Then, you can take that T-SQL code and schedule the action as a job.

To provide an example of a common T-SQL–based job, Exercise 13.1 steps you through the process of creating a job that will perform a backup of the AdventureWorks database and then create a snapshot of the same database. The job will include two steps: one for the backup and one for the snapshot. Do not worry about the concept of a snapshot at this time. Chapter 16, "Backup and Restoration," will cover snapshots in detail.

EXERCISE 13.1

Creating a T-SQL Job

In this exercise, you will create one of the most common job types: a backup job. The job creates a backup of the AdventureWorks database using standard T-SQL commands. The backup is performed in the first step of the job. The second step uses a T-SQL command to create a snapshot of the AdventureWorks database as it looks just after the backup completes.

To create the T-SQL–based job and job steps, perform the following:

1. Open the SSMS application and expand the SQL Server Agent node.

2. Right-click the Jobs node and select New Job.

3. Enter a job name of **Backup and Snapshot for AdventureWorks**, as in the following image:

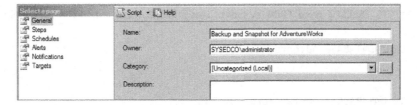

4. Accept all other defaults on the General page and click the Steps page to select it.

5. Click New to add a new step.

6. On the General page for the new step, enter the name of **Backup AdventureWorks**. Note that the default step type is Transact-SQL, and then enter the following code in the Command window:

```
BACKUP DATABASE AdventureWorks
TO DISK= 'C:\Program Files\Microsoft SQL Server\
MSSQL10.MSSQLSERVER\MSSQL\Backup\backup.bak'
GO
```

7. Click the Parse button to validate the code. In the Command window, the DISK parameter path should be typed without a line break. You should receive a message that reads, "The command was successfully parsed." If not, check the code for accuracy. The General page should look similar to the following image:

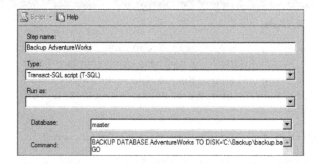

8. Click the OK button to save the step and accept all defaults for the Advanced page.

9. Click the New button to add the second step for the snapshot creation.

10. On the General page for the new step, enter the name of **CreateAdventureWorks Snapshot** and then enter the following code in the Command window:

```
IF EXISTS (SELECT name FROM sys.databases WHERE name = N'AdventureWorks_ss')
BEGIN
    DROP DATABASE AdventureWorks_ss
END
GO
CREATE DATABASE AdventureWorks_ss ON
( NAME = AdventureWorks_Data, FILENAME =
'C:\Program Files\Microsoft SQL Server\
MSSQL10.MSSQLSERVER\MSSQL\Data\AdventureWorks.ss' )
AS SNAPSHOT OF AdventureWorks;
GO
```

11. Click the Parse button to ensure accuracy of code entry. In the code, the FILENAME parameter path should be typed without a line break.

12. If the code parses correctly, the General page should look similar to the following image; if so, click OK to save the job step.

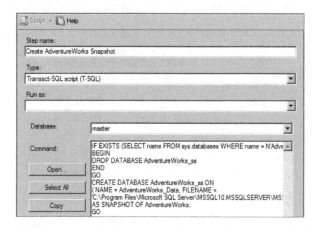

13. Select the Schedules page to configure a schedule for the Backup and Snapshot for AdventureWorks job.

14. Click the New button to create a new schedule.

15. Enter the schedule name of **Nightly-4-AM**.

16. Accept the default schedule type of Recurring.

17. For Frequency, choose Daily and then specify Occurs Once At: 4:00:00 AM. Your New Schedule screen should look similar to the following image. If so, click OK.

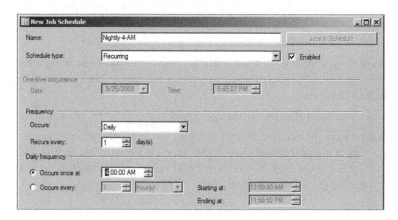

18. Click OK again to create the job.

In a production environment, you would create the operators before creating a job like the one in Exercise 13.1. You would take the extra steps to notify one or more operators for an important job like the backup of a database. If you want to run the job in order to verify that it works, follow these steps:

1. Right-click on the job and select Start Job at Step in SSMS.

2. Choose step 1 and click Start.

If everything goes well, you should see results similar to those in Figure 13.8.

FIGURE 13.8 Manually running the Backup and Snapshot for AdventureWorks job

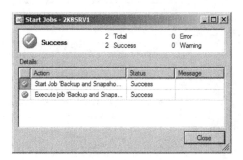

You can also navigate to the storage folders used in the job to verify that the files are there. A file named AdventureWorks.ss should be in the C:\Program Files\Microsoft SQL Server\MSSQL10.MSSQLSERVER\MSSQL\Data folder. Another file named backup.bak should be in the C:\Program Files\Microsoft SQL Server\MSSQL10.MSSQLSERVER\MSSQL\Backup folder.

Congratulations. You've successfully created your first and one of the most important job types you can create—a backup job. You'll learn much more about backups, including snapshots, in Chapter 16.

Once a job is created, however, it isn't set in stone. Jobs can be modified and monitored after you create them. For example, you may want to configure operators to be notified in relation to a job or you may need to change the steps in a job. You can modify a job easily by double-clicking it at any time. Here are a few quick and easy modifications:

- You can delete jobs by right-clicking the job and selecting Delete.

- If you want to prevent the job from automatically running—assuming it has been scheduled—without deleting it, you can prevent job execution by right-clicking the job and selecting Disable.

- Later, when you want the job to run again, just right-click the job and select Enable.

- You can also view the activity related to a job. For example, you can see if a job has run and, if so, if it was a success or failure. To view job activity, right-click the Job Activity Monitor in the SQL Server Agent node and select View Job Activity. You will see a screen similar to that in Figure 13.9.

FIGURE 13.9   Viewing job activity in the Job Activity Monitor

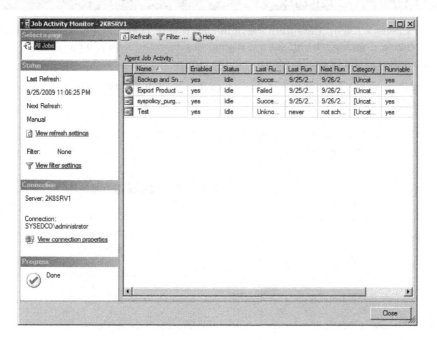

Creating SSIS Jobs

SSIS is very good at exporting and importing data. For this reason, you'll use the example of a data export job as the SSIS job. Exercise 13.2 steps you through the process of creating the SSIS export package with the Export Wizard.

EXERCISE 13.2

Creating the SSIS Export Package

In this exercise, you will use the Data Export Wizard in SSMS to generate a SSIS package that you can run as a job step. The package will export data in Excel format and store it in a file on the desktop of the server. The exported data will come from the Sales.SalesOrderHeader and Sales.SalesOrderDetail tables in the AdventureWorks database.

To create the SSIS Export package, follow these steps:

1.   Launch the SSMS application and expand the Databases node.

2.   Right-click on the database from which you want to export the data and right-click on the AdventureWorks database.

EXERCISE 13.2 *(continued)*

3. Choose Tasks ➢ Export Data from the right-click menu. The SQL Server Import and Export Wizard appears. If you see the Welcome screen because you have never checked the Do Not Show This Screen in the Future box, click Next.

4. On the Choose a Data Source screen, ensure that the AdventureWorks database is selected, as shown in the following image, and click Next.

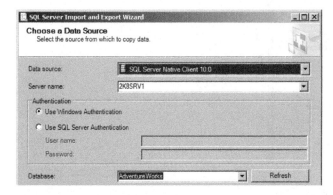

5. On the Choose a Destination screen, select the Microsoft Excel destination.

6. For the Excel file path, enter **C:\ExportData\Sales.xls**. (The C:\ExportData folder must exist. If it does not, launch a command prompt and execute **md C:\ExportData** to create it.)

7. Check the First Row Has Column Names option, as shown in the following image, and click Next.

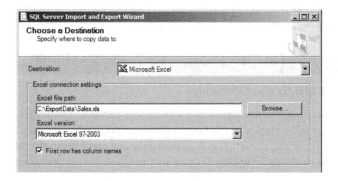

8. On the Specify Table Copy or Query screen, choose Copy Data from One Or More Tables or Views and click Next.

9. On the Select Source Tables and Views screen, scroll down and select (by checking the check box) the Sales.SalesOrderDetail and Sales.SalesOrderHeader tables, as in the following image, and then click Next.

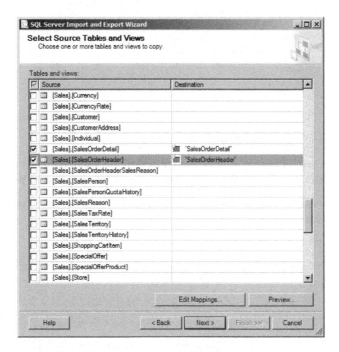

10. On the Review Data Type Mapping screen, review the settings, accept the defaults, and click Next. (Do not be alarmed if you see a warning on the Review Data Type Mapping screen. The warnings should not cause any problems for our purposes. They are usually related to data type conversion issues and should not corrupt data.)

11. On the Save and Run package screen, select Save SSIS Package and save the package in the SQL Server. For the Package Protection Level, choose "Rely on server storage and roles for access control." Deselect Run immediately, as in the following image, and then click Next.

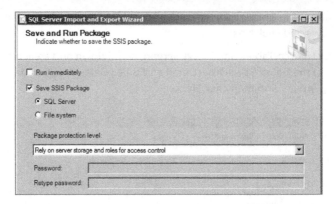

12. On the Save SSIS Package screen, enter the following parameters:

    a. In the Name field, enter **Export Sales Data**.

    b. In the Description field, enter **Export the Sales.SalesOrderDetail and Sales. SalesOrderHeader tables to an Excel spreadsheet named Sales.xls**.

    c. In the Server name field, select the name of your local server on which you are creating the package.

    d. For authentication security, choose Windows Authentication.

13. Once your Save SSIS Package screen looks similar to the following, click Next.

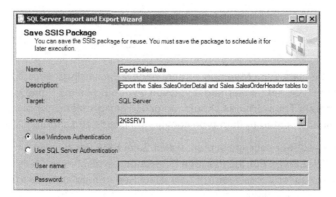

14. Review the chosen options on the Complete the Wizard screen and then click Finish to create the package. You should see results listing the value Success for each step similar to those in the following image.

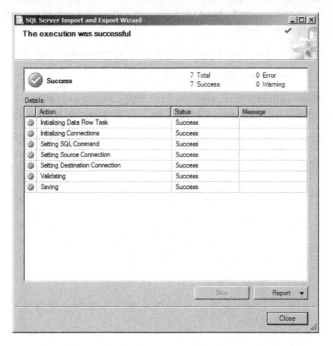

15. Click Close to close the Import and Export Wizard.

The Import and Export Wizard used in Exercise 13.2 is an important feature to remember because it provides an excellent way to import and export data from your SQL Servers dynamically as well as through an SSIS package.

In Exercise 13.3, you will create the actual job that calls on the SSIS package. The job creation process is very simple now that the SSIS package is doing all the work.

EXERCISE 13.3

Creating a SSIS Job

In this exercise, you will create the job to run the SSIS package generated in Exercise 13.2. If you have not performed exercise 13.2, you will not be able to complete this exercise.

To create the SSIS-based job, follow these steps:

1. Launch the SSMS and expand the SQL Server Agent node.

2. Right-click on the Jobs node and select New Job.

3. Enter a job name of **Export Sales Data Nightly** to indicate that the job is used to export sales data every night.

4. Accept the default for job ownership and enter any description you desire.

5. Ensure that the Enabled option is checked.

6. Accept the default value for the Category field. You can use the category to filter reports on the job history in production environments, but you'll leave it unassigned here.

7. Once your General page looks similar to the following image, click the Steps page.

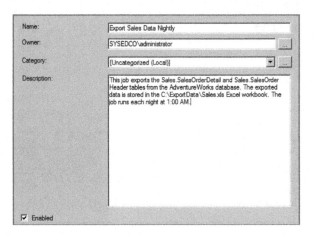

8. Click New to add a new job step.

9. Enter the step name of **Run the Export SSIS Package**.

10. Choose the step type of SQL Server Integration Services Package.

11. On the General tab, choose the server that you specified in step 12 of Exercise 13.2.

12. Again, on the General tab, click the select button (...),choose the Export Sales Data SSIS package, and click OK.

13. Once you have entered the information described and shown in the following image, click OK to create the step.

EXERCISE 13.3 *(continued)*

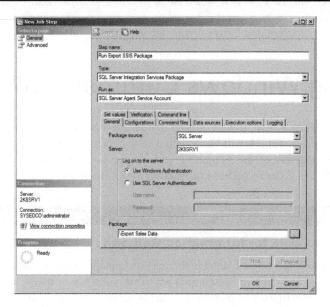

14. Select the Schedules page.

15. Click New to add a new schedule.

16. Enter a name of **Nightly at 1:00 AM**, choose the schedule type of Recurring, set the frequency to Daily, and choose Occurs Once At: 1:00:00 AM for the time. Once your New Job Schedule dialog looks similar to the following image, click OK to create the schedule.

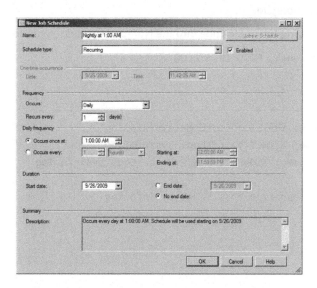

17. Click OK again to save the job.

As Exercise 13.3 shows, creating an SSIS job is very similar to creating a T-SQL job. If you want to delete the SSIS job that was created in Exercise 13.3, right-click the job and select Delete. You may want to do this for all of the jobs you create in this chapter so that they do not run on a scheduled basis on your lab server.

Creating Windows Command Jobs

In this final job example, you will learn how to create a job that calls on a Windows command. The purpose of this job will be to send a server status report to the DBA from the SQL Server. You will first create a batch file in Exercise 13.4. The batch file will execute several commands in order to gather information about the state of the server.

EXERCISE 13.4

Creating a Batch File for Information Gathering

In this exercise, you will create a batch file that can be launched from a job in Exercise 13.5. This batch file will run command-line commands to store the server name, IP configuration, network statistics, and more information in a log file named C:\Logs\%date%-sysinfo.log. In order for the batch file to work properly, the folder must exist. For this reason, the batch file first checks for the existence of the folder and creates it if it is missing. Next, several commands are executed to export information to the log file.

To create the batch file, follow these steps:

1. Launch the Notepad text editor by selecting Start ➢ All Programs (or Programs) ➢ Accessories ➢ Notepad.

2. Enter the following batch file code into the Notepad text editor window:

```
IF EXIST C:\Logs\. GOTO CREATELOG
MD C:\Logs
:CREATELOG
ECHO ---------------------------------------------------- >> c:\Logs\sysinfo.log
ECHO Log Date: %DATE% >> c:\Logs\sysinfo.log
ECHO Log Time: %TIME% >> c:\Logs\sysinfo.log
ECHO Server Name: %COMPUTERNAME% >> c:\Logs\sysinfo.log
ECHO.
ECHO IP Configuration >> c:\Logs\sysinfo.log
```

```
IPCONFIG >> c:\Logs\sysinfo.log
ECHO.
ECHO Running Tasks >> c:\Logs\sysinfo.log
TASKLIST /v >> c:\Logs\sysinfo.log
ECHO.
ECHO Network Stats >> c:\Logs\sysinfo.log
netstat -s >> c:\Logs\sysinfo.log
```

3. Click File Save to save the batch file.

4. Navigate to the C:\Program Files\Microsoft SQL Server\MSSQL10.MSSQLSERVER\ MSSQL\JOBS folder and save the file as GatherSysInfo.bat.

5. Click File ➢ Exit to exit Notepad.

You may want to run the batch file manually to verify that it works correctly on your server before proceeding to Exercise 13.5.

Now that the batch file is ready, it's time to start building the job. In Exercise 13.5, you will create a job that calls the batch file in the first step. Next, you will execute another step that sends the results of the batch file to the DBA as an email attachment. The exercise assumes that the DBA's email address is DBA@company.com. If you have not previously configured Database Mail, the job will not be able to send the email, but you can still create the job.

Creating a Windows Command Job

In this exercise, you will create the job that runs the batch file created in Exercise 13.4. To create the Windows command job, follow these steps:

1. Launch SSMS and expand the SQL Server Agent node.

2. Right-click the Jobs node and select New Job.

3. Enter a job name of **Generate System Information Log** to indicate that the job is used to export sales data every night.

4. Accept the default for job ownership and enter any description you desire.

5. Ensure that the Enabled option is checked.

6. Once your General page looks similar to the following image, click the Steps page.

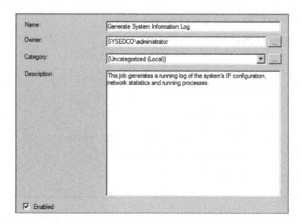

7. Click New to add a new job step.

8. Enter a name of **Run GatherSysInfo.bat**.

9. Choose the step type of Operating System (CmdExec).

10. In the command window, enter the following text all on one line:

`"C:\Program Files\Microsoft SQL Server\`
`MSSQL10.MSSQLSERVER\MSSQL\Jobs\GatherSysInfo.bat"`

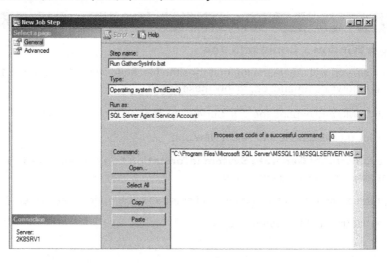

11. Click OK to save the job step.

12. Select the Schedules page.

13. Click New to add a new schedule.

14. Name the schedule **CPU IDLE**, and choose the schedule type of Start whenever the CPUs become idle as in the following image.

15. Click OK to save the new schedule.

16. Click OK to create the job.

After some time has passed and the CPUs have been idle, you should see a new folder named Logs in the root of your C: drive. In this folder will be an ever-growing log named syslog.log. To see if the Generate System Information Log job has executed, right-click the job and choose View History. From here, you can see any execution instances as represented in Figure 13.10.

FIGURE 13.10   Viewing the history of the Generate System Information Log job

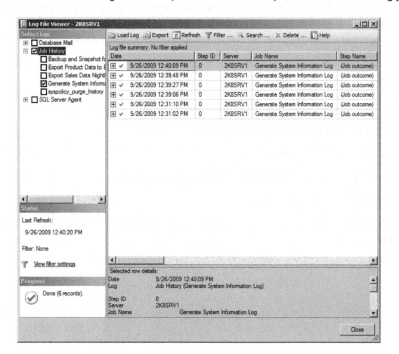

When you use a job schedule based on CPU idle time, you can adjust what is considered an idle CPU. Right-click the SQL Server Agent node and select Properties. From here, choose the Advanced page and set the CPU idle parameters as desired. You must restart the SQL Server Agent service for the CPU idle changes to work.

Creating and Using Operators

SQL Server *operators* are collections of contact information and contact time windows for individuals, groups, or systems. These individuals, groups, or systems can be referred to as points of contact. Operators are created to provide notifications to these points of contact. In most cases, jobs and alerts send the notifications. You create operators in SSMS by expanding the SQL Server Agent container in Object Explorer and then selecting the Operators container. From here you can create and manage operators. Exercise 13.6 steps you through the process of creating a fictitious operator named Fred Barney.

EXERCISE 13.6

Creating an Operator

In this exercise, you will create an operator for a fictitious individual named Fred Barney. Fred's fake email address will be configured as fredb@sqlserverdbabook.net. He will be available for net send messages at the NetBIOS name of fredb. In this case, the pager duty will not be applicable.

To create the operator, follow these steps:

1. Launch SSMS and expand the SQL Server Agent node.

2. Right-click the Operators node and select New Operator.

3. Enter the name of **Fred Barney**.

4. Enter the email address of **fredb@sqlserverdbabook.net**.

5. Enter the net send address of **fredb**.

6. Once the operator configuration looks like the following image, click OK to create the operator.

EXERCISE 13.6 *(continued)*

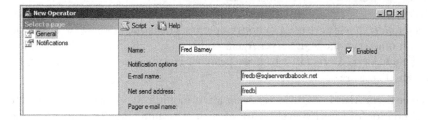

Note that you have created an operator, which means you can add the operator to any job for notification. To add an operator to a job, simply double-click the job and select the Notifications page. Choose the notification method and the appropriate operator. Figure 13.11 shows an example of this configuration.

FIGURE 13.11 Configuring an operator for notification within a SQL Server Agent job

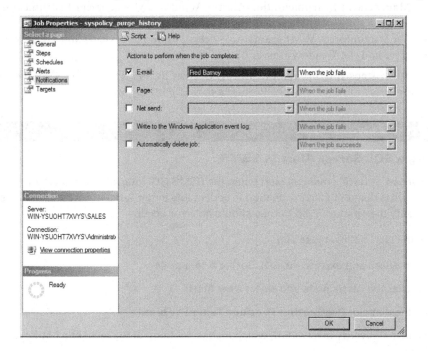

 You may create an operator so that the SQL Server can send notifications to another system. If the remote system monitors an email account or listens for incoming net send messages, it can receive notifications and take appropriate actions.

Creating and Using Alerts

SQL Server *alert objects* are used to notify operators or launch jobs when events occur. You create alert objects in the SQL Server Agent node by right-clicking the Alerts container and selecting New Alert. Alerts fall into three primary categories when creating a SQL Server alert object. These are

SQL Server Event Alerts   SQL Server event alerts monitor for errors within the SQL Server. You can monitor for severity levels or for explicit error numbers. You can also raise an alert when a message contains specific text. This latter option is most useful when you want to fire an alert if it mentions a particular object, such as a table or a database.

SQL Server Performance Condition Alerts   You can also indicate that an alert should fire based on a specific performance condition. You first specify the performance counter to monitor. Next, you set a threshold for the alert. Finally, you configure the behavior that the counter must show if the alert is to occur.

Windows Management Instrumentation Alerts   Windows Management Instrumentation (WMI) alerts monitor for WMI events. The WMI Query Language (WQL) is used to define the event that is monitored. WMI grants you access to internal systems and events within the SQL Server and the Windows server on which it runs.

Exercise 13.7 steps you through the process of creating an alert within SSMS. The alert monitors for errors in relation to the Production.Product table only.

EXERCISE 13.7

Creating a SQL Server Alert in SSMS

In this exercise, you will create an alert using the SSMS GUI interface. The alert will watch for errors related to the Production.Product table in the AdventureWorks database and will notify the operator Fred Barney should an error occur.

To create the alert, follow these steps:

1. Launch SSMS and expand the SQL Server Agent node.

2. Right-click the Alerts node and select New Alert.

3. Enter the name of **Production.Product Table Problem**.

4. Choose the Severity level of 007, which means anything at the level of a notification or higher.

5. Check the Raise Alert When Message Contains option and enter the text **Production.Product** into the text field.

6. Once your General page looks similar to the one in the following image, click the Response page.

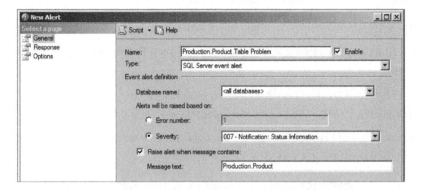

7. Select the Notify Operators option and check the E-mail notification for Fred Barney, as in the following image.

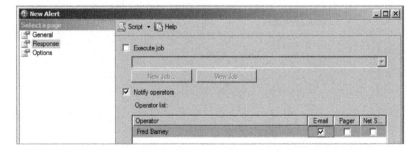

8. Click OK to create the new alert.

In addition to the alerts you create within SSMS, you can create alerts in the Performance Monitor (also known as the System Monitor). The Performance Monitor is part of the Windows server operating system itself and, in Windows Server 2008, it is part of the Reliability and Performance Monitor. Exercise 13.8 provides instructions for creating an alert within the Performance Monitor.

EXERCISE 13.8

Creating a Free Drive Space Alert

In this exercise, you will create a Performance Monitor alert using the Reliability and Performance Monitor in Windows Server 2008. You will first create a user-defined data collector set, which specifies the performance counter to monitor. Then, you will specify the threshold and action to take should the alert fire.

To create the counter-based alert, follow these steps:

1. Select Start ≻ All Programs ≻ Administrative Tools ≻ Reliability and Performance Monitor.

2. Expand the Data Collector Sets node.

3. Right-click the User Defined node and select New ≻ Data Collector Set.

4. Enter the name of **Free Drive Space on C**, select Create Manually (Advanced) as shown in the following image, and then click Next.

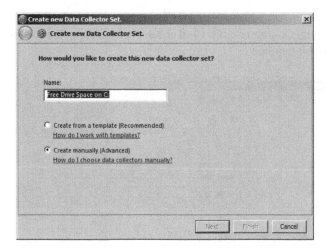

5. Select Performance Counter Alert, which is not the default, and then click Next.

6. Click Add to add the Logical Disk counter for drive C:.

7. Scroll through the list of available counters and expand Logical Disk.

8. Click on Free Megabytes within the Logical Disk object and choose C: in the instances of selected object section, as in the following image.

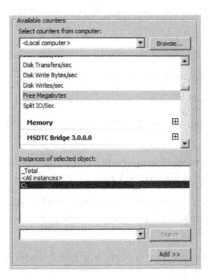

9. Click the Add button to add the counter and then click OK.

10. In the Create New Data Collector Set dialog, set the Alert When value to Below and the Limit value to **2000** so that the alert will fire when the drive is below 2,000 megabytes of free space. When your dialog looks similar to the following image, click Next.

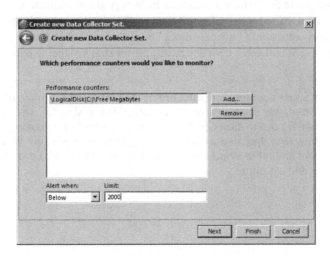

11. Click Finish to create the Data Collector Set.

At this point, the Data Collector Set named Free Drive Space on C exists; however, no actions are configured for when the alert fires. To configure these actions, follow these steps:

12. Expand the User Defined node within the Data Collector Sets node.

13. Click on the Free Drive Space on C set in the left pane.

14. Double-click on the DataCollector01 alert in the right pane.

15. Select the Alert Action tab and enable the Log An Entry In The Application Event Log option.

16. Notice that you can start a performance log Data Collector Set from the Alert Action tab as well and then click the Alert Task tab.

17. Notice that you can run programs in response to the firing of the alert from the Alert Task tab. Change nothing and click OK to save the event log notification change that you made in step 15.

Now, the alert is configured to log to the event log, but it is still not going to work until you start the Data Collector Set.

18. Right-click the Free Drive Space on C set in the left pane and select Start.

You have now stepped through the process of creating an alert in Windows Server 2008 with the Reliability and Performance Monitor for a very simple reason: it's much more complicated than it used to be in earlier versions of Windows server. However, it's also more powerful and consistent. This new model is also used in Windows Server 2008 R2, Windows Vista, and Windows 7, so it's very important that you get used to using it.

It's just a preference, but I prefer to create alerts outside of SQL Server when they are available in the Performance Monitor. The reason is simple: when I create alerts in the Performance Monitor, I'm using a consistent interface that also works on my Exchange servers, my IIS web servers, and any other Windows Server. It goes right back to the principle of standardization.

Using WSUS for SQL Server 2008

It would be nice if SQL Server 2008 were so flawless that Microsoft never needed to release an update for the product. However, Microsoft released service pack (SP) 1 on August 27, 2009. SQL Server 2008 was released to manufacturing in August of 2008. So, one year after its release, the first SP was available. A SP includes fixes for bugs in the application code and may introduce new features.

In addition to SPs, hotfixes are also released. *Hotfixes* repair, in most cases, individual problems. SPs repair the collected problems that may or may not have previously been fixed in hotfixes. You could choose to manually update all of your SQL Server 2008 installations and, if you only have a few, that may be the best choice. However, if you have dozens of SQL Server 2008 instances, you may need to implement a large-scale update infrastructure. That's where tools like Windows Server Update Services (WSUS) come into play.

WSUS is a free add-on to Windows servers. It allows you to configure an internal server for downloading of updates from Microsoft. The internal clients and servers on your network receive updates from the WSUS server. The benefits are several, but the following three benefits are the most important:

Reduced Internet Bandwidth Consumption   Because the internal clients and servers pull the updates from the WSUS server on your network, Internet bandwidth is utilized more efficiently. An update can be downloaded from the Microsoft Update website to the internal WSUS server once. This update can then be downloaded to any number of internal machines. The result is better Internet bandwidth utilization.

Redundancy Provides for Higher Update Uptime   In addition to the improved bandwidth utilization, updates are more likely to be available when you need them. When you rely on Microsoft Update, two things must always be available: your Internet connection and the Microsoft Update website. While both of these resources have very high uptime rates, you can install multiple internal WSUS servers that operate in a hierarchy resulting in even better uptime for new installs. Now, when a new server is installed, it can pull the updates or service packs from any of several internal update servers.

Selective Update Application   Other than Internet bandwidth savings, selective update application is probably my favorite benefit of WSUS. With selective update applications, you can choose which updates you want to install on your internal machines. If you rely on Automatic Updates through the Microsoft Update website, you can specify the type of updates to be applied automatically, but you have no way to massively select dozens or hundreds of updates while rejecting dozens or hundreds of others. WSUS gives you this capability.

Installing WSUS in a large-scale deployment is a very involved process. You must select the deployment model (hierarchical or flat) and the number of WSUS servers needed. You must then install the WSUS servers and configure them for their appropriate operations. In a large organization, this can be a multiweek or even multimonth project. You can download WSUS from the Microsoft website at `http://technet.microsoft.com/en-us/wsus`.

Summary

In this chapter, you learned about the SAU methodology for technology deployment: Standardize configuration settings and implementation procedures. Automate as much administration and maintenance as possible. Update the solution for durability and security. Standardize, automate, and update is SAU.

Next, you learned about several SQL Server features that can help you with the automation process. You learned about jobs and how to create T-SQL, SSIS, and Windows command-based jobs. Then you learned about operators and how to create and use them. Finally, you learned how alerts work and how to create them in both SSMS and the Performance Monitor. These skills will help you develop a fully standardized, automated, and updateable environment. Such an environment will cost less to support and result in reduced disruptions of service. In the next chapter, you will learn to use the performance monitoring and tuning tools to take your stable environment to greater levels of performance as well.

Chapter Essentials

Standardize, Automate, and Update   The SAU methodology provides a logical thinking structure for the implementation of any new technology. It begins with standardization of configurations and operational procedures. Next, you automate as much of the management and maintenance of the technology as possible. Finally, you plan and implement update procedures so that the durability of the technology is acceptable.

Understanding SQL Server Jobs   SQL Server jobs consist of one or more steps, schedules, alerts, and notifications. Jobs can be used to automate administrative and maintenance tasks. Standardization of generic job parameters, such as the job name, owner, and description, is very important.

Creating T-SQL Jobs   T-SQL job steps are used to run T-SQL commands within a job. A job does not have to be entirely one step type or another, but it is common to implement a job completely within the boundaries of a given step type when possible. Sticking with a single step type within a job can make it easier to understand and manage the job.

Creating SSIS Jobs   SSIS jobs run SSIS packages. The package is created using either wizards in SSMS or the Business Intelligence Development Studio (BIDS). Once the package is created, it can be executed as a job step in a SQL Server job. A job may run more than one package.

Creating Windows Command Jobs   Windows command or operating system command jobs run mostly Windows command-line commands and batch files. If you have a command-line utility that performs the work you need performed, this job step type is most useful. In this chapter, you learned to create a system information batch file and run it as a job step.

Creating and Using Operators   A SQL Server operator object is a collection of contact information for a person, group, or system that should be notified of specified events, alerts, or job results. Operators can also be configured for availability so that they will only be notified at proper times.

Creating Alerts   SQL Server alert objects are used to monitor for errors, events, or performance measurements and take action should they occur. Alerts can execute jobs when they fire. Alerts can also notify operators. In addition to the SQL Server alert objects, you can create alerts in the Performance Monitor within Windows Server itself.

Using WSUS for SQL Server 2008   Windows Server Update Services (WSUS) can be used to implement an update infrastructure within your organization. With WSUS, you have greater control over the updates that are automatically installed on your servers. SQL Servers may also be updated through WSUS, though the administrator should use great caution since an update could potentially prevent a mission-critical application from functioning properly.

Chapter 14

Performance Monitoring and Tuning

TOPICS COVERED IN THIS CHAPTER:

- ✓ Performance Tuning Principles
- ✓ Performance and Troubleshooting Tools
- ✓ Blocks, Locks, and Deadlocks
- ✓ SQL Server Profiler
- ✓ Database Engine Tuning Advisor
- ✓ Performance Monitoring with System Monitor
- ✓ Using the New Resource Governor
- ✓ Performance Studio
- ✓ Advanced Monitoring Tools

SQL Server 2008 database servers can be optimized to improve performance without requiring hardware upgrades; however, you must understand the tools used to analyze the performance of the server before you can decide whether or not a hardware upgrade is needed. In this chapter, you will learn about the performance monitoring tools available in SQL Server 2008 and Windows Server, and you will learn to use these tools for performance analysis and troubleshooting.

So that you can understand the proper application of the tools covered in this chapter, performance tuning principles will be reviewed first.

Performance Tuning Principles

This section will address two primary topics. First, you'll take a look at why performance tuning matters. What benefits can you gain through server performance analysis? Second, you'll look at some common myths related to performance tuning so you can both avoid them and understand how administrators often fall into their snares.

Why Performance Tuning Matters

Anyone can throw more hardware at a performance problem, but the most valuable DBAs can use performance tuning processes to save their organizations money, increase efficiency, and decrease frustration for database users. The following sections address each of these benefits.

Cost Savings

If the only solution you have to performance problems is a hardware upgrade, the performance enhancements you implement will be very costly. For example, if you have a database server that is performing poorly and you just assume that you have to upgrade to a new server, it may cost you thousands of dollars. By the same token, if you upgrade RAM in a server, it may cost you hundreds of dollars and you may have been able to achieve the needed performance gain by tweaking a few database queries or archiving some old data. The point is that by understanding the factors that impact the performance of a database, you can instead optimize existing software on existing hardware in order to improve performance.

🌐 **Real World Scenario**

ABC, Inc. Discovers Low-Cost Performance Enhancements

ABC, Inc. had a database server that had been in production for two years. The server provided exceptional performance for the first 18 months, but over the most recent 6 months users began to complain about delays in the system. When the DBA priced servers that were 50 percent more powerful than the existing machine, the price average was $6,700. She was sure that the hardware upgrade would resolve the performance problems, but the IT Director asked her to investigate other solutions first.

After attending a SQL Server class, she realized that she would be able to improve the performance of the database in several ways without hardware expenditures. First, because the database performed well for the first 18 months, the current problems appeared to be related to either data volume or transaction volume. The DBA analyzed the transactions per second and saw that they were not any higher than they were three months after implementation. However, the database had grown to be more than 12 gigabytes in size and it started as a 500 megabyte database.

Furthermore, she realized that no index maintenance procedures had been implemented. When she inspected the fragmentation level of the indexes, many showed fragmentation levels above 40 percent.

Based on this information, she implemented a new maintenance plan. First, she created a job that ran every six months and archived data that was more than one year old. Second, she created a job that defragmented the indexes once each week and reorganized them once each month with a rebuild. After performing these operations and implementing the automated maintenance, the database began to perform well again and no further cost investments were required.

The preceding scenario is based on a real-world situation. Only the company name was changed. The most important lesson to learn is that you can often improve the performance of your servers without costly expenditures.

Increased Efficiency

Not only will performance improvements initially save you money on hardware investments, but they will also allow you to save in other ways. Your users will get their jobs done faster, and this efficiency improvement means they will have more time for other responsibilities. However, increased efficiency is not just about saving money; it's also about increasing employee morale. The last thing you want as the DBA is a large group of frustrated users. Their increased efficiency results in your increased peace. The company's productivity will also increase, which can increase the profitability of the organization. Everyone looks better when this happens.

Decreased Frustration

As the preceding section notes, once efficiency is increased, the logical result is that frustration is decreased. Users are less frustrated because their tasks are completed in a timely manner. The DBA is less frustrated because she can spend her time dealing with issues other than user complaints related to performance. In the end, performance improvements provide value to everyone involved: the users, the organization, and the support staff.

Common Performance Tuning Myths

Before you investigate the specific tools used for performance monitoring and analysis, it's important that you understand the realities of performance testing and achieving a well-performing database implementation. To do this, you need to avoid falling into some of the myths that surround performance analysis and improvement. Table 14.1 lists the most common myths that seem to continually propagate through the systems administration and DBA world, along with their truth counterparts.

TABLE 14.1   Common Performance Tuning Myths

Myth	Truth
If processor utilization is high, a faster processor is needed.	One thing is seldom the culprit.
Eighty percent of the performance is determined by the application code.	Better code is better, but better design is best.
An optimized server is the only key to database performance.	It still has to travel the network.

The following sections cover the origins of the myths and the reasons the truths are more often the realities. These truths represent the common realities of performance tuning. That said, you should know that rare scenarios certainly exist where the myths are actually true, but these are the exception and not the rule.

One Thing Is Seldom the Culprit

When Microsoft introduced Windows 2000 Server, they made an adjustment to the System Monitor (which was called the Performance Monitor in Windows NT) so that it started with three default counters:

- % Processor Utilization
- Avg. Disk Queue Length
- Pages/sec

This change has been a tremendous help in overcoming the myth of the faster processor, but it does still lurk in the shadows. Sadly, Windows 7 has gone back to showing only the % Processor Utilization counter; hopefully, most administrators know that they must monitor more than this one counter. It's no question that scenarios exist where a faster processor is needed. However, it's also no question that a faster processor is usually not the thing that will provide the greatest performance gain. In fact, the culprit is seldom one thing but is usually two or more things that need to be addressed.

Here's an example to help you better understand this. Assume you have monitored the CPU utilization on your SQL Server, the virtual memory pages per second, and the length of the hard drive queue. Additionally, assume that CPU utilization is at an average of 82 percent. This reading would be rather high as an average, although not necessarily high as a single reading. You may decide to double the processor speed and notice that the average utilization only reduced to 80 percent. How could this happen? It could happen if the pages per second were really high. Such a pages-per-second reading would indicate that you do not have sufficient physical memory in the server.

In a scenario like this, you may be able to cut CPU utilization as much as 20 to 40 percent by simply doubling the memory. If pages per second are very high, memory is the likely culprit. If the hard drive queue length is high, then you could also look at getting faster hard drives or using a RAID 0 array to store the virtual memory file. This configuration change would allow for faster reads and writes to virtual memory and may also reduce CPU utilization.

As this example shows, if you look at one counter and make your performance judgment based on that single counter alone, you may well make an erroneous decision. It is usually best to monitor multiple counters and then consider them as an integrated whole to make your performance improvement decisions.

Better Code Is Better, But Better Design Is Best

It is very true that poorly written SQL statements and other code modules can reduce the performance of any database solution. However, the common thinking that 80 percent of a database system's performance comes from the code, which accesses the database, is frequently untrue. You can have the best written code in history and still have a poorly performing database if the physical and logical design is poorly implemented or created.

By improving the physical design, you can often double or triple the performance of a database system that already has perfectly coded modules and queries. For example, placing the physical data files on a stripe set RAID array can improve physical writes and reads. Database tables can be partitioned onto separate filegroups to control which data ends up on the different drives in your server. The point is that many things can be done in the physical design of a database system to improve its performance.

Additionally, the logical design—table structures, views, index choices, and data types—can greatly impact performance. As an example, consider a table where you've used the char(70) data type for a column that has variable-length data ranging from 10 characters to 70 characters. This data type choice may unnecessarily increase the database size and, therefore, reduce query performance regardless of how well the queries are written. Using the varchar(75) data type may improve performance in this scenario because the record sizes can vary based on the actual content of the data column. As you can see, there are many factors, other than the coding, that impact the performance of a database system and they usually add up to an equal—if not greater—amount of impact as the code.

It Still Has to Travel the Network

Finally, you can do everything to optimize the server, code, and design and still have a poorly performing database system if the network between the server and the clients is overloaded. Performance is both a measurable fact and a perceived reality. Stated differently, you can measure the server's potential and ensure that it is fast enough, but still receive communications from users who feel that the "server is slow" because the network cannot handle the bandwidth demanded. With a well-performing server, the data still has to travel across the network. Therefore, you will need to ensure that the network bandwidth is sufficient for your purposes. If you do not have control of the physical network, be sure to check with your infrastructure network administrators before you implement a database solution that is bandwidth-intensive.

Performance and Troubleshooting Tools

Several tools are available for performance analysis and troubleshooting. Some of these tools are Windows tools, meaning that they are part of the Windows operating system. Others are SQL Server tools and come with the SQL Server product. The following key tools should be considered for performance analysis:

Activity Monitor   The Activity Monitor is a SQL Server tool accessed from within the SQL Server Management Studio. With the Activity Monitor, you can view the processes used for connections to the SQL Server. Blocking can be monitored and locks can be viewed. The wait time can also be seen. The most common administrative task performed in the Activity Monitor is the killing of a stubborn connection that will not release resources. Thankfully, the Activity Monitor is very easy to use and is demonstrated in Exercise 14.1 later in this chapter.

Task Manager   The Task Manager is a process manager that ships with Windows operating systems. You can kill processes, set temporary process priorities, view performance information and, on newer Windows systems, launch the Resource Monitor for enhanced process and activity analysis. The Task Manager can be accessed by pressing Ctrl+Shift+Esc on any Windows system. Once in the Task Manager, you can see the processes and the overall performance of the system easily.

System Monitor   The System Monitor is known by many names based on the interfaces through which it is provided. It is technically an ActiveX control that can be loaded into any Microsoft Management Console (MMC), but it is loaded by default in the Performance console or the Reliability and Performance Monitor depending on the version of Windows utilized. The System Monitor is covered in detail in the later section of this chapter titled "Performance Monitoring with System Monitor."

SQL Server Profiler   The SQL Server Profiler is like a network protocol analyzer for SQL Server. It allows you to capture the events and requests related to SQL Server. You can use it to capture the actual SQL code executed against a database or to monitor for deadlocks and other negative events. It is covered in detail in the later section of this chapter titled "SQL Server Profiler."

Database Engine Tuning Advisor   The Database Engine Tuning Advisor (DTA) is a tool used to analyze the physical implementation of a database and recommend changes for performance improvement. A workload file is passed to the DTA tool in order to locate potential changes that will create a performance advantage. The tool is covered in the later section of this chapter titled "Database Engine Tuning Advisor."

DBCC   The DBCC Transact-SQL command is used to perform consistency checks against tables and databases. It is also used to perform management operations such as file shrinking and index defragmentation. The DBCC command is covered in more detail in the later section of this chapter titled "Advanced Monitoring Tools."

Event Logs and Error Logs   Finally, the event logs and error logs provide a useful source of information when analyzing both performance and functional problems. The event logs are found in the Event Viewer application, and the error logs are stored in the SQL Server instance's Logs subfolder. The logs can reveal problems resulting in the inability of the SQL Server services to start and errors that occur over time. If a SQL Server system experiences sporadic problems, check the Event Viewer logs and the SQL Server error logs to locate the problem. Chapter 15, "Policy-Based Management," provides more information on viewing and managing the Event Viewer log files.

Many of these tools are covered in greater detail throughout the remaining pages of this chapter. However, before you look too closely at the tools, you must first understand the basic concept of resource access in SQL Server databases. This resource access occurs using blocks, locks, and deadlocks.

Blocks, Locks, and Deadlocks

Concurrency, within the realm of database systems, is defined as the condition where multiple users or processes are accessing the same database at the same time. Because this condition will result in conflicts over resource access, some mechanism must be in place to address these conflicts. Conflicts will occur if two processes attempt to modify, or even access, the exact same data at the same time. Because two or more processes cannot possibly modify the same data at the same time, something must exist that provides the illusion of complete concurrency to the client applications while truly providing individual access to the data. In SQL Server, this illusion is created using locks. Locks result in blocks and may even create deadlocks in the right scenario.

Understanding Locks

In order to prevent data corruption or system errors, SQL Server uses locks. A lock is a mechanism used to disallow reads or modifications or both to a data object by other connections while the connection granted the lock reads or modifies the data. Depending on the locking model, processes may be prohibited from reading or writing to the data object until the locking process is finished (the lock is released) or they may be prohibited only from writing to the locked object. The locked object can be a row, page, or table depending on the locking level.

Versions of SQL Server preceding SQL Server 2005 supported only pessimistic locking inside the server, and optimistic locking had to be handled in the application code. SQL Server 2005 added support for optimistic locking inside the server using the new row versioning feature.

Pessimistic Concurrency Model In a *pessimistic* concurrency model, readers block writers and writers block readers and writers. Readers do not block other readers as shared locks can be acquired. Because row versioning is not used, writers block both readers and other writers.

Optimistic Concurrency Model In an *optimistic* concurrency model, writers do not block readers because the readers can read the version of the row before the writer began modifying it. This latter capability requires the row versioning feature that was new to SQL Server 2005 and, therefore, optimistic concurrency was a new capability in SQL Server 2005 that remains in SQL Server 2008.

Lock Types

Two types of locks exist that you need to be aware of for the Microsoft exams and to be able to administer SQL Server effectively. They are

- Shared
- Exclusive

Shared locks are created when a read request is made against an object. Multiple shared locks can be issued for a single object so that more than one process can read the data. Shared locks are usually released as soon as the read operation is completed and do not need to be held until the entire transaction, within which the read statement was executed, is completed. However, if the transaction isolation level is set to Repeatable Read or higher, the shared lock will remain until the transaction is completed.

An *exclusive* lock will lock the object so that it can be modified and will block all other readers and writers by default. The exception to this is when an isolation level of read uncommitted is used.

Granularity of Locks

Locks can occur at the row level, the data page level, and the table level. When a row is locked, other rows in the same table are unlocked. When a data page is locked, other pages are unlocked. Of course, when the table is locked, all data in that table is locked according to the lock type selected.

Locks can be escalated after they are instantiated. A page-level lock does not have to remain a page-level lock if a larger scope must be locked to meet the requirements of a transaction. Locks can escalate from page to table or from row to table. They do not escalate from row to page and then to table. This granularity of locking allows multiple rows to be locked by different processes at the same time; table-only locks would allow only one process to acquire a lock on the entire table at a time. SQL Server 2008 uses internal algorithms, which you will not need to know for the exams or basic administration, to determine the granularity of the locks.

Lock Isolation Levels

As you've seen in some of the previous paragraphs, the isolation level selected will help determine the behavior of the various locks. SQL Server supports five isolation levels. These isolation levels are defined here:

Read Uncommitted   Connections can read data that has not been committed.

Read Committed   Connections can read only committed data, and they cannot read data that is being modified.

Repeatable Read   Connections cannot read data that has already been read by other connections that have not completed the transactions from within which the read occurred.

Snapshot   Uses row versioning to read data as it existed prior to any ongoing modification operations. Also referenced as "writers don't block readers and readers don't block writers."

Serializable   Works like repeatable read and adds the limitation of row inserts. Rows cannot be inserted within the keyset range locked by the locking transaction.

Blocks and Deadlocks

A block occurs when a process has a lock on a resource that will not allow other processes to use the resources and another process attempts to use it. This behavior is a normal part of database operations and will impact the number of users that you can support concurrently. When blocking is minimized and server resources are sufficient to have a larger number of users connected and functioning, this is called high concurrency. When a high level of blocking occurs or server resources are insufficient so that you can support very few users, this is called low concurrency.

Your goal will be to have short block durations. A threshold often specified is one second. If your blocks last for more than one second, you will increase contention and lower concurrency. Users will feel that the system is sluggish or unresponsive. You can analyze blocking in your server with the `sys.dm_exec_requests` DMV by following these steps.

1. Look at the `blocking_session_id` column and seek for values greater than 0.

2. When you find a row that meets this filter, the value in the `blocking_session_id` column is the SPID of the blocking process.

3. At this point, if the process is very problematic, you can stop the process with the `KILL` *SPID* Transact-SQL command, where *SPID* is replaced with the numeric SPID value shown in the query results.

You can see the results of querying `sys.dm_exec_requests` in Figure 14.1. In Figure 14.1, the SPID of 57 is being blocked by 56.

FIGURE 14.1   Viewing the blocking processes in `sys.dm_exec_requests`

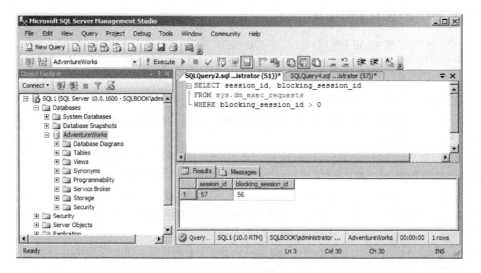

You can also use the Activity Monitor to stop a blocking process. To do this, follow these steps:

1. Right-click on the server instance you want to view and select Activity Monitor in the Object Explorer in SSMS.

2. Find the process you want to stop, right-click it, and select Kill Process.

3. You can also right-click a connection and select Details to see the actual code being executed, as shown in Figure 14.2.

FIGURE 14.2   Viewing the code executed by a connection or process in the Activity Monitor

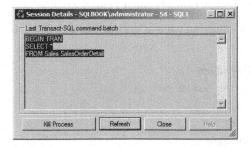

Unlike the blocks, which will go away eventually when the blocking process finishes with the tasks it is performing, deadlocks must be resolved by force—either random force or structured force. A *deadlock* occurs when process 1 has an exclusive lock on resource 1 and process 2 has an exclusive lock on resource 2. Then process 1 tries to access resource 2 during the execution of the transaction that has resource 1 locked and process 2 tries to access resource 1 during the execution of the transaction that has resource 2 locked. Do you see the picture? This could be called an infinite lock, but SQL Server will kill the process it feels has the lowest priority (random force). You can also specify the priority of a process so that SQL Server will give preference to it in a deadlock scenario (structured force). You use the SET DEADLOCK_PRIORITY statement to do this. Exercise 14.1 walks you through the process of creating a deadlock so you can see how they are automatically resolved by SQL Server.

EXERCISE 14.1

Generating a Deadlock Scenario

In this exercise, you will intentionally create a deadlock scenario to see the results.

1. Click Start and select All Programs ➤ Microsoft SQL Server 2008 ➤ SQL Server Management Studio.

2. Connect to your SQL Server instance.

3. Click the New Query window button.

4. Enter and execute the following code in the query window created in step 3:

```
Use AdventureWorks;
BEGIN TRANSACTION
UPDATE Person.Contact SET FirstName ='Gus'
WHERE ContactID = 1;
```

5. Click the New Query window button again to create another new window.

6. Enter and execute the following code in the query window created in step 5:

```
BEGIN TRANSACTION
UPDATE Production.Product
Set ProductNumber ='Ar-5381B'
WHERE ProductID = 1;
UPDATE Person.Contact
SET LastName = 'AchongGus'
WHERE ContactID=1;
```

7. Notice that the query seems to execute without end. You are now in a state of blocking, but it is not a deadlock. For this reason, SQL Server will not automatically kill either of these processes.

8. Right-click on your server instance in the Object Explorer and click on the Activity Monitor. In the Processes section, notice that one of the processes is suspended and has an hourglass icon. If you do not see an hourglass icon for the entry, simply press F5 to refresh. Do not kill the process.

9. Return to the first query window you created in step 3. Add and execute the following new code. Only execute this new code by selecting it before clicking the Execute button:

```
UPDATE Production.Product Set Name ='Adjustable Brace'
WHERE ProductID = 1;
```

10. One of the query windows will receive an error message similar to the following:

```
Msg 1205, Level 13, State 51, Line 7
Transaction (Process ID 57) was deadlocked on lock resources
with another process and has been chosen as the deadlock
victim. Rerun the transaction.
```

11. You may close the query windows. If asked to commit the transactions select No.

The steps in Exercise 14.1 showed a deadlock scenario; however, you do not create them intentionally in the real world. They do still happen, but the following tips can help to reduce them or mitigate their impact:

- Keep transactions as small as possible. Smaller transactions finish faster and cause fewer blocks and deadlocks.

- Limit the number of concurrent users on a single server. By distributing an application across multiple replicated databases, you can often all but eradicate deadlocks.

- Use the DEADLOCK_PRIORITY option to ensure that the more important transactions win in deadlock scenarios.

- Handle the 1205 errors that are returned when a process is killed by SQL Server to resolve a deadlock. This means writing your application code so that it can retry a transaction when it receives a 1205 error.

SQL Server Profiler

The SQL Server Profiler is a tool that is used to monitor database and server activity in a SQL Server environment. The DBA can use it to capture all the queries being executed against a database or just to capture the logins to the server or any number of other tasks. Literally, hundreds of columns (properties) and events (actions) can be traced to determine where problems or performance issues reside.

As an example, imagine you are the DBA for an outsourced application and you do not have the source code for the client application or the design plans for the database structure. In such a scenario, you have no knowledge of what exact queries are being executed against the database. However, you can discover these queries—and this is where the SQL Server Profiler really shines.

The SQL Server Profiler allows you to run a trace while the users are using the application. Though you were not involved in the programming of the application, you will now be able to see the exact SQL queries it executes against the database. The information can be used to add indexes or hardware where beneficial. Without this knowledge, you have no real way of knowing where to begin making performance improvements.

In addition to application monitoring, the SQL Server Profiler can be used to troubleshoot problems. For example, you can view capture and view deadlocks, *and* you can filter to a specific application, host, or user so that you can troubleshoot problems based on specific user complaints.

Exercise 14.2 steps you through the process of creating a trace with the SQL Server Profiler.

EXERCISE 14.2

Creating a Trace with SQL Server Profiler

In this exercise, you will create a basic trace file using the SQL Server profiler. You will look at the events that are available and the filtering options.

1. Select Start ➢ All Programs ➢ Microsoft SQL Server 2008 ➢ Performance Tools ➢ SQL Server Profiler to launch the SQL Server Profiler. You will see a screen similar to the following:

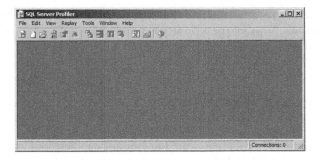

2. Click File ➢ New Trace.

3. Connect to the Database Engine on your SQL Server.

4. In the Trace Properties dialog, enter the trace name of **Trace1**. (You can enter any name you like when creating a trace.)

5. Select the Standard template, check the Save to File box, and provide a file name (Trace1 will be the default file name). If the Enable File Rollover check box is selected, deselect it and click Save.

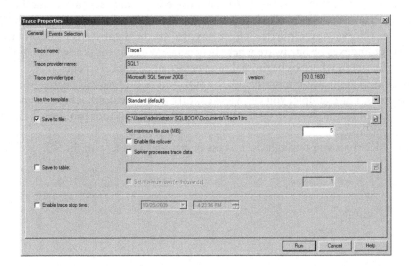

6. Accept all other defaults on the General tab and click on the Events Selection tab to view the available events.

7. Click the Show All Events check box in order to display all events.

8. Scroll through the additional events and browse the available events, but do not select any additional events.

9. Click the Column Filters button to view the available filtering options.

10. Notice that columns can be filtered based on values being like or not like specified criteria.

11. Click Cancel to avoid changing the filters in this case.

12. Click the Run button to begin capturing the trace file.

13. If you want to see SQL activity, run SSMS and then perform a query against a database.

14. Back in the SQL Server Profiler window, select File ➤ Stop Trace to stop the capture.

15. Scroll through the trace and view the results.

While Exercise 14.2 specified the use of the Standard template, several other templates are also provided in the SQL Server Profiler. Additionally, you can create your own templates by selecting File ➤ Templates ➤ New Template from within the SQL Server Profiler. By creating your own custom templates, you can reduce your work over time, if you find that you frequently customize the Standard template within the tool. The Standard template does not provide the individual T-SQL statements with their execution durations. You may want to create your own template, based on the Standard template, and add the individual events SQL:StmtStarting and SQL:StmtCompleted.

Database Engine Tuning Advisor

Another great tool provided with SQL Server is the Database Engine Tuning Advisor (DTA). The DTA will evaluate a workload file, which can be either a T-SQL script or a Profiler trace file, in order to generate recommendations for indexes and database structures that will improve the performance of the database. You must give the DTA what it needs to produce the best results. For instance, if you give it a workload file that does not represent real-world activity, you will not get recommendations that give improvements in your real-world database.

The DTA tool is used by creating a workload file, then running an analysis, and then either applying, saving, or saving and applying the recommendations it provides.

Creating a DTA Workload File

Using the DTA tool is a multistep process. First, you will need to create a workload file on an active SQL Server. Second, you will need to analyze the workload with the DTA tool in order to locate performance improvement options. Finally, you can apply the performance recommendations made by the DTA tool. Exercises 14.3 through 14.5 walk you through these three steps.

EXERCISE 14.3

Creating a DTA Workload File in SQL Server Profiler

In this first step to utilizing DTA, you will create a workload file for DTA to analyze. To get the best results, the workload file should be created on a production server. To create the workload file, follow these steps:

1. Select Start ➢ All Programs ➢ Microsoft SQL Server 2008 ➢ Performance Tools ➢ SQL Server Profiler.

2. Select File ➢ New Trace.

3. Connect to the target SQL Server for which you want to gain performance improvement recommendations in the DTA.

4. Name the new trace **DTAFILE** or any other name that will help you remember that it is a DTA workload file.

5. Select the Tuning template instead of the Standard template. The Tuning template captures the events needed by the DTA tool.

6. Check the Save to File option, provide a file name for the file or accept the default file name (DTAFILE), and click Save.

7. Click Run to begin the trace capture.

8. Allow the capture to run for several minutes to several hours of operation, depending on the scenario.

9. When the capture has run during a sufficient window of operation (determined by the way users use the system), select File ➢ Stop Trace to end the capture.

10. Close the SQL Server Profiler.

After completing Exercise 14.3, you will have a workload file that can be used to perform analysis in the DTA tool. But how do you determine how long the workload file should capture activity? The answer will depend on the scenario. If you have a database system with very similar activity from hour to hour, capturing a single hour's activity should be sufficient. However, if the database is used very differently in the morning than it is in the afternoon, you must be careful to capture both types of activity. Otherwise, if you capture only the morning's activity, the DTA tool may recommend performance changes that, while they help the morning performance, will hurt the afternoon performance.

In most cases, capturing an entire day's activity will be sufficient. Still some scenarios may demand a greater time window or different plans. For example, consider an accounting database that is used mostly the same from Monday through Wednesday and including Friday; however, on Thursday, massive reports are run for paycheck processing and accounts receivable. If these reports run against the same production database used every other day of the week and the database workload is captured on a day other than Thursday, you could receive recommendations from the DTA tool that will cause the reports to be delayed drastically. Realize that the DTA will provide one set of recommendations. That set of recommendations will be based on tuning settings for the specific workload analyzed. If the workload is not reflective of the real-world use for that database, the recommendations will actually hurt the performance of the database in many cases. Now, you can see why you usually need to capture a full day of activity.

In the end, the DTA tool is an excellent assistant, but your expertise as the DBA must be the deciding factor. This is most true during the application of the recommendations.

Analyzing Your Workload File

The next step, after capturing the workload, is to analyze it with the DTA tool. Exercise 14.4 steps you through this process.

EXERCISE 14.4

Analyzing the Workload File with the DTA Tool

In this exercise, you will analyze the workload captured in Exercise 14.3. To analyze the workload, follow these steps:

1. Select Start ➢ All Programs ➢ Microsoft SQL Server 2008 ➢ Performance Tools ➢ Database Engine Tuning Advisor.

2. Connect to the same server that you used for the workload capture in Exercise 14.3.

3. On the General tab, select the workload file you created in Exercise 14.3.

EXERCISE 14.4 *(continued)*

4. In the lower half of the General tab, select the target database or databases to tune.

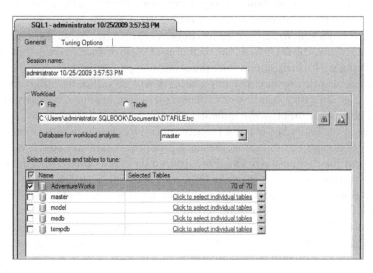

5. Select the Tuning Options tab.

6. If desired, set a tuning time limit. The analysis will stop when the time limit expires whether the analysis is complete or not.

7. Choose the recommendations you want the DTA tool to give.

8. Click the Start Analysis button on the toolbar.

9. When the analysis is complete, select Actions ➢ Save Recommendations, provide a file name, and click Save.

You may attempt an analysis with the DTA tool at times and receive an error indicating that too little storage space was available for processing the analysis. In this case, before step 8 in Exercise 14.4, you would click the Advanced Options button and increase the space for recommendations. You might want to just set this value to 1,024 megabytes to ensure that the process can complete.

The reason step 9 of Exercise 14.4 indicates that you should save the recommendation instead of applying the recommendation is simple. If you apply the recommendation blindly, you risk hurting the performance of your system. Even when you apply the recommendation, you can still save it; however, you should save the DTA recommendations and then open the T-SQL file in SSMS and analyze it for yourself. This latter method provides you with at least the following three benefits:

- You can review the changes recommended and apply only those with which you agree based on your expertise.

- You can save the T-SQL file for documentation purposes so that you will not forget the changes made by the DTA tool.

- You can rename the objects recommended by the DTA tool.

Why would you want to rename the objects? The answer is really simple: the names given by the DTA tool are horrible. They look like the odd cryptic names you'd expect a computer to come up with. Instead of names like _dta_index_SalesOrder_5_642101328__K7_ K1_2_3_4 (yes, that's really an example of an automatically generated index name from the DTA tool), wouldn't ix_SalesOrder make more sense? That's why renaming the objects in the saved recommendation script before you run the script is a good practice. Of course, you can always apply the recommendations exactly as they come out of the DTA tool.

Applying DTA Recommendations

If you save the DTA recommendations to a file, which most experts will recommend, you can apply the recommendations using SSMS. Although the recommendations could also be applied using SQLCMD at the command prompt, most DBAs will use the SSMS GUI interface. If you want to use SQLCMD, refer to Chapter 4, "SQL Server Command-Line Administration." Exercise 14.5 steps you through the process of applying the recommendations saved in Exercise 14.4.

EXERCISE 14.5

Applying the Saved DTA Recommendations

In this exercise, you will apply the recommendations saved in Exercise 14.4. In the real world, you may want to rename the objects in the CREATE statements before performing these steps:

1. Launch SSMS.

2. Connect to the target server.

3. Click File ➤ Open File and browse to and open the recommendations file saved in step 9 of Exercise 14.4.

4. Click the Execute button to execute the script and create the recommended changes.

Real World Scenario

Recommendations for Using DTA

With all this talk of recommendations, I have a few important ones to make as well. After using this tool on dozens, if not hundreds, of databases, I've found a few key best practices.

First, when using the DTA tool, always capture the workload file on the production database; however, you should always apply the recommended changes on a test server first. I learned this recommendation the hard way when using the tool for a company several years ago. I ran the recommendations on their production database and, while it did initially improve performance, a user ran a report (which he ran every few weeks) and the report took more than an hour to run. The report normally completed in less than five minutes. What had happened? The recommendation from DTA removed some key indexes the report needed because the report action was not included in my workload file.

Second, rename those pesky recommended objects. The names that the DTA tool suggests are necessarily ridiculous. The DTA tool has to ensure uniqueness of the object names so it uses really odd names for indexes and other objects. Just save the recommendation to a file and then rename the objects to something that is more meaningful to you before applying the recommendation.

Finally, here's the basic process I use with the DTA tool:

1. Capture the workload file on the production server during normal operational hours.

2. Run the DTA tool analysis against the workload file on the production server and save the recommendations.

3. Ensure that a recent copy of the production database is on a test server. You can do this by restoring from a recent full backup.

4. Inspect the recommendations file saved from the DTA analysis to locate tables targeted for performance gains.

5. Run some queries against those tables while capturing statistics and execution plans.

6. Rename the recommended objects and apply the recommendations (still on the test server).

7. Rerun the queries while capturing statistics and execution plans.

After going through this process, I can determine whether the recommendations will provide value to my production system or not. If they will provide value, I can apply the recommendations and monitor to ensure that stability has not been diminished and that performance has increased.

Please, learn from my failures and successes and use these recommendations. You'll be glad you did.

Performance Monitoring with System Monitor

The System Monitor provides a tool that is used to analyze live performance data, log performance data over time, log performance data when events occur, and fire alerts when performance counters report outside of specified thresholds. Over the years, Microsoft has changed the name used to refer to the System Monitor shortcut. For example, in Windows NT it was known as the Performance Monitor and it was a standalone application. In Windows 2000 and Server 2003, it was simply called Performance, and the shortcut named Performance was actually a link to an MMC that loaded the System Monitor ActiveX control among other snap-ins. In Windows Server 2008, it was called the Reliability and Performance Monitor and the System Monitor was a very small subset of the default snap-ins in the console. Now, in Windows Server 2008 R2, it is known as Performance Monitor once again, so it's gone full circle. Isn't life with Microsoft wonderful?

The System Monitor is actually an ActiveX control that ships with Windows servers and clients. The control can be used from within applications as well as the Microsoft Management Console (MMC) that exists by default after installation. Additionally, you can snap it into a custom console that you use with other snap-ins to build a performance and troubleshooting environment that meets your needs.

Configuring the System Monitor will vary depending on your objectives. When you want to monitor live activity, you will use it in one way, and when you want to log activity to be analyzed at a later time, you will use it in another way. Newer Windows systems use data collector sets instead of individual performance logs, but the old performance logs are still buried in there. You'll see how to get to them in the section titled "Data Collection in Windows Server 2008" later in this chapter.

When you want to include the System Monitor in a customized Microsoft Management Console (MMC), you will add it as a snap-in. The process is not as intuitive as you might first think, but it becomes clearer when you remember that the System Monitor is really just an ActiveX control.

Installing the System Monitor

To install the System Monitor into your custom MMC, follow the steps in Exercise 14.6.

EXERCISE 14.6

Installing the System Monitor in a Custom MMC

1. Open an existing MMC or create a new one by either double-clicking the existing MMC or by clicking Start and selecting Run and then running MMC.EXE from the Run dialog.

2. Click the File menu and select Add/Remove Snap-in.

3. Click the Add button.

4. Select ActiveX Control in the Available Stand-Alone Snap-ins area and click the Add button.

5. Click Next in the Insert ActiveX Control Wizard.

6. In the Control Type area, scroll down to and select the System Monitor Control and then click the Next button.

7. Type a name for the System Monitor or accept the default of System Monitor Control and click Finish.

8. Click Close in the Add Stand-Alone Snap-In dialog.

9. Click OK in the Add/Remove Snap-in dialog.

After completing the steps in Exercise 14.1, you can click on the System Monitor control in the left pane and then use it in the right pane. You will need to add the performance counters you want to view. In this mode, you cannot log data; you can only view live results. The following section will cover more about viewing live results and when it would be beneficial.

In keeping with the SAU (Standardize, Automate, and Update) model introduced in Chapter 13, "Creating Jobs, Operators, and Alerts," you should standardize on a MMC configuration that you will make available on all Windows servers. Microsoft has made this a little more difficult with the changes in Windows Server 2008 and then again in Windows Server 2008 R2, but one thing is consistent: you can load the System Monitor into a custom MMC on any of these systems.

Viewing Live Performance Data

When you want to view live performance counter data with Windows Server 2003 or Windows Server 2008 systems and you want to use the built-in tools without creating a custom console, you actually have two different procedures to follow. Exercise 14.7 steps you through the process on a Windows Server 2003 server.

Viewing Live Performance Data on Windows Server 2003

In this exercise, you will view live performance data on Windows Server 2003. To view the live performance data with the Performance console, follow these steps:

1. Select Start ➢ Programs ➢ Administrative Tools ➢ Performance.

2. Click the Add counter button or press Ctrl+I to add a new counter.

3. Choose the desired counter and click Add.

4. Click Close to view live information about the selected counters.

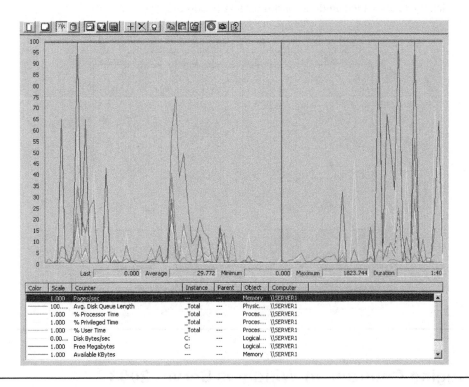

Exercise 14.8 steps you through the process of monitoring live performance data on a Windows Server 2008 server. As you will see, the process has changed a bit since Windows Server 2003. Because both Windows Server 2003 and 2008 can run SQL Server 2008, you will need to understand the processes for both server platforms.

Viewing Live Performance Data on Windows Server 2008

In this exercise, you will view live performance data on Windows Server 2008. To view the live data with the Reliability and Performance Monitor console:

1. Select Start ➢ All Programs ➢ Administrative Tools ➢ Reliability and Performance Monitor.

2. In the Monitoring Tools node, select the Performance Monitor child node.

3. Click the Add counter button or press Ctrl+I to add a new counter.

EXERCISE 14.8   *(continued)*

4. Choose the desired counter in the left half of the Add Counters dialog and click Add to add the counter. Repeat until all desired counters have been added.

5. Click OK to view the live data for the selected counters.

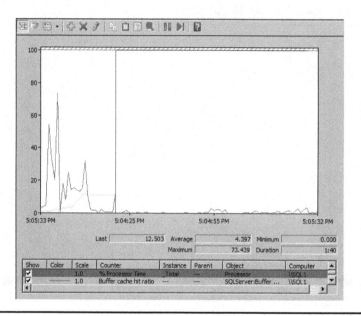

Logging Counters in Windows Server 2003

Just as the viewing of live performance data is different in Windows Server 2003 than it is in Windows Server 2008, the logging of performance data differs too. In Windows Server 2003, you create counter logs. In Windows Server 2008, you create data collector sets. In Exercise 14.9, you will create a performance counter log in Windows Server 2003.

EXERCISE 14.9

Creating a Performance Counter Log in Windows Server 2003

In this exercise, you will use the Performance console to create a counter log in Windows Server 2003.

1. Select Start ➢ Programs ➢ Administrative Tools ➢ Performance.

2. Expand the Performance Logs and Alerts node in the left pane.

3. Right-click Counter Logs and select New Log Settings.

4.   Enter a name for the log such as **Baseline 1**.

5.   Click the Add Counters button on the General tab and add the counters you wish to log.

6.   After adding the counters, select the Log Files tab and select the log file format you desire (I prefer the comma delimited text file so that I can analyze the data easily in Excel).

7.   On the Schedule tab, either schedule a start and stop time for the log or set it to start manually. Note that you can run a command after the log is created.

8.   Click OK.

9.   If prompted to create the log directory, click Yes.

One of the benefits of saving the counter logs as CSV files is the simplicity it provides for use within Excel and other data analysis tools. You can simply double-click on the CSV file to open it in Excel and then create charts and line graphs to show the performance of the server. Line graphs are excellent tools for displaying downward trends for management. For example, if you can show that the free memory on a given server was 17 megabytes six months ago and it was 14 megabytes three months ago and it is 11 megabytes today, what is the trend? The answer is that the trend is a loss of 3 megabytes of free memory every three months. At this rate, you may be experiencing memory problems on the server in another 9 to 12 months. This kind of trend analysis can be very helpful in predicting when new upgrades or scale-outs may be required.

Another important feature that was first introduced in SQL Server 2005 is performance log correlation. This feature allows you to take the performance logs you create and view them alongside SQL Server Profiler traces created during the same window of time. To use this feature, you must start a performance log capture first, and then start a SQL Server Profiler trace. When you've monitored everything you want to analyze, stop the trace first and then stop the performance log. Now you can load the performance log into the SQL Server Profiler and view them side-by-side. This may seem trivial at first, but it is very valuable and time-saving to the performance tuning process.

An interesting quirk exists in SQL Server Profiler. When attempting to correlate performance log data with a trace file, you will sometimes have to close and reopen the trace file before the Import Performance Data option becomes available on the File menu. We'll call this a Microsoft feature.

Data Collection in Windows Server 2008

Data collection in Windows Server 2008 is used to provide similar benefits to counter logs in Windows Server 2003. However, in addition to the counter logs, you can gather more information about the system, such as trace events and configuration parameters. The performance counters, trace events, and configuration parameters are gathered together into what is called a data collector set. The data collector set can be executed in order to generate a report. Figure 14.3 shows a partial representation of the built-in System Diagnostics data collector set.

FIGURE 14.3 Viewing the default System Diagnostics data collector set

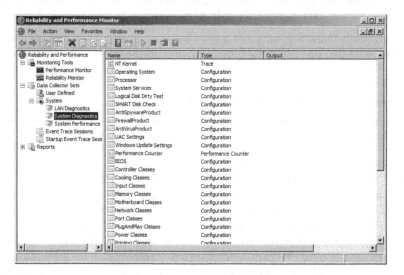

When you right-click a data collector set, you can select to Start the data collection. The result of the data collection run will be a report in the Reports section of the Reliability and Performance monitor. Figure 14.4 shows an example of the report from the System Diagnostics data collector set.

FIGURE 14.4 Viewing a report in the Reliability and Performance Monitor

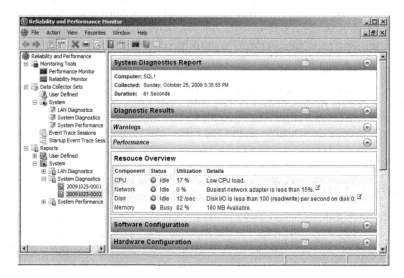

Exercise 14.10 steps you through the process of creating a basic data collector set for a typical SQL Server 2008 analysis.

EXERCISE 14.10

Creating a Data Collector Set in Windows Server 2008

In this exercise, you will create a data collector set in Windows Server 2008 that can be used to gather important performance information for a SQL Server 2008 installation. To create the collector set:

1. Select Start ➢ All Programs ➢ Administrative Tools ➢ Reliability and Performance Monitor.

2. Double-click the Data Collector Sets node in the left pane to expand it.

3. Double-click the User Defined node to expand it.

4. Right-click the User Defined node and select New ➢ Data Collector Set.

5. Name the new set **SQL Server Analysis** and select Create from a template and click Next.

6. Choose the System Performance template and click Next.

7. Accept the default location for saving the data and click Next.

8. Click Finish to create the data collector set.

While the default System Performance template used in Exercise 14.10 includes valuable performance counters, it does not include any SQL Server specific counters. In Exercise 14.11, you will add counters to the SQL Server Analysis data collector set so that it is more useful for SQL Servers.

EXERCISE 14.11

Adding SQL Server Counters to a Data Collector Set

In this exercise, you will add the SQL Server connections and buffer cache hit ratio counters in order to make the SQL Server Analysis data collector set more useful for SQL Server analysis. To add the counters, follow these steps:

1. In the Reliability and Performance Monitor, expand the Data Collector Sets ➢ User Defined nodes, if they are not already expanded.

2. Select the SQL Server Analysis data collector set in the left pane.

3. Double-click on the Performance Counter object in the right pane to open its properties dialog.

EXERCISE 14.11 *(continued)*

4. Click the Add button to add new counters.

5. In the left half of the Add Counters dialog, scroll to and double-click the SQL Server:Buffer Manager object.

6. Scroll further down in the list, click on the Buffer Cache Hit Ratio counter, and then click the Add button. The counter should be added to the right half of the dialog in the Added counters pane.

7. Scroll further down in the list and expand SQL Server:General Statistics.

8. From within SQL Server:General Statistics, click on User Connections and click the Add button. Your Add Counters dialog should look similar to the following:

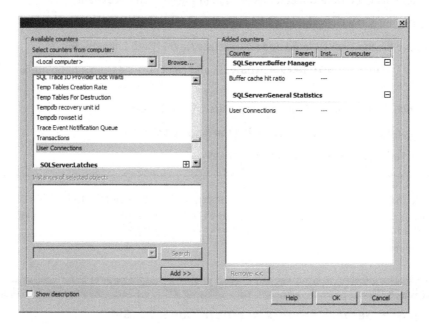

9. Click OK to save the changes.

10. Back in the Performance Counters properties dialog, change the Log format to Comma Separated so that you can use the data outside of the Reliability and Performance Monitor as well.

11. Click OK to save the changes.

You now have a data collector set that you can use for SQL Server performance analysis anytime you like. Simply right-click the data collector set and select Start. By default, it will run for one minute. You can change this default by right-clicking on the data collector set, selecting Properties and then clicking on the Stop Condition tab. From here, you can set the run time as in Figure 14.5.

FIGURE 14.5   Configuring the stop condition for a data collector set

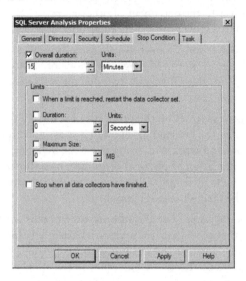

Using the New Resource Governor

The Resource Governor is new to SQL Server 2008 and provides an internal mechanism for the control and management of resource consumption by connections and processes. In the past, you had to use the external Windows System Resource Manager (WSRM) to get any reasonable amount of control over resource management. Now, with the Resource Governor, most resource management tasks can be handled within SQL Server 2008 itself.

The Resource Governor is comprised of resource pools, workload groups, and classifications. Resource pools collect the physical resources of the server and allow them to be used for assignment to workload groups. Microsoft suggests that a resource pool can be thought of as a virtual SQL Server inside the real SQL Server instance. The workload groups are collections of connections based on classification. To make it clear, when a user connects to the SQL Server 2008 instance that is using the Resource Governor, the connection is classified and based on that classification it is placed in a single workload group. The workload group belongs to one and only one resource pool. The resource pool has limits on the consumption of physical resources that it can perform. The end result is fine control over the level of impact that a given user connection can have on the server.

To get a better idea for how the Resource Governor can really shine, think back to a time when you experienced a situation with SQL Server, or any other database system for that matter, where a single user ran a report and brought the rest of the users to a practical halt. With Resource Governor, you can classify that report user so that his or her report will not overutilize the server to the detriment of other users.

Implementing the Resource Governor is a three-step process.

1. Enable the Resource Governor. Thankfully, this step is very easy. You simply right-click the Resource Governor in the Management node of SSMS and select Enable. When you enable the Resource Governor, two default workload groups and two default resource pools are created.

2. Use these workload groups to set up the properties for members of the groups. The first workload group is called the Internal group, and it is assigned to the Internal resource pool. The Internal pool and workload group is for the SQL Server process itself. It uses this pool for its own allocation of physical resources. It is allowed to consume from 0 to 100 percent of the CPU by default. The second workload group is called Default, and it is assigned to the Default resource pool.

3. Work with your resource pools. The Default resource pool is configured in the same manner as the Internal pool so that resources are basically balanced between the two. While you cannot delete or move the Default workload group, you can adjust it if you desire. If you want to use the Resource Governor in the simplest manner, you will simply enable it and then make adjustments to the Default resource pool.

 It's important to know that the Resource Governor works only with the Database Engine. It does not provide support for Integration Services, Analysis Services, or Reporting Services processes.

Performance Studio

Earlier in this chapter, you looked at the Reliability and Performance Monitor as it exists in Windows Server 2008. The Reliability and Performance Monitor is there whether SQL Server 2008 is installed on the system or not. However, SQL Server 2008 introduces its own performance toolset that Microsoft calls the Performance Studio in their various exam objectives. The Performance Studio is really just a hook into this underlying performance-gathering technology in Windows Server and the implementation of a storage mechanism known as the Management Data Warehouse (MDW). The good news is that you can set it all up in just a few minutes.

SSIS is required for Performance Studio to work. The SQL Server Agent service must be running to upload the data to the MDW, and the SSIS service must be installed because it is used for the ETL work of the Performance Studio's data collection processes. If you did not install SSIS during the installation of SQL Server 2008, simply rerun the installation and add the Integration Services component.

In Exercise 14.12, you will enable the Performance Studio by creating the MDW. Once enabled, you can begin using it for ongoing performance analysis and troubleshooting.

EXERCISE 14.12

Creating the MDW for Performance Studio

In this exercise, you will use the wizard in the SQL Server Management Studio to generate the MDW required for the Performance Studio functions. To create the MDW, follow these steps:

1.   Launch SSMS.

2.   In the Object Explorer, expand the Management node.

3.   Right-click the Data Collection node and select Configure Management Data Warehouse.

4.   Click Next to begin working through the Configure Management Data Warehouse Wizard.

5.   On the Select configuration task screen, choose to Create or Upgrade a Management Data Warehouse and click Next.

6.   On the Configure Management Data Warehouse Storage screen, click the New button to create a new database.

7.   Name the database **MDW** and click OK to create it.

8.   Back in the wizard, click Next to continue the configuration process.

9.   On the Map Logins and Users screen, accept the default and click Next.

10. Click Finish to generate the MDW database.

11. Click Close to close the wizard.

Once you've performed the actions in Exercise 14.12, you're ready to configure how the data collection will transpire. Exercise 14.13 then steps you through the process of setting up the data collection options.

E X E R C I S E   1 4 . 1 3

Setting Up Data Collection Options

In this exercise, you will rerun the Configure Management Data Warehouse Wizard in order to set up data collection options. To configure data collection, follow these steps:

1. Right-click Data Collection and select Configure Management Data Warehouse.

2. Click Next if the Welcome screen is displayed.

3. Select Set Up Data Collection and click Next.

4. Click the Build button (the button with the ellipses) and select to connect to the same server instance on which you created the MDW database in Exercise 14.12.

5. Select the MDW database from the drop-down list and click Next.

6. Click Finish to enable the data collection configuration you've selected.

7. Click Close to close the wizard.

Now that you have enabled the data collection, you can view reports at any time. Three sets of statistics are gathered: disk usage, query statistics, and server activity. The disk usage statistics are gathered and uploaded to the MDW every six hours by default. The query statistics and server activity information are cached during normal operations and uploaded to the MDW every 15 minutes. You can change these settings by right-clicking on the desired System Data Collection Set and selecting Properties. You'll see a screen similar to the one in Figure 14.6 and you can reconfigure the data collection from there.

To view a report provided by the Performance Studio, follow the steps in Exercise 14.14.

E X E R C I S E   1 4 . 1 4

Viewing Performance Studio Reports

To view the reports in SSMS, follow these steps:

1. Right-click the Data Collection node and select Reports ➢ Management Data Warehouse ➢ Disk Usage Summary (to view the other two reports, you select them in the same way).

2. Scroll through the report as desired.

3. Click a specific database name to view detailed report information about that database.

If you ever decide that the data collection is no longer needed, simply right-click the Data Collection node and select Disable Data Collection.

FIGURE 14.6   Viewing the properties for the Query Statistics System Data Collector Set

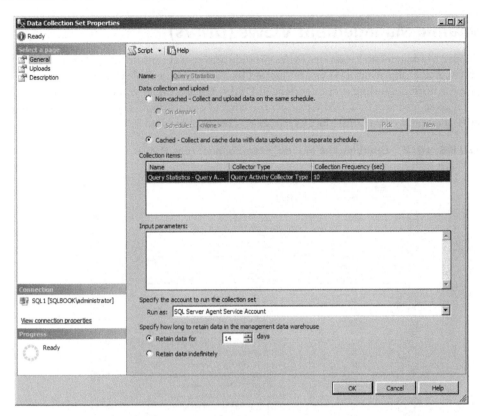

    I recommend that you standardize the configuration for the Performance Studio and the Resource Governor as much as possible. Working with a standardized environment is always much easier because you know what to expect when you're troubleshooting a problem.

Advanced Monitoring Tools

In addition to the standard monitoring tools you've explored so far in this chapter, several tools and features of SQL Server 2008 and the Windows operating system may prove beneficial in performance analysis and general troubleshooting. These tools include:

- Dynamic Management Views (DMVs)
- DBCC
- Resource Monitor

The following sections will cover each of these topics fully.

Dynamic Management Views (DMVs)

Dynamic Management Views or DMVs provide server state information for health and performance monitoring. DMVs are queried like SQL Server tables, making them easy to use for both beginning and experienced DBAs. For example, you can query the sys.dm_exec_connections DMV to view the current connections. Figure 14.7 shows the results of a query run against the sys.dm_exec_connections DMV.

FIGURE 14.7   Querying the sys.dm_exec_connections DMV

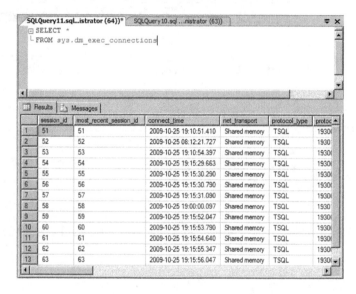

Over 140 total DMVs exist in SQL Server 2008. The best way to find the DMV with the information you're looking for would be to either look in the SQL Server 2008 Books Online for Dynamic Management Views and Functions or simply enter a SELECT statement into a query window in SSMS and let the autocomplete feature show you a list of available DMVs. Books Online categorizes the DMVs and provides examples for accessing them. Other than sys.dm_exec_connections, here are a few that you might want to take a look at:

sys.dm_exec_cached_plans   Shows a list of the execution plans cached in the SQL Server memory for faster query execution times.

sys.dm_exex_query_stats   Pay close attention to the execution_count column because it reveals how many times the query has been executed.

`sys.dm_os_loaded_modules`   Shows a list of the various DLLs and system modules loaded with the version numbers.

`sys.dm_os_performance_counters`   Shows the SQL Server–related performance counters and their values at the time of the query.

To illustrate the benefit of the DMVs, consider the following code:

```
SELECT TOP 5 total_worker_time/execution_count AS [Avg CPU Time],
    SUBSTRING(st.text, (qs.statement_start_offset/2)+1,
        ((CASE qs.statement_end_offset
        WHEN -1 THEN DATALENGTH(st.text)
        ELSE qs.statement_end_offset
        END - qs.statement_start_offset)/2) + 1) AS statement_text
FROM sys.dm_exec_query_stats AS qs
CROSS APPLY sys.dm_exec_sql_text(qs.sql_handle) AS st
ORDER BY total_worker_time/execution_count DESC;
```

If you execute this code in SSMS, you will see that it shows the top five queries (including the actual SQL statements) with the average CPU time consumed. The result is a prime target list of queries for optimization analysis. If you can improve the performance of these queries, you know that you are likely to improve the performance of the database overall.

As with all other management features of SQL Server 2008, I recommend the application of the SAU methodology. Standardize the DMV information you want to gather on your SQL Servers. Automate the information-gathering with jobs. Update the standard as needed when the environment demands a change.

DBCC

The DBCC command has been in SQL Server since the original Sybase days before Microsoft parted ways with that company. DBCC is the database consistency checker, and it can be used for several performance and troubleshooting tasks, including:

- Analyzing the consistency of databases, tables, and indexes.
- Shrinking files that have grown out of control.
- Defragmenting indexes.
- Showing information, such as statistics and index fragmentation.

While DBCC commands like DBCC CHECKDB and DBCC CHECKTABLE are well known, valuable commands like DBCC SHOWCONTIG are less well known. Figure 14.8 shows the output of the DBCC SHOWCONTIG command run against the Production.Product table in the AdventureWorks database.

FIGURE 14.8   Running DBCC SHOWCONTIG against the Production.Product table

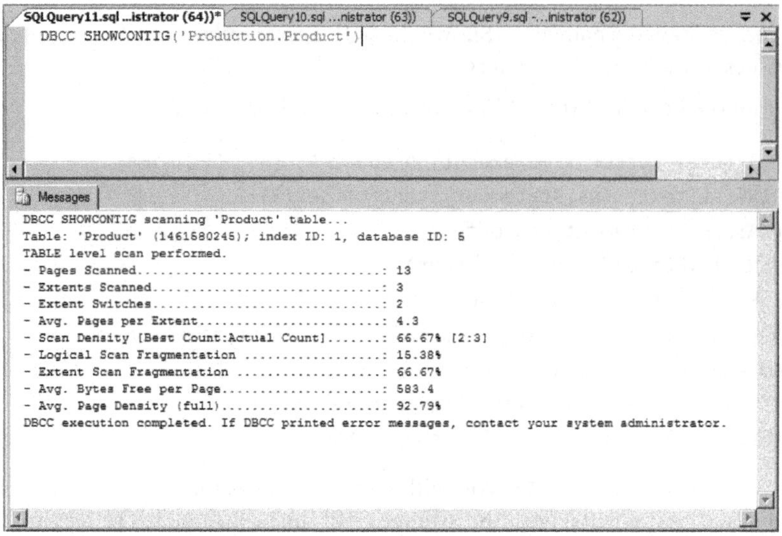

From Figure 14.8 you can see the value of this uncommonly referenced DBCC command. You can see the average free bytes per page, the fragmentation of the clustered index data (index ID 1), and more valuable information you can use to determine whether an index rebuild is in order or not. To view the fragmentation information for a specific index on a table, execute a command like the following:

```
DBCC SHOWCONTIG ('Production.Product',AK_Product_Name)
```

The preceding DBCC command would show fragmentation information about the AK_Product_Name index on the Production.Product table.

Table 14.2 lists several of the important DBCC commands and what they offer. Use this table as a reference when you need to determine the right DBCC command for the job.

TABLE 14.2   DBCC Commands with Examples

DBCC Command	Description	Example
DBCC CHECKDB	Used to validate the consistency and integrity of a database.	DBCC CHECKDB (AdventureWorks);
DBCC CHECKTABLE	Used to validate the consistency and integrity of a specific table.	DBCC CHECKTABLE ('Production.Product');

TABLE 14.2   DBCC Commands with Examples *(continued)*

DBCC Command	Description	Example
DBCC SHOWCONTIG	Used to determine the fragmentation level of a table or index. Will be replaced with the sys.dm_db_index_physical_stats in a future SLQ Server version.	DBCC SHOWCONTIG ('Production.Product');
DBCC SHINKFILE	Used to shrink a file, such as a transaction log file, after data is removed.	DBCC SHRINKFILE (DataFile1, 7);
DBCC SHOW_STATISTICS	Used to view information about statistics for a table or indexed view.	DBCC SHOW_STATISTICS ('Person.Address', AK_Address_rowguid);
DBCC HELP	Get help with the specified DBCC subcommand.	DBCC HELP ('CHECKDB');

Resource Monitor

The Resource Monitor was new to Windows Server 2008 and still exists in Windows Server 2008 R2. In both systems, you access the Resource Monitor from within the Task Manager. The Resource Monitor is the Task Manager all grown up. This metaphor simply means that it is more powerful and provides more valuable information than the Task Manager ever has.

To access the Resource Monitor, you have two basic options. The first option is to launch the Task Manager, click the Performance tab, and then click the Resource Monitor button. While this first option works just fine, you may prefer the Start and Type method for launching applications. The Start and Type method is simply the process of bringing up the Start menu (with the Windows key on the keyboard) and then typing the command you want. To give this method a try, perform Exercise 14.15.

Launching the Resource Monitor Directly

In this exercise, you will learn to launch the Resource Monitor without having to first launch the Task Manager. To quickly launch the Resource Monitor:

1. Press the Windows key on your keyboard (if you do not have a keyboard with the Windows key, press Ctrl+Esc to get the same results).

2. You will default to the Search field on the Start menu.

3. Type the following command: **perfmon /res**.

4. Press Enter.

At this point, you should see a screen similar to the following:

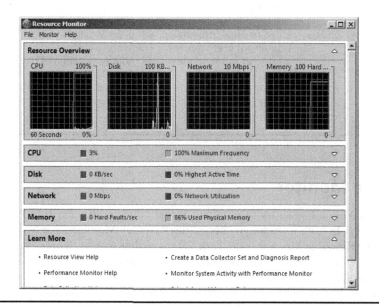

Now, for some really great news. The steps in Exercise 14.15 work in Windows Vista, Windows 7, Windows Server 2008, and Windows Server 2008 R2. The Resource Monitor has been greatly enhanced in Windows 7 and Windows Server 2008 R2, but it still supports this same command-line parameter.

To see another interesting feature of the Resource Monitor, execute the following command:

perfmon /report

You'll see a screen indicating that the performance analysis will run for approximately 60 seconds. When the analysis is complete, you will see a report like the one in Figure 14.9. Does this report look familiar? For that matter, does the Resource Monitor itself look familiar? Well, if you worked through the exercises earlier in this chapter related to the Reliability and Performance Monitor, it should. The Resource Monitor is one of the components of the Reliability and Performance Monitor. Now you know how to access it directly.

FIGURE 14.9   Viewing the Resource Monitor report

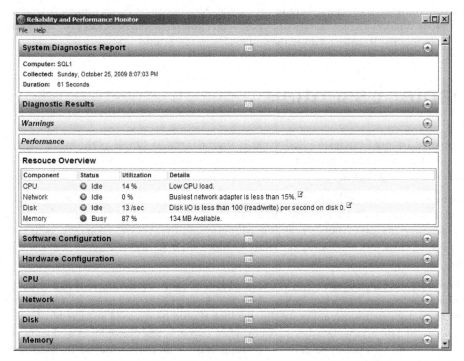

You can also view the reliability report for a Windows Vista, Windows 7, or Windows Server 2008 and 2008 R2 machine with the following command:

perfmon /report

This is most useful because the reliability report was obvious and easy to find in Windows Vista, but it's a bit more buried in Windows 7 and Windows Server 2008 R2.

Summary

In this chapter, you learned about the different performance tools that are available in SQL Server 2008 and Windows Server systems. You began by reviewing important performance tuning principles and then you explored the concurrency mechanisms of SQL Server. Next, you looked at the SQL Server Profiler and learned to create trace files with this powerful tool. Then the Database Engine Tuning Advisor was explained and demonstrated. With this tool, you can get recommendations to help improve the performance of your existing databases. You moved on from there to the System Monitor in its many implementations in the different Windows Server systems. Finally, you explored some new tools in SQL Server 2008, including the Resource Governor and Performance Studio.

Chapter Essentials

Performance Tuning Principles   Performance tuning is not as simple as throwing more hardware at a performance problem. You must use systems thinking and avoid the common performance tuning myths.

Performance and Troubleshooting Tools   If you're going to do much performance analysis and enhancement, you'll have to understand the available tools. Windows provides several tools, including the Task Manager, System Monitor, and Event Viewer log files. SQL Server 2008 also provides tools including the Activity Monitor, SQL Server Profiler, Database Engine Tuning Advisor, and DBCC.

Blocks, Locks, and Deadlocks   Locks are normal in a multiuser database system and will result in blocking. Blocking occurs when one connection has a resource locked that is requested by another resource. Eventually, the lock should be released and the blocked connection should gain access. Deadlocks occur when two processes have locks and want to access the resource locked by each other. Deadlocks occur in most systems, but high numbers should be avoided.

SQL Server Profiler   The SQL Server Profiler is like a network protocol analyzer specifically tuned and adjusted to capture only SQL Server events and actions. The SQL Server Profiler can be used to discover the T-SQL code being executed by many applications. It is used to build the workload for the Database Engine Tuning Advisor as well.

Database Engine Tuning Advisor   The Database Engine Tuning Advisor (DTA) is a simple program that can provide recommendations for performance tuning within your SQL Server databases. Caution should be taken with the recommendations because the DTA is not a human DBA and it can make mistakes.

Performance Monitoring with System Monitor   The System Monitor is actually an ActiveX control that can be added to custom MMCs and utilized within custom developed applications. The Performance tool and the Reliability and Performance Monitor provide access to the System Monitor in Windows Server 2003 and Windows Server 2008, respectively. In Windows Server 2003, you create performance counter logs and in Windows Server 2008, you create data collector sets.

Using the New Resource Governor   The Resource Governor is like having a set of virtual SQL Servers inside of your SQL Server instances. The Resource Governor can classify connections and place them in workload groups (also known as resource groups). The workload groups are assigned to resource pools, and the resource pools limit the consumption of the physical resources.

Performance Studio   The Performance Studio is a Management Data Warehouse (MDW) and a set of reports that can be viewed against the MDW. The MDW is a SQL Server 2008 database. Wizards are available for assistance in creating and configuring the MDW.

Advanced Monitoring Tools   In addition to the traditional tools used to monitor SQL Server, you should be aware of the Dynamic Management Views (DMVs), the powerful DBCC commands, and the Resource Monitor.

Policy-Based Management

TOPICS COVERED IN THIS CHAPTER:

✓ Policy-Based Management

✓ Centralized Server Management

✓ Standardizing with PBM

Microsoft first introduced management by policy in Windows 95 all the way back in 1995. Back then, they were called system policies. The system policies in Windows 95 systems were simply stored in a network share and pulled down to the Windows 95 clients automatically. The policies were all contained in a single file and no real hierarchy existed. Eventually, these policies evolved into group policies with the release of Windows 2000, and group policies are still heavily used to centrally manage and administer Microsoft Operating Systems. Group policies added a new hierarchical structure so that you could apply them locally, through an Active Directory site, through the Active Directory domain, or through an organizational unit within the domain. Now, SQL Server 2008 finally has *Policy-Based Management,* which allows for the enforcement of configuration standards and naming conventions—among other things—in an automated and centralized manner. Like group policies, they provide a hierarchy of application and great flexibility.

This chapter will introduce you to Policy-Based Management (PBM) and the components that comprise a PBM solution in the latest version of SQL Server. Next, it will step you through the process of creating a policy from start to finish. After you've created a policy or two, you will see how to centralize the management of policies using a Central Management Server. Finally, you'll learn about some recommendations for standardizing, automating, and updating your PBM environment.

Policy-Based Management (PBM)

Policy-Based Management (PBM) is also known as the Declarative Management Framework (DMF). You might say that PBM is implemented through the DMF. This all gets very interesting very quickly because Microsoft uses different terms for the technology depending on the certification exam objectives you're reading. In the TS exam (also knows as the Microsoft Certified Technology Specialist (MCTS): Microsoft SQL Server 2008, Implementation and Maintenance exam number 70–432) objectives, Microsoft asks you to implement the DMF. The objective may include, but is not limited to, the following:

- Create a policy
- Verify a policy
- Schedule a policy compliance check

- Enforce a policy
- Create a condition

This means the exam asks you to implement DMF by working with policies. Now, the PRO exam (also known as the PRO: Designing, Optimizing and Maintaining a Database Administrative Solution Using Microsoft SQL Server 2008 exam number 70–450) asks you to design policies using Policy-Based Management (PBM). The objective may include but is not limited to designing policies and conditions. Does that sound eerily familiar? It should because both Policy-Based Management and the Declarative Management Framework allow you to implement management through policies.

Although Microsoft seems to treat the two different phrases as one, the rest of this chapter will use only PBM. Just remember that PBM and DMF are one and the same.

PBM brings several advantages to the SQL Server DBA. Examples include:

Automatic Evaluation   The policies can be evaluated using automation. You can schedule the policies for evaluation using the same scheduling engine that you use for SQL Server jobs. By automating the evaluation, you ensure that you are in compliance with the policies and remove the human component called forgetfulness. (Exercise 15.9, later in this chapter, provides you with instructions for creating an example automatic evaluation policy.)

Policy Reuse   Even if you are not using a Centralized Management Server, you can still reuse policies. A policy can be exported as an XML data file and then imported into one or more other servers. Once a policy is imported, it can be scheduled for evaluation on the server.

Automatic Enforcement   Many policies can be enforced automatically. Some policies can be configured to disallow an action that would breach the policy. For example, you can reject a new login if it doesn't meet a policy's requirements. This enforcement is actually accomplished with DDL triggers, but the triggers are created for you automatically during the policy creation process. (Exercise 15.9 also provides an example of automatic enforcement.)

Surface Area Configuration   Many DBAs have asked why Microsoft removed the Surface Area Configuration tool that was introduced in SQL Server 2005 from SQL Server 2008. The answer is that PBM is intended to provide Surface Area Configuration features now. You can use `sp_configure` directly or you can configure the surface area through PBM. (Exercise 15.7 provides an example of surface area configuration through PBM.)

Centralized Policy Management   When you use one or more Central Management Servers, you can centralize the management of policies. The policies can be configured to apply automatically to a single server or to a server group. By placing servers in server groups, you make it much easier to manage similar servers. The later section of this chapter titled "Centralized Server Management" provides details on how to implement and configure Central Management Servers.

As you can see from this brief list of advantages, PBM has a lot to offer to a SQL Server DBA. When you must implement and administer hundreds of SQL Servers, PBM will make your life much easier.

One of the most exciting things about PBM is that it is really not that hard to learn and use. You must understand the components that make up the PBM architecture; but once you've mastered these components, implementation is very straightforward.

To help you master PBM and implement it properly, the following key topics will be covered in this section:

- PBM components
- Creating conditions
- Creating policies
- Evaluating policies

If you're wondering where centralized policy management is in this list, don't worry. An entire section titled "Centralized Server Management" is devoted to this topic later in the chapter.

PBM Components

PBM is comprised of several components including facets, conditions, policies, categories, and targets. Figure 15.1 represents the first four of these components and the hierarchy within which they operate. You will notice that conditions operate on facets and policies operate on conditions. You can categorize the policies and apply an entire category of policies to a server or server group.

FIGURE 15.1 PBM components represented hierarchically

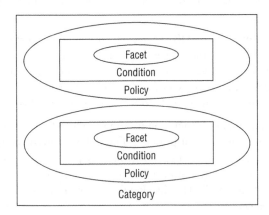

The following sections address each component individually.

Facets

Think of facets as configurable objects in SQL Servers. The *Oxford American College Dictionary* defines a facet as a particular aspect or feature of something. In PBM, the *facet* is the elemental object that contains configuration properties. It is elemental because you cannot really work with a more basic component than the property of a facet, but you must access the property through the facet.

SQL Server 2008 was initially released with 74 facets out-of-the box. These facets cannot be removed or modified by the DBA, but they can be checked and constrained by creating conditions within the PBM hierarchy. Microsoft may choose to release new facets through service packs or patches.

Facets can be read/write or they may be read-only. Read/write facets can be configured through PBM. Read-only facets are used to monitor the state of an object. For example, the Database Performance facet includes a Size property. You may want to ensure that a particular database never exceeds a specified size. You can use the Size property of the Database Performance facet to evaluate this constraint. You cannot change the size of the database to a smaller size, however, because this would require removing data pages. The only way you can see that the database is too large is through the evaluation of your specifications. Read-only facet properties are used in this way. Exercise 15.1 steps you through a process that reveals the read-only versus read/write properties of facets.

EXERCISE 15.1

Determining Read-Only Properties of Facets

In this exercise, you will locate the facets for a SQL Server object and then determine which properties of a facet are read-only. To view the read-only properties of a facet:

1. Launch SSMS.

2. In the Object Explorer, right-click a server instance root node and select Facets.

3. In the Facets selection box, choose the facet you want to view.

4. In the Facet properties list, note that the read-only properties are gray and the read/write properties are black, as in the following image:

EXERCISE 15.1 *(continued)*

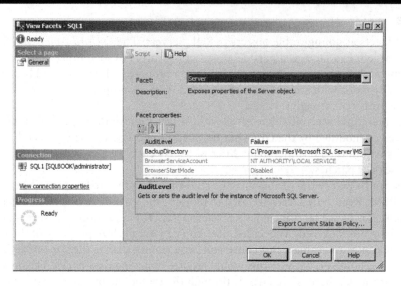

5. Click OK to close the View Facets window.

6. Expand the Databases container, right-click the AdventureWorks database, and select Facets.

7. In the Facets selection box, choose the facet you want to view.

8. In the Facet properties list, note that the read-only properties are again gray and the read/write properties are again black.

The steps used in Exercise 15.1 to view the facet properties can be used with any valid PBM target. A PBM target is the item to be evaluated by a policy. PBM targets include:

- Server instances
- Databases
- Tables
- Indexes
- Logins and database users
- Audit objects
- Linked servers
- Triggers
- Resource Governor and its objects
- Schemas

With most of these targets, you can right-click the target in SSMS and select Facets to view the list of facets and facet properties available. Remember, if the property is gray, it is read-only. If the property is black, it is read/write.

You can view a list of available facets by expanding the Management node in Object Explorer and then expanding the Policy Management and Facets nodes to see a list similar to the one in Figure 15.2.

Conditions

You've undoubtedly heard questions like the following:

- What are the weather conditions like today?
- In what condition is that used automobile?
- Under what conditions should the machine work?

As you've probably noticed, all of these questions have something in common: they are all seeking information about conditions. A *condition* is defined as the state of something. The three questions listed previously ask about the state of the weather, the automobile, and the environment. In a PBM implementation, conditions define the desired state of a single facet property.

FIGURE 15.2   Viewing the list of available facets in Object Explorer

A SQL Server 2008 condition has four properties, all of which are listed here along with their conditions:

Name   The Name property is what you would expect: the name for the condition.

Facet   The Facet property defines the actual facet evaluated in the condition.

Expression   The Expression property defines the property of the facet and the evaluated state.

Description   The Description property is used to describe the condition.

A large text box is provided in the GUI interface for entering the Description property data. You should use this area to provide information for management purposes. It's a good idea to standardize (remember, SAU?) on the contents of the Description property and the convention for the Name property. It will make life much easier. Figure 15.3 shows the Create New Condition dialog's General page and Figure 15.4 shows an example Description page.

FIGURE 15.3 The General page of the Create New Condition dialog

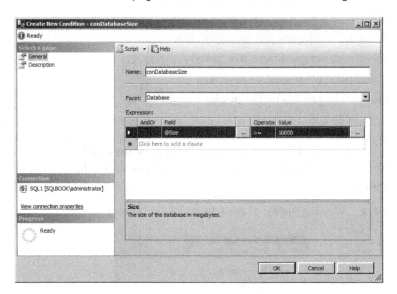

FIGURE 15.4 The Description page of the Create New Condition dialog

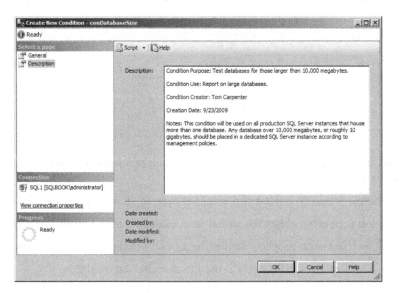

Policies

Policies are used to test for conditions. Remember, you start with a prebuilt facet. The facet is then linked with a desired or undesired state in a condition. The policy goes to the next step and checks to see if the condition is True or False and acts according to the evaluation mode specification. A policy includes the following properties:

- Name
- Enabled
- Check condition
- Targets
- Evaluation mode
- Server restriction
- Category
- Description
- Additional help hyperlink

The first six of these properties will be located on the General page of the Create New Policy dialog, as shown in Figure 15.5.

Let's discuss each of these in depth.

FIGURE 15.5   The General page of the Create New Policy dialog

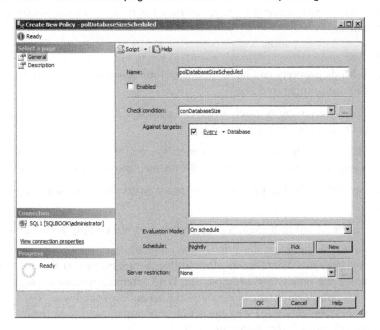

Name

As with the conditions, the Name property is simply the name of the policy. Again, creating a naming convention for these objects is a good idea. For example, you could require that all policy names begin with the pol prefix and then name the condition name without the prefix (con) and then the way in which the policy should be evaluated.

To illustrate this, imagine you're creating a policy that checks the conDatabaseSize condition. You will evaluate this policy on a schedule. So the name might be polDatabaseSizeScheduled. Do you see how the name alone tells us much about the policy? One of the driving benefits behind naming conventions is that the names mean something to us.

Enabled

The Enabled property determines whether the policy is on or off. If the Enabled check box is checked, the policy is on and will be evaluated at the scheduled time or when a change event occurs (for facets that support the On Change evaluation modes). The Enabled check box will not be available with policies configured for the On Demand evaluation mode.

Check Condition

The Check Condition property determines the condition that is evaluated by the policy. In Figure 15.5, the conDatabaseSize condition is evaluated. Once the Check Condition property is set, you can then determine the configuration for the Targets property. In Figure 15.5, the target is Every database, which means that the policy can be evaluated against a server and every database on that server will be tested for compliance with the conDatabaseSize condition specifications.

Evaluation

The Evaluation Mode property can be set to one of four possible values. The values and their descriptions are summarized here:

On Demand   Used for testing or rarely evaluated policies. The DBA must initiate the evaluation with the On Demand evaluation mode.

On Schedule   Used to evaluate a policy on a specific schedule. Uses the scheduling engine used for jobs. Commonly used to evaluate read-only facet properties through PBM.

On Change: Log Only   Used to log when a change is made that does not comply with a policy.

On Change: Prevent   Used to prevent a change that does not comply with a policy.

The most important thing you must do is determine which evaluation mode to use based on the outcome you desire. Some facets allow rollback capabilities so that you can undo actions that breach the policy. For example, if a DBA attempts to create a login that does not comply with a condition, you can disallow the creation of the login. The DBA will receive an error message indicating why the action was not allowed, and the message will include the policy that restricted the action.

Only a select group of facets may be used with the two On Change evaluation modes. The following list of facets may be used with both the On Change: Log Only and On Change: Prevent evaluation modes:

- Application Role
- Asymmetric Key
- Database Role
- Endpoint
- Login Options
- Multipart Name
- Resource Pool
- Schema
- Stored Procedure
- Table Options
- User Defined Function
- User Options
- View Options
- Workload Group

In addition to these facets that can be evaluated on a change for both logging and prevention, several facets can be used only with On Change: Log Only. These logging only facets include:

- Database Option
- Server Configuration
- Surface Area

All other facets are limited to the On Demand and On Schedule evaluation modes.

Server Restriction

You can use the Server Restriction property of the policy to analyze a condition and determine, by that condition, whether the policy should apply to a given server. Sadly, the Server Restriction property is limited to conditions that evaluate facets supporting On Change: Prevent evaluation modes. The result is that you are very limited in the properties you can evaluate.

Description Page Policies

The next three policy properties—Category, Description, and Additional Help Hyperlink—are found on the Description page of the Create New Policy dialog and they are shown in Figure 15.6.

FIGURE 15.6   The Description page of the Create New Policy dialog

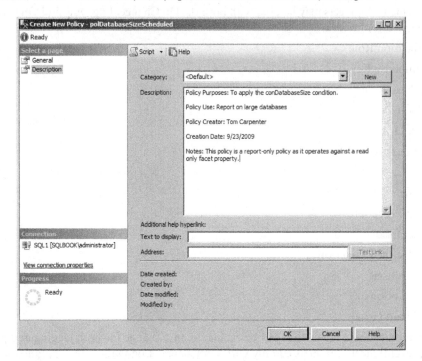

The Category policy allows you to group policies into categories. Categories are covered in more detail in the next subsection titled "Categories." For now, just know that you can specify a category here and that you can create the category by clicking the New button, if it does not already exist.

The next property is the Description property. Like the condition, this should be used to specify details about the policy that will be useful to future administrators. It may be helpful to include the name of the policy creator, the purpose for the policy, and any other notes you think are relevant and meaningful.

The Additional Help hyperlink includes two fields: the text to display and the HTTP link to the information page. This property is useful for providing links to more information related to this policy. The link can be to an internal Intranet document that defines the organization's policies that impact this particular policy. Alternatively, you may decide to link to a Microsoft web page that provides technical information. The choice is yours, but you will want to ensure that the link provides useful information for the viewer in relation to this specific policy. You can also use a mailto: link in this area so that the viewer can send an email to an administrator who can assist with the policy.

Categories

If you have done any administration in a modern Windows domain-based network, you can think of the categories in SQL Server's PBM like the organizational units (OU) in Active Directory. Like the OUs, you can link multiple policies with a single category. Once you've placed the policies in the category, you can then assign an entire category of policies to a target database.

No categories exist by default. If you want to use categories, you have two primary options:

- Import a set of categories by importing the Microsoft sample policies
- Create your own categories with the category management features of SSMS

The sample policies provided by Microsoft can be very useful in the learning process. Exercise 15.2 steps you through the process of loading the sample policies. Do not load the policies into your production environment because they will unnecessarily clutter your SSMS interface, but they are useful in the lab for learning purposes. Additionally, you can import them into the lab environment to locate the ones that would indeed be useful for your production environment.

EXERCISE 15.2

Importing the Microsoft Sample Policies

In this exercise, you will import the sample policies for the database engine. To import the policies, follow these steps:

1. Launch SSMS.

2. In Object Explorer, expand Management ➤ Policy Management ➤ Policies.

3. Right-click the Policies node and select Import Policy.

4. Click the build or selection button to the right of the Files to Import field.

5. Navigate to the C:\Program Files\Microsoft SQL Server\100\Tools\Policies\ DatabaseEngine\1033 folder.

6. Single-click on any file in the list and then press Ctrl+A to select all the files.

7. Click the Open button to return to the Import dialog.

8. Under Options, for the Policy State option, choose Preserve Policy State on import (don't worry; the policies are all disabled by default).

9. Your Import dialog should look similar to the following; if it does, click OK to import the sample policies.

EXERCISE 15.2 *(continued)*

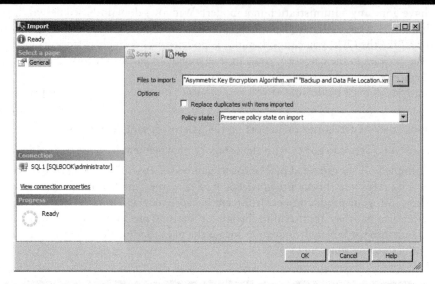

10. When the import is complete, you will see a new list of policies in the Policies node. Expand the Conditions node and note the new conditions that match with the new policies.

11. Right-click on the Policy Management node and select Manage Categories. You will see a screen similar to the following.

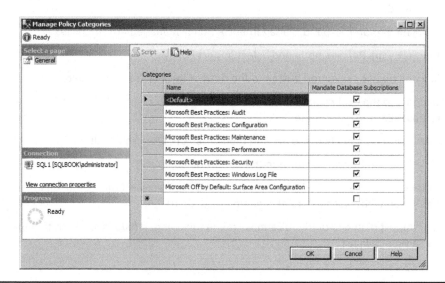

Two significant lessons can be learned from Exercise 15.2. First, Microsoft has provided several sample policies from which to learn. Second, when you export a policy and then import it into another server, if that target server does not already have a category defined in the policy, the category will be created automatically. The categories added during the processes in Exercise 15.2 were in the sample policies.

In addition to the Database Engine policies demonstrated in Exercise 15.2, sample policies exist for Analysis Services and Reporting Services. Just change the DatabaseEngine portion of the C:\Program Files\Microsoft SQL Server\100\Tools\Policies\DatabaseEngine\1033 path to AnalysisServices or ReportingServices to access the additional sample policies.

You may also create categories manually. Exercise 15.3 steps you through the process of creating your own categories.

EXERCISE 15.3

Creating Custom Categories for Policies

In addition to creating categories by clicking the New button from the Create New Policy dialog, you can create categories in the Manage Policy Categories dialog. To do this, follow these steps:

1. Right-click on the Policy Management node within the Management node of Object Explorer and select Manage Categories.

2. In the Manage Policy Categories dialog, click on the next available row and enter a name for the category, such as **Company: Security**, as shown in the following image:

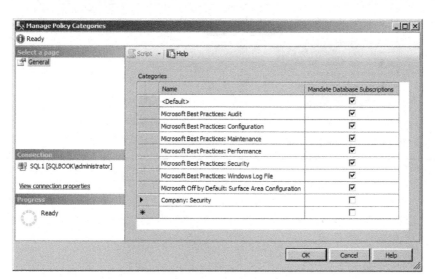

EXERCISE 15.3   *(continued)*

3. Check the Mandate Database Subscriptions check box, if you want to require all databases on the target server to adhere to this category of policies. Keep in mind that if you mandate subscriptions, all databases must adhere to this policy.

4. Click OK to save the new category.

At this point you have created a new category. Now, you can subscribe to the category, if it is not a mandated subscription, at the database level. If the category is a mandated subscription, you do not have to subscribe because all databases must subscribe automatically. A mandated subscription is a required policy. When mandated, all databases must adhere to the policy. Exercise 15.4 provides the steps required to subscribe to a nonmandated category in SQL Server 2008.

EXERCISE 15.4

Subscribing to a Category

In this exercise, you will subscribe the AdventureWorks database to the Company: Security category created in Exercise 15.3. To do this, follow these steps:

1. Expand the Databases node in Object Explorer.

2. Right-click on the AdventureWorks database and select Policies ≻ Categories.

3. In the Categories dialog, check the Subscribed check box for the Company: Security category as in the following image.

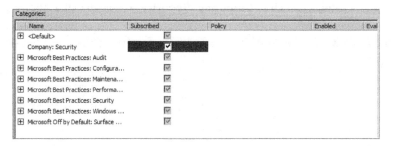

4. Click OK to save the changes.

Because the Company: Security category does not contain any categories, no new policies will be applied to the AdventureWorks database. However, now that the database is subscribed to the category, any future policies will be applied automatically.

Targets

The final component of the PBM architecture is the target. The available targets are too numerous to list in entirety, but a partial list containing many of the most important targets follows:

- Server
- Database
- Schema
- Table
- View
- Logins
- Users
- Trigger
- Stored procedure
- User-defined function
- Audit
- Backup device
- Data file

The most confusing part of PBM to new DBAs seems to be the matching of policies to targets. This confusion comes from the fact that facets control or limit the targets and not policies. A facet may be applicable to one or more targets. For example, the Multipart Name facet may apply to multiple targets. The good news is that the vast majority of facets apply to only one target type.

Now, let's consider the inverse. Can a target type be evaluated based on more than one facet? The answer is a resounding Yes. In this case, the number of many-to-one relationships is greater. For example, the Server target type can be evaluated based on eight different facets. If you double-click on any facet in the Facets node, you can see a list of applicable target types as shown in Figure 15.7.

FIGURE 15.7   Viewing the applicable target types by facet

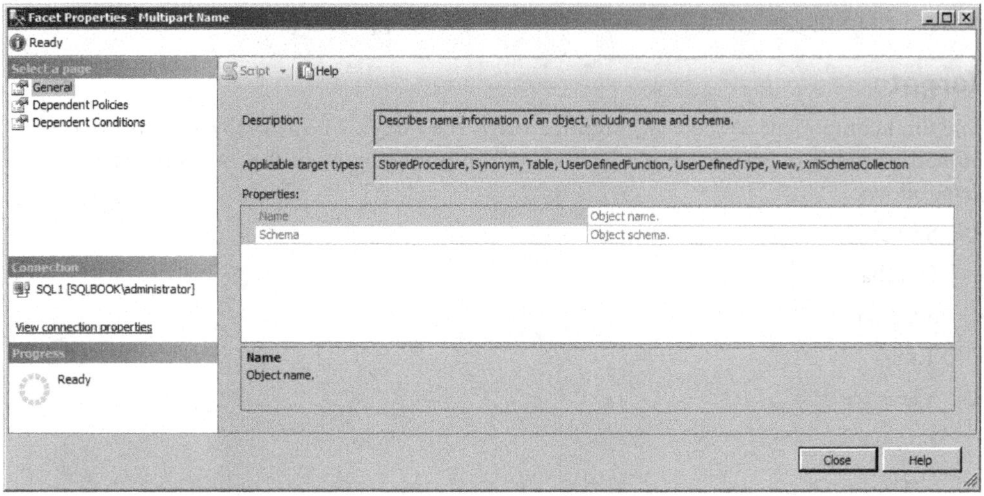

Creating Conditions

The first step you must take to implement a policy is to create a condition. Remember, the facets already exist and you must create a condition that defines a desired or undesired state for a facet property. In this section, you will create three different conditions. The three conditions will demonstrate the use of the On Schedule, On Change: Log Only, and On Change: Prevent evaluation modes, when they are used in the next section titled Creating Policies. If you do not create the three conditions as instructed in Exercises 15.5, 15.6, and 15.7, you will not be able to perform the Exercises in the "Creating Policies" section.

The first condition you will create will work with the Database facet and the Size property. You will define a condition that expects the database to be less than 10,000 megabytes in size. Exercise 15.5 steps you through the process.

EXERCISE 15.5

Creating the conDatabaseSize Condition

In this exercise, you will create a condition named conDatabaseSize. The condition will use the Database facet. The Size property of the facet will be evaluated. You will expect the value of the Size property to be less than 10,000 megabytes. To do this, follow these steps:

1. In the Object Explorer Management node, right-click the Conditions node within Policy Management and select New Condition.

2. For the Name field, enter **conDatabaseSize**.

3. For the Facet, choose Database.

4. In the Expression builder, click in the Field column and choose @Size from the list.

5. For the operator, choose less than or equal to (<=).

6. In the criteria field, enter **10000**.

7. Click the pencil button to the left of the row you've just added to save the expression.

8. Click OK to save the condition.

Keep in mind that you would normally want to go to the Description page and enter a standardized description value. For these exercises, you will leave the Description blank.

The second condition you will create will use the Login Options facet and will require that the PasswordExpirationEnabled and PasswordPolicyEnforced properties be set to True. Exercise 15.6 steps you through the process.

Creating the conPasswordRules Condition

In this exercise, you will create a condition named conPasswordRules. The condition will use the Login Options facet. The PasswordExpirationEnabled and PasswordPolicyEnforced properties of the facet will be evaluated. To do this, follow these steps:

1. In the Object Explorer Management node, right-click the Conditions node within Policy Management and select New Condition.

2. For the Name field, enter **conPasswordRules**.

3. For the Facet, choose Login Options.

4. In the Expression builder, click in the Field column and choose @PasswordExpirationEnabled from the list.

5. For the operator, choose equal to (=).

6. In the criteria field, enter **True**.

7. Click in the Field column for the next row and choose @PasswordPolicyEnforced from the list.

8. For the operator, choose equal to (=).

9. In the criteria field, enter **True**.

10. Click the pencil button to the left of the row you've just added to save the expression.

11. Click OK to save the condition.

The third and final condition you will create will use the Surface Area Configuration facet and will expect the property of XPCmdShellEnabled to be False. Exercise 15.7 steps you through the process.

Creating the conSurfaceArea Condition

In this exercise, you will create a condition named conSurfaceArea. The condition will use the Surface Area Configuration facet. The XPCmdShellEnabled property of the facet will be evaluated. To do this, follow these steps:

1. In the Object Explorer Management node, right-click the Conditions node within Policy Management and select New Condition.

2. For the Name field, enter **conSurfaceArea**.

3. For the Facet, choose Surface Area Configuration.

4. In the Expression builder, click in the Field column and choose @XPCmdShellEnabled from the list.

5. For the operator, choose equal to (=).

6. In the criteria field, enter **False**.

7. Click the pencil button to the left of the row you've just added to save the expression.

8. Click OK to save the condition.

Notice that you chose the criteria of False for the conSurfaceArea condition. In most cases, you still specify the condition as what you want it to be when creating a condition that is based on a read-only property. The reason is simple: you want the evaluation process to indicate a problem if the condition is not the way you've specified it. In this case, you want to see a problem indication if the XP CMD Shell feature is enabled so you set the condition to look for XPCmdShellEnabled to equal False. If the property is equal to True, the condition will not be True and you will see a nice red circle and a white X letting you know something is off from the intended condition.

Now that you've created the three conditions, you can move on to create the policies that will evaluate these conditions.

Creating Policies

You create policies in the SSMS GUI just as you do conditions. The policies are created in the Policies node within the Policy Management node in Object Explorer. No real limit exists on the number of policies you can create, but the policies are stored in the master database, so creating unnecessary policies would increase the size of the master database without benefit. You should only create the policies that you need. This is the reason you were cautioned against importing the sample Microsoft policies into a production SQL Server 2008 instance. This section will provide exercises that create the policies to match the conditions created in the preceding section.

 WARNING   If you have not created the conditions by performing Exercises 15.5, 15.6, and 15.7, the exercises in this section will not work.

In Exercise 15.8, you will create a policy that evaluates the conDatabaseSize condition. The policy will be configured to evaluate on a schedule and the schedule will be every night at 4 A.M. The policy will be named polDatabaseSizeScheduled.

EXERCISE 15.8

Creating the polDatabaseSizeScheduled Policy

In this exercise, you will create the polDatabaseSizeScheduled policy. To do this, follow these steps:

1. In Management ➤ Policy Management, right-click on Policies and then select New Policy.

2. Enter the policy name of **polDatabaseSizeScheduled**.

3. For the Check condition property, choose conDatabaseSize.

4. Accept the default target of Every Database.

5. Set the Evaluation Mode to On Schedule.

6. Click the New button to create a new schedule.

7. Enter the schedule name of **Nightly-4-AM**.

8. For the Frequency, choose Occurs Daily.

9. For the Daily Frequency, choose Occurs Once At: 4:00:00 AM, as in the following image:

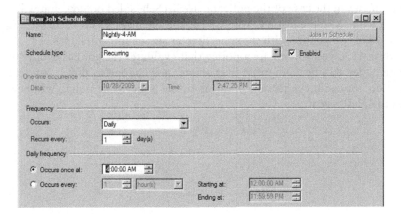

EXERCISE 15.8   *(continued)*

10. Click OK to save the schedule.

11. Check the Enabled check box so that the Create New Policy screen looks like the following image:

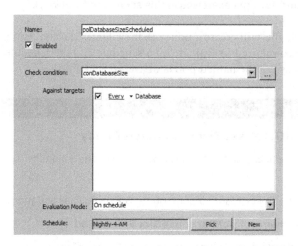

12. Click OK to create the new policy.

The policy created in Exercise 15.8 will run automatically every night at 4 A.M. You can view the results of a scheduled policy run by looking at the history of the policy. Simply right-click the policy in SSMS and choose View History to see the results of the policy's evaluation. As long as the policy evaluated to True (for example, the Database size was less than 10,000 megabytes in the case of the polDatabaseSizeScheduled policy), the history will show only that the evaluation ran and a green check mark will indicate that everything was OK.

When a scheduled evaluation does not check out (for example, the database is more than 10,000 megabytes in the case of the polDatabaseSizeScheduled policy), you will see a red circle with a white X in the history. You can expand the history entry and see exactly which target was not in compliance with the condition, as shown in Figure 15.8.

In Exercise 15.9, you will create a policy that evaluates the conPasswordRules condition. The policy will be configured to evaluate on a change so that it can reject new logins that do not comply with the condition of the policy. The policy will be named polPasswordRulesPrevent.

FIGURE 15.8   Viewing the history of an evaluation showing noncompliant targets

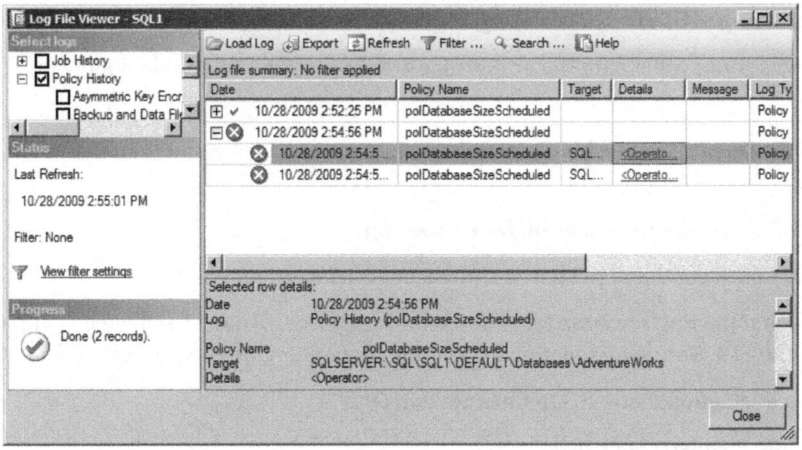

EXERCISE 15.9

Creating the polPasswordRulesPrevent Policy

In this exercise, you will create the polPasswordRulesPrevent policy. To do this, follow these steps:

1. In Management ➢ Policy Management, right-click on Policies and then select New Policy.

2. Enter the policy name of **polPasswordRulesPrevent**.

3. For the Check Condition property, choose conPasswordRules.

4. Accept the default target of Every Login.

5. Set the Evaluation mode to On Change: Prevent.

6. Check the Enabled check box.

7. Click OK to save the new policy.

In Exercise 15.10, you will create a policy that evaluates the conSurfaceArea condition. The policy will be configured to evaluate on a change and log the results of the evaluation. The policy will be named polSurfaceAreaLog.

EXERCISE 15.10

Creating the polSurfaceAreaLog Policy

In this exercise, you will create the polSurfaceAreaLog policy. To do this, follow these steps:

1. In Management ➢ Policy Management, right-click on Policies and then select New Policy.

2. Enter the policy name of **polSurfaceAreaLog**.

3. For the Check condition property, choose conSurfaceArea.

4. Notice that the Surface Area facet does not list a target. That's because it is applicable to the SQL Server installation as a whole, depending on the property evaluated.

5. Set the Evaluation mode to On Change: Log Only.

6. Check the Enabled check box.

7. Click OK to save the new policy.

Because the policy created in Exercise 15.10 is an On Change: Log Only policy, you must check the Event Viewer logs to see if a breach in policy has occurred. Of course, you can also view the internal history by right-clicking the policy and selecting View History. Figure 15.9 shows the log in the Event View. The proper log to view is the application log.

FIGURE 15.9   Viewing On Change: Log Only entries in the Event Viewer application log

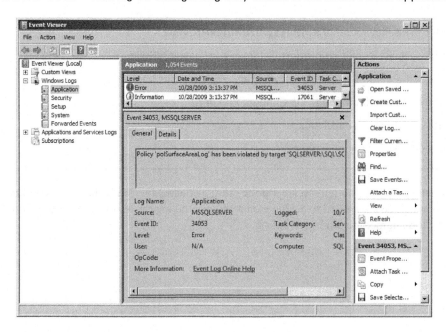

Evaluating Policies

Policies can be evaluated using different evaluation modes. The available modes include On Demand, On Schedule, On Change: Log Only, and On Change: Prevent. The modes available for a given policy will depend on the facet specified in the condition evaluated by the policy. The evaluation mode, as you saw in the preceding section, is configured as part of the policy. If you open a policy and do not see one or more of the four evaluation modes, it simply means that the facet on which the policy is based does not support the missing evaluation modes.

When you use the On Change: Prevent Evaluation mode, a trigger is created to process the evaluation. The trigger actually calls on a system stored procedure named `sp_syspolicy_dispatch_event` that is located in the dbo schema of the MSDB database. Because the code used for PBM is stored throughout the MSDB and master databases, it is very important to back up these databases whenever you make changes to the policies in your environment.

You can evaluate On Demand policies, by right-clicking the policy and selecting evaluate. When you evaluate an On Demand policy, you will see a report indicating whether the object is in compliance with the policy or not. You can also do this with On Schedule or On Change policies, but it will not be necessary in most production implementations with On Schedule or On Change policies. You will simply allow the policies to work on the schedule or change events on which they are intended to work.

Centralized Server Management

Now that you've seen how to create conditions and policies, you're probably excited to learn how you can centralize the management of these policies. The key to centralization is the creation of a Central Management Server or CMS. In this section, you'll see how to create a CMS and how to register subscriber servers or instances with the CMS.

Major Benefits and Requirements

Before you see the steps for creating a CMS, you should understand the benefits of having one and the requirements for having one.

The requirement is that the CMS must be a SQL Server 2008 server or later. While a SQL Server 2005 server can be registered with the CMS, it cannot act as the CMS. In fact, SQL Server 2000 and later servers can be registered as members of the server groups managed by the CMS.

The benefits are several. First, you can run T-SQL statements against a server group created in the CMS. This feature is very useful because SQL Server 2000 and 2005 do not really support PBM. You can create a T-SQL statement to execute against a server group that contains all of your down-level SQL Servers. As long as the statement is syntactically correct for both SQL Server 2000 and 2005, you can massively change your down-level servers in this way.

Second, you can evaluate policies against a server group. Instead of going to each server and manually importing and evaluating the policies, you can create the policies on the CMS server and then evaluate them against a group of SQL Server 2008 or later servers.

Third, you can import policies into the server group. Of course, the end result is that the policies are actually imported into each server in the group. Now, policies that evaluate on change, for example, will all be running on each server within that server group.

Creating a Centralized Management Server

Creating a CMS is a simple process. Exercise 15.11 provides the instructions for creating a CMS.

EXERCISE 15.11

Creating a CMS in SSMS

In this exercise, you will create a CMS. To do this, follow these steps:

1. Launch SSMS.

2. From the top menus, select View ➤ Registered Servers.

3. In the Registered Servers window, expand the Database Engine root node.

4. Right-click Central Management Servers and select Register Central Management Server.

5. In the New Server Registration dialog, enter **localhost** into the Server name field and click the Test button.

6. Click OK on the successful test report.

7. Click Save to create the local server as a CMS.

After completing the steps in Exercise 15.11, you've created the CMS. This is the first step in using centralized management in SQL Server 2008. But your work is not yet complete; you must now register servers with the CMS, if you want to centrally manage them. Additionally, you may want to create server groups so that the servers can be managed in collections.

Registering Subscriber Servers

With the CMS created, the next step is to register subscriber servers. These servers are SQL Server 2000 and later servers that will be managed by the CMS. Remember that the PBM functions are intended for SQL Server 2008 and later servers; however, if you connect to a SQL Server 2000 or 2005 server, some manual policy evaluations can be performed.

Because you may want to create server groups, you should follow the steps in Exercise 15.12.

EXERCISE 15.12

Creating Server Groups in the CMS

In this exercise, the steps for creating a server group are provided. Just follow these steps:

1. In the Registered Servers window, right-click on the CMS server and select New Server Group.

2. In the New Server Group dialog, enter a name and description as shown in the following image. (The name High Security is used out of preference. You can name the groups to your liking.)

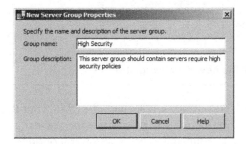

3. Click OK to create the new server group.

You can cycle through the three steps in Exercise 15.12 as many times as required to create the needed server groups. Remember that you have three main motivators for creating a server group:

- To collect servers together that should have the same configurations
- To collect servers together that do not support fully centralized PBM
- To collect servers together that must comply with different regulatory policies

Once you have your server groups, you can begin adding registered servers (or subscriber servers) to the groups. Exercise 15.13 provides the steps required to register a server.

EXERCISE 15.13

Custom Categories for Policies

In this exercise, the steps for creating a server group are provided. To create a server group, follow these steps:

1. In the Registered Servers window, right-click on the CMS server or the server group to which you want to add the new server and select New Server Registration.

2. In the New Server Registration dialog, type in the name or IP address of the new server to be registered and click the Test button.

3. Assuming the test is successful, click OK to indicate The Connection Was Tested Successfully in the New Server Registration dialog, which looks like the following image:

4. Click Save to create the new server registration.

After you've registered one or more servers with the CMS, your Registered Servers window should look similar to that in Figure 15.10. In this state, you can right-click on a specific registered server or a server group and select from several options.

FIGURE 15.10   Viewing the registered servers in the Registered Servers window of SSMS

In Figure 15.11, you can see the different options that you can select by right-clicking on a server group.

FIGURE 15.11   Viewing the options available when right-clicking a server group

🌐 Real World Scenario

Even Small Businesses Can Benefit from PBM and CMS Servers

I was working with a small business located just outside of Dayton, Ohio. They only had three SQL Server 2008 servers, but they were running into a repeated problem. Two different DBAs were creating objects in the SQL Servers and they were using different naming constructs. One DBA seemed to randomly choose names of objects, and the other had a nice naming convention that he always used. The result, however, was a confusing mess of a database server.

I was asked to come into the organization and assist in the implementation of a wireless intrusion-detection system that logged information into a SQL Server database. While I was there, I noticed the naming inconsistencies and mentioned it to one of the DBAs. He said that it frustrated him as well and he wanted to have a consistent naming convention.

I met with both DBAs (if you didn't catch it, the DBA who was frustrated was the one with the nice naming convention) and explained the benefits of using a naming convention. Some of the benefits I mentioned included:

- You know what you're looking at when you see an object.

- New administrators can more quickly learn the system.

- Visiting consultants, such as myself, are less likely to mess things up.

After reviewing these benefits and a few others, the other DBA agreed that a naming convention was needed. I sat down with them and we developed a plan similar to what the frustrated DBA had already been using.

Then I dropped the bombshell. "Have you implemented PBM?" I asked. "We haven't even heard of it," they responded. Were they ever in for a treat. I connected to my lab servers using a VPN connection and showed them the potential. After just a few minutes of demonstration, they agreed that PBM was very needed in their organization.

In the end, we implemented their naming convention through PBM policies so that the convention would be enforced and not just given lip service. Today, they have a well-oiled machine and they use PBM for several dozen other things as well. Even if you are in a small SQL Server shop, I would encourage you to give PBM a serious look.

Standardizing with PBM and CMS

So far, in this chapter, you've learned the mechanics of setting up PBM and centralized management with a CMS. You should standardize your implementations of PBM and CMS and use them to standardize your SQL Server 2008 instances. The benefits of standardization are many and include consistency, simplified troubleshooting, and a general feeling of awareness. Why this feeling of awareness? Because you know what you're up against when you face a problem and must come up with a solution. In order to help you develop standards for PBM and CMS, this chapter will conclude by addressing the topics you've covered from the perspective of the SAU model that you first learned in Chapter 13, "Creating Jobs, Operators, and Alerts." First, you'll learn about some recommendations for the items you should standardize in relations to both PBM and CMS servers. Next, you'll read some tips on how to automate things using these solutions. Finally, you'll briefly address considerations for updating your standard of use for PBM and CMS servers to wrap things up.

Standardizing

After reading Chapter 13 of this book, you probably realized that standardization of information systems and technologies is a big deal. When it comes to PBM and CMS servers, several items should be considered for standardization because developing standards will help you implement a more consistent and simpler environment.

PBM Standardizations

First, here's a list of items you should standardize for your environment with PBM implementations:

   Names: Develop a standard naming convention for each of the following items: conditions, policies, and categories. You may be able to borrow from existing naming conventions you've developed for other database schema items.

Descriptions: Provide a list of items that should be in the description for conditions and policies. Items that you may decide to include would be creator name, purpose, expiration date (if it should be later removed), and notes.

Processes: What will be your process for creating a new condition/policy pair? Make it a required practice to immediately export the policy after it is created. This action will give you a good backup of the policy should you later need it.

CMS Standardizations

For the CMS, a few items should be considered as well:

Number of CMS Servers: How many CMS servers will you require? This question might be best answered by considering whether you want one CMS server for the enterprise or several created based on departments, locations, security requirements, or some other criteria.

Down-Level Support Policy: Will you allow SQL Server 2008 CMS servers to manage SQL Server 2000 and 2005 servers? If so, for what can the CMS server be used? You may choose to allow running queries against the down-level servers but not other actions.

Dedicated CMS Servers: Will you create dedicated CMS servers or will the CMS role be employed on production servers? If the CMS role is deployed on a production server, will you limit the production database activity on that server?

As you can see, for both the PBM infrastructure and the CMS servers, you have some important decisions to make.

Please understand that I am in no way saying that you will be able to create a standard that could address every possible scenario. Rules are made to be broken, as they say, and sometimes you will have to go against your own standards. But such scenarios should be the exception and not the rule.

Automating

Equally important to standardization is automation. When you automate your standards, you make it more likely that they will be implemented. If you do not automate, many of the administrators and support professionals will sneak in shortcuts that hinder your standardized environment.

As you created the various policies in this chapter, you may have noticed a key problem. Several facets only allow you to log an event when a configuration value is changed. So what can you do to receive automatic notification of such changes? Several answers to this question exist, but here you'll focus on one great feature of the Event Viewer that many administrators do not realize it has: Task Scheduling. You can configure the Event Viewer to monitor for a particular log entry and to take action should that log entry be added to the log.

For example, in Figure 15.12 you can see an entry in the application log for the polSurfaceAreaLog policy created in Exercise 15.10. In Exercise 15.14, you see how to create an automated monitoring solution for this entry.

FIGURE 15.12   Viewing the polSurfaceAreaLog entry in the application log

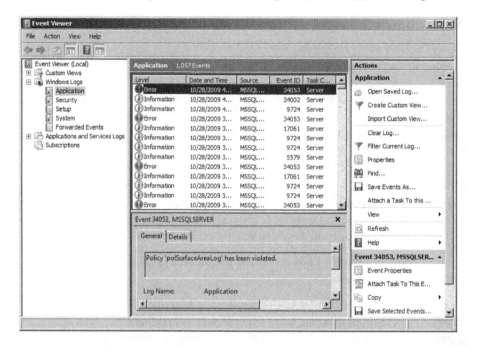

EXERCISE 15.14

Creating an Automated Event Log Monitoring Solution

In this exercise, you will create an automated task that watches the application event log for the polSurfaceAreaLog entry. To do this, follow these steps:

1. Click Start ➤ All Programs ➤ Administrative Tools ➤ Event Viewer.

2. Expand the Windows log and then the application log.

3. Right-click on the log item for the polSurfaceAreaLog policy entry and select Attach Task to this Event.

4. Name the task **polSurfaceAreaLog Monitor** and click Next.

5. Note that the task will monitor for the event log entry based on the ID value of the selected entry, and then click Next.

6. Select Send an E-Mail from the list of available actions and click Next. (Notice that you can also run a program or simply display a message.)

7. On the Send an E-Mail screen, configure it so you replace values with your email address and server information, and click Next.

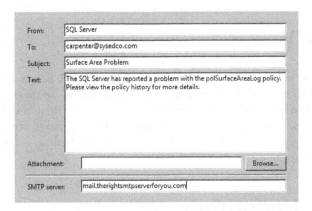

8. Click Finish on the Summary screen to create the monitoring solution.

The ability to attach scheduled tasks to event entries is new in Windows Server 2008 and a long-awaited feature. One thing to consider with this feature is the ability to run a program. You could launch a batch file from the Event Viewer log entry that would send an email, but also call on the SQLCMD tool to reconfigure the surface area with the sp_configure command. Can you imagine the power? Do you sense my excitement? There's a reason for this excitement: a feature like this (built into the Event Viewer) has been needed since Windows NT 4.0 was released in 1996. Finally, it's here.

Updating

As with any product, you should keep an eye out for changes that are made to the system. As of this writing, no new facets have been released for SQL Server 2008. However, this does not mean that there will be no new facets in SQL Server 2008 R2 or a later version of SQL Server. Whenever a new version is implemented in your environment, you should always check for changes. If such changes are noticed, will they impact the standards by which you manage PBM or CMS servers? If they will, you should evaluate your standards and make the appropriate changes.

As an example, SQL Server 2008 R2 includes a new feature called the SQL Server Utility. This tool allows you to centrally monitor and report on the health of your SQL Servers. With the introduction of this tool, several of the methods you use today for monitoring automation may no longer be required. If so, your standard should be updated to include the new automation techniques accordingly.

To update a new version of SQL Server, you will have to go through the rigorous process of testing, backing up, and upgrading your servers. However, when you are installing a service pack, the process is much simpler. You still need to test and have a new backup handy, but you can usually get by with much less lab testing time.

Summary

In this chapter, you learned how to implement and manage SQL Server 2008 Policy-Based Management (PBM) and a Central Management Server (CMS). You learned that PBM is the new term for the Declarative Management Framework (DMF) and that it is comprised of facets, conditions, policies, categories, and targets. You learned to create a CMS and register servers with the CMS. Finally, you learned how to standardize, automate, and update a PBM and CMS environment.

Chapter Essentials

Policy-Based Management   PBM is the new term for DMF, or you might say that PBM implements the DMF. PBM is based on facets that are controlled by conditions, which are evaluated by policies. Policies can use one of four evaluation modes including On Demand, On Schedule, On Change:Log Only, and On Change:Prevent. The facet will dictate which evaluation modes may or may not be utilized.

Centralized Server Management   A CMS can be used to centrally control or manage multiple server instances. The CMS can manage both local instances and remote server instances. You begin using centralized management by registering a CMS and then registering servers with the CMS. You can place servers in server groups so that they may be managed as a collection. You can run queries against a server group, evaluate policies against a server group, import policies into a server group, and even launch the Object Explorer with a view for all servers in the group.

Standardizing with PBM   As you implement PBM and CMS servers, it's important to consider the SAU process. Standardize on implementation and operational procedures. Automate as much as you can and update your standards as required with new releases of the product or updates to the existing release.

Chapter

16

Backup and Restoration

TOPICS COVERED IN THIS CHAPTER:

- ✓ Back Up a Database
- ✓ Back Up System Databases
- ✓ Restore a Database
- ✓ Back Up the Environment

Why create a backup? Numerous reasons exist and some are obvious. First of all, hard drives do not last forever—even when they are configured for fault tolerance. If the hard drive you're using to store your database fails and you do not have a backup of the database, you may lose all the data in the database. Backing up the data regularly is one way to ensure you can recover in the event of a hard-drive failure. Secondly, data can be corrupted through server failures or code mistakes, among other things. Additionally, someone with the proper privileges can accidentally delete a few thousand records. If you don't have a backup, you may have no way to restore this data. What if someone accidentally (or maliciously) deletes all of the customer records from your database? Without a backup, your job itself could be in jeopardy. In addition to these scenarios, natural disasters do occur. Tornados, floods, fires, and more can destroy a datacenter and often all the data in it.

In this chapter, you'll learn all about backup and restoration so you can avoid these grim prospects of losing data. First, you'll get a feel for the various backup methods provided in SQL Server 2008, and then you'll learn to back up a database and restore that database in the event of hardware or software failures. You'll then explore how to back up the system databases, which contain the configuration settings for the database server as well as the many server-level objects you might have created, such as jobs, operators, alerts, triggers, and Resource Governor configuration objects. Finally, you'll gain an understanding of the backup options provided in Windows Server for backing up the environment so that the entire server can be recovered in the worst-case scenarios.

Now that you are good and scared, read on so you can learn how to protect all that valuable data with proper backup procedures.

Backing Up a Database

Unlike a typical operating system backup that can be performed only when major changes are made to an installation, your databases must be backed up regularly. The more heavily the databases are modified, the more frequently they must be updated. In this section, you'll see why you need backup and restoration plans. You'll also learn about recovery models, the different backup types, and how to perform the actual backups. If you abide by the recommendations in this section, your user data will be safe.

Creating a Backup Plan

An effective backup plan will include what data should be backed up, how it should be backed up, when it should occur, and how it will be restored in the event of an emergency. SQL Server provides the tools you can use to perform the backups and restorations, but it is up to you to determine how to best use these tools. The following key questions should be asked:

- Which databases should be backed up?

- How frequently should they be backed up?

- Should the transaction logs be backed up as well?

- Will any encryption keys need to be backed up in addition to the databases?

- Should the backups be compressed or uncompressed?

These are all questions that only you can answer. Although it may seem like a difficult task to do this, everything you need to answer these questions will be covered in the following pages.

To get started, you need to detail the process for creating a backup plan. The process can be summarized in the following steps:

1. Determine the business requirements.

2. Choose the recovery model.

3. Specify the backups required.

4. Identify the backup frequency.

5. Determine the security needs for backups.

Determine the Business Requirements

In order to determine business requirements related to a specific database, you will need to answer at least two questions: What is the acceptable level of data loss and what is the acceptable recovery cost? When dealing with acceptable levels of data loss, you are determining your requirements in relation to transaction recoverability. How many transactions can be lost without causing damage to the business that is greater than the cost of preventing transaction loss? For example, if you implement a system that guarantees no transactions are lost, will it cost more than the loss of the transactions that could otherwise be lost? If it does, the business may determine that an acceptable level of loss can be tolerated and the perfect system, which guarantees no loss whatsoever, is just too expensive. This decision will impact the way you implement database recovery models and backup types and schedules.

When dealing with acceptable recovery costs, you are determining the acceptable recovery time. For example, if the database is down for more than an hour in order to perform a restoration from backup, is this too long? If the database is down for more than 30 minutes, is this too long? Of course, these questions must be balanced with the database size. If the database is 30 gigabytes in size, it may not be possible to recover it in less than 20 to 30 minutes. On the other hand, you may be able to implement special backup procedures that allow you to recover only damaged files or sections of the database. This decision will also impact the way you implement recovery models and backup types and schedules.

Choose the Recovery Model

A little later in this chapter, you'll learn how to choose a recovery model. For now, you should simply know that part of your database backup plan will include the selection of the appropriate recovery model. For example, if you determine that you must recover to the point of failure, you will have to use the full recovery model because it allows for the backup of transaction logs, which is required in order to recover to the point of failure. However, running a database in the simple recovery model can result in performance improvements during heavy write operations and may be desired. You must understand these choices and the impact they will have on your system.

Specify the Backups Required

After you've determined the recovery model in relation to your business requirements, you must determine the required backups that will be implemented. Do you need full backups only or will you require differential and transactional log backups as well? The answer to this question will be determined by your acceptable recovery costs and acceptable transaction losses. Each organization will have its own set of required backup types.

Generally speaking, a more incremental backup solution will result in more flexible recovery options. If you perform a full backup every night and that's all, you will be limiting your recovery options. For example, in most scenarios, you will not be able to recover to a point in time previous to the most recent full backup. However, if you back up with a full backup every night and a transaction log backup every hour, you will be able to recover to any point in time covered by the backup files you have on hand. For example, if you have all the full backups and transaction log backups for the past two weeks, you can recover to any point in time during that two-week window.

Identify the Backup Frequency

Some databases may require a full backup only once a week, while others will demand full backups nightly. In addition to full backups, you may determine that you need to implement differential backups in between the full backups, and you may even decide to implement transaction log backups between the differential backups. Again, the solution will be determined by your acceptable recovery costs and acceptable transaction losses.

When the recovery cost tolerance is low (meaning you must recover as fast as possible), you will need more frequent backups. You do not necessarily have to perform a full backup on some frequent interval, but you will need to perform at least a transaction log backup with some frequency.

The issue of recovery cost is the major reason behind SQL Server's lack of support for incremental backups. An *incremental backup* backs up only the data that has changed since the last incremental backup. If you had a full backup from a week ago and five incremental backups since that time, you would have to restore the full backup and then each of the incremental backups in sequence in order to restore that database. Differential backups are different (no pun intended). A *differential backup,* as explained later in this chapter, backs up everything that has changed since the last full backup. Therefore, recovery is achieved by restoring the most recent full backup and then the most recent differential backup. Only two restoration processes are required regardless of how many differential backups have been taken since the most recent full backup.

When choosing between full or differential backups, you will need to consider the following factors:

Backup Time Windows   You may not have a sufficient backup time window to perform a full backup every night. In such cases, you can perform a full backup only once each week and then perform differential backups (which will take less time) every night.

Recovery Time Requirements   If you must recover the database quickly, a single, full backup restore with a quick restoration of the transaction logs since the full backup will be the fastest recovery method. With differential backups, you always have to recover the most recent full backup first and then the most recent differential backup before recovering the transaction logs.

Data Change Rate   Not every database is updated every day. If your database has very few changes from day to day, you may be much better off with a monthly full backup and nightly differential backups. Even after several weeks, the differential backup will likely be very small because the database changes slowly over time rather than drastically on a daily basis.

As you can see from these example considerations, choosing the backup type is a bit more complex than simply saying, "I prefer full backups because they're easier to restore." It's always important to meet the requirements of the business over your own preferences.

Determine Security Needs for Backups

Just as you must secure your data while it is online and being accessed by users, you must secure the data backups that you create. This effort includes security against physical damage as well as security against theft. The backup media—whether it is tape, DVD, or otherwise—must be handled, transported, and stored with security in mind. For the most sensitive data, the backups should be stored on secure media located in secure offsite storage sites that are accessible while maintaining high levels of security. Less sensitive data may be stored onsite on secure media—usually in a fireproof and waterproof container. Generated data (data that can be regenerated from the original sources) may not need to be backed up or it may need to be backed up less often. The latter situation would assume that the data is publicly available and is, therefore, not considered sensitive.

Choosing a Recovery Model

Now that you understand the decisions required to create a backup plan at a high level, it's time to take a deep dive into some of the most important decisions you'll have to make. The first one is the recovery model under which the database will operate.

The primary role of a recovery model's configuration is to determine how the transaction log will be used by a database. This setting also determines the types of backups you can perform against a database. Some backup types cannot be performed on databases that use specific recovery model settings. For example, you cannot perform a transaction log backup against a database that is configured for the simple recovery model. The previous section pointed out that choosing the recovery model is part of the backup plan development process for any database. Now, you'll look at the three different recovery models to ensure that you understand the implications of choosing each one. The three recovery models are

- Simple
- Full
- Bulk-Logged

You will also discover setting the recovery models at the end of the section.

Simple Recovery Model

When using the simple recovery model, SQL Server minimally logs the transactions that occur and then truncates the transaction log at each checkpoint. In other words, the transaction log is not maintained until it is backed up, but instead it is emptied each time the server writes the data from buffered memory to the actual database files. The server then writes to the database during a checkpoint. For this reason, the simple recovery model will not allow transaction log backups and a database using this model cannot be recovered to a point in time or to the point of failure.

The simple recovery model should be used only for development databases, test databases, or read-only databases. It should not be used for production databases, with the exception of the read-only databases mentioned previously. Of course, read-only databases don't really matter (from a backup and recovery perspective) because they are never modified. If a database using the simple recovery model is modified through a bulk insert or update, it should usually be backed up immediately after the large modification occurs. The AdventureWorks sample database uses the simple recovery model by default.

 The MSDB, master, and tempdb databases use the simple recovery model by default. The model database uses the full recovery model by default. Because new databases use the model database settings as their defaults, a new database will default to the full recovery model.

To see the recovery model for all databases, execute the following query from a query window in SSMS:

```
SELECT name, recovery_model_desc FROM master.sys.databases;
```

The results of this command are shown in Figure 16.1.

FIGURE 16.1   Querying the database recovery models of all databases

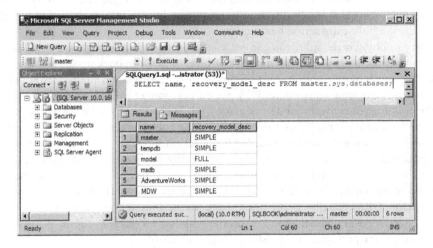

Full Recovery Model

The full recovery model provides complete transaction logging. All transactions, bulk or otherwise, are logged into the transaction log and the log is never truncated during normal operations. For this reason, you must ensure that the transaction log is large enough to handle all the transactions that will occur between backups. The full recovery model is the model that should be used for most OLTP (online transaction processing) databases. The exception to this recommendation may be a temporary change during bulk operations, as you'll see in the following description of the bulk-logged recovery model.

WARNING   If you have a database configured with the full recovery model and you do not back up the transaction log, the transaction log can grow to be extremely large. I've seen 100-megabyte databases with 20-gigabyte transaction logs. Make sure you are either backing up the transaction log or truncating it during full database backups to keep it from consuming all of your valuable drive space.

Bulk-Logged Recovery Model

The bulk-logged recovery model provides a mechanism for minimally logging information to the transaction log during bulk operations such as BULK INSERT statements, SELECT INTO statements, and BCP (bulk copy program) program-based inserts. (BCP is a command-line program used to import or export data.) A database can be placed permanently in bulk-logged mode; however, it is more common to use the full recovery model and switch to bulk-logged before a bulk transaction and then switch back to the full recovery model afterward. A database that is in bulk-logged recovery mode cannot be recovered to a specific point in time if a bulk transaction has occurred.

Contrary to popular thought, you can back up the transaction log when a database is running in the bulk-logged recovery model. However, when you back up the transaction log, it will be much more resource-consuming (processor, memory, and disk resources) and, therefore, more time-consuming. Why does it take longer to back up the transaction log in the bulk-logged recovery model? Because SQL Server 2008 tracks the pages that are changed by bulk operations. When the transaction log backup occurs, SQL Server 2008 encounters the bulk-logged action in the log (bulk transactions are minimally logged) and knows to look at the bulk changed map (BCM) to locate any pages modified with a bulk operation. When it backs up those BCM identified pages, it has no idea what specific data changed on those pages, so each entire page must be backed up with the transaction log. For this reason, DBAs usually choose not to back up the transaction log for a database in the bulk-logged recovery model—but, again, the bulk-logged recovery model is usually used only as a temporary performance booster for bulk operations.

 **Real World Scenario**

Selecting the Right Recovery Model

After years of working with SQL Server, I've found that many DBAs still have an improper understanding of the recovery models. Recently, while working with another DBA, I was reminded of this fact when he told me, "Tom, we aren't using the transaction log for this database because it's in the simple recovery model." This event only reminded me that misinformation is common in the industry, and the process of learning how things really work can often be very difficult.

I informed the DBA that, first, the transaction log is still used in the simple recovery model. It is used during the normal processing of the database. However, it is not retained for very long. As soon as a checkpoint occurs, the changed data pages that are stored in the buffer memory are copied into the data file and the transactions that created those changes are truncated from the transaction log. For this reason, you cannot back up the transaction log when in the simple recovery model and you cannot restore to a point in time (unless of course the point in time you want to restore to happens to be the exact moment when you created a full or differential backup, but that doesn't really count, does it?).

Next, I let the DBA know that the recovery model has absolutely no impact on how the data is stored in the database or the atomicity of the data or the recoverability of the system, should it lose power or otherwise crash during normal operations. Remember, regardless of the recovery model used, during normal non–bulk-logged transactions, the transaction log is used for crash recoverability and to enforce atomicity of the data.

Finally, I told him that the recovery model does impact how you can restore your database. For example, with the simple recovery model, you can only restore to a full or differential backup point. With the bulk-logged recovery model, you can recover to a point in time only if you have not performed any bulk operations since that last full backup; however, the bulk-logged recovery model can improve the performance of bulk operations. Finally, with the full recovery model, you can recover to any point in time (as long as you are regularly backing up your transaction logs) regardless of the type of operations performed against the database.

The next time you hear someone say that the transaction logs are not used when the simple recovery model is selected, please let them know how SQL Server really handles such a configuration. If we can clear up the confusion on this matter, we can do a better job of selecting the appropriate recovery model for the right reasons.

Setting the Recovery Model

Now that you understand your three recovery model choices, it's time to learn how to actually set the recovery model. You can set the recovery model for the model or any user database in one of three ways:

- Using the ALTER DATABASE command
- Using the sp_dboption system stored procedure
- Using the GUI interface in SSMS

If you want to use the direct T-SQL command method, you will need to use the ALTER DATABASE command. For example, the following T-SQL statement would set the recovery model of the AdventureWorks database to FULL:

```
ALTER DATABASE AdventureWorks SET RECOVERY Full;
```

To set the recovery model to bulk-logged, you would change the FULL keyword to BULK_LOGGED. To set the recovery model to simple, you would change the FULL keyword to SIMPLE.

If you want to use the sp_dboption system stored procedure to set the recovery model, you would need to configure one of the following database options:

- select into/bulkcopy
- trunc. log on chkpt

The sp_dboption method goes all the way back to SQL Server 7.0 and earlier. With SQL Server 2000, Microsoft released support for the easier recovery model selection methods used today. However, if you set the select into/bulkcopy database option to True, the recovery model will be changed to bulk-logged. If you set the trunc. log on chkpt database option to True, the recovery model will be changed to simple.

It's best to use the ALTER DATABASE method or the GUI to change the recovery model. You saw how to use the ALTER DATABASE method in the preceding paragraphs. In Exercise 16.1, you'll step through setting the database recovery model using the GUI interface in SSMS.

EXERCISE 16.1

Setting the Recovery Model in SSMS

In this exercise, you will set the recovery model for the AdventureWorks database to Full. To do this, follow these steps:

1. Open the SQL Server Management Studio.

2. Expand the Databases node.

3. Right-click on the AdventureWorks database and select Properties.

4. Select the Options page from the list on the left.

5. Set the Recovery Model setting to Full. Notice that you can also set it to Bulk Logged or Simple in the same location.

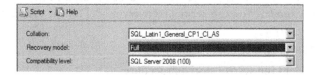

6. Click OK to apply the change.

Using the Different Backup Types

With the appropriate recovery model configured for your database, you can begin performing backups. Yet before you begin, it is important that you understand the different backup types that are available. The three major types are full, differential, and transactional log backups, and they are covered in this section. Remember that these backup types can be considered internal backups because they back up the data within the database files, but they do not actually back up the database files themselves. This backup methodology keeps you from having to take the database offline before you can actually perform the backups.

What you might call an external backup can be performed by taking the database offline or stopping the entire database server service and then backing up the physical files.

Full Backups

A full backup extracts all the data pages out of the physical database files and stores them on the backup media. Note that the backup does not include unused or empty pages within the database files. To see how much space is consumed in a database, follow these steps:

1. Launch a new query window.

2. Change the context to the database you want to analyze.

3. Once you have the proper context, execute the following statement in the query window:

```
EXECUTE sp_spaceused;
```

The results will include the reserved space, the data space, the index size, and the unused space, as shown in Figure 16.2. To determine the consumed space that must be backed up, subtract the unused space from the reserved space. While some extra information may be stored with the backup, the result of this formula will be very close to the backup space required.

FIGURE 16.2   Viewing the approximate consumed space in a database

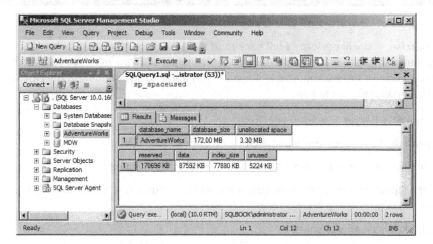

A full backup can be performed with a T-SQL command, such as the following:

```
BACKUP DATABASE database_name TO device_name;
```

This command is used to back up a database to a device, and you can alternatively specify a file path instead of a device. The command to back up to a file looks like this:

```
BACKUP DATABASE database_name TO DISK='c:\folder\file.bak';
```

`c:\folder` should be replaced with the drive and folder into which you want to place the backup, and `file.bak` should be replaced with the desired backup filename.

You may also back up databases in the SSMS by right-clicking the database and selecting Tasks and then Back Up. From the graphical Backup dialog, you can configure the backup and then choose to script the backup configuration to a new job so that it can be scheduled to run as needed.

A full backup is the foundation of your backup plans. Differential backups provide no value without the full backup on which they are based. In addition, transaction log backups can only be used—when a database fails—in conjunction with a full backup or a full and differential backup combination. Some databases may need only a weekly full backup, and others may need a full backup every night. It really depends on the size of the database and the backup window you have available on a nightly basis. Many variables are involved in this decision, but you must remember that a full backup must exist in order to benefit from the other backup types. The preceding section titled "Identify the Backup Frequency" outlined the considerations you must review when choosing the backup type.

Exercise 16.2 provides step-by-step instructions for creating a full backup of the AdventureWorks database. These same steps can be used for any database you want to back up.

EXERCISE 16.2

Creating a Full Backup of the Database

In this exercise, you will perform a full backup of the AdventureWorks database. You will back up the database to the default directory for backups, and you will back up to a file. Before you perform the backup, you will ensure that the recovery model for the AdventureWorks database is set to Full.

1. Launch SQL Server Management Studio.

2. Expand the Databases container in Object Explorer.

3. Right-click the AdventureWorks database and select Properties.

4. On the Options page, change the Recovery Model to Full if it is not already configured as such.

5. Click OK to save this change.

6. Right-click the AdventureWorks database, and select Tasks and then Backup.

7. In the Backup Database dialog, ensure that the Backup Type is set to Full and accept the default Database of AdventureWorks, the default Backup Type of Full, and the default Backup Component of Database.

EXERCISE 16.2   (continued)

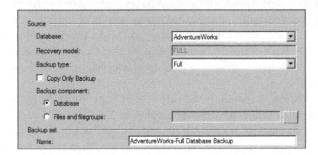

8. Under Destination, accept the default location, but notice that it will back up the database to a disk file.

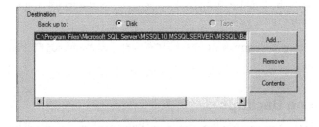

9. Select the Options page and browse the optional parameters available there. Note that you can verify the backup after it completes in the Reliability section of the Options page. This is a good idea for production backup jobs because it verifies that the data is on the backup media after the backup. Without this, the backup is simply assumed to have taken place.

10. Without making any other changes, click the OK button to perform the Full backup.

Remember that you can schedule a configured backup by clicking the Script button and selecting Script Action to Job. Using this method, you will not have to remember all of the required syntax for the BACKUP DATA-BASE or BACKUP LOG commands.

Differential Backups

When a full backup is performed, all the data pages are marked as having been backed up. When these pages are modified either with new inserts or updates, they are changed to a mark of modified. A differential backup backs up these pages (actually, the extents that contain the pages are backed up) and does not mark them as having been backed up. For this reason, each differential backup is a backup of everything that has been changed since the last full backup.

If you do a full backup on Sunday and differential backups on Monday and Tuesday, Tuesday's backup will contain the same data pages as Monday's backup plus any new data pages that have been modified or created since Monday's backup. This functionality allows you to restore a database by restoring the full backup and then the most recent differential backup. You will not have to restore differential backups in sequence.

A differential backup is performed in the same way as a full backup from within SSMS with the exception of setting the Backup Type to Differential. You can also perform a differential backup with the BACKUP DATABASE statement, as the following command illustrates (the C:\backups folder must exist.):

```
BACKUP DATABASE AdventureWorks TO Disk='C:\backups\AWorksDiff.bak'
WITH DIFFERENTIAL;
```

Transaction Log Backups

When you back up the transaction log, the log is truncated by default. The space that has been consumed by transactions is freed once those transactions are backed up. Backing up the transaction log of a database throughout the day allows you to recover to the point of failure or to any point in time. In addition, because databases set to full or bulked-log recovery models do not truncate the transaction log during full or differential backups, it may be essential to back up the transaction log periodically just to truncate the log.

If you allow the transaction log of a database to become completely filled, users will be denied write access to the database until you clear the transaction log. Scheduling regular backups of the transaction log can prevent this from happening. When the log is full, users may still execute read-only SELECT statements against the database. You can also prevent the transaction log from filling up by enabling autogrowth on the transaction log.

Just as you can back up the database with a full or differential backup type using SSMS, you can back up a transaction log in the graphical interface. Just be sure to select the Backup Type of Transaction Log. The T-SQL command for backing up the transaction log for the AdventureWorks database is as follows:

```
BACKUP LOG AdventureWorks TO DISK='C:\BACKUPS\AWorksTlog.bak';
```

The BACKUP T-SQL command is a key command used to back up databases and transaction logs. The complete syntax of the command is as follows:

```
BACKUP DATABASE { database_name | @database_name_var }
  TO <backup_device>
  [ <MIRROR TO clause> ]
  [ WITH { DIFFERENTIAL | <general_WITH_options> [ ,...n ] } ]
[;]
```

The BACKUP DATABASE command shown is used to back up an entire database or a specific file or filegroup in the database. The database_name parameter is simply the name of the database. If a database is named Marketing, you would type **BACKUP DATABASE Marketing** to begin the BACKUP command.

The backup_device will either be the name of a backup device or the path to a backup file. When a backup device is used, the name of the device is listed. For example, if a backup device named MktBackup exists, the BACKUP statement will look like this:

```
BACKUP DATABASE Marketing TO MktBackup;
```

If a backup device is not used and a file is used instead, the DISK keyword must be specified like this:

```
BACKUP DATABASE Marketing TO DISK='path_name';
```

The path_name variable should be equal to the folder path and filename used for the backup. For example, if you want to store the backup in a file named MktBackup.bak that is located in the C:\Backups folder, you would execute the following statement:

```
BACKUP DATABASE Marketing TO DISK='C:\Backups\MktBackup.bak';
```

The MIRROR TO clause is used to make duplicate copies of the backup during the process. For example, to store a backup in the MktBackup.bak file in the C:\Backups folder and also store a backup in the MktBackupM.bak file in the E:\Backups folder, you would execute the following command:

```
BACKUP DATABASE Marketing TO DISK='C:\Backups\MktBackup.bak'
MIRROR TO DISK='E:\Backups\MktBackupM.bak'
WITH FORMAT;
```

The benefit of the MIRROR TO command is that a single backup process can create duplicate copies of the backup automatically. You can mirror to as many as three separate backup devices or destinations in addition to the initially specified backup location. Stated differently, three MIRROR TO clauses can be used to achieve a total of four backup locations.

The WITH FORMAT clause is required only if the *mirror set* (the two *.bak files) has not been previously formatted. On all succeeding backups, you can leave the WITH FORMAT clause off and the command will run fine. For this reason, when using mirror backups, you will usually create the first backup manually and then allow successive backups to be scheduled.

Working with Backup Devices and Files

The commands in the previous section show the T-SQL backup commands that are used to back up to disk. You can back up to disk files directly, but you can also create a device and then back up to that device. These devices should not be confused with physical backup devices, such as tape drives. These devices are really nothing more than logical names used to reference files on the disk drive. For example, it is easier to reference a device named MyDevice than it is to reference C:\BackupFolder\Database1\MyFullBackups.bak. The good news is that you can configure the device named MyDevice to reference the file C:\BackupFolder\Database1\MyFullBackups.bak.

Because you can use files and devices that reference files for backups, it is important that you keep a few guidelines in mind when backing up to these files.

- The backup files should not be stored on the same physical hard drive as the actual database.

- The files should be stored on a secure media, such as a hard drive that uses the NTFS file system.

- You may consider performing the backup with a password required to restore it and then encrypting the backup file itself.

- You could encrypt the backup file with the Windows Encrypting File System (EFS) or use a third-party encryption solution.

The following code shows how to back up the AdventureWorks database to a file while using a password for security:

```
BACKUP DATABASE AdventureWorks TO DISK='C:\backups\AdvFullBack.bak'
WITH PASSWORD = 'fghytZ123';
```

Backup devices can be created with the SSMS or T-SQL commands. Exercise 16.3 covers the latter.

EXERCISE 16.3

Creating a Backup Device That Points to a File

To create a backup device in SSMS, follow these steps:

1. Launch SQL Server Management Studio.

2. Expand the Server Objects container.

3. Right-click the Backup Devices container and select New Backup Device.

4. Enter the backup device name of your choice.

5. Add the path to the actual backup file you want to have the backup device represent and click OK to create the device.

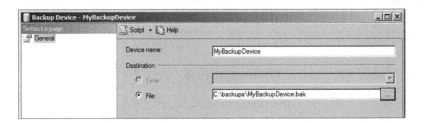

When you want to create a backup device with T-SQL code, you will use the following syntax:

```
USE master;
GO
EXEC master.dbo.sp_addumpdevice  @devtype = 'disk',
@logicalname = 'MyBackupDevice',
@physicalname = 'C:\backups\MyBackupDevice.bak';
```

This code will create a backup device similar to the one being created in the graphical interface in Exercise 16.3. Notice that a stored procedure named sp_addumpdevice is actually doing the work of adding the device.

Once you've created a device, even if it is a DISK device such as the one created here, you can treat it like a tape drive. This means that you can format the media, append to the media, and even overwrite the media. The following code samples show how to do all three:

```
--The following code formats the device before creating the backup:
BACKUP DATABASE AdventureWorks TO MyBackupDevice
WITH FORMAT;

--The following code appends to an existing backup device:
BACKUP DATABASE AdventureWorks TO MyBackupDevice
WITH NOINIT; --this is an optional clause since NOINIT is the default

--The following code overwrites an existing backup device:
BACKUP DATABASE AdventureWorks TO MyBackupDevice
WITH INIT;
```

In effect, both the WITH FORMAT and WITH INIT clauses will overwrite the existing backups within a device. The benefit of these features is that you can create scheduled backup procedures that reuse existing backup files or devices. For example, you may choose to create a structure similar to that in Table 16.1.

TABLE 16.1   Backup Device Rotation Structure

Device Name	Purpose	Rotation Group
BackDev1	Full Backups	1
BackDev2	Differential Backups	1
BackDev3	Transaction Log Backups	1
BackDev4	Full Backups	2
BackDev5	Differential Backups	2
BackDev6	Transaction Log Backups	2

With a structure like that in Table 16.1, you could perform all backups from one week using the rotation group 1 devices and then perform all backups from the next week using the rotation group 2 devices. These devices could be stored on different physical drives, and this will provide you with extra levels of redundancy and recoverability. If the database drive fails and the drive on which rotation group 1 is stored happens to fail at the same time, you can still recover using rotation group 2. You may lose some data, but you'll have something to recover. If this system were used in conjunction with storing the transaction logs separately, you could achieve an even higher likelihood that you would be able to restore your data in a disaster scenario.

 SQL Server 2008 also supports copy-only backups. A copy-only backup is a backup that does not interrupt your backup cycles. You can create a copy-only backup of the transaction log, and it will not truncate the transaction log. You can create a copy-only backup of the database, and it will not show in the backup history. The copy-only backup is used to make a copy of the database for another server without interrupting the backup cycles.

Compressing Backups

SQL Server 2008 now supports compressed backups. Compressed backups require less storage space, but they will increase CPU utilization. You will have to decide whether the reduction in storage space is worth the cost in CPU time. SQL Server 2008 Enterprise edition can create and read compressed backups. Other editions of SQL Server 2008 can only read compressed backups.

Compressed backups do have some constraints, however, so familiarize yourself with them before you make any decisions:

- You cannot store both compressed and uncompressed backups on the same media or in the same backup file. This limit is imposed because compressed backups use a different storage format.

- Backups created by NT backup (the backup software built into Windows servers from Windows NT 4.0 through Windows Server 2003) cannot exist on the same media as SQL Server 2008 compressed backups.

- SQL Server 2008 compressed backups cannot be read by previous versions of SQL Server.

You can set up a SQL Server 2008 Enterprise Edition instance to default to compressing all backups. The following command will configure this as an instance-level default:

```
EXEC sp_configure 'backup compression default', '1';
```

Setting the value back to 0, at any time, will revert to the default, which is that backups are not compressed.

If you prefer to specify compression during backups, you can do so with the WITH COMPRESSION clause of the BACKUP DATABASE or BACKUP LOG statements. If the default has been changed so that compressed backups are now the default behavior, you can override this with the WITH NO_COMPRESSION clause.

Performing File and Filegroup Backups

In addition to backing up the entire database, you can back up just a file or filegroup within a database. This is useful with very large databases. For example, you may have a database that is more than 500 gigabytes in size. With a large database like this, it may be helpful to split the tables across multiple filegroups and then back up one of the filegroups on one night and another on another night, and so forth. This backup type is still performed with the BACKUP DATABASE statement and the syntax is as follows:

```
BACKUP DATABASE database_name
FILEGROUP=filgroup_name
TO device_name | disk_file_path;
```

As you can see, three parts are needed—at a minimum—to perform a filegroup backup. You need to know the database name, the filegroup name, and the backup destination. For example, the following code would back up the SECONDARY filegroup in the Marketing database to the disk file named Marketing_Secondary.bak in the C:\backups directory:

```
BACKUP DATABASE Marketing FILEGROUP=SECONDARY
TO DISK='C:\backups\Marketing_Secondary.bak';
```

To back up a file instead of a filegroup, you would simply replace the FILEGROUP keyword with the FILE keyword. The logical name of the data file must be specified in place of the filegroup name as well. If you have a data file that contains read-only data, you can back up this file once and not include it in nightly backups. This can reduce the time required to perform backups.

WARNING   SQL Server does not allow you to back up a single file if the data in the file is read/write data. Only read-only data files may be backed up individually and restored individually.

Back Up System Databases

All of the backup issues discussed in the previous section apply equally to the system databases (master, model, and MSDB). You can back up these databases using the same methods. However, it is more common to back up these databases with only full backups because they usually do not become extremely large and they are usually backed up once each day at most. The system databases should be backed up at a few other times as well. These additional times include:

- Back up the master database any time you change metadata. This would mean that you've issued any kind of DDL statement in relation to database and database object structures.

- Back up the MSDB database any time you add or alter jobs, alerts, or operators.

- Back up the model database each time you make a change to it.

- Back up all three databases regularly. For some systems, this will mean monthly; and for others, it will mean nightly.

You will seldom a need to back up the tempdb database because it is re-created each time the SQL Server service starts and is primarily based on the model database.

Restore a Database

The reason so much effort should be put into backing up your databases is to provide you with the ability to recover from these backups in the event of failures. This section provides the basic information you'll need to be able to restore your databases completely to a point in time or to the point of failure. It will also review the methods you can use to restore the system databases should they become corrupted.

Choosing a Restore Method

You can restore databases to a point in time, to the point of failure, or to a full backup made at a specific point. Before you begin, however, it is important that you understand the limitations you impose on yourself through your backup plan. Here are some examples:

- If your backup plan includes only performing full backups, you'll only be able to restore to the latest full backup.

- If your backup plan includes performing differential backups, you'll be able to restore to the most recent differential backup after restoring the most recent full backup.

- If you want to restore to a point in time, you'll also need to be backing up your transaction logs.

- Finally, if the database storage drive fails, you can restore to the point of failure as long as the database uses the full recovery model and the transaction logs are stored on a separate drive from the database. In this situation, when the database fails, you can back up the transaction log and then recover to the most recent full and/or differential backups and then recover the newly backed-up transaction log to arrive at the point of failure.

Again, what you can do in the restoration process will be limited by what you have done in the backup process.

Restoring to a Point in Time

To restore to a point in time, you will need a full backup and transaction log backups at a minimum. You may also need differential backups if they are included in your backup plan and you want the recovery process to occur more quickly. In Exercise 16.4, you will perform the steps required to restore to a point in time.

EXERCISE 16.4

Restoring to a Point in Time

To recover to a point in time, follow these steps:

1. Right-click the database you want to restore to a point in time and select Tasks ➤ Restore ➤ Database. This database is likely to be flagged as suspect at this time because this is often the reason for performing a restore.

2. Click the button to the right of the Point in Time field.

EXERCISE 16.4 *(continued)*

3. Select the specific Date and Time to which you want to restore and click OK.

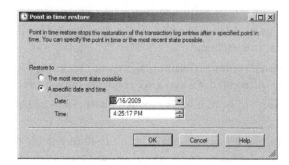

4. Click OK again to begin the restoration to the specified point in time.

If you attempt the steps in Exercise 16.4 while the database is online or while a user is connected to it, you will receive an error. Click the Options page in the dialog shown in Figure 16.3 and check the Overwrite Existing Database option to force the restore to take place.

FIGURE 16.3 Forcing a database overwrite during a restoration

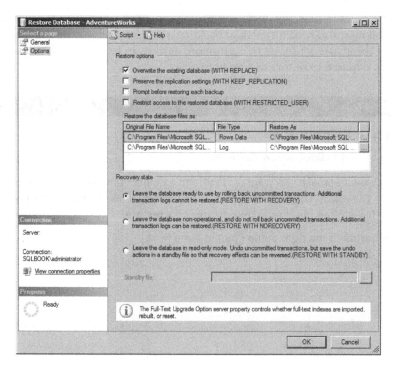

Restoring to the Point of Failure

In order to restore to the point of failure, you will need to back up the transaction log before beginning the restoration. If you do not back up the transaction log before you begin the restoration process, you will receive an error informing you that you will lose the data in the transaction log. Of course, if the failure is due to hard-drive failure and the transaction log is stored on the same drive as the database, you will not be able to restore to the point of failure. This is why you should store the transaction log on a separate drive from the database files.

Microsoft refers to the transaction log transactions that have not been backed up when a failure occurs as the tail log. The name *tail log* comes from the fact that you are backing up the transactions that are at the "tail end of the log" when you perform this backup.

Exercise 16.5 provides the steps required to back up the transaction log (tail log) for a failed database and then restore to a new drive once it has been installed.

EXERCISE 16.5

Backing Up the Tail Log After a Database File Storage Failure

This exercise provides the steps required to both back up the tail log and restore the database should the database file storage volume fail. The steps are generic so that they can be applied to any database requiring recovery.

1. Back up the transaction log for the failed database with a command like the following:

    ```
    BACKUP LOG database_name TO device_name WITH NO_TRUNCATE;
    ```

    The NO_TRUNCATE option is required because the database is currently in a failed state.

2. Begin the restoration of the database by restoring the full backup with a command like the following:

    ```
    RESTORE DATABASE database_name FROM device_name WITH NORECOVERY;
    ```

3. Finally, you can restore the transaction log with a command like this:

    ```
    RESTORE LOG database_name FROM device_name WITH RECOVERY;
    ```

Remember that your restoration process may look different than the one represented in Exercise 16.5. The basic process outlined in Exercise 16.5 would work for a database that is backed up using only full backups and transaction log backups. If you perform differential backups, you may choose to restore those as well. In such a backup plan, you would usually restore the most recent full backup first and then the most recent differential backup and then all transaction log backups in sequence up to the point of failure.

WARNING

Document your restoration procedures in excruciating detail before you need to use them. You will probably be very stressed when you do need to recover from a database failure. Times of stress are not usually the best times to rely on your memory alone. Additionally, the documentation could be used by someone else if you are unavailable to perform the restoration.

Restoring System Databases

System databases are restored in a similar manner to user databases except you cannot restore them while the database service is running in multiuser mode. You must first start the SQL Server Database Engine service in single-user mode before you can restore the system databases from a backup. To start the service in single-user mode, stop the service and then start it from the command line with the −m switch. Exercise 16.6 provides the instructions required to start SQL Server in single-user mode.

EXERCISE 16.6

Starting the SQL Server Database Engine in Single-User Mode

In this exercise, you will learn to start the SQL Server Database Engine service in single-user mode. First, you must stop the service if it is running; however, in most cases, when you want to start the service in single-user mode, it will not be running because the system databases have been lost or corrupted. To start the service in single-user mode, follow these steps:

1. Launch the Windows command prompt by clicking Start, selecting Run, and then entering **CMD** as the command to run.

2. Change to the SQL Server directory by typing the following command:

    CD\Program Files\Microsoft SQL Server\MSSQL10.MSSQLSERVER\MSSQL\BINN

    This command assumes a default install and that you are working with the default instance that was installed first. If this is not true, you will need to change to the appropriate directory for your installation.

3. Enter the command: **SQLSERVR −m**

4. The server will start in single-user administration mode.

After you've performed the steps in Exercise 16.6, you can connect to the server with SSMS and launch a new query window to execute RESTORE commands against the master or MSDB databases. You could also use the SQLCMD command-line tool to execute RESTORE DATABASE and RESTORE LOG commands. When you are finished restoring the SQL Server, go back to the command prompt window where you initially launched the service in single-user mode and press Ctrl+C to stop the single-user mode server. You can now start the service normally.

Back Up the Environment

Up to this point, you've focused on backing up the SQL Server databases. However, the SQL Server services do not run in isolation. They run on a Windows server that has been configured over time to meet the needs of the organization. In addition to the database backups, the administrator must ensure that a recovery solution is available for the entire server. You really have three options for these types of environment backups:

- Built-in backup tools
- Imaging tools
- Third-party tools

Built-In Backup Tools

Windows Server Backup (WSB) is the built-in tool provided in Windows Server 2008 and Windows Server 2008 R2. WSB is not installed by default. You will have to install it using the Server Manager interface. Exercise 16.7 provides instructions for installing WSB in Windows Server 2008.

EXERCISE 16.7

Installing Windows Server Backup

In this exercise, you will install the Windows Server Backup feature of Windows Server 2008. To install this feature, follow these steps:

1. Log on to the Windows Server 2008 server as an administrator.

2. Select Start ➤ Server Manager.

3. Select the Features node in the left pane.

4. In the right pane, select Add Features.

5. In the Add Features Wizard, scroll down the list of available features and expand Windows Server Backup Features.

6. Select Windows Server Backup and Command-Line Tools and click Next.

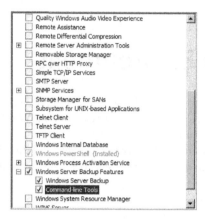

7. Click Install to begin the installation of the Windows Server Backup toolset.

If you performed the steps in Exercise 16.7, you probably noticed that you were installing both Windows Server Backup and a set of command-line tools. You can perform backups, using WSB, with either the GUI interface or the command line. The choice is yours.

With either tool, you should back up the entire volume on which the Windows Server operating system is installed. If the SQL Server services are installed on the same volume, your environment backup will be complete. If the SQL Server services are installed on a separate volume, you should back up that volume as well. WSB supports scheduling backups.

Imaging and Third-Party Tools

Imaging tools, such as Ghost and DriveImage, can also be used to back up the environment. These tools are not usually used for incremental backups, but they provide an excellent method of fast recovery. In most cases, imaging tools can be used to create a restore point and then WSB or some other third-party backup software will be used to create incremental backups from the time of the restore point.

The process of backing up your server with an imaging or cloning tool is really quite simple. First, you will need to boot the machine from a CD or DVD with the imaging software on it. Second, run the imaging software and dump an image to another hard drive in the computer or to a network share. It's really that simple. These imaging solutions are used to restore the environment within which SQL Server databases operate and not to back up and restore the databases themselves. However, if you have an image backup of the server and nightly backups of the databases (including the system databases), you could recover the entire server from a massive driver failure in less than an hour in many cases and certainly in a few hours in most cases.

Third-party backup tools should be selected with caution. For example, some tools will allow you to back up the environment as well as the SQL Server databases and others will not. Check with the backup software vendor to see if they offer a SQL Server connector or a SQL Server module that allows for database backups while the databases are online. If such a module is provided, the backup software can back up the environment and the live databases on a scheduled basis.

Among the third-party backup tools for Windows systems and SQL Servers, the following are very common:

- Backup Exec
- ARCServe
- NovaBackup
- Acronis Backup & Recovery

Summary

Creating a backup plan and choosing a recovery model is an essential part of the DBA's role. You must have a plan that allows for recovery within business constraints. These business constraints may include short recovery windows and complete recoverability, and they will dictate the backup types you select. The recovery model is also important because it will determine how you can recover your databases. With the right recovery model and a solid backup plan, you can sleep peacefully at night knowing that your data is safe.

Backing up the SQL Server is one of the most important tasks the DBA must perform. In addition to the user databases, the system databases and the environment must be backed up. SQL Server supports three main types of backups. The first backup type is the full backup, and it is used to back up every used data page in the database. The second backup type is the differential backup, and it is used to back up the data pages that have been added or changed since that last full backup. The third backup type is the transaction log backup, and it is used to back up the transaction log so that you can recover to a point in time or the point of failure. In addition to these three main types, SQL Server also offers file and filegroup backups, as well as copy-only backups.

A new feature in SQL Server 2008 is compressed backups. You can enable backup compression as an instance-level default. You can also specify that backups should be compressed with the `WITH COMPRESSION` clause of the `BACKUP` command.

Chapter Essentials

Back Up a Database   Databases can be backed up in SQL Server 2008 using full, differential, transaction log, filegroup, file, or copy-only backups. The backup types available will depend on the recovery model used and whether the data is flagged as read-only data or not. User databases should be backed up on a regular basis.

Back Up System Databases   The system databases include master, model, and MSDB. The system databases should be backed up either on a schedule or any time they are modified. Because the databases can be modified daily through new job or object creation, the best practice is to back up the system databases on a schedule.

Restoring a Database   User databases can be restored while the SQL Server service is running in normal mode. However, system databases can only be restored if the SQL Server is running in single-user mode. The `RESTORE DATABASE` command is used to restore a database.

Back Up the Environment   In addition to the SQL Server databases, you should consider backing up the SQL Server environment. The environment includes the operating system and services running on the same server as the SQL Server services. You can back up the environment using the Windows Server Backup software on Windows Server 2008 or using imaging tools or third-party backup solutions.

SQL Server Security

Chapter

17

Security Threats and Principles

TOPICS COVERED IN THIS CHAPTER:

- ✓ Security Defined
- ✓ Security Threats
- ✓ Security Principles

Understanding the foundations of security is essential to understanding any specific security solution. For this reason, this chapter is divided into three sections that will provide a solid foundation for understanding the specific security features of SQL Server covered in Chapter 18, "Authentication and Encryption," and Chapter 19, "Security Best Practices."

The first section is titled "Security Defined." Although it is the shortest section of the chapter, it is an important foundational concept. If you do not understand what you are attempting to achieve, it will be very difficult to achieve it. You'll begin by exploring a basic definition of security and then break this definition into its parts to clearly understand what security is. Often it is easiest to understand what something is by also understanding what it is not, so you'll explore what security is not.

The second section of this chapter looks at security threats. Because this book focuses on SQL Server, you will look at the threats from four perspectives related to the SQL Server product. The first perspective is the Windows Server operating system on which SQL Server runs. After that you'll look at the SQL Server service itself. Then you'll analyze the network between the SQL Server and its clients. Finally, you'll review client security issues as they relate to SQL Server.

The third and final section of this chapter covers common security principles. These principles help you conceptualize security solutions and understand their most beneficial applications. You'll explore core security principles, such as defense in depth and least privilege, in this section.

Security Defined

Security is a difficult concept to define as it relates to computers and information systems. This is, in part, because security may involve many disciplines. For example, to secure a SQL Server 2008 instance, you must understand SQL Server, Windows Server, networking, and even client operating system security. If the SQL Server is accessed through a web application, you'll need to understand Internet security. Are you beginning to see the complexity? However, we should not lose hope because security can be defined and this section will do just that.

Real World Scenario

Mission Almost Impossible

To illustrate why security is so hard to define, consider an exploratory adventure I went on just a few moments before writing this section. I pulled out two different Security+ certification study guides to see how security was defined in their glossaries. Each book indeed had a glossary. Each book was designed to prepare candidates for a certification that has one single word in the title and that word is security. Yet, neither book defines security in the glossary. The word is simply missing from their lists.

I didn't want to give up there, so I pulled out the study guide for another certification exam. This time, the certification was the CCNA Security exam from Cisco Systems. The book, again, has a glossary. Do you want to guess whether the word *security* was defined? If you guessed that the word was missing from this glossary too, you were correct. If you knew me well, you would know that I don't give up easily. I left the certification books with the word *security* in the certification name and decided to look at other resources. After seeking through the glossary of 11 books on the topic of security, I finally found one that included the word *security* in the glossary. It was the *Certified Ethical Hacker (CEH) Prep Guide* (Wiley, 2008) by Ronald L. Krutz and Russell Dean Vines. Now, I'm sure that many other security books on the market include the definition for the term in their glossaries, but I was surprised at the effort it took to find one in my library of more than 1,100 books on computer-related topics (yes, I love books and have a library of more than 4,000 books in total).

Just in case you're wondering, the definition in the CEH Prep Guide book was, "Measures and controls that ensure the confidentiality, integrity, availability, and accountability of the information processed and stored by a computer." I agree with this specific computer-related definition and have found this book exceptional in its coverage of hacking techniques, whether you're interested in gaining the CEH certification or not.

Why is the term *security* so hard to define in relation to computer and systems security for so many people? In part, it is probably because the term represents an impossible dream. Consider the definition of security as found in *The Oxford American College Dictionary*:

> The state of being free from danger or threat.

Can this state of freedom really be achieved? Probably not. Even in everyday life you cannot really be free from danger or threat. You can only manage the level of risk you accept in relation to dangers and threats. The same is true for computer and network security. So let's use the following as our working definition of security in relation to SQL Server:

> SQL Server security is the state in which an acceptable level of risk is achieved through the use of policies and procedures that can be monitored and managed.

The phrase "acceptable level of risk" establishes a foundation that is both achievable and measurable. You can achieve an acceptable level of risk by creating and documenting policies, implementing procedures in compliance with those policies, and ensuring the adherence to the policies through auditing and enforcement.

In a SQL Server environment, security is about data protection. The procedures should result in a state that ensures the following:

- The data can be accessed by authorized users only.
- The data is secure in storage.
- The data is secure in transit.
- The data is recoverable.

Now let's cover each of these more fully:

The data can be accessed by authorized users only.   To ensure that the data can be accessed by only authorized users, a strong authentication system must be utilized. SQL Server 2008 provides both SQL logins and Windows authentication, which are covered in Chapter 18. Windows authentication should be used whenever possible as it provides better security than SQL logins.

The data is secure in storage.   The data is secure in storage when the database files are stored in a secure file system. A secure file system requires that a user be authenticated before he can access any files. The NTFS file system provides such security for internal drives and many external drive systems as well. Storage area networks (SANs) may also provide such security using different file systems.

The data is secure in transit.   When you want to secure data in transit, you must consider the path between the SQL Server and the requesting client. You must also remember that the requesting client is not always an end-user system, such as Windows XP or Windows 7. Often, the requesting client is another server. Regardless of the client used, the key to secure transit is encryption. If the data is traversing a wired network, it may be less vulnerable to easy interception; however, even wired communications should be encrypted for the most sensitive information that travels across the wires. In a wireless environment, encryption is essential to data security. If you do not encrypt the data, anyone with a free copy of WireShark and the right wireless network adapter can sniff the data right out of the air (or at least off the RF signals). Encryption is the only way to protect this wireless data.

The data is secure in transit.   Data recoverability is essential to data security. Some attackers will want to steal your data. This desire can be thwarted with authentication, authorization, and encryption. Other attackers will only want to prevent you from accessing the data. For them, data destruction is sufficient. To ensure recoverability, the data must be backed up and the backup storage must be secured. The procedures for backing up the data were covered in Chapter 16, "Backup and Restoration." Chapter 19 will review the best practices for securing the backup storage media and location.

How to Classify Data for Security Purposes

The importance of security varies by organization. The variations exist due to the differing values placed on information and networks within organizations. For example, organizations involved in banking and healthcare will likely place a greater priority on information security than organizations involved in selling greeting cards. However, in every organization there exists a need to classify data so that it can be protected appropriately. The greeting card company will likely place a greater value on its customer database than it will on the log files for the Internet firewall. Each of these data files has value, but one is more valuable than the other and should be classified accordingly so that it can be protected properly. This process is at the core of information security and it can be itemized as follows:

1. Determine the value of the information in question.

2. Apply an appropriate classification based on that value.

3. Implement the proper security solutions for that classification of information.

As an example, your organization may choose to classify information in three categories: internal, public, and internal sensitive. Information classified as internal information may require only appropriate authentication and authorization. Information classified as public information may require neither authentication nor authorization. The internal sensitive information may require authentication, authorization, and storage-based encryption.

From this very brief overview of information classification and security measures, you can see why different organizations have different security priorities and needs. It is also true, however, that every organization is at risk for certain threats. Threats like Denial of Service (DoS), worms, and others are often promiscuous in nature. The attacker does not care what networks or systems are damaged or made less effective in a promiscuous attack. The intention of such an attack is often only to express the attacker's ability or to serve some other motivation for the attacker, such as curiosity or need for recognition. Because many attacks are promiscuous in nature, it is very important that every organization place some level of priority on security regardless of the intrinsic value of the information or networks they employ.

Various organizations perform surveys and gather statistics that are useful in gaining an understanding of the need for security. *InformationWeek* magazine performs an annual security survey. Their 2008 security survey (2008 Security Survey, June 2008) showed that complexity is the greatest difficulty in securing systems. A whopping 62 percent of respondents cited complexity as the biggest security challenge. Administrators are dealing with many different data types, and that data is often unclassified. Without classification, it's difficult to determine how to protect the data. Good news exists, however, in *InformationWeek*'s survey: solutions exist that can help reduce the likelihood of a security incident. According to the survey, the following solutions were selected by the indicated percentage of respondents:

- Firewalls (63%)

- Antivirus (59%)

- Encryption (46%)

- VPNs (45%)

- Strong passwords (40%)

- Spam filtering (35%)

- E-mail security (34%)

The Computer Security Institute (CSI) is another organization that reports on the state of information and systems security. CSI has performed their annual security survey for more than 10 years and the statistics show that security should be a very important part of any organization's budget and plans. For the five years preceding the 2007 survey, the results showed a drop in the average organization's losses due to cybercrime; however, the 2007 survey reported a significant rise in estimated losses. The only good news is that the spike in the 2007 survey resulted in financial losses that were still lower than those reported in 2002. This continued lower financial loss rating may indicate that companies are doing a better job of securing their data and assets, or it may only indicate that they are spending less on hardware and software and, therefore, losing less when these assets are stolen or compromised.

The following statistics represent just a few of the important reports from the 2007 CSI Computer Crime and Security Survey:

- 25 percent of responding organizations spend between 6 and 10 percent of the annual IT budget on security.

- 61 percent of responding organizations still outsource no security functions.

- 46 percent indicated that they had experienced a security incident in the previous 12 months and 10 percent indicated that they were unsure.

- 26 percent of the total responding pool indicated that there had been more than 10 incidents in the previous 12 months.

- Only 36 percent indicated that they accrued no losses due to insider threats, which means that 64 percent experienced an insider attack that led to losses.

- The most common type of attack was the simple abuse of Internet access by valid users.

- Viruses were also a common attack problem with 52 percent reporting such attacks.

- Only 5 percent reported telecom fraud and 13 percent reported system penetration; however, it is important to know that some experts estimate as many as 85 percent of all attacks go undetected.

It is very clear from these statistics that threats are real, security is important, and actions should be taken to improve the security of your systems, including your database systems. The statistics show you what is happening, but the theory can help you understand why these attacks occur.

Security in Theory

Why does a seemingly unprovoked attacker attack? This is an important question, but it is very difficult to answer with certainty. After all, you are dealing with human nature in these circumstances. It is very easy to understand why an employee who is terminated decides to attack: that employee is not thinking rationally. He or she is upset and angry. Such emotions often lead to actions that he or she would never take in a more stable state of mind. It is even easy to understand why a competitor might attack: to gain the upper hand on your organization. But why does a *script kiddy* (one who lacks deep technical understanding but has the ability to run scripts or follow instructions) choose to attack your organization? Why does a skilled attacker attack your organization? The next few paragraphs will attempt to answer those questions.

One theory says that they don't choose your organization. Instead, the suggestion is that the attacker is promiscuous. In the realm of network and systems security, the term *promiscuous* simply means that the attacker does not care who the target is, but will attack any target that is vulnerable to a particular exploit. Attacks from script kiddies often fall into this category. These attackers will scan hundreds or even thousands of networks looking for any network that is vulnerable or any system that is vulnerable on that network. When a vulnerable network or system is found, the attacker will launch other scripts or utilities against the network to penetrate it and gain access to data and resources. This method may also be used by skilled crackers who wish only to gain control of the network and resources so that an attack may be launched against a primary target using these easily penetrated resources. A distributed DoS (DDoS) would be an example of just such an attack. Script kiddies may launch a DoS attack just for fun, or they may be unskilled crackers who want to harm your organization. The important point to remember is that a DoS is easy to launch against an insecure server.

At the same time, the threat of script kiddies is more than a theory; it is a reality. Script kiddies exist in the many thousands (possibly millions) and are a prime threat for any organization. Because attacks are often promiscuous, each organization must protect its data regardless of the likelihood of an attack intended to harm them. Remember, attackers are very likely to use your network and system as a point of attack against another target. Therefore, networks and servers must be protected even in smaller businesses and organizations.

But there are threats other than the promiscuous attacker; usually these attacks are ideological and driven with underlying motives that move the attacker against your organization. For example, the attacker may be motivated by any of the following common drivers as well as hundreds of others not listed here:

- Direct financial gain
- Opposition to your political positions
- Opposition to your environmental impacts

- Retaliation for some perceived self-harm
- Devaluing your business for their own profit

Whether the attacker's thinking is correct or incorrect doesn't matter. All that matters is that the attacker perceives your organization to be a threat to something he or she values. These values may include environmental concerns, freedom of speech concerns, freedom from government, or any other value that the attacker holds in high esteem. If the attacker sees your organization as a threat to the realization of these values, this perception may be the motivation for the attack. Depending on the attacker's value system, he or she may attempt only to deface your website or could completely destroy all your data and systems. Either way, you must protect against these individuals as well.

What is the difference between these two attacker types and why does it matter? The big difference is the answer to the question, "Why?" Why does the attacker want to attack your network or systems? If it is promiscuous in nature, traditional protection mechanisms will likely suffice. If it is targeted, the attacker will most likely be willing to spend much more time attempting to penetrate your network and stronger security mechanisms will be needed. You will need to evaluate your organization's risk of being an intentional target based on strong motivations or a promiscuous target based on weak motivations. Additionally, you must remember that even an attack that is promiscuous in nature may be intended to harm another organization through the utilization of your resources.

 Regardless of the primary reason behind the attack, script kiddies and skilled crackers can be motivated by similar drives. Protecting against the script kiddy is a little easier, because you only have to protect against known attacks, while protecting against the skilled crackers may require advanced intrusion-monitoring solutions as well.

Security in the Real World

Every organization must deal with information, network, and systems security. If you have a network, database system, or information, you must protect it. Protection methods must be considered for the information. These methods will include authentication, authorization, accounting, and encryption—and each need requires different action.

For the network systems, you will need to implement authentication and authorization to ensure that only the assigned personnel may administer the devices. For the database systems security, you should ensure secure management of your application code base and secure programming practices, as well as secure administration. From this big-picture perspective, you must drill down to the specific actions required to protect these different attack points.

Now that you have the definition for security under your belt, you can move on to look at the drivers behind security. Why is security so important? This question is answered in the following section as you explore the four areas of threat to a SQL Server implementation: the Windows server, the SQL Server, the network, and the client.

Security Threats

Some people call them *hackers*; others prefer to call them *crackers* or *attackers*. Regardless of the name they are assigned, they are an evolving and morphing collective. This group of technically savvy and intensely creative individuals continues to surprise us as they develop new techniques for penetrating networks and systems. While you spend your days implementing, maintaining, and troubleshooting these networks and systems, the attackers spend their time for very different ends. They are developing new methods for mayhem and mischief nearly every day. Database administrators and security practitioners must evolve with them. Because such a time-investment disparity exists, it is essential that systems professionals collaborate to share their collective protection knowledge. You may not have the time to perform the research that leads to vulnerability discovery and protection against those vulnerabilities, but you must make the time to learn of these vulnerabilities and solutions through books, websites, magazines, and conferences.

To understand security threats, you'll need to understand how a threat leads to an exploitation. This section contains six subsections to help you understand this. The first subsection explains threats, vulnerabilities, and exploits. The next four subsections help you understand the primary points of entry or attack that a cracker may choose to exploit, which are the Windows server, the SQL Server, the network, and the clients. Finally, the sixth subsection provides examples of cracks so that you can understand the concepts covered from a practical perspective.

Threats, Vulnerabilities, and Exploits Defined

Understanding threats, vulnerabilities, and exploits is the beginning of network security evaluation. You must understand how these three things connect with each other and how a threat can take advantage of a vulnerability in order to exploit it. The following sections step through this knowledge base.

Threats

A *threat* is defined as an individual, group, circumstance, or event with potential to cause harm to a system. The only requirement for a person or event to be considered a threat is the potential for harm. Certainty is not required. Threats fall into two general categories: intentional and unintentional.

Intentional threats   include all threats that have human intelligence behind them. Stated differently, intentional threats are those threats that are planned and executed by an individual or a group of people.

Unintentional threats   include those events or circumstances that are often called acts of God. Lightning strikes, hurricanes, accidents of any kind, and other similar events are unintentional threats; however, these unintentional threats must be accounted for as well. Additionally, human stupidity threats would fall into this category. These are the threats that exist because we humans make mistakes.

Vulnerabilities

A *vulnerability* is defined as a weakness in a system or object. The object may be part of a system or it may be an independent entity. For example, a SQL Server database server may be considered as an independent entity or as part of a larger networked system. As an independent entity, the server must be secured to protect the data it stores; however, if the SQL Server accesses other systems, you must consider this system and the potential threat it introduces to the system by the SQL Server. What if an attacker gains control of the SQL Server? Can she gain access to the other resources accessible by the SQL Server? The result is that new vulnerabilities, which were nonexistent in individual objects, are often discovered when those objects are used together as a system. A given software module may have no vulnerabilities when used alone, but when that module communicates with another module, the communication channel may introduce a new vulnerability.

The discovery of vulnerabilities is known as *vulnerability analysis*. Vulnerability analysis may be performed by a software or hardware vendor in order to test its solutions. It may also be performed by organizations implementing the solution in order to ensure the privacy and protection of their data. In most cases, it will be performed by both the vendor and the implementing organization. This dual testing is needed because the implementing organization will be deploying the solution in an environment that is foreign to the vendor and may, therefore, introduce new vulnerabilities. Additionally, the implementing organization will write code for its specific needs. In SQL Server, this means stored procedures, user-defined functions, and triggers, among other things.

Exploits

An *exploit* is a specific method used to expose and take advantage of a vulnerability. Exploits introduce threats because of vulnerabilities. An exploit may be a procedure that an attacker must perform, or it may come in the form of source code that must be executed.

When an attacker wishes to gain access to a network or systems on a network, he will go through the following basic steps:

1. Scan for devices on the network.

2. Scan for services on those devices.

3. Discover the versions of the running services.

4. Research vulnerabilities.

5. Launch an exploit based on one or more vulnerabilities.

This step-by-step process shows that attacking a network or system is a simple process. You just have to have the right tools. For instance, on a Windows system, you could use nmap or Angry IP Scanner to find the devices, services, and versions. These Windows tools are free to download. Next, you can search the Internet for known vulnerabilities and then you can take advantage of those vulnerabilities through exploits. In many cases, you can download free applications that are specially designed to launch the exploit. As an illustration, AirCrack is a program designed specifically for cracking WEP keys on wireless networks. If you're using WEP to protect sensitive SQL Server data that is transferred across wireless links, you're relying on an insecure security solution (scary, right?).

When the tools are easy to get and the instructions are easy to follow, the threat increases. This threat increase is due to the fact that script kiddies can easily launch the exploit. For this reason, WEP cracking must be considered a valid threat to all organizations implementing wireless networks because promiscuous attackers can use the exploit against them. WEP cracking is used as an example here, but any other exploit that is similar in nature (it can be acquired and executed without in-depth technical knowledge) should be considered a threat and protection against it should be part of all security policies and procedures. One common example in the SQL Server world is the SQL injection attack. Several websites provide step-by-step instructions for performing injection attacks and they should not be taken lightly.

Attack Point One: Windows Server

Windows servers are used to store data, provide services to users, or provide services to other systems. Many servers are running Linux or Windows operating systems, and these systems are heavily targeted by attackers because of their heavy use. Windows Server is used to run SQL Server. If an attacker can penetrate or otherwise damage the Windows server, he can effectively hinder SQL Server operations.

Attack methods include:

- Exploiting known vulnerabilities
- Exploiting configuration errors
- Exploiting running services

Attackers can locate known vulnerabilities using search engines, discussion forums, and many other websites. Common websites used for vulnerability discovery include:

```
http://www.microsoft.com/security/
```

```
http://milw0rm.com/
```

```
http://zone-h.org/
```

```
http://hackerwatch.org/
```

```
http://secunia.com/advisories/product/
```

As a database administrator, you should visit these websites regularly to keep your knowledge up-to-date in the hardware, operating systems, and applications you are utilizing. You should specifically look for issues related to SQL Server. At the Secunia.com website, for instance, you can browse the vulnerability database and drill down by product to the SQL Server product line. Figure 17.1 shows the SQL Server 2005 vulnerability report for the year 2009 generated by Secunia. At the time of this writing, no reports were entered in the Secunia database for SQL Server 2008.

FIGURE 17.1 Viewing the Secunia.com SQL Server 2005 vulnerability report for the year 2009

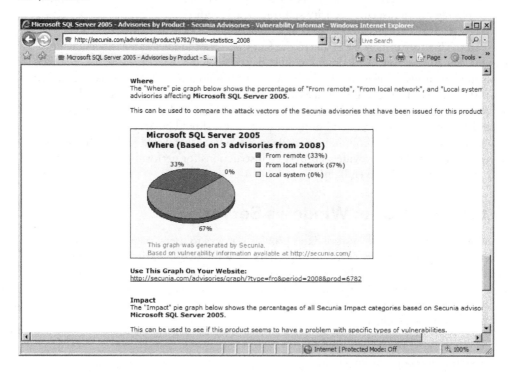

Configuration error exploits can often be avoided by implementing a strong security management process. This process would include threat and vulnerability analysis, security policy development, and policy implementation. By implementing configurations based on solid security policies, you reduce the likelihood of configuration errors. However, it does require a team effort because each technician must abide by the policies when configuring a device. An attacker requires only one improperly configured device to gain entry to the network. Auditing and security assessments may also be used to ensure proper configuration.

Using the Microsoft Baseline Security Analyzer (MBSA)

Using the Microsoft Baseline Security Analyzer (MBSA) on your Windows servers that run SQL Server is a good place to start. Exercise 17.1 steps you through the process of downloading, installing, and running the MBSA application.

EXERCISE 17.1

Using the MBSA Utility from Microsoft

In this exercise, you will download and install the MBSA utility from Microsoft and then run the utility to analyze a SQL Server. To do this, follow these steps:

1. Log on to the Windows server that is running SQL Server 2008 as an administrator.

2. Launch Internet Explorer and navigate to the following URL:

   http://www.microsoft.com/downloads/details.aspx?familyid=B1E76BBE-71DF-41E8-8B52-C871D012BA78&displaylang=en

3. Click the proper download link for your edition of Windows to start the download. Be sure to choose x64 if you're running a 64-bit version of Windows and x86 if you're running a 32-bit version of Windows. Additionally, be sure to choose the proper language.

4. When the File Download dialog appears, choose to Save the file. Select the desired location for file saving and click Save again.

5. Close Internet Explorer.

6. Navigate to the location where the MBSA download was saved in step 4 and execute the downloaded file by double-clicking on it.

7. If a security warning is displayed, click the Run button; otherwise, move on to step 8.

8. Click Next to begin the installation.

9. Agree to the license agreement and click Next.

10. Click Next to accept the default installation location and then click Install to begin the installation.

11. Click OK to complete the installation.

12. On the desktop, double-click the MBSA icon to launch the utility.

13. In the MBSA utility, choose to Scan a Computer.

14. Accept the default computer name, which will be the local computer, and all other default options and click Start Scan. The scanning process can take anywhere from a few seconds to several minutes depending on the system speed and the number of scanned elements.

EXERCISE 17.1   *(continued)*

15. View the scan results report. The following image shows an example of the SQL Server section of the MBSA report.

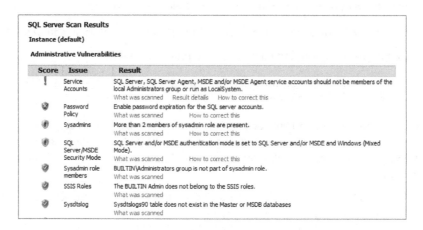

Many services are insecure regardless of the implementation method used. For example, telnet sends authentication credentials as cleartext when implemented according to the standards. Therefore, a telnet server does not provide a secure management interface unless it supports SSH or some other security solution. FTP also sends the username and password in the clear. Passwords sent as cleartext can be easily retrieved using protocol analyzers. This statement is particularly true of wireless networks that do not implement encryption, such as wireless hotspots and older networks. It is more difficult to sniff the data on wired networks than on unencrypted wireless networks. The increased difficulty is due to the requirement of physical access to the wired network.

Utilizing Authentication Systems

In addition to the service and configuration problems, the authentication system used must be considered. Chapter 18 addresses authentication in detail, but it must be considered here from a Windows Server perspective as well. Authentication systems are used to validate user identities and allow for authorization of the users for access to resources. Authentication systems are based on credentials. Windows Server uses authentication and, if it is implemented improperly, this can provide a point of attack on the Windows server.

Credentials can include any of the following three types:

Something You Know: This includes passwords and personal identification numbers (PINs).

Something You Have: This includes keys, smart cards, and RFID chips.

Something You Are: This includes biometrics such as fingerprint scanners, retina scanners, and even weight measurements

Windows Server can support any or all of the three types of credentials mentioned.

Authentication systems can be attacked by exploiting weak protocols, weak credential stores, or weak credentials. Weak protocols are protocols that are implemented poorly. The passwords may actually be sent across the network or another vulnerability may be inherent in the system. Weak credentials stores are exploited by cracking the encryption used on the store or simply accessing the credential store when no encryption is implemented. Weak credentials are usually weak passwords. Today, weak passwords are passwords that contain fewer than eight characters and those passwords that do not include multiple character types. However, a password such as "thehorsejumpedoverthemoononabroom" is very secure even though it does not contain multiple character types. The ultimate indicators of the strength of a password, with few exceptions, are the size of the password pool and the complexity of the password. The unusually long password referenced previously is more than 30 characters long. A 30-character password with only lowercase letters is part of a password pool that includes 254,186,582,832,900,000,000,000,000,000,000,000 possible passwords. This number represents more than 254 undecillion passwords. To put it into perspective, you could guess 100 trillion passwords each second and it would take more than 40 quadrillion years to guess the password on average. These numbers assume a blind brute force attack, but clearly even with advanced methods including rainbow tables and intelligent algorithms, it would take far too long to make it worth the attempt.

There's probably a cracker out there saying, "Wait a minute. I can use a dictionary attack method against that horse jumped mess of a password." The cracker is correct. However, it's still a rather difficult process. Unlike simple dictionary cracking methods that combine a single word with a number or two or three words together, cracking this password requires putting nine words together. Let's look at the math. The average English word is 5.1 characters long. If the average passphrase includes just seven words, it would give us a password length of 35 characters, rounding down. Looking at the number of characters, it would seem to be an insurmountable passphrase, if brute force were used. However, if dictionary cracking is used, it's simple, right?

Let's see. To use dictionary cracking when seven words are in the password using a moderate dictionary size of 100,000 words, more than 100 nonillion possible passwords would exist. That's the number 100 followed by 33 zeros. Yes, it's another really big number. If a cracking program processed 100 trillion possible passwords per minute, it would still take many trillions of years to guess all the passwords. Divide this time in half and add in some fancy commonly used word filters (such as the word "the" and the word "a") and you might reduce this to a few million years. The point is that the size of the password pool has a huge impact on the "crackability" of the password.

However, improper password storage or transmission makes all this theory null and void. If the hashing algorithm is weak or the challenge/response mechanism is flawed, the password can be gained in a few moments even if it's 100 characters long.

Still, the point with these examples is simple: if you have strong enough passwords, you will be safe enough for most data. If you feel passwords cannot be made strong enough, due to the human element (writing passwords on sticky notes), you should consider other authentication methods such as smart cards or biometrics. Authentication will be covered in much more detail in Chapter 18.

Encryption

In addition to the need for authentication to access data, sensitive data should be encrypted. The encryption may take place in two places: during transit and during storage. Encryption for transmitted data is processor intensive and may introduce additional processing delays in database systems; however, the tradeoff may be worth it if security is of utmost importance to your organization. In-transit encryption solutions are vulnerable to various sniffing attacks. For example, WEP encrypts traffic for WLANs, but the algorithm and keys were improperly implemented resulting in the ability to easily crack the WEP key and then gain access to the transmitted data.

Storage encryption is most frequently attacked by attacking the key store. You may have noticed that brute force methods were mentioned with encryption. Brute force is seldom used to crack any encryption scheme due to the time required. Even DES (Digital Encryption Standard) at 40 bits takes too long for most attacks. For this reason, attackers will usually look for vulnerabilities in the key store or the method used to access the key store. An example of this is given in the "Cracking Examples" section later in this chapter under the title "Encryption Cracks."

Many storage attacks are really authentication attacks. The attacker performs password guessing, password sniffing, or offline password cracking in order to gain access to the storage location. Once access is granted, the system treats the attacker as an authorized user.

In addition to authentication attacks against Windows servers, an attacker may take advantage of vulnerabilities inherent in the embedded operating system of a storage device used on a Windows network. For example, many Network Attached Storage (NAS) devices use embedded Linux. Because the operating system is implemented through firmware, the administrator may fail to update the operating system as often as normal computers running the same operating system. This delay can result in vulnerabilities being exposed for longer periods of time. The moral of the story is simple: Update the firmware on your devices whenever a security vulnerability is patched and the firmware does not introduce problems into the system. If you cannot update the firmware because the vendor is no longer updating it, consider placing the device behind a router or firewall that can be used to block all traffic that may result in the exploiting of the vulnerability.

Attack Point Two: SQL Server

The SQL Server service itself is an important attack point to consider. The Windows Server supports Windows authentication—either local accounts or Active Directory domain accounts. In addition to these logins, the SQL Server service supports SQL logins. SQL logins are used for non-Windows clients that must access the SQL Server. Linux machines and MAC OS machines may require SQL logins. Because SQL logins are password-only logins, while Windows accounts can log in with smart cards and biometrics, they will never be as secure as Windows authentication. Additionally, the SQL logins are considered insecure even for password-based authentication. SQL logins and the security flaws they introduce will be covered in more detail in Chapter 18.

In addition to the SQL logins, SQL Server introduces potential vulnerabilities through a large number of services that are included with the product. You have the SQL Server Database Engine service, the SQL Server Agent service, the SQL Browser service, the Full-Text Filter Daemon Launcher service, and many more. If all of these services are enabled when they are not needed, they unnecessarily introduce potential security problems. They may not have known vulnerabilities today, but they could have them tomorrow. A quick perusal of Microsoft's site shows that several security vulnerabilities are indeed discovered each year in the SQL Server product. For examples, refer to the following security bulletins in your favorite web browser:

- `http://www.microsoft.com/technet/security/Bulletin/MS09-004.mspx`
- `http://www.microsoft.com/technet/security/bulletin/ms08-040.mspx`

One thing to note about these security bulletins is that the discovered problems go all the way back to SQL Server 7.0. Such discoveries are not uncommon in the computer industry. Many times vulnerabilities are discovered in products many years after they were released. Vulnerabilities in network protocols such as SSL and TCP have been discovered many years after they were put into use. The only thing you can really do about these is to implement recommended protection mechanisms when such vulnerabilities are discovered. In the case of SQL Server, this usually means applying a patch to the system.

To be clear, several vulnerabilities are also discovered each year in Oracle, MySQL, and other databases as well. While Microsoft's security problems tend to receive large press coverage, the truth is that every product must be maintained to protect against newly discovered vulnerabilities.

Attack Point Three: the Network

The earliest networks were wired only; however, with the standardization of wireless technologies in the late 1990s, wireless networks have become very popular. Therefore, the potential vulnerabilities introduced by both wired and wireless networks must be considered.

Why all this information about the network? Simple, it's what you use to get to the SQL Server. If the network is not secure, the clients and the servers may be more easily attacked.

Wired Networks

Wired networks may be exploited by gaining access to an unsecured port or by penetrating the network through a secured port. If the network is connected to the Internet, the

Internet connection may also be exploited. The last method of exploit is through dial-up connections. Dial-up connections are becoming increasingly rare, but they do still exist.

An unsecured wired port is an Ethernet (or some other wired network standard) port that is enabled and not protected with authentication. IEEE 802.1X is a standard that defines mechanisms for securing such a port. Some organizations choose to implement 802.1X while others choose to resolve the issue by disabling any unused ports until they are needed. The latter method leaves the network vulnerable to human error or forgetfulness. What if the network administrator fails to disable the port after the authorized user is finished using it? The result is an open port available for an internal attacker. The 802.1X solution is preferred as long as a secure extensible authentication protocol (EAP) implementation is used.

If a port is unsecured, an attacker may connect to the port and begin scanning and ultimately attacking the network. Prime targets include ports in conference rooms, unused offices, and remote areas of warehouses or manufacturing plants. These ports should certainly be secured or disabled any time they are not in use. The fact that these ports can be located anywhere in the facility and will provide access to the enterprise network makes it quickly apparent that they can be used as an attack point to gain access to SQL Server data.

Another method used by attackers, in relation to wired ports, is the installation of a rogue wireless access point (AP). When the rogue AP is installed, the attacker can gain access to the network from outside the facility. One quick and undetected trip into the building is all it takes to implement an inexpensive rogue AP. This rogue AP is not likely to cost the attacker anything because he will simply steal the AP so that he incurs no loss when you do eventually find and confiscate it.

One of the most commonly used wired attack points is an organization's Internet connection. Many administrators have noted more than 1,000 attack attempts in a single day. If you have an Internet connection (hopefully, a good firewall) and the connection attempts can be logged, you should enable this logging. After a few days you can look at the log to see how many connection attempts are being made against ports that are commonly attacked. You may be surprised by the number of attempts. You may also be surprised at how many attempts are made to connect to TCP port 1433 (the default SQL Server port).

 One of the most basic security solutions that will help to protect your SQL Servers is to place them in a locked server room or network operations center. Physical security is still a very important part of network security.

Wireless Networks

Wireless networks are vulnerable to penetration through Internet-facing connections just like wired networks; however, wireless networks also introduce entirely new vulnerabilities. Instead of focusing on ports, you must focus on connections. Wireless networks allow client devices to connect to the network without the use of preassigned ports. For this reason, disabling ports is not an option. MAC filtering has been used in the past in an attempt to accomplish security at the same level as port management; however, MAC filtering is very weak because an attacker may monitor the network and discover valid MAC addresses. Once the valid addresses are known, the attacker may reconfigure her device to use an allowed MAC address. For this reason, you should consider MAC filtering as a security myth and not as a security solution.

In fact, many myths are associated with wireless security. While the primary focus of this book is on SQL Server, a few of those security myths related to wireless networks will be addressed so that your SQL Servers will not be made more vulnerable to client-side exploits due to improper wireless implementations. The wireless security myths briefly covered here include:

- MAC filtering
- SSID hiding
- All modern equipment uses "better WEP."
- Wireless networks can't be secured.

MAC Filtering

Vendors of wireless devices and books on wireless networking often provide a list of the "Top 5" or "Top 10" things you should do to secure your WLAN (wireless LAN). This list usually includes MAC filtering and SSID hiding or cloaking. The reality is that neither of these provides a high level of security. MAC addresses can easily be spoofed and valid MAC addresses can be identified in just a few moments. For example, an attacker can eliminate the AP in an infrastructure BSS by looking for the MAC address that sends out Beacon frames. This will always be the AP in the BSS. With this filtered out of the attacker's protocol analyzer, he has only to find other MAC addresses that are transmitting with a destination MAC address equal to that of the AP. Assuming the captured frames are data frames, the attacker now knows a valid MAC address.

There is no question that MAC filtering will make it more difficult for an attacker to access your network. The attacker will have to go through the process just outlined (or a similar process) in order to obtain a valid MAC address to spoof. However, you are adding to your workload by implementing such MAC filtering and you have to ask, "Am I getting a good return on investment for my time?" The answer is usually "No." Using Temporal Key Integrity Protocol (TKIP) or Counter Mode with Cipher Block Chaining Message Authentication Code Protocol (CCMP) with a strong EAP type for authentication (or even pre-shared keys) will be so much more secure than MAC filtering could ever hope to be that it makes the extra effort of MAC filtering of minimal value. Do not concern yourself with MAC filtering in an enterprise or SMB implementation. It may be useful in a SOHO (small office/home office) implementation, but even then its value is questionable.

If you rely on MAC filtering to protect your network and wireless clients, you're relying on the wrong solution. In a business environment, WPA or WPA2 should always be used and, preferably, the enterprise edition, which uses network-based authentication instead of pre-shared keys.

SSID Hiding

Hiding or cloaking the Service Set Identifier (SSID) of your WLAN falls into a similar category as MAC filtering. Both provide very little in the way of security enhancement. Changing the name of your SSID from the vendor defaults can be very helpful because it will make dictionary attacks against pre-shared key implementations more difficult. This is because the SSID is used in the process of creating the pairwise master key. Hiding the SSID only makes it difficult for casual eavesdroppers to find your network.

Hiding the SSID also forces your valid clients to send out probe requests in order to connect to your WLAN, whether using the Windows Wireless Zero Configuration (WZC) utility or your vendor's client software. This activity means that, when the user turns on his or her laptop in a public place, the laptop is broadcasting your SSID to the world. This could be considered a potential security threat because a rogue AP of any type can be configured to the SSID that is being sent out in the probe requests. Software-based APs can respond to random SSIDs generated by WZC, but hiding your SSID effectively makes every WLAN client in existence vulnerable to such attacks since they will all have to send probe requests with the SSID.

For security purposes, you should always change the SSID from the default, but never hide it. Some people will hide the SSID for usability purposes. Turning off the SSID broadcast in all AP's Beacon frames will prevent client computers from "seeing" the other networks to which they are not supposed to connect. This may reduce confusion, but SSID hiding should not be considered a security solution.

All Modern Equipment Uses "Better WEP"

In the past, when an initial WEP vulnerability scare hit, many vendors looked for solutions to the weak Initialization Vectors (IVs) used in the WEP implementations that existed at the time. Eventually, many vendors began implementing newer WEP solutions that attempted to avoid the weak IVs. You simply cannot trust that a vendor has actually implemented algorithms that protect you against WEP weaknesses just because the hardware is newer. Instead, you would need to monitor the communications with the device in order to determine if weak IVs are being used. It's easier to implement WPA or WPA2.

 As early as 2003, I noticed people on the Internet saying that the newer hardware didn't have this problem. In fact, I have a network attached storage device that was purchased in 2005 that includes a built-in AP. This device is running the most recent firmware from the vendor (D-Link, in this case), and I can connect a brand new Intel Centrino chipset laptop to the device using WEP. While monitoring from another computer, I am able to capture weak IVs and crack the WEP key in a matter of minutes.

Wireless Networks Can't Be Secured

Don't allow these last few ineffective security methods to keep you from implementing a wireless LAN. Wireless LANs can be implemented in a secure fashion using IEEE 802.11i (now clause 9 of 802.11-2007) and strong EAP types. In fact, they can be made far more secure than many wired LANs, because many wired LANs do not implement any real authentication mechanisms at the node level. If you buy into the concept that wireless LANs cannot be secured and you decide not to implement a wireless LAN for this reason, you will likely open your network up to more frequent rogue AP installations from users who want to have wireless access to the network. The simplest way to avoid or at least diminish the occurrence of user-installed rogue APs is to implement a secure wireless network for the users. In the end, wireless LANs can be secured, but you must be aware of the security myths surrounding them.

Attack Point Four: the Client

The client is probably the most overlooked attack point in a database system. The assumption is that, if the server is secure and the network is secure, the database will be secure. This assumption could not be further from the truth. Depending on the design of your database client application, it could become the easiest point of attack for an intruder.

Here's one way to think about this. Have you heard of the SQL injection attack? If you have, you know that an SQL injection attack is a cracking method that is used to penetrate or damage any SQL-based server that is accessed through a client with poorly written code. Now, if you've studied SQL injection attacks, you're probably thinking, "Wait a minute. Don't injection attacks take place mostly on web servers and aren't they, therefore, server attacks instead of client attacks?" At first glance, you would be correct, but consider the typical architecture used for a website. The website runs a web server such as Internet Information Services (IIS) or Apache. The database may be installed on the same server, but it is more common for large websites to access a separate database server. In such a configuration, the website (an application running in a web server) is the client to the database server.

Even if the database server is installed on the same physical server as the web server software, the web server is still a client to the database. Regardless of the distribution or nondistribution of services, the website is always a client to the database; therefore, a SQL injection attack is a client attack.

But let's take this a step further. If you have a client application written in Visual Studio .NET 2008 and that application accesses a SQL Server from a Windows XP client, SQL injection attacks can still occur. Remember, an *SQL injection attack* is simply any attack where extra information is injected (inserted) into the SQL request strings or statements. If someone can inject SQL code into the requests of the .NET client application before the requests are submitted to the server, they can perform an injection attack. The question is this: can you inject extra code into a client application request? The answer is "Yes."

You can insert extra code into a client application, which is not a website application, by using man-in-the-middle attacks or by installing a malicious software program (malware) onto the client machine. The malware would need to look for SQL Server requests and then reform these requests before allowing them to be sent to the database server. In effect, this would be a type of client proxy. Instead of acting as a web proxy, it is acting as a SQL

Server proxy. This attack method is not common, but it is possible. Just because it is not common today, no guarantee exists that ensures it will not be sweeping across the Internet tomorrow.

In addition to injection attacks, session hijacking can be attempted. *Session hijacking* simply means that the attacker takes over the session of the valid SQL Server user or at least uses the user's session alongside him. Through this action, the attacker is not required to know the user's password. This attack method is not a direct SQL Server attack, but is an attack against the standard operation of the TCP protocol. You may remember from previous chapters that SQL Server's default instance uses TCP port 1433 by default. Of course, this fact means that TCP is used for communications. If the highway on which SQL Server is communicating (TCP) can be exploited, someone may be able to exploit SQL Server. This attack method may be better categorized as a network attack since they're actually going underneath SQL Server in the OSI model. However, they are hijacking a client session so it's also possible to categorize this as a client attack.

Understanding all the details of a specific hack is beyond the scope of this book; however, I encourage you to explore the concept of session hijacking further. One of the easiest ways to counter session hijacking is to use IPSec between the client and the SQL Server.

Of course, one of the simplest methods an attacker can use is social engineering against a database user. *Social engineering* is an attack method that relies on human manipulation to gain information that should not be given to the attacker. With social engineering, the attacker is not required to sniff packets off the network or install malware on the user's machine. Instead, the attacker can ask the valid user to perform actions that would result in the theft or destruction of data.

Real World Scenario

Stealing Data Through Social Engineering

I've dealt with several security incidents where social engineering was used to penetrate a network or database system. Social engineering is a powerful attack method. You cannot protect against it using technical measures. Only user education can help to protect your databases from social engineering attacks. For example, consider the following telephone conversation where Amy is the target of a social engineering attack:

"Hello, this is Amy. How may I help you?" queries Amy, as she answers the telephone.

"Hi, this is Dale from the Help Desk. We're having a problem with the Sales Automation program and I need you to perform some actions on your system to help us resolve the problem," states the attacker. He then queries, "Can you give me about five minutes of your time right now?"

Amy wants to be helpful so she quickly replies, "Yes, what do you need?"

The attacker responds, "First, remember not to give out your password. When I ask you to perform the steps, please do not say your password out loud, just enter it in with the commands. That way we can maintain security. OK?"

"OK," is Amy's brief response.

"Now, I need you to click the Start button and then select Run. Please, let me know when you see the Run dialog on your screen," says the attacker.

"Just a sec. OK, it's there. What do I do now?" asks Amy.

The attacker requests, "The next part is a little technical so feel free to verify the command before you press the Enter key. Type in NET SEND Dale and then enter your username and password to recommission the database server. I'll know when you've typed it because the server session will become active again for your login."

Amy uncertainly responds, "I think I've typed it right. Did you see the recommission thing?"

The attacker, now giddy with joy over the success of his attack, responds, "Yes. It looks like everything is OK. Thanks for your help."

"No problem," replies Amy, feeling that she has been both helpful and technically proficient.

Now, in this scenario, the attacker would have to be on a computer that could be reached with the NET SEND command, so he would be on the internal network. However, the attacker could have also had Amy install a program on her computer and then send the credentials using email. The victim, in this case Amy, would have likely followed these instructions as well.

The point of this illustration is simple: You cannot protect against social engineering attacks with technical methods. For every technical solution you can come up with to protect against the scenario presented here, I can simply come up with another social engineering script that gets the same data or information in a different way. End-user training is essential.

I recommend that my clients provide user education on the topic of social engineering. I don't recommend that they teach them things like, "Don't give your password to anyone," but instead teach them why they shouldn't give their password to anyone.

The fictional scenario I've presented here is loosely based on real-world situations that have occurred. Don't be fooled into thinking that you won't be the target of a social engineering attack. Instead, provide the proper training and help to protect against it.

Cracking Examples

With an awareness of the common attack points, you're ready to investigate a few hacking examples. You will improve your understanding of security by learning about specific hacking methods. The next few pages will present various hacks that can be used against a selection of the attack points previously discussed.

If you are using this book as a study guide for exams 70–432 or 70–450 and want to optimize your study time, you can move on to Chapter 18 at this point. The remaining examples and topics covered in this chapter are not likely to appear on the exam and you can understand Chapters 18 and 19 without mastering the concepts covered in the rest of this chapter.

Network Cracks

Cracking WEP is a perfect example of a network hack. The Wired Equivalent Privacy (WEP) protocol is used to encrypt data on wireless LANs and authenticate users to the wireless LAN based on the fact that the user knows the WEP key. Numerous problems exist with the WEP protocol that result in the ability to crack it easily.

An understanding of the basic WEP process will help you to understand the weaknesses that are covered next. The WEP process starts with the inputs to the process. These inputs include the data that should be encrypted (usually called plaintext), the secret key (40-bits or 104-bits), and the IV (24-bits). These inputs are passed through the WEP algorithms to generate the output (the ciphertext or encrypted data).

Because WEP is a Layer 2 security implementation, it doesn't matter what type of data is being transmitted as long as it originates above Layer 2 in the OSI model. In order to encrypt the data, the RC4 algorithm is used to create a pseudorandom string of bits called a keystream. The WEP static key and the IV are used to seed the pseudorandom number generator used by the RC4 algorithm. The resulting keystream is XORed against the plaintext to generate the ciphertext. The ciphertext alone is transferred without the keystream; however, the IV is sent to the receiver. The receiver uses the IV that was transmitted and the stored static WEP key to feed the same pseudorandom number generator to regenerate the same keystream. The XOR is reversed at the receiver to recover the original plaintext from the ciphertext.

WEP was never intended to provide impenetrable security, but was only intended to protect against casual eavesdropping. With the rapid increase in processor speeds, cracking WEP has become a very short task and it can no longer be considered for protection against any organized attack.

In late 2000 and early 2001, the security weaknesses of WEP became clear. Since then many attack methods have been developed and tools have been created that make these attack methods simple to implement for entry-level technical individuals. The weaknesses in WEP include the following:

- Brute force attacks
- Dictionary attacks

- Weak IV attacks
- Reinjection attacks
- Storage attacks

Brute Force Attacks The *brute force* attack method is a key guessing method that attempts every possible key in order to crack the encryption. With 104-bit WEP, this is really not a feasible attack method; however, 40-bit WEP can usually be cracked in one or two days with brute force attacks using more than 20 distributed computers. The short timeframe is accomplished using a distributed cracking tool like jc-wepcrack. jc-wepcrack is actually two tools: the client and the server. The cracker would first start the tool on the server and configure it for the WEP key size he thinks the target WLAN uses and provide it with a *pcap file* (a capture of encrypted frames) from that network. Next, he would launch the client program and configure it to connect to the server. The client program will request a portion of the keys to be guessed and will attempt to access the encrypted frames with those keys. With the modern addition of Field Programmable Gate Arrays (FPGAs), which are add-on boards for hardware acceleration, the time to crack can be reduced by more than 30 times. In fairness, the 20 computers would have to be P4 3.6 GHz machines or better. If a cracker chose to go the FPGA route, he would be spending a lot of money to crack that WEP key. Smart enterprises will no longer be using WEP, so the cracker will not likely gain access to any information that is as valuable as his hacking network.

Dictionary Attacks The *dictionary attack* method relies on the fact that humans often use words as passwords. The key is to use a dictionary cracking tool that understands the conversion algorithm used by a hardware vendor to convert the typed password into the WEP key. This algorithm is not part of IEEE 802.11 and is implemented differently by the different vendors. Many vendors allow the user to type a passphrase that is then converted to the WEP key using the Neesus Datacom or MD5 WEP key generation algorithms. The Neesus Datacom algorithm is notoriously insecure and has resulted in what is sometimes called the Newsham-21-bit attack because it reduces the usable WEP key pool to 21 bits instead of 40 when using a 40-bit WEP key. This smaller pool can be exhausted in about 6–7 seconds on a P4 3.6 GHz single machine using modern cracking tools against a pcap file. Even MD5-based conversion algorithms are far too weak and should not be considered secure because they are still used to implement WEP, which is insecure due to weak IVs as well.

Weak IV Attacks *Weak IV attacks* are based on the faulty implementation of RC4 in the WEP protocols. The IV is prepended to the static WEP key to form the full WEP encryption key used by the RC4 algorithm. This means than an attacker already knows the first 24 bits of the encryption key because the IV is sent in cleartext as part of the frame header. Additionally, Fluhrer, Mantin, and Shamir (the original experts who identified early vulnerabilities in WEP) identified "weak" IVs in a paper released in 2001. These weak IVs result in certain values becoming more statistically probable than others and make it easier to crack the static WEP key. The 802.11 frames that use these weak IVs have come to be known as *interesting frames*. With enough interesting frames collected, someone can crack the WEP key in a matter of seconds. This reduces the total attack time down to less than five to six minutes on a busy WLAN.

The weak IVs discovered by Fluhrer, Mantin, and Shamir are now among a larger pool of known weak IVs. Since 2001, another 16 classes of weak IVs have been discovered by David Hulton (h1kari) and KoreK.

Reinjection Attacks   What if the WEP-enabled network being attacked is not busy and you cannot capture enough interesting frames in a short window of time? The attacker can use a *reinjection attack*. This kind of attack usually reinjects Address Resolution Protocol (ARP) packets onto the WLAN. The program Aireplay can detect ARP packets based on their unique size and does not need to decrypt the packets. By reinjecting the ARP packets back onto the WLAN, it will force the other clients to reply and cause the creation of large amounts of WLAN traffic very quickly. For 40-bit WEP cracking, you usually want around 300,000 total frames to get enough interesting frames and for 104-bit WEP cracking you may want about 1,000,000 frames.

Storage Attacks   *Storage attacks* are those methods used to recover WEP or WPA keys from their storage locations. On Windows computers, for example, WEP keys have often been stored in the Registry in an encrypted form. An older version of this attack method was the Lucent Registry Crack, which was a tool used to read the WEP keys right out of the Windows Registry; however, it appears that the problem has not been fully removed from our modern networks. An application named *wzcook* can retrieve the stored WEP keys used by Windows' Wireless Zero Configuration. This application recovers WEP or WPA-PSK keys (since they are effectively the same, WPA just improves the way the key is managed and implemented) and comes with the Aircrack-ng tools used for cracking these keys. The application only works if you have administrator access to the local machine, but in an environment with poor physical security and poor user training, it is not difficult to find a machine for this attack that is logged on and using the WLAN.

WEP makes up the core of pre-RSNA security in IEEE 802.11 networks. The reality that WEP can be cracked in less than five minutes should be enough to make you realize that you shouldn't be using it on your networks. The only exception would be an installation where you are required to install a WLAN using older hardware and you have no other option. This scenario has occurred in a few church network implementations. The problems were not with the infrastructure equipment in any of the scenarios. The problems were with the client devices that the church members wanted to use to connect to the WLAN. These devices did not support WPA or WPA2, and they were forced to use either WEP or no security at all. While WEP can certainly be cracked quickly, at least it has to be cracked. Open System authentication with no WEP, WPA, or WPA2 security is just that: open.

In the end, businesses and organizations that have sensitive data to protect must take a stand for security and against older technologies. This means that you should not implement WEP anywhere in your organization. When you have the authority of a corporation, the government, or even a nonprofit oversight board, you can usually sell them on the need for better security with a short (five minutes or less) demonstration of just how weak WEP is. If you're implementing Voice over WLAN, these insights will be tremendously valuable.

Password Cracks

Most computer access controls are based on passwords. Weak passwords cause one of the most serious security threats in networking, for obvious reasons. Intruders easily guess commonly used and known passwords, such as `password`, `admin`, `drowssap`, `Password1`, etc. Short words or strings of characters are often at risk from a brute force password-attack program, and passwords made from words found in the dictionary can be guessed using dictionary attacks as mentioned previously in this chapter.

All of this information is common knowledge to security administrators, but what is not commonly considered is that passwords flow from client to server across unsecured networks all the time. In the past, there was a common misconception that wired networks were secure, but wireless LANs have opened the eyes of many administrators and attackers that networking systems using passwords passed in cleartext across any medium are vulnerable to interception. For this reason, password encryption has become very popular along with security mechanisms, such as Kerberos (which is used in Windows Active Directory domains), that implement such encryption. Two auditing tools often used by administrators and hackers alike to view cleartext passwords are Win Sniffer and ettercap. The following sections address the following tools for password capture and cracking:

- Win Sniffer
- Revelation
- ettercap
- L0phtCrack

As you read through these sections, remember this common fact: Users often use the same passwords with multiple systems. If someone wants to get a user's password for the SQL Server, they can often find it by sniffing that user's FTP, telnet, SMTP, or HTTP passwords.

Win Sniffer

Win Sniffer is a password-capture utility capable of capturing FTP, HTTP, ICQ, Telnet, SMTP, POP3, and NNTP, and IMAP usernames and passwords in shared-medium networking environments such as wireless APs or wired hubs. If you use telnet to gain command-line access to your SQL Servers, this tool could be used to sniff the password off the network. Win Sniffer is installed on a Windows-based computer, usually a laptop being used to audit wireless networks. In a switched network, Win Sniffer can only capture passwords that originate from either the client that sent the password or the server that sent the client the information directly. Win Sniffer can be used to capture your own passwords (when saved in applications) when you forget them. Sample output from Win Sniffer is shown in Figure 17.2.

FIGURE 17.2   Using Win Sniffer to capture passwords

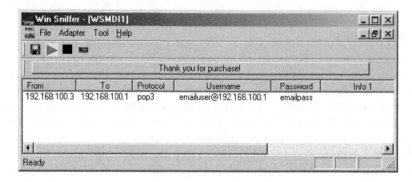

Consider Figure 17.3 in which the user is checking email over an unencrypted wireless LAN segment. An attacker is scanning the wireless segment using a password sniffer and picks up the user's email login information and the domain from which the user is checking the email. The attacker now has access to the user's email account and can read all of the user's email.

FIGURE 17.3   Sniffing a user's email password from a wireless network connection

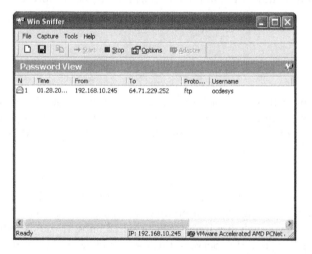

Public access wireless networks (hotspots), such as those found in airports or in metropolitan areas, are some of the most vulnerable areas for user attacks. Users that are not familiar with how easy it is to obtain their login information through a peer-to-peer attack unknowingly check their email or access their corporate network—even VoIP systems—and end up giving access to their accounts to a hacker. Once the hacker obtains a valid login to a corporate account, she is now well equipped to try to obtain further access into the network to locate more sensitive information.

Revelation

On Windows systems, a tool that can be used to discover passwords is Revelation. This program will allow you to drag a curser over a password field in any login dialog or a web page and have the password revealed. Of course, to use this tool, the user would have to have left his or her computer logged on and you will have to have the ability to run the tool. However, with users saving their passwords in web forms so frequently today, this tool can reveal passwords for many situations. To protect against it, you can disallow the tool from running through Windows Group Policies or disallow users from saving their passwords. While neither method will provide complete protection, they can provide extra protection and make it more difficult for the attacker. For example, the attacker would have to use a hex editor to modify the binary file (revelation.exe) in order to get around the hash-based Group Policies in Windows Server 2003 and supported by Windows XP clients. Revelation can be used on wired and wireless systems in order to discover passwords.

ettercap

ettercap is one of the most powerful password capture and auditing tools available today. ettercap supports almost every operating system platform, and it can be found at http://ettercap.sourceforge.net. ettercap is capable of gathering data even in a switched environment, which far exceeds the abilities of most other audit tools. ettercap uses a menu-style user interface, making it user friendly. Some of the features available in ettercap include:

Character Injection into an Established Connection: A user can inject characters into a server (emulating commands) or into a client (emulating replies) while maintaining a live connection.

SSH1 Support: A user can analyze usernames and passwords and even the data of the SSH1 connection. ettercap is the first software capable of analyzing an SSH connection in full-duplex mode.

HTTPS Support: A user can sniff HTTP-SSL data even if the connection is made through a proxy.

Remote Traffic Through a GRE Tunnel: A user can analyze remote traffic through a GRE tunnel from a remote router.

PPTP Broker: A user can perform man-in-the-middle attacks against PPTP tunnels.

Plug-In Support: A user can create her own plug-in using ettercap's API. Many plug-ins are included in the base package.

Password Collector for: TELNET, FTP, POP, RLOGIN, SSH1, ICQ, SMB, MySQL, HTTP, NNTP, X11, NAPSTER, IRC, RIP, BGP, SOCKS-5, IMAP4, VNC, LDAP, NFS, SNMP, HALF LIFE, QUAKE 3, MSN, and YMSG.

Packet Filtering/Dropping: A user can configure a filter that searches for a particular string (even hex) in the TCP or UDP payload and replace it with a new string or drop the entire packet.

OS Fingerprinting: A user can fingerprint the operating system of the victim host and its network adapter.

Kill a Connection: From the connections list, a user can kill all the connections he or she chooses.

Passive Scanning of the LAN: A user can retrieve information about any of the following: hosts in the LAN, open ports, services version, host type (gateway, router, or simple host), and estimated distance (in hops).

Check for Other Poisoners: ettercap has the ability to actively or passively find other poisoners on the LAN. These would be devices that have hacked the ARP cache to point to improper devices, a process known as *ARP poisoning*.

Bind Sniffed Data to a Local Port: A user can connect to a port on a client and decode protocols or inject data.

In addition to these features, the newer versions of ettercap support internal WEP decryption for wireless packets. When you provide the WEP key, which you must know or have previously cracked, the packets can be decrypted on-the-fly for storage and later viewing.

 ettercap requires another free add-on for Windows called WinPcap, which allows you to capture low-level network communications. You can download WinPcap from http://www.winpcap.org/.

L0phtCrack

In many cases, operating systems implement password authentication and encryption at the application layer. Such is the case with Microsoft Windows file sharing and NetLogon processes. The challenge/response mechanism used by Microsoft over the years (and over several operating system and service pack upgrades) has changed from LM (weak), to NTLM (medium), to NTLMv2 (strong). Before NTLMv2, tools such as L0phtCrack could easily crack these hashes. It is important to properly configure your Windows operating system to use NTLMv2 and not to use the weaker versions. This process must be accomplished manually, and instructions can be found at www.technet.com.

L0phtCrack is a password auditing and recovery tool originally created by L0pht Heavy Industries. The tool passed through several hands, including @stake and Symantec, before landing in the current organization, which is L0pht Holdings, LLC. The newest version, at the time of this writing is version 6, but the functional purpose remains the same. You can often find older versions on download sites such as Download.com and Tucows.com. L0phtCrack can capture passwords in many different ways, but two methods that auditors frequently attempt are file share authentication and network logons. L0phtCrack can capture these challenge/response conversations and derive the password. The strong the challenge/response mechanism used, the more difficult it is for L0phtCrack to crack them. The output of a password recovery session in L0phtCrack version 4 (LC4) is shown in Figure 17.4.

FIGURE 17.4   Cracking passwords with L0phtCrack

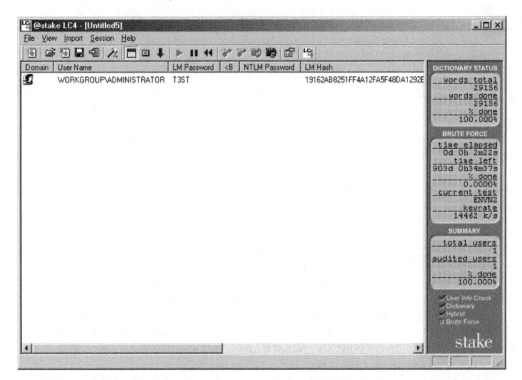

Once the intruder has captured the targeted password hashes (as many as deemed appropriate in a given audit), the hashes are imported into LC4's engine, and a dictionary attack automatically ensues. If the dictionary attack is unsuccessful, a brute force attack automatically begins thereafter. The processing power of the computer doing the audit will determine how fast the hash can be broken. L0phtCrack has many modes for capturing password hashes and dumping password repositories. One mode allows for sniffing in a shared medium (such as wireless), while another goes directly after the Windows Security Access Manager (SAM).

Windows 2000 service pack 3 introduced a new feature called SysKey, which is short for System Key. This feature, implemented by running the syskey.exe executable file, encrypts the SAM such that L0phtCrack cannot extract passwords from it as was possible before it was encrypted. L0phtCrack has the capability of letting the auditor know that he or she is auditing a SAM that has been encrypted so the auditor will not waste much time attempting to extract that password.

L0phtCrack is managed and updated by L0pht Holdings, LLC at the time of this writing. If the history of the tool is any indicator of its future, it may change hands several more times. For now, you can download a trial version at L0phtCrack.com.

Encryption Cracks

The Encrypting File System (EFS) in Windows 2000 and later operating systems is an example of storage encryption. It is also an example of potential weaknesses in encryption systems. EFS is vulnerable to key store attacks.

In any encryption system, the most difficult thing to do is protect the key store. The problem is found in the method used to access the keys. If a user needs to decrypt data she previously encrypted, she must be able to retrieve the encryption key. With EFS, data is encrypted with a file encryption key (FEK). The EFS encrypts the FEK with the user's public key. This process means that the user's private key will be needed in order to decrypt the FEK, which will be used to decrypt the file. The question is this: how does the user access her private key? The answer is simple: automatically.

By default, when the user opens a file that is encrypted by EFS, the user's private key is automatically retrieved and the FEK is then decrypted followed by the decryption of the data file. As long as the user is logged on, it all happens automatically. This process reveals the potential weakness, which is that the user's authentication credentials establish the true security of EFS (or any other encryption solution that uses automatic encryption and decryption once the user is authenticated).

The EFS uses a solid encryption algorithm with a sufficient key length; however, the user's password may be very weak and this reality introduces an important vulnerability into the system. If the attacker can guess the user's password, all of the data encrypted by that user will now be accessible to the attacker in many, if not most, scenarios. However, this is not a unique problem with EFS. If a user implements the very popular Pretty Good Privacy (PGP) Desktop encryption system and uses weak passphrases, the data may be equally vulnerable.

The solution is to implement strong passwords and solid user education. Strong passwords can be required using Group Policies in Windows Server domain environments. Exercise 17.2 steps you through configuring strong password rules for an Active Directory domain. User education is required in order to protect against social engineering. A password can be a very strong password, such as Byrt6uyo78H, and still be vulnerable to social engineering. Social engineering will be discussed in more detail in the next section.

EXERCISE 17.2

Creating Strong Password Policies in Windows Domains

In this exercise, the steps to implement a strong password policy in an Active Directory domain are provided. These steps work on a Windows Server 2008 domain controller. To implement strong password policies:

1. Select Start ➢ All Programs ➢ Administrative Tools ➢ Group Policy Management.

2. Expand the forest, the domains container, and the target domain in which you want to implement secure password policies.

3. Expand Group Policy Objects.

4. Right-click on the Default Domain Policy and select Edit.

5. In the GPO Editor, expand Computer Configuration ➢ Policies ➢ Windows Settings ➢ Security Settings ➢ Account Policies ➢ Password Policy.

6. Configure the password policies as desired.

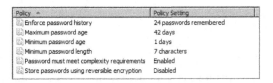

Social Engineering

Social engineering is defined as persuading someone to give you or tell you something that they should not give you or tell you through the manipulation of human or social interactions. Successful social engineering attacks occur because the target may be ignorant of the organization's information security policies or intimidated by an intruder's knowledge, expertise, or attitude. Social engineering is one of the most dangerous and successful methods of hacking into any IT infrastructure. If defeating SQL Server's security directly has stumped the cracker, she might try to trick an employee who is authorized to access the SQL Server into giving up his authentication credentials. Once the cracker has the credentials, she will enter them into her own computer and use the credentials to log on to the SQL Server, just as though there was no security. For this reason, social engineering has the potential of rendering even the most sophisticated security solution useless.

Crackers are not always as they are portrayed in movies: the cigarette-smoking, caffeine-loaded teenager in a dark room in a basement with multiple high-speed connections to the Internet, loud music, and plenty of spare time. Many times the most successful and damaging network intrusion is accomplished in broad daylight through the clever efforts of someone who walks into a business as if he owns it. In the very same manner, a hired professional security auditor should openly attempt intrusion as one tactic of testing security policy adherence.

There are some well-known targets for this type of attack:

- The Help Desk
- On-site contractors
- Employees (end users)

The Help Desk

The Help Desk is in place to assist those individuals who need help with some aspect of a computer or network. It becomes quite awkward in many situations for the Help Desk not to provide answers to questions when the person on the other end of the line seems to know what they need. It is not an easy task to train Help Desk personnel not to be helpful in certain situations; nevertheless, this type of education is crucial to corporate network security. The Help Desk should be trained to know exactly which pieces of information related to the wireless network should not be given out without the proper authorization or without following specific processes put in place by security policy. Items that might be marked for exclusion are

- SSID of access points
- WEP key(s)
- SQL Server credentials
- Usernames and passwords for network access and services (e.g., email)
- Passwords and SNMP strings for infrastructure devices

To test your exposure to potential social engineering attempts, auditing may be performed. The auditor should (and the hacker will) use two particular tactics when dealing with Help Desk personnel:

- Forceful, yet professional language
- Playing dumb

Both of these approaches have the same effect: getting the requested information. Help Desk personnel understand that their job is to help people with their problems. They also understand that their manager will not be happy with them if their customers are not happy with the service they are receiving. By threatening to speak with, or write a letter to, the manager, the social engineer can get the Help Desk person to give over the requested information just to appease and settle down the social engineer. Some people are just naturally inept at handling personal conflict, and some people are easily intimidated by anyone with an authoritative voice. Both of these situations can be used to the advantage of the social engineer. The human factor has to be overcome with training, discipline, and repetitively following documented procedures.

Playing dumb is a favorite of many social engineers. The Help Desk attendant is usually disarmed and stops paying attention when they figure out that the person to whom they are speaking knows very little. This situation is exacerbated when the "dumb" customer is overly polite and thankful for the help. It's important that a Help Desk person be alert to this tactic at all times. A social engineer is likely to call over and over, hoping to speak with different representatives and taking different approaches with each.

On-Site Contractors

IT contractors are commonplace at many businesses today, and very few, if any, are put through organizational security training. Few are given a copy of the company security policy or required to sign privacy agreements. For this reason, and because IT contractors, like the Help Desk, are there to help, IT contractors can be especially good targets for social engineers. Contractors are aware of the specific details about network resources because they are often on-site to design or repair the network. In wanting to be helpful to their customers, contractors often give out too much information to people who are not authorized to have such information. For this reason, strong security solutions that rely on multifactor authentication are recommended.

As an example, if you require smart card authentication for all contractors who access the SQL Server, it will not be possible for these contractors to give out their credentials over the phone to an attacker. Fingerprint scanners would provide a similar benefit. The complete removal of all password-based authentication systems and the replacement of these systems with smart cards and biometrics can greatly reduce the potential for a social engineering attack. Of course, this would also be very expensive and the cost must be weighed against the benefit.

Employees

Because people spend many hours each day with each other at their work location, they often share private information—such as network login information—with one another. It is also common to see that same login information on sticky notes under keyboards and on monitors. Another problem is that most computer users are not computer network or security savvy. For this reason, they might not recognize spyware, hack attempts, or social engineering.

If your SQL Server databases are new to your environment, employees may need to be reminded to protect the authentication information used with the SQL Server. Employees who are not educated about network security may not realize the dangers that unauthorized access via the network can pose to the organization and to them personally. Specifically, nontechnical employees who use the network should be aware of the fact that their computers can be attacked in a peer-to-peer fashion at work, at home, or on any public wireless network if the device uses wireless networking. Social engineers take advantage of all of these facts and even engineer elaborate stories that would fool almost anyone not specifically trained to recognize social engineering attacks.

Similar to social engineering is shoulder surfing. *Shoulder surfing* is a nontechnical way of capturing information. As its name implies, you will simply watch over the user's shoulder to see what information you can gather. Frequently, users enter their passwords slowly enough that you can see what they are typing. If the attacker is watching at the right moment, he may be able to see the user typing in her password as she accesses the SQL Server. Once again, this can be prevented with smart cards or fingerprint scanners.

In the preceding section, I mentioned smart cards and fingerprint scanners a few times. Smart cards usually require the entry of a PIN—effectively a password—in addition to the scanning of the smart card. This way, if the card is stolen, the cracker will still need the PIN. Be sure to remind your users that they should not write their PINs on their smart cards with a marker.

0-Day Hacks

In the end, you must stay up-to-date on the various vulnerabilities that may pose a threat to your network. You may have noticed that most of this chapter was not specific to Voice over Internet Protocol (VoIP) networks. VoIP networks are vulnerable to the same exploits as traditional wired and wireless networks. This does make your efforts somewhat easier if you're already familiar with network security; however, you must remember that the impact of security technologies can be detrimental on VoIP networks. As an example, the implementation of encryption for VoIP calls could be just enough to take your network latency to an unacceptable level. Balancing between security and performance is an important issue in VoIP networks.

The phrase *0-day hacks* is a reference to the newest attack methods in use. You will need to frequent websites mentioned in this chapter in order to keep your knowledge fresh.

Security Principles

Security principles lay the foundation of thinking on which all security solutions are based. So far, in this chapter, you've looked at the dark side of security. The focus has been on the threats and dangers that must be addressed. The next two chapters will deal with specific steps you can take to improve the security of your SQL Servers, so this chapter will leave you with a review of commonly recommended security principles and practices. The principles covered include:

- Start with good design.
- Trust, but monitor.

- Defense-in-depth
- Least privilege

Start with Good Design

The principle embodied in the phrase "start with good design" simply means that you should implement systems that are secure by default. You should implement systems that must be opened up in order to allow features and functions that are required. This is also called a *closed-to-open system*. At least three areas of the network should be considered:

- Network design and security
- Perimeter security solutions
- Connectivity solutions

Network Design and Security

Security should be designed into a system or network. It should not be an afterthought. You will have a more secure network when security is designed into the implementation from the start. Instead of thinking of specific attacks and specific countermeasures alone, you may want to consider security as a system, or rather as a group of independent but interrelated elements that form a whole.

A good example of the fact that security is a system is a bank vault. A bank vault is usually thought of as a single entity that helps to protect valuables, but it is actually a group of independent and interrelated elements. The vault combination lock is combined with procedures and policies as well as alarms and response mechanisms to form the whole of the bank vault. Additionally, many vaults are layered: one door opens the vault and smaller doors may open compartments within the vault.

Security design is about building systems and implementing layers that help to protect valuable assets. When you design a security system, you are designing a unique system that is aimed at keeping certain actions—attacks—from working. You are designing a system to protect against intelligent, intentional, and malicious attacks. This process is very different than safety management where you are protecting against unintentional problems that occur randomly. Security attacks may be intentional and occur during specially selected times that provide the attacker with the greatest opportunity.

Two key principles assist in security design: layered security and isolation. Layered security implies that more than one protection mechanism is used between an attack point and a valued resource. Layered security is sometimes called defense in depth. Isolation provides virtual or literal separation of one set of users or services from another set of users or services.

Perimeter Security Solutions

A demilitarized zone (DMZ) is a concept borrowed from military operations. It defines a portion of the network that is not as secure as the rest of the network. The DMZ is usually located between the private network and the Internet or another external network. DMZs are also known as perimeter networks because they exist at the edge of the private network. The DMZ acts as a location for Internet service servers and as a point of inspection and authentication for access into the internal or private network.

Most organizations will choose to place a firewall between the Internet and the DMZ. An additional firewall will usually be placed between the DMZ and the private network. This dual-firewall implementation allows for reduced restrictions at the ingress to the DMZ from the Internet and increased restrictions at the ingress from the DMZ to the private network.

Connectivity Solutions

Once a client is connected to the network, you can use virtual LANs (VLANs) to segment a physical network into multiple logical networks. VLANs operate within the switches and routers on your network, and client computers are usually unaware of their participation in a VLAN. To the client computers, the VLANs look and operate just like a physically segmented LAN. For this reason, VLANs can be used to provide increased security on converged networks.

If you've worked with VLANs, you know that devices in one VLAN cannot communicate with devices in another VLAN without the configuration of some sort of trunking protocol or routing solution. However, you should not assume that the segregation provided is a solid security solution by itself. VLAN protocols were not designed with security as the primary intent and can be compromised with the right knowledge.

An additional connectivity solution, discussed earlier in this chapter, is 802.1X port-based authentication. This security solution will disable an Ethernet port unless a user passes approved authentication data through the port. Once the client is authenticated, other nonauthentication data may be transferred through the port.

Trust, but Monitor

The security technologies presented in this chapter and the next two can help to protect your network from an attack; however, new attack methods are continually being developed and you must have a solution that allows you to monitor for both the older and newer attacks. The technologies that assist you with this effort include:

- Intrusion detection and intrusion prevention systems
- Antivirus and antispyware solutions

Intrusion Detection and Intrusion Prevention Systems

An intrusion detection system (IDS) detects many security-related incidents and logs the information. An IDS may notify an administrator of suspect activity. Incidents that may be detected by an IDS include unwanted connections, high bandwidth consumption, attacks based on signatures, and anomalies in network activity. Signature-based detection relies on patterns that exist within attack scenarios. Anomaly-based detection relies on comparisons with the baseline (normal operations) of network activity.

An intrusion prevention system (IPS) goes one step further than the IDS solution. Intrusion prevention systems may prevent an attack by disallowing connections from suspect devices or even shutting down services that are under attack.

 To see an example of an intrusion-detection or intrusion-prevention system, check out www.snort.org. Snort is an open source Linux and Windows IDS/IPS solution.

Antivirus and Antispyware Solutions

Although *virus* is a global term for a software-based attack, there are really individual types of attacks and it's important to understand each. Here are a few that you should become familiar with:

Virus: A computer program with the ability to regenerate itself is called a *virus*. A virus may or may not harm the infected computer. Viruses may lie dormant for some period of time before they attack the infected host machine.

Worm: A *worm* is a self-replicating application that requires no user action for reproduction. Viruses usually require human interaction in some way whereas worms do not.

Trojan Horse: Another type of malware is the Trojan horse (or simply the trojan). Named after the fabled gift in Homer's Odyssey that allowed the Greek army to conquer the Trojans, the Trojan horse enters the computer under the guise of a useful program or utility. Once in the machine, it may infect the machine with a virus or worm or it may download other trojans.

Spyware and Adware: Similar to the Trojan horse is the spyware or adware villain. Spyware is installed on your computer and reports back to the source. Adware is installed on your computer and causes unwanted ads to display on your screen. Additionally, spyware and adware combinations are common.

To protect your network from these malware applications, you will need to run antivirus and antispyware applications. There are two basic types of antimalware applications:

Ingress Applications: These reside at the entry point of the data.

Host-Based Antimalware Applications: These run on the host devices.

An example of an ingress antimalware application would be an email server scanner. This software would scan email messages as they enter (and possibly exit) the email server. If malware is detected, the message can be rejected, flagged as malware infected, or passed on without attachments.

Antivirus software must be maintained. You will need to download and apply new definition files frequently. Many antivirus applications include automatic update features so that the definitions can be maintained without the need for user interaction. The definition file includes the signatures that are used to identify known malware.

Choosing an antivirus solution is a complicated matter. Consider the following guidelines to help you in the decision process:

- Choose antivirus vendors that have quick response times. You don't want to be left without protection against a new virus for long periods of time.

- Choose antivirus software that is compatible with your environment. Many times antivirus software can cause stability problems for your servers. Make sure the software you choose does not cause system crashes.

- Choose antivirus software that can also protect against spyware and other malware if possible. Typically, antivirus and antispyware applications from different vendors do not play well together.

 I've had very good experiences with Symantec and Avast antivirus and antispyware products. However, it's important to test the products you choose against your production configurations.

Defense-in-Depth

Defense-in-depth (DiD) can be summarized by simply stating that you should never rely on one security solution alone. Do not rely only on your firewall for protection from Internet attacks. Do not rely only on Active Directory domain authentication to protect against internal attacks. Layer your security solutions to provide DiD. Layered security is a synonym for DiD. Consider the following list:

- User awareness
- Client security
- Network security
- Server security
- Perimeter security

Do you see the layers in this list? If the attacker gets through the perimeter security (firewall), maybe the internal client, network, or server security will stop him. If the attacker gains access to an internal client, maybe the network security will stop him. If the network security doesn't stop him, maybe the server security will. With DiD, the attacker must successfully penetrate through multiple layers of security in order to gain access to sensitive information.

Least Privilege

Least privilege is easily defined. When you abide by the principle of least privilege, you never give a user or system more access than it needs. Implementing least privilege is not always so easy. The SQL Server Agent is a perfect example of this. For example, assume that the SQL

Server Agent service account must be able to access the following resources in order for your jobs to work properly:

\\Server13\DataBack—Change permissions

\\Server19\Reporting—Read permissions

\\Server19\Analysis—Change permissions

\\Server23\Eng—Change permissions

\\Acct\FY09—Read permissions

\\Acct\FY10—Change permissions

\\Server13\SShot—Change permissions

\\Server4\Mkt—Read permissions

\\Server7\Mkt—Read permissions

Now, if you don't already have a group that has this exact permission set, it means you'll either have to create one just for the SQL Server Agent service account or provide these permissions to the account directly. Either way, it means adding nine different permissions. Imagine having to do this for a few thousand accounts for a few thousand users and services. It's time-consuming even if you abide by recommendations like Microsoft's that you assign permissions through groups as much as possible.

If you give the SQL Server Agent service account membership in the Domain Admins group, the service will be able to do everything it needs on all of these listed servers (assuming they are all members of the domain and default permissions are inherited and not overridden). That would be the easy road. It would also be amazingly insecure. Now, if an attacker does gain access to the SQL Server with the ability to create jobs, those jobs will run as a domain administrator—shiver at the thought. When running as a domain administrator, the attacker can do just about anything he desires.

Please, always abide by the principle of least privilege.

Summary

In this chapter, you built a foundation of fundamentals. You explored what security really is and what it is not. You discovered the threats, vulnerabilities, and exploits that can be used to attack your SQL Servers either directly or indirectly. Finally, you reviewed several security principles that can act as guiding navigators through the myriad of security technologies available today. In the next chapter, you'll look specifically at authentication and encryption. The topics are covered from both a theoretical and a very practical standpoint as related to SQL Server 2008.

The fact that vulnerabilities may be exploited by anyone who can read and follow instructions shows that system cracking is a science. It is a repeatable process that can be learned. Crackers are not some special genetic mutation in the human gene pool that have abilities others do not—as television shows and movies often portray them. Crackers are just normal people, usually with average IQs, who have focused their learning on the science of computing technology. Ask a cracker to plant a 400-acre farm and nurture it to harvest and, more often than not, very little of the crop will make it to market.

The preceding paragraph is not intended to belittle crackers, but to empower security practitioners. Many network administrators, DBAs, and PC technicians look at crackers as a mystical group with an ability they lack. The result is that they often throw up their hands in defeat and give up on providing strong security for their systems. This seems particularly true in smaller organizations where the IT professional is already stretched very thin.

There is hope. By frequenting security-related websites and reading books, like the one you're reading now, you can stay informed and better protect your systems. If you implement the best practices for securing SQL Server that are presented in Chapters 18 and 19, you will immediately have a much more secure environment. While this chapter lays a solid foundation to help you understand the fundamentals of security, the next two chapters give you the practical steps to implement secure SQL Server systems.

Chapter Essentials

Security Defined   Security is a complex topic that was briefly introduced in this chapter. If security is defined as an acceptable level of risk, rather than no risk, it may be achieved. Security involves the systems, people, and processes working together to achieve this acceptable level of risk.

Security Threats   Security threats are many. SQL Servers may be attacked from four major attack points. The first is the Windows Server operating system on which the SQL Server runs. The second is the SQL Server service itself. The third is the network infrastructure that allows for communications with the SQL Server. The final and fourth attack point is the client. The client may be a desktop or laptop computer or it may be another server that acts as the client to the SQL Server.

Security Principles   Security principles can act as guiding foundations as you build secure networks. Important security principles include: Start with good design; Trust, but monitor; Defense-in-Depth; and Least Privilege.

Chapter 18

Authentication and Encryption

TOPICS COVERED IN THIS CHAPTER:

- ✓ Understanding Authentication
- ✓ SQL Server Authentication Methods
- ✓ Logins, Users, and Roles
- ✓ Encryption

Two important components of security are authentication and confidentiality, which are accomplished through the use of encryption in data storage. *Authentication* helps to prove the identity of a user or system, and *encryption* helps to protect data and prevent unauthorized users from accessing or viewing it. This chapter will address authentication as a concept and how it is implemented in SQL Server specifically. Then it will turn to encryption, first addressing the concept of encryption to ensure your understanding of the basic concepts involved, and then exploring encryption solutions and implementation methods available in SQL Server 2008. When you've finished this chapter, you'll have a solid understanding of secure authentication and secure data storage in SQL Server.

Understanding Authentication

You use authentication every day of your life. When you are at a seminar or training event and the speaker says he is an expert on the topic of his speech, you use authentication mechanisms to verify this information. You listen to the information he delivers and use it to determine if he is truly an expert. You practice authentication in casual interactions too. For example, suppose someone walked up to you and said, "Hi, my name is Susan and I am tall." You would look at her and compare her height with a height you consider to be tall and authenticate whether she is truly tall or not. If she is not tall, by your standards, she will lose credibility with you.

Remember the word *credentials*? Consider other important "cred" words: credit and credibility. Do you see how they are related? They all have to do with having proof of something. When you have good credit, you have proof of your trustworthiness to pay debts. When you have credibility, you have proof that you are authentic, persuasive, and dynamic. When you have credentials, you have an object or the experience that proves your skill or identity. Authentication results in the verification of credentials.

Authentication should not be confused with authorization. *Authentication* can be defined as proving a person or object is who or what he or it claims to be. *Authorization* is defined as granting access to a resource by a person or object. Authorization assumes the identity has been authenticated. If authentication can be spoofed or impersonated, authorization schemes fail. From this, you can see why authentication is such an integral and important part of network and information security. When an attacker breaks your authentication system so that he is seen as an authenticated user, the authorization becomes irrelevant. Authentication must be strong if authorization is to serve its purpose.

One of the most important components of a security strategy is, therefore, an identity management system (IMS). An IMS provides a storage location for identity objects, typically called user accounts, and one or more methods for connecting to that storage location and proving identity ownership—a process known as authentication. User accounts are objects that identify users and are owned by users. The user accounts provide properties for use by authentication systems and network operating systems. Besides user accounts, certificates, biometrics, tokens, and other credentials may also be used for authentication or identity management.

Without a clear understanding of authentication and identity management, you will have difficulty installing a secure database system. Both basic and advanced authentication systems exist and many systems include the ability to support both. Windows Server systems allow for advanced authentication mechanisms through the Internet Authentication Service (Microsoft's RADIUS implementation) and basic authentication using simple passwords against the Active Directory database. Each method serves a valid purpose and is best for certain scenarios. When you determine which method is right for your scenario, you have taken the first step to secure authentication. The actual selection of the core authentication system, which is used to initially authenticate to the network, is a choice outside the scope of the SQL Server DBA's responsibility, but as the SQL Server DBA you must choose how users will authenticate to the SQL Server. Specific guidance for this decision is provided in the later section of this chapter titled "SQL Server Authentication Methods."

Once you've selected the appropriate advanced or basic authentication method, you must determine whom to authenticate. Will you only authenticate known or identified users or will you allow some level of anonymous access? In most cases, SQL Server is used only by identified users; however, the identified user may actually be a middle-tier application (such as a web application), which receives anonymous connections itself. The connection between the web application and the SQL Server is authenticated and is limited through authorization to only the needed data tables.

Advanced authentication systems generally utilize stronger credentials and better protection of those credentials than basic authentication systems. The strength and protection of the credential is determined by the effort it takes to exploit it. A password-protected credential is usually considered weak when compared with biometric-protected credentials. This, in some cases, is a misconception, because strength of authentication really depends on how the authentication information (the credential and proof of ownership) is sent across the network. If you were to implement a biometric system, such as a thumb scanner, and the client sent the credentials and proof of ownership (a unique number built from the identity points on the user's thumb) to the server in cleartext, it would be no more secure than a standard password-based system.

 I am not aware of any biometric authentication system that sends the authentication data as cleartext; however, if such a system existed, it would certainly offset any gains achieved through biometric credentials.

The key element, which will provide a truly strong authentication pathway, is the encryption or hashing of the user credentials, or at least the proof of identity information (for example, the password). This can be accomplished with Virtual Private Networking (VPN) technology or with well-designed authentication systems. One example of a well-designed authentication system is 802.1X with a strong EAP (extensible authentication protocol) type. 802.1X and EAP types are used to secure both wired and wireless connections at the network access level.

Advanced authentication is more secure than basic authentication because advanced mechanisms are used to protect the user's credentials. This usually means protecting a username and password pair, but it can also include protecting a user/certificate combination, a user/machine combination, or any other user/object combination used to identify a specific user. In addition to the extra protection offered by advanced authentication systems, when 802.1X-based systems are used, you have the benefit of standards-based technology. This means that hardware from many different vendors is likely to support the authentication process. Sometimes driver or firmware upgrades are required, but there is often a path which can be taken to implement the authentication mechanism.

Credentials

Many different credential solutions are available for securing your networks. It's important that you select the right solution for your needs. In this process, you will consider the primary features of a credential solution and whether you need a multifactor authentication system. In addition, you should be aware of the various credential types available to you.

A credential solution should provide a means of user or computer identification that is proportional to your security needs. You do not want to select a credential solution that places unnecessary burdens on the users and results in greater costs (of both time and money) than the value of the information assets you are protecting. You should evaluate whether the selected authentication solution provides for redundancy and integration with other systems, such as Active Directory. The system should also support the needed credential types, such as smart cards and/or biometrics. In addition, consider the following factors when selecting a credential solution:

- The method used to protect the credentials
- The storage location of the credentials
- The access method of the credential store

If an authentication system sends the credentials as cleartext, a protection method is effectively nonexistent. Advanced authentication systems will protect the user credentials by encrypting them or avoiding the transmission of the actual credentials in the first place. Instead of transmitting the actual credentials, many systems use a hashing process to encode at least the password. *Hashing* the passwords means that the password is passed through a one-way algorithm resulting in a fixed-length number. This number is known as the hash of the password or the message digest. The hash is stored in the authentication database and can be used as an encryption key for challenge text in a challenge/response authentication system. Traditional Windows domain authentication systems store password hashes in this way.

The credentials, both username and password (or hash) or certificates, must be stored in some location. This storage location should be both secure and responsive. It must be secure to protect against brute force attacks and it must be responsive to service authentication requests in a timely fashion. Certificates are usually stored in a centralized certificate store (known as a certificate server or certificate authority) as well as on the client using the certificate for authentication. Both locations must be secure or the benefit of using certificates is diminished. In addition to the standard certificate store, users may choose to back up their certificates to disk. These backups are usually password protected, but brute force attacks against the media store may reveal the certificate given enough time. For this reason, users should be well-educated in this area and understand the vulnerability presented by the existence of such backups.

Access methods vary by authentication system and storage method, but there are standards that define credential access methods. One example is LDAP (Lightweight Directory Access Protocol). LDAP is a standard method for accessing directory service information. This information can include many objects, but it usually includes authentication credentials. LDAP is used by Microsoft's Active Directory domain service, among other network operating systems.

 **Real World Scenario**

Choosing a Credential Solution

I was working with a warehousing service provider in western Ohio on a database project that involved users accessing the server from Windows and Linux machines. The organization needed to implement an authentication solution that was both secure and easy for the users to utilize. In order to comply with these demands, we had to implement Mixed Mode authentication and support both Windows logins and SQL logins. Of course, the internal administrators were concerned about the security of the SQL logins, so we called a meeting.

During the meeting I explained several methods that could be used to make the SQL logins just as secure as the Windows logins. The options I recommended included:

- Creating a VPN connection to the SQL Server before authenticating to the SQL Server

- Requiring IPSec associations to the SQL Server before authentication begins

- Using SQL Server through a secure web interface for the Linux clients

In the end, the organization chose to use the IPSec recommendation. IPSec is a standards-based solution that provides secure channels across which standard communications can flow. Windows servers support IPSec according to the standards, and this makes the solution an excellent one for organizations that must support Linux clients.

Sometimes, one type of authentication alone is not sufficient. In these cases, multifactor authentication can be used. Multifactor authentication is a form of authentication that uses more than one set of credentials. An example of a multifactor authentication process would be the use of both passwords and thumb scanners. Usually, the user would place her thumb on the thumb scanner and then be prompted for a password or PIN (personal identification number) code. The password may be used for network authentication or it may only be used for localized authentication before the thumb data is used for network authentication. However, in most cases the password and thumb data are used to authenticate to the local machine and then the network or just to the network alone. A common example of multi-factor authentication would be your ATM card. You have the card and you know the PIN (something you have and something you know).

Common Authentication Methods

Many common credential types and, therefore, authentication types exist. They include:

- Username and password
- Certificates
- Biometrics

Username and Password   Username and password pairs are the most popular type of credential. They are used by most network operating systems, including Novell Netware, Linux, Unix, and Windows. Of course, SQL Server supports password-based authentication—either indirectly through Windows logins or directly through SQL logins. Due to the human factor involved in the selection of the password, they often introduce a false sense of security. This is because the chosen password is usually too weak to withstand dictionary attacks and, depending on the length of the password, certainly brute force attacks. In addition, the passwords are often written down or stored in plaintext files on the system and then changed infrequently, resulting in a longer attack opportunity window. Usernames and passwords are addressed in detail in Chapter 17.

It is not uncommon to see passwords written down on notes and then attached to the display monitor of the user's computer. To prevent this, implement password use policies and educate users about the problems caused by such actions. Additionally, teach the users to create passwords that are easy to remember. See the sidebar in this chapter titled "Creating Strong Passwords" for more information.

Certificates   Certificates provide an alternative to username and password pairs. In order to use certificates throughout an organization, a certificate authority must exist. This certificate authority can be operated by the organization or an independent third party. In either case, the costs are often prohibitive to widespread use due to the need for an extra server or even a hierarchy of servers. Small and medium-sized organizations usually opt for server-only certificates or no certificates at all because of the cost of implementation. A full PKI (Public Key Infrastructure) would usually consist of more than one certificate authority. Each certificate authority would be a single server or cluster of servers. The PKI is the mechanism used for generation, renewal, distribution, verification, and destruction of user and machine certificates.

Biometrics   Yet another authentication credential is you. Biometrics-based authentication takes advantage of the uniqueness of every human and uses this for authentication purposes. For example, your thumb can be used as a unique identifier, as can your retina. The balancing of cost and security is important with biometric credentials. While hair analysis could potentially be used to authenticate a user, the cost and time involved is still too high for practical use. Today, both thumb scanners and retina scanners are becoming more popular.

Creating Strong Passwords

If you've been reading closely up to this point, you know that passwords can be a point of weakness in your SQL Server security. For that matter, they can be a point of weakness in the security of any system. If you must use passwords (and most of us must), there are three rules to making your passwords as secure as possible.

Create Password Policies   You should write password policies. Password policies describe an acceptable password from the perspective of number of characters, complexity, and length of life. Here's an example statement: A strong password is a complex password (including uppercase letters, lowercase letters, and digits or special characters) that is at least eight characters long and is changed every 30 days. This is just one example. For a more detailed example, see the Password Protection Policy template at http://www.sans.org/security-resources/policies/.

Enforce Your Password Policies   You should enforce the password policies where possible. Windows Active Directory Domain Service (AD DS) allows you to force users to create strong passwords. In Chapter 17, "Security Threats and Principles," I showed you how to access the password policies in a Windows domain. If you use the SQL Server Windows authentication mode, you can force these policies on the users for SQL Server as well. Starting with SQL Server 2005, you can also force SQL logins to use these same password rules.

Teach Users to Create Memorable Passwords   Although you can tell users a thousand times to keep their passwords secure and secret, people will continue to write them on sticky notes on monitors if they don't think they'll remember them. The best way to rectify this problem is to teach users to create passwords that are easy to remember. By doing this, you will reduce the number of passwords set out in the open for anyone to see. Here's an example of a password that is easy to remember: 9apec18C.

Now, you're probably wondering how 9apec18C is a password that is easy to remember. Let me help you out. It's my last name. Well, it's my last name passed through an algorithm. The algorithm is as follows. Start with a word that is at least six characters in length. Count the number of vowels in the word and multiply the number by 3. This is the first part of the password; when using carpenter as the input, the answer is equal to 9. Next, take the second, fourth, fifth, and first characters in the word for the second, third, fourth and fifth positions of the password, which is equal to apec, in this case. The next step is to count the total number of letters in the word and multiply by 2, which is equal to 18 for the word "carpenter." Finally, take the first letter of the starting word and capitalize it for the final character of the password. The end result is 9apec18C.

I know you're probably thinking that this is very time-consuming. Instead, it's actually very liberating. Here's why. You can write down the word that you use as the source of your password and never have to worry about it causing a security problem. Why? Because you're not going to use the exact algorithm I mentioned here. You may count the vowels and multiply by 4. Or you may use the word for the total number of vowels. Or you may count the vowels and divide by 2 and then multiply by 3 and then round down. Get the point? Just this one part of the algorithm could be altered in hundreds of ways. Literally trillions of possible algorithms exist.

In summary, teach users to create their own algorithm for password generation. Then, in the best scenario, they pick a word each month that they don't have to write down and pass it through the algorithm to reset their password. For the first week after changing the password, they may have to think for 30 to 45 seconds to regenerate the password—depending on the complexity of their algorithm, but they will have it memorized after that first week and will simply be able to log in. It's a simple method but very powerful and it's why I haven't forgotten a password in the last 10 years—I haven't memorized one. I simply have a few algorithms that I apply to the appropriate systems.

Regulatory Compliance

When implementing authentication, as well as other components of SQL Server security, you must consider applicable regulations. Governing bodies define and enforce regulations related to many different knowledge domains. Information has evolved to become an extremely valuable resource in modern economies. With this fact in mind, many regulatory agencies have defined regulations related to information management. For example, in the United States, the government has passed health information management policies as the HIPAA guidelines. As a database administration professional, you must understand the basics of these regulations in order to implement SQL Server solutions that comply with them. The PCI and HIPAA regulations demonstrate how you must be aware of regulatory compliance issues. PCI is common in the payment-processing industry, and HIPAA is very important in the healthcare industry.

WARNING You should know the basics of the PCI and HIPAA requirements for the 70-450 exam. You may see a few questions based on these regulations and the impact they have on your SQL Server database implementations.

PCI Compliance

Payment Card Industry (PCI) compliance is a statement of conformity to the PCI Data Security Standard (DSS), a worldwide information security standard. PCI DSS is a set of standards that help to ensure that companies processing payment cards (credit cards, debit cards, etc.) do so in a secure manner. The standards encompass payment card processing, storage, and information transfer, but they are also a great example for how an organization can institute good security practices.

The PCI DSS document is a 73-page document (version 1.2) that outlines the process of implementing a secure payment card processing environment. The document covers the following components:

- Building and maintaining a secure network

- Protecting cardholder data

- Maintaining vulnerability management programs

- Implementing strong access control measures

- Regularly monitoring and testing networks

- Maintaining an information security policy

After reading the security sections of this book, you'll immediately recognize most of these components as standard security best practices. Indeed, the only unique component is that of protecting cardholder data, and even that can be classified under the normal heading of protecting valuable data. In the end, there is nothing new in the PCI DSS document; however, more and more states and credit card companies are requiring compliance with it in order to process payment cards. At this point, the United States government does not require compliance with PCI DSS, but it probably will in the future. The good news is this: If you implement security best practices, you'll have very little to change in order to comply with PCI DSS.

The PCI DSS lists both recommended practices and required practices. The standard lists the following requirements for secure data storage:

- Keep cardholder data storage to a minimum. Develop a data retention and disposal policy. Limit storage amount and retention time to that which is required for business, legal, and/or regulatory purposes, as documented in the data retention policy.

- Do not store sensitive authentication data after authorization (even if encrypted).

- Do not store the full contents of any track from the magnetic stripe (located on the back of a card, contained in a chip, or elsewhere).

- Do not store the card-verification code or value (three-digit or four-digit number printed on the front or back of a payment card) used to verify card-not-present transactions.

- Do not store the personal identification number (PIN) or the encrypted PIN block.

- Render primary account number (PAN), at minimum, unreadable anywhere it is stored (including on portable digital media, backup media, in logs) by using any of the following approaches: one-way hashes based on strong cryptography, truncation, index tokens and pads (pads must be securely stored), or strong cryptography with associated key-management processes and procedures.

- If disk encryption is used (rather than file- or column-level database encryption), logical access must be managed independently of native operating system access control mechanisms (for example, by not using local user account databases). Decryption keys must not be tied to user accounts.

- Protect cryptographic keys used for encryption of cardholder data against both disclosure and misuse. Restrict access to cryptographic keys to the fewest number of custodians necessary. Store cryptographic keys securely in the fewest possible locations and forms.

- Fully document and implement all key-management processes and procedures for cryptographic keys used for encryption of cardholder data.

As you can see, to comply with PCI DSS, a database system that stores payment card processing must store as little information as possible about the payment card. The stored information should be encrypted, and the encryption should be based on a network authentication system outside of the single SQL Server (for example, Active Directory). The key-management processes should be documented in a policy, and the policy should be followed and audited.

 If you're interested in reviewing the PCI DSS standards more fully, you can do so at their website at https://www.pcisecuritystandards.org/.

HIPAA Compliance

The HIPAA regulations require that healthcare organizations (including hospitals, doctors, and any other organization that handles health information) implement policies and procedures to ensure that only authorized individuals may access patient health information. HIPAA stands for Health Insurance Portability and Accountability Act, and it was enacted within the United States in 2006. Organizations covered by the act and, therefore, required to comply include:

- Health plan providers

- Healthcare clearinghouses

- Any healthcare provider who transmits health information in electronic form

The health information protected by HIPAA includes all individually identifiable health information. This information is identified as information that is unique to an individual and related to the health of that individual. Examples include:

- Past, present, or future mental or physical health condition
- Healthcare that has been provided to the individual
- Healthcare payment information

Information classified as de-identified does not require compliance with HIPAA regulations. *De-identified* information is information that neither identifies a patient nor provides a foundational knowledge base on which a patient may be identified.

The HIPAA regulations are nonspecific, allowing organizations of differing sizes to implement appropriate security measures that result in the protection of health information. The general requirements include:

- Privacy policies and procedures must be documented.
- A privacy official must be designated to oversee the HIPAA regulation implementation and maintenance.
- All workforce members must be trained to understand and comply with the privacy policies.
- Mitigation efforts must be taken when privacy policies are breached.
- Effective data safeguards must be implemented.
- Complaint-processing procedures must be implemented.
- Patients must not be asked to waive privacy rights, and retaliation against complaints is not allowed.
- Privacy policies and incident documentation must be maintained for six years.

With an understanding of the HIPAA regulations, the only remaining question is this: How do these regulations apply to a SQL Server solution? The answer is simple. They apply to SQL Servers in the same way they apply to any database system. Regardless of the database system used, the following five security solutions should be used in order to effectively comply with HIPAA regulations:

- Authentication
- Authorization
- Confidentiality
- Integrity
- Nonrepudiation

All of these requirements can be met with SQL Server. Authentication is best provided through Windows Active Directory. Authorization is achieved through the use of roles or direct authorizations for logins and users. Confidentiality is accomplished through the use of encryption in data storage. Integrity is accomplished through consistency checks within the database. Nonrepudiation can be achieved with a combination of strong authentication and database auditing. Authentication, authorization, and encryption are covered in the remaining sections of this chapter. Integrity is an automatic part of the SQL Server database engine, and nonrepudiation is addressed through the use of auditing in Chapter 19, "Security Best Practices."

> HIPAA regulations are among the most commonly tested regulations on vendor exams when they mention things like "regulatory requirements," as exam 70–450 does. I've provided an overview of the HIPAA regulations here because you are likely to see them mentioned in a question or two, if you choose to take the exam.

SQL Server Authentication Methods

SQL Server supports two authentication modes: Windows mode and mixed mode. Here's a definition of each:

Windows Mode   When in Windows mode, a SQL Server only allows connections by users who are authenticated through the Windows Active Directory service or the local user account database on the SQL Server machine.

Mixed Mode   When in mixed mode, Windows users can be mapped to SQL Server logins, and SQL logins can be created directly in SQL Server. SQL logins are used, and therefore, mixed mode is required, when non-Windows clients need access to the SQL Server. For example, if a Linux or MAC OS client needs to access the SQL Server, SQL logins will usually be required.

SQL logins are not considered as secure as Windows logins. Windows users, for the most part, use Kerberos authentication today. Without getting into all the details of Kerberos authentication, let's just say that it is a very strong authentication system originally developed by MIT (Massachusetts Institute of Technology) in the early 1980s, and it has evolved since that time. Kerberos uses mutual authentication to validate clients and servers, and it is a token-based system. You receive a token when you log on and can utilize resources based on the information within the token. All Windows clients, since Windows 2000 Professional, may use Kerberos. If they log on to a Windows 2000 or later domain, they will be logging on with Kerberos authentication.

SQL logins do not use the strong authentication used by Kerberos-based Windows clients. First, SQL logins store the login name and password (although in an encrypted format) in the master database on the SQL Server. Second, SQL Server handles the authentication directly.

You should avoid SQL logins when you can. If you must use SQL logins, consider using some form of lower-layer network encryption, such as IPSec. For example, with the proper client software installed, a Linux or MAC client could create an IPSec association with the SQL Server before logging into the SQL Server. The IPSec association would secure the channel across which the SQL login authentication occurs. Now, the authentication will be as secure as Kerberos because the authentication takes place in a secure channel.

You can also use Secure Sockets Layer (SSL) to secure SQL Server connections. SSL is less flexible, in my opinion, than IPSec from a SQL Server perspective, but it is an option. You can enable SSL in the SQL Server Configuration Manager once you've imported a Server Authentication certificate into the local certificate store.

Logins, Users, and Roles

You will ultimately build your authentication and authorization solution for SQL Server through the use of logins, users, and roles. The logins will get the users into the SQL Server system. The user objects will get the users into the databases, and the roles will define what they can do in the databases. When the rubber meets the road and you're ready to start configuring authentication for SQL Server 2008, you will need to be able to perform three basic tasks:

1. Configure the authentication mode.
2. Create and manage principals and roles.
3. Create and manage database users.

Before you can begin granting permission to securables in your databases, you will need to have some principals to which you can grant the permissions. *Principals* are the entities that access the resources within the SQL Server. The principals access securables. *Securables* are the entities that exist in the SQL Server, such as databases, tables, and views. You grant permissions to principals on securables. For example, you may grant the SELECT permission to a user named Fred on the dbo.Sales table in a database. In this section, you will learn how to configure the authentication mode and create SQL logins, Windows logins, and SQL Server roles.

Configuring the Authentication Mode

In order to create and use SQL logins as opposed to Windows logins, you must be running SQL Server in mixed mode. Whether the SQL Server is running in mixed mode or

Windows mode is determined by a Registry entry. You can modify this Registry entry with SQL Server Management Studio, as you will see later in Exercise 18.1, or it can be viewed using REGEDIT from the Start ➢ Run option. Figure 18.1 shows this Registry entry. The full location on a default instance of SQL Server 2008 is as follows:

```
HKEY_LOCAL_MACHINE\SOFTWARE\Microsoft\Microsoft SQL Server\
MSSQL10.MSSQLServer\MSSQLServer
```

FIGURE 18.1   Viewing LoginMode in REGEDIT

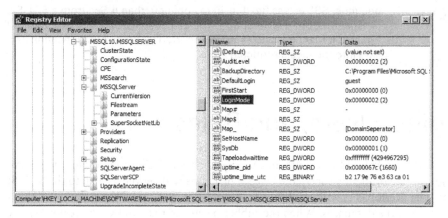

The value at this location is LoginMode. When this Registry entry is set to 1, the SQL Server is in Windows authentication mode. When it is set to 2, it is in mixed authentication mode and can support SQL logins.

On Windows XP machines running SQL Server Express edition, this Registry key path may vary slightly, but you will find it in a similar location and it will be named LoginMode. The best thing to do in such situations is to search the Registry for the value named LoginMode. This book assumes you are running SQL Server on Windows Server. Remember, if you do not have full versions of these products, both the SQL Server and Windows Server software packages are available in trial editions from Microsoft.

Because different instances of SQL Server 2008 will use a different Registry path, you can use the following little-known stored procedure to modify the Registry entry if you must do it through code:

```
EXEC xp_instance_regwrite 'HKEY_LOCAL_MACHINE',
'Software\Microsoft\MSSQLServer\MSSQLServer',
'LoginMode', REG_DWORD, 2
```

You may notice that the stored procedure is called xp_instance_regwrite. The procedure name gives away its purpose. It is used to modify a Registry entry related to the configuration of the currently accessed instance. The code here will configure the authentication mode to mixed mode. If you want to set the authentication mode to Windows only, change the 2 to a 1 at the end of the command. You will need to stop and restart the SQL Server service after making this change.

This Registry setting can also be configured in SSMS. Exercise 18.1 steps you through the process of configuring the authentication mode in the SSMS application. This is the preferred way to modify this Registry entry because there is less risk of a mistake that could cause a major problem on your system. If you configure the server to support mixed logins, you can create SQL logins using either SSMS or SQL statements.

EXERCISE 18.1

Configuring the Authentication Mode in SSMS

In this exercise, you will configure the authentication mode for the SQL Server instance. You will ensure that the authentication mode is set to mixed mode so that the remaining exercises in this chapter will function properly. To do this:

1. Launch SSMS.

2. Right-click on the SQL Server instance you want to configure and select Properties.

3. Select the Security page to view the authentication mode settings.

4. Ensure that the authentication mode is set to SQL Server and Windows authentication mode, which is mixed mode.

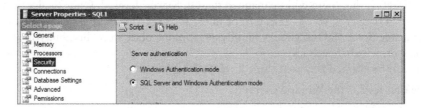

5. Click OK to save the changes.

6. If you see a message indicating that the service must be restarted, right-click on the instance and select Restart.

Creating and Managing Principals and Roles

Principals are referenced in SQL Server 2008 in different ways depending on the level at which they exit. You manage two general categories of principals: indivisible and collections.

Indivisible Principals   An *indivisible principal* is an entity that exists independently of other entities. Examples of indivisible principals include SQL logins and Windows logins.

Collection Principals   A *collection principal* is a principal that actually represents a collection of entities that are treated as one even though each entity exists as an individual. A Windows group is an example of a collection principal.

Three layers (levels) of security can be managed in SQL Server deployments: Windows, SQL Server, and the databases. At each of these levels, the following principals can be defined and managed.

- Windows-level principals
    - Domain logins
    - Local system logins
- SQL Server–level principals
    - SQL logins
    - Windows mapped logins
- Database-level principals
    - Users
    - Roles
    - Application roles

It is important to keep in mind that a principal is only represented at each of these levels. For example, if you are a user who has access to a SQL Server database, you will be referenced—either individually or through a collection—at the SQL Server– and database-levels at a minimum. You may be referenced at all three levels. If you log in to a Windows domain (level 1), that login will be mapped to SQL Server (level 2). Once the login is mapped to SQL Server, you will need to be given access to the database either as a user or through a role (level 3). Of course, you only exist in one place in reality, but you are refer-enced as a principal at each level.

Users can be granted access at three levels in SQL Server:

- The first level is the Windows server.
- The second level is the SQL Server service.
- The third level is the individual database to which the user is granted access.

Remember that security starts at the operating system level. It is also important to remember that it is possible to give a user access to one database on a SQL Server instance and not give access to any others.

A large part of your job as a DBA or developer will be to ensure that the right users have the right access in the right way. To do this, you will need to know about the functionality and implementation of the following principal management objects:

- SQL logins
- Windows logins
- Fixed server roles
- Fixed database roles
- Custom database roles
- Application roles

You will use SQL Logins for users who do not access the SQL Server from a Windows domain client. You will use Windows logins for users who access the SQL Server from a Windows domain client. Windows logins are more secure due to the improved authentication systems employed in Windows Active Directory domains. You will need to understand how to create these objects, configure them, and apply them to the appropriate locations. You will find details on how to do this in the sections that follow.

SQL Logins

SQL logins are created in, and only exist in, the SQL Server service. These logins are actually stored in the master system database, so you have another good reason for backing up the database. You can query the view related to SQL logins by opening a new query window and executing the following code:

```
USE master;
SELECT * FROM sys.syslogins;
```

Figure 18.2 shows the results of this query. As you can see, the passwords are stored in an encrypted format that cannot be viewed directly. However, you should not be fooled by this. The password is sent across the network in a basic format that is generated by XORing the password. An XOR algorithm simply flips bits at the binary level, and you don't really have to understand the complexities of the algorithm to understand that it is really a simple process. Ones become zeros and zeros become ones, depending on the pattern matches. The process is easily reversed. If you must use SQL logins, remember to use SSL or IPSec to encrypt the channel before the login occurs.

FIGURE 18.2   Viewing the sys.syslogins table that contains the logins within the SQL Server

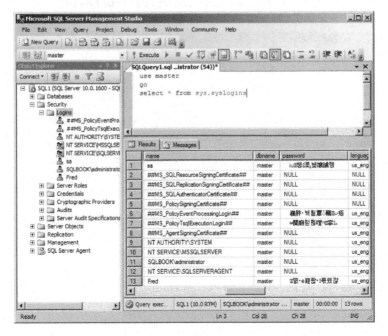

SQL logins are useful when you are not in a Windows domain, do not want to use a domain, do not want to use local system logins, or need to support clients that cannot log in with Windows accounts, as with some non-Microsoft operating systems.

The basic command to create a SQL login using SQL statements is

```
CREATE LOGIN fred WITH PASSWORD = '87967fb7Hr4Z';
```

This command will create a SQL login for fred with a password of 87967fb7Hr4Z. You can also specify that the user must change his password at the first login using the MUST_CHANGE option. In order for the MUST_CHANGE option to work, CHECK_EXPIRATION must be set to ON.

Creating logins in the SSMS GUI is also very simple. Exercise 18.2 provides the instructions for creating SQL logins.

EXERCISE 18.2

Creating a SQL Login

In this exercise, you will create a SQL login for a user named Monty with a password of 7Pass8now.

1. Launch SSMS.

2. Expand the Security section in Object Explorer.

3. Right-click the Logins container and select New Login.

4. Enter the word **Monty** in the Login name field.

5. Check the SQL Server authentication radio button.

6. Enter **7Pass8now** in both the Password and Confirm Password fields.

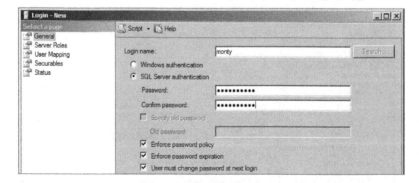

7. Accept all other defaults, click the selector arrow next to the Script button, and choose Script Action to New Query Window.

8. Click the OK button. (If you are running SQL Server on Windows XP, you may have to clear the User Must Change Password at Next Login check box.)

9. Notice the code in the new query window is similar to the following:

```
CREATE LOGIN [monty] WITH PASSWORD=N'7Pass8now ' MUST_CHANGE,
DEFAULT_DATABASE=[master], CHECK_EXPIRATION=ON, CHECK_POLICY=ON
```

As you can see, after performing the steps in Exercise 18.1, you can specify the default database and determine how you will use password policies. It is important to note the Enforce Password Policy check box. If it is checked, the password you enter must meet the requirements of the Windows password policies—even though the login is a SQL login and not a Windows login. These policies will either come from the domain in which the SQL Server is a member or, if it's not in a domain, the local password policies. Local password policies can be viewed by performing the steps in Exercise 18.3.

EXERCISE 18.3

Viewing Local Password Policies

In this exercise, you will view the password policies on a non–domain member server that is running SQL Server 2008. Domain member SQL Servers receive their password policies from the domain. Only the Domain Admins and the Enterprise Admins group members can manage the domain password policies. To view the local password policies, follow these steps:

1. Click Start and select Run.

2. Type **gpedit.msc** into the Open field and click OK.

3. In the Local Computer Policy\Computer Configuration section, expand the Windows Settings container.

4. Expand the Security Settings container.

5. Expand the Account Policies container.

6. Click on the Password Policy container. From here, you can view and manage the local password policies.

While Exercise 18.3 will get you to the location of the password policies, it is also important that you know what these policies mean. Table 18.1 provides descriptions of each password policy available; these are also shown in Figure 18.3. If you need to manage domain policies, you will have to be a Windows domain administrator. If you are, you can use the Group

Policy feature in the Windows domain to administer the policies. If you are not, you will need to ask the Windows domain administrator to inform you of the policies. You can also use the Windows XP command-line tool GPRESULT to generate a list of the applied policies.

FIGURE 18.3   Viewing the local password policies

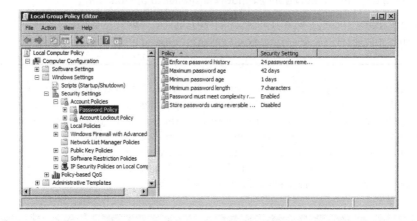

TABLE 18.1   Password Policy Descriptions and Recommendations

Policy	Description	Recommendation
Enforce password history	Determines the number of unique new passwords that must be associated with a user account before an old password may be reused. The value must be between 0 and 24 passwords.	Typically, three or more unique passwords are required in order to prevent users from reusing passwords too soon after the first use.
Maximum password age	Determines the period of time (in days) that a password can be used before the system requires that it be changed. A password can be set to expire after a number of days between 1 and 999, or the value can be set to 0, which indicates that passwords do not expire.	The passwords are usually set to expire somewhere between 30 and 60 days.
Minimum password age	Determines the period of time the user must wait before voluntarily changing the password. This setting is used to prevent users from quickly resetting their passwords the number of times required to set it right back to what it was.	The minimum password age is typically set to be something more than five days, but it must be less than the maximum password age.

TABLE 18.1   Password Policy Descriptions and Recommendations *(continued)*

Policy	Description	Recommendation
Minimum password length	Determines the minimum length that the password must be. If Password Must Meet Complexity Requirements is enabled, the password length must be at least 6 characters or the value of this setting, whichever is greater	In secure environments, this setting is typically set to a value between 6 and 10 characters. Highly secure environments will usually require between 8 and 10 characters.
Password must meet complexity requirements	Requires that passwords be at least 6 characters and contain three of four character types: upper case letters, lower case letters, digits, and special characters (i.e., $, #, !, etc.).	It is recommended that this setting be enabled. Otherwise, users can use words, which can be cracked in just a few minutes—even seconds—with dictionary cracking techniques.
Store passwords using reversible encryption	Determines whether the operating system stores passwords using reversible encryption. If an application uses protocols that require knowledge of the user's password for authentication purposes, this setting must be enabled. This policy is required when using Challenge-Handshake Authentication Protocol (CHAP) authentication through remote access or Internet Authentication Services (IAS). It is also required when using Digest Authentication in Internet Information Services (IIS).	Storing passwords using reversible encryption is essentially the same as storing plaintext versions of the passwords. For this reason, this policy should never be enabled unless application requirements outweigh the need to protect password information. SQL Server 2008 does not require that this setting be enabled.

Windows Logins

Windows logins take advantage of the Windows Server Active Directory Domain Services (or simply Active Directory). Active Directory logins originating from Windows 2000 and later client systems use Kerberos authentication, which is a very secure authentication solution. For this reason, Windows logins are considered more secure than SQL logins.

Windows logins are created in the local system database or the domain database and are then mapped to SQL Server for treatment as principals. Windows logins are considered to be more secure than SQL logins because they can use Kerberos for authentication and are restricted by all the policies and parameters of Windows logins. Of course, if you are not using a Windows domain and Windows clients, this becomes irrelevant very quickly.

If you plan to take the 70-432 and 70-450 exams, remember that Windows logins are considered more secure than SQL logins. If you can use Windows logins, you should always choose them over SQL logins.

Windows logins, created in SQL Server, can map to a Windows user account or a Windows group account. When using a Windows user account, a single user is granted the right to access the SQL Server service. When using a Windows group account, all members of the group are granted the right to access the SQL Server service unless they are restricted by their user accounts. In other words, a user may be mapped to the SQL Server service by both his user account and a group to which he belongs. In this case, he can be denied access as a user, which will override any access rights given through the group. Exercise 18.4 provides instructions for creating Windows logins in SQL Server 2008.

EXERCISE 18.4

Creating Windows Logins

In this exercise, you will create a Windows login by first creating a Windows user account and then a Windows group account. Next, you will map these accounts to a Windows login in SQL Server 2008. To do this, follow these steps. Please note that this exercise assumes the use of local users and groups on Windows Server 2008.

1. Right-click My Computer on your SQL Server machine's desktop and select Manage.

2. Expand the Configuration container and then the Local Users and Groups container.

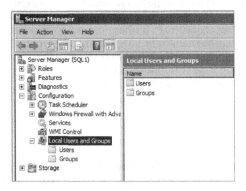

3. Right-click the Users container and select New User.

4. Enter **Jeremy** in the User Name field.

5. Enter **7Pass8now** in both the Password and Confirm Password fields.

6. Deselect the User Must Change Password at Next Logon check box.

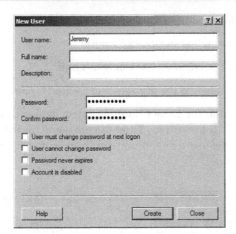

7. Click the Create button to create the user account. Click the Close button to close the dialog.

8. Right-click the Groups container and select New Group.

9. For the Group name field, enter **SQLUsers**.

10. In the Description field, enter **Users with access to SQL Server**.

11. Click the Create button to create the group.

12. Click the Close button to close the New Group dialog.

13. Close the Server Manager application.

EXERCISE 18.4 *(continued)*

14. Launch SQL Server Management Studio.

15. Expand the Security container in Object Explorer.

16. Right-click the Logins container and select New Login.

17. Click the Search button to find the account you created for Jeremy.

18. Type **Jeremy** in the Enter the Object Name to Select field and click the Check Names button. The dialog will automatically enter the full name for the user, which includes the server name and the username. A domain user would have a format like this: *domainName\userName*.

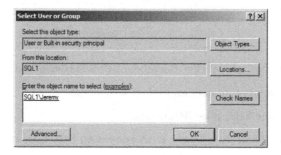

19. Click OK.

20. In the New Login dialog, click OK again to create the mapping to the Windows user account.

21. To create the mapping for the SQLUsers group, right-click the Logins container and select New Login.

22. Click the Search button to search for the SQLUsers group.

23. Click the Object Types button to bring up the Object Types dialog box and then check the Groups check box (the other check boxes will already be checked) and then click OK.

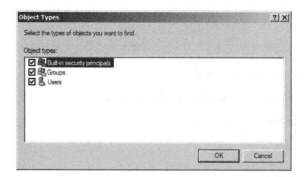

24. Type **SQLUsers** in the Enter the Object Name to Select field and click the Check Names button.

25. Click the OK button.

26. Click the OK button in the New Login dialog to create the group-based login.

Fixed Server Roles

Users and groups are principals that can be given rights to access the SQL Server and, eventually, permissions to access databases and database securables, such as tables and views. You can also use roles to make it easier to manage security inside of SQL Server. Three basic types of roles are available: server roles, database roles, and application roles (application roles are really just a type of database role). All server roles are fixed roles. They exist as soon as you've finished installing SQL Server 2008 and allow you to grant various administrative-type capabilities to the users and groups that access your SQL Server instance.

Fixed server roles are permission and rights collections that apply to the entire SQL Server instance. Fixed server roles cannot be modified or deleted, but you can add new members to the roles. Following is a list that summarizes the fixed server roles.

BulkAdmin: Can launch the BULK INSERT statement.

DBCreator: Can create and alter the user databases.

DiskAdmin: Can manage the files on disk.

ProcessAdmin: Can manage the processes running as part of the instance of SQL Server.

Public: Provides universal roles for all logins. When no other permissions are granted, the permissions of the public role will provide a minimum set of capabilities.

SecurityAdmin: Can manage server logins.

ServerAdmin: Can manage server-wide settings.

SetupAdmin: Can execute the stored procedure sp_serveroption and create or remove linked servers.

SysAdmin: Can do anything in SQL Server. This role is equivalent to all other fixed server roles combined.

You can add a login, either SQL logins or Windows logins, to a fixed server role using the sp_addsrvrolemember stored procedure. For example, to add the user Jeremy to the bulkadmin role, issue the following SQL command:

```
EXEC sp_addsrvrolemember [servername\Jeremy], bulkadmin;
```

You will need to change servername to the name of your server because Jeremy is a Windows login.

You can also add a user to a fixed server role by double-clicking on the user and then selecting the Server Roles page. Here you can check the role you want the user to fill, as shown in Figure 18.4.

FIGURE 18.4 Managing Server Role membership within user properties

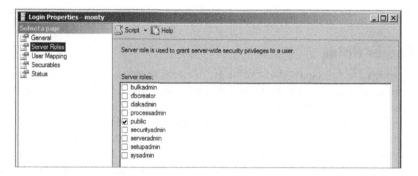

Fixed Database Roles

A fixed database role is a collection of permissions and rights that exist at the database level. Just as the SQL Server has fixed roles at the server level, pre-existing fixed database roles exist in every database you create. These roles are explained in the following list:

DB_AccessAdmin: Can alter any user and create schemas.

DB_BackupOperator: Can back up the database or the log, or force a checkpoint to occur.

DB_DataReader: Can execute SELECT statements against the database.

DB_DataWriter: Can execute INSERT, UPDATE, and DELETE statements against the database.

DB_DDLAdmin: Can execute most CREATE and ALTER statements against the database.

DB_DenyDataReader: Cannot execute SELECT statements against the database.

DB_DenyDataWriter: Cannot execute INSERT, UPDATE, or DELETE statements against the database.

DB_Owner: Can perform all configuration and maintenance activities on the database including the DROP DATABASE command.

DB_SecurityAdmin: Can ALTER application roles or custom roles and execute CREATE SCHEMA.

Public: All users belong to this role, and the public role cannot perform any actions on a newly created database by default.

The special guest user account is also a member of the public role and, therefore, anything the public role can do the guest user can do. By default, there is no guest account in a newly created database.

It is important to note that members of both the db_owner and db_securityadmin roles can manage memberships in the fixed database roles, but the db_owner is the only role that can add or remove members from the db_owner role. To add a user to a role, use the sp_addrolemember stored procedure, as shown here:

```
EXEC sp_addrolemember db_securityadmin, 'servername\Jeremy';
```

Finally, in relation to fixed database roles, it is essential that you understand how you would use the db_denydatareader and db_denydatawriter roles. You may wonder why you would need to deny access to a user by placing him in these roles, but the answer lies in the hierarchical structure of security. Imagine a user named Barney belongs to a group named Redrock. Now imagine that the Redrock group has been added to the SQL Server as a Windows login and has been granted membership in the db_datareader role for a database. Further imagine that Barney should not have access to the data in this database. You can add Barney to the db_denydatareader role and effectively deny him access while easily granting all other members access to the data through the Redrock login. Deny always wins. This is an important security standard to keep in mind throughout your Microsoft-based systems.

Custom Database Roles

Sometimes the fixed database roles are not specific enough for your needs. In these situations, you can create a custom database role and grant to the role only the permissions you desire. To create a custom database role, use the simple CREATE ROLE command from a new query window in SSMS. For example, if you want to create a new role called accountants, just issue this command:

```
CREATE ROLE accountants;
```

This creates the role, and you would then use the same sp_addrolemember stored procedure referenced in the fixed database roles section earlier.

Application Roles

Application roles are useful when you want to ensure that users are using no other application to access the SQL Server database. You first create the application role and then configure the application to use the role. In your role as the DBA, you will not have to configure the application to use the role, but the client application will make a call to the sp_setapprole stored procedure to authenticate as the application role. Applications roles simply have a name and a password. They are then managed, as far as permissions, like any other role. To create an application role as the DBA, use the following code as an example:

```
CREATE APPLICATION ROLE app_role_name WITH PASSWORD='7Pass8now';
```

So far you have focused on creating all the roles, custom and application, using SQL code. In Exercise 18.5, you'll see the step-by-step instructions for creating a database role using SSMS.

EXERCISE 18.5

Creating a Database Role with SSMS

In this exercise, you will perform the simple steps required to create a database role using SSMS. To do this:

1. Expand the Databases container.

2. Expand the container for the database in which you want to create a custom or application role.

3. Expand the Security container and right-click on the Roles container to select New ≻ Database Role or New ≻ Application Role.

The following graphic shows the results of creating a new database role in SSMS.

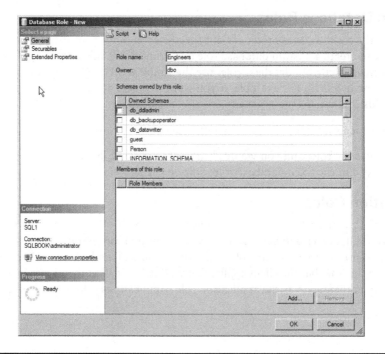

Creating Database Users

In order for the users to access a database, they must have a login and a user account in the database. The user account in the database is mapped to the login of the same name, by default, in the server instance. You can map a user to a different login name, but the most common action is to create a login at the instance level and then create a user with the same name at the database level.

Database users are created using the same basic process as logins. Instead of creating the account at the instance level, using the Security node, you will create the account at the database level. Exercise 18.6 provides instructions for creating a database user.

EXERCISE 18.6

Creating a Database User

In this exercise, you will create a database user. You will create the user with the CREATE USER T-SQL command. You will also create an account for a user named Fred in the database named Books. To do this, follow these steps:

1. Launch SQL Server Management Studio.

2. Connect to the SQL Server instance containing the database in which you want to create a user. Log in as an administrator.

3. Click the New Query button.

4. In the new query window, enter the following code.

```
USE Books;
GO
CREATE USER fred;
GO
```

5. Click the Execute button to run the code.

Understanding Encryption

The process of converting data from its normal state to an unreadable state is known as *encryption*. The unreadable state is known as ciphertext (or cipherdata), and the readable state is plaintext (or plaindata). The normal way to encrypt something is to pass the data through an algorithm using a key for variable results. For example, say you want to protect the number 108. Here is an algorithm for protecting numeric data:

```
original data / crypto key + (3 x crypto key)
```

Using this algorithm to protect (encode or encrypt) the number 108 with a key of 3, you come up with this:

```
108 / 3 + (3 x 3) = 45
```

In order to recover the original data, you must know both the algorithm and the key. Needless to say, modern crypto algorithms are much more complex than this, and keys are much longer, but this overview gives you an idea of how things work with data encryption.

Encryption is used in SQL Server to secure data in storage. You can encrypt data through application code or you can encrypt data transparently. In addition, you can use operating system–level encryption solutions such as BitLocker and the Encrypting File System (EFS).

SQL Server has not always supported encryption out-of-the-box. In fact, before SQL Server 2005, you had to use third-party add-ons to encrypt any data at all. SQL Server 2005 introduced column-level encryption and then SQL Server 2008 added Transparent Data Encryption (TDE).

Whatever encryption solution you choose, it is essential that the encryption key store be protected. For this reason, many organizations choose to implement a public key infrastructure (PKI), which is used to securely store encryption keys in certificates using a hierarchy of authentication and authorization that is difficult to penetrate.

SQL Server Encryption Solutions

Encryption is provided at three levels in SQL Server: the Windows operating system, the SQL Server, and the databases. In addition, SQL Server can take advantage of a Public Key Infrastructure in your environment or use externally signed keys from third-party cryptographic providers. SQL Server provides encryption in one of two ways today: column-level encryption and Transparent Data Encryption (TDE). In order to understand the requirements for encryption in SQL Server 2008, you must understand the basics of encryption hierarchies and Public Key Infrastructures. These topics are addressed in the following two sections.

Encryption Hierarchies

Windows provides the DPAPI (data protection application programming interface) for encryption of the SQL Server master key. The SQL Server master key, known as the service master key, is used to encrypt and secure all database keys and certificates for extra security. This service master key should be backed up to avoid a situation where the master key is lost, making all other keys inaccessible. This key can be backed up using the BACKUP SERVICE MASTER KEY command.

Each database can also have a master key known as the database master key. This key is used to generate and secure symmetric and asymmetric keys for the actual encryption of data. Symmetric keys are more efficient for encryption, but asymmetric keys are considered to be more secure. A certificate is a digitally signed statement that binds the value of a public key to the identity of a person, device, or service that holds the corresponding private key. Data encrypted with a private key can be decrypted with the complementary public key, and the same is true in reverse. Certificates usually contain the following:

- Public key
- Identity information for the owner such as name and/or email address
- A validity period
- Identity and digital signature of the issuer

At the database level, functions are provided that allow for the encryption and decryption of data using the keys generated for encryption in the database. In the end, the service master key secures the database master keys and the database master keys secure the encryption keys and certificates used to actually encrypt the data.

As you can imagine, with this hierarchy, encryption will demand an overhead beyond normal server operations. This means you will have to consider the impact encryption will have on the performance of your databases. Sometimes, using a lesser strength encryption (DES instead of AES), you can strike a balance between performance and security. Ultimately, you must provide encryption strengths that comply with three demands:

Regulations   If you are required to comply with HIPAA or PCI regulations, you must implement an encryption solution that meets the minimum requirements of these regulations. You may also have to comply with additional regulations not mentioned here. In the end, you must implement hardware and software that can comply with regulation demands and the performance you require.

Policies   Many organizations have security policies. If your organization has such policies, you must comply with the requirements they set forth. It is common for security policies to require 128-bit encryption solutions today.

Performance   You must ensure that the encryption you implement does not result in a poorly performing system. Encryption will always degrade the performance of any system when compared to the same system on the same hardware without encryption; therefore, you must counter the performance impact with increased hardware capacity to compensate for it.

Public Key Infrastructures

Microsoft's Certificate Services, which runs on Windows 2000, Windows 2003, and Windows 2008 servers, can be used to implement a public key infrastructure (PKI). SQL Server can take advantage of such a PKI and use the certificates it provides for encryption purposes. However, installation and management of Certificate Authorities is beyond the scope of this resource. For more information see the book *Mastering Windows Server 2008 R2*.

Implementing Application-Level Encryption

Now that you understand the features related to encryption that are available in SQL Server 2008, you will need to understand how to utilize them. First, you *must* back up the service master key before encrypting any data. This allows you to prevent massive re-encryption of data, which can be very processor-intensive. Here's how you do that (the c:\data folder must exist):

```
USE master;
BACKUP SERVICE MASTER KEY TO FILE='c:\data\keybak.key'
ENCRYPTION BY PASSWORD='2006Sept01tdc';
```

This code, issued in a new query window, will back up the service master key to the file keybak.key in the root of the C: drive. You should probably store this file on a secure media in a secure location. The file will be protected by the password 2006Sept01tdc. To restore this key, use the following code in a new query window:

```
USE master;
RESTORE SERVICE MASTER KEY FROM FILE='c:\data\keybak.key'
DECRYPTION BY PASSWORD='2006Sept01tdc';
```

Please back up this service master key before you start using encryption. If you do not back up this key, the data will have to be encrypted again in order to maintain security.

You can optionally encrypt data in a database using application code. The first thing you will have to do is create a master key for encryption in the database. The following code provides an example:

```
USE Books;
IF NOT EXISTS
    (SELECT * FROM sys.symmetric_keys WHERE symmetric_key_id=101)
    CREATE MASTER KEY
        ENCRYPTION BY PASSWORD='938498937#$jHJh7YUsy7jjj$#nj';
```

This code results in an encryption master key that uses the string 938498937#$jHJh7YUsy7jjj$#nj to encrypt. Next, you'll need to create a certificate that will be used to encrypt the symmetric key, which is the key that will actually encrypt the data. The following code will generate a certificate:

```
USE Books;
CREATE CERTIFICATE BookCert
WITH SUBJECT='For encryption in Books DB';
```

The certificate will be named BookCert and is described as providing encryption in Books DB. You created the Books database earlier in the book. Now you can create the symmetric key that will be used to encrypt data columns:

```
Use Books;
CREATE SYMMETRIC KEY colEncrypt
WITH ALGORITHM=AES_256
ENCRYPTION BY CERTIFICATE BookCert;
```

The key is named colEncrypt and uses AES encryption at 256 bits. You will store the symmetric key with encryption using the BookCert certificate. At this point, the encryption key hierarchy is in place and data can be encrypted.

 If you attempt to create a symmetric encryption key on Windows XP running SQL Server, you will have to change WITH ALGORITHM=AES_256 to WITH ALGORITHM=DES.

If you have created a table named Encryption with a column named Test and another named Unencrypted, you encrypt the data in that column using the following code:

```
USE Books;
OPEN SYMMETRIC KEY colEncrypt
DECRYPTION BY CERTIFICATE BookCert;
UPDATE dbo.Encryption
SET Test = EncryptByKey(Key_GUID('colEncrypt'), 'This will be encrypted');
```

The code will store the text This will be encrypted in the Test column for every row in the table. Figure 18.5 shows the results of a query against this table once encryption is in place. Notice the encrypted data in the Test column.

FIGURE 18.5   Viewing encrypted data without decrypting it

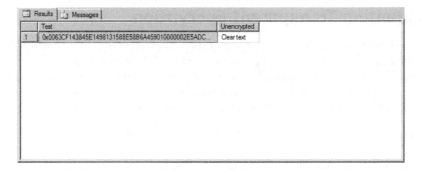

You're probably wondering how you would access this encrypted information. The solution is to use the DecryptByKey function as in the following code:

```
OPEN SYMMETRIC KEY colEncryption
DECRYPTION BY CERTIFICATE BookCert;


SELECT  Unencrypted,
        CONVERT(varchar, DecryptByKey(Test)) As 'Plain Text Test'
FROM dbo.Encryption;
```

Figure 18.6 shows the results of running the SELECT statement with the DecryptByKey function.

It's very important that you keep in mind the fact that every example within this section depends on changes to the application code in order for the encryption to work. If you want to encrypt data without changing application code, consider the Transparent Data Encryption option covered in the next section.

FIGURE 18.6 Viewing encrypted data with the DecryptByKey function

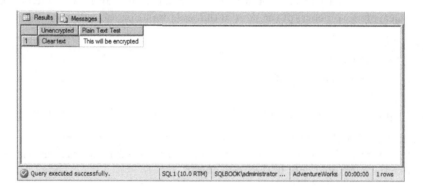

Implementing Transparent Encryption

Transparent Data Encryption (TDE) is a new feature in SQL Server 2008. With TDE, you can encrypt data without modifying application code. While certificate and encryption key hierarchies still play important roles, because TDE is enabled once for the database and no application changes are required, it is much simpler to implement. For example, the following code implements TDE for the AdventureWorks database:

```
USE master;
GO
CREATE MASTER KEY ENCRYPTION BY PASSWORD = '<UseStrongPasswordHere>';
GO
```

```
CREATE CERTIFICATE MyServerCert WITH SUBJECT = 'My TDE Certificate';
GO
USE AdventureWorks;
GO
CREATE DATABASE ENCRYPTION KEY
WITH ALGORITHM = AES_128
ENCRYPTION BY SERVER CERTIFICATE MyServerCert;
GO
ALTER DATABASE AdventureWorks
SET ENCRYPTION ON;
GO
```

From this example code, you can see that the basic process of implementing TDE is as follows:

1. Create a master key for the database.

2. Create a certificate to protect the database encryption key.

3. Create a database encryption key.

4. Set ENCRYPTION to equal ON for the database.

 When you back up a database that has TDE enabled, the backup is also encrypted. You must have access to the encryption keys in order to restore the backup. Additionally, remember that FILESTREAM data does not support encryption.

Summary

In this chapter, you learned about authentication and encryption in SQL Server 2008. Hopefully, one thing you took away from this discussion was the importance of strong authentication and information about how to provide this through SQL Server features and functions. You also learned how to create and manage principals and roles. Integral to this discussion was information on creating logins—both SQL logins and mapped Windows logins. You also learned about the server and database roles and how they provide simpler security management for SQL Servers. Finally, you explored the encryption options available in SQL Server 2008. These options include application-level encryption and transparent data encryption. In the next chapter, you'll learn how to manage permissions, secure the Windows Server itself, implement auditing, and configure the surface area in SQL Server 2008.

Chapter Essentials

Understanding Authentication   Authentication is the process used to validate a user or system identity. Strong authentication systems include both secure storage of credentials and secure validation processes. SQL Server supports strong authentication methods.

SQL Server Authentication Methods   SQL Server allows both Windows authentication and internal SQL Server authentication. SQL logins are processed by SQL Server internally and should be processed across secure channels that use encryption. Windows logins are processed by the Windows domain or the local Windows server and are passed through the SQL Server. Windows logins are considered more secure.

Logins, Users, and Roles   Logins are created using the CREATE LOGIN T-SQL command or created with the GUI in SSMS. Roles can be fixed or they can be user-created. Only database roles can be created by the database administrator. All server roles are fixed roles. Users must be created in the databases and mapped to a login in order for users to have access to the database. Otherwise, only guest access can be provided.

Understanding Encryption   Encryption is the process by which plaintext is converted into ciphertext. Encryption uses a two-way process. The data can be both encrypted and decrypted. Hashing algorithms are sometimes confused with encryption algorithms, but technically, hashing algorithms do not provide encryption—they provide encoding as the process is one-way. SQL Server provides encryption internally using two methods: application-level encryption or transparent data encryption. Application-level encryption with the EncryptByKey and DecryptByKey requires that the application internally implement the encryption using code. TDE allows for data encryption without requiring changes to the application code. Both methods are storage-only encryption. It is important to remember that the data is decrypted before it is sent across the network. In order to implement application-level encryption, you will have to alter the code of your applications. Anytime encrypted data is accessed, the application must call the DecryptByKey function in the SQL SELECT statements. Anytime data is encrypted, the EncryptByKey function will be called. TDE is implemented once for the database and no application changes are required. Once the key hierarchy is created, database encryption can be implemented with a simple ALTER DATABASE command.

Chapter

19

Security Best Practices

TOPICS COVERED IN THIS CHAPTER:

- ✓ Establishing Baselines
- ✓ Implementing Least Privilege
- ✓ Auditing SQL Server Activity
- ✓ Configuring the Surface Area
- ✓ Understanding Common Criteria and C2

As you saw in Chapter 17, "Security Threats and Principles," and Chapter 18, "Authentication and Encryption," securing any technology is more complex than many people think it is. You know that authentication and encryption are important components of SQL Server security, but security doesn't stop with them. The process includes more than just the technical steps required to turn off a feature or configure a security solution. Security really begins with the establishment of baselines, which provide a starting point from which you can further secure a system for specific uses. You can think of these baselines as best practices. In this chapter, you will learn the importance of establishing security best practices and how to use Windows Server features to create them. Of course, each organization establishes its own set of best practices, but the best practice baselines you learn here will provide a solid foundation for your security.

You will learn the methods used to implement least privilege through the internal authorization solutions in SQL Server 2008. Least privilege is achieved by limiting a user's access to the lowest level of access required for him to achieve his work objectives. This section will explore how to create permissions, manage ownership chains, establish credentials, and properly configure service accounts.

Then you will learn about auditing, which is one of the ways in which SQL Server 2008 adds functionality. In this section, you will review the methods available to audit activity in SQL Server. These methods will include audits, extended events, notifications, logon triggers, and DDL triggers.

Another key security issue involves surface area configuration, which has changed once again in SQL Server 2008. In SQL Server 2005, the Surface Area Configuration Manager was introduced. SQL Server 2008 removes this tool and gives preference to surface area configuration through two means: the sp_configure stored procedure and SQL Server policies. Both are explored in this chapter.

Finally, you'll need to understand how to ensure compliance with internal and external policies and regulations. This chapter will wrap up with C2 compliance and the Common Criteria. With everything you have to cover, you should jump right in and get started.

Establishing Baselines

Security baselines are used to establish minimum requirements for a system or a server. It's good to think of these minimum requirements or baselines as the enforcement of best practices. While the phrase *best practice* may be taken to mean a suggested practice, secure organizations actually enforce the best practice through the use of baselines. Different types of servers will require different baselines. Database servers, for example, are accessed using different ports and protocols than file and print servers. For this reason, many organizations establish baseline security configurations based on the server type. Server types requiring baselines may include:

- Authentication servers
- File and print servers
- Email servers
- Database servers
- Application servers

When you create a baseline for a server type, you reduce the likelihood that minimum security settings will be forgotten during the installation process. When you implement automation for these baseline settings, you further reduce the likelihood that these settings will be forgotten. Windows servers can use security templates to implement these baselines.

Security templates are simple INF files that contain security settings to be applied to target machines. Once you've created your database server security template, you can apply it to an organizational unit (OU) in Active Directory. If you place all of the SQL Servers in your organization in this OU, the security settings will apply automatically.

The following sections will describe the use of security templates, how to analyze a server's security settings, and how to use the Security Configuration Wizard. In these sections, you'll review recommendations for security template settings that would work well as a baseline for your SQL Servers.

Working with Security Templates

Security templates were first introduced with the release of Windows 2000 in 1999. They have been used to secure both clients and servers since that time. The security templates still exist in Windows Server 2008 R2 and Microsoft has provided new ways to utilize them over the years.

The GPO Accelerator

One of the newest tools Microsoft released is the GPO Accelerator tool. The GPO Accelerator is a download available at Microsoft's website, and it was not released with a specific operating system release. You can use it to generate security settings for several versions of Windows servers and clients. GPO Accelerator makes it easy to implement Microsoft's recommended security baselines for Windows servers and clients. You can run a wizard and automatically deploy group policy objects (GPOs) that incorporate security settings required to implement minimum security or even high security.

Exercise 19.1 steps you through the process of downloading and installing the GPO Accelerator.

EXERCISE 19.1

Installing the GPO Accelerator

In this exercise, you will download and install the GPO Accelerator from the Microsoft website. Please note that these steps assume you are running Windows Server 2008 on the server.

1. Log on to the Windows server as an administrator.

2. Open your web browser and navigate to `http://download.microsoft.com`.

3. Search for Security Compliance Management Toolkit.

4. Follow the link to download the Security Compliance Management Toolkit.

5. Scroll down the page and download the file named `Security Compliance Management Toolkit - All.zip`.

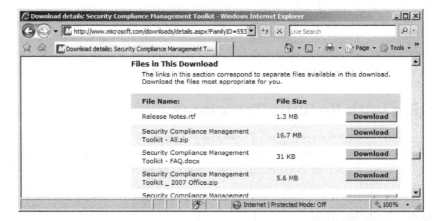

6. When the download completes, double-click on the `Security Compliance Management Toolkit - All.zip` file to open it.

7. Right-click on the Security Compliance Management Toolkit - All folder and select Copy.

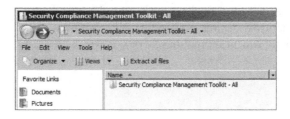

8. Click the Start button and select Computer.

9. Right-click on the C: drive and select Paste to place the folder from the downloaded zip file onto the C: drive. At this point, you should have a folder named "Security Compliance Management Toolkit - All" in the root of your C: drive. This folder contains everything you need to install the GPO Accelerator.

10. Navigate to the Security Compliance Management Toolkit - All folder in the root of the C: drive and then open the folder named GPOAccelerator.

11. Double-click on the GPOAccelerator installation application to begin the installation.

12. You may need to click Run to approve the execution of the installation application.

13. Click Next on the Welcome screen in the Installation Wizard.

14. Agree to the license terms and click Next.

15. On the Features screen, simply accept the defaults and click Next.

16. Click the Install button to perform the installation.

17. When the installation is finished, click the Finish button.

The steps for Windows Server 2003 vary only slightly. For example, you will not have to click Run in step 12 of Exercise 19.1 to approve the application's execution.

If you followed the steps in Exercise 19.1, you now have the GPO Accelerator on your server. At this point, you can run the program to install the necessary GPOs for Microsoft recommended baseline security. You should use the GPO Accelerator in a lab in order to ensure that the settings it enforces are compatible with your environment before you actually use it in your work environment. You should also be very cautious about the baseline you select. The GPO Accelerator includes two sets of baselines for each target operating system:

The Enterprise Computing Settings: The security settings applied through this set are very typical of enterprise environments.

The Specialized Security Limited Functionality Settings: The security settings applied through this set are highly restrictive and should be used with great caution.

The GPO Accelerator requires the Group Policy Management Console (GPMC). If you have not installed the GPMC, you will not be able to push the policies to a domain environment. However, you can test the policies on a local machine without the GPMC tool, but you will be limited to the client policies.

The Security Templates Snap-in of the Microsoft Management Console (MMC)

Of course, you are not required to use Microsoft's recommended security baselines provided through the GPO Accelerator. Depending on your needs, you may implement more restrictive or less restrictive settings. The tool you use to create your own templates, which can then be imported into GPOs in the Active directory domain, is the Security Templates snap-in of the Microsoft Management Console (MMC). Figure 19.1 shows the security template snap-in with the categories displayed.

FIGURE 19.1   The Security Templates snap-in showing expanded categories

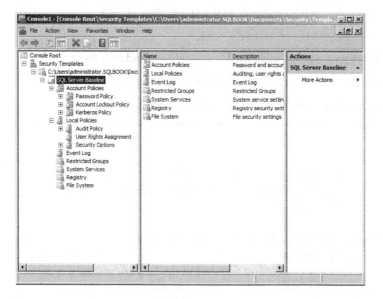

The Security Templates snap-in provides access to several categories of security settings on a Windows server that can impact the security of the SQL Server installation. These settings include:

Account Policies   The account policy settings include password rules, lockout rules, and Kerberos authentication settings. All of these settings are typically managed through the

Active Directory domain. However, if you do have standalone SQL Servers, you may want to consider creating a security baseline template for them that imposes strict password rules.

Local Policies   The local policies include audit policies for the Windows server (not for SQL Server itself), user rights assignments, and general security options. In this section of the template, consider the "Access This Computer from the Network" policy and the "Network Access: Do Not Allow Anonymous Enumeration of SAM Accounts and Shares" policy. The first policy controls who can access this server from the network, and it should be implemented in a domain environment as well as a standalone environment. Through this policy, you can limit access to the server to only those needing access to the SQL Server service (assuming the server is dedicated to running SQL Server). The second policy allows you to restrict the viewing of user lists and shares to authenticated users. By default, even anonymous users can see the logon names and the share names on the server.

Event Log   The event log policies are very important for a SQL Server in an enterprise environment. These policies allow you to configure the event log size and retention method. The best practice is to implement a log size that allows for infrequent backups of the logs; however, the most important thing is that the logs are indeed backed up for documentation purposes. It's not really that beneficial to log access to the server (through auditing) if you're not going to retain those logs.

Restricted Groups   The restricted group policy is used to add a group and limit the users or groups who can have membership in the group. This is a useful policy for powerful groups such as Administrators, Domain Admins, and Backup Operators—to name a few.

System Services   The system services portion of the template provides for automatic service startup configuration. If you want the SQL Server Agent to start automatically, for example, you can enable this through the system services section of the template. Only the services installed on the machine on which the template is created will be available for configuration within the template through this interface.

Registry   If you have special permission requirements for Registry keys, you can configure these permissions here. These settings can be used to provide read-only access to certain keys, for example, so that the server may not be reconfigured.

File System   The final category of the template file is the file system section. This category provides the functionality required to control permissions on the file system. You may want to enforce permission on the SQL Server data store (both the default data location and the user database file locations) using this category.

Exercise 19.2 provides the steps required to create a security template. This security template can be imported into a local machine (using the Security Configuration and Analysis snap-in in the MMC) or it can be imported into a GPO for distribution through Active Directory.

EXERCISE 19.2

Creating a Custom Security Template

In this exercise, you will create a custom security template. This template will ensure that auditing is enabled for failed logons to the server and that the security event log is sufficiently large to handle the extra auditing information. This action prevents undetected operations after the log has filled. To do this, follow these steps:

1. Click Start and type **MMC** into the search field and press the Enter key.

2. Click File ⪼ Add/Remove Snap-in.

3. Scroll down in the Available snap-ins list until you see Security Templates.

4. Select Security Templates and click the Add button.

5. Now select the Security Configuration and Analysis snap-in and click the Add button again. These two snap-ins are best used together.

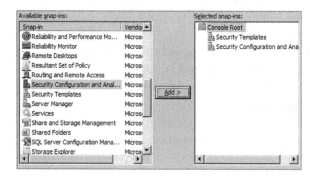

6. Click OK to add the two snap-ins.

7. Expand the Security Templates node and then the default file location, as in the following image.

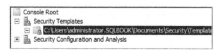

8. Right-click on the default file location and select New Template.

9. Name the template **SQL Server Baseline** and click OK.

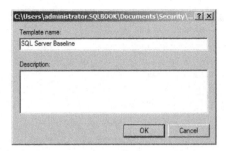

10. Expand the new SQL Server Baseline template.

11. Expand the Local Policies ➢ Audit Policy node.

12. Double-click the Audit logon events policy to configure it.

13. Select Define These Policy Settings in the Template, choose both Success and Failure, and click OK.

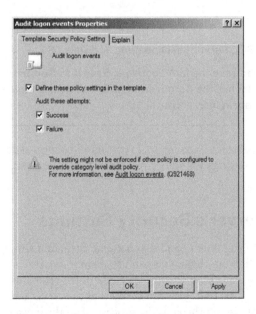

14. To configure the security event log, expand the Event logs node and double-click on the Maximum Security Log Size policy.

15. Check Define this policy setting in the template.

16. Set the value to **200000** kilobytes, which is roughly 200 megabytes, and click OK.

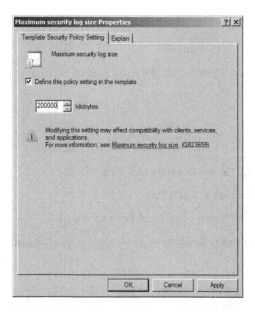

17. Right-click on the SQL Server Baseline node and select Save.

18. Select File ➢ Save to save the MMC console. Save it as **Security Templates** in the default location, which is the Administrative Tools folder on the Start menu. This MMC will be used again in Exercise 19.3.

If you followed the steps in Exercise 19.2, you should have a security template file. You may choose additional settings for your environment, but the process for creating the template will be the same.

Analyzing a Server's Security Settings

The templates won't do you much good if you create them and simply store them on a hard drive. In order to benefit from them, you can use them to analyze a computer to determine if it is configured according to the settings specified in the template. For example, using the template created in Exercise 19.2, you can verify that the server has auditing enabled for logons. Exercise 19.3 steps you through the process of analyzing security settings based on a template.

EXERCISE 19.3

Analyzing Security with Templates

In this exercise, you will analyze the security of the local SQL Server based on the template created in Exercise 19.2. To do this, follow these steps:

1. Select Start ➤ All Programs ➤ Administrative Tools ➤ Security Templates (if this shortcut does not exist, you must perform Exercise 19.2).

2. Expand the Security Configuration and Analysis node.

3. Right-click on the Security Configuration and Analysis node and select Open Database (the security analysis process uses a database to analyze security settings).

4. Enter the filename of **SQL Analysis** and click Open.

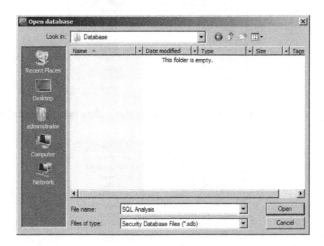

5. Choose the SQL Server Baseline template and click Open.

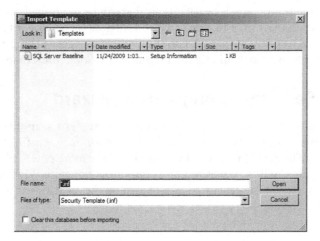

EXERCISE 19.3 *(continued)*

6. Right-click the Security Configuration and Analysis node and select Analyze Computer Now.

7. Accept the default error log path and click OK.

8. When the processing is complete, expand the Security Configuration and Analysis node. The categories that were in the security template are now listed.

9. Expand Local Policies ➢ Audit Policy.

10. If the Audit Logon Events policy has a red circle with a white X, this indicates that the policy is not currently enforced on the local server.

Policy ▲	Database Setting
Audit account logon events	Not Defined
Audit account management	Not Defined
Audit directory service access	Not Defined
Audit logon events	Success, Failure
Audit object access	Not Defined
Audit policy change	Not Defined
Audit privilege use	Not Defined
Audit process tracking	Not Defined
Audit system events	Not Defined

11. Expand the Event Logs node and note whether the policy is enforced there or not.

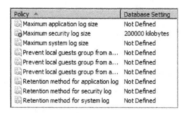

Policy ▲	Database Setting
Maximum application log size	Not Defined
Maximum security log size	200000 kilobytes
Maximum system log size	Not Defined
Prevent local guests group from a...	Not Defined
Prevent local guests group from a...	Not Defined
Prevent local guests group from a...	Not Defined
Retention method for application log	Not Defined
Retention method for security log	Not Defined
Retention method for system log	Not Defined

In addition to the security analysis operations that can be performed using the Security Configuration and Analysis snap-in, you can also configure the security of the local machine to match that of the security template. To do this, instead of right-clicking and selecting Analyze Computer Now, you would right-click and select Configure Computer Now.

Using the Security Configuration Wizard

The Security Templates and Security Configuration and Analysis snap-ins have been with us for over 10 years, and they provide a valuable toolset for implementing best practices as security baselines. The new kid on the block—and also the more powerful—is the Security Configuration Wizard (SCW). The SCW comes out-of-the-box with Windows Server 2008, and it can be used to create a security baseline based on the security settings in your existing server. Imagine you've spent hours locking down your SQL Server machine. You've configured port filtering in the firewall, file and Registry permissions, and many more settings. Now, you must do all that again on several other SQL Servers. The SCW is there to rescue you from all that extra work.

Exercise 19.4 steps you through the process of creating a baseline from the current configuration of the local server.

EXERCISE 19.4

Creating a Baseline from Current Settings with SCW

In this exercise, you will use the SCW tool to create a baseline from the server's current settings. This exercise should be performed on a Windows Server 2008 machine. To do this:

1. Select Start ➢ All Programs ➢ Administrative Tools ➢ Security Configuration Wizard.

2. On the Welcome to the Security Configuration Wizard screen, click Next.

3. Choose to Create a New Security Policy and click Next.

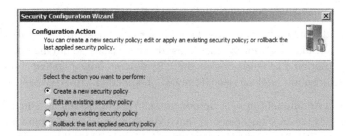

4. On the Select Server screen, accept the default of the local server name and click Next.

5. Once the processing of the configuration database is complete, click Next (you may want to click View Configuration Database to explore beyond this exercise).

6. The next phase of SCW is the role configuration. Click Next on the Role-Based Service Configuration introduction screen to continue.

7. On the Select Server Roles screen, the currently installed roles are displayed by default. You may choose additional roles if the server will require them. Otherwise, click Next.

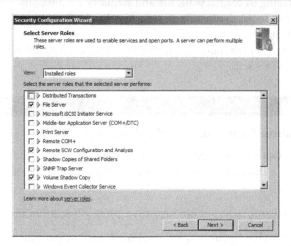

8. On the Select Client Features screen, the currently installed features are displayed by default. Again, you may choose additional features if you plan to add them later so that they are included in the security baseline. Otherwise, click Next.

9. The Select Administration and Other Options screen is used to configure services and ports for out-of-the-box Windows services (these services do not include add-ons such as SQL Server, Exchange Server, etc.). By default, only installed components are selected. Select additional services if they will be needed. Otherwise, click Next.

10. On the Select Additional Services screen you can configure the default settings for any non–out-of-the-box services that may exist in the current machine. In the following image, the SQL Server services are shown. Make sure you've selected the SQL Server services you require in the baseline and then click Next.

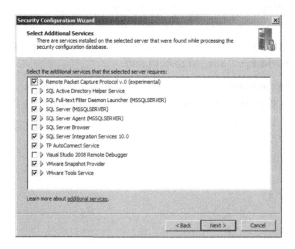

11. On the Handling Unspecified Services screen, choose Disable the Service to ensure that no services are allowed to run on other servers to which this baseline is applied. Then click Next.

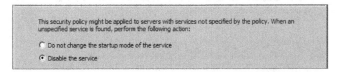

This security policy might be applied to servers with services not specified by the policy. When an unspecified service is found, perform the following action:

○ Do not change the startup mode of the service

◉ Disable the service

12. View the selected changes on the Confirm Service Changes screen. If everything looks acceptable, click Next.

13. The next phase of SCW is the Network Security phase. Click Next on the Network Security screen to begin this phase.

14. On the Network Security Rules screen, notice the first firewall rule for SQL Server. You can click on the rule and then click the Edit button to view the parameters if you desire. Otherwise, click Next.

15. The next phase of SCW is the Registry settings phase. You're going to accept all defaults for this phase. So, you should check Skip This Section and click Next.

☑ Skip this section
If you skip this section, this security policy will not configure registry settings.

16. The next phase is the Audit Policy section. Click Next to enter this section.

17. Choose Audit Successful and Unsuccessful Activities on the System Audit Policy screen and click Next.

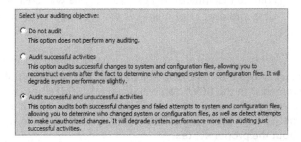

Select your auditing objective:

○ Do not audit
This option does not perform any auditing.

○ Audit successful activities
This option audits successful changes to system and configuration files, allowing you to reconstruct events after the fact to determine who changed system or configuration files. It will degrade system performance slightly.

◉ Audit successful and unsuccessful activities
This option audits both successful changes and failed attempts to system and configuration files, allowing you to determine who changed system or configuration files, as well as detect attempts to make unauthorized changes. It will degrade system performance more than auditing just successful activities.

18. On the Audit Policy Summary screen, review the audit setting and then click Next.

19. The final phase of SCW is the Save Security Policy section. Click Next to enter this section.

EXERCISE 19.4 *(continued)*

20. Enter a name and description for the security policy, as shown in the following image, and then click Next.

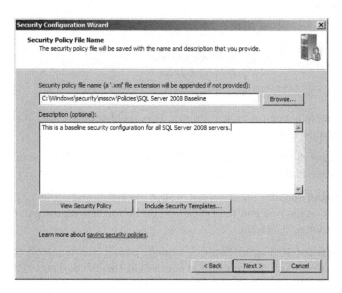

21. Choose to Apply Later and click Next.

22. Click Finish to exit the wizard.

If you followed the instructions in Exercise 19.4, you should now have a file named SQL Server 2008 Baseline.xml in the C:\Windows\Security\msscq\Policies folder. You can use this file with the SCW on other machines to automatically configure them according to the security settings on the machine on which the baseline was created. This activity can save you hours of time and dozens of mistakes when compared to manual security configurations.

You can use the command line to work with security policies (baselines) created with the SCW. You will use the SCWCMD command from the command line. To learn more about the command, type it at the command line. You can then type **SCWCMD** and any of its subcommands to learn more about the proper syntax.

Implementing Least Privilege

The principle of least privilege says simply that users and systems should have no greater access than is required to perform their intended duties. This means that users can do what they need to do and nothing more. Other systems can access the secured system to perform their intended operations and can do nothing more. In SQL Server 2008, least privilege is implemented through permissions; however, you must understand several objects and concepts in order to ensure that least privilege is properly implemented. These topics include:

- Permissions and authorization
- Ownership chains
- Credentials

Permissions and Authorization

Permissions are used to authorize the action of users. If a user has the permissions to perform an action, when the user attempts the action, it will be authorized. Permissions within a database system are different than those used in a file system or on a network. In a Microsoft Windows environment, administrators are used to granting permissions such as Read, Change, Full Control, Write, etc. In SQL Server, you will grant the permission to execute particular statements against specific securables. For example, you can grant a user Select permissions on the Accounting table in the Balance database. The Accounting table is the securable and Select is the permission or capability provided to the user.

When you set permissions using T-SQL, you use the GRANT, REVOKE, and DENY statements. You can also manage permissions using the SSMS graphical administration interface. In fact, one of the best ways for learning how to create T-SQL permission statements is to configure permissions in the GUI and then view the resulting T-SQL code using the Script button. Exercise 19.5 shows you how to use the Script button to view the T-SQL code for GRANT, REVOKE, and DENY statements.

EXERCISE 19.5

Permission Management in SQL Server Management Studio

In this exercise, you will practice permission management using the AdventureWorks database. To do this, follow these steps:

1. Launch SQL Server Management Studio.

2. Expand the Databases container in the Object Explorer window.

3. Expand the AdventureWorks database.

4. Expand the Tables within AdventureWorks.

5. Right-click on the Production.Product table and select Properties.

6. Select the Permissions page.

7. Click the Search button to add users or roles.

8. Click the Browse button, choose the [guest] user, click OK, and then click OK again in the Select Users or Roles dialog to add the user.

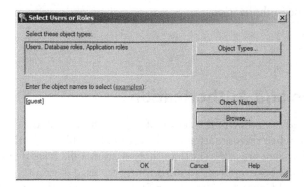

9. In the Permissions for Guest section, select the Control, Insert, and Select rows in the Grant column, but select the Delete permission in the Deny column as in the following image.

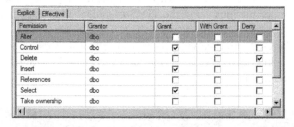

10. Choose the down arrow next to the Script button, and select Script Action to New Query Window.

11. Click Cancel to avoid applying the permission changes from within the GUI.

12. In the new query window, you should see code similar to the following:

```
use [AdventureWorks]
GO
GRANT CONTROL ON [Production].[Product] TO [guest]
GO
```

```
use [AdventureWorks]
GO
GRANT INSERT ON [Production].[Product] TO [guest]
GO
use [AdventureWorks]
GO
GRANT SELECT ON [Production].[Product] TO [guest]
GO
use [AdventureWorks]
GO
DENY DELETE ON [Production].[Product] TO [guest]
GO
```

13. If you want to apply the permissions, you can execute the code. Otherwise, close SSMS without saving anything. The main purpose of this exercise is to see the code generated when applying permissions.

To best manage the permissions to database securables, you will need to understand the scope of those permissions and how they pass down through the securable hierarchies. Additionally, you will need to differentiate between statement and object permissions and know how to manage both permission types. Finally, it is important to grasp the relationship between schemas and security. All of these topics are covered in the following sections.

Permission Scopes

SQL Server 2008 groups securables at three scope levels: server, database, and schema. Table 19.1 lists the securables that are managed at each scope level. All securables, regardless of scope, are secured by the application of appropriate permissions. When you assign permissions, you are enforcing least privilege—assuming that the configured permissions are indeed providing only required capabilities.

TABLE 19.1 Securables and Scope Level

Securable	Scope Level
Server	Server
Endpoint	Server
Logins	Server

TABLE 19.1   Securables and Scope Level *(continued)*

Securable	Scope Level
Database Users	Database
Database Roles	Database
Application Roles	Database
Assemblies	Database
Services	Database
Service Contracts	Database
Schemas	Database
Tables	Schema
Views	Schema
Functions	Schema
Procedures	Schema
Queues	Schema
Rules	Schema
Synonyms	Schema

Statement Permissions

Two major categories of permissions apply in SQL Server. The first category is statement permissions and the second is object permissions. *Statement permissions* are not related to the data, but to the structure of the data. These permissions apply to statements that are used to create or alter server, database, or schema securables. Object permissions are used to control who can access the data in the created securables.

Examples of statement permissions include CREATE TABLE, CREATE DATABASE, CREATE VIEW, and CREATE INDEX. The ability to execute any of these statements can be granted, denied, or revoked. Consider the following code:

```
GRANT CREATE TABLE TO [Server1\Jeremy];
```

This statement provides the user `Jeremy` on the computer `Server1` the ability to create tables in the database. The following code takes this ability away:

```
REVOKE CREATE TABLE TO [Server1\Jeremy];
```

The difference between `REVOKE` and `DENY` is that `REVOKE` takes away a privilege that has been granted and `DENY` is used to override a privilege coming from some other area related to the user, like a Windows group. In fact, the `REVOKE` statement can be used to take away a negative permission assigned with the `DENY` statement.

Object Permissions

While statement permissions control the ability to create the structure of a database, the object permissions control the ability to access the data stored within the structure. This includes the ability to read, write, and otherwise alter the data. Following is a list of the 12 object permissions and what abilities the permissions provide.

Control: Provides ownership-like capabilities on the assigned objects and all objects beneath it in the hierarchy. When the Control permission is granted to a user on the database, the user will, by default, have the Control permission on all database objects such as tables and views.

Alter: Interestingly, the Alter permission can grant the Create permission. This happens when you grant the Alter permission on an object which is a scope-level object containing other objects. For example, by granting Alter to a user on a schema, you grant Create to that user for the objects in the schema. Alter provides the ability to alter, drop, or create objects. Alter does not provide the ability to change ownership.

Take Ownership: Gives the granted user the ability to take ownership of the object.

Impersonate: Can be granted on a login to another user or role. Allows the granted user to act as the impersonated login.

Create: Allows the granted user to create objects.

View Definition: Provides the granted user with the ability to see the SQL code that was used to create the object being secured.

Select: Allows the granted user to issue `SELECT` statements and read data from the object.

Insert: Grants the ability to create new records in a table.

Update: Grants the ability to modify records in a table.

Delete: Grants the ability to delete records from a table.

References: Grants the ability to select data from a table that references another table without having the Select permission granted on the referenced table.

Execute: Provides the user with the ability to execute the stored procedure on which the permission is granted.

Object permissions can be granted using SQL code similar to statement permissions. Consider the following code:

```
USE music;
GRANT SELECT ON OBJECT::albums TO [Server1\Jeremy];
```

This will grant the Select permission to Jeremy for the albums table in the music database.

> The object you are dealing with really doesn't matter. Tables, views, and stored procedures, for example, all receive the same core GRANT, REVOKE, and DENY statements. Of course, the only permissions that can be granted, revoked, or denied are those that apply to the object. For example, a stored procedure can be executed, but a table cannot.

Schemas and Security

A *schema* is a collection of database objects grouped together under the umbrella of a schema name. Microsoft's official definition is that a schema is a collection of database entities that form a single namespace. For example, dbo.sales and dbo.salespersons may refer to two tables—sales and salespersons—in the dbo schema. SQL Server 2005 introduced the concept of named schemas and the separation of the schema from the user. In SQL Server 2000 and earlier, a schema was named for the owner of the schema. Now, in SQL Server 2005 and 2008, you can create schema names, such as sales or marketing, and then assign ownership of the schema to any user. The benefits of the separation of the user from the schema include:

- Several schemas can be owned by a single principal.
- When you delete a user, you do not have to rename the objects that were part of that user's schema.
- Multiple principals can own a single schema through role or Windows group memberships.

SQL Server 2008 will utilize the four-part naming convention even more than past versions of SQL Server due to the introduction of schemas that are separate from the users. For example, a database table named "sales" in a database named "tracking" on a schema named "reports" on a server named "SQL1" would be referenced as "SQL1.reports.tracking.sales." If you are in the context of the reports database (for example, you've executed a USE reports statement), you can reference the same table as simply tracking.sales.

> Understanding the role of the schema in the four-part names is important—particularly if you plan to take Microsoft certification exams. You may encounter questions that will stump you on the schema issue, if you fail to remember concepts such as the default schema for a user (which is usually dbo) and the current database context.

In addition, the concept of a default schema was introduced with SQL Server 2005. This is an important feature in light of the fact that a single database can have two tables with the same table-level name that belong to two different schemas. For example, you can have a table named sales.results and another named marketing.results and store them both in the database named `campaigns`. You can configure the users who are from marketing to use the `marketing` schema by default and the users from sales to default to the `sales` schema. Now, an application that issues a command like `SELECT * FROM results` will not need to specify the schema in order to get the right table information for the user. The following code demonstrates how you configure the default schema for a user during creation and after creation:

```
USE music;
CREATE USER barney WITH DEFAULT_SCHEMA = sales;
ALTER USER barney WITH DEFAULT_SCHEMA = marketing;
```

The first command creates a user named `barney` while setting his default schema to `sales`. The second command modifies the user named `barney` and sets his default schema to `marketing`. In order for the first command to work, a login named `barney` must exist at the server level.

It is also important to note that members of the `sysadmin` fixed server role will have a default schema of `dbo` regardless of the previous commands. Also, the default `default_schema` setting is `dbo` for users that are created without an alternative schema specification. Schemas are created with the `CREATE SCHEMA` command.

 It's worth calling attention to the fact that schemas changed drastically in SQL Server 2005 in that they were completely disassociated from users and roles. In the past, a user or role owned the schema and the schema had the same name as the owning user or role. Now, because of named schemas, a schema can be created and then owned by any specified individual or collective principal.

Ownership Chains

When implementing least privilege, you must consider ownership chains because they can result in the granting of permissions that you may not intend to grant. Ownership chaining is a simple concept to understand; however, the implications are far-reaching in your databases, and they can make a big difference in security and whether users can access needed resources or not. To understand ownership chains, you must first understand ownership.

When a user owns a database, schema, or object, that user has full management capabilities on the principal. The user can assign permissions, alter the structure of the object, or even delete an object. Ownership is powerful.

An ownership chain exists when an object references another object that is also owned by the same user. For example, if the dbo owns the vmarketing view, which is based on the marketing table, and the marketing table is also owned by the dbo, an ownership chain exists.

So, who cares about these ownership chains and why do they matter? You will care when you understand the impact. If the ownership chain exists, it means you can grant a permission on the vmarketing view, such as SELECT, to any user and no additional permissions will be required on the marketing table. The authorization passes along the chain as long as the ownership chain is not broken. This makes security management much easier. Of course, it also means you need to make sure that only the proper people are given access to higher level objects—such as views or stored procedures—that utilize lower level objects, such as tables.

To understand the benefit fully, consider this example: Imagine you have a stored procedure named usp_MarketingUpdate that reads from the vmarketing view that is based on the marketing table. Further, assume that each object is owned by a different user. Because no ownership chain exists, you will need to grant additional permissions at the view and table level to anyone requiring execute permissions on the usp_MarketingUpdate stored procedure. If the ownership chain existed—meaning that all three objects were owned by the same user—you would set the permission once and forget it.

 In SQL Server 2005 and 2008, the primary ownership point is the schema. In other words, you assign ownership at the schema level and this ownership is inherited by all objects within the schema. To change the ownership of a specific object, such as a table, you use the ALTER AUTHORIZATION command.

Credentials

User credentials are used to validate the identity of a user. The user credentials provide the first step required to implement least privilege, which is user identification. When users connecting to your SQL Server need to access resources outside of the SQL Server, credentials may be used. A SQL Server credential object is usually just a Windows username and password pair stored within the SQL Server. The username and password set is used to access the external resources as needed.

The most common use of credentials in SQL Server 2008 is with the SQL Server Agent proxy objects. A proxy object must be created in order to run a job step as some user other than the SQL Server Agent service account. To use these proxy objects, you must first create a credential object. The process is generically outlined as follows:

1.   Create a credential that references a standard Windows user account.
2.   Create the proper proxy object that references the credential object.
3.   Create the job step and configure it to run as the created proxy object.

These proxy and credential objects can be very useful for providing access to resources that would not normally be accessible to the SQL Server Agent account.

As an example, consider the following code, which creates a credential named Jeremy:

```
USE master;
GO
CREATE CREDENTIAL Jeremy
    WITH IDENTITY = 'SQL1\Jeremy',
    SECRET = 'Password1';
GO
```

In this code, notice that the Windows account is SQL1\Jeremy and the password (the secret) is Password1. Once the credential is created, you can create the proxy. For example, the following code would create a proxy for running operating system commands:

```
USE msdb;
GO
EXEC msdb.dbo.sp_add_proxy
    @proxy_name='OSCommands',
    @credential_name=N'Jeremy',
    @enabled=1;
GO
EXEC msdb.dbo.sp_grant_proxy_to_subsystem
    @proxy_name='OSCommands',
    @subsystem_id=3;
GO
```

As you can see, the creation of the proxy object is a bit more complicated. You must call on stored procedures to do this through code. Of course, you can always create a proxy in the SQL Server Management Studio graphical interface, if you prefer.

 Real World Scenario

Ensuring Least Privilege with Service Accounts

The service accounts used to run SQL Server make up an important area that cannot be overlooked. I was once in a meeting with the internal DBAs for a large United States-based organization. We were discussing security requirements for a project they were planning, and I was there to help with the SQL Server planning. The project involved building an Internet-facing application. As you might have guessed, we were discussing the need to implement least privilege.

After more than an hour of discussions related to logins, users, and permissions, I asked them how they planned to protect the SQL Servers from the most common attack type for Internet-servicing database servers—injection attacks. They indicated that they would protect against such attacks with secure code. I asked, "But what about the mistakes that will creep into the code that you don't catch?" They said that they hadn't really considered that issue. Of course, that's why I was there, to remind them of just such realities.

 I reminded them that the best way to ultimately protect against unknown injection attacks (those that you miss when testing your code) is to use least privilege at the SQL Server service account level. If the SQL Server service is running with minimal privileges, even if a cracker does find a way to inject code into their SQL Server, at least she won't be able to do major damage. She could only do what the SQL Server service account can do. This is why I encouraged them to create special accounts just for the SQL Server service and the SQL Server Agent service. I suggested they create one for each service so that each account could provide only the privileges needed for that service. By implementing my suggestion, they have helped protect themselves from unforeseen attacks that will certainly be developed in the future.

This does not mean that they don't need to keep up with the current news related to attacks and implement the appropriate countermeasures. Indeed, they should update their server and correct errors in their code; however, even with these efforts, they will miss some potential entry points. Least privilege helps to protect them in such cases. This particular organization has experienced no serious security incidents on their SQL Servers since the time of implementation.

Auditing SQL Server Activity

While the Windows servers on which SQL Server 2008 run can implement auditing, SQL Server also supports internal auditing. The auditing can be accomplished using traditional methods, such as DDL triggers, or new methods in SQL Server 2008, such as audits and logon triggers. Notifications can also be configured so that SQL trace events or DDL triggers have a method for notifying administrative personnel. The following sections address these various methods and the steps required to implement them.

Using Audits

Those of you who implement and support SQL Server have been waiting a long time for the new audit architecture in SQL Server 2008. Now you finally have the ability to set up automatic auditing without the requirement of creating dozens of custom triggers. Of course, triggers are still there and they can be very useful (they will be covered later in this chapter), but the ability to implement standard and automated auditing is a big leap forward.

SQL Server Audit, the new feature in SQL Server 2008, uses extended events to implement an audit. The audit can be a server-level audit (more specifically, the instance-level) or a database-level audit. At either level, the audit is assigned a target. The *target* is the storage location for the audit details. The target can be a file, the Windows Security log in the Event Viewer, or the Windows application log in the Event Viewer.

When you're ready to implement SQL Server Audit, you must perform four tasks:

1. Create the audit, which points to a target.
2. Create the server (instance) audit and specification.
3. Enable the audit.
4. Monitor the log files or Event Viewer logs.

Creating an Audit   The first step is to create an audit. An *audit* is basically a name and a target. The name is used to identify the audit, and the target specifies one of three targets. The first target is the file system. By default, a new audit points to a file system file; however, you can change this so that it points to the application log or the security log in the Event Viewer. For security purposes, you can point the audit to the security log so you can monitor with tasks scheduled to notify you of an audit event.

You can create multiple audits. For example, you could create an audit named File, another named Application, and another named Security. With these named audits, you can use them to direct captured events to the appropriate output. This naming scheme is just a suggestion and not at all required. You can develop your own audit-naming structure.

A rumor is floating around on the Internet that says you can have only one audit per instance. This is simply not the case. To prove that point, go ahead and create more than one. SQL Server 2008 will certainly allow you to create multiple audit objects.

Creating the Server (Instance) Audit and Specification   The second step is to create the audit specification. The audit *specification* defines the events you want to audit. As examples, you can audit for ownership changes or for instance logins.

Enabling the Audit   The third step is to enable the audit and the audit specification. By default, when audits and audit specifications are first created, they are disabled. You will need to enable both in order for auditing to begin.

Monitoring the Log Files or Event Viewer Logs   The fourth and final step is to monitor the log files or Event Viewer logs. SQL Server provides no simple way to do this. Instead, you must use third-party Event Viewer log monitoring applications or scripts that you create yourself. You can certainly create SQL Server jobs that monitor for audit events and then email an operator or take some other action should an audit event occur.

Interestingly, it's not that complicated to set up auditing. Just remember that you are first creating an audit output definition that can be used by multiple audit specifications. Then you will create the specifications. Finally, you will enable both objects so that auditing can begin. Exercise 19.6 provides instructions for creating a basic auditing configuration.

EXERCISE 19.6

Enabling SQL Server 2008 Audit

In this exercise, you will create an audit object and an audit specification. You will then enable both in order to turn on the auditing feature. The audit object will be named Application Log and will output any audit events to the application log in the Event Viewer. The audit specification will monitor the FAILED_LOGIN_GROUP audit action, which will fire if a failed login occurs. To do this, follow these steps:

1. Launch SSMS and connect to the SQL Server 2008 instance on which you want to enable auditing.

2. Expand Security ➢ Audits in the Object Explorer.

3. Right-click the Audits node and select New Audit.

4. Name the new audit object **Application Log** to indicate that the audit target will be the application log in the Event Viewer.

5. Select Application Log for the Audit destination field.

6. Accept all other defaults and click OK to create the audit object.

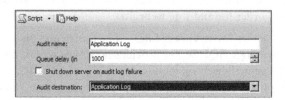

7. Right-click the new Application Log Audit object and select Enable Audit. Click Close upon success of the Enable Audit operation.

EXERCISE 19.6 *(continued)*

8. Right-click on the Server Audit Specifications node and select New Server Audit Specification.

9. Enter the name of **Failed Logins**.

10. Choose the Application Log Audit object from the Audit drop-down list.

11. For the Audit Action Type, choose FAILED_LOGIN_GROUP.

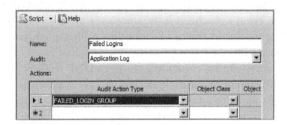

12. Click OK to create the audit specification.

13. Right-click the new Failed Logins audit specification and choose Enable Server Audit Specification.

14. Click Close upon success of the Enable Specification operation.

If you've performed the steps in Exercise 19.6 and want to see an audit event generated and stored in the application log of the Event Viewer, simply open a new query window in SSMS and then disconnect and reconnect. You'll be prompted for logon credentials. Intentionally enter a login name and password pair that is incorrect. Now, go to your application log and you'll see the new entry in the log. You may also right-click on the audit object, in this case the one named Application Log, and select View Audit Logs. You'll see a screen similar to the one in Figure 19.2.

FIGURE 19.2   Using the log file to view the audit logs within SSMS viewer

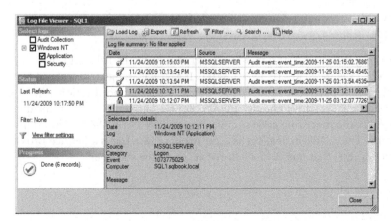

Notifications

The Service Broker component of SQL Server was first introduced in SQL Server 2005. The Service Broker allows for asynchronous communications within the database system through the use of queues. Messages are stored in queues and can be processed as needed by stored procedures or .NET CLR code. The new event notifications in SQL Server 2008 take advantage of the Service Broker.

Event notifications work by sending information about SQL traces or DDL trigger events to Service Broker services. Event notifications are usually used to track database changes or to perform some action in response to an event. The benefit of event notifications is that they can respond to an event asynchronously, since they use Service Broker, instead of synchronously. The end result is that you use event notifications when you do not require an instant response to the event.

Event notifications offer similar capabilities to both DDL triggers and SQL traces; however, differences do exist. For example, a DDL trigger is synchronous and runs in the resource space of the firing transaction; an event notification is asynchronous and runs outside the resource space of the transaction that created the event. Unlike SQL traces, event notifications can respond to an SQL trace and perform an action inside of SQL Server.

SQL Trace is a new internal component of SQL Server 2008 that allows applications to initiate traces inside of the SQL Server Database Engine. In the past, SQL traces were created using the SQL Server Profiler and could not be easily created within T-SQL application code. Now, stored procedures (such as sp_trace_create) can be used to perform this action.

Event notifications are created with the CREATE EVENT NOTIFICATION statement. The following code provides an example of an event notification statement:

```
USE AdventureWorks;
GO
CREATE EVENT NOTIFICATION NotifyAlterTables
    ON DATABASE
    FOR ALTER_TABLE
    TO SERVICE '//Adventure-Works.com/ArchiveService',
    '8140a771-3c4b-4479-8ac0-81008ab17984';
```

The first thing the code performs is a context change to the AdventureWorks database. When you execute a CREATE EVENT NOTIFICATION statement, you should be in the context of the target database. In this code sample, the event notification will be named NotifyAlterTables, and it watches for an ALTER TABLE statement within the database. You'll notice that the preceding code sample specified ON DATABASE, but it did not specify a database name. The //Adventure-Works.com/ArchiveService is a Service Broker service (an endpoint address) that must exist before executing the statement.

DDL Triggers

Data Definition Language (DDL) triggers monitor for schema changes. Schema changes are performed with CREATE, ALTER, and DROP statements. You can monitor for any of these statements with DDL triggers and then take any desired action. From a security perspective, DDL triggers are frequently used to log actions that users take (or attempt to take) on the server. They can also be used to prevent specific actions. For example, the following DDL trigger would prevent any tables from being deleted from the AdventureWorks database:

```
USE AdventureWorks;
GO


CREATE TRIGGER PrevTableDrop
    ON DATABASE
    FOR DROP_TABLE
    AS
    BEGIN
        PRINT 'Table drops or deletions are not allowed';
        ROLLBACK TRANSACTION;
    END;
GO
```

The preceding code simply informs the user that table drops or deletions are not allowed and then prevents the transaction from completing. Such DDL triggers have been common over the years in SQL Server. They may begin to fade into the background as newer solutions, such as event notifications and SQL Audit, take hold.

Logon Triggers

The final audit tool that you will address in this chapter is the logon trigger. Logon triggers are new to SQL Server 2008 and form a special class of trigger that can be used to monitor logins. Microsoft defines *logon triggers* as objects that fire stored procedures in response to logon events. Of course, traditional triggers do the same in response to code execution events, but they can not track logons. To create a logon trigger, execute code similar to the following sample found in SQL Server Books Online:

```
CREATE TRIGGER connection_limit_trigger
    ON ALL SERVER WITH EXECUTE AS 'login_test'
    FOR LOGON
    AS
    BEGIN
        IF ORIGINAL_LOGIN()= 'login_test' AND
```

```
(SELECT COUNT(*) FROM sys.dm_exec_sessions
    WHERE is_user_process = 1 AND
    original_login_name = 'login_test') > 3
ROLLBACK;
END;
```

This creative example uses the logon trigger object to limit the number of concurrent connections allowed for the user named `login_test`. This example shows that logon triggers can be used for more than just auditing logons. You can use them for any of the following creative uses as well:

- Limit the number of concurrent logons for a user

- Automatically launch a service on the server when a specific user, who would require that service for his actions, logs onto the server

- Email the administrator automatically if a user logs on with the administrator's SQL Server login

You are sure to see even more creative uses of logon triggers over the next few years. A new feature like this is certain to be tested and stretched to meet the needs of different organizations.

Configuring the Surface Area

One of the primary components in SQL Server used to implement best practices is surface area configuration. In the world of computer security, the *surface area* is a reference to the attack points exposed on the system. For example, a system with more services running and more open network ports has a larger attack surface than a system with fewer services and fewer open network ports. The goal of the security administrator is to reduce the attack surface of each and every node on his network and, therefore, of his entire network. Attack surface reduction should be performed for every SQL Server machine in your environment.

 If you have created a secure baseline for your SQL Server 2008 deployments, you will already have a reduced attack surface. Reducing the attack surface should be part of the security baseline and not an afterthought.

In SQL Server 2008, the Surface Area Configuration Manager is removed. Instead, you will use the `sp_configure` stored procedure or Policy-Based Management (PBM) to configure the surface area.

SP_Configure for Surface Area Management

The sp_configure stored procedure is not new to SQL Server 2008, but using it to configure the surface area is new, since the Surface Area Configuration Manager was available in SQL Server 2005. You can use the sp_configure stored procedure to configure any Database Engine settings that impact the security of the system. Examples include:

- Turning off xp_cmdshell, which is an extended stored procedure used to run operating system commands and can introduce a big security problem for your SQL Servers

- Disabling cross-database ownership chaining to increase security

- Preventing the execution of the SQL Mail extended stored procedures on the server

Exercise 19.7 provides instructions for using the sp_configure stored procedure to turn off xp_cmdshell and disable all SQL Mail stored procedures.

EXERCISE 19.7

Using *sp_configure* to Configure the Surface Area

In this exercise, you will use sp_configure to turn off the xp_cmdshell stored procedure and disable all SQL Mail stored procedures. To do this, follow these steps:

1. Launch SSMS and connect to the target instance of SQL Server 2008 as an administrator.

2. Click the New Query button to open a Query Editor window.

3. Enter and execute the following code to disable xp_cmdshell:

```
EXEC sp_configure 'show advanced options', 1;
GO
RECONFIGURE;
GO
EXEC sp_configure 'xp_cmdshell', 0;
GO
RECONFIGURE;
GO
```

4. Now that the xp_cmdshell stored procedure is disabled, enter and execute the following code to turn off the SQL Mail stored procedures:

```
sp_configure 'show advanced options', 1;
GO
RECONFIGURE;
GO
```

```
sp_configure 'SQL Mail XPs', 0;
GO
RECONFIGURE;
GO
```

At this point, the surface area is configured to disallow both the xp_cmdshell stored procedure and any of the SQL Mail stored procedures.

Policy-Based Management Surface Area Options

Chapter 15, "Policy-Based Management," introduced you to PBM. Within PBM, the Surface Area Configuration facet is used to manage the surface area of the SQL Server Database Engine service. Analysis Services' surface area can be managed with the Surface Area Configuration for Analysis Services facet and the Reporting Services' surface area can be managed with the Surface Area Configuration for Reporting Services facet.

Instructions for configuring the surface area of SQL Server using PBM are provided in Exercise 19.8. This exercise will implement a portion of the surface area options available. Most of the surface area management features that were available in the Surface Area Configuration Manager in SQL Server 2004 are available within PBM.

If you have not read Chapter 15, you may want to do so before performing Exercise 19.8 in this section. Reading it will ensure that you understand the steps you take in the exercise.

Configuring the Surface Area with PBM

In this exercise, you will disable xp_cmdshell and SQL Mail stored procedures using PBM. You will first create a condition that uses the Surface Area Configuration facet. Next, you will create a policy that can be used to enforce the condition. To do this, follow these steps:

1.   Launch SSMS and connect to the SQL Server as an administrator.

2.   In Object Explorer, expand Management ➢ Policy Management.

EXERCISE 19.8 *(continued)*

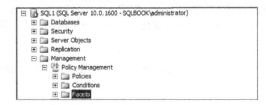

3. Right-click the Conditions node and select New Condition.

4. Name the condition object **Surface Area**.

5. Choose the Surface Area Configuration facet.

6. In the Expression area, choose @XPCmdShellEnabled and set it to equal False.

7. Additionally, choose @SqlMailEnabled and set it to equal False as in the following image.

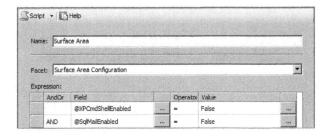

8. Click OK to save the condition object.

9. Right-click on the Policies node and select New Policy.

10. Name the policy object **Surface Area**.

11. For the Check Condition, choose the Surface Area condition you just created.

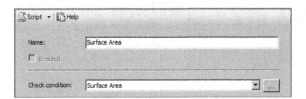

12. Click OK to save the policy.

13. Right-click on the Surface Area policy object and choose Evaluate.

If you performed the steps in Exercise 19.8 on a SQL Server 2008 machine configured with default settings, the policy should evaluate to True because xp_cmdshell and SQL Mail stored procedures are disabled by default. Figure 19.3 shows the results of the evaluation on a default install of SQL Server 2008. Figure 19.4 shows the detailed view of the evaluation results.

FIGURE 19.3   Evaluating the surface area policy on a SQL Server 2008 default installation

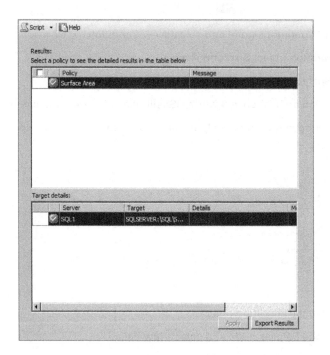

FIGURE 19.4   Viewing the details of the evaluation

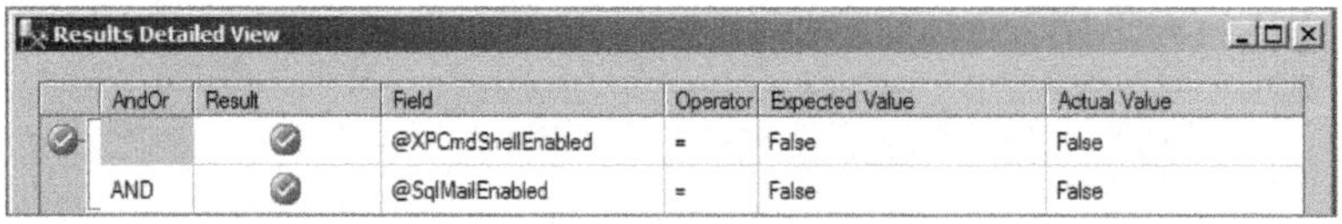

	AndOr	Result	Field	Operator	Expected Value	Actual Value
✓		✓	@XPCmdShellEnabled	=	False	False
	AND	✓	@SqlMailEnabled	=	False	False

Understanding Common Criteria and C2

Information Systems (IS) have become more and more complex over time. To ensure the security of these systems, matching complexity was introduced to the management processes. The governance, risk management, and compliance process is used to govern and manage IS risk and mitigation techniques. The Common Criteria and C2 provide a foundation on which to build secure systems.

So why bother to talk about C2 security? Take a look at the Microsoft objectives for exam 70-432. You'll notice that C2 is mentioned along with Command Criteria. The Common Criteria is so new that C2 compliance is still an important consideration. Additionally, many security professionals argue that C2 is still better because it is more specific than the Common Criteria.

GRC

The acronym GRC, which stands for governance, risk management, and compliance, is often used to describe the management processes used to ensure the security of complex and interoperating IT solutions. SQL Server 2008 may also be managed with GRC.

 If you want to read additional information related to GRC, you might be interested in the Wikipedia article titled "Governance, risk management, and compliance" located at http://en.wikipedia.org/wiki/ Governance,_risk_management,_and_compliance.

The *G* in GRC stands for governance and is a reference to the processes and tools used to create and implement policies that will help to remove or mitigate security risks (as well as nonsecurity risks) to the system. The simplest way to remember what governance is about is to say that governance equals policies. More specifically, governance equals the policies and the management structure employed to implement, enforce, and evaluate these policies.

The *R* in GRC stands for risks or risk management. Risk management is the process used to identify and address risks. From a security perspective, this means evaluating the potential attack points and ensuring that the risk of attack through those points is either removed, reduced, or dealt with otherwise. As you can see in the following list, there are five primary risk responses that can be taken. The risk response you choose will depend on the scenario and, in many cases, the budget.

> **Eradicate:** When you can eradicate a risk, it means you can completely remove the risk. In these cases, you've usually identified something you should already be doing. For example, if you are not performing backups and you identify total data loss as a risk, you can eradicate the possibility of total data loss by implementing backups and offsite storage.

Mitigate: To mitigate a risk, you must reduce the likelihood or the impact of the risk. For example, if you use only Windows authentication and not SQL logins, you mitigate the risk of credential theft (though it is not completely removed).

Transfer: Insurance is the best example of risk transference. If you have homeowner's insurance, you are transferring all of the risk of home damage to the insurance company with the exception of your deductible. Of course, you carry the risk of paying for the insurance with no claims over the lifetime of the policy.

Develop Contingencies: If you cannot eradicate, mitigate, or transfer the risk, you may need to develop contingency plans. A contingency plan is simply an alternative plan that will be implemented should the risk occur.

Accept: As a last resort, you may simply have to accept the risk. Sometimes you cannot do anything to reduce the likelihood or impact of a risk, you cannot transfer it, and no alternative plans can be implemented. In these cases, acceptance is the only option.

This brings us to the final letter in the GRC acronym, which is the letter C. The letter C stands for compliance. Compliance references the processes and tools used to ensure that the policies created in order to reduce the risks identified are being implemented appropriately. Many consider compliance to be a subset of governance. Whether you agree or disagree with this understanding of compliance, you must accept that some form of compliance checking should exist.

C2 Compliance

So that you can better understand GRC, take C2 compliance as an example. A C2-compliant system is one that enforces controlled access protection. *C2 compliance* is defined in The Trusted Computing System Evaluation Criteria (TCSEC), which is sometimes called the Orange Book because the original book was, well, orange. The standard was published as United States Department of Defense (DoD) document 5200.28 in 1983. While the TCSEC defined security levels above C2 (for example, B1, B2, B3, and A1), few systems were developed to meet the requirements of these higher levels due to cost constraints. It is generally accepted that a C2-secure system is the baseline for security. Building on this foundation is required to secure a system for a specific purpose.

 In addition to the information presented here, you can read more about C2 and the TCSEC in the Wikipedia article titled, "Trusted Computer System Evaluation Criteria" located at http://en.wikipedia.org/wiki/ Trusted_Computer_System_Evaluation_Criteria.

The three key levels within the TCSEC document are

D: Minimum protection or unsecured

C1: Discretionary security protection

C2: Controlled access protection

Of course, any system can comply with D-level assurance. C1-level assurance requires that resource access authorization take place. C2-level assurance requires that authentication take place.

A C2-certified system is different than a C2-compliant system. If a system is C2 certified, it means that an independent organization tested the system and verified that it meets C2 compliance. If a system is only C2 compliant, it simply means that actions were taken to ensure that the system was configured to meet the requirements of C2 assurance. Your organization's policies will dictate whether you can implement a system that is simply C2 compliant or not. For example, some government installations may require C2-certified products.

A later DoD standard, known as the Trusted Network Interpretation of the TCSEC (TNI), was published as the Red Book in 1987. Little known to many systems administrators and security professionals, a C2-secure system under TCSEC (the Orange Book) was not intended to be connected to a network. The Red Book sought to remedy this. However, most evaluations that rate a system as C2 certified will also indicate whether it applies to a network connected implementation or not.

So, what are the basic requirements of C2 security? The specific language about C-level assurance in the original 1983 Orange Book is as follows:

> Classes in this division provide for discretionary (need-to-know) protection and, through the inclusion of audit capabilities, for accountability of subjects and the actions they initiate.

From this definition, you can see that discretionary access must be implemented in some way. Additionally, you must be able to track actions taken and prove the identity of the actor. You could wrap up C2 compliance in the following simple phrase: discretionary access with nonrepudiation. Simply put, a system that meets C2-level security must implement the following:

Protected Authentication   Protected authentication indicates that user identification and the logon process will be protected sufficiently. For example, SQL logins, without SSL or IPSec security, would not meet C2-level security. The SQL logins do implement authentication, but it is not protected authentication.

Discretionary Access Control Through Authorization   Discretionary access control indicates that authenticated users cannot access everything and anything. The authenticated users can access only those items to which explicit access is granted. For example, in SQL Server, this means that you are not using the guest account for access to any resources.

Accountability Through Auditing   Finally, C2 requires accountability through auditing. SQL Server does provide auditing capabilities, which were covered earlier in this chapter. The key for C2 compliance is that the auditing process must identify the specific user who took the action. This requires careful thought as many jobs and stored procedures are configured to run in the context of a user other than the calling user. Log chaining, which is a simple phrase used to reference the multitiered reference required to track actions back to the source user, may be required to identify the acting user in such scenarios. For example, you may identify that the account context used to run a stored procedure did indeed perform some action. Now, you must look at the log to see exactly what user called the stored procedure to execute the action.

Now that you understand the basic requirements of C2 compliance, you can explore the implementation of it through the GRC methodology. The first step is to create the policies that will protect against the risks. The nice thing about using a baseline like C2 is that the risk analysis portion is done and the C2 criteria defines the actual policies. In fact, you could borrow the exact language from the Orange Book and use that as the language for your SQL Server policies. Consider the following rewrite of the Orange Book's C2 definitions:

2.2 CLASS (C2): SQL Server Controlled Access Protection

SQL Servers in this class enforce a more finely grained discretionary access control than C1 systems, making logins individually accountable for their actions through login procedures (using only Windows authentication), auditing of security-relevant events (using triggers and/or audits), and resource isolation (using ownership and authorization).

The preceding is a paraphrase of the opening paragraph in the Orange Book's C2 section, but it could be continued to cover the entire requirement set from a SQL Server perspective. With the policies written, the next step is to ensure compliance (remember the *C* in GRC?). Thankfully, SQL Server 2008 makes this very easy with PBM (covered in detail in Chapter 15 and briefly referenced for surface area configuration in this chapter). You can create conditions and policies on those conditions to watch for noncompliance with the C2-level policies you create for SQL Server.

SQL Server 2008 also supports enabling a feature called C2 audit trace. This feature was also available in SQL Server 2005. The C2 audit trace is enabled at the instance level and can be enabled for a single instance or for as many instances as you have installed on a single Windows Server installation. When you enable the C2 audit trace feature, you are actually configuring SQL Server to create a SQL Server Profiler trace file that will be stored in the instance's default data directory. Exercise 19.9 steps you through the process of enabling the C2 audit trace feature.

EXERCISE 19.9

Enabling the C2 Audit Trace

In this exercise, you will enable the C2 audit trace for a SQL Server 2008 instance. To do this, follow these steps:

1. Launch the SQL Server Management Studio.

2. Connect to the instance on which you want to enable the C2 audit trace.

3. Right-click on the root of the SQL Server instance and select Properties.

4. Select the Security page.

5. Choose Enable C2 Audit Tracing.

6. Click OK to save the changes.

7. Click OK when informed that the changes will require a server instance restart.

8. Right-click the root of the SQL Server instance and select Restart.

When the service finishes restarting, the C2 auditing will be enabled.

If you enable C2 auditing, you should know two additional and very important things.

- You can use the SQL Server Profiler to view the audit trace. Simply open the trace file, which is created in the instance's default data directory, using SQL Server Profiler.

- The trace file will continue to grow and may grow very quickly on some systems. If the server runs out of space on the drive where the default data store is located, the SQL Server service will shut down. Do not allow this to happen. Make sure you create a Windows Server alert that monitors the free drive space on this drive to ensure continued operation (Exercise 13.8 in Chapter 13, "Creating Jobs, Operators, and Alerts," provides instructions for doing this).

Common Criteria

One of the things you probably noticed while reading the preceding section was that the C2 criteria were defined in 1983. What else happened in 1983? Well, the top-earning movie of 1983 was *Return of the Jedi,* with *Flashdance* coming in at a very distant second place. The Cabbage Patch dolls were released, and "Just Say No" became the United State's rallying cry against illegal drugs. Oh, and it was also the year that a lot of people acquired Commodore 64s (what a great machine). The point is simple: 1983 was a long time ago. Since that time a lot of things have changed related to computers and security. While the Orange Book was updated in 1985 (let's not get into what happened during that year), it certainly needed an update for the new millennium. In 2005, the Common Criteria was released as the replacement for the Orange Book and, therefore, C2 security.

The Common Criteria (CC) is an international security standard that was created by merging the European, Canadian, and United States security standards together and then evolving them to meet current needs. The CC is far more complex than the old Orange Book, but so are today's modern systems and networks. Interestingly, the greater complexity is not due to more specific technology requirements but rather to the greater ambiguity in the standard. If that sentence sounded ambiguous, you should read the CC itself.

If you would like to download and read the CC, you can get it here: `http://www.commoncriteriaportal.org/thecc.html`. However, the most important thing to know in relation to SQL Server and the CC is that you should still implement the basic security requirements of C2 security in order to meet CC EAL4+. Do you see what I mean when I said that C2 still applies?

The CC provides for evaluation assurance levels (EALs) ranging from 1 to 4. SQL Server 2005 can meet the EAL4+ assurance level if the Common Criteria compliance feature is enabled and the provided configuration script available at `http://go.microsoft.com/fwlink/?LinkId=79877` is executed on the server. At the time of this writing, SQL Server 2008 meets only EAL1+ certification according to the Microsoft website. The Common Criteria compliance feature is enabled on the Security page of the SQL Server instance Properties dialog box, just as the C2 auditing feature is enabled.

Summary

In this chapter, you learned about the best practices related to SQL Server 2008 security. First, you learned about the importance of creating security baselines and the tools available for creating them. These tools included the GPO Accelerator, the Security Templates and Security Configuration and Analysis snap-ins, and the Security Configuration Wizard.

Next, you learned about the actions required to implement the best practice of least privilege. These actions included implementing proper authorization schemes, using credentials, and understanding ownership chains. From here, you moved on to auditing SQL Server. You learned about SQL Server Audits, event notifications, DDL triggers, and logon triggers.

You also learned about surface area configuration and the tools used to perform this action. You learned that the Surface Area Configuration Manager, which was introduced in SQL Server 2005, is no longer available in SQL Server 2008. Then you explored the `sp_configure` stored procedure and the Policy-Based Management Surface Area Configuration facet.

Finally, you learned about the Common Criteria (CC) and C2-level security certifications. You learned that C2 has been superseded by CC and that CC is a bit more vague than C2. Even though CC was introduced in 2005 and is therefore newer, C2 is still very popular as a starting point for security implementation even though it was first created in 1983 and is older.

Chapter Essentials

The Importance of Establishing Baselines   Security baselines provide the minimum security configuration settings required to implement a given system type. As a best practice, you should create a security baseline for SQL Server 2008 servers in your environment. Once the baseline is implemented, you can then harden each SQL Server 2008 server for its specific intent.

Implementing Least Privilege   Least privilege simply says that a user or system should never have more access than that required of the user or system to perform its intended actions. Least privilege is implemented by using authorization schemes. SQL Server 2008 supports authorization through object and statement permissions. Object permissions are used to protect objects like tables, views, and stored procedures. Statement permissions are used to prevent unauthorized users from executing statements like CREATE TABLE and DROP TABLE.

Auditing SQL Server Activity   SQL Server 2008 introduced several new features for auditing. The new SQL Server Audit components allow you to enable automatic auditing without having to create complex DDL triggers. Of course, SQL Server 2008 still supports DDL triggers. Additionally, SQL Server 2008 introduced the new logon trigger so that you can automatically audit or respond to logon events.

Configuring the Surface Area   Surface area reduction is a very important part of your security procedures. The Surface Area Configuration Manager is no longer in SQL Server 2008. Instead of using this tool, you will use the sp_configure stored procedure or Policy-Based Management (PBM) for surface area configuration. Within PBM, you can use the Surface Area Configuration facet to manage most of the items available in the old Surface Area Configuration Manager that was in SQL Server 2005.

Understanding the Common Criteria and C2   Both C2 and the Common Criteria (CC) provide guidelines for secure system implementation. GRC is a process that is used to manage the risk and security of systems. C2 was originally developed in the 1980s and is still applicable today. CC was released in 2005 and is the new international standard for system security evaluation.

High Availability and Data Distribution

Chapter

20

SQL Server Failover Clustering

TOPICS COVERED IN THIS CHAPTER:

✓ Understanding Windows Failover Clustering Service

✓ Implementing a Windows Cluster

✓ Installing SQL Server 2008 to a Cluster

✓ Monitoring and Managing a SQL Server Cluster

SQL Server 2008 supports the Windows Failover Clustering service for fault tolerance and high availability. SQL Server does not implement the clustering, but it operates on the clustering provided by Windows Server. In this chapter, you will learn about the Failover Clustering service and the features it provides. You will also learn of the steps required to implement a cluster and the way in which a cluster operates. Both topics are part of the 70-432 and 70-450 exams from Microsoft.

Once you've implemented Windows Failover Clustering, you'll see how you can install SQL Server 2008 to a cluster. The SQL Server cluster installation process is very simple and is no more complex than a standard nonclustered installation. Finally, you'll explore the tools used to monitor and manage a SQL Server cluster.

Understanding Windows Failover Clustering Service

The Windows Failover Clustering service provides server clustering for Windows-based servers. A *cluster* is a collection of servers that work together to provide services to the network. The unique thing about a cluster of servers, as opposed to separate servers performing independent functions, is that the collection of clustered servers is accessed as a single server. You may have two servers in a cluster, but they appear as one to the users.

Clusters share storage. For example, if you have two physical servers that you want to use as a cluster for SQL Server 2008, both servers must have access to shared storage. It is this shared storage that allows both servers to access the same data and for services to failover from one server to another rapidly. The shared storage should be a fault-tolerant storage solution in order to prevent downtime from storage failures. Fault-tolerant storage solutions include the following:

RAID Cabinets: These are storage devices that support various implementations of RAID, such as RAID 0 (striping), RAID 1 (mirroring), and RAID 5 (striping with parity). Only RAID 1 and RAID 5, of the mentioned RAID levels, support fault tolerance.

Storage Area Networks (SANs): SANs may include multiple physical drive enclosures, but they provide access to the drives in the SAN through logical mappings (usually called LUNs). SANs are typically accessed with either Fibre Channel or iSCSI connections.

Distributed Storage: Distributed storage solutions provide for network-based redundancy. In a distributed storage solution, each storage location will use RAID for fault tolerance, but the data is distributed to multiple RAID locations. Distributed storage solutions preceded SANs and have been largely replaced by SANs today.

When considering a SQL Server cluster installation, you must be aware of the end goal, which is to provide high availability. The goal of a load-balancing cluster is to provide high availability with performance. SQL Server 2008 supports only failover clustering. The performance must be achieved using separate measures such as increased hardware capacity in each clustered server or distribution of the workload among multiple clusters. The point is that high availability does not automatically equate to high performance. If you have a single server that is not performing well and you add another identical server and configure the two as a failover cluster, you will achieve no better performance than that which the single server provided. In a failover cluster, only one server is working with the users at a time. The backup server in the cluster becomes active only if the primary server fails. Hence, high availability is not equal to high performance.

You must also differentiate between high availability and disaster recovery. High availability ensures that the resource is available with as little downtime as possible. Disaster recovery ensures that down time is as short as possible. Do you see the difference? Another way of saying it is to say that disaster recovery helps you get things back up and running and high availability helps you keep things running.

Even with high availability solutions, such as the Failover Clustering service, you must plan for disaster recovery. In most cases, the servers in a cluster will be located in the same physical space, such as a server room or network operations center. Because this is true, a fire or flood could easily take out both servers. This is where disaster recovery kicks in. The Windows Failover Clustering service cannot help you when the server room is full of water.

It is important that you remember the following rule of high availability: *Your system is only as available as its weakest link.*

What does this mean? It means that you have to look at the cluster nodes, the network between these nodes, the shared storage, and the stability of hardware components. This is why Microsoft only recommends using the Failover Clustering service with validated hardware. Validated hardware has been tested by Microsoft or service providers to ensure stability and compatibility with the Failover Clustering service.

 Many organizations that implement Microsoft Failover Clustering will purchase entire solutions from vendors. The solution will include the servers, the storage, and the Windows Server licenses. This ensures compatibility and can reduce complexity during installation and management.

As an example of this "weakest link" concept, consider the Windows Vista and Windows 7 feature called the Windows Experience Index (WEI). WEI rates various hardware components and uses these ratings to determine the performance expectations of the system. Microsoft knew that a system with a very fast processor, but a very slow hard drive would still have performance problems. In the same way, a system with a very fast hard drive and very fast memory, but a very slow processor will also have performance problems. For this reason, the WEI is actually based on the weakest link or the lowest performing component.

This paragraph was typed on a machine with a WEI of 5.9 in Windows 7. The 5.9 rating comes from the hard disk. All other evaluated components (graphics, memory, and processor) are rated from 6.0 to 7.3; however, the Windows 7 report is more realistic than the evaluation of a single component. The same is true for your clusters. If you have expensive and stable servers but faulty storage, the cluster will not live up to your expectations.

Ultimately, four things impact the availability of your systems. These four things are security, stability, life expectancy, and redundancy.

Security   Security must be considered as an availability issue because a security incident can indeed make a resource unavailable. For example, a denial of service (DoS) attack against a SQL Server can make it unavailable to the users regardless of clustering or other availability technologies utilized.

Stability   Stability is a factor of hardware and software quality. Quality hardware should not overheat and should operate effectively for long periods of uninterrupted time. Poorly designed systems often suffer from heat problems and shut themselves off or damage hardware components, resulting in down time.

Life Expectancy   Hard drives have a value called MTBF. MTBF stands for mean time between failures and indicates the life expectancy of the drive. While it is important to purchase drives that will last a long time, it is more important to know when drives are expected to fail. Many organizations plan for drive replacements just before the MTBF is reached. In RAID systems with dynamic data regeneration, the drives can be replaced one-by-one with no down time at all. For other hardware, check with the vendor to determine life expectancy.

Redundancy   The key to high availability is redundancy. This is true in every area of life. For example, if you are designing an application and the application is due in 30 days, and you are the only programmer working on the application, you carry great risk. If you are sick and unable to work for a week, the deadline is sure to be missed; however, if you have other programmers who can take up the work when you are unavailable, the work of the project continues. In the same way, redundant hardware helps keep systems running and available for user access.

Now that you understand what clustering is and the important factors related to high availability, you can move on to explore the specific features and functionality of the Windows Failover Clustering service.

 Windows servers also offer a feature called network load balancing (NLB) that should not be confused with failover clustering. NLB is used to distribute workloads across multiple servers on a session-by-session basis. NLB is not used directly with SQL Server 2008, although it may be used with a web-based front end that accesses a SQL Server 2008 cluster on the back end.

Implementing a Windows Cluster

Before you can jump in and start creating and working with the Failover Cluster service in Windows Server 2008, you must understand the different components that make up a cluster. This section is divided into two parts. First, you'll learn about the components and terminology involved in Windows Failover Clustering. Then, you'll explore the steps required to install the Failover Clustering service and implement a failover cluster.

Failover Clustering Components

The Windows Failover Clustering service can be installed and configured using simple wizards; however, the simple installation process belies a more complicated set of tools and concepts that must be understood by the server administrator. As the DBA, you are more likely to be required to support a SQL Server 2008 instance that is installed on a cluster than to create the initial cluster. Even with this reality, it is important for you to understand what's going on under the hood of that cluster so that you can help the server administrators and network administrators troubleshoot problems with the server. Of course, if you work in a smaller organization, you are most likely the DBA, the network administrator, and anything else the company needs you to be, so you'll certainly benefit from this knowledge.

The first thing you should understand is the terminology related to clustering. For this, you should understand the following terms:

Node   A cluster *node* is a single server that participates in the cluster. Failover clusters must have at least two nodes. One node will be the active node, and the other will be the passive node. Should the active node fail, the services are provided by the passive node and the passive node automatically becomes the active node.

Shared Storage   The nodes in a cluster must have access to centralized and shared storage. Windows Failover Clustering supports Fibre Channel, internet SCSI (iSCSI), or Serial Attached SCSI (SAS) for the shared storage. These storage options fall into the category of storage area networks and are the only shared storage formats supported by Windows Server 2008 and Windows Server 2008 R2 Failover Clustering.

Clustered Services   Clustered services are cluster-aware services. Cluster-aware services can operate on a cluster and communicate with the Failover Clustering service. SQL Server 2008 is such a cluster-aware service.

Quorum   The final element is the quorum. The quorum is used to decide which node should be active at any time in the cluster. The *Oxford American College Dictionary* defines a *quorum* as the minimum number of members of an assembly that must be present to make a meeting valid. You can see how this term is borrowed for clustering. The *quorum* is the minimum number of cluster components (storage, services, nodes) that must be available to offer services. If the quorum is intact, the cluster is available. If it is not intact, the cluster is unavailable.

The concept of the quorum may require further explanation. As an analogy, consider a board of trustees. If the charter for an organization indicates that at least five trustees must exist on the board and at least four must attend a meeting for board activities to occur, the quorum for that board is any four trustees. Decisions can be made even if one trustee is unavailable. However, if two of the five trustees are unavailable, quorum is not met and decisions cannot be made. With Windows clustering, the quorum works in a similar manner. As long as the minimum components are present, the cluster can provide services.

The quorum in Windows Server 2008 and 2008 R2 is based on votes. Nodes, shared disks, and even file shares—depending on the quorum mode—get to vote. If sufficient votes are available, the cluster is active. If the votes are not there, the cluster is not available. The process used to establish quorum is as follows:

1. A cluster node starts and looks for other nodes with which it may communicate.

2. The nodes agree on the cluster configuration and determine if sufficient quorum votes are available to bring the cluster online.

3. If the quorum votes are insufficient (too few voting resources are available), the nodes enter a dormant state and wait for more votes to arrive.

4. If sufficient quorum votes are available, the nodes bring the appropriate resources and applications online (based on active and passive node configurations) and start monitoring the health of the cluster.

5. At this point, quorum is attained and the cluster is online and functioning.

Failover Clustering supports four different quorum modes in Windows Server 2008 and 2008 R2. These modes are outlined in Table 20.1.

TABLE 20.1   Failover Clustering Quorum Modes and Functionality

Mode	Functionality	Best Use
Node Majority	Clustered nodes have the only votes. When half or more of the nodes are online, quorum is achieved.	Used when an odd number of nodes exist in the cluster.
Node and Disk Majority	Clustered nodes have a vote and a witness disk also has a vote. When more than half the votes are online, quorum is achieved.	Used when an even number of nodes exist in the cluster.
Node and File Share Majority	Clustered nodes have a vote and a witness file share has a vote. When more than half the votes are online, quorum is achieved.	Only used when the clustered nodes are spread over some distance. For example, one server may exist at one WAN location and the other exists at a separate WAN location. In this configuration, a file share is often used to provide quorum since strict shared storage is not used.

TABLE 20.1   Failover Clustering Quorum Modes and Functionality (continued)

Mode	Functionality	Best Use
No Majority: Disk Only	The shared disk has the only vote. If the shared disk is online, quorum is achieved.	Used when you want the cluster to be available as long as one node and the shared storage are online. No Majority: Disk only is common for small-scale SQL Server 2008 clusters with only two nodes.

When you think of the votes in the quorum, do not think of them as actions taken by the voting components. Instead, realize that the cluster service looks for these items and if they exist (are online) their vote is counted.

When implementing a multisite cluster across WAN links, one site will be the read/write site and the other site will be a read-only site. All changes happen to the storage at the read/write site and are replicated to the read-only site. The replication may be synchronous or asynchronous. With synchronous replication, changes are made at the primary site and the process is not considered complete until the changes are replicated to the secondary site. Asynchronous replication allows the process to continue as soon as the change is written at the primary site.

In addition to the terms used in relation to clustering, you should understand the networks used. Three networks will typically exist in a failover clustering solution.

Public Network: This is used by clients to access the cluster. The public network is the same as any other network used to connect to a standard single server installation.

Private Network: This exists only between the clustered nodes. You will usually use separate network cards for the public and private networks.

Storage Network: This is used to connect with the shared storage location. A specialized adapter (known as a host bus adapter) may be required for Fibre Channel or SAS, but iSCSI may be accessed using standard network cards. Special iSCSI adapters also exist that offload the TCP/IP process from the operating system in order to improve performance when accessing iSCSI storage devices.

Multiple network cards are not required for the public and private networks; however, it is recommended that you use multiple network cards for performance enhancement.

Once the server cluster is in place, cluster resources must be managed. These resources include shared storage, IP addresses, and network names. Clients will connect to the cluster using network names, which are resolved to IP addresses. Only one node in the cluster can respond to a request. The node currently configured to respond is the active node. In order for other nodes to respond, the active node must fail—intentionally or unintentionally—and the resources will then failover to the alternative node.

The Failover Clustering Installation Process

Installing Windows Failover Clustering can be a time-consuming process requiring much planning. You'll need to ensure that the hardware selected is supported by Microsoft for clustering purposes. You'll also need to ensure that the vendor provides quick and secure updates for the hardware device drivers and software. The most important thing to keep in mind during the planning process that leads up to installation is the issue of up time or availability. If you implement Windows Failover Clustering on a machine that is not supported by Microsoft or maintained well by the vendor, you are just asking for trouble on a machine that you apparently need to be highly available. The following sections provide an overview of the planning and installation process.

Meeting Requirements Before Installing

Before you can install a Windows failover cluster, you must ensure that your systems meet the requirements of the Failover Clustering service. In order to have support from Microsoft for your cluster solution, the following hardware requirements must be met:

- The server hardware must be marked with the Certified for Windows Server 2008 logo.

- All server nodes should have the same configuration and contain the same components and features.

- The Validate a Configuration Wizard must pass all tests. This wizard is executed as part of the service installation and configuration process.

In addition to the hardware requirements, the following network requirements must be met:

- The network hardware must be marked with the Certified for Windows Server 2008 logo.

- The server nodes should be connected to multiple networks to provide communication resiliency.

- The network infrastructure must not contain single points of failure (for example, a single router that connects a network segment to the rest of the infrastructure).

- Network adapters must be configured with the same IP version, speed settings, duplex, and flow control capabilities.

It doesn't stop with the network requirements. You must also ensure that the following storage requirements are met:

- The cluster storage device controllers must be identical and have the same firmware versions installed on each node.

- You must use separate networks for client access and iSCSI storage, if iSCSI is utilized instead of Fibre Channel or SAS.

- The Microsoft Storport driver model must be used in the development of the storage drivers.

- Basic disks should be configured on the storage.

- Multipath solutions must be based on MPIO (Microsoft Multipath I/O).

Next, you'll need to ensure that your infrastructure meets the following requirements:

- All cluster nodes must use DNS for name resolution and, therefore, a DNS server must be available.

- All cluster nodes must be members of the same Active Directory domain.

- Administrator rights must be granted on all cluster nodes to the user account that creates the cluster, and this account must have Create Computer Object permissions within the Active Directory domain.

Finally, you must consider the software requirements to implement the failover cluster. The following software requirements must be met:

- All nodes must run the same edition of Windows Server 2008 and only Enterprise and DataCenter editions support the Failover Clustering service.

- All nodes must run the same processor type (for example, 32-bit, 64-bit, etc.).

- All nodes should be updated to the same level with service packs and updates.

 It's important to remember that Microsoft only supports failover clustering on hardware marked with the Certified for Windows Server 2008 logo. Additionally, all tests in the Validate a Configuration Wizard must pass to get support for the cluster from Microsoft. You may be able to install the Failover Clustering service without these items in place, but you will not get support from Microsoft Support Services.

Installing Failover Clustering

Once you've ensured that your hardware and software meet the requirements for the Failover Clustering service and the network connections and shared storage have been installed and configured, you are ready to install the Failover Clustering feature. Exercise 20.1 provides the steps required to install Failover Clustering.

EXERCISE 20.1

Installing Windows Failover Clustering

In this exercise, you will install the Failover Clustering service on a Windows Server 2008 node. To do this, follow these steps:

1. Log on to the Windows Server 2008 machine as a domain administrator.

2. Select Start ➢ Server Manager to open the Server Manager window.

3. In the left pane, select the Features node.

4. In the Features Summary window, click the Add Features link.

5. In the list of features, choose Failover Clustering, as in the following image, and click Next.

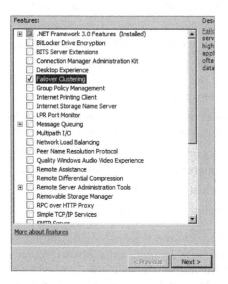

6. Click the Install button to begin the installation.

7. When the installation is complete, you may need to restart your server. If prompted, select to restart now. If a prompt does not appear, click Close to complete the installation.

8. You may close the Server Manager window at this point.

As Exercise 20.1 shows, installing the Failover Clustering service is a very simple process.

Validating Your Configuration

Now that Failover Clustering is installed, you'll need to validate your configuration. The validation is performed from the Failover Cluster Management tool found in Administrative

Tools on the Start menu. From here, you can run the Validate a Configuration Wizard. Keep the following facts about the Validate a Configuration Wizard in mind:

- The wizard verifies that Microsoft will support the configuration.
- The wizard requires that the Failover Clustering feature be installed on each node to be tested.
- The wizard should be executed before you actually create the failover cluster.
- Each test will result in one of four outcomes: pass, pass with warnings, fail, or test not run.
- Anytime major cluster changes are made, you should run the wizard again.
- The wizard confirms that the cluster hardware and software is compatible with the Failover Clustering service.

When the Validate a Configuration Wizard runs, it performs four primary tests. The descriptions and actions for these are listed in Table 20.2.

TABLE 20.2   Validate a Configuration Wizard Tests and Actions

Test	Description	Actions
Inventory Test	This ensures that the required components exist in order for clustering to work.	Reports on BIOS information, environment variables, Fibre Channel HBAs, iSCSI HBAs, SAS HBAs, memory, OS information, plug-and-play devices, running processes, services running, software updates, system information, drivers, and unsigned drivers.
Network Test	This is used to make sure the network connections are configured appropriately.	Network configuration is verified for the cluster network, IP settings, network communications, and Windows firewall settings.
Storage Test	This is used to ensure that the nodes can all contact and access the shared storage.	The storage test verifies disk failover, disk access latency, file system selection, MPIO version, SCSI-3 persistent reservation, and simultaneous failover.
System Configuration Test	This ensures that the nodes are all running the same operating systems, service packs, updates, and components.	The system configuration analysis includes Active Directory configuration, all drivers are signed, operating system versions match, required services are installed, processor types match, service pack levels are consistent, and software update levels are consistent.

Exercise 20.2 provides the steps for running the Validate a Configuration Wizard.

Running the Validate a Configuration Wizard

In this exercise, you will run the Validate a Configuration Wizard and view the resulting report. In order to perform these steps, you will need two Windows Server 2008 servers with the Failover Clustering feature installed as described in Exercise 20.1. To run the wizard, follow these steps:

1. Log on to one of the intended nodes as a domain administrator.

2. Select Start ➤ All Programs ➤ Administrative Tools ➤ Failover Cluster Management.

3. In the Management pane, choose Validate a Configuration.

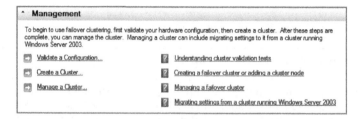

4. Read the information on the Before You Begin page of the wizard and then click Next.

5. On the Select Servers or a Cluster page, click Browse to choose the servers to be validated as functional for a cluster.

6. In the Select Computers window, click Advanced.

7. Click Find Now to list all servers available in the domain.

8. While holding down the Ctrl key, click the servers you want to become part of the cluster and then click OK.

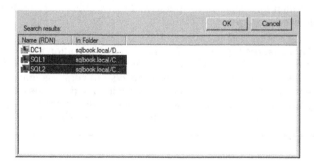

9. Click OK again to add the servers. If you receive an error indicating that Failover Clustering is not installed on one of the nodes, you must log on to that node and install Failover Clustering before proceeding. Click Next.

10. On the Testing Options page, accept the default option to Run All Tests and click Next.

11. Click Next on the Confirmation page to begin the actual validation process. As the process runs, you will see a screen similar to the following:

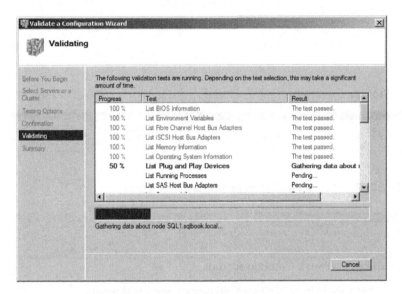

12. When the validation completes and you are taken to the Summary page, click View Report to read the HTML report created by the wizard.

When reading the report generated by the Validate a Configuration Wizard, look for the items with a warning description. Click the link for any such items to find out what caused the warning. For example, Figure 20.1 shows a report with a warning for the Validate Network Communications item. Figure 20.2 shows the detailed information for this warning.

FIGURE 20.1 Viewing the warnings in a Validate a Configuration Wizard report

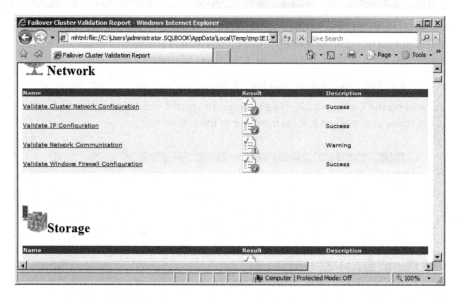

FIGURE 20.2 Viewing the warning details in the report

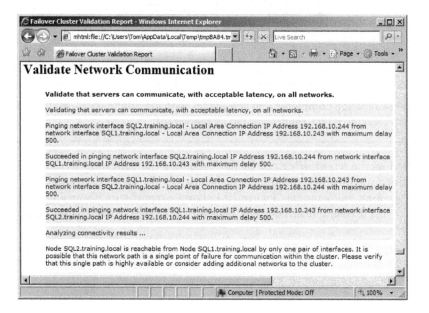

If you find warnings in the report, you should read the warning details and then take any necessary actions to resolve the problem. For example, the warning pictured in Figure 20.1 is related to the fact that the servers are connected to each other using a single network and not multiple networks. Clustering will work with a single network, but it will not provide the higher levels of availability you may require (because the single network is a single point of failure). If the single point of failure in the network is acceptable to you, you can ignore the warning.

Creating the Cluster

With the Validate a Configuration Wizard completed and assuming no significant problems were encountered, you're ready to create the cluster. You create cluster configurations with the Create Cluster Wizard in the Failover Cluster Management tool. Exercise 20.3 provides the steps required to create a cluster.

EXERCISE 20.3

Creating a Failover Cluster

In this exercise you will create a cluster using the Failover Cluster Management tool. To do this, follow these steps:

1. Log on to a cluster node as a domain administrator.

2. Select Start ➤ All Programs ➤ Administrative Tools ➤ Failover Cluster Management.

3. In the Management pane, choose the Create a Cluster option to launch the Create Cluster Wizard.

4. On the Before You Begin page, read the information and then click Next to begin the creation process.

5. Click Browse to select the Windows Server 2008 instances with the Failover Clustering service installed.

6. Click the Advanced button and then Find Now to list all available Windows servers.

7. Press Ctrl and then click on each of the servers to be included in the cluster. With the servers selected, click OK.

8. Click OK again to add the servers.

9. When you're returned to the Select Servers page, click Next.

10. On the Access Point for Administering the Cluster page, enter the name you want to use for the cluster and the IP address (if only one network adapter exists in each node, the IP address option will not be displayed) and then click Next.

11. Click Next to create the cluster.

12. When the cluster creation is complete, you'll see the Summary page. Click Finish to finish the wizard.

Cluster Resources

After the cluster is created using the steps in Exercise 20.3, you can begin assigning resources to the cluster. Several resource types can be assigned to the cluster right out-of-the-box. The resources include:

- DHCP Service
- Distributed File System
- Distributed Transaction Coordinator
- File Server
- File Share Quorum Witness
- Generic Application
- Generic Script
- Generic Service
- IP Address
- IPv6 Address
- IPv6 Tunnel Address
- iSNSClusRes
- Network Name
- NFS Share
- Physical Disk
- Print Spooler
- Volume Shadow Copy Service Task
- WINS Service

When you look through this list, it becomes apparent that the resources that can be assigned to the cluster are very similar to resources that are assigned to a standalone server. For example, just as you can have multiple IP addresses assigned to a single network adapter in a server, you can have multiple IP addresses assigned to a cluster as well. As another example, just as you can install and manage printers on standalone servers, you can install the Print Spooler service and share printers through the cluster. This collection of resources is known as a *cluster resource group*.

 Real World Scenario

Clustering in a Virtual Environment

When you implement a cluster using physical hardware, the process is very straightforward. But what if you want to implement a cluster using virtualization? I was working on a project recently that required just such a solution. The short answer to the question is that you can, but the long answer is that it's not quite as easy as having the real physical equipment. To implement clustered virtual machines (VMs) with Windows Server 2008, I needed four VMs.

The first VM was the Active Directory domain controller, since the new Failover Clustering service in Windows Server 2008 requires a domain. For this VM, I used 1024MB (1GB) of RAM. You should provide more RAM to this machine if you plan to have virtual or physical clients connecting to the machine, but I was not allowing clients to connect in my situation.

The second VM ran the iSCSI service software. This software is needed because Windows Server 2008 no longer allows you to configure attached disks as the "shared storage" within a virtual environment. The best solution is, therefore, iSCSI. Two excellent free software-based iSCSI solutions are FreeNAS (www.FreeNAS.org) and OpenFiler (www.OpenFiler.org). I used OpenFiler for my virtual environment because it can be downloaded as a VMware appliance. This made the setup much easier.

Finally, the last two VMs ran Windows Server 2008 Enterprise Edition and acted as the Failover Clustering nodes. These nodes connected through iSCSI with the second VM for shared storage. With a configuration like this, I was able to build a clustered test environment for certification preparation or lab testing without the expense of a hardware-based SAN. The nice thing is that all the virtual machines are backed up so I can rebuild a virtual clustered environment within a few hours anytime I need it.

Installing SQL Server 2008 to a Cluster

Once you have created the Windows failover cluster, you can install SQL Server 2008 to the cluster. The installation process is not much different from the one described in Chapter 2, "Installing SQL Server 2008," when you learned to install SQL Server 2008 on a standalone server in the sections titled "Installing a Default Instance" and "Installing Named Instances." This time around during the installation process, you will choose New SQL Server failover cluster installation to begin the installation process. Then, during the install, in addition to the standard decisions made in a normal standalone installation, you'll need to make the following decisions:

- What will you name the SQL Server failover cluster instance? This name will be used to access the clustered SQL Servers from the network.

- What resource group will you use for the cluster? The resource group collects the resources (such as names, IPs, etc.) that will be needed for the SQL Server cluster to function.

- What storage resource will you use for the SQL Server cluster? The storage or drive resource must be shared among all nodes in the cluster, and the databases will be physically installed to this drive in order to be accessed from the cluster.

- What network settings should be used for the failover cluster? These settings will determine the IP address used to access the cluster.

With these questions answered, you will be ready to begin the installation process. You can actually follow the standard installation instructions provided in Chapter 2, but remember that you'll need to provide these four items in addition to the standard set of information.

Monitoring and Managing a SQL Server Cluster

Once you have the SQL Server cluster installed and operational, you will have to consider management and monitoring of the cluster. Several issues must be considered including:

- Service packs and update management
- Failover management
- Cluster troubleshooting

You must plan for all three in order to maintain the high availability of the failover cluster. The following sections provide an overview of these three factors.

Service Packs and Update Management

One of the most common questions DBAs have about SQL Server 2008 clusters is related to maintenance. The question usually goes something like this: "How do I apply service packs to the nodes in the cluster since they are all separate computers?" The answer lies in a little-known secret related to SQL Server service packs. SQL Server service packs and updates are cluster aware. This cluster awareness simply means that the service pack will automatically install to the nodes in the cluster in order to keep them synchronized. You will not have to install the service pack on each node individually. Individual patches released for SQL Server 2008 are also cluster aware. Service packs and updates are installed in the normal fashion; the installation packages themselves have the logic to detect a cluster and install properly for it.

Failover Management

One of the key tasks you must perform as the server administrator and possibly as the DBA is failover management. Failover management is all about deciding which server should be active in a failover cluster. Failover clustering can be implemented in one of two ways including:

Active/Passive   An Active/Passive failover cluster uses one active node and one or more passive nodes. In other words, if you have three nodes in a cluster, only one node can be active for any service at any time. The other nodes wait in the wings for the active node to fail and then one of the passive nodes may become active. Of course, you can manually failover to one of the passive nodes if you need to for maintenance purposes or any other purpose.

Active/Active   An Active/Active failover cluster allows different services to be active on different nodes at the same time. For example, if you have a three-node cluster (Node A, Node B, and Node C), you could run a different service actively on each node. Node A may run a SQL Server instance. Node B may run file and print services, and Node C may run a third-party service. If Node A fails, then Node B or Node C could become active for SQL Server; however, SQL Server is only running on a single node at any given time.

In addition to needing to choose between Active/Passive and Active/Active, you should test failover to make sure everything is working properly. You can test failover using several methods including:

Move resource groups.   You can use the Failover Clustering Management tool to move a resource group from the active node to a passive node. When you do this, you provide that the resource group can be moved to the passive server node and that failover can occur. If the move from the active node to the passive node works, you may want to move the resource group back again—assuming that the previously active node was indeed the one you want to use as the primary node in the cluster.

Manually break the network.   This method may seem odd, but you can force an automatic failover by breaking the network connection to the public network. Just unplug the Ethernet cable from the currently active node's public network adapter. You will see the resource group failover to the passive node. When you plug the network cable back into the server, you can move the resource group back using the Failover Clustering Management tool.

Shut down the active node.   Several Internet-based resources say to turn off the active node for this type of test, but presumably their intention is that you shut them down. If you power off the node, you risk system corruption. If you shut down the node, you should see that the resource group moves to the passive node automatically.

Ultimately, you can use any method that causes the active node to be removed from the quorum. If the active node is moved from the quorum, the failover to the passive node should occur automatically.

Cluster Troubleshooting

If you attempt a manual failover from the active to the passive node and the failover does not work, check for one of the following problems:

- Is the public network connection functioning for the passive node? If the public network is down, Failover Clustering cannot fail to that node. Get the public network up and running on the passive node and try again.

- Can the passive node access and use the shared storage? Failover Clustering will be unable to fail to the passive node if the passive node cannot access the needed data. Resolve any connection problems related to the shared storage and try the failover again.

As another troubleshooting trick, use the Validate a Configuration Wizard again as covered in Exercise 20.2. This wizard can usually locate the problems that would prevent the failover from occurring. Run the wizard and then view the report. Does the report show new problems that did not exist during the initial installation of the cluster? If so, resolve these problems and you will most likely resolve the failover issue.

Summary

In this chapter, you learned how to implement a Windows Server cluster. You first learned what clustering is and the different terms used to describe and work with clustering solutions. Next, you learned how the Windows Server 2008 Failover Clustering service functions and how to plan for its installation. You then installed the Failover Clustering service and ran the Validate a Configuration Wizard to ensure that the targeted servers could indeed operate as a cluster. Finally, you explored the process required to install SQL Server 2008 to a cluster and to maintain and support that cluster after installation.

Chapter Essentials

Understanding Windows Failover Clustering Service   The Windows Failover Clustering service provides the core functionality required for SQL Server 2008 clustering. In fact, SQL Server 2008 installs to a Windows cluster in much the same way as it installed to a standalone machine. The Failover Clustering service provides the monitoring and automatic failover from an active to a passive node within the cluster.

Implementing a Windows Cluster   If you are required to implement a Windows cluster, you must first ensure that your hardware and software meet the minimum requirements. If you will require Microsoft support, you should only use hardware that is marked with the Certified for Windows Server 2008 logo and completely passes all tests in the Validate a Configuration Wizard.

To install a Windows cluster, you must first establish the appropriate network connection between the intended cluster nodes. The best practice is to implement one network for the public network accessed by the clients and another network for the private network between the cluster nodes. You will also need to configure the connections to the appropriate shared storage devices on each node.

Once the nodes are configured, you should install the Failover Clustering feature on each node. With the Failover Clustering feature installed, run the Validate a Configuration Wizard and resolve any problems detected by the wizard. Finally, you can use the Create a Cluster Wizard to create the actual cluster across the nodes.

Installing SQL Server 2008 to a Cluster   Installing SQL Server 2008 to a cluster is not much different from installing to a standalone machine. You will need to identify a cluster name, the IP configuration used in the cluster, the resource group used for the cluster, and the shared storage. Aside from these four items, the installation is the same as that of a standalone install.

Monitoring and Managing a SQL Server Cluster   Once SQL Server 2008 is installed to the cluster, you will have to consider how you will monitor and maintain the cluster. Service packs are cluster aware so they can be installed to all nodes in the cluster at once. You should test failover using either manual resource-group copy methods or automated methods through forced failure. Regardless of the testing method you choose, always be careful not to do permanent damage to a cluster node with actions such as powering off the node instead of shutting it down. Remember that most problems that keep a failover from occurring can be identified by running the Validate a Configuration Wizard.

Chapter 21

Database Mirroring and Snapshots

TOPICS COVERED IN THIS CHAPTER:

- ✓ Data Redundancy
- ✓ Using Database Mirroring
- ✓ Understanding Log Shipping
- ✓ Implementing Database Snapshots

The typical DBA must concern himself with not only administration of data in a single server, but the distribution of that data to multiple servers. This chapter will cover replication, but first it will discuss some other forms of data distribution, which are database mirroring and log shipping. Additionally, you should understand database snapshots; although they are not used to distribute data across different servers, they can be used to retain copies of data as it exists at specific points in time. Data is distributed for two main reasons. The first is to get the data to the user in the most efficient way possible. Replication and ETL tools perform this function well. The second reason is to distribute the data for redundancy purposes. This chapter will focus on the methods SQL Server 2008 provides for data distribution with the intent of redundancy.

Data redundancy actually begins at the hardware level with redundant storage. Redundant storage usually means RAID, and this topic is addressed first in this chapter. Next, three of SQL Server 2008's data redundancy solutions will be addressed. They are

Database Mirroring: Allows a database to exist and be automatically maintained on two SQL Server 2008 instances at the same time

Log Shipping: Allows a database to be duplicated on a second instance with high levels of latency (delays between updates)

Database Snapshots: Do not typically involve a second instance, but are created on the local instance to provide point-in-time access to data

All three solutions are addressed in this chapter.

Some databases require very little down time, while others can allow for much more down time. If you can accept system outages of an hour or more, you may be able to use a single server with effective backup and restoration plans using some form of redundancy in the hardware, such as RAID controllers. This chapter will detail how to handle down times of minutes or less. You will learn about the technologies provided by SQL Server that will help you accomplish such up time. You will also learn the difference between hot, warm, and cold standby servers, along with how to implement and maintain them.

RAID-Based Data Redundancy

Data availability technologies are used to keep data online and available with little or no down time. Data redundancy is essential to recoverability. If your data exists only in one place, it cannot be recovered should that storage location fail. Availability is provided through internal server techniques as well as through the use of multiple servers. Internal server techniques include component-level redundancy solutions such as RAID and software solutions. Multiple-server techniques include mirroring, log shipping, replication, and clustering.

RAID (redundant array of independent disks) is one such internal server or external storage technology that may be hardware or software based. Hardware-based RAID uses hardware drive controllers that have the RAID processing software built in. Software-based RAID uses standard hard-drive controllers and handles the RAID processing as a software layer that is either built into the operating system or installed as an extra feature. There are many different RAID levels, but the most commonly used RAID levels are listed here:

- RAID 0
- RAID 1
- RAID 5
- RAID 0+1
- RAID 1+0 or RAID 10

Figure 21.1 shows the various RAID levels in a graphical representation. RAID 0 is depicted as three physical drives acting as one virtual drive. Under the hood, data is striped evenly across the three drives. For example, if 99KB of data is being written to the D: drive using RAID 0, one third would be written to Drive 1, one third to Drive 2, and the final third to Drive 3. By itself, RAID 0 does not provide any fault tolerance. RAID 0 is used to improve read and write performance only. Most controllers require two drives to create a stripe set without parity or a RAID 0 array. Some will require three drives in the array. The negatives of RAID 0 include the fact that one drive failure makes the entire array unavailable and that the large amount of storage represented by the physical drives now aggregates into one, possibly difficult-to-manage, storage location. The positives include faster data access and storage, as well as no loss of storage space.

The next level of RAID represented is RAID level 1. At level 1, data is mirrored to two physical drives, but the user only sees one drive at the operating system level—if the RAID is implemented through hardware as opposed to software. Software-based RAID levels 0, 1, and 5 are supported through the Disk Management snap-in in Windows Server. RAID 1 provides fault tolerance through the fact that all data is written twice. The data is written once to the "visible" drive and once to the "invisible" drive. There is no striping of data during writes, but some RAID controllers (hardware drive controllers that support RAID configurations) will read the data from both drives. RAID 1 is used to provide fault tolerance and quick failover. The negatives of RAID 1 include the loss of half of your storage space and the reduced performance of writes. The positive is that RAID 1 provides the highest level of data availability because all the data is completely written to two separate physical devices.

RAID 5 attempts to balance RAID 0 and 1. RAID 5 arrays stripe data across the drives in the array. However, unlike RAID 0, RAID 5 arrays also provide fault tolerance. This is done through the generation of parity bits. For example, assume there are three physical drives (see Figure 21.1) that make up the logical drive array. When data is written to the array, half the data will be written to one drive, half the data to another, and then parity bits will be written to the third drive. In most implementations, the parity bits are stored evenly across the drives in the array. Now, if any single physical drive fails, the controller or software can regenerate the data that was stored on the failed drive. This regeneration generally occurs on-the-fly with no administrative intervention. Of course, should another drive fail at this time, the entire array will be lost.

FIGURE 21.1   RAID levels 0, 1, and 5

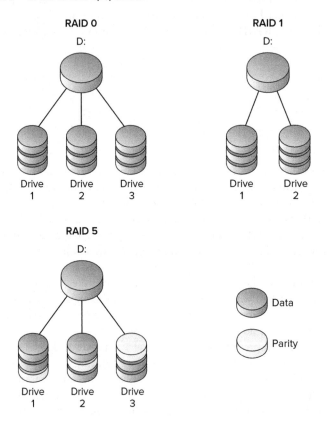

To understand how RAID 5 functions, consider this simple analogy. Imagine you want to store the numbers 5 and 7. If you store 5 in one notebook and 7 in another, when either notebook is lost, you've lost the ability to recover all of your meaningful data. However, imagine you have a third notebook. In this third notebook, you store the number 12 (5+7). Now, if you lose one of the three notebooks, you will always be able to get your data back. For example, if you lose the second notebook, you can subtract 5 (the number in notebook 1) from 12 and recover the number 7 that was in the second notebook. While RAID 5 striping and parity algorithms are more complex than this, it should help you to conceptualize how the RAID level functions. It is also important to keep in mind that when you add more drives to your system, you increase the likelihood that one of those drives will fail on any given day and actually increase the need for fault tolerance.

RAID 0+1 combines the stripe sets with mirroring. You would configure two stripe sets first and then configure those two stripe sets to show up as one drive that is a RAID 1 implementation. For example, you might have three drives in each stripe set and, in the end, all six drives would show up as one virtual drive. This gives you a balance between the performance of RAID 0 and the complete fault tolerance of RAID 1.

RAID 1+0, also known as RAID 10, is just the opposite of RAID 0+1. In this case, you will actually implement two or three mirror sets first and then stripe data across those mirror sets. This provides fault tolerance as the foundation and performance as an added layer.

Understanding the various levels of RAID is important, and you will use this knowledge as you make decisions related to the server hardware that you purchase. If you determine that you will need fault tolerance at the drive level, you will want to be sure and purchase a server that provides this feature through hardware. Although you can implement RAID through software, the performance is not generally as high and it will take away processing power from the database server software.

RAID is one method of providing fault tolerance for your databases. You can also achieve this with many of the built-in features of SQL Server. Data redundancy is provided through database mirroring, log shipping, and replication. Data availability is enhanced through these as well as database snapshots. In addition, there are manual methods that you can perform or automate through Integration Services packages or jobs that allow bulk transfer of data for redundancy purposes or for other data distribution needs, such as data warehousing and business analysis databases.

Using Database Mirroring

Unlike RAID mirroring, which is a drive-level concept, database mirroring is a transaction-level concept within a SQL Server architecture. Database mirroring provides a mechanism for duplicating databases across servers and is a low-latency solution. With this technology, you can create a warm standby server using just two servers or a hot standby server using a third server. A *warm* standby server is one that can be brought online with some effort in a manual fashion. A *hot* standby server is one that is enabled automatically when the primary server fails. You create the warm standby server with a production server, where the user interactions occur, and another server that is receiving the transactions but is not available for user access. You create a hot standby server by implementing a third instance of SQL Server that monitors the previously mentioned two servers for failure and automatic failover. Regardless of which implementation method you choose, this section will give you the information you need to understand and implement database mirroring.

Database Mirroring Components

Database mirroring is a process provided by SQL Server that maintains two copies of one database with each copy stored in a separate instance of SQL Server. At least two server instances are involved in every mirroring configuration and up to three servers can be used. These three servers are:

Principal: The principal server instance houses the active database that is accessed by the users. This principal instance contains the database that is modified through normal application usage and is treated much like a normal single database server instance. This principal instance is said to be serving the database because it allows transactions to be performed against the database.

Mirror: The mirror server instance houses the second copy of the database and is not accessed by users or applications while in the mirror role. This mirror instance contains the database that is modified only by the principal instance.

Witness: The witness server instance is the optional server and, when it is provided, is used to provide automatic failover. This witness instance does not contain a copy of the database being mirrored, but instead it monitors the primary instance and, should it fail, it switches the mirror instance to act as the primary instance and in so doing provides automatic failover.

The principal and mirror instances must be running either SQL Server Standard or Enterprise Edition. The witness instance, if used, can run any edition of SQL Server except the Mobile Edition. This means you could use the free edition—SQL Server Express—to act as the witness instance for an automatic failover configuration of database mirroring. Database mirroring roles defined at the database level include the principal and mirror roles; however, the witness role is configured at the instance level, as there is no actual copy of the database on the witness server.

 Both copies of the database in a mirror set are exact copies. They are synchronized with each other automatically, so either instance can play the principal or mirror role at any time. For this reason, the principal and mirror roles are considered transient operating states—*transient* meaning temporary or not lasting. Therefore, these operating states do not have to be considered permanent.

An interesting and useful feature of the mirror instance in the mirror set is the ability to create a snapshot on the mirror instance. You can allow users to query this snapshot on the mirror instance for reporting against point-in-time data. Snapshots are covered later in this chapter. Because you cannot actually query the mirror instance, this provides an interesting benefit when it comes to getting more use out of a server running a mirror instance.

Understanding Mirror Operating Modes

Database mirroring supports two different operating modes. These operating modes determine the way transactions are transferred between the principal and mirror databases and the failover mechanism that will be used. The two operating modes are

- High Safety
- High Performance

High Safety

The high safety operating mode requires all three server roles. This operating mode provides guaranteed transaction committal on both the principal and the mirror. The guaranteed transaction committal is provided through synchronous operations. All committed transactions are committed on both partners (synchronous), which provides the guarantee of committal at both the principal and the mirror instance. In high safety mode, the transactions are written to memory and then to the transaction log. When the transaction is written to the transaction log, database mirroring transfers these transactions to the mirror instance. When a commit transaction is executed, the transaction is first committed on the mirror and then the mirror instance sends an acknowledgement of committal to the principal. At this time, the principal commits the transactions and notifies the application of the results. As you can guess, this can result in performance issues, but the transactions are guaranteed to be committed in both the principal and the mirror or not committed anywhere. When you need to guarantee synchronicity between the principal and the mirror more than you need to provide high performance, you will want to use the high safety operating mode.

High Performance

The high performance operating mode uses asynchronous transaction committal. When a transaction is submitted to the principal, it is processed in the same way a standalone instance would process the transaction. The mirroring service is also monitoring these transactions and sending them to the mirror instance. There is no verification that the transaction has been written to the mirror database before more transactions are accepted at the principal. This may result in a lag on the mirror instance and a risk of data loss in the event of principal database failure; however, the performance gains can be substantial—and when you are implementing mirroring across WAN links or other slower connections, it may be the only option you have.

Planning for Role Switching

Role switching is used to convert a mirror server to the primary server or vice versa. This may be required to perform maintenance or because of a failure in system components. The transient operating states (principal and mirror) can be changed in one of three ways:

- Automatic failover
- Manual failover
- Forced service

Automatic failover requires the use of a witness server, and it also requires that you use the high safety operating mode. The witness server monitors the partner server in the mirroring relationship. If the witness server detects that the partner server has failed, it will automatically switch the mirror instance to act as the principal instance. This actually works in a little more complicated fashion as outlined next.

1. The mirroring partners (principal and mirror) continually ping each other.

2. The witness intermittently pings the partners.

3. When the principal fails, the mirror instance detects this, in that the principal is no longer responding to the pings.

4. The mirror sends a request to the witness to be promoted to the principal.

5. The witness pings the principal and gets no response so it agrees with the mirror and authorizes the promotion.

6. The mirror instance promotes itself to become the principal.

After this process, when the principal comes back online, it detects that the mirror has become the principal and it automatically demotes itself to playing the mirror role. As you can see, the witness server is crucial to this process. If the witness server is unavailable, the mirror instance will not promote itself. This implementation prevents split-brain problems where you have two instances trying to act as the principal at the same time. This could occur, without the use of a witness server, if the mirror could not reach the principal, but it was actually still functioning.

When using manual failover, a witness server is not required, but high safety mode is still required. In manual failover mode, you will have to see that the principal instance has failed and then manually promote the mirror instance to become the principal. The forced service failover is used when in high performance mode. Because some transactions may not be committed on the mirror instance, you have to force it to act as the primary and indicate that data loss is allowed.

Implementing Database Mirroring

To implement database mirroring, you will need to perform a number of tasks and ensure that the databases involved in the mirroring processes are configured correctly. It is very important to remember that a database participating in database mirroring must use the full recovery model. Then you'll need to back up the database on the principal instance and recover the database to the intended mirror instance. When you recover the database to the intended mirror instance, be sure to use the NORECOVERY option so that the database is left in the proper state to begin mirroring operations.

In addition to the backup and restore of the database, you should also be sure that any system objects in existence on the principal server are also created on the mirror server. These may include users, roles, custom error messages, Integration Services packages, SQL Server Agent jobs, and linked servers. Remember, you only need to create the system objects on the mirror instance that are actually used by the database being mirrored. The principal instance may have other databases as well, and the system objects those databases use exclusively will not need to be created on the mirror instance.

After you've performed these initial steps, you'll need to do the following:

- Create endpoints for the mirroring configuration.

- Configure the mirroring partners, which means backing up the database on the primary server and restoring it to the mirror server with NORECOVERY.

- Configure a witness server, if needed, which can be done with SQL Server Express Edition.

Configure operating modes according to the guidelines suggested in the previous section of this chapter titled "Understanding Mirror Operating Modes." Each instance in the database mirroring partnership requires a mirroring endpoint. Endpoints were covered with a fair amount of detail in Chapter 2, "Installing SQL Server 2008," so there is no need to go into detail here. However, you will need to know how to create the endpoints for the principal and the mirror servers. The endpoints can use either Windows authentication or certificate-based authentication. Most implementations will choose to use Windows authentication. In addition, only one mirroring endpoint can exist in each SQL Server instance. Because of this limitation, you will want to ensure that no mirroring endpoints exist on your SQL Server before actually creating an endpoint. The following code can be used to test for the existence of a mirroring endpoint:

```
SELECT name, role_desc, state_desc
FROM sys.database_mirroring_endpoints;
```

If you get zero results, you are ready to execute code like that in Exercise 21.1 to create the mirroring endpoints. If you find existing endpoints, you may have to delete them using the DROP ENDPOINT statement or create new additional endpoints specifically for mirroring. You will need to execute the code that is shown in Exercise 21.1. For example, you should only run the principal code on the principal instance.

EXERCISE 21.1

Creating the Mirroring Endpoints

In this exercise, the code needed to create mirroring endpoints is presented. This code may require modification in order to work on your specific system. To create mirroring endpoints:

1. Log on to the principal server as an administrator and connect to the SQL Server, using SSMS, as an administrator.

2. Execute the following code in a new query window:

```
--Endpoint for principal server instance.
CREATE ENDPOINT mirroring
    STATE = STARTED
```

```
        AS TCP ( LISTENER_PORT = 7575 )
        FOR DATABASE_MIRRORING (ROLE=PARTNER);
    GO
```

3. Log on to the mirror server as an administrator. Using SSMS, connect to the SQL Server as an administrator.

4. Execute the following code in a new query window:

```
--Endpoint for mirror server instance.
CREATE ENDPOINT mirroring
    STATE = STARTED
    AS TCP ( LISTENER_PORT = 7575 )
    FOR DATABASE_MIRRORING (ROLE=PARTNER);
GO
```

5. Log on to the witness server as an administrator. Using SSMS, connect to the SQL Server as an administrator.

6. Execute the following code in a new query window:

```
--Endpoint for the witness server instance.
CREATE ENDPOINT mirroring
    STATE = STARTED
    AS TCP ( LISTENER_PORT = 7575 )
    FOR DATABASE_MIRRORING (ROLE=WITNESS);
GO
```

Keep in mind the fact that you can use any available TCP port for the listener_port parameter shown in Exercise 21.1, and the name mirroring can be changed to any valid and available name you choose. Notice that no authentication setting is specified. This is because Windows authentication is the default and that's exactly what you want to use.

You can also configure the endpoints in a more automated fashion by using the Mirroring page of the Database Properties dialog box. To access this page, right-click the database you want to mirror and select Properties. From here, click the Mirroring page. You should see something similar to Figure 21.2.

The Configure Security button on the Mirroring page allows you to execute code that will create the appropriate endpoints on the servers involved in the mirroring partnership. After you set up the endpoints, using this feature, you will want to fill in the IP addresses of the participating servers. You could also use the FQDN (fully qualified domain name) if you have a DNS infrastructure, which is likely in modern networks. Finally, you will need to select the operating mode. Notice that the available operating modes change depending on whether you specify a witness server or not. When everything is configured, click Start Mirroring.

FIGURE 21.2   The Mirroring page in the Database Properties dialog

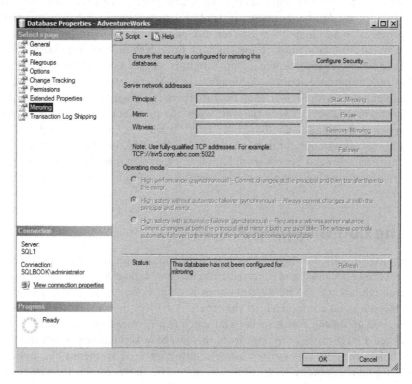

Should you need to manually failover a mirrored database to the mirror server from the primary, you can do so with code like the following on the mirror instance:

```
USE database_name;
GO
ALTER DATABASE database_name SET PARTNER FAILOVER;
```

If you use this code, the variable that reads *database_name* should be changed to the name of your database. Remember that this code should be executed on the mirror database instance and not on the primary database instance. When you execute this code, users will be automatically disconnected from the primary database instance.

Finally, SQL Server 2008 Standard and Enterprise Editions provide a Database Mirroring Monitor so that you can verify mirroring operations. The Database Mirroring Monitor is accessed by right-clicking on a mirrored database and selecting Tasks ➤ Launch Database Mirroring Monitor.

Understanding Log Shipping

Log shipping is used to provide high-latency redundant storage for your databases. You could call log shipping *database copying* instead of *database mirroring*. While database mirroring provides an automated way to keep a duplicate copy of your database and optionally provide automatic failover, log shipping provides only the first benefit and does not offer the same low-latency benefits. Database mirroring is said to have low latency because the transactions are applied to the mirrored database very quickly. Log shipping is usually implemented with high latency because there is a longer interval, usually measured in minutes or greater, between the time when the production database is updated and the time when the standby database is updated. When you can accept high latency and need a standby server without automatic failover, log shipping may be the better choice. In fact, certain scenarios can benefit from high latency, as you'll see later. In this section, you will learn about how log shipping works and the steps required to implement it in your environment.

Inside the Log-Shipping Process

The fact that log shipping is a high-latency data redundancy technology causes some administrators to be alarmed and deterred from using it. However, there are certain situations where high latency can be a tremendous benefit. For example, imagine that you enable log shipping and configure it so that there is a 15-minute delay between when the log is backed up on the active server and when it is restored on the standby server. If a user deleted a large amount of data from the database accidentally, you would have 15 minutes before the data was written to the standby server. This means you could back up the database on the standby server and restore it to the active server, thereby reverting to the previous state before the data was deleted. While there are other methods that could be implemented to prevent this scenario, log shipping certainly provides an alternative solution.

In addition, log shipping is not used by itself when the data is critical to business continuity. In these situations, you may choose to implement redundant hard drives, frequent transaction log backups, and even mirrored databases for low-latency data redundancy solutions. However, you could also implement log shipping alongside these technologies. This gives you the ability to have the database online, though representing an older state of the data, while you work on recovering the active server in the event of server failure or, when using mirroring, in the very unlikely event of total mirror partnership unavailability.

Log shipping occurs in three phases.

Phase 1: In the first phase, the transaction log is backed up on the primary server.

Phase 2: The log is then copied to the secondary server in the second phase.

Phase 3: The third phase is where the log is restored on the secondary server.

While you could accomplish the actions implemented by log shipping through manually created jobs, you can also configure log shipping using the Database Properties dialog, as shown in Figure 21.3.

FIGURE 21.3   The Transaction Log Shipping page in the Database Properties dialog

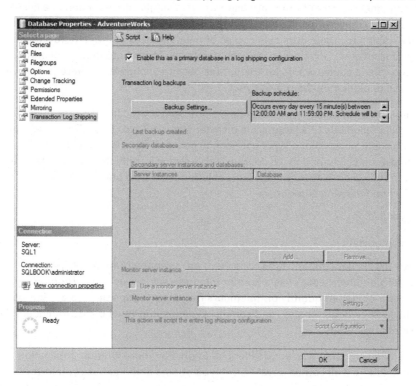

The database that is to be configured as the primary database in a log-shipping configuration must be using either the full or bulk-logged recovery model. In addition, log shipping does not provide automatic failover from the primary to the secondary database. You can also configure one SQL Server to be the secondary database server to multiple primary servers. This allows for reduced cost while implementing a fault-tolerant solution. However, if multiple databases exist on the primary server, you must configure log shipping to ship the logs to the same secondary server—if you want to use log shipping for more than one of the databases. Log shipping is now supported on Standard, Workgroup, and Enterprise Editions of SQL Server.

> ### 🌐 Real World Scenario
>
> **Log Shipping to a Remote Site**
>
> Most log-shipping implementations are used within a single site, but I had one client who needed a remote site-creation solution for their business critical databases. We were able to use log shipping to create duplicate copies of the databases at the remote site. The log shipping occurred every 15 minutes for each database. This meant that in a worst-case scenario, the offsite copies would be 15 minutes out-of-synch, but on average they would be only seven or eight minutes out-of-synch.
>
> The primary goal of this client was to create a warm standby location in case their primary network facility failed due to a large-scale disaster such as fire or flood. The benefit of the log-shipping solution was that a WAN connection could be used without concern for continuous bandwidth consumption. Of course, in this scenario, only three databases were shipped offsite. I would not recommend this solution if the data being transferred fit into either of the two following categories:
>
> - Low-latency data
>
> - High-change data
>
> *Low-latency data* is data that must be consistent between the primary site and the standby site. *High-latency* data has a greater tolerance for lost updates. *High-change data* is data that is modified frequently or that incurs frequently added new data. High-change data results in large data transfers and can quickly consume WAN bandwidth needed for other business processes.
>
> For my client, log shipping was an excellent solution. For your situation, replication may be a better solution. It all comes down to the type of data and database you have.

Configuring Log Shipping and Monitoring

To configure log shipping, you will need to take three major steps:

1. Create a share on the secondary system to which the transaction logs can be shipped and give the SQL Server service accounts access to this share.

2. Create a share on the primary system to which the transaction logs can be backed up and give the SQL Server service accounts access to this share.

3. This is the step that implements the log-shipping configuration You will use the Database Properties dialog to configure log shipping. Once the shares are created, it is as simple as specifying backup intervals on the Transaction Log Shipping page and the location where the logs should be backed up. The final configuration item, in the Transaction Log Shipping dialog, configures the secondary servers to which you want to ship the logs.

You can also configure a monitoring server to use with all of your log-shipping configurations. In this method, unlike mirroring, the monitoring server will not automatically failover to the secondary server; however, it can be used to send alerts related to the log-shipping activities. To set up the monitoring server, you simply create scripts on any Windows server that periodically check for Event Viewer log entries on the SQL Servers involved in the log shipping, and then email a report to the appropriate administrators when problems occur.

Once the shares are created, you can follow the steps in Exercise 21.2 to implement log shipping.

EXERCISE 21.2

Implementing Log Shipping

In this exercise, you will implement log shipping. To do this, follow these steps:

1. On the primary server, right-click the database on which you want to configure log shipping and select Properties.

2. Click on the Transaction Log Shipping page.

3. Check the Enable This as a Primary Database in a Log Shipping Configuration check box.

4. Click the Backup Settings button to configure the share to which you want to send the transaction log backups that are used in the log-shipping process.

5. Configure the network path similar to what you see in the following image, changing the network path to the appropriate path for your configuration, which includes the server name and the share name.

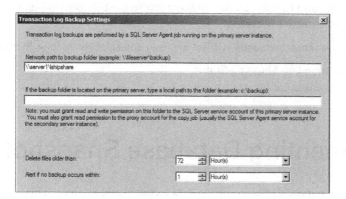

6. Click OK.

7. Click the Add button to add in the secondary server.

8. In the resulting dialog, click the Connect button and select the appropriate server to use as the secondary server. This is the server where you configured the secondary share.

9. Configure the Initialize Database options as needed.

10. Select the Copy Files tab and enter the network share name that you created on the secondary server in the Destination Folder field.

11. Click OK.

12. Click OK to implement the log-shipping configuration.

If you initialized the database on the remote secondary server during the process provided in Exercise 21.1, it can take some time as the database is backed up on the primary, copied to the secondary, and then restored there. In the future, only new transactions will be sent to the secondary server.

Once you've implemented log shipping, you can check the status of shipping processes and the health of the system by generating a Log Shipping Report. Exercise 21.3 provides instructions for generating a Log Shipping Report.

Generating a Log Shipping Report

To generate a Log Shipping Report in SQL Server Management Studio, perform these steps:

1. Launch SSMS and connect as an administrator to the SQL Server instance on which the mirrored database is stored.

2. Right-click the server instance in Object Explorer and select Reports ➢ Standard Reports.

3. Click Transaction Log Shipping Status.

Implementing Database Snapshots

Database snapshots provide point-in-time data recovery and analysis. They do not provide for standby database access in that the original database must be available, as the data set is built partly from the snapshot files and partly from the original database files. This behavior will become clearer as you read through this section. Database snapshots are useful for recovering from data entry or data processing errors, and they are also beneficial for data reporting.

Database Snapshot Functionality

Database snapshots are created almost instantaneously. This is because the snapshot of the original database contains no data at its initial creation. Instead, SQL Server takes advantage of a technology known as sparse files. *Sparse files* are files stored on NTFS partitions that allow unallocated space to be made available for use very quickly. These files are empty when the snapshot is first created and only contain real data when modifications are made to the original database. Before a data page is modified in the original database, that page is copied into the sparse files used by the snapshot. The interesting thing is that future changes to the page require no actions in the snapshot as the original page is already preserved. This makes for a very efficient and well-performing system.

When the snapshot is queried, SQL Server uses a list of pages known as the *catalog of changed pages* to determine if the data being requested is in the snapshot sparse files or in the original database. All pages that have not been changed since the snapshot was created will still be in the original database. All pages that have been changed will now be in the snapshot. From these two data sources, the result set is generated for query response.

Snapshots are read-only and the structure of the source (original) database cannot be changed as long as the snapshot exists. This means you cannot add new filegroups to the original database without first dropping the snapshot or snapshots based on it. In addition, the following restrictions apply:

- You cannot create full-text indexes against a snapshot.

- Backups, restores, and detachments of the original database are not supported as long as the snapshot exists.

- System databases do not support snapshots.

- Snapshots prevent the dropping of the original database.

- Snapshots must exist within the same instance of SQL Server as the original database.

- The maximum size of the snapshot will be the size of the original database at the time the snapshot was created, so you will need to ensure that you have at least that much space on the drive where you create the snapshot.

You can create a snapshot of a mirror copy of a principal database. You cannot query the mirror copy of a database mirroring partnership, but you can create a snapshot of the mirror and then query the snapshot. While this will only give you read-only access to the database through the mirror instance, it at least provides some access to the mirrored data.

As you can see from these capabilities, there are many possible uses for database snapshots. They can be used to protect against user or administrative errors. They can be used to offload reporting to mirror servers in a mirroring partnership. They can be used to maintain historical data for reporting purposes, and they can be used to implement a test database.

Implementing a Snapshot

Database snapshots are created with the standard CREATE DATABASE command using a special AS DATABASE SNAPSHOT clause. The following code will create a snapshot of the standard installation of AdventureWorks. If you have the AdventureWorks database installed and have not added any new filegroups, you should be able to run this code:

```
CREATE DATABASE AWSnapshot
ON (
        NAME = 'AdventureWorks_Data',
        FILENAME='c:\data\AWSnapshot.ds'
)
AS SNAPSHOT OF AdventureWorks;
```

This code assumes that the directory C:\DATA exists and that the SQL Server service has access to that directory. Note that the NAME option references the logical data file name of the original database and not a new name for the snapshot. However, the FILENAME option does define the data file for the snapshot.

Querying a Snapshot

While you can create snapshots for the purpose of data recovery (you can revert to the data state represented in the snapshot), you can also query the snapshot. For example, imagine a user wants to query the previous day's data every morning, but she does not want to see any of the changes made to the data so far that morning. You can create a snapshot every night at midnight and allow her to query the snapshot, which will provide a representation of the data as it was when the snapshot was created. You query a database snapshot in exactly the same way you query a database. For example, the following code returns all rows from the Sales.SalesOrderDetail table in the snapshot where the ProductID is equal to 889:

```
USE AWSnapshot;
GO
SELECT *
FROM Sales.SalesOrderDetail
WHERE ProductID = 889;
```

Reverting to a Snapshot

Reverting to a snapshot is as simple as restoring to it using the RESTORE DATABASE command. Before you can revert to a snapshot, you must drop all other database snapshots. Here is an example command that would revert the AdventureWorks database to the previously created snapshot:

```
RESTORE DATABASE AdventureWorks
FROM DATABASE_SNAPSHOT='AWSnapshot';
```

In addition to reverting to a snapshot, you can selectively restore data to that which is in the snapshot. You do this by using INSERT or UPDATE statements that pull their values from the database snapshot, but insert those values into the original database. For example, imagine that a user inadvertently deleted a few hundred rows from a table. You could restore just those rows by applying the same filter the user applied to the snapshot data and inserting the results back into the original database.

Summary

In this chapter, you learned to implement several high-availability and redundancy features. First, you learned about the importance of internal availability through the illustration of hard drive RAID configurations. Next, you learned to implement database mirroring for data redundancy. Database mirroring is considered a low-latency availability feature because the updates to the mirror database are transactional in nature—meaning they happen as they occur on the primary server. The next topic addressed was log shipping. Log shipping also provides data redundancy, but it is considered high latency. Finally, you learned to implement snapshots, which can be used to provide copies of your database at points in time. The snapshots can be used for reporting or for data recovery.

Chapter Essentials

The Importance of Data Redundancy   Data redundancy is essential to recoverability. If your data exists only in one place, it cannot be recovered should that storage location fail. Internal data redundancy is provided using hard disk RAID. RAID levels 1 and 5 provide redundancy. RAID level 0 does not. RAID level 0 only provides for performance improvements.

Using Database Mirroring   Database mirroring should not be confused with RAID mirroring. RAID mirroring is a drive-level concept. Database mirroring is a transaction-level concept within a SQL Server architecture. When mirroring is enabled, the mirror database receives updates on a transaction-by-transaction basis. For this reason, database mirroring is considered a low-latency solution. If you want to enable automatic failover, you must implement a witness server as well. SQL Server Express Edition can act as a witness server.

Understanding Log Shipping   Log shipping uses transaction log backups and restorations to keep a second copy of a database synchronized on a standby server. Log shipping is considered high latency because the time between the change on the primary database and the application of that change on the receiving database is often more than 10 or 15 minutes. The receiving database can have snapshots created on it to allow for reporting.

Implementing Database Snapshots   A database snapshot provides a point-in-time view of your database. Snapshots are created with the CREATE DATABASE statement, but the statement employs an AS SNAPSHOT clause. You can create multiple snapshots on a single database, but you must drop all snapshots other than the one to which you want to revert before you can revert a database to a snapshot. Snapshots are excellent for time-based reporting.

Chapter 22

Implementing Replication

TOPICS COVERED IN THIS CHAPTER:

✓ SQL Server Replication

✓ Importing and Exporting Data

While Chapter 21, "Database Mirroring and Snapshots," covered database mirroring and log shipping, which can both be used to perform data distribution, this chapter focuses first on the most common method used to distribute data for active use. In most cases, the mirror copy of a database is used only if the primary copy fails. Also, when log shipping is used, the receiving server is typically used to bring the database copy online only when the sending server fails. The point is that both mirroring and log shipping are usually used to provide backups of the data for failover purposes. SQL Server replication is used to copy data to multiple subscribers that will actively use the data, which is quite different from the technologies covered in Chapter 21.

Data can be imported to a SQL Server or exported from a SQL Server using several methods. One automated method is replication. *Replication* can be used to automatically export data for delivery to multiple clients. In addition to replication, data can be imported or exported from files. As the DBA for your organization, you may be called upon to implement a replication strategy. To do this, you must understand the replication model implemented in SQL Server 2008 and the steps required to enable it. You may also need to import data from CSV files (or other file types), and you should be aware of the methods and tools used for this process as well. Both replication and data import and export are addressed in this chapter.

If you are preparing for the 70-432 or 70-450 exam, it is important that you know how to choose the proper replication type and implement replication for a specified database. You should also know how to import and export data from SQL Server 2008 databases.

SQL Server Replication

When you want the same data to be available in multiple physical locations or on multiple server instances, you may choose to implement data replication. Data replication, in SQL Server 2008, should not be conceptualized as database replication, because you can replicate part of the database and you are not required to replicate the entire database. Instead, you create publications that include articles. The articles are tables and other objects that you want to replicate. A publication could include an entire database, but it doesn't have to; this is why you should think of it as data replication and not database replication. In this section, you'll learn about the different replication types, replication roles (such as publisher and distributor), and replication models, as well as how to implement the different roles used to provide the replication architecture. You'll also learn to monitor replication and replication performance.

SQL Server Replication Roles and Concepts

Microsoft has implemented the replication in SQL Server using a magazine publishing metaphor. Your replication infrastructure will include publishers, distributors, and subscribers. These roles are involved in the replication of publications that include articles, and the articles describe and contain the data to be replicated. Here are some key descriptions for this process:

Publisher: A publisher is a SQL Server instance that is configured to distribute data using data replication and possibly receive and merge data from subscribers. A publisher is an instance of SQL Server.

Subscriber: A subscriber is a SQL Server instance, which can include portable editions of SQL Server for PDAs as well as the other server and express editions, that receives data from a publisher and possibly submits data for merge processing.

Distributor: A distributor is a machine that is configured to respond to subscriber requests for publications and distribute these publications from the publishers to the subscribers. The same server can be both the publisher and the distributor.

Publication: A publication consists of one or more articles.

Article: An article is a collection of described and possibly filtered data that is flagged for replication with the publication.

Subscribers subscribe to publications and not articles. This constraint is consistent with the magazine publishing metaphor, because you do not subscribe to articles in a traditional magazine but rather the entire magazine.

Replication Types

SQL Server supports three main replication types:

- Transactional
- Snapshot
- Merge

As the DBA, the selection of the appropriate replication type is important. If you choose snapshot replication when you need the lowest latency levels, you've made a bad decision. In order to choose the best replication type, you'll need to understand the way each replication type operates.

Transactional Replication   Transactional replication starts with a snapshot of the published (designated to be replicated) data for the initial data distribution to subscribers and then replicates future changes as they occur or in near-real-time. Transactional replication is usually implemented as one-way replication from the publisher to the subscriber. The subscriber is usually considered to be read-only, although you can use transactional replication types that replicate in both directions. Transactional replication is generally used when:

- Changes should be replicated to subscribers as they happen.
- The data source (publisher) has much activity (modifications, deletions, and insertions).
- There is a low tolerance for latency between the time of change and the time of replication (the subscriber must be as current as possible).

Snapshot Replication   Snapshot replication uses point-in-time replication and does not track changes as they occur. When it is time for a snapshot to be taken, the data to be published is selected at that time and the subscriber receives the full copy of the replicated data—whether it is one change or 1,000 changes—every time. Snapshot replication is generally used when:

- Delays in data replication are acceptable.
- Data is seldom modified and these modifications are not large.
- The data set being replicated is small.

Merge Replication   Merge replication allows data to be modified at either end of the replication link. The publisher and the subscribers can modify the data. Merge replication uses triggers to make the replication happen where transactional replication is based on the Snapshot Agent, Log Reader Agent, and the Distribution Agent. Merge replication is generally used when:

- You need to update data at both the publisher and the subscribers.
- Each subscriber receives a different subset of the data.
- Subscribers replicate while online and modify data while offline.

Table 22.1 provides a reference for these replication types. You can use it as a guide to help you select the appropriate replication type for your needs.

TABLE 22.1   Replication Types and Their Applications

Type	Definition	Applications
Transactional	The initial subscription pulls a snapshot of the publication and then ongoing changes are typically sent to the subscriber as they occur.	Provides for lower latency and faster replication of changes. Useful when the data source processes a large number of transactions.
Snapshot	Publishes data exactly as it exists at a point-in-time and does not publish updates transactionally as they occur.	Used when higher latency is acceptable or changes happen less frequently at the publisher.

TABLE 22.1   Replication Types and Their Applications *(continued)*

Type	Definition	Applications
Merge	Publishes a snapshot to start the replication partnership with a subscriber and then changes are made at the publisher and subscriber. These changes are merged into the publisher.	Used when data changes should be allowed and retained at both the publisher and the subscriber.

Replication Latency

Latency is a very important issue to consider in database replication scenarios. *Latency* is defined as the amount of time it takes for data to travel from source to destination. High latency indicates that the time is longer, and low latency indicates that the time is shorter. Lower latency is usually considered to be better.

SQL Server 2008 offers the three basic replication types referenced in this chapter, and they provide different levels of latency. With the right hardware and configuration, transactional and merge replication can provide low latency. Snapshot replication provides high latency. However, it is only high in comparison to some threshold—and that threshold is the "other way of doing it." In other words, snapshot replication has a higher latency than transactional or merge replication.

The Replication Monitor, referenced later in this chapter, can be used to monitor tracer tokens. These tracer tokens can be used to monitor replication latency. A *tracer* is basically dummy data that is written to the transaction log of the publisher so that its performance can be traced throughout the networked system to measure latency.

Replication Models

Replication models are used to conceptualize how you will implement the various replication components (publishers, subscribers, publications, etc.). One model uses a local distributor and another uses a remote distributor.

> **Local Distributor Model:** When a local distributor is used, the same SQL Server 2008 instance plays the role of the publisher and the distributor.
>
> **Remote Distributor Model:** When a remote distributor is used, one SQL Server 2008 instance plays the role of publisher and another plays the role of distributor. The remote distributor model is useful when you have more than one publisher and you want to have all the publications from these publishers available to subscribers through a single server instance.

As an analogy for the remote distributor model, consider an online book store. You can go to an online book store and purchase books from many different publishers. Imagine how difficult it would be for you if you had to remember which publisher published the various books you wanted to purchase and then you had to go to each publisher's website to purchase the different books. Through centralized distribution, access is simplified.

An additional benefit of the remote distributor model is that it offloads the distribution workload to a different server. The publisher is often the OLTP (online transaction processing) copy of the database, and replication is used to distribute the data for analysis or reporting purposes. To improve the performance of the OLTP server, you can perform only the publishing functions there and offload the distribution to a remote server.

In addition to the models related to the publisher and distributor relationship, you have two basic models for the subscriber and distributor relationship:

Single Subscriber: In the single subscriber model, there is only one subscriber for each publication.

Multiple Subscriber: In the multiple subscriber model, there are multiple subscribers for each publication. If you want to distribute data to multiple remote servers, you will likely implement a multiple subscriber model.

Configuring a Publisher and Distributor

When configuring a publisher and distributor, you must consider three things. First, you will need to configure the publisher and distributor for replication. Second, you will need to understand how to deal with conflicts. Third, you should understand replication security issues. All three are addressed in this section.

Configuring replication starts with the configuration of the publisher and distributor roles. Depending on whether you are implementing a local or remote distributor model, you can configure both roles at the same time (local) or separately (remote). The publisher and distributor roles are configured in SQL Server Management Studio (SSMS) by right-clicking on the Replication container and selecting Configure Distribution. Don't let this confuse you. Once you get into the wizard, you will see that it is used to configure only the distribution role, both the distribution and publisher roles, or only the publisher role. Exercise 22.1 provides the steps required to configure a publisher/distributor model (local) on a single instance of SQL Server 2008.

EXERCISE 22.1

Configuring the Publisher and Distributor

In this exercise, you will enable a single instance to act as a publisher and a distributor. To do this, follow these steps:

1. Launch SSMS and connect to the target instance as an administrator.

2. Right-click on the Replication node in the Object Explorer and select Configure Distribution.

3. You will see the Configure Distribution Wizard; click Next on the Welcome screen.

4. On the Configure Distribution Wizard, accept the default to use the local server as its own distributor and click Next.

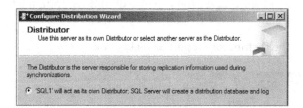

5. Either accept the default snapshot folder (the place to store replication data to be replicated) or specify a different location. The warning in the following image indicates you will need to use a network path (UNC path) if you want to support pull subscriptions from the client. Click Next.

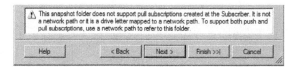

6. Accept the default replication database name, as in the following image, or specify a different name and location. This is the database that will be used to store information related to replication. Click Next.

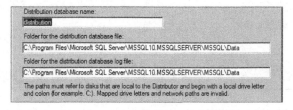

7. Select the servers that you want to allow access to this distributor server as a publisher. Because you are configuring a local distribution model, the local server will be in the list by default. Click Next when you are finished.

8. You can generate a script that will enable distribution or you can accept the default to do it immediately. When you've made your selection, click Next.

9. Click Finish to configure the local server as a distributor and publisher.

10. When the process completes, click Close.

After you've completed this process, you can right-click the Replication container and select Publisher Properties or Distributor Properties to manage the properties of the two roles. The Distributor Properties dialog, shown in Figure 22.1, allows you to specify how long transactions will be retained on the distributor and which publishers are allowed to use the distributor. The Publisher Properties dialog allows you to configure which databases are allowed to use replication and whether they are enabled for transactional or merge replication, as shown in Figure 22.2. You can also disable replication by right-clicking the Replication container and selecting Disable Publishing and Distribution.

FIGURE 22.1   The Distributor Properties dialog box

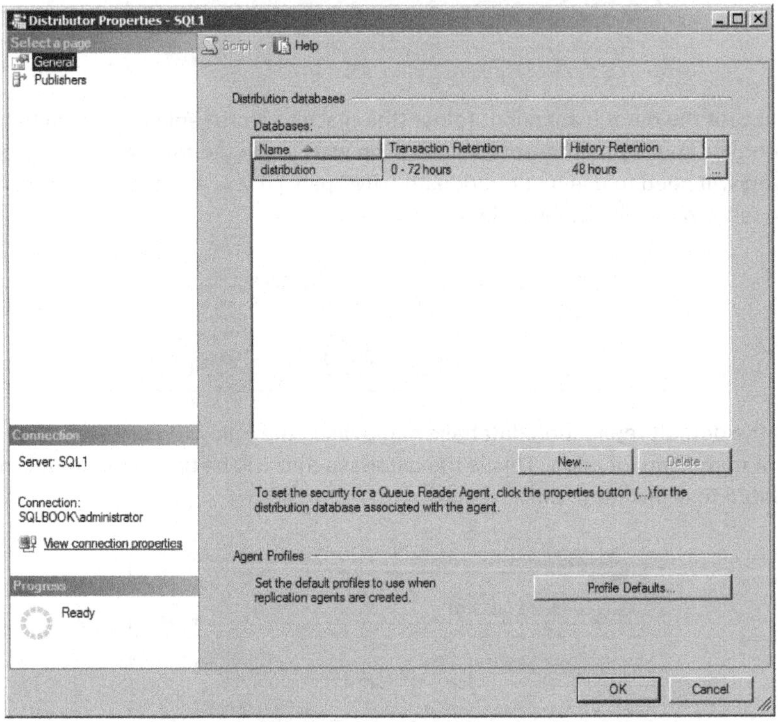

After you've enabled the publisher and distributor role and enabled databases for replication, you can begin creating publications. Here are some details for how to do this. New publications are created by right-clicking the Local Publications node in the Replication container and selecting New Publication. In the resulting wizard, you can select the database on which the publication will be based and the publication type. Next, you will configure the articles to be included in the publication by selecting the tables or views to include. After you've selected the tables to include, you can employ filters to limit the replicated data to only specific columns or rows. These filters are simple WHERE filters like the ones you would use in standard SELECT statements. Exercise 22.2 provides the steps required to create a basic publication with a single table being replicated from the AdventureWorks database.

FIGURE 22.2   The Publisher Properties dialog box used to select replication databases

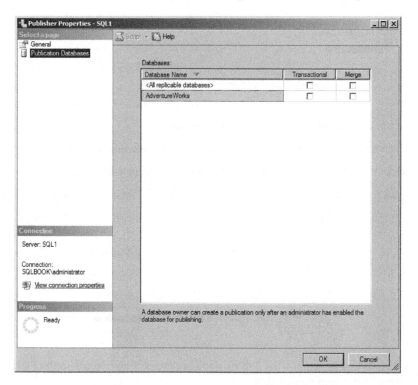

EXERCISE 22.2

Creating a Publication with a Single Table to Replicate the Production.Product Table

In this exercise, you will create a publication to replicate the Production.Product table in the AdventureWorks database. To perform this exercise, you must first perform Exercise 22.1 and have the AdventureWorks OLTP sample database installed.

1.   Launch SSMS and connect to the target instance as an administrator.

2.   Right-click on the Replication node and select Publisher Properties.

3.   Select the Publication Databases page.

EXERCISE 22.2 *(continued)*

4. Ensure that the AdventureWorks database is enabled for Transactional replication, as in the following image, and click OK.

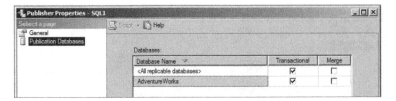

5. Expand the Replication node by double-clicking on it.

6. Right-click on the Local Publications node and select New Publication.

7. Click Next in the New Publication Wizard to move past the Welcome page.

8. Select the AdventureWorks database on the Publication Database page and click Next.

9. On the Publication Type page, choose Transactional Publication and click Next.

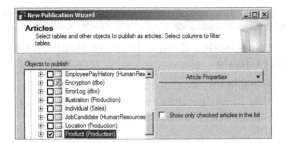

10. On the Articles page, expand the Tables node and scroll down to select the Product (Production) table and then click Next.

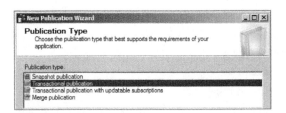

11. On the Filter Table Rows page, accept the default and do not add any filters. Click Next.

12. On the Snapshot Agent page, choose to create a snapshot immediately and click Next.

EXERCISE 22.2 *(continued)*

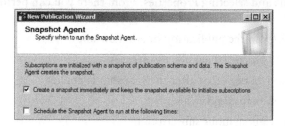

13. On the Agent Security page, click the Use the Security Settings from the Snapshot Agent button, choose Run under the SQL Server Agent service account, click OK, and then click Next to save the Agent Security settings.

14. On the Wizard Actions page, ensure that Create the Publication is checked and click Finish.

15. Enter the publication name of **Products Table** and click Finish.

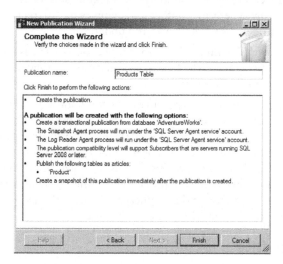

16. Click Close when the process completes.

Once a publication has been created, you can modify the settings by right-clicking it in Local Publications and selecting Properties. From there you can perform the following operations:

- Modify the articles in the publication or add new ones
- Change the filters processed against the articles
- Specify scripts to run before or after the snapshot is applied
- Enable FTP-based snapshot downloads
- Allow or disallow anonymous subscriptions
- Determine the accounts allowed to create or synchronize subscriptions
- Reconfigure the agents accounts
- Determine retention rules for snapshots

Conflict Resolution

Resolving conflicts is an important part of configuring the publisher and distributor and replication in general. When using merge replication or transactional replication with updates, conflicts can occur. SQL Server provides three levels of conflict detection. Here's a description of each:

Row-Level Tracking: When row-level tracking is used, any change to any column in a row will generate a conflict if any other replication partner has changed any column in that same row.

Column-Level Tracking: When column-level tracking is used, only changes to the same column within a row generate a conflict and changes to different columns within a record will be considered separate and valid updates.

Logical Record-Level Tracking: When your replication article is based on a JOIN statement between multiple tables, the logical record can be evaluated for conflicts and this is called logical record-level tracking.

You can also have conflicts resolved automatically with notification or manually. When a subscription to a publication is created, it can be assigned a priority. Conflicts can be resolved automatically based on the change-location with the higher priority, and this is known as the additive resolver or the averaging resolver. The *additive resolver* uses the sum of the source and destination values, and the *averaging resolver* uses the average of the two values. You can also specify that the subscriber or the publisher always wins. If you configure conflicts to be managed manually, you must look at the conflicts and choose the accepted change. Conflicts management rules are configured within each publication.

Replication Security

The final topic you'll need to address when configuring a publisher and distributor for replication is security. Replication security is configured by setting the appropriate limits on the accounts that are used by the various replication agents and ensuring that only valid users can access publications or subscribe to them. Remember that snapshots are stored in standard shares and, therefore, normal Windows security permission management guidelines apply.

Publications have a Publication Access List that determines which users can access the publication. All users in the access list can subscribe to and synchronize publications. You can also manage this list with the following stored procedures:

sp_help_publication_access: Provides a list of all granted logins for a publication.

sp_grant_publication_access: Adds a login to the access list for a specified publication.

sp_revoke_publication_access: Removes a login from the access list for a specified publication.

Configuring a Subscriber

The replication subscriber is configured in a similar method as the publisher and distributor. The subscriber can be configured through the use of a wizard. Exercise 22.3 provides the steps required to subscribe to the publication created in Exercise 22.2 from a different server.

EXERCISE 22.3

Creating a Subscription

In this exercise, you will perform the steps used to create a subscription to the publication created in Exercise 22.3. To do this, follow these steps:

1. Launch SSMS on the subscribing SQL Server instance and connect as an administrator.

2. Expand the Replication node in Object Explorer.

3. Right-click on Local Subscriptions and select New Subscriptions.

4. Click Next to move beyond the New Subscription Wizard Welcome page, if you have not previously selected to turn off the Welcome page.

5. On the Publication page, select the Publishing instance of SQL Server that was used in Exercise 22.2. Additionally, select the Products Table publication and then click Next.

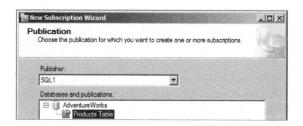

6. On the Distribution Agent Location page, choose Run Each Agent at Its Subscriber (Pull Subscriptions) and click Next.

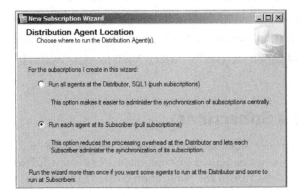

7. On the Subscribers page, select <New Database> in the Subscription Database field for the local instance.

8. In the New Database dialog that appears, enter the name Subscriptions for the database (if you prefer, you can use any local database name you desire here) and then click OK to create the new database.

9. When you are returned to the Subscribers page, ensure that the Subscription Database is set to the database name you created in step 8 and click Next.

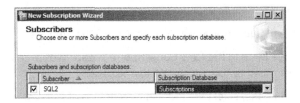

10. On the Distribution Agent Security page, click the dotted button to configure the security settings.

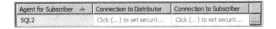

11. On the Distribution Agent Security dialog that appears, choose Run under the SQL Server Agent service account (in a production environment, you would create a Windows domain account for this purpose instead) and click OK.

12. On the Distribution Agent Security page, click Next.

13. Accept the default setting to run continuously on the Synchronization Schedule page and click Next.

14. Accept the default setting to initialize immediately on the Initialize Subscriptions page and click Next.

15. Ensure that Create the Subscription(s) is checked and click Next.

16. Click Finish to create the subscription.

17. Click Close when the process completes.

Monitoring Replication

You can view the replication activity at the publisher by right-clicking the Replication container and selecting to Launch Replication Monitor. From here you can see the subscriptions as well as which subscriptions have been initialized. The Replication Monitor can also be used to configure alerts for proactive replication management. When monitoring replication, you are looking for the following events:

New Subscription Requests: You can determine if a subscription request made it through to the publisher if a subscriber is reporting a failure.

Replication Actions: You can see when a subscriber pulls a replication update and if any errors occur.

Conflict Events: You can see when conflicts occur and determine if the appropriate resolution action is taken.

Replication Performance

When you are using replication, you can monitor it with the System Monitor instead of the Replication Monitor. Although the Replication Monitor shows replication events and errors, it does not show statistics such as the number of replication updates per second or the number of conflicts occurring. The System Monitor can be used to view such information. This is the Windows tool that allows you to monitor performance counters to determine where bottlenecks might exist or to pin down problematic configurations and services. The System Monitor is covered extensively in Chapter 14, "Performance Monitoring and Tuning."

Replication performance, like all database access from the network, will be impacted by the speed of the server as well as the bandwidth or speed of the network. For example, if you are replicating across a WAN connection, you can expect performance to be poor in comparison to replication across a LAN connection or within a server across instances. By setting greater intervals for replication or reducing the publication size to include only the essential data, you can work around some of the limitations imposed by limited bandwidth.

Replication Recovery

Like all other SQL Server 2008 features and functions, it's important to provide recoverability for your implementation. Replication recovery is all about having good backups of the replication configurations on each server involved in the replication topology. In order to ensure that you can recover your replication configuration, you must back up the following databases regularly:

- The distribution database on the distributor

- The primary database on the publisher, also known as the publication database

- The secondary database on the subscriber, also known as the subscription database

- The MSDB and master databases on the distributor, publisher, and subscribers

   Although you could restore your actual data with a full backup of the publication database, you will have to re-create your entire replication topology if you have not backed up all of these databases. To learn about the actions that can require a new backup of these databases, search for "Common Actions Requiring an Updated Backup" in SQL Server 2008 Books Online.

Importing and Exporting Data

Another method used to distribute data is to export the data from one database and import it into another. This can be accomplished using different methods in SQL Server, and this section will introduce you to the basic techniques at your disposal. These techniques are also used to import data from flat text files. These text files may be generated from mainframes or legacy database systems and then imported into SQL Server for ongoing modification or for analysis purposes.

   When importing data from flat files, you should consider the following factors:

Source Location   If the data is located on a network share, the limitations of the network may slow the bulk import of the data. This can happen when the data is being pulled from Internet websites or WAN locations. When the data is being imported from the local network, the process can be faster. Of course, the fastest method is to import the data from the local hard drive. In fact, it is often better to first copy the data from the remote location to the local hard drive when the data actually originates outside of the SQL Server computer.

Import Method   The import method can also impact performance. For example, the BCP utility is an external process to the SQL Server service and is slower than a BULK INSERT statement for this reason. However, while BCP may be slower at data import, it supports data export where the BULK INSERT command does not. Integration Services can do both the importing and exporting of data.

Data Destination   Finally, you must consider the data destination. Do the tables already exist or will they need to be created? Do the databases exist for that matter? Will you be appending to existing data or overwriting any data that exists? To which database server will you import the data and to which database? Lastly, you must ensure that the permissions are set appropriately so that the import process works as expected. This means the user context you choose to use for the insert process must be given the appropriate permissions in the databases and tables.

Using *BCP*

Whether using BCP (the bulk copy program) or some of the other methods that follow, you should consider switching to the bulk-logged recovery model just before the import takes place and then changing back to the full recovery model when it is finished. This will make the import process go much faster. To switch to the bulk-logged recovery model using T-SQL code, execute the following code:

```
ALTER DATABASE dBname
SET RECOVERY BULK_LOGGED;
```

When you are finished with the import and ready to switch back to the full recovery model, use the following T-SQL code:

```
ALTER DATABASE dBname
SET RECOVERY FULL;
```

BCP is a program that allows you to import and export data to and from SQL Server databases. The program existed in previous versions of SQL Server and is still provided in SQL Server 2008. The program is not capable of complex transformations during data import. For this you will need to use either BULK INSERT commands or Integration Services. In addition, BCP has limited error correction; however, you can set the error count threshold with the -m switch.

The BCP command is used from the Windows command line and not from within a new query window in SSMS. This means the tool can be used in batch files along with other commands to include capabilities that may be more difficult if coded from the ground up in T-SQL. The BCP command uses the following syntax:

```
bcp {[[database_name.][owner].]{table_name | view_name} | "query"}
    {in | out | queryout | format} data_file
    [-mmax_errors] [-fformat_file] [-x] [-eerr_file]
    [-Ffirst_row] [-Llast_row] [-bbatch_size]
    [-n] [-c] [-w] [-N] [-V (60 | 65 | 70 | 80)] [-6]
    [-q] [-C { ACP | OEM | RAW | code_page } ] [-tfield_term]
    [-rrow_term] [-iinput_file] [-ooutput_file] [-apacket_size]
    [-Sserver_name[\instance_name]] [-Ulogin_id] [-Ppassword]
    [-T] [-v] [-R] [-k] [-E] [-h"hint [,...n]"]
```

This may seem complex at first; however, the following example command illustrates how simple the usage of the tool can be:

```
bcp theDatabase.dbo.theTable in data.dat -T -c
```

This command would import data from a file named `data.dat`, which resides in the directory where BCP is being executed, into a table named `theDatabase.dbo.theTable`. In this case, the `-T` switch informs BCP to use a trusted connection so that network credentials are not required. Of course, you must be logged on as a user with the rights to perform the action in SQL Server to use this switch. The `-c` switch indicates that the data type for all columns should be the `char()` data type.

Other switches that are important to know, but not represented in this example include:

-fformat_file: This switch is used to provide custom data formats.

-tcolumn_separator: This switch specifies the column separator to use during operations.

-mmax_errors: This switch determines the number of errors that will be allowed before the BCP command is cancelled.

Bulk Insert Commands

The BULK INSERT statement is used to import data only. While BCP can export data as well, BULK INSERT lacks this capacity. However, BULK INSERT works from within the SQL Server instance and is therefore faster than BCP. All bulk-logged recovery model issues apply to using the BULK INSERT statement as they do to the BCP command. Because BULK INSERT is a T-SQL command, it can be executed from a new query window. The syntax is as follows:

```
BULK INSERT database_name.schema_name. [ table_name | view_name ]
    FROM 'data_file'
  [ WITH
  (
  [ [ , ] BATCHSIZE = batch_size ]
  [ [ , ] CHECK_CONSTRAINTS ]
  [ [ , ] CODEPAGE = { 'ACP' | 'OEM' | 'RAW' | 'code_page' } ]
  [ [ , ] DATAFILETYPE =
    { 'char' | 'native'| 'widechar' | 'widenative' } ]
  [ [ , ] FIELDTERMINATOR = 'field_terminator' ]
  [ [ , ] FIRSTROW =first_row ]
  [ [ , ] FIRE_TRIGGERS ]
  [ [ , ] FORMATFILE = 'format_file_path' ]
  [ [ , ] KEEPIDENTITY ]
  [ [ , ] KEEPNULLS ]
  [ [ , ] KILOBYTES_PER_BATCH =kilobytes_per_batch ]
```

```
[ [ , ] LASTROW = last_row ]
[ [ , ] MAXERRORS = max_errors ]
[ [ , ] ORDER ( { column [ ASC | DESC ] } [ ,...n ] ) ]
[ [ , ] ROWS_PER_BATCH = rows_per_batch ]
[ [ , ] ROWTERMINATOR = 'row_terminator' ]
[ [ , ] TABLOCK ]
[ [ , ] ERRORFILE = 'file_name' ]
 )]
```

Like the BCP command, the BULK INSERT statements can be either very complex or moderately simple. The following code inserts data into a table named theDatabase.dbo.theTable from a file called c:\theData.dat using a field separator of the piping (|) symbol:

```
BULK INSERT theDatabase.dbo.theTable
    FROM 'c:\theData.dat'
    WITH
      (
          FIELDTERMINATOR =' |'
      );
```

Real World Scenario

Exporting Data Easily from the Command Line

I frequently need to export data from SQL Server tables. I've done it with the BCP command and with SQL Server Integration Services; however, I find it more convenient to use the SQLCMD command at the command line in many cases.

Recently, I received a call from a client who wanted an easy way to dump data from a sales tracking table to a comma-separated, flat text file. He wanted his users to be able to dump the data by double-clicking on a simple shortcut on their desktops. While I could have told this client to use SQL Server Integration Services or the BCP command, it would have been more difficult for him to learn how to do that in a short window of time. Instead, I directed him to the SQLCMD command.

With a single command line, he could easily export data with SQLCMD and he could also use it for many other tasks. That's the benefit of SQLCMD over BCP. The SQLCMD command can do much more than just export data; it can do the data exports too. BCP is limited to imports and exports of data. Although SSIS can do more than import and export data, it is much more complicated than SQLCMD.

The next time you need to export or import some data, consider using the SQLCMD command. I introduced the command in Chapter 4, "SQL Server Command-Line Administration," and you can always learn more about it by typing SQLCMD /? at the command prompt of any SQL Server 2008 machine.

Using SQL Server Integration Services (SSIS)

A final method of data transport is the built-in ETL (extract, transform, and load) tool called SQL Server Integration Services (SSIS). While you can perform extremely complex data transformations with this tool, you can also call upon its power with the Import/Export Wizard through SSMS. You can start this wizard from within the management studio interface or from within the Business Intelligence Development Studio (BIDS). BIDS is beyond the scope of this book, but you should learn how to use the wizard from within SSMS.

> Here's a great tip for you. If you find that you use the Import/Export a lot and in a manual fashion, you should learn the fast way to access it. When sitting at the SQL Server, click Start and select Run. From there, enter **DTSWizard** and press the Enter key to launch the tool.

Exercise 22.4 provides step-by-step procedures for exporting data with the Import/Export Wizard. You can just as easily import data with the tool.

EXERCISE 22.4

Exporting Data with the Import/Export Wizard

In this exercise, you will export the HumanResources.Employee table from the AdventureWorks sample database. To do this, follow these steps:

1. As an administrator, launch SSMS and connect to the SQL Server instance containing the AdventureWorks database.

2. From within SSMS, right-click the AdventureWorks database and choose Tasks ➢ Export Data. The first time you run the tool, you will receive a Welcome screen. To avoid seeing this screen in the future, check the box that reads Do Not Show This Starting Page Again.

3. After you click Next on the Welcome screen, go to the Choose a Data Source page where you must select a data source. Depending on whether you are importing data into SQL Server or exporting data out, the data source will either be an external data source (importing) or a SQL Server data source (exporting). Select the AdventureWorks database as the data source. Once you've selected the data source, click Next.

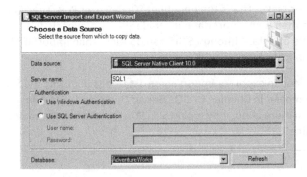

4. The next task will be to choose the data destination. Again, if you are importing data, the destination will be SQL Server. If you are exporting data, the destination will be another SQL Server or some other data destination. Choose a Flat File Destination as in the following image. Once you've selected the data destination, click Next.

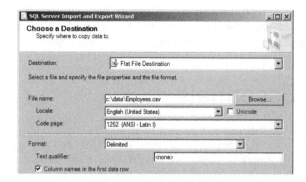

5. You can select to copy data from specific tables or views or you can write a SELECT statement to choose the exact data you want. Choose to Copy Data From One Or More Tables Or Views and then click Next.

6. You can select the table and the row or column delimiters. Select the [HumanResources.Employee] table and the default delimiters used by the wizard.

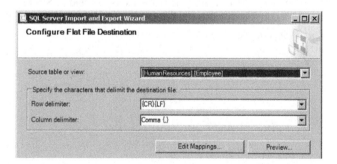

7. You can execute your data import/export immediately or you can save it as an Integration Services package, which can be scheduled or launched as part of another job. Choose Run immediately and then click Next.

8. Click Finish to export the data.

Summary

In this chapter, you learned to move data in and out of SQL Server 2008 databases using two key methods: replication and import/export. You learned that you can use replication for low-latency updates, high-latency updates, and bidirectional (merge) updates. You configured a publisher, a distributor, and a subscriber in a replication implementation. You also learned to deal with replication conflicts, security, and monitoring.

Finally, you learned about the different methods available for data import and export. These methods include BCP, the BULK INSERT command, and SSIS.

Chapter Essentials

SQL Server Replication   SQL Server 2008 replication, like the versions of SQL Server before it, is based on a magazine publishing model. You must configure the publisher, distributor, and subscriber to complete a replication configuration.

Replication can be implemented using one of three core replication methods. The first is transactional replication and offers near real-time updates. The second is snapshot replication, and it has lower latency but only consumes network bandwidth periodically. The third is merge replication and is used when updates must be allowed at both the publisher and the subscriber.

Importing and Exporting Data   Data can be imported and exported using several methods in SQL Server 2008. The Import/Export Wizard is used to create SSIS packages that can import or export data. You can also use the BCP command at the command line or the BULK INSERT command in T-SQL code.

Appendix

A

Microsoft's Certification Program

Since the inception of its certification program, Microsoft has certified more than two million people. As the computer network industry continues to increase in both size and complexity, this number is sure to grow—and the need for *proven* ability will also increase. Certifications can help companies verify the skills of prospective employees and contractors.

Microsoft has developed its Microsoft Certified Professional (MCP) program to give you credentials that verify your ability to work with Microsoft products effectively and professionally. Several levels of certification are available based on specific suites of exams. With the release of Windows Vista, Microsoft created a new generation of certification programs:

Microsoft Certified Technology Specialist (MCTS)   The MCTS can be considered the entry-level certification for the new generation of Microsoft certifications. The MCTS certification program targets specific technologies instead of specific job roles. You must take and pass one to three exams.

Microsoft Certified IT Professional (MCITP)   The MCITP certification is a Professional Series certification that tests network and system administrators on job roles rather than only on a specific technology. The MCITP certification program generally consists of one to three exams in addition to obtaining an MCTS-level certification.

Microsoft Certified Professional Developer (MCPD)   The MCPD certification is a Professional Series certification for application developers. Similar to the MCITP, the MCPD is focused on a job role rather than on a single technology. The MCPD certification program generally consists of one to three exams in addition to obtaining an MCTS-level certification.

Microsoft Certified Architect (MCA)   The MCA is Microsoft's premier certification series. Obtaining the MCA requires a minimum of 10 years of experience and passing a review board consisting of peer architects.

How Do You Become Certified on SQL Server 2008?

Attaining Microsoft certification has always been a challenge. In the past, students have been able to acquire detailed exam information—even most of the exam questions—from online "brain dumps" and third-party "cram" books or software products. For the new generation of exams, this is simply not the case.

Microsoft has taken strong steps to protect the security and integrity of its new certification tracks. Now prospective candidates should complete a course of study that develops detailed knowledge about a wide range of topics. It supplies them with the true skills needed, derived from working with the technology being tested.

The new generations of Microsoft certification programs are heavily weighted toward hands-on skills and experience. It is recommended that candidates have troubleshooting skills acquired through hands-on experience and working knowledge.

MCITP: Database Administrator 2008 must pass a total of two exams:

- TS: Microsoft SQL Server 2008, Installation and Maintenance (70-432)

- Pro: Designing, Optimizing and Maintaining a Database Server Infrastructure using Microsoft SQL Server 2008 (70-450)

 The detailed exam objectives, and the chapters in which those objectives are discussed, can be found in the section "Certification Objectives Map" later in this appendix.

For a more detailed description of the Microsoft certification programs, including a list of all the exams, visit the Microsoft Learning website at www.microsoft.com/learning.

Tips for Taking a Microsoft Exam

Here are some general tips for achieving success on your certification exam:

- Arrive early at the exam center so that you can relax and review your study materials. During this final review, you can look over tables and lists of exam-related information.

- Read the questions carefully. Don't be tempted to jump to an early conclusion. Make sure you know *exactly* what the question is asking.

- Answer all questions. If you are unsure about a question, mark it for review and come back to it at a later time.

- On simulations, do not change settings that are not directly related to the question. Also, assume default settings if the question does not specify or imply which settings are used.

- For questions you're not sure about, use a process of elimination to get rid of the obviously incorrect answers first. This improves your odds of selecting the correct answer when you need to make an educated guess.

Exam Registration

You may take the Microsoft exams at any of more than 1,000 Authorized Prometric Testing Centers (APTCs) around the world. For the location of a testing center near you, call Prometric at 800-755-EXAM (755-3926). Outside the United States and Canada, contact your local Prometric registration center.

Find out the number of the exam you want to take, and then register with the Prometric registration center nearest to you. At this point, you will be asked for advance payment for the exam. The exams are $125 each and you must take them within one year of payment. You can schedule exams up to six weeks in advance or as late as one working day prior to the date of the exam. You can cancel or reschedule your exam if you contact the center at least two working days prior to the exam. Same-day registration is available in some locations, subject to space availability. Where same-day registration is available, you must register a minimum of two hours before test time.

You may also register for your exams online at www.prometric.com. As of this writing, VUE no longer offers Microsoft exams. If you have taken Microsoft exams with VUE, continue to watch VUE's website (www.vue.com) to see if it starts offering Microsoft exams again.

When you schedule the exam, you will be provided with instructions regarding appointment and cancellation procedures, ID requirements, and information about the testing center location. In addition, you will receive a registration and payment confirmation letter from Prometric.

Microsoft requires certification candidates to accept the terms of a nondisclosure agreement before taking certification exams.

Certification Objectives Map

Table A.1 provides objective mappings for the 70-432 exam. Table A.2 provides objective mappings for the 70-450 exam. In addition to the book chapters, you will find coverage of exam objectives in the flashcards, practice exams, and videos on the book's accompanying CD.

TABLE A.1   Exam 70-432 Objectives Map

Objectives	Chapter
Installing and Configuring SQL Server 2008	**Chapters 2, 3, 4, and 12**
Install SQL Server 2008 and related services	Chapter 2
Configure SQL Server instances	Chapters 2, 3
Configure SQL Server services	Chapters 2, 3, 4
Configure additional SQL Server components	Chapter 12
Implement database mail	Chapter 12
Configure full-text indexing	Chapter 12

TABLE A.1   Exam 70-432 Objectives Map *(continued)*

Objectives	Chapter
Maintaining SQL Server Instances	**Chapters 13, 14, and 16**
Manage SQL Server Agent jobs	Chapter 13
Manage SQL Server Agent alerts	Chapter 13
Manage SQL Server Agent operators	Chapter 13
Implement the declarative management framework (DMF)	Chapter 14
Back up a SQL Server environment	Chapter 16
Managing SQL Server Security	**Chapters 14, 18, and 19**
Manage logins and server roles	Chapter 18
Manage users and database roles	Chapter 18
Manage SQL Server instance permissions	Chapter 18
Manage database permissions	Chapter 18
Manage schema permissions and object permissions	Chapter 18
Audit SQL Server instances	Chapters 14, 19
Manage transparent data encryption	Chapter 18
Configure surface area	Chapter 19
Maintaining a SQL Server Database	**Chapters 5, 6, 7, 8, 15, 16, and 21**
Back up databases	Chapter 16
Restore databases	Chapter 16
Manage and configure databases	Chapters 5, 6, 7, 8
Manage database snapshots	Chapters 8, 21
Maintain database integrity	Chapter 15
Maintain a database by using maintenance plans	Chapter 16

TABLE A.1   Exam 70-432 Objectives Map *(continued)*

Objectives	Chapter
Performing Data Management Tasks	**Chapters 3, 4, 9, 10, 16, and 22**
Import and export data	Chapters 3, 4, 22
Manage data partitions	Chapter 9
Implement data compression	Chapter 16
Maintain indexes	Chapter 10
Manage collations	Chapter 9
Monitoring and Troubleshooting SQL Server	**Chapters 1, 3, 4, and 14**
Identify SQL Server service problems	Chapter 3
Identify concurrency problems	Chapters 1, 14
Identify SQL Agent job execution problems	Chapter 13
Locate error information	Chapters 3, 4
Optimizing SQL Server Performance	**Chapters 3 and 14**
Implement Resource Governor	Chapter 14
Use the Database Engine Tuning Advisor	Chapter 14
Collect trace data by using SQL Server Profiler	Chapters 3, 14
Collect performance data by using Dynamic Management Views	Chapters 3, 4
Collect performance data by using System Monitor	Chapter 14
Use Performance Studio	Chapter 14
Implementing High Availability	**Chapters 20, 21, and 22**
Implement database mirroring	Chapter 21
Implement a SQL Server clustered instance	Chapter 20

TABLE A.1   Exam 70-432 Objectives Map *(continued)*

Objectives	Chapter
Implement log shipping	Chapter 21
Implement replication	Chapter 22

TABLE A.2   Exam 70-450 Objectives Map

Objective	Chapter
Designing a SQL Server Instance and a Database Solution	**Chapters 2 and 8**
Design for CPU, memory, and storage capacity requirements	Chapter 2
Design SQL Server instances	Chapter 2
Design physical database and object placement	Chapter 8
Design a migration, consolidation, and update strategy	Chapter 2
Designing a Database Server Security Solution	**Chapters 17, 18, and 19**
Design instance authentication	Chapter 18
Design instance-level security configurations	Chapters 17, 18, 19
Design database, schema, and object security parameters	Chapters 18, 19
Design a security policy and audit plan	Chapters 17, 18, 19
Design an encryption strategy	Chapter 18
Designing a Database Solution for High Availability	**Chapters 20, 21, and 22**
Design a failover clustering solution	Chapter 20
Design database mirroring	Chapter 21
Design a high-availability solution that is based on replication	Chapter 22
Design a high-availability solution that is based on log shipping	Chapter 21
Select high-availability technologies based on business requirements	Chapters 20, 21, 22

TABLE A.2 Exam 70-450 Objectives Map *(continued)*

Objective	Chapter
Designing a Backup and Recovery Solution	**Chapter 16**
Design a backup strategy	Chapter 16
Design a recovery strategy	Chapter 16
Design a recovery test plan	Chapter 16
Designing a Monitoring Strategy	**Chapter 14**
Design a monitoring solution at the operating system level	Chapter 14
Design a monitoring solution at the instance level	Chapter 14
Design a solution to monitor performance and concurrency	Chapter 14
Designing a Strategy to Maintain and Manage Databases	**Chapters 14, 15, and 16**
Design a maintenance strategy for database servers	Chapters 15, 16
Design a solution to govern resources	Chapter 14
Design policies by using policy-based management	Chapter 15
Design a data compression strategy	Chapter 16
Design a management automation strategy	Chapter 15
Designing a Strategy for Data Distribution	**Chapters 12 and 22**
Administer SQL Server Integration Services (SSIS) packages	Chapter 12
Design a strategy to use linked servers	Chapter 22
Design a replication strategy for data distribution	Chapter 22

Exam objectives are subject to change at any time without prior notice and at Microsoft's sole discretion. Please visit Microsoft's website (www.microsoft.com/learning) for the most current listing of exam objectives.

Appendix
B

About the Additional Bonus Materials

IN THIS APPENDIX:

- What You'll Find
- System requirements
- Using the Bonus Materials
- Troubleshooting

What You'll Find

The following sections are arranged by category and summarize the software and other goodies you'll find. If you need help with installing the items, refer to the installation instructions in the "Using the Bonus Materials" section of this appendix.

Video Walkthroughs

The bonus materials include over an hour of video walkthroughs from author Tom Carpenter. Tom shows readers how to perform some of the more difficult tasks that they will encounter.

Sybex Test Engine

For Windows
The bonus materials include the Sybex test engine with two bonus exams.

Electronic Flashcards

For PC
These handy electronic flashcards are just what they sound like. One side contains a question or fill-in-the-blank question, and the other side shows the answer.

To download the bonus materials, visit booksupport.wiley.com, and plug in the book's ISBN: 9780470554203. From there, click on ISBN, and then download the zip file to your hard drive.

System Requirements

Make sure your computer meets the minimum system requirements shown in the following list. If your computer doesn't match up to most of these requirements, you may have problems using the software and files. For the latest and greatest information, please refer to the ReadMe file located at the root of the downloads.

- A PC running Microsoft Windows 98, Windows 2000, Windows NT4 (with SP4 or later), Windows Me, Windows XP, Windows Vista, or Windows 7
- An Internet connection

Using the Bonus Materials

To install the items to your hard drive, follow these steps:

1. Once you download the zip file, unzip and click the start.exe file. The license agreement appears.

2. Read the license agreement, and then click the Accept button.

    The interface appears. The interface allows you to access the content with just one or two clicks.

Troubleshooting

Wiley has attempted to provide programs that work on most computers with the minimum system requirements. Alas, your computer may differ, and some programs may not work properly for some reason.

The two likeliest problems are that you don't have enough memory (RAM) for the programs you want to use or you have other programs running that are affecting installation or running of a program. If you get an error message such as "Not enough memory" or "Setup cannot continue," try one or more of the following suggestions and then try using the software again:

Turn off any antivirus software running on your computer. Installation programs sometimes mimic virus activity and may make your computer incorrectly believe that it's being infected by a virus.

Close all running programs. The more programs you have running, the less memory is available to other programs. Installation programs typically update files and programs; so if you keep other programs running, installation may not work properly.

Have your local computer store add more RAM to your computer. This is, admittedly, a drastic and somewhat expensive step. However, adding more memory can really help the speed of your computer and allow more programs to run at the same time.

Customer Care

If you have trouble with the book's bonus materials, please call the Wiley Product Technical Support phone number at (800) 762-2974.

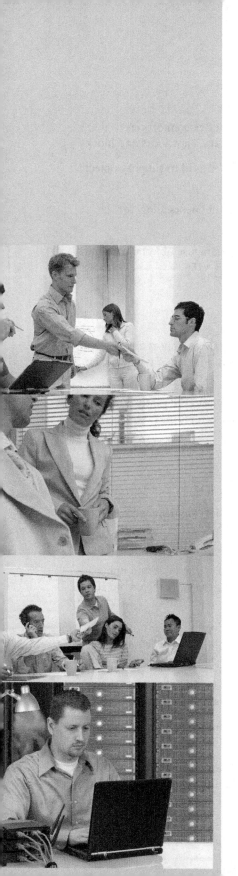

Glossary

A

Activity Monitor   An application used to monitor and manage active connections to the SQL Server. With the Activity Monitor, you can kill connections and view locks and blocks.

Alias   An alternative name for a SQL Server object. Aliases can be used to simplify object access.

Analysis Services   The SQL Server Analysis Services (SSAS) components allow for the analysis of data for business intelligence (BI) and decision support.

ALTER   A Transact-SQL keyword or command used to modify database objects. Examples include ALTER DATABASE, ALTER TABLE, ALTER TRIGGER, and ALTER VIEW.

B

BCP   Bulk copy program (BCP) is a command-line application used to import and export data to or from a SQL Server database. With the IN switch, you can import data. With the OUT switch, you can export data.

BULK INSERT   A Transact-SQL command that can be used to import data into SQL Server database tables from flat text files. The database and table targets must be specified, as well as the data source file.

C

CLR   The Common Language Runtime (CLR) is an application development environment that supports multiple languages, such as Visual Basic and C#. The CLR is integrated into the SQL Server engine so that CLR stored procedures may be developed.

Clustered Index   A table index that dictates the ordering of data in the table and implements a b-tree index structure for rapid location of records (rows) based on the record ID column (field).

Clustering   A method that allows multiple servers to act as one logical server on the network so that clients may access the logical server with high availability. SQL Server supports failover clustering.

Column   The term used to reference a vertical collection of data values in a table. Often called a domain, the column defines the data type and any constraints required.

CPU affinity   A feature that allows processes to be assigned to individual processors in multiprocessor systems.

CREATE   A Transact-SQL keyword or command used to create database objects. Examples include CREATE DATABASE, CREATE TABLE, CREATE LOGIN, CREATE INDEX, and CREATE VIEW.

D

Data   The actual values stored in a table. The data may be of binary, character, or numeric type and may be defined by several data types in SQL Server 2008.

Data Type   A specification that determines the type of characters or information that may be placed in a table column. SQL Server supports numeric, character, and binary data types.

Database   A collection of organized data that is stored in a digital format within a computer system. A database may be stored in one or more physical files on the hard drive.

Database Engine   The service that provides access to and management of the actual databases in SQL Server. The Database Engine service is usually configured to run as a Windows user account.

Database Engine Tuning Advisor   A tool used to analyze a workload file (a T-SQL script or a SQL Server Profiler trace) and recommend database changes to improve performance. Recommendations may include the creation of indexes, partitions, or indexed views.

Database Mirroring   A technology that allows a duplicate (mirror) copy of a database to be maintained on a separate instance of SQL Server. Database mirroring provides for high availability and data redundancy.

Database Snapshot   A picture of the database at the point-in-time when the snapshot was taken. Multiple snapshots can be taken against a single database at the same time. The administrator can revert the database to a snapshot.

Data Definition Language (DDL)   The subset of the ANSI SQL language that is used to define database structures such as tables and indexes. Example DDL commands include CREATE, ALTER, and DROP.

Data Control Language (DCL)   The subset of the ANSI SQL language that is used to define database permissions. Examples include GRANT, REVOKE, and DENY.

Data Manipulation Language (DML)   The subset of the ANSI SQL language that is used to work with data in databases. Examples include SELECT, INSERT, UPDATE, and DELETE.

Declarative Management Framework   A policy-based management model that allows for centralized configuration management of all SQL Servers in an organization. Also known as policy-based management.

DELETE   A SQL statement used to remove records from a database table. Multiple records may be deleted with a single DELETE statement.

DENY   A SQL command used to deny a permission. The DENY statement is a negative permission statement. It always results in the removal of the permission from the target login, user, or role.

Differential Backup   A database backup that only backs up the data pages that have changed since the last full backup.

DROP   The Transact-SQL keyword or command used to delete database objects. Examples include DROP DATABASE, DROP TABLE, DROP INDEX, and DROP VIEW.

Dynamic Management View   A special view that provides access to configuration information and internal SQL Server 2008 statistics that may be helpful for the management of the server.

E

Encryption   The process used to convert plaintext or readable text into ciphertext. Encryption may be used on any data because all data is represented by binary numbers within computer systems. The input to the encryption algorithm is one set of binary numbers and the output is another. The algorithm can both scramble and descramble the data.

F

Filegroup   A logical collection of one or more files used to store database table data. Every database has at least one filegroup in SQL Server 2008 and may have more than one filegroup. The administrator can specify that an object should be stored in a specific filegroup.

Filestream   A new feature in SQL Server 2008 that allows for the external storage of data. The filestream data is accessed as if it were stored in the standard database files.

Full Backup   A database backup that backs up every data page in the database.

Full-Text Index   A special index that allows for faster searches against text data columns. Search features provided include word forms and plurality.

G

GRANT   A SQL command used to grant a permission to a login, user, or role. The GRANT command may not always result in a positive permission condition. The DENY command can overrule the GRANT command.

I

Index   A database object that provides for faster searches on data tables. Indexes may be clustered, nonclustered, or full-text in SQL Server 2008.

INNER JOIN   The Transact-SQL clause used to join to separate tables together in a query statement. An INNER JOIN only includes rows that exist in both the first and second named tables in the statement.

INSERT   A SQL command used to add data to a SQL Server database table.

Integration Services   An optional service that allows for data extraction, transformation, and loading (ETL). Also known as SQL Server Integration Services or SSIS. SSIS is required for the creation of database maintenance plans.

L

Log Shipping   A data redundancy feature that provides a secondary copy of the shipped database on another server instance. Log shipping is considered a high latency redundancy feature because the logs are shipped every few minutes and are not shipped as transactions occur.

N

Nonclustered Index   An index that is stored separately from the data table within the same database. Nonclustered indexes are used to improve query results when non-key columns are used in WHERE clauses of SELECT statements.

O

OUTER JOIN   The Transact-SQL clause used to join rows from multiple tables and include rows that exist in only one of the tables. The LEFT outer join includes all rows in the first named table and the RIGHT outer join includes all rows in the second named table of the OUTER JOIN statement.

P

Policy-Based Management   Also known as the Declarative Management Framework (DMF), a SQL Server management feature that allows centralized management of multiple SQL Servers through policies.

R

RAID   Redundant Array of Independent Disks (RAID) is used to provide improved performance or storage fault tolerance. RAID 0 provides striping and improves drive performance. RAID 1 provides mirroring and improves fault tolerance. RAID 5 provides striping with parity and provides fault tolerance and sometimes a performance gain as well.

Replication   A SQL Server technology that allows data to be distributed automatically. The replication system includes publishers, distributors, and subscribers. Articles are published and the articles include entire tables or portions of tables.

Reporting Services   A SQL Server component that allows for the generation of data reports. The reports may be viewed through a web browser. SQL Server Reporting Services is known as SSRS.

Resource Governor   A new SQL Server 2008 feature that provides the DBA with flexible resource scheduling through resource pools and workload groups.

REVOKE   A SQL command that removes a GRANT or DENY permission.

Row   The horizontal collection of columns that comprise a record.

S

Security   The state in which an acceptable level of risk is achieved through the use of policies and procedures that can be monitored and managed.

SELECT   The most commonly used SQL command. Used to read data from a table or select data from one table into another.

SQL   The database communications language managed by the ANSI organization. SQL provides common commands such as SELECT, INSERT, UPDATE, DELETE, GRANT, REVOKE, DENY, CREATE, ALTER, and DROP. The SQL language is divided into three subsets: Data Manipulation Language (DML), Data Control Language (DCL), and Data Definition Language (DDL).

SQL Server Agent   The SQL Server service that is responsible for jobs and monitoring of the other SQL Server services. The SQL Server Agent service must be running for scheduled SQL Server jobs to run on schedule.

SQL Server Profiler   An application that is used to monitor the activity taking place in the target SQL Server instance. Used to monitor for T-SQL transactions and deadlocks among other actions.

SQLCMD   A command-line utility used to execute SQL commands against a SQL Server database. SQLCMD replaced OSQL in SQL Server 2005.

Stored Procedure   A collection of T-SQL statements used to perform an administrative or application-level action within a SQL Server database. Stored procedures are used to abstract security, improve performance, and centralize business rule logic within SQL Server 2008 databases.

T

Table   A collection of columns and rows of data. SQL Server tables are stored as heaps or clustered indexes. A heap is a disorganized collection of rows as no clustered index exists.

Transaction   In a SQL Server database, an action that results in changed or added data. Transactions may be implicit or explicit. Implicit transactions include any actions that result in a change but do not include BEGIN TRAN and COMMIT TRAN statements. Explicit transactions do include BEGIN TRAN and COMMIT TRAN statements.

Transaction Log   A database log file or files used to track changes as they are made to the database. The transaction log can be used to recover data in the event of a storage drive loss. The transaction log should be stored on a separate physical drive from the database files.

Transparent Data Encryption   Transparent Data Encryption (TDE) can be applied to an existing database without requiring changes to the client access applications. TDE decrypts the data automatically when the data is accessed. The encryption is used to protect the data when stored on backups or should the physical database file be stolen.

Trigger   A collection of T-SQL statements executed automatically when an event occurs. Triggers may be INSTEAD OF triggers or AFTER triggers. Both DDL and DML triggers are supported in SQL Server 2005 and later versions.

T-SQL   Transact-SQL is the Microsoft implementation of the SQL language. T-SQL includes enhancements to the ANSI SQL language for specific use with the Microsoft SQL Server database system.

U

UPDATE   A SQL statement used to modify existing data in a SQL Server database table.

User Defined Function   A function developed within SQL Server for use within ad hoc SQL statements or stored procedures. User-defined functions (UDF) should not be confused with T-SQL functions, which are part of the T-SQL language.

V

View   A stored SELECT statement that is used to simplify access to data in SQL Server database tables. Views may also improve the performance of data access. SQL Server 2005 and later versions support indexed views.

X

XML   The extensible markup language (XML) is a portable data description language supported by SQL Server. SQL Server supports the XML data type for XML data storage and the XQuery language for access to the XML data.

Index

Note to the Reader: Throughout this index **boldfaced** page numbers indicate primary discussions of a topic. *Italicized* page numbers indicate illustrations.

S

T

X

Z

Wiley Publishing, Inc. End-User License Agreement

The Perfect Companion for All SQL Server 2008 DBAs

Includes over an hour of video walkthroughs with author Tom Carpenter.

- Tom walks you through some of the more difficult tasks you can expect to face as a SQL Server 2008 DBA.
- See firsthand how to install a named instance, create an ER file, create a DML or DDL trigger, and much more.

For certification candidates, we've included practice tests for both required exams for the IT Pro: SQL Server 2008 Database Administration certification

- Microsoft SQL Server 2008, Installation and Maintenance (70-432)
- Designing, Optimizing and Maintaining a Database Server Infrastructure using Microsoft SQL Server 2008 (70-450)

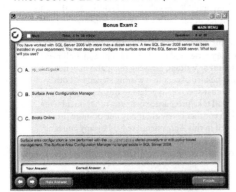

Electronic Flashcards to jog your memory of topics covered in the book!

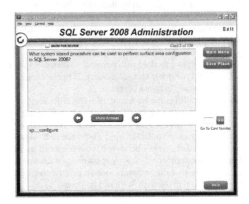

To download the bonus materials, visit booksupport.wiley.com, and plug in the book's ISBN: 9780470554203. From there, click on ISBN, and then download the zip file to your hard drive.

CPSIA information can be obtained at www.ICGtesting.com
Printed in the USA
LVOW03s1949050215

425888LV00005B/142/P

9 780470 554203